Business
Plans
Handbook

Business Plans

A COMPILATION OF BUSINESS PLANS DEVELOPED BY INDIVIDUALS THROUGHOUT NORTH AMERICA

Handbook

VOLUME

26

**Sonya D. Hill,
Project Editor**

GALE
CENGAGE Learning·

Detroit • New York • San Francisco • New Haven, Conn • Waterville, Maine • London

Business Plans Handbook, Volume 26

Project Editor: Sonya D. Hill

Product Manager: Jenai Drouillard

Product Design: Jennifer Wahi

Composition and Electronic Prepress: Evi Seoud

Manufacturing: Rita Wimberley

Gale, a part of Cengage Learning
27500 Drake Rd.
Farmington Hills, MI 48331-3535

ISBN-13: 978-1-4144-6838-9
ISBN-10: 1-4144-6838-5
1084-4473

Printed in Mexico
1 2 3 4 5 6 7 16 15 14 13

Contents

Highlights vii
Introduction ix

BUSINESS PLANS

Airport Shuttle
Prestige Car Service. 1

Baby Furniture Rental
Baby, Baby. 17

Banquet Facility
Sycamore Hills Banquet Center. 25

Catering Service
Creative Catering 41

Children's Hair Salon
Kool Kidz 49

Consignment Shop
Upscale Resale 55

Copy Shop
Pronto Printing. 61

Custom Paint and Body Shop/Classic Car Restorations
Racing Stripes 77

Dance Studio
Dancing Divas 85

Dollar Store
Dollar Daze 93

Food Truck
Suerte Cuban Cuisine 109

General Staffing Company
GENRX LLC 115

Gift Basket Service
Sunrise Gift Baskets 123

Handmade Writing Instruments & Accessories Business
StanMark Gifts Inc. 133

Hedge Fund
Oxford Advisors 143

Home Accessibility Services Provider
AccessibilityWorx Inc. 159

Paintball Store and Field
X-Treme Paintball 165

Real Estate Investment Company
Schroeder Real Estate 181

CONTENTS

Resume Writing Business
    Nieberger Career Consulting, LLC 197

Solar Panel Installation Service
    Living Green Energy Services. 205

APPENDIXES

Appendix A
    Business Plan Template 221
    Fictional Plan 1 - Food Distributor 225
    Fictional Plan 2 - Hardware Store 229

Appendix B
    Associations. 233
    Consultants 235
    SBA Regional Offices. 250
    Small Business Development Centers 251
    Service Corps of Retired Executives Offices 255
    Venture Capital & Financing Companies 280

Appendix C
    Glossary of Small Business Terms. 311

Appendix D
    Cumulative Index. 335

Highlights

Business Plans Handbook, Volume 26 (BPH-26) is a collection of business plans compiled by entrepreneurs seeking funding for small businesses throughout North America. For those looking for examples of how to approach, structure, and compose their own business plans, BPH-26 presents 20 sample plans, including plans for the following businesses:

- Airport Shuttle
- Baby Furniture Rental
- Banquet Facility
- Catering Service
- Children's Hair Salon
- Consignment Shop
- Copy Shop
- Custom Paint and Body Shop/Classic Car Restorations
- Dance Studio
- Dollar Store
- Food Truck
- General Staffing Company
- Gift Basket Service
- Handmade Writing Instruments & Accessories Business
- Hedge Fund
- Home Accessibility Services Provider
- Paintball Store and Field
- Real Estate Investment Company
- Resume Writing Business
- Solar Panel Installation Service

FEATURES AND BENEFITS

BPH-26 offers many features not provided by other business planning references including:

- Twenty business plans, each of which represent an attempt at clarifying (for themselves and others) the reasons that the business should exist or expand and why a lender should fund the enterprise.
- Two fictional plans that are used by business counselors at a prominent small business development organization as examples for their clients. (You will find these in the Business Plan Template Appendix.)

- A directory section that includes listings for venture capital and finance companies, which specialize in funding start-up and second-stage small business ventures, and a comprehensive listing of Service Corps of Retired Executives (SCORE) offices. In addition, the Appendix also contains updated listings of all Small Business Development Centers (SBDCs); associations of interest to entrepreneurs; Small Business Administration (SBA) Regional Offices; and consultants specializing in small business planning and advice. It is strongly advised that you consult supporting organizations while planning your business, as they can provide a wealth of useful information.

- A Small Business Term Glossary to help you decipher the sometimes confusing terminology used by lenders and others in the financial and small business communities.

- A cumulative index, outlining each plan profiled in the complete *Business Plans Handbook* series.

- A Business Plan Template which serves as a model to help you construct your own business plan. This generic outline lists all the essential elements of a complete business plan and their components, including the Summary, Business History and Industry Outlook, Market Examination, Competition, Marketing, Administration and Management, Financial Information, and other key sections. Use this guide as a starting point for compiling your plan.

- Extensive financial documentation required to solicit funding from small business lenders. You will find examples of Cash Flows, Balance Sheets, Income Projections, and other financial information included with the textual portions of the plan.

Introduction

Perhaps the most important aspect of business planning is simply doing it. More and more business owners are beginning to compile business plans even if they don't need a bank loan. Others discover the value of planning when they must provide a business plan for the bank. The sheer act of putting thoughts on paper seems to clarify priorities and provide focus. Sometimes business owners completely change strategies when compiling their plan, deciding on a different product mix or advertising scheme after finding that their assumptions were incorrect. This kind of healthy thinking and re-thinking via business planning is becoming the norm. The editors of *Business Plans Handbook, Volume 26* (*BPH-26*) sincerely hope that this latest addition to the series is a helpful tool in the successful completion of your business plan, no matter what the reason for creating it.

This twenty-sixth volume, like each volume in the series, offers business plans used and created by real people. *BPH-26* provides 20 business plans. The business and personal names and addresses and general locations have been changed to protect the privacy of the plan authors.

NEW BUSINESS OPPORTUNITIES

As in other volumes in the series, *BPH-26* finds entrepreneurs engaged in a wide variety of creative endeavors. Examples include a proposal for a Dance Studio, a Landscaping Business, and Concierge Service. In addition, several other plans are provided, including a Produce and Flower Market, a Digital Asset Management Consultant, and a Massage Therapist, among others.

Comprehensive financial documentation has become increasingly important as today's entrepreneurs compete for the finite resources of business lenders. Our plans illustrate the financial data generally required of loan applicants, including Income Statements, Financial Projections, Cash Flows, and Balance Sheets.

ENHANCED APPENDIXES

In an effort to provide the most relevant and valuable information for our readers, we have updated the coverage of small business resources. For instance, you will find a directory section, which includes listings of all of the Service Corps of Retired Executives (SCORE) offices; an informative glossary, which includes small business terms; and a cumulative index, outlining each plan profiled in the complete *Business Plans Handbook* series. In addition we have updated the list of Small Business Development Centers (SBDCs); Small Business Administration Regional Offices; venture capital and finance companies, which specialize in funding start-up and second-stage small business enterprises; associations of interest to entrepreneurs; and consultants, specializing in small business advice and planning. For your reference, we have also reprinted the business plan template, which provides a comprehensive overview of the essential components of a business plan and two fictional plans used by small business counselors.

SERIES INFORMATION

If you already have the first twenty-five volumes of *BPH*, with this twenty-sixth volume, you will now have a collection of over 524 business plans (not including the updated plans); contact information for hundreds of organizations and agencies offering business expertise; a helpful business plan template; more than 1,500 citations to valuable small business development material; and a comprehensive glossary of terms to help the business planner navigate the sometimes confusing language of entrepreneurship.

ACKNOWLEDGEMENTS

The Editors wish to sincerely thank the contributors to *BPH-26*, including:

- BizPlanDB.com
- Heidi Denler
- Fran Fletcher
- Paul Greenland
- Kimberly C. Herrera
- Kari Lucke
- Claire Moore
- Zuzu Enterprises

COMMENTS WELCOME

Your comments on *Business Plans Handbook* are appreciated. Please direct all correspondence, suggestions for future volumes of *BPH*, and other recommendations to the following:

Managing Editor, Business Product
Business Plans Handbook
Gale, a part of Cengage Learning
27500 Drake Rd.
Farmington Hills, MI 48331-3535
Phone: (248)699-4253
Fax: (248)699-8052
Toll-Free: 800-347-GALE
E-mail: BusinessProducts@gale.com

Airport Shuttle
Prestige Car Service

33978 1st Ave.
New York, NY 10001

BizPlanDB.com

The purpose of this business plan is to raise $150,000 for the development of an airport shuttle company while showcasing the expected financials and operations over the next three years. Prestige Car Service, Inc. is a New York based corporation that will provide for the transportation of people from terminals to rental car locations to customers in its targeted market on an outsourced basis. The Company was founded by Vince Green.

1.0 EXECUTIVE SUMMARY

The purpose of this business plan is to raise $150,000 for the development of an airport shuttle company while showcasing the expected financials and operations over the next three years. Prestige Car Service, Inc. is a New York based corporation that will provide for the transportation of people from terminals to rental car locations to customers in its targeted market on an outsourced basis. The Company was founded by Vince Green.

1.1 The Services

As mentioned above, the business is a transportation service company that will primarily provide for the transportation of individuals to and from the airport to local rental car agencies as well as hotels (from time to time). The business will generate its income from ongoing contracts with major car rental agencies and hotels on a monthly basis.

The Company will generate secondary revenues from fuel surcharges based upon the daily usage of the Company's fleet of transportation vehicles.

The third section of the business plan will further describe the services offered by Prestige Car Service.

1.2 Financing

Mr. Green is seeking to raise $150,000 from as a bank loan. The interest rate and loan agreement are to be further discussed during negotiation. This business plan assumes that the business will receive a 10 year loan with a 9% fixed interest rate. The financing will be used for the following:

- Development of the Company's office location.
- Financing for the first six months of operation.
- Capital to finance deposits for leasing of three transportation vehicles.

Mr. Green will contribute $25,000 to the venture.

1.3 Mission Statement

The mission of Prestige Car Service is to become the recognized leader in its targeted market for airport shuttling services.

1.4 Management Team

The Company was founded by Vince Green. Mr. Green has more than 10 years of experience in the transportation industry. Through his expertise, he will be able to bring the operations of the business to profitability within its first year of operations.

1.5 Sales Forecasts

Mr. Green expects a strong rate of growth at the start of operations. Below are the expected financials over the next three years.

Proforma profit and loss (yearly)

Year	1	2	3
Sales	$973,590	$1,168,308	$1,366,920
Operating costs	$297,003	$ 310,535	$ 324,590
EBITDA	$ 79,734	$ 141,549	$ 204,349
Taxes, interest, and depreciation	$ 52,155	$ 70,101	$ 93,348
Net profit	$ 27,579	$ 71,448	$ 111,001

Sales, operating costs, and profit forecast

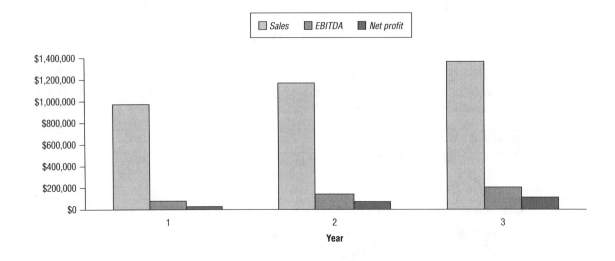

1.6 Expansion Plan

As time progresses, Management intends to aggressively expand each segment of the Company's operations especially as it relates to working with hotels and car rental agencies. The Company will also extensively develop ongoing relationships with additional airlines and airports.

2.0 COMPANY AND FINANCING SUMMARY

2.1 Registered Name and Corporate Structure

Prestige Car Service, Inc. is registered as a corporation in the State of New York.

2.2 Required Funds

At this time, Prestige Car Service requires $150,000 of debt funds. Mr. Green will make a $25,000 capital contribution. Below is a breakdown of how these funds will be used:

Projected startup costs

Initial lease payments and deposits	$ 15,000
Working capital	$ 35,000
Inventory	$ 25,000
Leasehold improvements	$ 7,500
Security deposits	$ 12,500
Insurance	$ 5,000
Vehicle deposits	$ 50,000
Marketing budget	$ 17,500
Miscellaneous and unforeseen costs	$ 7,500
Total startup costs	**$175,000**

Use of funds

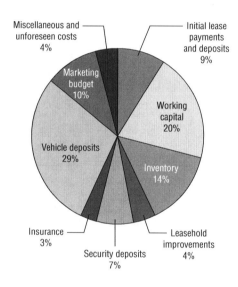

2.3 Investor Equity

Mr. Green is not seeking an investment from a third party at this time.

2.4 Management Equity

Vince Green owns 100% of Prestige Car Service, Inc.

2.5 Exit Strategy

If the business is very successful, Mr. Green may seek to sell the business to a third party for a significant earnings multiple. Most likely, the Company will hire a qualified business broker to sell the business on behalf of Prestige Car Service.

Based on historical numbers, the business could fetch a sales premium of up to 6 times earnings. However, with recent fuel costs rising, the premiums for transportation support businesses have declined due to the volatility of the oil markets. It should be noted that Mr. Green intends to operate this business for a significant period of time, and a potential exit strategy would not be executed for at least five to seven years.

3.0 PRODUCTS AND SERVICES

Below is a description of the services offered by Prestige Car Service:

3.1 Outsourced Transportation Services

As stated in the executive summary, the business intends to immediately acquire three van type transportation vehicles that will make ongoing routes through the Company's targeted airport on a 24 hour a day basis. The business will generate all of its income from relationships that are to be developed with car rental agencies as well as local hotels. The business will use specialized signage on its initial vehicles so that individuals that are in need of transportation to these hotel and car rental locations can quickly find the business. The Company will employ three to four drivers from the onset of operations that will operate the three vehicles on a round the clock basis.

During busy seasons and during busy traveling hours, the Company will charge surcharges for fuel that are related to having to provide more frequent trips to the airport coupled with returns to the contracted hotel or car rental agency.

4.0 STRATEGIC AND MARKET ANALYSIS

4.1 Economic Outlook

This section of the analysis will detail the economic climate, the airline support industry, the customer profile, and the competition that the business will face as it progresses through its business operations.

Currently, the economic market condition in the United States is sluggish. This slowdown in the economy has also greatly impacted real estate sales, which has halted to historical lows. Many economists expect that this sluggish growth will continue for a significant period of time, at which point the economy will begin a prolonged recovery period with more normalized growth.

A primary concern for the Company is its ability to price its services affordably during times of economic recession or spikes of oil prices. As of 2012, the price of oil and its associated refined energy products have reached multi-year highs. As such, the demand for travel may decline and the business' revenues may decline.

4.2 Industry Analysis

There are 1,500 companies in the United States that on ground services to airports (and related companies near airports). In each of the last five years, these businesses have aggregate generated $3.7 billion dollars. The industry employs 60,000.

As transportation costs have increased, airports, car rental agencies, and local hotels have sought to reduce their overhead expenditures by outsourcing management services to third party companies. As such, Prestige Car Service is an excellent position to expand within this market over the next five years.

The growth of this industry is expected to equal that of the US economy in general.

4.3 Customer Profile

Among the Company's corporate airline clients, Management has outlined the following demographics:

- Has gross revenues in excess of $20 million dollars
- Is seeking to reduce costs related to non-core on ground services
- Operates within the State of New York

4.4 Competition

Due to the ongoing contracts that are provided to airport shuttle businesses, competition within this market is fierce. Within the Company's target market of the New York metropolitan area, there are 20 businesses that operate in a similar capacity. One of the ways that Mr. Green intends to differentiate his business from that of the competition is to remain pricing competitive, operating a streamlined infrastructure to reduce cost, provide unparalleled support to customers (air ports and car rental agencies), and provide friendly customer service to passengers.

5.0 MARKETING PLAN

Prestige Car Service intends to maintain an extensive marketing campaign that will ensure maximum visibility for the business in its targeted market. Below is an overview of the marketing strategies and objectives of Prestige Car Service.

5.1 Marketing Objectives

- Develop strong contractual relationships with airports (via their car rental agencies and local hotels) within New York.

- Establish a large web presence to promote traffic to the Company's website.

- Maintain proper licensure for operating an on ground airport related support service business.

5.2 Marketing Strategies

At the onset operations, a sales representative hired by the Company will aggressively pursue clients so that the business can provide airport shuttle services. These sales agent(s) will be heavily rewarded for closing contracts with car rental agencies and local hotels. Mr. Green will also develop extensive sales literature and sales brochures that will showcase the cost effectiveness, relevant licensure, and contact information for the business. Once these relationships are in place, very little ongoing marketing will be required.

5.3 Pricing

Management expects that the business will receive a per diem fee of $750 for operating a vehicle. The business intends to operate three airport shuttles at the onset of operations.

6.0 ORGANIZATIONAL PLAN AND PERSONNEL SUMMARY

6.1 Corporate Organization

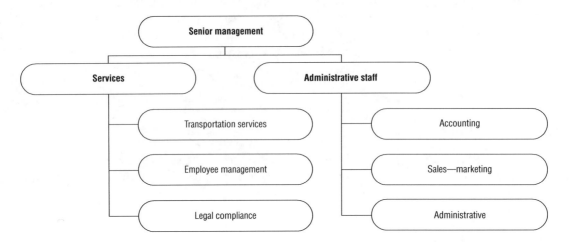

6.2 Organizational Budget

Personnel plan—yearly

Year	1	2	3
Owner	$ 40,000	$ 41,200	$ 42,436
Assistant manager	$ 29,000	$ 29,870	$ 30,766
Drivers	$ 93,000	$ 95,790	$ 98,664
Bookkeeper (P/T)	$ 9,000	$ 9,270	$ 9,548
Administrative (P/T)	$ 17,000	$ 17,510	$ 18,035
Total	**$188,000**	**$193,640**	**$199,449**

Numbers of personnel

Owner	1	1	1
Assistant manager	1	1	1
Drivers	3	3	3
Bookkeeper (P/T)	1	1	1
Administrative (P/T)	1	1	1
Totals	**7**	**7**	**7**

Personnel expense breakdown

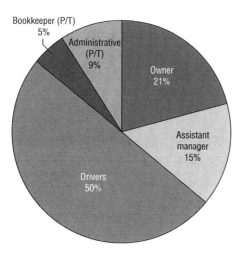

7.0 FINANCIAL PLAN

7.1 Underlying Assumptions

The Company has based its proforma financial statements on the following:

- Prestige Car Service will have an annual revenue growth rate of 14.5% per year.

- The Owner will acquire $150,000 of debt funds to develop the business.

- The loan will have a 10 year term with a 9% interest rate.

7.2 Sensitivity Analysis

The Company's revenues are sensitive to a number of external environmental factors that are beyond its control. Airport shuttle service revenues are not subject to changes in the general economy as companies will continue to need these services despite deleterious economic changes. As such, the business (despite increasing energy costs) should be able to remain profitable and cash flow positive at all times.

7.3 Source of Funds

Financing

Equity contributions	
Management investment	$ 25,000.00
Total equity financing	**$ 25,000.00**
Banks and lenders	
Banks and lenders	$ 150,000.00
Total debt financing	**$150,000.00**
Total financing	**$175,000.00**

7.4 General Assumptions

General assumptions

Year	1	2	3
Short term interest rate	9.5%	9.5%	9.5%
Long term interest rate	10.0%	10.0%	10.0%
Federal tax rate	33.0%	33.0%	33.0%
State tax rate	5.0%	5.0%	5.0%
Personnel taxes	15.0%	15.0%	15.0%

7.5 Profit and Loss Statements

Proforma profit and loss (yearly)

Year	1	2	3
Sales	**$973,590**	**$1,168,308**	**$1,366,920**
Cost of goods sold	$596,853	$ 716,224	$ 837,982
Gross margin	38.70%	38.70%	38.70%
Operating income	**$376,737**	**$ 452,084**	**$ 528,939**
Expenses			
Payroll	$188,000	$ 193,640	$ 199,449
General and administrative	$ 25,200	$ 26,208	$ 27,256
Marketing expenses	$ 4,868	$ 5,842	$ 6,835
Professional fees and licensure	$ 5,219	$ 5,376	$ 5,537
Insurance costs	$ 1,987	$ 2,086	$ 2,191
Vehicle maintenance costs	$ 17,596	$ 19,356	$ 21,291
Rent and utilities	$ 14,250	$ 14,963	$ 15,711
Miscellaneous costs	$ 11,683	$ 14,020	$ 16,403
Payroll taxes	$ 28,200	$ 29,046	$ 29,917
Total operating costs	**$297,003**	**$ 310,535**	**$ 324,590**
EBITDA	**$ 79,734**	**$ 141,549**	**$ 204,349**
Federal income tax	$ 26,312	$ 42,686	$ 63,738
State income tax	$ 3,987	$ 6,468	$ 9,657
Interest expense	$ 13,107	$ 12,197	$ 11,202
Depreciation expenses	$ 8,750	$ 8,750	$ 8,750
Net profit	**$ 27,579**	**$ 71,448**	**$ 111,001**
Profit margin	**2.83%**	**16.12%**	**8.12%**

Sales, operating costs, and profit forecast

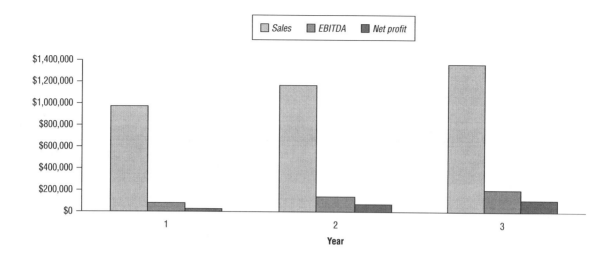

7.6 Cash Flow Analysis

Proforma cash flow analysis—yearly

Year	1	2	3
Cash from operations	$ 36,329	$ 80,198	$119,751
Cash from receivables	$ 0	$ 0	$ 0
Operating cash inflow	**$ 36,329**	**$ 80,198**	**$119,751**
Other cash inflows			
Equity investment	$ 25,000	$ 0	$ 0
Increased borrowings	$150,000	$ 0	$ 0
Sales of business assets	$ 0	$ 0	$ 0
A/P increases	$ 37,902	$ 43,587	$ 50,125
Total other cash inflows	**$212,902**	**$ 43,587**	**$ 50,125**
Total cash inflow	**$249,231**	**$123,786**	**$169,876**
Cash outflows			
Repayment of principal	$ 9,695	$ 10,605	$ 11,599
A/P decreases	$ 24,897	$ 29,876	$ 35,852
A/R increases	$ 0	$ 0	$ 0
Asset purchases	$122,500	$ 20,050	$ 29,938
Dividends	$ 25,430	$ 56,139	$ 83,826
Total cash outflows	**$182,522**	**$116,669**	**$161,214**
Net cash flow	**$ 66,708**	**$ 7,116**	**$ 8,662**
Cash balance	**$ 66,708**	**$ 73,825**	**$ 82,487**

Proforma cash flow (yearly)

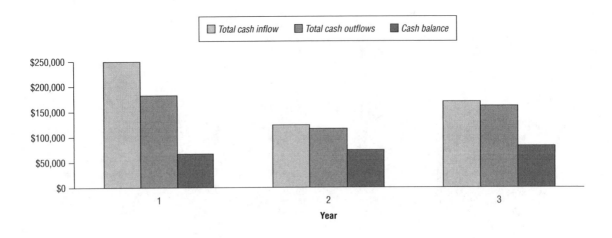

7.7 Balance Sheet

Proforma balance sheet—yearly

Year	1	2	3
Assets			
Cash	$ 66,708	$ 73,825	$ 82,487
Amortized expansion costs	$ 47,500	$ 49,505	$ 52,499
Vehicle deposits	$ 50,000	$ 65,037	$ 87,490
Inventory	$ 25,000	$ 28,007	$ 32,498
Accumulated depreciation	($ 8,750)	($ 17,500)	($ 26,250)
Total assets	**$180,458**	**$198,874**	**$228,724**
Liabilities and equity			
Accounts payable	$ 13,005	$ 26,716	$ 40,990
Long term liabilities	$140,305	$129,700	$119,096
Other liabilities	$ 0	$ 0	$ 0
Total liabilities	**$153,310**	**$156,416**	**$160,085**
Net worth	**$ 27,149**	**$ 42,458**	**$ 68,639**
Total liabilities and equity	**$180,458**	**$198,874**	**$228,724**

Proforma balance sheet

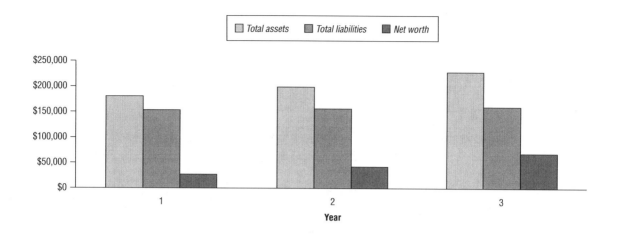

7.8 Breakeven Analysis

Monthly break even analysis

Year	1	2	3
Monthly revenue	$ 63,961	$ 66,876	$ 69,902
Yearly revenue	$767,536	$802,507	$838,828

Break even analysis

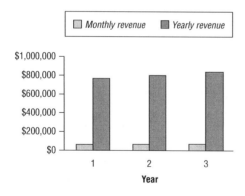

7.9 Business Ratios

Business ratios—yearly

Year	1	2	3
Sales			
Sales growth	0.00%	20.00%	17.00%
Gross margin	38.70%	38.70%	38.70%
Financials			
Profit margin	2.83%	6.12%	8.12%
Assets to liabilities	1.18	1.27	1.43
Equity to liabilities	0.18	0.27	0.43
Assets to equity	6.65	4.68	3.33
Liquidity			
Acid test	0.44	0.47	0.52
Cash to assets	0.37	0.37	0.36

7.10 Three Year Profit and Loss Statement

Profit and loss statement (first year)

Months	1	2	3	4	5	6	7
Sales	**$80,500**	**$80,615**	**$80,730**	**$80,845**	**$80,960**	**$81,075**	**$81,190**
Cost of goods sold	$49,350	$49,421	$49,491	$49,562	$49,632	$49,703	$49,773
Gross margin	38.70%	38.70%	38.70%	38.70%	38.70%	38.70%	38.70%
Operating income	**$31,150**	**$31,195**	**$31,239**	**$31,284**	**$31,328**	**$31,373**	**$31,417**
Expenses							
Payroll	$15,667	$15,667	$15,667	$15,667	$15,667	$15,667	$15,667
General and administrative	$ 2,100	$ 2,100	$ 2,100	$ 2,100	$ 2,100	$ 2,100	$ 2,100
Marketing expenses	$ 406	$ 406	$ 406	$ 406	$ 406	$ 406	$ 406
Professional fees and licensure	$ 435	$ 435	$ 435	$ 435	$ 435	$ 435	$ 435
Insurance costs	$ 166	$ 166	$ 166	$ 166	$ 166	$ 166	$ 166
Vehicle maintenance costs	$ 1,466	$ 1,466	$ 1,466	$ 1,466	$ 1,466	$ 1,466	$ 1,466
Rent and utilities	$ 1,188	$ 1,188	$ 1,188	$ 1,188	$ 1,188	$ 1,188	$ 1,188
Miscellaneous costs	$ 974	$ 974	$ 974	$ 974	$ 974	$ 974	$ 974
Payroll taxes	$ 2,350	$ 2,350	$ 2,350	$ 2,350	$ 2,350	$ 2,350	$ 2,350
Total operating costs	**$24,750**	**$24,750**	**$24,750**	**$24,750**	**$24,750**	**$24,750**	**$24,750**
EBITDA	**$ 6,400**	**$ 6,444**	**$ 6,489**	**$ 6,533**	**$ 6,578**	**$ 6,622**	**$ 6,667**
Federal income tax	$ 2,176	$ 2,179	$ 2,182	$ 2,185	$ 2,188	$ 2,191	$ 2,194
State income tax	$ 330	$ 330	$ 331	$ 331	$ 332	$ 332	$ 332
Interest expense	$ 1,125	$ 1,119	$ 1,113	$ 1,107	$ 1,101	$ 1,095	$ 1,089
Depreciation expense	$ 729	$ 729	$ 729	$ 729	$ 729	$ 729	$ 729
Net profit	**$ 2,040**	**$ 2,087**	**$ 2,134**	**$ 2,181**	**$ 2,228**	**$ 2,274**	**$ 2,321**

Profit and loss statement (first year cont.)

Month	8	9	10	11	12	1
Sales	$81,305	$81,420	$81,535	$81,650	$81,765	$973,590
Cost of goods sold	$49,844	$49,914	$49,985	$50,055	$50,126	$596,853
Gross margin	38.70%	38.70%	38.70%	38.70%	38.70%	38.70%
Operating income	$31,462	$31,506	$31,551	$31,595	$31,640	$376,737
Expenses						
Payroll	$15,667	$15,667	$15,667	$15,667	$15,667	$188,000
General and administrative	$2,100	$2,100	$2,100	$2,100	$2,100	$25,200
Marketing expenses	$406	$406	$406	$406	$406	$4,868
Professional fees and licensure	$435	$435	$435	$435	$435	$5,219
Insurance costs	$166	$166	$166	$166	$166	$1,987
Vehicle maintenance costs	$1,466	$1,466	$1,466	$1,466	$1,466	$17,596
Rent and utilities	$1,188	$1,188	$1,188	$1,188	$1,188	$14,250
Miscellaneous costs	$974	$974	$974	$974	$974	$11,683
Payroll taxes	$2,350	$2,350	$2,350	$2,350	$2,350	$28,200
Total operating costs	$24,750	$24,750	$24,750	$24,750	$24,750	$297,003
EBITDA	$6,711	$6,756	$6,800	$6,845	$6,889	$79,734
Federal income tax	$2,197	$2,200	$2,204	$2,207	$2,210	$26,312
State income tax	$333	$333	$334	$334	$335	$3,987
Interest expense	$1,083	$1,077	$1,071	$1,065	$1,059	$13,107
Depreciation expense	$729	$729	$729	$729	$729	$8,750
Net profit	$2,368	$2,415	$2,463	$2,510	$2,557	$27,579

Profit and loss statement (second year)

Quarter	Q1	2 Q2	Q3	Q4	2
Sales	$233,662	$292,077	$315,443	$327,126	$1,168,308
Cost of goods sold	$143,245	$179,056	$193,380	$200,543	$716,224
Gross margin	38.70%	38.70%	38.70%	38.70%	38.70%
Operating income	$90,417	$113,021	$122,063	$126,584	$452,084
Expenses					
Payroll	$38,728	$48,410	$52,283	$54,219	$193,640
General and administrative	$5,242	$6,552	$7,076	$7,338	$26,208
Marketing expenses	$1,168	$1,460	$1,577	$1,636	$5,842
Professional fees and licensure	$1,075	$1,344	$1,451	$1,505	$5,376
Insurance costs	$417	$522	$563	$584	$2,086
Vehicle maintenance costs	$3,871	$4,839	$5,226	$5,420	$19,356
Rent and utilities	$2,993	$3,741	$4,040	$4,190	$14,963
Miscellaneous costs	$2,804	$3,505	$3,785	$3,926	$14,020
Payroll taxes	$5,809	$7,262	$7,842	$8,133	$29,046
Total operating costs	$62,107	$77,634	$83,845	$86,950	$310,535
EBITDA	$28,310	$35,387	$38,218	$39,634	$141,549
Federal income tax	$8,537	$10,672	$11,525	$11,952	$42,686
State income tax	$1,294	$1,617	$1,746	$1,811	$6,468
Interest expense	$3,138	$3,080	$3,020	$2,959	$12,197
Depreciation expense	$2,188	$2,188	$2,188	$2,188	$8,750
Net profit	$13,154	$17,832	$19,739	$20,724	$71,448

Profit and loss statement (third year)

Quarter	Q1	Q2	Q3	Q4	3
Sales	$273,384	$341,730	$369,068	$382,738	$1,366,920
Cost of goods sold	$167,596	$209,495	$226,255	$234,635	$ 837,982
Gross margin	38.70%	38.70%	38.70%	38.70%	38.70%
Operating income	$105,788	$132,235	$142,813	$148,103	$ 528,939
Expenses					
Payroll	$ 39,890	$ 49,862	$ 53,851	$ 55,846	$ 199,449
General and administrative	$ 5,451	$ 6,814	$ 7,359	$ 7,632	$ 27,256
Marketing expenses	$ 1,367	$ 1,709	$ 1,845	$ 1,914	$ 6,835
Professional fees and licensure	$ 1,107	$ 1,384	$ 1,495	$ 1,550	$ 5,537
Insurance costs	$ 438	$ 548	$ 591	$ 613	$ 2,191
Vehicle maintenance costs	$ 4,258	$ 5,323	$ 5,749	$ 5,962	$ 21,291
Rent and utilities	$ 3,142	$ 3,928	$ 4,242	$ 4,399	$ 15,711
Miscellaneous costs	$ 3,281	$ 4,101	$ 4,429	$ 4,593	$ 16,403
Payroll taxes	$ 5,983	$ 7,479	$ 8,078	$ 8,377	$ 29,917
Total operating costs	$ 64,918	$ 81,147	$ 87,639	$ 90,885	$ 324,590
EBITDA	$ 40,870	$ 51,087	$ 55,174	$ 57,218	$ 204,349
Federal income tax	$ 12,748	$ 15,935	$ 17,209	$ 17,847	$ 63,738
State income tax	$ 1,931	$ 2,414	$ 2,607	$ 2,704	$ 9,657
Interest expense	$ 2,897	$ 2,834	$ 2,769	$ 2,702	$ 11,202
Depreciation expense	$ 2,188	$ 2,188	$ 2,188	$ 2,188	$ 8,750
Net profit	$ 21,106	$ 27,717	$ 30,401	$ 31,777	$ 111,001

7.11 Three Year Cash Flow Analysis

Cash flow analysis (first year)

Month	1	2	3	4	5	6	7
Cash from operations	$ 2,770	$ 2,816	$ 2,863	$ 2,910	$ 2,957	$ 3,004	$ 3,051
Cash from receivables	$ 0	$ 0	$ 0	$ 0	$ 0	$ 0	$ 0
Operating cash inflow	$ 2,770	$ 2,816	$ 2,863	$ 2,910	$ 2,957	$ 3,004	$ 3,051
Other cash inflows							
Equity investment	$ 25,000	$ 0	$ 0	$ 0	$ 0	$ 0	$ 0
Increased borrowings	$150,000	$ 0	$ 0	$ 0	$ 0	$ 0	$ 0
Sales of business assets	$ 0	$ 0	$ 0	$ 0	$ 0	$ 0	$ 0
A/P increases	$ 3,159	$ 3,159	$ 3,159	$ 3,159	$ 3,159	$ 3,159	$ 3,159
Total other cash inflows	$178,159	$ 3,159	$ 3,159	$ 3,159	$ 3,159	$ 3,159	$ 3,159
Total cash inflow	$180,928	$ 5,975	$ 6,022	$ 6,068	$ 6,115	$ 6,162	$ 6,209
Cash outflows							
Repayment of principal	$ 775	$ 781	$ 787	$ 793	$ 799	$ 805	$ 811
A/P decreases	$ 2,075	$ 2,075	$ 2,075	$ 2,075	$ 2,075	$ 2,075	$ 2,075
A/R increases	$ 0	$ 0	$ 0	$ 0	$ 0	$ 0	$ 0
Asset purchases	$122,500	$ 0	$ 0	$ 0	$ 0	$ 0	$ 0
Dividends	$ 0	$ 0	$ 0	$ 0	$ 0	$ 0	$ 0
Total cash outflows	$125,350	$ 2,856	$ 2,862	$ 2,867	$ 2,873	$ 2,879	$ 2,885
Net cash flow	$ 55,578	$ 3,119	$ 3,160	$ 3,201	$ 3,242	$ 3,283	$ 3,324
Cash balance	$ 55,578	$58,697	$61,857	$65,058	$68,300	$71,583	$74,906

Cash flow analysis (first year cont.)

Month	8	9	10	11	12	1
Cash from operations	$ 3,098	$ 3,145	$ 3,192	$ 3,239	$ 3,286	$ 36,329
Cash from receivables	$ 0	$ 0	$ 0	$ 0	$ 0	$ 0
Operating cash inflow	**$ 3,098**	**$ 3,145**	**$ 3,192**	**$ 3,329**	**$ 3,286**	**$ 36,329**
Other cash inflows						
Equity investment	$ 0	$ 0	$ 0	$ 0	$ 0	$ 25,000
Increased borrowings	$ 0	$ 0	$ 0	$ 0	$ 0	$150,000
Sales of business assets	$ 0	$ 0	$ 0	$ 0	$ 0	$ 0
A/P increases	$ 3,159	$ 3,159	$ 3,159	$ 3,159	$ 3,159	$ 37,902
Total other cash inflows	**$ 3,159**	**$ 3,159**	**$ 3,159**	**$ 3,159**	**$ 3,159**	**$212,902**
Total cash inflow	**$ 6,256**	**$ 6,303**	**$ 6,350**	**$ 6,397**	**$ 6,445**	**$249,231**
Cash outflows						
Repayment of principal	$ 817	$ 823	$ 829	$ 835	$ 842	$ 9,695
A/P decreases	$ 2,075	$ 2,075	$ 2,075	$ 2,075	$ 2,075	$ 24,897
A/R increases	$ 0	$ 0	$ 0	$ 0	$ 0	$ 0
Asset purchases	$ 0	$ 0	$ 0	$ 0	$ 0	$122,500
Dividends	$ 0	$ 0	$ 0	$ 0	$25,430	$ 25,430
Total cash outflows	**$ 2,892**	**$ 2,898**	**$ 2,904**	**$ 2,910**	**$28,346**	**$182,522**
Net cash flow	**$ 3,365**	**$ 3,406**	**$ 3,446**	**$ 3,487**	**−$21,902**	**$ 66,708**
Cash balance	**$78,271**	**$81,676**	**$85,123**	**$88,610**	**$66,708**	**$ 66,708**

Cash flow analysis (second year)

Quarter	Q1	2			2
		Q2	Q3	Q4	
Cash from operations	$16,040	$20,050	$21,654	$22,456	$ 80,198
Cash from receivables	$ 0	$ 0	$ 0	$ 0	$ 0
Operating cash inflow	**$16,040**	**$20,050**	**$21,654**	**$22,456**	**$ 80,198**
Other cash inflows					
Equity investment	$ 0	$ 0	$ 0	$ 0	$ 0
Increased borrowings	$ 0	$ 0	$ 0	$ 0	$ 0
Sales of business assets	$ 0	$ 0	$ 0	$ 0	$ 0
A/P increases	$ 8,717	$10,897	$11,769	$12,204	$ 43,587
Total other cash inflows	**$ 8,717**	**$10,897**	**$11,769**	**$12,204**	**$ 43,587**
Total cash inflow	**$24,757**	**$30,946**	**$33,422**	**$34,660**	**$123,786**
Cash outflows					
Repayment of principal	$ 2,563	$ 2,621	$ 2,680	$ 2,741	$ 10,605
A/P decreases	$ 5,975	$ 7,469	$ 8,067	$ 8,365	$ 29,876
A/R increases	$ 0	$ 0	$ 0	$ 0	$ 0
Asset purchases	$ 4,010	$ 5,012	$ 5,413	$ 5,614	$ 20,050
Dividends	$11,228	$14,035	$15,157	$15,719	$ 56,139
Total cash outflows	**$23,776**	**$29,137**	**$31,318**	**$32,439**	**$116,669**
Net cash flow	**$ 981**	**$ 1,809**	**$ 2,104**	**$ 2,221**	**$ 7,116**
Cash balance	**$67,690**	**$69,499**	**$71,604**	**$73,825**	**$ 73,825**

Cash flow analysis (third year)

Quarter	Q1	3 Q2	Q3	Q4	3
Cash from operations	$23,950	$29,938	$32,333	$33,530	$119,751
Cash from receivables	$ 0	$ 0	$ 0	$ 0	$ 0
Operating cash inflow	**$23,950**	**$29,938**	**$32,333**	**$33,530**	**$119,751**
Other cash inflows					
Equity investment	$ 0	$ 0	$ 0	$ 0	$ 0
Increased borrowings	$ 0	$ 0	$ 0	$ 0	$ 0
Sales of business assets	$ 0	$ 0	$ 0	$ 0	$ 0
A/P increases	$10,025	$12,531	$13,534	$14,035	$ 50,125
Total other cash inflows	**$10,025**	**$12,531**	**$13,534**	**$14,035**	**$ 50,125**
Total cash inflow	**$33,975**	**$42,469**	**$45,867**	**$47,565**	**$169,876**
Cash outflows					
Repayment of principal	$ 2,803	$ 2,867	$ 2,932	$ 2,998	$ 11,599
A/P decreases	$ 7,170	$ 8,963	$ 9,680	$10,038	$ 35,852
A/R increases	$ 0	$ 0	$ 0	$ 0	$ 0
Asset purchases	$ 5,988	$ 7,484	$ 8,083	$ 8,383	$ 29,938
Dividends	$16,765	$20,956	$22,633	$23,471	$ 83,826
Total cash outflows	**$32,726**	**$40,270**	**$43,328**	**$44,890**	**$161,214**
Net cash flow	**$ 1,249**	**$ 2,199**	**$ 2,539**	**$ 2,675**	**$ 8,662**
Cash balance	**$75,074**	**$77,273**	**$79,812**	**$82,487**	**$ 82,487**

Baby Furniture Rental

Baby, Baby

799 S. Main St.
Sarasota, Florida 34236

Heidi Denler

Located in the Bradenton-Sarasota, Florida area, Baby, Baby will offer baby furniture and related accessories for those visiting the area. Alex and Jenny Johnston will be full owners and partners of Baby, Baby.

EXECUTIVE SUMMARY

Baby, Baby is a planned extension of a currently known, successful children's toy and game rental business called Granny's Attic. Located in the Bradenton-Sarasota, Florida area, Baby, Baby will offer baby furniture and related accessories for those visiting the area. Alex and Jenny Johnston will be full owners and partners of Baby, Baby.

The Bradenton-Sarasota, Florida region is a highly popular vacation destination for families. The success of Granny's Attic has encouraged the Johnstons to expand their current store, which offers baby and children's toys and games. Baby, Baby's location, adjoining Granny's Attic, will serve further needs of traveling families and families being visited by families with babies by offering safety-tested, disinfected cribs, high chairs, strollers, and other items too large to pack in the car or take on a plane. At least 1 percent of hotel rooms are booked by families with babies according to statistics. Baby, Baby will seek contracts with area hotels to rent baby furniture and accessories to their clientele.

Relationships have been secured with Graco and Fisher Price to offer cribs, playpens, strollers, high chairs, and walkers, in addition to such related items as crib sheets, floor mats, and stroller umbrellas.

COMPANY SUMMARY

Baby, Baby is an expansion of Granny's Attic, which has proven extremely successful in the Bradenton-Sarasota, Florida, area after only a year in existence. The Johnstons bring not only experience with Granny's Attic, along with that shop's reputation for high-quality, sanitized, safe product rental, but also Johnston's background in law and his parent's expertise in accounting (father Jim was a CPA) and education/early childhood (mother Kay was an elementary school teacher and principal). Although Jim and Kay Johnston are co-owners with the younger Johnstons for Granny's Attic, Baby, Baby will be a partner ownership of Alex and Jenny Johnston.

MANAGEMENT SUMMARY

Jenny and Alex Johnston will assume full ownership of Baby, Baby and will be the primary employees of the shop for the first six months, along with a permanent delivery team of two men who can carry and set up the furniture at the rental location. During high-volume vacation times they will hire part-time staff to assist with rentals, cleaning and sanitizing, and delivery.

As at Granny's Attic, Jenny will handle research and purchasing and Alex will handle legal and in-store responsibilities. Both will train employees to provide high-quality, efficient, friendly service.

MISSION STATEMENT

The mission of Baby, Baby is to provide visitors with babies to the Sarasota-Bradenton area with high-quality, safety tested and inspected, clean furniture for the duration of their stay, whether it comprise a weekend, a week, or an extended stay, or in a hotel, resort, or home of a friend or family member.

VISION STATEMENT

The Johnstons will build on their customer base from Granny's Attic and expand to include local hotels and resorts that will subcontract rentals of baby furniture and accessories for their guests with babies. They will extend their customer loyalty club cards from Granny's Attic and continue to advertise via flyers, newspaper advertising, and word of mouth.

VALUES STATEMENT

The baby furniture available for rental from Baby, Baby will comprise high-quality, name brand products that will be well-maintained and sanitized between uses. Whether a customer arranges a rental via the store web site or in person, a warm, congenial atmosphere will be readily apparent, encouraging return business on a visitor's next trip to the area.

The risk inherent in renting baby furniture can be significant as malfunctions can cause injuries that lead to lawsuits. For that reason, major manufacturers will be the only suppliers of items to be rented. In addition, inspections will be made at the end of each rental, with maintenance or replacement occurring as necessary. Anything deemed even slightly defective will be replaced or, if possible, repaired, before being leased to another customer. Liability insurance will be in place based on the recommendations of Baby, Baby's lawyer and insurance carrier. Safety is a primary concern, and this policy will be prominently displayed in the store and on all advertising and brochures.

BUSINESS PHILOSOPHY

Baby, Baby will offer a welcoming, congenial atmosphere and high-quality products. The Johnstons recognize that return business relies on customer service and goodwill as much as it does on advertisements in local print, radio, and television media. Building on the success of Granny's Attic, the Johnstons expect growth in customer base along with profitability within six to eight months.

A sufficient inventory and assistance in selection of baby furniture needs, along with friendly, efficient customer service, are key components of a successful enterprise.

GOALS AND OBJECTIVES

Goals and objectives for Baby, Baby include:

- Providing high-quality, safe, sanitized furniture for families traveling with babies to rent while visiting family and friends or simply on vacation

- Creating additional working relationships with more manufacturers of baby furniture and accessories

- Increasing inventory to increase potential rentals

- Hiring additional employees

- Increasing advertising

- Creating additional working relationships with local hotels, resorts, and condo associations to increase potential rentals

- Achieving profitability on

- To be profitable within a year

ORGANIZATION STRUCTURE

Baby, Baby is a partnership between Jenny and Alex Johnston, who share ownership in Granny's Attic with Alex's parents, Jim and Kay Johnston. Granny's Attic, a toy and game rental company, has been operating for 18 months, having achieved profitability within the first six months of business.

While Alex and Jenny will be the front of the business, they will have a staff of two assistants to man the shop and check the computer for requests, as well as a delivery team comprised of two employees to carry and set up rented furniture at its destination. Initially, Alex and Jenny will verify pricing and review contracts, but as the assistants gain experience, they will assume full responsibility for those tasks.

At peak vacation times, including Thanksgiving, school holidays, Christmas, Hanukkah, Easter, and spring break, part-time help will be hired to assist, particularly with deliveries.

ADVERTISING AND PROMOTION

Baby, Baby will serve two customer bases: families on vacation or visiting family and friends who can't haul cribs, strollers, and other large needs for babies, and hotels, resorts, and rental properties who can call on Baby, Baby for guest needs instead of bearing the burden of the expense of maintaining their own inventory.

Advertising will be easily tied to a strong customer base from partner store, Granny's Attic. The two stores will combine to serve families with children of all ages, which will be heavily promoted in the two main local newspapers and in community publications. Brochures will be available at local stores and will be placed with hotel and resort concierge and reservations desks.

Because most visitors to the Sarasota-Bradenton area return on a regular basis, Baby, Baby will use the same tracking program as Granny's Attic's Loyalty Club card. That card has a magnetic strip that saves information to track rentals and offer discounts on future rentals. It will also enable staff to offer suggestions for rentals on return trips based on ages of children that are easily seen on the database.

Advertising will also include press releases to local media outlets and radio and TV spots promoting both Granny's Attic and Baby, Baby, with testimonials from satisfied families and hotel and resort concierges. The web site for both stores will allow customers to ask questions and easily pre-order so they can move right in to their accommodations with everything ready for baby.

CUSTOMER BASE

Families who travel have had to rely on rickety portable cribs from a hotel's housekeeping service, or putting their infants to bed in a cumbersome pack n' play playpen. With the use of the latter, a baby doesn't know if he or she is being put in the space to sleep or to play. By renting baby furniture similar to what they have at home avoids that confusion and makes it easier for baby to sleep and nap.

The customer base for Baby, Baby will be based on that for Granny's Attic, including hotel and resort concierge/reservations desks, and rental property managers and owners. The Johnstons will make personal contact with these people to secure contracts for baby furniture rentals through Baby, Baby.

PRODUCTS AND SERVICES

Products offered for rental to area visitors include:

- Cribs
- Rollaways for toddlers
- Bassinet
- Pack and Ply
- Portacrib
- High chairs
- Booster seats
- Youth chair
- Changing table
- Baby monitors
- Safety gates
- Walkers
- Bouncy seats
- Baby swings
- Umbrella strollers
- Twin stroller
- Swivel wheel jogger
- Double stroller
- Double jogger

All items available for rental will be purchased new from reputable manufacturers of baby products, including Graco, Fisher Price, and Childcraft, among others.

Delivery service and set up will be included in the rental pricing. Clients will be able to pick up most items if they so desire. Staff will be available to help clients select needed items and set up delivery or pick up via the telephone, fax, and web site order form. The option to bundle high-traffic furniture and equipment will offer added convenience along with discounted pricing.

LOCATION

Baby, Baby will be located immediately adjacent to Granny's Attic. The site has proven to be successful for the original toy and game rental shop and is centrally located for delivery to local hotels, resorts, and rental properties in the Bradenton-Sarasota area.

STORE DESIGN AND EQUIPMENT

Most customers will not be walking in to the store to secure their rentals, most of which will be finalized over the phone or online. Those who do come in will find a professional, businesslike atmosphere with samples of clean, sanitized, baby furniture shrink-wrapped on the floor. The majority of the furniture available for rent will be stored at the rear of the store for ease of loading onto the delivery van at the back alley loading dock.

There will be two desks and accompanying chairs for staff and customers at each where rentals will be finalized. A laptop will be available for each desk, along with a shared printer.

Shelving will be placed along the wall separating Baby, Baby from Granny's Attic, next to the archway joining the two stores. Baby furniture accessories, including sheets, bath towels, stroller and bouncy seat covers, and stroller umbrellas/toys will be shrink-wrapped and stored on these shelves, ready for families to rent.

Baby, Baby will share office space and employee break space with Granny's Attic. A desk will be added to the office, along with a second all-in-one printer.

The back two-thirds of the storefront will serve sanitizing, shrink-wrapping, storage, and maintenance needs for Baby, Baby.

FINANCIAL

Baby, Baby will require a 50 percent deposit plus a security deposit of 25 percent of the value of the rental on booking a rental, with the remainder to be paid on delivery or pickup. There is one other baby rental company in the immediate area, and pricing will be competitive.

Start-up costs for inventory will include:

- Purchase of a dozen cribs, half a dozen high chairs, two dozen strollers of various styles (umbrella, twin, individual), half a dozen bouncy seats,

- Purchase of sheets, stroller and bouncy seat covers, etc.

- Purchase of stroller umbrellas and toys

Start-up costs for the office will include:

- Two laptops

- One black and white printer

- Letterhead

- Brochures

- Business cards

- Flyers

- Addition of a dedicated phone/fax line

- Expanded Internet access

- Security deposits

- Licensing and registration fees with local, state, and federal governments

- Shrink-wrapping machine

- Sanitizing machine

Ongoing expenses will include:

- Rent

- Utilities

- Payroll, benefits, taxes, etc.

- Delivery van lease(s)

- Insurance (liability, key man, property-casualty)

- Alarm system

- Advertising

- Web site maintenance

PROFESSIONAL AND ADVISORY SUPPORT

Baby, Baby will share the professional support system of Granny's Attic. Legal issues will be handled by local small business attorney Leonard Sales. Financial matters will be handled by CPA Edgar Lytle. Granny's Attic and Baby, Baby will enjoy a discounted fee scale from both professionals because much of the work will be overlapping.

BUSINESS AND GROWTH STRATEGY

By forging contracts with major baby furniture manufacturers Baby, Baby will be able to offer high-quality, reliable rentals to its customers. Contracts with area hotels, resorts, condo associations, and rental property owners/managers will build on the customer base from partner store Granny's Attic.

As with Granny's Attic, Baby, Baby's focus will be on client needs:

- High quality furniture and accessories

- Reasonable, competitive pricing

- Short-term or long term rentals

- Delivery and set up

- Sanitized, shrink-wrapped items

- Customer service whether in person, on the phone, or via fax or interactive web site
- Attention to safety

At the end of the first year of operation, the owners will assess needs and make adjustments. Among things to be considered adding would be a diaper service and diaper pails, as well as disposable diapers and baby foods.

COMPETITION

As of late 2012, there is one other baby furniture rental business in the area. ABC Rentals has been in business more than 30 years, with an established clientele. However, it is limited to furniture and toys for babies. Because Baby, Baby is directly linked to Granny's Attic, it has the competitive advantage of being a one-stop shop for families with children of all ages. The ability to build on the customer base of Granny's Attic will be a competitive edge as well.

The Johnstons will develop relationships initially with two major baby furniture manufacturers: Graco and Fisher Price. Both are well-known names that are quickly recognized by anyone who has small children. Maintenance will be of the utmost priority in addition to sanitizing after each use.

Pricing will be competitive and affordable for traveling families, and will be available on the web site or by contacting the store directly. To build clientele, the Johnstons will be relying on word of mouth advertising, particularly from current customers of Granny's Attic, along with brochures distributed at local hotels, resorts, and rental properties and advertisements in *The Bradenton Herald* and *The Sarasota Herald Tribune*.

WEB SITE

The current web site for Granny's Attic will include a page about Baby, Baby, as well as a link to the actual Baby, Baby web site. They have contracted with the builders of the Granny's Attic web site to complete the update and new site for Baby, Baby. Potential clients can access these sites from anywhere on the globe to preview and even combine rental requests for babies and children. Because the sites for the two shops are interactive, keywords must be selected carefully to encourage search engine results.

CONCLUSION

The Johnstons project that Baby, Baby will follow the success of Granny's Attic by being profitable with six to nine months of operation. The customer base of the latter store will be used to build a clientele for the new store, combining to form a unique option for traveling families. Convenience, reliability, and safety, while reducing and even eliminating the hassles and headaches of traveling with a baby, are expected to ensure new and repeat business. Bundle options of furniture and equipment will offer added convenience along with discounted pricing.

Banquet Facility

Sycamore Hills Banquet Center

99011 W. 57th St.
New York, NY 10001

BizPlanDB.com

Sycamore Hills Banquet Center, Inc. is a New York based corporation that will provide banquet hall rental and catering services to customers in its targeted market. The company was founded by Vernon Niebauer.

1.0 EXECUTIVE SUMMARY

The purpose of this business plan is to raise $500,000 for the development of a banquet hall while showcasing the expected financials and operations over the next three years. Sycamore Hills Banquet Center, Inc. is a New York based corporation that will provide banquet hall rental and catering services to customers in its targeted market. The company was founded by Vernon Niebauer.

1.1 The Services

Management intends to acquire and develop a wedding and events venue that will act as a standalone site for major parties. The business will only host one event per day, which will allow clients privacy while they celebrate their wedding or event. The venue will feature a beautiful banquet hall that will be developed from a converted home. The grounds will feature immaculate grounds keeping and landscaping.

The third section of the business plan will further describe the services offered by Sycamore Hills Banquet Center.

1.2 Financing

Mr. Niebauer is seeking to raise $500,000 from as a bank loan. The interest rate and loan agreement are to be further discussed during negotiation. This business plan assumes that the business will receive a 10 year loan with a 9% fixed interest rate. The financing will be used for the following:

- Development of the Sycamore Hills Banquet Center location.
- Financing for the first six months of operation.
- Capital to purchase FF&E.

Mr. Niebauer will contribute $100,000 to the venture.

1.3 Mission Statement

Management is committed to providing the highest quality venue for wedding and events planning within the New York area.

25

1.4 Management Team

The company was founded by Vernon Niebauer. Mr. Niebauer has more than 10 years of experience in the events planning and management industry. Through his expertise, he will be able to bring the operations of the business to profitability within its first year of operations.

1.5 Sales Forecasts

Mr. Niebauer expects a strong rate of growth at the start of operations. Below are the expected financials over the next three years.

Proforma profit and loss (yearly)

Year	1	2	3
Sales	$567,378	$612,768	$661,790
Operating costs	$299,647	$310,343	$321,482
EBITDA	$182,837	$210,741	$241,288
Taxes, interest, and depreciation	$118,356	$115,493	$126,856
Net profit	$ 64,481	$ 95,248	$114,431

Sales, operating costs, and profit forecast

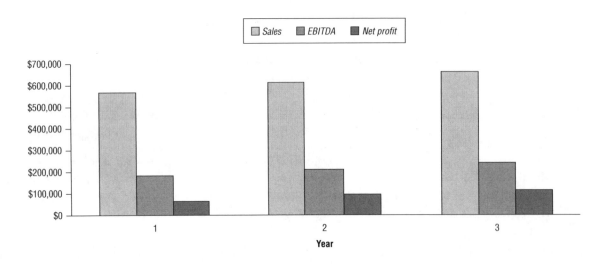

1.6 Expansion Plan

In the future, Management will begin to develop ancillary and complimentary services such as bar, catering, and complete events planning services that will provide clients with a complete wedding or event hosting package. Once operations commence, the business will begin to apply for an onsite alcohol license that will allow the business to offer beer, wine, and liquor on the venue's premises.

2.0 COMPANY AND FINANCING SUMMARY

2.1 Registered Name and Corporate Structure

Sycamore Hills Banquet Center, Inc. is registered as a corporation in the State of New York.

2.2 Required Funds

At this time, Sycamore Hills Banquet Center requires $500,000 of debt funds. Mr. Niebauer will provide $100,000 to the venture. Below is a breakdown of how these funds will be used:

Projected startup costs

Facility acquisition	$450,000
Working capital	$ 35,000
FF&E	$ 20,000
Facility improvements	$ 30,000
Security deposits	$ 5,000
Insurance	$ 2,500
Kitchen FF&E	$ 35,000
Marketing budget	$ 17,500
Miscellaneous and unforeseen costs	$ 5,000
Total startup costs	**$600,000**

2.3 Investor Equity

Mr. Niebauer is not seeking an investment from a third party at this time.

2.4 Management Equity

Vernon Niebauer owns 100% of Sycamore Hills Banquet Center, Inc.

2.5 Exit Strategy

If the business is very successful, Mr. Niebauer may seek to sell the business to a third party for a significant earnings multiple. Most likely, the Company will hire a qualified business broker to sell the business on behalf of Sycamore Hills Banquet Center. Based on historical numbers, the business could fetch a sales premium of up to 4 times earnings.

3.0 SERVICES

Below is a description of the services offered by Sycamore Hills Banquet Center.

3.1 Venue Hosting

The business will only host one event per day so that each of the clients has exclusive access to the facility and its premises. Sycamore Hills Banquet Center will also feature separate rooms for the bride and grooms in the event that the wedding is held on the Company's premises. The facility will feature an immaculate garden and landscaping.

3.2 Event Planning

The Company, in addition to acting as the hosting venue, will help wedding couples, businesses, and other people hosting events, arrange for all of the catering, entertainment, and alcohol services that will be hosted on site. The business will also partner with events and wedding planners that operate within the New York area.

4.0 STRATEGIC AND MARKET ANALYSIS

4.1 Economic Outlook

This section of the analysis will detail the economic climate, the banquet hall industry, the customer profile, and the competition that the business will face as it progresses through its business operations.

Currently, the economic market condition in the United States is moderate. The meltdown of the sub prime mortgage market coupled with increasing gas prices has led many people to believe that the US is on the cusp of a double dip economic recession. This slowdown in the economy has also greatly impacted real estate sales, which has halted to historical lows. This may impact Sycamore Hills Banquet Center's revenues as people will host less luxurious or fewer events.

4.2 Industry Analysis

The leasing of banquet halls in the United States is an extremely large business. The US Economic Census indicates that there are approximately 5,000 companies that specialize in the rental of banquet halls and event locations. Each year, these businesses aggregately generate more than $5 billion dollars a year of revenue and provide jobs for more than 40,000 people. The growth of this industry has remained in lockstep with the growth of the economy in general. The number of facilities operating within this industry has increased 15% over last five years while gross receipts have increased almost two fold.

4.3 Customer Profile

Sycamore Hills Banquet Center anticipates that its average client will be a couple seeking to get married or a local business (or corporation) seeking to host a large scale event. Management has outlined several demographics among its target client market, including:

- Has an annual household income of $50,000 or more.

- Is seeking to spend approximately $20,000 on their wedding or event

- Wants privacy within a venue (i.e. one event hosted per day)

- Needs an event or wedding planner

Manhattan is an island borough of New York City, New York, USA, coterminous with New York County. According to the U.S. Census Bureau estimates, there were 1,720,867 people residing in the borough. Manhattan's population is spread out with 16.8% under the age of 18, 10.2% from 18 to 24, 38.3% from 25 to 44, 22.6% from 45 to 64, and 12.2% who were 65 years of age or older. The median age is 36 years. For every 100 females, there were 90.3 males. For every 100 females age 18 and over, there were 87.9 males. The annual household income for an average individual within Manhattan is $49,000 while median family income is $75,000.

4.4 Competition

Banquet halls and venues have significant competitive issues that must be dealt with on an ongoing basis. Foremost, the facility must be immaculate as people (or businesses) are spending large sums of money on important events. As such, Management has found an outstanding property within the New York metropolitan area that will attract the above mentioned demographics for hosted events.

5.0 MARKETING PLAN

Sycamore Hills Banquet Center intends to maintain an extensive marketing campaign that will ensure maximum visibility for the business in its targeted market. Below is an overview of the marketing strategies and objectives of Sycamore Hills Banquet Center.

5.1 Marketing Objectives

- Develop an online presence by developing a website and placing the Company's name and contact information with online directories.

- Establish connections with local event and wedding planners.

- Develop relationships with local businesses for their event planning and corporate event needs.

5.2 Marketing Strategies

Sycamore Hills Banquet Center, Inc. will promote the business through a number of traditional marketing and advertising channels. The foremost marketing strategy that the business will use, will be to develop connections with local event and wedding planners so that the business can continually book events through these planners. This will greatly decrease the amount of advertising required by the business as once a rapport is established with these vendors, they will continually refer business to the Company.

Sycamore Hills Banquet Center will also maintain a strong level of print and media advertising among local newspapers, event planning publications, and other news medium. The business will also maintain listings in the local Yellow Books.

The facility will also maintain a website that has a virtual tour of the facility in addition to standard contact information and booking resources.

5.3 Pricing

Management anticipates that each event will generate approximately $20,000 to $30,000 for the business. The anticipated gross margins will be 85 cents for each dollar of revenue.

6.0 ORGANIZATIONAL PLAN AND PERSONNEL SUMMARY

6.1 Corporate Organization

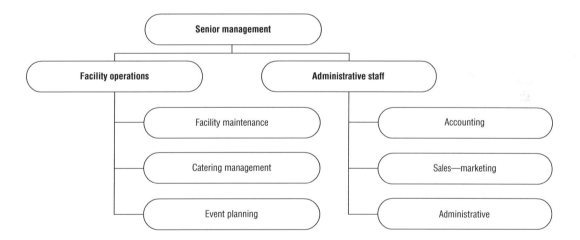

6.2 Organizational Budget

Personnel plan—yearly

Year	1	2	3
Owner	$ 40,000	$ 41,200	$ 42,436
General manager	$ 35,000	$ 36,050	$ 37,132
Owner's assistant	$ 32,500	$ 33,475	$ 34,479
Bookkeeper (P/T)	$ 12,500	$ 12,875	$ 13,261
Facility staff	$ 80,000	$ 82,400	$ 84,872
Total	**$200,000**	**$206,000**	**$212,180**

Numbers of personnel

Owner	1	1	1
General manager	1	1	1
Owner's assistant	1	1	1
Bookkeeper (P/T)	1	1	1
Facility staff	4	4	4
Totals	**8**	**8**	**8**

Personnel expense breakdown

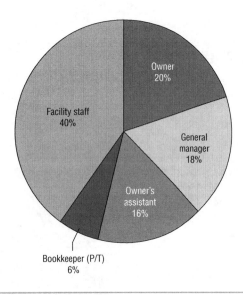

7.0 FINANCIAL PLAN

7.1 Underlying Assumptions

The Company has based its proforma financial statements on the following:

- Sycamore Hills Banquet Center will have an annual revenue growth rate of 13.4% per year.

- The Owner will acquire $500,000 of debt funds to develop the business.

- The loan will have a 10 year term with a 9% interest rate.

7.2 Sensitivity Analysis

In the event of an economic downturn, the business may have a decline in its revenues. Sycamore Hills Banquet Center, Inc. is offering a reasonably priced venue for wedding and banquet events. However, in the event of a steep economic decline, Management expects that its revenue will decrease as people host events at alternative, less expensive venues. In the event of a decline in revenues, the business will be able to maintain profitability (after debt service is paid) because the business generates significantly high gross margins from the rental of its facility.

7.3 Source of Funds

Financing

Equity contributions

Management investment	$ 10,000.00
Total equity financing	**$ 10,000.00**

Banks and lenders

Banks and lenders	$ 100,000.00
Total debt financing	**$100,000.00**
Total financing	**$110,000.00**

7.4 General Assumptions

General assumptions

Year	1	2	3
Short term interest rate	9.5%	9.5%	9.5%
Long term interest rate	10.0%	10.0%	10.0%
Federal tax rate	33.0%	33.0%	33.0%
State tax rate	5.0%	5.0%	5.0%
Personnel taxes	15.0%	15.0%	15.0%

7.5 Profit and Loss Statements

Proforma profit and loss (yearly)

Year	1	2	3
Sales	**$567,378**	**$612,768**	**$661,790**
Cost of goods sold	$ 84,893	$ 91,685	$ 99,020
Gross margin	85.04%	85.04%	85.04%
Operating income	**$482,485**	**$521,083**	**$562,770**
Expenses			
Payroll	$200,000	$206,000	$212,180
General and administrative	$ 25,200	$ 26,208	$ 27,256
Marketing expenses	$ 2,837	$ 3,064	$ 3,309
Professional fees and licensure	$ 5,219	$ 5,376	$ 5,537
Insurance costs	$ 1,987	$ 2,086	$ 2,191
Travel and vehicle costs	$ 7,596	$ 8,356	$ 9,191
Utilities	$ 20,000	$ 21,000	$ 22,050
Miscellaneous costs	$ 6,809	$ 7,353	$ 7,941
Payroll taxes	$ 30,000	$ 30,900	$ 31,827
Total operating costs	**$299,647**	**$310,343**	**$321,482**
EBITDA	**$182,837**	**$210,741**	**$241,288**
Federal income tax	$ 60,336	$ 58,169	$ 68,379
State income tax	$ 9,142	$ 8,813	$ 10,360
Interest expense	$ 34,839	$ 34,472	$ 34,078
Depreciation expenses	$ 14,038	$ 14,038	$ 14,038
Net profit	**$ 64,481**	**$ 95,248**	**$114,431**
Profit margin	**11.36%**	**15.54%**	**17.29%**

Sales, operating costs, and profit forecast

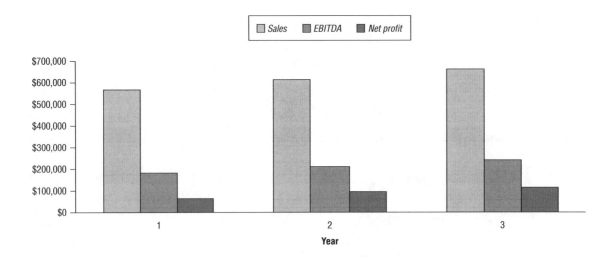

7.6 Cash Flow Analysis

Proforma cash flow analysis—yearly

Year	1	2	3
Cash from operations	$ 78,520	$109,287	$128,470
Cash from receivables	$ 0	$ 0	$ 0
Operating cash inflow	**$ 78,520**	**$109,287**	**$128,470**
Other cash inflows			
Equity investment	$100,000	$ 0	$ 0
Increased borrowings	$500,000	$ 0	$ 0
Sales of business assets	$ 0	$ 0	$ 0
A/P increases	$ 37,902	$ 43,587	$ 50,125
Total other cash inflows	**$637,902**	**$ 43,587**	**$ 50,125**
Total cash inflow	**$716,422**	**$152,874**	**$178,595**
Cash outflows			
Repayment of principal	$ 5,079	$ 5,446	$ 5,840
A/P decreases	$ 24,897	$ 29,876	$ 35,852
A/R increases	$ 0	$ 0	$ 0
Asset purchases	$547,500	$ 16,393	$ 19,270
Dividends	$ 62,816	$ 87,429	$102,776
Total cash outflows	**$640,292**	**$139,145**	**$163,738**
Net cash flow	**$ 76,130**	**$ 13,729**	**$ 14,857**
Cash balance	**$ 76,130**	**$ 89,859**	**$104,716**

Proforma cash flow (yearly)

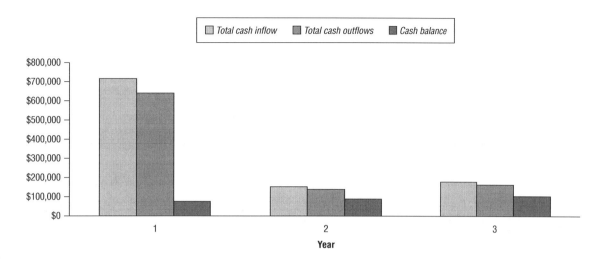

7.7 Balance Sheet

Proforma balance sheet—yearly

Year	1	2	3
Assets			
Cash	$ 76,130	$ 89,859	$104,716
Amortized development/expansion costs	$ 42,500	$ 44,139	$ 46,066
Kitchen equipment	$ 20,000	$ 32,295	$ 46,748
FF&E	$ 35,000	$ 37,459	$ 40,350
Plant, property, and equipment	$450,000	$472,500	$496,125
Accumulated depreciation	($ 14,038)	($ 28,077)	($ 42,115)
Total assets	**$609,591**	**$648,175**	**$691,889**
Liabilities and equity			
Accounts payable	$ 13,005	$ 26,716	$ 40,990
Long term liabilities	$494,921	$489,475	$484,029
Other liabilities	$ 0	$ 0	$ 0
Total liabilities	**$507,926**	**$516,191**	**$525,018**
Net worth	**$101,666**	**$131,984**	**$166,871**
Total liabilities and equity	**$609,591**	**$648,175**	**$691,889**

Proforma balance sheet

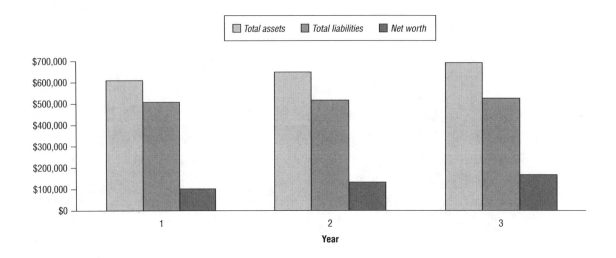

7.8 Breakeven Analysis

Monthly break even analysis

Year	1	2	3
Monthly revenue	$ 29,364	$ 30,412	$ 31,504
Yearly revenue	$352,371	$364,948	$378,047

Break even analysis

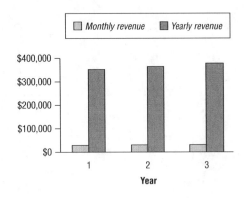

7.9 Business Ratios

Business ratios—yearly

Year	1	2	3
Sales			
Sales growth	0.00%	8.00%	8.00%
Gross margin	85.00%	85.00%	85.00%
Financials			
Profit margin	11.36%	15.54%	17.29%
Assets to liabilities	1.20	1.26	1.32
Equity to liabilities	0.20	0.26	0.32
Assets to equity	6.00	4.91	4.15
Liquidity			
Acid test	0.15	0.17	0.20
Cash to assets	0.12	0.14	0.15

7.10 Three Year Profit and Loss Statement

Profit and loss statement (first year)

Months	1	2	3	4	5	6	7
Sales	**$46,550**	**$46,683**	**$46,816**	**$46,949**	**$47,082**	**$47,215**	**$47,348**
Cost of goods sold	$ 6,965	$ 6,985	$ 7,005	$ 7,025	$ 7,045	$ 7,065	$ 7,084
Gross margin	85.00%	85.00%	85.00%	85.00%	85.00%	85.00%	85.00%
Operating income	**$39,585**	**$39,698**	**$39,811**	**$39,924**	**$40,037**	**$40,151**	**$40,264**
Expenses							
Payroll	$16,667	$16,667	$16,667	$16,667	$16,667	$16,667	$16,667
General and administrative	$ 2,100	$ 2,100	$ 2,100	$ 2,100	$ 2,100	$ 2,100	$ 2,100
Marketing expenses	$ 236	$ 236	$ 236	$ 236	$ 236	$ 236	$ 236
Professional fees and licensure	$ 435	$ 435	$ 435	$ 435	$ 435	$ 435	$ 435
Insurance costs	$ 166	$ 166	$ 166	$ 166	$ 166	$ 166	$ 166
Travel and vehicle costs	$ 633	$ 633	$ 633	$ 633	$ 633	$ 633	$ 633
Utilities	$ 1,677	$ 1,677	$ 1,677	$ 1,677	$ 1,677	$ 1,677	$ 1,677
Miscellaneous costs	$ 567	$ 567	$ 567	$ 567	$ 567	$ 567	$ 567
Payroll taxes	$ 2,500	$ 2,500	$ 2,500	$ 2,500	$ 2,500	$ 2,500	$ 2,500
Total operating costs	**$24,971**	**$24,971**	**$24,971**	**$24,971**	**$24,971**	**$24,971**	**$24,971**
EBITDA	**$14,614**	**$14,727**	**$14,841**	**$14,954**	**$15,067**	**$15,180**	**$15,293**
Federal income tax	$ 4,950	$ 4,964	$ 4,979	$ 4,993	$ 5,007	$ 5,021	$ 5,035
State income tax	$ 750	$ 752	$ 754	$ 756	$ 759	$ 761	$ 763
Interest expense	$ 2,917	$ 2,914	$ 2,912	$ 2,909	$ 2,907	$ 2,905	$ 2,902
Depreciation expense	$ 1,170	$ 1,170	$ 1,170	$ 1,170	$ 1,170	$ 1,170	$ 1,170
Net profit	**$ 4,828**	**$ 4,927**	**$ 5,026**	**$ 5,125**	**$ 5,224**	**$ 5,324**	**$ 5,423**

Profit and loss statement (first year cont.)

Month	8	9	10	11	12	1
Sales	$47,481	$47,614	$47,747	$47,880	$48,013	$567,378
Cost of goods sold	$ 7,104	$ 7,124	$ 7,144	$ 7,164	$ 7,184	$ 84,893
Gross margin	85.00%	85.00%	85.00%	85.00%	85.00%	85.00%
Operating income	$40,377	$40,490	$40,603	$40,716	$40,829	$482,485
Expenses						
Payroll	$16,667	$16,667	$16,667	$16,667	$16,667	$200,000
General and administrative	$ 2,100	$ 2,100	$ 2,100	$ 2,100	$ 2,100	$ 25,200
Marketing expenses	$ 236	$ 236	$ 236	$ 236	$ 236	$ 2,837
Professional fees and licensure	$ 435	$ 435	$ 435	$ 435	$ 435	$ 5,219
Insurance costs	$ 166	$ 166	$ 166	$ 166	$ 166	$ 1,987
Travel and vehicle costs	$ 633	$ 633	$ 633	$ 633	$ 633	$ 7,596
Utilities	$ 1,677	$ 1,677	$ 1,677	$ 1,677	$ 1,677	$ 20,000
Miscellaneous costs	$ 567	$ 567	$ 567	$ 567	$ 567	$ 6,809
Payroll taxes	$ 2,500	$ 2,500	$ 2,500	$ 2,500	$ 2,500	$ 30,000
Total operating costs	$24,971	$24,971	$24,971	$24,971	$24,971	$299,647
EBITDA	$15,406	$15,519	$15,632	$15,745	$15,858	$182,837
Federal income tax	$ 5,049	$ 5,063	$ 5,078	$ 5,092	$ 5,106	$ 60,336
State income tax	$ 765	$ 767	$ 769	$ 771	$ 774	$ 9,142
Interest expense	$ 2,900	$ 2,897	$ 2,895	$ 2,892	$ 2,890	$ 34,839
Depreciation expense	$ 1,170	$ 1,170	$ 1,170	$ 1,170	$ 1,170	$ 14,038
Net profit	$ 5,522	$ 5,622	$ 5,721	$ 5,820	$ 5,920	$ 64,481

Profit and loss statement (second year)

Quarter	Q1	2 Q2	Q3	Q4	2
Sales	$122,554	$153,192	$165,447	$171,575	$612,768
Cost of goods sold	$ 18,337	$ 22,921	$ 24,755	$ 25,672	$ 91,685
Gross margin	85.00%	85.00%	85.00%	85.00%	85.00%
Operating income	$104,217	$130,271	$140,693	$145,903	$521,083
Expenses					
Payroll	$ 41,200	$ 51,500	$ 55,620	$ 57,680	$206,000
General and administrative	$ 5,242	$ 6,552	$ 7,076	$ 7,338	$ 26,208
Marketing expenses	$ 613	$ 766	$ 827	$ 858	$ 3,064
Professional fees and licensure	$ 1,075	$ 1,344	$ 1,451	$ 1,505	$ 5,376
Insurance costs	$ 417	$ 522	$ 563	$ 584	$ 2,086
Travel and vehicle costs	$ 1,671	$ 2,089	$ 2,256	$ 2,340	$ 8,356
Utilities	$ 4,200	$ 5,250	$ 5,670	$ 5,880	$ 21,000
Miscellaneous costs	$ 1,471	$ 1,838	$ 1,985	$ 2,059	$ 7,353
Payroll taxes	$ 6,180	$ 7,725	$ 8,343	$ 8,652	$ 30,900
Total operating costs	$ 62,069	$ 77,586	$ 83,792	$ 86,896	$310,343
EBITDA	$ 42,148	$ 52,685	$ 56,900	$ 59,007	$210,741
Federal income tax	$ 11,634	$ 14,542	$ 15,706	$ 16,287	$ 58,169
State income tax	$ 1,763	$ 2,203	$ 2,380	$ 2,468	$ 8,813
Interest expense	$ 8,653	$ 8,630	$ 8,606	$ 8,582	$ 34,472
Depreciation expense	$ 3,510	$ 3,510	$ 3,510	$ 3,510	$ 14,038
Net profit	$ 16,589	$ 23,800	$ 26,699	$ 28,161	$ 95,248

Profit and loss statement (third year)

Quarter	Q1	3 Q2	Q3	Q4	3
Sales	**$132,358**	**$165,447**	**$178,683**	**$185,301**	**$661,790**
Cost of goods sold	$ 19,804	$ 24,755	$ 26,735	$ 27,726	$ 99,020
Gross margin	85.00%	85.00%	85.00%	85.00%	85.00%
Operating income	**$112,554**	**$140,693**	**$151,948**	**$157,576**	**$562,770**
Expenses					
Payroll	$ 42,436	$ 53,045	$ 57,289	$ 59,410	$212,180
General and administrative	$ 5,451	$ 6,814	$ 7,359	$ 7,632	$ 27,256
Marketing expenses	$ 662	$ 827	$ 893	$ 927	$ 3,309
Professional fees and licensure	$ 1,107	$ 1,384	$ 1,495	$ 1,550	$ 5,537
Insurance costs	$ 438	$ 548	$ 591	$ 613	$ 2,191
Travel and vehicle costs	$ 1,838	$ 2,298	$ 2,482	$ 2,574	$ 9,191
Utilities	$ 4,410	$ 5,513	$ 5,954	$ 6,174	$ 22,050
Miscellaneous costs	$ 1,588	$ 1,985	$ 2,144	$ 2,224	$ 7,941
Payroll taxes	$ 6,365	$ 7,957	$ 8,593	$ 8,912	$ 31,827
Total operating costs	**$ 64,296**	**$ 80,371**	**$ 86,800**	**$ 90,015**	**$321,482**
EBITDA	**$ 48,258**	**$ 60,322**	**$ 65,148**	**$ 67,561**	**$241,288**
Federal income tax	$ 13,676	$ 17,095	$ 18,462	$ 19,146	$ 68,379
State income tax	$ 2,072	$ 2,590	$ 2,797	$ 2,901	$ 10,360
Interest expense	$ 8,558	$ 8,533	$ 8,507	$ 8,481	$ 34,078
Depreciation expense	$ 3,510	$ 3,510	$ 3,510	$ 3,510	$ 14,038
Net profit	**$ 20,442**	**$ 28,595**	**$ 31,871**	**$ 33,523**	**$114,431**

7.11 Three Year Cash Flow Analysis

Cash flow analysis (first year)

Month	1	2	3	4	5	6	7
Cash from operations	$ 5,997	$ 6,097	$ 6,196	$ 6,295	$ 6,394	$ 6,494	$ 6,593
Cash from receivables	$ 0	$ 0	$ 0	$ 0	$ 0	$ 0	$ 0
Operating cash inflow	**$ 5,997**	**$ 6,097**	**$ 6,196**	**$ 6,295**	**$ 6,394**	**$ 6,494**	**$ 6,593**
Other cash inflows							
Equity investment	$100,000	$ 0	$ 0	$ 0	$ 0	$ 0	$ 0
Increased borrowings	$500,000	$ 0	$ 0	$ 0	$ 0	$ 0	$ 0
Sales of business assets	$ 0	$ 0	$ 0	$ 0	$ 0	$ 0	$ 0
A/P increases	$ 3,159	$ 3,159	$ 3,159	$ 3,159	$ 3,159	$ 3,159	$ 3,159
Total other cash inflows	**$603,159**	**$ 3,159**	**$ 3,159**	**$ 3,159**	**$ 3,159**	**$ 3,159**	**$ 3,159**
Total cash inflow	**$609,156**	**$ 9,255**	**$ 9,354**	**$ 9,454**	**$ 9,553**	**$ 9,652**	**$ 9,751**
Cash outflows							
Repayment of principal	$ 410	$ 412	$ 415	$ 417	$ 419	$ 422	$ 424
A/P decreases	$ 2,075	$ 2,075	$ 2,075	$ 2,075	$ 2,075	$ 2,075	$ 2,075
A/R increases	$ 0	$ 0	$ 0	$ 0	$ 0	$ 0	$ 0
Asset purchases	$547,500	$ 0	$ 0	$ 0	$ 0	$ 0	$ 0
Dividends	$ 0	$ 0	$ 0	$ 0	$ 0	$ 0	$ 0
Total cash outflows	**$549,985**	**$ 2,487**	**$ 2,489**	**$ 2,492**	**$ 2,494**	**$ 2,497**	**$ 2,499**
Net cash flow	**$ 59,171**	**$ 6,768**	**$ 6,865**	**$ 6,962**	**$ 7,059**	**$ 7,155**	**$ 7,252**
Cash balance	**$ 59,171**	**$65,940**	**$72,804**	**$79,766**	**$86,825**	**$93,980**	**$101,233**

Cash flow analysis (first year cont.)

Month	8	9	10	11	12	1
Cash from operations	$ 6,692	$ 6,791	$ 6,891	$ 6,990	$ 7,089	$ 78,520
Cash from receivables	$ 0	$ 0	$ 0	$ 0	$ 0	$ 0
Operating cash inflow	**$ 6,692**	**$ 6,791**	**$ 6,891**	**$ 6,990**	**$ 7,089**	**$ 78,520**
Other cash inflows						
Equity investment	$ 0	$ 0	$ 0	$ 0	$ 0	$100,000
Increased borrowings	$ 0	$ 0	$ 0	$ 0	$ 0	$500,000
Sales of business assets	$ 0	$ 0	$ 0	$ 0	$ 0	$ 0
A/P increases	$ 3,159	$ 3,159	$ 3,159	$ 3,159	$ 3,159	$ 37,902
Total other cash inflows	**$ 3,159**	**$ 3,159**	**$ 3,159**	**$ 3,159**	**$ 3,159**	**$637,902**
Total cash inflow	**$ 9,851**	**$ 9,950**	**$ 10,049**	**$ 10,149**	**$10,248**	**$716,422**
Cash outflows						
Repayment of principal	$ 427	$ 429	$ 432	$ 434	$ 437	$ 5,079
A/P decreases	$ 2,075	$ 2,075	$ 2,075	$ 2,075	$ 2,075	$ 24,897
A/R increases	$ 0	$ 0	$ 0	$ 0	$ 0	$ 0
Asset purchases	$ 0	$ 0	$ 0	$ 0	$ 0	$547,500
Dividends	$ 0	$ 0	$ 0	$ 0	$62,816	$ 62,816
Total cash outflows	**$ 2,502**	**$ 2,504**	**$ 2,507**	**$ 2,509**	**$65,328**	**$640,292**
Net cash flow	**$ 7,349**	**$ 7,446**	**$ 7,543**	**$ 7,639**	**−$55,080**	**$ 76,130**
Cash balance	**$108,582**	**$116,027**	**$123,570**	**$131,210**	**$76,130**	**$ 76,130**

Cash flow analysis (second year)

Quarter	Q1	2 Q2	Q3	Q4	2
Cash from operations	$21,857	$27,322	$29,507	$30,600	$109,287
Cash from receivables	$ 0	$ 0	$ 0	$ 0	$ 0
Operating cash inflow	**$21,857**	**$27,322**	**$29,507**	**$30,600**	**$109,287**
Other cash inflows					
Equity investment	$ 0	$ 0	$ 0	$ 0	$ 0
Increased borrowings	$ 0	$ 0	$ 0	$ 0	$ 0
Sales of business assets	$ 0	$ 0	$ 0	$ 0	$ 0
A/P increases	$ 8,717	$10,897	$11,769	$12,204	$ 43,587
Total other cash inflows	**$ 8,717**	**$10,897**	**$11,769**	**$12,204**	**$ 43,587**
Total cash inflow	**$30,575**	**$38,218**	**$41,276**	**$42,805**	**$152,874**
Cash outflows					
Repayment of principal	$ 1,326	$ 1,349	$ 1,373	$ 1,397	$ 5,446
A/P decreases	$ 5,975	$ 7,469	$ 8,067	$ 8,365	$ 29,876
A/R increases	$ 0	$ 0	$ 0	$ 0	$ 0
Asset purchases	$ 3,279	$ 4,098	$ 4,426	$ 4,590	$ 16,393
Dividends	$17,486	$21,857	$23,606	$24,480	$ 87,429
Total cash outflows	**$28,066**	**$34,774**	**$37,472**	**$38,833**	**$139,145**
Net cash flow	**$ 2,509**	**$ 3,444**	**$ 3,804**	**$ 3,972**	**$ 13,729**
Cash balance	**$78,639**	**$82,083**	**$85,887**	**$89,859**	**$ 89,859**

Cash flow analysis (third year)

Quarter	Q1	Q2	Q3	Q4	3
Cash from operations	$25,694	$32,117	$ 34,687	$ 35,972	$128,470
Cash from receivables	$ 0	$ 0	$ 0	$ 0	$ 0
Operating cash inflow	**$25,694**	**$32,117**	**$ 34,687**	**$ 35,972**	**$128,470**
Other cash inflows					
Equity investment	$ 0	$ 0	$ 0	$ 0	$ 0
Increased borrowings	$ 0	$ 0	$ 0	$ 0	$ 0
Sales of business assets	$ 0	$ 0	$ 0	$ 0	$ 0
A/P increases	$10,025	$12,531	$ 13,534	$ 14,035	$ 50,125
Total other cash inflows	**$10,025**	**$12,531**	**$ 13,534**	**$ 14,035**	**$ 50,125**
Total cash inflow	**$35,719**	**$44,649**	**$ 48,221**	**$ 50,007**	**$178,595**
Cash outflows					
Repayment of principal	$ 1,422	$ 1,447	$ 1,472	$ 1,498	$ 5,840
A/P decreases	$ 7,170	$ 8,963	$ 9,680	$ 10,038	$ 35,852
A/R increases	$ 0	$ 0	$ 0	$ 0	$ 0
Asset purchases	$ 3,854	$ 4,818	$ 5,203	$ 5,396	$ 19,270
Dividends	$20,555	$25,694	$ 27,749	$ 28,777	$102,776
Total cash outflows	**$33,002**	**$40,922**	**$ 44,105**	**$ 45,710**	**$163,738**
Net cash flow	**$ 2,717**	**$ 3,727**	**$ 4,116**	**$ 4,297**	**$ 14,857**
Cash balance	**$92,576**	**$96,304**	**$100,419**	**$104,716**	**$104,716**

Catering Service

Creative Catering

5678 Kercheval
Grosse Pointe Park, MI 48236

Heidi Denler

Creative Catering will be a full-service catering company that will serve the Grosse Pointe community for food service needs for private home and small business parties, including holiday, graduation, engagement parties and weddings. Within the first six months of operation, owners Jack and Cindy Morris plan to have the company running in the black, which will be accomplished by efficient service; reasonably priced, high-quality, innovative foods and beverages; referrals; an easy-to-navigate web site; and a personal, friendly staff.

EXECUTIVE SUMMARY

Creative Catering will be a full-service catering company that will serve the Grosse Pointe community for food service needs for private home and small business parties, including holiday, graduation, engagement parties and weddings. Within the first six months of operation, owners Jack and Cindy Morris plan to have the company running in the black, which will be accomplished by efficient service; reasonably priced, high-quality, innovative foods and beverages; referrals; an easy-to-navigate web site; and a personal, friendly staff. The Morrises are planning to build on the informal catering services that Cindy has been offering for local schools and children's birthday parties. Jack's master's degree in hotel and restaurant management, along with 14 years as a motel manager and restaurant manager for an area golf club, will provide needed business expertise. Although Cindy has a degree in education, she has been a stay-at-home mom for the last seven years and has become an active volunteer at her child's school. That volunteering has led to a plethora of contacts on which the Morrises can begin to build their expanding business. Cindy has also been taking culinary classes at the local community college in preparation to take a long-time love of cooking and baking for others to a bigger stage in the community.

The Morrises will hire a staff that will include an event manager and event staff. Until the operation is fully successful for at least 12 months, they will subcontract floral design and musicians/DJ services. Once the company is showing a profit, they will contract with those floral designers and musicians/DJs who have worked best within the mission and value statements of Creative Catering. The Morrises will offer varied menus for breakfasts, brunches, lunches, and dinners, as well as cocktail parties with alcoholic and non-alcoholic beverages. Table settings, space design, décor, invitations, and event favors will be available for client selection.

COMPANY SUMMARY

Creative Catering is a small, growing catering company that serves the private household and small business market in the suburban Detroit communities that comprise the Grosse Pointes. In 2008, Cindy Morris began catering small Parent Teacher Organization (PTO) events at her son's school. That informal start launched an ever-increasing client list of parents for whom she catered children's parties and adult cocktail and holiday parties. When a few of those parent clients approached her to cater events for their small businesses, Cindy and her husband Jack decided it was time to formalize the business.

They have been renting the health inspector-approved kitchen at their church to handle the cooking end of the business. They have realized that to keep the company growing they need a space of their own not only for cooking and preparation of food to be served at the events they cater, but also to store such needed items as tablecloths, napkins, stemware, plates, silverware, serving trays, and staff uniforms, among others. They have found and secured a local rental property with a professional kitchen, storage space, and office space. Eventually they would like to expand to the rental property next door so they can have their own event space rather than relying on renting such space for business events. Private clients would then have the option of hosting the event in their own home or renting Creative Catering's space. Currently, the Morrises subcontract outside vendors for photography, floral design, and music, as well as rentals for tables, chairs, and tents. However, they plan to have those vendors under contract to Creative Catering to provide those services for all their events within the next two years. They also will be able to buy their own tables, chairs, and tents once they move into the rental property and have a place to store them.

The Morrises project that Creative Catering, which is currently recording a profit, to return to profitability within six to eight months as the client list grows and they begin to repay the loan to Cindy's parents. They foresee hiring a full-time staff from their current pool of part-time employees, including a manager to assume many of the responsibilities Cindy and Jack currently are undertaking, allowing them some free time.

MANAGEMENT SUMMARY

Creative Catering was founded by Cindy and Jack Morris. A loan from Cindy's parents gave them 25 percent ownership of the company as silent partners until the loan is repaid, at which time Cindy and Jack will have full ownership of the company.

Plans for the company include hiring an office manager and one event manager within six months. During the following six months, an additional event manager will be hired. Until these managers are in place, Cindy Morris will be in charge of food service, tables and floral decorations, and dealing with clients, while Jack will be responsible for the business aspects of Creative Catering and working with prospective clients. Once managers are trained and cooks are hired, Cindy and Jack will train them in their respective responsibilities, which will allow the employees to assume much of the day-to-day operations of the company, allowing Cindy to concentrate on the food preparation and Jack to oversee the business end of the company on a weekly, rather than daily, basis.

Legal matters will be handled by a local attorney who specialized in start-ups and small businesses. When Cindy first began catering, the Morrises turned over all financial duties to a local CPA who also specializes in small business and family accounting.

MISSION STATEMENT

The mission of Creative Catering is to provide local residents and small businesses with delicious food, served by an efficient, friendly staff, at the client's venue that will include all the necessary extras to create a perfect party.

VISION STATEMENT

Creative Catering will build a customer base of local residences and small businesses in the Grosse Pointes. With innovative advertising, incentives for return business, and an Internet presence, the company will be poised for further expansion into neighboring suburbs of Harper Woods, St. Clair Shores, and Eastpointe.

VALUES STATEMENT

Jack and Cindy Morris recognize the value of delicious food; customer service; and efficient, friendly staff and subcontractors, providing their clients with a memorable event on every level.

Customer service is the number one priority of Creative Catering. To that end, the Morrises and their employees are dedicated to serving local corporate owners and managers efficiently and cheerfully. Employees will be highly trained to not only meet, but also exceed, client expectations. Employees will be empowered to take pride in their service to the clients.

BUSINESS PHILOSOPHY

Creative Catering will provide a memorable event for all clients, in their home or at an outside venue, with friendly, efficient, service and delicious food. Return business and client referrals are recognized as key to the success of Creative Catering.

GOALS AND OBJECTIVES

Short term goals for Creative Catering are:

- Moving business into rental property
- Building a customer base through the company web site, word-of-mouth, and advertising in local papers
- Making working connections with event locations, floral designers, musicians and DJs
- Hiring permanent full-time staff, including an office manager and an event manager
- Purchase event equipment, including tables, chairs, tablecloths, napkins, flatware, stemware, and dishware
- Be profitable within six months

Long-term goals include:

- Buying a permanent location, possibly the rental property

- Having a neighboring building to hold events that would be used 60 percent of the year

- Expansion to neighboring suburbs of St. Clair Shores and Harper Woods

The Morrises plan to build their customer base via friendly staff; delicious, competitively priced food; full-service party plans; and marketing. Promotion will be through referrals, advertising in **The Grosse Pointe News,** web site, and follow-up with current clients.

ORGANIZATION STRUCTURE

Jack and Cindy Morris are 75 percent owners of Creative Catering. Cindy's parent, Tina and Sam Zarema, have loaned the couple $50,000 for a 25 percent silent partnership stake in the company. When the loan has been repaid, the Morrises will assume 100 percent ownership of the company.

Personnel for Creative Catering other than Jack and Cindy will include:

- Office manager

- Marketing manager

- Event manager

- Two cooks

- Serving staff

- Bartenders

Staff under contract will include:

- Musicians

- DJs

- Floral designer

As owners, Jack and Cindy will have the final say in all matters pertaining to Creative Catering, although most responsibilities will be slowly assumed by the managers who will consult with the Morrises.

ADVERTISING AND PROMOTION

Creative Catering's expanded business and new location will be promoted via personal letters to current clients, including brochures that will outline the services being offered. In addition, ads will be placed in **The Grosse Pointe News,** which is read by virtually everyone living in the Grosse Pointes. These ads will include a coupon for 10 percent off the first event catered by Creative Catering by a new client. The web site will offer a form for prospective clients to ask questions of the staff and set up appointments to consult with Creative Catering's owners or staff to contract for an event. A brochure will be created that will feature the web site URL, services offered, favorite menu items, and photos of past events. Contact information will be prominent.

An e-mail blast will be sent to current and prospective clients with an attached e-brochure and offer for 10 percent off the first event catered. Personal calls from Jack, Cindy, the office manager, or the event manager will be made to follow-up on past events and to secure future bookings.

CUSTOMER BASE

Creative Catering will serve a small geographical area comprising the five Grosse Pointes for individuals and small local businesses whether they want to celebrate a special occasion or host a meeting.

The primary customer base will expand from the current private, family party to include small businesses who want to have a breakfast, lunch, and/or dinner meeting or a seminar/workshop with light refreshments during a break. The target base for private clients is households with a median income of $90,000. Small business owners with locations in the Downtown Park, the Village, the Hill, and the shops along Mack Avenue will offer the opportunity for a higher profit margin than private events.

Parties and banquets to celebrate birthdays, showers, weddings, bar/bat mitzvahs, and retirement are currently among the events Cindy Morris has catered and planned. Holiday, product launch, and retirement parties, as well as business meetings, will join the portfolio of offerings of Creative Catering.

Approximately a dozen other formal caterers are operating in the Grosse Pointes as of mid-2012, but as businesses expand, and more dual income families are the norm, an increase in the number of clients is projected as catering companies assume the responsibilities of planning, preparing, and executing family and business parties and events for busy families and business owners.

PRODUCTS AND SERVICES

Products and services offered by Creative Catering will include (but are not limited to):

- Planning
- Management
- Servers
- Food (from appetizers to multi-course meals)
- Valet parking
- Coat check
- Alcoholic and non-alcoholic beverages
- Tablescape design
- Floral design
- Musician/DJ
- Equipment, furniture, and tent rentals
- Audio-visual equipment
- Security
- Invitations
- Photographers/videographers

LOCATION

The owners of Creative Catering, Jack and Cindy Morris, plan to move their business from their home and their church kitchen to a rental property they have found on Kercheval in Grosse Pointe Park. The new location has a commercial kitchen and room for storage of equipment, tables, chairs, tablecloths, silverware, stemware, and all other party/even necessities, as well as office space. They are considering renting the property next door that can be turned into meeting space or an event hall to offer clients the option of hosting their event outside their home or business without having to incur the expense of finding and renting an outside hall.

OFFICE DESIGN AND EQUIPMENT

The rental property that the Morrises have chosen for Creative Catering has a commercial kitchen at the back of the space, allowing deliveries through a door to the alley and parking area behind the storefront. The front of the space will be the location for the offices, where there will be three laptops, an all-in-one printer for faxing, copying, and printing, including invitations and other print items requested by the clients. The front of the store will also be the site of a conference room for meetings with clients to discuss and determine menus, color schemes, and other party planning details.

The office computers will have software for graphics for print items, as well as standard office software. Jack Morris will record business expenses and accounting information on an Excel program that can be shared with the CPA. An inventory program that has been used successfully thus far in the informal business will be used on the office computers, although Cindy is open to finding a different program if it will be more effective. The CPA will handle payroll, all taxes, rental payments, insurance, employee benefits, and all expenses related to the business.

FINANCIAL

Ongoing expenses include:

- Rent

- Utilities

- Payroll, including taxes and benefits

- Insurance (property, liability, key man, auto for delivery vans)

- Office expenses (computer maintenance, printer ink, stationery, postage, software, paper, brochures, etc.)

- Cleaning supplies

- Advertising

- Health department requirements

- Alarm system

- CPA fees

- Food

- Beverages

One-time major expenses include:

- Banquet tables and chairs

- Outdoor event tents

- Tablecloths and napkins

- Additional flatware, stemware, and dinnerware
- Uniforms for staff
- Washer/dryer set up
- Two additional vans equipped to carry food, trays, tables, tents, etc.
- Web site creation
- Legal fees for start-up paperwork filings

PROFESSIONAL AND ADVISORY SUPPORT

Cindy Morris has established a relationship with a CPA and an attorney, both of whom specialize in small business start ups. Those relationships will continue for Creative Catering.

The Morrises will also continue to work with John Howard to provide life, health, and dental insurance options for the owners and employees, as well as retirement planning. Other insurance, such as liability and auto, will be covered by the Howard Agency as well.

Cindy's parents have loaned the couple $50,000 for a 25 percent stake in the company that will cease upon repayment of the loan. The Morrises plan to work with Fifth Third Bank in the future to secure a line of credit to cover additional expenses as the company grows.

BUSINESS AND GROWTH STRATEGY

The establishment of Creative Catering represents the first phase of growth for the company. Phase two of the Morrises growth plan is to obtain neighboring property that will house actual event space. Phase three is to expand the business into neighboring suburbs of Harper Woods and St. Clair Shores.

Advertising and promotion will figure significantly into the growth of the business. The Morrises plan to hire a marketing manager to handle this aspect of Creative Catering, but they will work with current clients and all future clients by making personal contacts throughout the planning, execution, and follow-up phases of the event being catered.

COMPETITION

There are some dozen other catering companies within a 25-mile radius of Creative Catering. Some are upscale with private event space, some only offer drop-off or pick-up service, some are within restaurants and bakeries.

Creative Catering will provide high-quality food and service at competitive prices. Clients will be able to get everything they need for their events at one place, without having to shop around at different vendors to put together a party.

WEB SITE

Creative Catering has hired a local high school computer whiz to create a company web site to promote the business. It includes contact information and a description of event services available, as well as sample menus. One page of the site is dedicated to reviews and references, and another is a form that can be completed requesting estimates and additional information. Until an office manager is hired, Jack will check the web site every hour or so to ensure prompt responses to queries from clients and potential clients.

CONCLUSION

Creative Catering will offer "one-stop-shopping" for private and small business clients who want to host a party or business event at their own venues. Within three years the company will offer its own venue for such events. A full-time staff will provide efficient, friendly service with high-quality, delicious food and beverages. Creative Catering has all elements of a party for any size group to be successful and memorable at competitive prices.

Success will depend on exceeding client expectations; listening to client preferences and executing them; and professionalism in every aspect of planning, executing, and following up on events.

Children's Hair Salon

Kool Kidz

Shops on the Circle
3500 Ross Clark Circle
Dothan, AL 36303

Fran Fletcher

Kool Kidz is a hair salon with kids in mind. It is the brainchild of Brandi Sharpe, Brianna Smith, and Shannon Mears, three licensed cosmetologists who met while classmates at Wiregrass Technical College.

BUSINESS OVERVIEW

Kool Kidz is a hair salon with kids in mind. It is the brainchild of Brandi Sharpe, Brianna Smith, and Shannon Mears, three licensed cosmetologists who met while classmates at Wiregrass Technical College.

Starting a hair salon exclusively for kids was first discussed in 2008 while the friends were still in school. All three friends had babysitting jobs and often heard the parents describing the horror of taking their children to get a haircut. Each went her own way after graduation and the idea of a kids' salon was forgotten until recently, while having dinner together, the subject was once again brought to light. The friends know that they have the experience necessary to finally make their dream a reality. Each brings a wealth of knowledge gained from working in various salons over the last three years.

Kool Kidz will be a place where kids love to get their hair cut. There will be a small flat screen television by each chair with DVD capabilities. Clients may bring a favorite movie from home or choose one from the salon's library. While waiting on siblings to get a hair cut, children can play video games, watch movies, play board games, read books, or play with a variety of other toys.

The co-owners are seeking financing for this venture and have an opportunity to rent a 2,000 sq. ft. space in a high traffic location. The space needs some structural and aesthetic modifications for salon use and for kid appeal. The co-owners are confident that within a matter of months, their salon will be overflowing with happy kids, resulting in enough profits to effortlessly pay back the financing within two years.

COMPANY DESCRIPTION

Location
Kool Kidz will be conveniently located in the Shops on the Circle, a strip mall that is also home to the family clothing retail giant Old Navy, PetSmart, and Party City. The owners strategically picked this location for its high visibility and for the volume of family shopping that the three large stores will bring.

Hours of Operation

The company will operate as follows:

Tuesday-Saturday 10 AM—6 PM

Personnel

Brandi Sharpe, Brianna Smith, and Shannon Mears will perform all duties associated with Kool Kidz. The three co-owners bring nine total years experience in the hair industry. Brandi and Shannon have been self-employed since graduation and know the ins and outs of marketing themselves and their businesses. Brianna brings her managerial experience to the table and will serve both as a stylist and the office manager. Additionally, the co-owners plan to hire a full time receptionist and a part time nail tech after the salon is off the ground and is financially able.

Brianna Smith (co-owner, stylist, office manager)

Brianna is a licensed cosmetologist with the state of Alabama and is currently the manager of Regis Salon in the Wiregrass Commons Mall. Prior to Regis, she worked as a stylist with JCPenney Styling salon.

Brandi Sharpe (co-owner, stylist)

Brandi is a licensed cosmetologist with the state of Alabama and is currently a self-employed stylist at Hair Force Salon in Dothan, AL.

Shannon Mears (co-owner, stylist)

Shannon is a licensed cosmetologist with the state of Alabama and is currently a self-employed stylist at Extreme Expressions Hair Salon in Dothan, AL.

Products and Services

Services

- Haircuts

- Hair styling for special occasions (pageants, dance recitals, etc.)

- Highlights/coloring

- Perms

Products

- General hair accessories

- Custom hair accessories (custom hair bows, hair bands)

- Baby hair accessories (hair bows, hair bands)

- Hair pieces

- Washing and styling products

- Bath accessories (soaps, fizzes)

- First haircut keepsake kits

MARKET ANALYSIS

Industry Overview

According to the Bureau of Labor Statistics, the hairstyling industry is set to increase by 14% over the next ten years. Forty-four percent of hairstylists were self-employed and the median salary was $26,510 in 2010 according to the Labor Bureau.

Target Market

The target market for Kool Kidz will be kids from birth to teens in the Dothan, AL and surrounding areas. The University of Alabama estimates that as of 2011, there are approximately 19,410 children in Houston County, AL under the age of 13. The owners of Kool Kidz plan to obtain as many of these kids as possible.

Competition

There are no other salons in the area that cater solely to children.

GROWTH STRATEGY

The overall strategy of Kool Kidz is to be the premiere place for Dothan-area kids to go for all of their hair-care needs. Additionally, it is the goal of Kool Kidz to obtain and retain a loyal customer base and to achieve strong financial growth during the first year of operation. During the second year, the owners hope that additional stylists will be needed due to customer demand.

Sales and Marketing

The owners have identified key tactics to support the salon's growth strategy.

Initial advertising/marketing will include:

- Running half-page newspaper ads in the Dothan Eagle, Early County News, and the Donalsonville News prior to the grand opening.
- Word of mouth—the owners expect current customers to transfer to the new salon and are telling their clients about their new venture

Ongoing advertising/marketing will include:

- Using social media such as Face Book.
- Sponsoring local beauty pageants
- Offering free "first haircuts"
- Sending out colorful appointment reminder cards two weeks before scheduled appointment
- Creating a Birthday club in which kids will get a birthday card, sticker, and a coupon for a free ice cream cone on their birthday

FINANCIAL ANALYSIS

Start-up Costs

The rent for this location is higher than other commercial properties the owners viewed, but the owners think that this will pay off in terms of the large amount of family traffic brought into the strip mall by Old Navy, and other stores. The building owner is offering $6,000 toward renovating the space into a salon in return for signing a 3-year lease. The owners have spoken with LRA Construction Company and will need an additional $4,000 dollars to complete the renovation.

Kool Kidz will need approximately $10,000 to purchase salon fixtures. This includes:

- Three barber shop chairs
- Three 16 inch flat screen TVs with DVD players

- Two salon sinks

- Two driers

- Three mirrors

- Booster seats

- Capes

- Coloring and perm supplies

- Tools (curling irons, flat irons, hair dryers, scissors)

- Sanitation equipment

Initial advertising in the newspapers and the grand opening will cost around $2,000. Kool Kidz plans to take out half page ads in the Dothan Eagle, the Donalsonville News, and the Early County News. The grand opening will be a fun- filled event for the kids. Plans include face painting, games, snacks, drinks, and lots of prizes.

In addition to salon fixtures, furniture for the salon will be needed. This includes:

- Desk and chair for the reception area

- Two cordless phones

- Answering machine

- Computer and printer

- Couches for parents

The kids play area will be equipped with:

- One large rug

- Two kid tables with chairs

- Two bean bags

- One 60 inch flat screen TV

- DVD player

- Wii gaming system

- Video rocker chairs

- Books and art supplies

Start-up Costs

Building renovation	$ 4,000
Salon fixtures	$10,000
Supplies/tools	$ 500
Business license	$ 200
Initial advertising	$ 2,000
Salon furniture	$ 5,000
Kids play area	$ 2,000
Total	**$23,700**

Estimated Monthly Expenses

Generally, the cost of monthly expenses is fixed. Monthly rent is $2,500 and includes electricity and water. The owners will sign a three-year lease and rent will not increase during this period. A monthly advertising budget of $150 will be used for the birthday club, to showcase specials, and for sponsorships.

The co-owners will initially be paid $20 per hour. The wages of workers will be re-evaluated at six-month intervals and again after the business loan is repaid. Brianna will perform office management duties during business hours when possible. Brandi and Shannon will perform duties such as mailing out appointment reminders and birthday club cards. Each stylist will work approximately forty hours per week. If extra hours are needed for administrative duties, employees will be paid $20 an hour for those as well.

Monthly Expenses

Rent	$ 2,500
Phone/Internet	$ 150
Advertising	$ 150
Insurance	$ 100
Wages	$ 9,600
Total	**$12,500**

Estimated Monthly Income

The number of clients will determine estimated income. If the three stylists are fully booked, the salon has the potential to make a minimum of $120.00 per hour or $960.00 per day. This estimate uses the least expensive service (girls trim only) and the maximum number of this service that can be performed by each stylist in an hour (4).

Price Schedule

Prices for Services

First hair cut	$ 0
Boys cuts	$15
Girls trim only	$10
Girls bangs only	$10
Girls cut/style	$20
Highlights	$50
Color	$60
Crazy color streaks	$30
Perms	$60
Special occasion styling	$30

The chart titled "Estimated Appointments" is a conservative estimate of appointments per stylist. Appointments increase from 776 total appointments in Month 1 until Month 6 at which time the owners estimate that each stylist will be booked solid with 1,440 total appointments.

Estimated Appointments

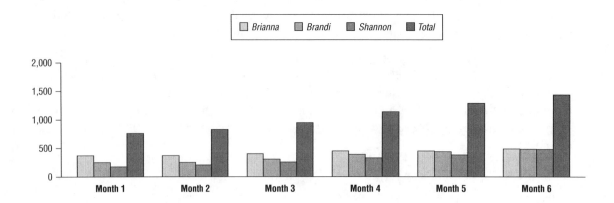

Profit/Loss

The chart titled "Monthly Profit/Loss" uses the "Estimated Appointments" chart data to estimate monthly income. $15 is the median service price and is therefore used for the Profit/Loss data and chart. The estimated income in the chart does not include product sales because the owners consider that income negligible. The chart shows monthly income increasing from $11,400 in Month 1 to $21,600 in Month 6 and profits increasing from −$1,100 in Month 1 to $9,100 in Month 6. The chart estimates that monthly expenses will be fixed at $12,500.

Monthly profit/loss

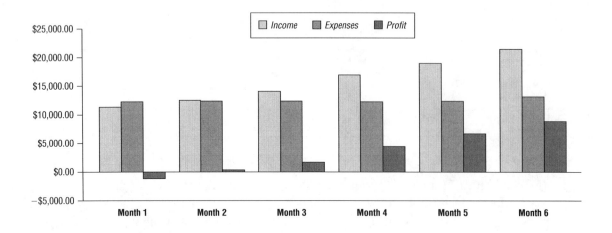

Financing

The owners of Kool Kidz wish to obtain financing in the form of a business loan or line of credit for the amount needed to cover the start up costs and operating expenses for the first three months. This loan would be in the amount of $61,200. According to the estimated expenses vs. income, Kool Kidz should be able to pay back the loan by the end of year two.

Consignment Shop

Upscale Resale

12345 Emerald Parkway
Dublin, Ohio 43017

Heidi Denler

Upscale Resale is a new consignment and resale shop in Dublin, Ohio that will feature high-quality, gently-used garments and accessories.

EXECUTIVE SUMMARY

Upscale Resale is a new consignment and resale shop in Dublin, Ohio that is owned solely by Gary Smith. Smith recently took early retirement after 30 years in a marketing position for a major national retailer. He chose Dublin for the site of his shop because of its upper middle class family demographics. He has secured a storefront in a strip mall with high foot traffic that is near office complexes and restaurants. Smith understands the need for attention to details within the store as well as in the items he will accept for consignment sales, which he will translate to profitability within the first six to nine months of operation.

COMPANY SUMMARY

Upscale Resale will be a consignment shop for high-quality, gently-used garments and accessories. Pricing will be higher than thrift stores, based on the quality of the merchandise, but substantially lower than retail. After cleaning out a closet, people will be able to bring clean items to the shop where Smith will price them and keep them on display for 90 days. When the item sells, the consignor will receive 40 percent of the sale price. At the end of the 90 days, Smith will notify the customer if the item has not been sold and allow seven days to pick up the items before Smith donates it to a local charity. Smith will also offer manufacturers' closeouts for which he will retain the full selling price.

Management Summary

Upscale Resale will be 100 percent owned by Gary Smith as an Ohio LLC. Smith has an MBA from Wharton and 30 years of experience in marketing for a national clothing retailer, having started his career in sales for that company while pursuing his undergraduate degree from Ohio State University. His experience dealing with customers will work with his understanding of marketing and experience in all aspects of retail sales to create an inviting, friendly environment in which his customers can shop. After taking early retirement, Smith found himself with too much time on his hands. His passion for the business, as well as an understanding of the human desire to find a bargain, led him to the decision to open a consignment/resale shop.

MISSION STATEMENT

Gary Smith will offer customers high-quality fashion and accessories at modest prices.

VALUES STATEMENT

Upscale Resale will surpass local competition in the consignment/retail industry in attention to both the buying and selling customer, display of merchandise, pricing, and store layout.

VISION STATEMENT

Profitability will be achieved through quality merchandise and friendly, efficient customer service. The customer base is expected to expand through word-of-mouth advertising, flyers, advertising in local media, and outstanding selection at reasonable prices.

BUSINESS PHILOSOPHY

Attention to detail in display, store layout, merchandise, and customer service are the key components to a successful business. Marketing and promotion will promote these components, creating a pleasant environment for employees and customers alike.

GOALS AND OBJECTIVES

Within nine months, Upscale Resale will be showing a profit due to the low overhead allowed by not pre-paying for merchandise.

Future plans include offering items via a web site and establishing a service for those who want to sell items on e-Bay in addition to the brick-and-mortar shop.

Expansion of the customer base will be a primary objective upon the opening of the store. This will be accomplished through word-of-mouth advertising, flyers, ads in local publications, and press releases sent to the local cable station and network affiliates.

Owner Gary Smith is projecting a 10 percent growth rate per month for the first year of operation.

Within 10 years, Smith plans to take full retirement, at which point he plans to sell Upscale Resale to an employee or third party.

ORGANIZATION STRUCTURE

Gary Smith is the sole proprietor of Upscale Resale. He will hire three sales associates and train them to accept responsibility for tagging and stocking items, cleaning the store, and assisting customers. The top worker will be promoted to assistant manager of the shop and will be given the additional responsibilities of overseeing staff and accepting consignments from customers.

ADVERTISING AND PROMOTION

As a former marketing executive with 30 years of experience with a national retailer, Upscale Resale owner Gary Smith has been preparing a campaign for television, radio, and print media. That campaign will be supplemented with flyers delivered doo-to-door in the immediate neighborhood, particularly at the office complexes. Smith will approach neighboring shop owners/managers to arrange an exchange of flyers/brochures to have available near the cash register, promoting each others' stores. Word-of-mouth advertising will account for additional promotion of the store. A web site will be developed that will initially include hours of operation and contact information. Pages of items for sale will be offered, along with photos of the storefront and display areas.

Signage on the front of the building will be dynamic in order to increase foot traffic from those shopping or dining at the strip mall as well as those working in nearby office complexes.

CUSTOMER BASE

Upscale Resale's target market will be women living within a 20-mile radius of the shop who are seeking a bargain or, in some cases, vintage clothing. Also part of the target market will be sorority women at Ohio State University who seek bargain prices for stylish, up-to-the-minute clothing for formal dances and other special occasions, as well as graduating senior women from the University who require a professional wardrobe for their job hunting days following graduation.

The economy in the early 2010s continues to be difficult, creating a climate ripe for bargains in the clothing and accessory sector. Consignors are able to garner cash for items they are no longer wearing and buyers are able to dress for success at lowered prices. The resulting exchange stands to support profitability for Upscale Resale.

PRODUCTS AND SERVICES

A highly diversified selection of gently used and, in some cases, new merchandise will be available on a seasonal basis. Those leaving items on consignment will receive the standard 40 percent of the final sale price for their item. Women's clothing and accessories will be featured in the store.

Sources for consignment will primarily be individuals who live, work, and shop in the area. These women are mindful of recycling and repurposing clothing and accessories in order to find a bargain.

In the future, retailers will be contacted with offers to purchase remainders at bargain prices. These items will be resold at a profit by Upscale Resale.

LOCATION

Owner Gary Smith has secured a storefront in a strip mall in Dublin on a main road. The mall boasts a high degree of foot traffic and about a dozen stores, none of which are in close competition to the merchandise available at Upscale Resale. The location is close to a handful of office and medical complexes, whose employees frequent the mall stores on their lunch hours and after work. Several restaurants are also nearby, and diners stop at the stores before or after eating.

SHOP DESIGN AND EQUIPMENT

The front two-thirds of the store will be dedicated to display and shopping space with display cases for accessories, racks and mannequins for clothing, and three partitioned dressing rooms along a wall. There will be a small area with two chairs and a lamp table where patrons (or spouses) can take a break from shopping or sit to choose accessories.

A stock room, employee break room, and Smith's office will share the back one-third of the store. The stock room will open to the back door where customers bringing items to consign will be served. The break room will be furnished with a table and chairs, small cupboard, microwave, refrigerator, and a sink. An employee restroom will also be in the back of the store.

The office will have a laptop, all-in-one printer, file cabinet, desk, desk chair, side chair, and cabinet for storage of blank contracts, tags, and office supplies.

FINANCIAL

Start up costs for Upscale Resale will include:

- Purchase of display racks and cases, hangers, shelves
- Laptop, Internet access, all-in-one printer
- Bar code label software
- Inventory management software
- Consignment contracts
- Hang tags for pricing
- Furniture for office
- Mirrors on walls in dressing rooms; cheval mirrors on sales floor
- Office supplies (paper, stapler, pens, pencils, etc.)
- Letterhead/envelopes
- Promotional items including advertising in local media and flyers for neighborhood door-to-door delivery
- Dynamic signage for storefront to attract customers
- Legal fees to set up the business (DBA, state and local permits, tax ID number, etc.)

Ongoing expenses will include:

- Rent
- Utilities (phone, gas, electric)
- Internet access
- Web site maintenance
- Advertising in local print media
- Office supplies
- Employee break room stock (paper towels, mugs, toilet paper, soap, etc.)
- Legal and accounting fees

PROFESSIONAL AND ADVISORY SUPPORT

Gary Smith has signed a contract with an attorney who specializes in start-ups and has an understanding of the retail clothing market. Fees for legal work are set by work done rather than by an hourly rate. A retainer has been paid.

The Dublin Agency has been selected to handle life, key man, health, and dental insurance options for Smith and his employees at their own expense. The Agency also handles property-casualty, liability, and business interruption insurance.

In addition, Smith will work with the local office of the Small Business Administration to ease the transition from working for a national retailer to being a local retailer.

BUSINESS AND GROWTH STRATEGY

Gary Smith's 30 years of experience in retail and marketing are reflected in the design of the shopping area of the store. Displays will be well-lit, price tags will be easy to read, top selling and new items will be at the front of the store and in the windows, and those items that are close to having been on sale for 90 days will be at the rear of the store.

Inventory-control will be managed by bar code labels and cash register software. Stock will constantly be changing due to the 90 day limit for consignments, after which time the items are to be picked up by the consignor or be donated to charity. That turnover will ensure frequent return customers who want to find the latest bargain among new stock on display.

Advertising will not only be important for sales, but for stock. Initial flyers and advertising will focus on consignment acquisitions. To encourage people to bring their clothing and accessories to Upscale Resale, an offer for 50 percent on the sale of the items will be extended to anyone bringing in items in the first month the store is open. Following that period, the percentage will be the standard 40 percent offered by most other consignment stores.

COMPETITION

Upscale Resale will be set apart from the competition with its selection of upscale, designer clothing and accessories. Personalized customer service, combined with unique merchandise, will ensure repeat business. In addition, Gary Smith will maintain a database of customers that will include such personal information as sizes, color preferences, and favorite designers to enable him and his staff to directly contact customers when an item comes in that might appeal to a customer.

As some charity thrift stores begin to separate high-end items from their donations and offer them in separate shops, competition will increase for Upscale Resale. However, by that time, Smith should have established a clientele that will come to him first thanks to competitive pricing, friendly service, and a welcoming shopping experience.

WEB SITE

Future plans call for development of a web site that will highlight special items that have arrived in the shop on consignment. The web site will also include hours of operation, a map and written directions, and contact information. An interactive form will be available for prospective customers and consignors to ask question 24/7 instead of waiting for the shop to be open to make queries over the phone.

CONCLUSION

High-quality, designer clothing and accessories will be the key component to attracting not only consignors but also buyers to Upscale Resale. The competitive edge of owner Gary Smith's experience in retail and marketing will combine with attractive, well-lit displays of merchandise; 90-day rotation of all items; modest pricing; a welcoming staff; and personalized customer service and a customer profile database to create a welcoming environment in which to shop. The Dublin, Ohio, area is poised to support a consignment shop for designer items, which will create a profitable store within six to nine months.

Copy Shop
Pronto Printing

8878 E. Washington Ave.
New York, NY 10001

BizPlanDB.com

The purpose of this business plan is to raise $100,000 for the development of copy shop while showcasing the expected financials and operations over the next three years. Pronto Printing, Inc. is a New York based corporation that will provide sales of basic printing and business services to customers in its targeted market. The Company was founded by Dave Schmidt.

1.0 EXECUTIVE SUMMARY

The purpose of this business plan is to raise $100,000 for the development of copy shop while showcasing the expected financials and operations over the next three years. Pronto Printing, Inc. is a New York based corporation that will provide sales of basic printing and business services to customers in its targeted market. The Company was founded by Dave Schmidt.

1.1 The Services

The Company's retail business center will provide a number of services needed by local businesses, professionals, and individuals. The Company's offerings include:

- Color, Black and White, and Large Format Copies

- Fax Services

- Binding and Lamination

- Volume printing and copying

- Office Supply Products (limited)

Section three of the business plan will further detail the services offered by the Company.

1.2 Financing

Mr. Schmidt is seeking to raise $100,000 from as a bank loan. The interest rate and loan agreement are to be further discussed during negotiation. This business plan assumes that the business will receive a 10 year loan with a 9% fixed interest rate. The financing will be used for the following:

- Development of the Pronto Printing location.

- Financing for the first six months of operation.

- Capital to purchase copying equipment.

Mr. Schmidt will contribute $10,000 to the venture.

1.3 Mission Statement

Pronto Printing's mission is to become the recognized leader in its targeted market for general printing services.

1.4 Management Team

The Company was founded by Dave Schmidt. Mr. Schmidt has more than 10 years of experience in the retail management industry. Through his expertise, he will be able to bring the operations of the business to profitability within its first year of operations.

1.5 Sales Forecasts

Mr. Schmidt expects a strong rate of growth at the start of operations. Below are the expected financials over the next three years.

Proforma profit and loss (yearly)

Year	1	2	3
Sales	$420,750	$462,825	$509,108
Operating costs	$241,508	$250,272	$259,417
EBITDA	$ 86,678	$110,731	$137,686
Taxes, interest, and depreciation	$ 45,782	$ 51,226	$ 61,058
Net profit	$ 40,895	$ 59,505	$ 76,628

Sales, operating costs, and profit forecast

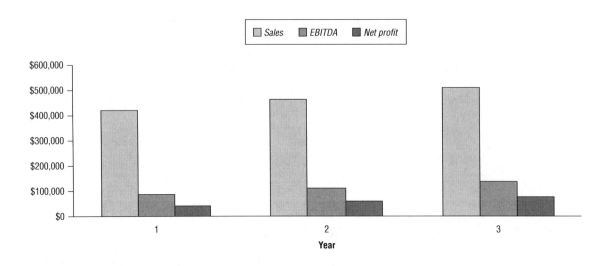

1.6 Expansion Plan

The Founder expects that the business will aggressively expand during the first three years of operation. Mr. Schmidt intends to implement marketing campaigns that will effectively target individuals and businesses within the target market.

2.0 COMPANY AND FINANCING SUMMARY

2.1 Registered Name and Corporate Structure

Pronto Printing, Inc. is registered as a corporation in the State of New York.

2.2 Required Funds

At this time, Pronto Printing requires $100,000 of debt funds. Mr. Schmidt will contribute $10,000 to the development of the business. Below is a breakdown of how these funds will be used:

Projected startup costs

Initial lease payments and deposits	$ 10,000
Working capital	$ 35,000
FF&E	$ 23,000
Leasehold improvements	$ 5,000
Security deposits	$ 5,000
Insurance	$ 2,500
Copy machine equipment	$ 17,000
Marketing budget	$ 7,500
Miscellaneous and unforeseen costs	$ 5,000
Total startup costs	**$110,000**

Use of funds

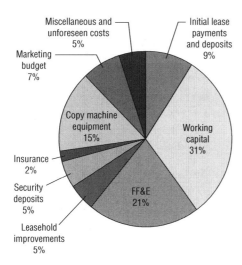

2.3 Investor Equity

Mr. Schmidt is not seeking an investment from a third party at this time.

2.4 Management Equity

Dave Schmidt owns 100% of Pronto Printing, Inc.

2.5 Exit Strategy

If the business is very successful, Mr. Schmidt may seek to sell the business to a third party for a significant earnings multiple. Most likely, the Company will hire a qualified business broker to sell the business on behalf of Pronto Printing, Inc. Based on historical numbers, the business could fetch a sales premium of up to 4 times earnings.

3.0 PRODUCTS AND SERVICES

Below is a description of the products and services offered by Pronto Printing.

3.1 Business and Printing Services

The business will provide a number of printing related services needed by local businesses, professionals, and individuals. Management feels that offering these services will provide the business with a predictable stream of revenue. All businesses require specialized business/printing services from time to time, and as the Company develops its local affinity with consumers, Management feels that the will become the number one service provider for these people. The services that the Company will offer include, but are not limited to:

- Business card printing (outsourced)

- Color, Black and White, and Large Format Copies

- Fax Services

- Binding and Lamination

- Volume printing and copying

As time progresses, Management may begin to offer several services that meet the continually changing needs of clients.

3.2 Sales of Office Supplies

The secondary revenue center for the business will be the sale of general office supplies including paper, binders, thumbtacks, folders, and small office electronics. Mr. Schmidt is currently sourcing a number of suppliers that can provide the business with its inventories before the onset of operations.

4.0 STRATEGIC AND MARKET ANALYSIS

4.1 Economic Outlook

This section of the analysis will detail the economic climate, the copy shop industry, the customer profile, and the competition that the business will face as it progresses through its business operations.

Currently, the economic market condition in the United States is sluggish. This slowdown in the economy has also greatly impacted real estate sales, which has halted to historical lows. Many economists expect that this sluggish growth will continue for a significant period of time, at which point the economy will begin a prolonged recovery period with more normalized growth. However, business owners and individuals will continue to need copy shop services. As such, the business should be able to remain profitable and cash flow positive at all times.

4.2 Industry Analysis

There are over 100,000 businesses that operate retail locations that provide small office business and printing related services identical or substantially similar to that of the Company. The industry generates more than $91 billion dollars a year in gross receipts. Additionally, copy and business service centers employ more than 290,000 people and the industry pays over $20 billion dollars a year in average annual payrolls. The growth rate of the industry has remained unusually high over the last ten years. With more and more people developing entrepreneurial ventures, the demand for office supplies and related services has increased.

Retail sales operations are a significantly riskier operation to maintain. This is due to the fact that there are significant costs in maintaining a high end retail location in an urban or upscale suburban market. There failure rate for these businesses is approximately 65% for the first five years of operations. Management is currently building a number of proprietary marketing and pricing models to help ensure the success of the Company.

4.3 Customer Profile

Pronto Printing's average client will be a middle to upper middle class man or woman (or small business owner) living in the Company's target market. Common traits among clients will include:

- Annual household income exceeding $50,000.

- Lives or works no more than 15 miles from the Company's location.

- Will spend $25 to $50 per visit to the location among individuals.

- Will spend $50 to $150 per month with Pronto Printing among business owners.

4.4 Competition

Within the Company's target market radius (approximately 10 miles), there are six other businesses that provide similar business services and sales of office supplies. The primary way that the business will differentiate itself from competitors is that the Company will use a number of vendors as it relates to specialty printing. As such, the business will be able to provide a much greater range of services to customers.

5.0 MARKETING PLAN

Pronto Printing, Inc. intends to maintain an extensive marketing campaign that will ensure maximum visibility for the business in its targeted market. Below is an overview of the marketing strategies and objectives of Company.

5.1 Marketing Objectives

- Develop an online presence by developing a website and placing the Company's name and contact information with online directories.

- Implement a local campaign with the Company's targeted market via the use of flyers, local newspaper advertisements, and word of mouth advertising.

- Develop ongoing relationships with Chambers of Commerce so that new businesses can become aware of the Company through local directories and referrals.

5.2 Marketing Strategies

Mr. Schmidt intends on using a number of marketing strategies that will allow Pronto Printing to easily target individuals and business owners within the target market. These strategies include traditional print advertisements and ads placed on search engines on the Internet. Below is a description of how the business intends to market its services to the general public.

Pronto Printing, Inc. will also use an internet based strategy. This is very important as many people seeking local retailers, such as copy shops, now the Internet to conduct their preliminary searches. Mr. Schmidt will register the Company with online portals so that potential customers can easily reach the business. The Company will also develop its own online website.

The Company will maintain a sizable amount of print and traditional advertising methods within local markets to promote the business/printing services and products that the Company is selling.

5.3 Pricing

As the business will provide a broad range of printing services and office supply products, it is difficult to determine pricing at this time. However, Mr. Schmidt anticipates that the business will generate gross margins of 78 cents on each dollar of revenue generated.

6.0 ORGANIZATIONAL PLAN AND PERSONNEL SUMMARY

6.1 Corporate Organization

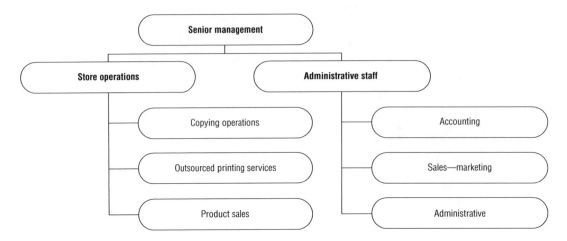

6.2 Organizational Budget

Personnel plan—yearly

Year	1	2	3
Owner	$ 40,000	$ 41,200	$ 42,436
Manager	$ 32,500	$ 33,475	$ 34,479
Copy shop employees	$ 57,000	$ 58,710	$ 60,471
Bookkeeper (P/T)	$ 12,500	$ 12,875	$ 13,261
Administrative	$ 20,000	$ 20,600	$ 21,218
Total	**$162,000**	**$166,860**	**$171,866**

Numbers of personnel

Owner	1	1	1
Manager	1	1	1
Copy shop employees	3	3	3
Bookkeeper (P/T)	1	1	1
Administrative	1	1	1
Totals	**7**	**7**	**7**

Personnel expense breakdown

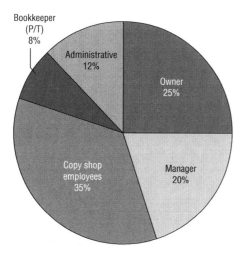

7.0 FINANCIAL PLAN

7.1 Underlying Assumptions

The Company has based its proforma financial statements on the following:

- Pronto Printing, Inc. will have an annual revenue growth rate of 10% per year.

- The Owner will acquire $100,000 of debt funds to develop the business.

- The loan will have a 10 year term with a 9% interest rate.

7.2 Sensitivity Analysis

In the event of an economic downturn, the business may have a decline in its revenues. However, small business/printing services are demanded regardless of the general economy. As such, only a severe economic drawback would result in a decline in revenues for the business.

7.3 Source of Funds

Financing

Equity contributions	
Investor(s)	$ 10,000.00
Total equity financing	**$ 10,000.00**
Banks and lenders	
Banks and lenders	$ 100,000.00
Total debt financing	**$100,000.00**
Total financing	**$110,000.00**

7.4 General Assumptions

General assumptions

Year	1	2	3
Short term interest rate	9.5%	9.5%	9.5%
Long term interest rate	10.0%	10.0%	10.0%
Federal tax rate	33.0%	33.0%	33.0%
State tax rate	5.0%	5.0%	5.0%
Personnel taxes	15.0%	15.0%	15.0%

7.5 Profit and Loss Statements

Proforma profit and loss (yearly)

Year	1	2	3
Sales	**$420,750**	**$462,825**	**$509,108**
Cost of goods sold	$ 92,565	$101,822	$112,004
Gross margin	78.00%	78.00%	78.00%
Operating income	**$328,185**	**$361,004**	**$397,104**
Expenses			
Payroll	$162,000	$166,860	$171,866
General and administrative	$ 12,500	$ 13,000	$ 13,520
Marketing expenses	$ 2,104	$ 2,314	$ 2,546
Professional fees and licensure	$ 3,500	$ 3,605	$ 3,713
Insurance costs	$ 2,000	$ 2,100	$ 2,205
Outsourced labor costs	$ 8,000	$ 8,800	$ 9,680
Rent and utilities	$ 25,000	$ 26,250	$ 27,563
Miscellaneous costs	$ 2,104	$ 2,314	$ 2,546
Payroll taxes	$ 24,300	$ 25,029	$ 25,780
Total operating costs	**$241,508**	**$250,272**	**$259,417**
EBITDA	**$ 86,678**	**$110,731**	**$137,686**
Federal income tax	$ 28,604	$ 33,858	$ 42,972
State income tax	$ 4,334	$ 5,130	$ 6,511
Interest expense	$ 8,738	$ 8,131	$ 7,468
Depreciation expenses	$ 4,107	$ 4,107	$ 4,107
Net profit	**$ 40,895**	**$ 59,505**	**$ 76,628**
Profit margin	**9.72%**	**12.86%**	**15.05%**

Sales, operating costs, and profit forecast

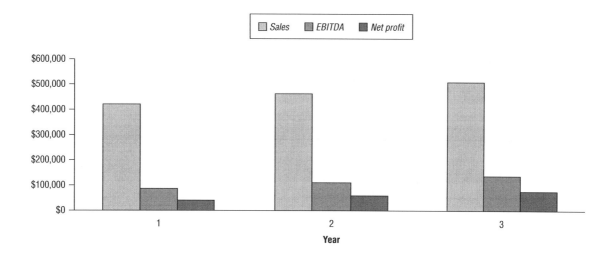

7.6 Cash Flow Analysis

Proforma cash flow analysis—yearly

Year	1	2	3
Cash from operations	$ 45,002	$ 63,612	$ 80,735
Cash from receivables	$ 0	$ 0	$ 0
Operating cash inflow	**$ 45,002**	**$ 63,612**	**$ 80,735**
Other cash inflows			
Equity investment	$ 10,000	$ 0	$ 0
Increased borrowings	$100,000	$ 0	$ 0
Sales of business assets	$ 0	$ 0	$ 0
A/P increases	$ 37,902	$ 43,587	$ 50,125
Total other cash inflows	**$147,902**	**$ 43,587**	**$ 50,125**
Total cash inflow	**$192,904**	**$107,199**	**$130,861**
Cash outflows			
Repayment of principal	$ 6,463	$ 7,070	$ 7,733
A/P decreases	$ 24,897	$ 29,876	$ 35,852
A/R increases	$ 0	$ 0	$ 0
Asset purchases	$ 57,500	$ 15,903	$ 20,184
Dividends	$ 31,502	$ 44,528	$ 56,515
Total cash outflows	**$120,362**	**$ 97,377**	**$120,283**
Net cash flow	**$ 72,542**	**$ 9,822**	**$ 10,578**
Cash balance	**$ 72,542**	**$ 82,364**	**$ 92,942**

Proforma cash flow (yearly)

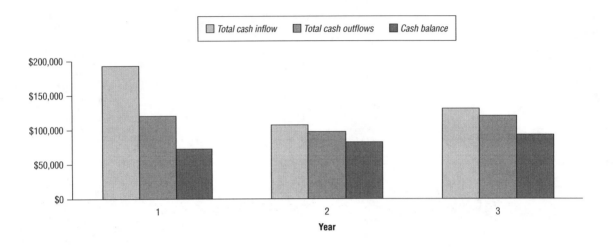

7.7 Balance Sheet

Proforma balance sheet—yearly

Year	1	2	3
Assets			
Cash	$ 72,542	$ 82,364	$ 92,942
Amortized development costs	$ 17,500	$ 19,090	$ 21,109
FF&E	$ 23,000	$ 34,927	$ 50,065
Copy machine equipment	$ 17,000	$ 19,385	$ 22,413
Accumulated depreciation	($ 4,107)	($ 8,214)	($ 12,321)
Total assets	**$125,935**	**$147,553**	**$174,207**
Liabilities and equity			
Accounts payable	$ 13,005	$ 26,716	$ 40,990
Long term liabilities	$ 93,537	$ 86,467	$ 79,397
Other liabilities	$ 0	$ 0	$ 0
Total liabilities	**$106,542**	**$113,183**	**$120,387**
Net worth	**$ 19,394**	**$ 34,370**	**$ 53,820**
Total liabilities and equity	**$125,935**	**$147,553**	**$174,207**

Proforma balance sheet

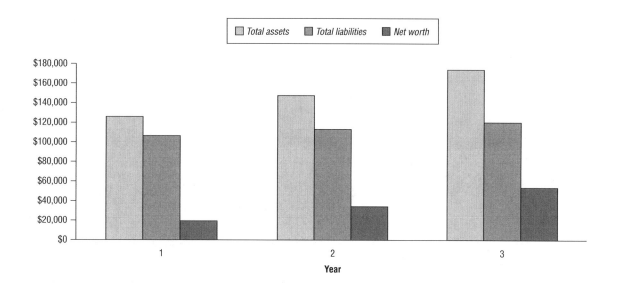

7.8 Breakeven Analysis

Monthly break even analysis

Year	1	2	3
Monthly revenue	$ 25,802	$ 26,738	$ 27,716
Yearly revenue	$309,625	$320,862	$332,586

Break even analysis

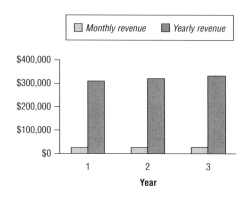

7.9 Business Ratios

Business ratios—yearly

Year	1	2	3
Sales			
Sales growth	0.00%	10.00%	10.00%
Gross margin	78.00%	78.00%	78.00%
Financials			
Profit margin	9.72%	12.86%	15.05%
Assets to liabilities	1.18	1.30	1.45
Equity to liabilities	0.18	0.30	0.45
Assets to equity	6.49	4.29	3.24
Liquidity			
Acid test	0.68	0.73	0.77
Cash to assets	0.58	0.56	0.53

7.10 Three Year Profit and Loss Statement

Profit and loss statement (first year)

Months	1	2	3	4	5	6	7
Sales	$34,375	$34,500	$34,625	$34,750	$34,875	$35,000	$35,125
Cost of goods sold	$ 7,563	$ 7,590	$ 7,618	$ 7,645	$ 7,673	$ 7,700	$ 7,728
Gross margin	78.00%	78.00%	78.00%	78.00%	78.00%	78.00%	78.00%
Operating income	$26,813	$26,910	$27,008	$27,105	$27,203	$27,300	$27,398
Expenses							
Payroll	$ 13,500	$ 13,500	$ 13,500	$ 13,500	$ 13,500	$ 13,500	$ 13,500
General and administrative	$ 1,042	$ 1,042	$ 1,042	$ 1,042	$ 1,042	$ 1,042	$ 1,042
Marketing expenses	$ 175	$ 175	$ 175	$ 175	$ 175	$ 175	$ 175
Professional fees and licensure	$ 292	$ 292	$ 292	$ 292	$ 292	$ 292	$ 292
Insurance costs	$ 167	$ 167	$ 167	$ 167	$ 167	$ 167	$ 167
Outsourced labor costs	$ 667	$ 667	$ 667	$ 667	$ 667	$ 667	$ 667
Rent and utilities	$ 2,083	$ 2,083	$ 2,083	$ 2,083	$ 2,083	$ 2,083	$ 2,083
Miscellaneous costs	$ 175	$ 175	$ 175	$ 175	$ 175	$ 175	$ 175
Payroll taxes	$ 2,025	$ 2,025	$ 2,025	$ 2,025	$ 2,025	$ 2,025	$ 2,025
Total operating costs	$20,126	$20,126	$20,126	$20,126	$20,126	$20,126	$20,126
EBITDA	$ 6,687	$ 6,784	$ 6,882	$ 6,979	$ 7,077	$ 7,174	$ 7,272
Federal income tax	$ 2,337	$ 2,345	$ 2,354	$ 2,362	$ 2,371	$ 2,379	$ 2,388
State income tax	$ 354	$ 355	$ 357	$ 358	$ 359	$ 361	$ 362
Interest expense	$ 750	$ 746	$ 742	$ 738	$ 734	$ 730	$ 726
Depreciation expense	$ 342	$ 342	$ 342	$ 342	$ 342	$ 342	$ 342
Net profit	$ 2,904	$ 2,995	$ 3,087	$ 3,179	$ 3,270	$ 3,362	$ 3,454

Profit and loss statement (first year cont.)

Month	8	9	10	11	12	1
Sales	$35,250	$35,375	$35,500	$35,625	$35,750	$420,750
Cost of goods sold	$ 7,755	$ 7,783	$ 7,810	$ 7,838	$ 7,865	$ 92,565
Gross margin	78.00%	78.00%	78.00%	78.00%	78.00%	78.00%
Operating income	$27,495	$27,593	$27,690	$27,788	$27,885	$328,185
Expenses						
Payroll	$13,500	$13,500	$13,500	$13,500	$13,500	$162,000
General and administrative	$ 1,042	$ 1,042	$ 1,042	$ 1,042	$ 1,042	$ 12,500
Marketing expenses	$ 175	$ 175	$ 175	$ 175	$ 175	$ 2,104
Professional fees and licensure	$ 292	$ 292	$ 292	$ 292	$ 292	$ 3,500
Insurance costs	$ 167	$ 167	$ 167	$ 167	$ 167	$ 2,000
Outsourced labor costs	$ 667	$ 667	$ 667	$ 667	$ 667	$ 8,000
Rent and utilities	$ 2,083	$ 2,083	$ 2,083	$ 2,083	$ 2,083	$ 25,000
Miscellaneous costs	$ 175	$ 175	$ 175	$ 175	$ 175	$ 2,104
Payroll taxes	$ 2,025	$ 2,025	$ 2,025	$ 2,025	$ 2,025	$ 24,300
Total operating costs	$20,126	$20,126	$20,126	$20,126	$20,126	$241,508
EBITDA	$ 7,369	$ 7,467	$ 7,564	$ 7,662	$ 7,759	$ 86,678
Federal income tax	$ 2,396	$ 2,405	$ 2,413	$ 2,422	$ 2,430	$ 28,604
State income tax	$ 363	$ 364	$ 366	$ 367	$ 368	$ 4,334
Interest expense	$ 722	$ 718	$ 714	$ 710	$ 706	$ 8,738
Depreciation expense	$ 342	$ 342	$ 342	$ 342	$ 342	$ 4,107
Net profit	$ 3,545	$ 3,637	$ 3,729	$ 3,821	$ 3,913	$ 40,895

Profit and loss statement (second year)

Quarter	Q1	2 Q2	Q3	Q4	2
Sales	$92,565	$115,706	$124,963	$129,591	$462,825
Cost of goods sold	$20,364	$ 25,455	$ 27,492	$ 28,510	$101,822
Gross margin	78.00%	78.00%	78.00%	78.00%	78.00%
Operating income	$72,201	$ 90,251	$ 97,471	$101,081	$361,004
Expenses					
Payroll	$33,372	$ 41,715	$ 45,052	$ 46,721	$166,860
General and administrative	$ 2,600	$ 3,250	$ 3,510	$ 3,640	$ 13,000
Marketing expenses	$ 463	$ 579	$ 625	$ 648	$ 2,314
Professional fees and licensure	$ 721	$ 901	$ 973	$ 1,009	$ 3,605
Insurance costs	$ 420	$ 525	$ 567	$ 588	$ 2,100
Outsourced labor costs	$ 1,760	$ 2,200	$ 2,376	$ 2,464	$ 8,800
Rent and utilities	$ 5,250	$ 6,563	$ 7,088	$ 7,350	$ 26,250
Miscellaneous costs	$ 463	$ 579	$ 625	$ 648	$ 2,314
Payroll taxes	$ 5,006	$ 6,257	$ 6,758	$ 7,008	$ 25,029
Total operating costs	$50,054	$ 62,568	$ 67,574	$ 70,076	$250,272
EBITDA	$22,146	$ 27,683	$ 29,897	$ 31,005	$110,731
Federal income tax	$ 6,772	$ 8,464	$ 9,142	$ 9,480	$ 33,858
State income tax	$ 1,026	$ 1,282	$ 1,385	$ 1,436	$ 5,130
Interest expense	$ 2,092	$ 2,053	$ 2,013	$ 1,973	$ 8,131
Depreciation expense	$ 1,027	$ 1,027	$ 1,027	$ 1,027	$ 4,107
Net profit	$11,230	$ 14,856	$ 16,330	$ 17,088	$ 59,505

Profit and loss statement (third year)

Quarter	Q1	3 Q2	Q3	Q4	3
Sales	**$101,822**	**$127,277**	**$137,459**	**$142,550**	**$509,108**
Cost of goods sold	$ 22,401	$ 28,001	$ 30,241	$ 31,361	$112,004
Gross margin	78.00%	78.00%	78.00%	78.00%	78.00%
Operating income	**$ 79,421**	**$ 99,276**	**$107,218**	**$111,189**	**$397,104**
Expenses					
Payroll	$ 34,373	$ 42,966	$ 46,404	$ 48,122	$171,866
General and administrative	$ 2,704	$ 3,380	$ 3,650	$ 3,786	$ 13,520
Marketing expenses	$ 509	$ 636	$ 687	$ 713	$ 2,546
Professional fees and licensure	$ 743	$ 928	$ 1,003	$ 1,040	$ 3,713
Insurance costs	$ 441	$ 551	$ 595	$ 617	$ 2,205
Outsourced labor costs	$ 1,936	$ 2,420	$ 2,614	$ 2,710	$ 9,680
Rent and utilities	$ 5,513	$ 6,891	$ 7,442	$ 7,718	$ 27,563
Miscellaneous costs	$ 509	$ 636	$ 687	$ 713	$ 2,546
Payroll taxes	$ 5,156	$ 6,445	$ 6,961	$ 7,218	$ 25,780
Total operating costs	**$ 51,883**	**$ 64,854**	**$ 70,043**	**$ 72,637**	**$259,417**
EBITDA	**$ 27,537**	**$ 34,422**	**$ 37,175**	**$ 38,552**	**$137,686**
Federal income tax	$ 8,594	$ 10,743	$ 11,602	$ 12,032	$ 42,972
State income tax	$ 1,302	$ 1,628	$ 1,758	$ 1,823	$ 6,511
Interest expense	$ 1,932	$ 1,889	$ 1,846	$ 1,802	$ 7,468
Depreciation expense	$ 1,027	$ 1,027	$ 1,027	$ 1,027	$ 4,107
Net profit	**$ 14,682**	**$ 19,135**	**$ 20,942**	**$ 21,869**	**$ 76,628**

7.11 Three Year Cash Flow Analysis

Cash flow analysis (first year)

Month	1	2	3	4	5	6	7
Cash from operations	$ 3,246	$ 3,337	$ 3,429	$ 3,521	$ 3,612	$ 3,704	$ 3,796
Cash from receivables	$ 0	$ 0	$ 0	$ 0	$ 0	$ 0	$ 0
Operating cash inflow	**$ 3,246**	**$ 3,337**	**$ 3,429**	**$ 3,521**	**$ 3,612**	**$ 3,704**	**$ 3,796**
Other cash inflows							
Equity investment	$ 10,000	$ 0	$ 0	$ 0	$ 0	$ 0	$ 0
Increased borrowings	$100,000	$ 0	$ 0	$ 0	$ 0	$ 0	$ 0
Sales of business assets	$ 0	$ 0	$ 0	$ 0	$ 0	$ 0	$ 0
A/P increases	$ 3,159	$ 3,159	$ 3,159	$ 3,159	$ 3,159	$ 3,159	$ 3,159
Total other cash inflows	**$113,159**	**$ 3,159**	**$ 3,159**	**$ 3,159**	**$ 3,159**	**$ 3,159**	**$ 3,159**
Total cash inflow	**$116,404**	**$ 6,496**	**$ 6,588**	**$ 6,679**	**$ 6,771**	**$ 6,863**	**$ 6,954**
Cash outflows							
Repayment of principal	$ 517	$ 521	$ 525	$ 528	$ 532	$ 536	$ 540
A/P decreases	$ 2,075	$ 2,075	$ 2,075	$ 2,075	$ 2,075	$ 2,075	$ 2,075
A/R increases	$ 0	$ 0	$ 0	$ 0	$ 0	$ 0	$ 0
Asset purchases	$ 57,500	$ 0	$ 0	$ 0	$ 0	$ 0	$ 0
Dividends	$ 0	$ 0	$ 0	$ 0	$ 0	$ 0	$ 0
Total cash outflows	**$ 60,092**	**$ 2,595**	**$ 2,599**	**$ 2,603**	**$ 2,607**	**$ 2,611**	**$ 2,615**
Net cash flow	**$ 56,313**	**$ 3,901**	**$ 3,988**	**$ 4,076**	**$ 4,164**	**$ 4,251**	**$ 4,339**
Cash balance	**$ 56,313**	**$60,214**	**$64,202**	**$68,278**	**$72,442**	**$76,693**	**$81,032**

Cash flow analysis (first year cont.)

Month	8	9	10	11	12	1
Cash from operations	$ 3,888	$ 3,979	$ 4,071	$ 4,163	$ 4,255	$ 45,002
Cash from receivables	$ 0	$ 0	$ 0	$ 0	$ 0	$ 0
Operating cash inflow	**$ 3,888**	**$ 3,979**	**$ 4,071**	**$ 4,163**	**$ 4,255**	**$ 45,002**
Other cash inflows						
Equity investment	$ 0	$ 0	$ 0	$ 0	$ 0	$ 10,000
Increased borrowings	$ 0	$ 0	$ 0	$ 0	$ 0	$100,000
Sales of business assets	$ 0	$ 0	$ 0	$ 0	$ 0	$ 0
A/P increases	$ 3,159	$ 3,159	$ 3,159	$ 3,159	$ 3,159	$ 37,902
Total other cash inflows	**$ 3,159**	**$ 3,159**	**$ 3,159**	**$ 3,159**	**$ 3,159**	**$147,902**
Total cash inflow	**$ 7,046**	**$ 7,138**	**$ 7,230**	**$ 7,322**	**$ 7,414**	**$192,904**
Cash outflows						
Repayment of principal	$ 545	$ 549	$ 553	$ 557	$ 561	$ 6,463
A/P decreases	$ 2,075	$ 2,075	$ 2,075	$ 2,075	$ 2,075	$ 24,897
A/R increases	$ 0	$ 0	$ 0	$ 0	$ 0	$ 0
Asset purchases	$ 0	$ 0	$ 0	$ 0	$ 0	$ 57,500
Dividends	$ 0	$ 0	$ 0	$ 0	$31,502	$ 31,502
Total cash outflows	**$ 2,619**	**$ 2,623**	**$ 2,627**	**$ 2,632**	**$34,138**	**$120,362**
Net cash flow	**$ 4,427**	**$ 4,515**	**$ 4,602**	**$ 4,690**	**−$26,724**	**$ 72,542**
Cash balance	**$85,459**	**$89,974**	**$94,576**	**$99,266**	**$72,542**	**$ 72,542**

Cash flow analysis (second year)

Quarter	Q1	2 Q2	Q3	Q4	2
Cash from operations	$12,722	$15,903	$17,175	$17,811	$ 63,612
Cash from receivables	$ 0	$ 0	$ 0	$ 0	$ 0
Operating cash inflow	**$12,722**	**$15,903**	**$17,175**	**$17,811**	**$ 63,612**
Other cash inflows					
Equity investment	$ 0	$ 0	$ 0	$ 0	$ 0
Increased borrowings	$ 0	$ 0	$ 0	$ 0	$ 0
Sales of business assets	$ 0	$ 0	$ 0	$ 0	$ 0
A/P increases	$ 8,717	$10,897	$11,769	$12,204	$ 43,587
Total other cash inflows	**$ 8,717**	**$10,897**	**$11,769**	**$12,204**	**$ 43,587**
Total cash inflow	**$21,440**	**$26,800**	**$28,944**	**$30,016**	**$107,199**
Cash outflows					
Repayment of principal	$ 1,708	$ 1,747	$ 1,787	$ 1,827	$ 7,070
A/P decreases	$ 5,975	$ 7,469	$ 8,067	$ 8,365	$ 29,876
A/R increases	$ 0	$ 0	$ 0	$ 0	$ 0
Asset purchases	$ 3,181	$ 3,976	$ 4,294	$ 4,453	$ 15,903
Dividends	$ 8,906	$11,132	$12,023	$12,468	$ 44,528
Total cash outflows	**$19,770**	**$24,324**	**$26,170**	**$27,113**	**$ 97,377**
Net cash flow	**$ 1,670**	**$ 2,476**	**$ 2,774**	**$ 2,902**	**$ 9,822**
Cash balance	**$74,212**	**$76,688**	**$79,462**	**$82,364**	**$ 82,364**

Cash flow analysis (third year)

Quarter	Q1	Q2	Q3	Q4	3
Cash from operations	$16,147	$20,184	$21,799	$22,606	$ 80,735
Cash from receivables	$ 0	$ 0	$ 0	$ 0	$ 0
Operating cash inflow	**$16,147**	**$20,184**	**$21,799**	**$22,606**	**$ 80,735**
Other cash inflows					
Equity investment	$ 0	$ 0	$ 0	$ 0	$ 0
Increased borrowings	$ 0	$ 0	$ 0	$ 0	$ 0
Sales of business assets	$ 0	$ 0	$ 0	$ 0	$ 0
A/P increases	$10,025	$12,531	$13,534	$14,035	$ 50,125
Total other cash inflows	**$10,025**	**$12,531**	**$13,534**	**$14,035**	**$ 50,125**
Total cash inflow	**$26,172**	**$32,715**	**$35,332**	**$36,641**	**$130,861**
Cash outflows					
Repayment of principal	$ 1,869	$ 1,911	$ 1,954	$ 1,999	$ 7,733
A/P decreases	$ 7,170	$ 8,963	$ 9,680	$10,038	$ 35,852
A/R increases	$ 0	$ 0	$ 0	$ 0	$ 0
Asset purchases	$ 4,037	$ 5,046	$ 5,450	$ 5,651	$ 20,184
Dividends	$11,303	$14,129	$15,259	$15,824	$ 56,515
Total cash outflows	**$24,379**	**$30,049**	**$32,343**	**$33,513**	**$120,283**
Net cash flow	**$ 1,793**	**$ 2,667**	**$ 2,989**	**$ 3,128**	**$ 10,578**
Cash balance	**$84,157**	**$86,824**	**$89,813**	**$92,942**	**$ 92,942**

Custom Paint and Body Shop/Classic Car Restorations

Racing Stripes

3014 Hwy 441
Douglas, Georgia 31535

Fran Fletcher

Racing Stripes is an auto paint and body shop owned and operated by Trey Jackson. Racing Stripes will provide customers with customized paint jobs, total classic car restorations, and collision repairs.

EXECUTIVE SUMMARY

Racing Stripes is an auto paint and body shop owned and operated by Trey Jackson. Racing Stripes will provide customers with customized paint jobs, total classic car restorations, and collision repairs.

Mr. Jackson, a native of Douglas, Georgia, has 25 years experience in the industry as the sole proprietor of Jackson Paint and Body. His mainstay over the years has been collision work; however, his passion is custom work. Due to the time involved and the space required for long-term projects, he has not been able to meet customer demand for restoring cars over the years.

What makes Racing Stripes stand out from the rest?

1. It will be an environmentally friendly shop using waterborne paint.

2. It will offer customized graphics, including murals.

3. It will provide show-quality restorations of classic cars.

4. It will have space to accommodate tractor-trailers, who currently have to go out of the area for service.

Mr. Jackson wishes to purchase land and construct a new shop on a major roadway to increase visibility and for customer convenience. Mr. Jackson is seeking financing in the form of a business line of credit. Financial projections indicate that Racing Stripes will be able to pay back the line of credit in three years.

COMPANY DESCRIPTION

Location

Mr. Jackson is considering purchasing land on Hwy. 441 South, just outside of the Douglas, GA city limits. Hwy. 441 is a four-lane highway that will allow him to accommodate tractor-trailers. This space is large enough to allow for a large fenced area, parking lot, and a large metal building.

Hours of Operations

Tuesday-Saturday 8 AM—5 PM

Sunday-Monday by appointment only

Personnel

Trey Jackson (Owner/Operator)

Mr. Jackson will perform all operations for the first six months including collision repair, custom paint jobs, and office management.

Autobody technician/Painter

A full-time technician will be hired after six months, if business allows, or sooner if two total restorations are scheduled.

Products and Services

Products

- Running boards
- Euro tail lights
- Vent shades
- Pinstripes
- Under-car neon lights
- HID headlight conversion kits

Services

- Collision Repair
- Customized Paint jobs
- Classic car restorations
- Air brushed graphics
- Wrapping
- Tractor-trailer painting
- Spray-in bedliners
- Pin striping

MARKET ANALYSIS

Industry Overview

According to the Bureau of Labor Statistics, jobs in the automotive body and glass repairers industry is expected to increase 19% from 2010 to 2020.

Racing Stripes will be located in Coffee County, Georgia just outside the city limits of Douglas, the county seat. Coffee County has a population of 40,868. According to the Georgia Department of Transportation, there were 420 crashes in Coffee County in 2006. This does not include citizens who had crashes elsewhere. According to the 2011 Georgia County Guide compiled by the University of Georgia, 21.1% of Coffee County's workforce commute from surrounding counties and will serve as an additional customer base.

Target Market

Racing Stripes will have three target markets in the first three years of business. Each target will be marketed in different ways.

- Classic car restoration—adult males from the southeastern U.S.

- Customized paint jobs—OTR truck drivers and teenagers

- Collision—drivers whose vehicles have suffered damage

Competition

There are currently six automotive paint and body shops within the city limits of Douglas, Georgia. None of these shops currently use waterborne paint, accommodate tractor-trailers, or perform classic car restorations.

- Jones Paint and Body, Hwy 221 North, Douglas, GA—Performs collision work

- Primo Paint and Body, North Patterson Ave., Douglas, Georgia—Performs collision work; custom paint

- Henderson GMC Body Shop, 206 Connector, Douglas, Georgia—Performs collision work

- King Ford Body Shop, South King Street, Douglas, Georgia—Performs collision work

- Buddy's Body Shop, Hazlehurst Hwy, Douglas, Georgia—Performs collision work; spray in bed-liners

- Extreme Excellence Paint and Body, West Ward Street, Douglas, Georgia—Performs collision work; custom paint

GROWTH STRATEGY

The overall strategy of the company is to attract new customers and to retain the loyal customer base that Mr. Jackson has gained over the years. Racing Stripes wishes to achieve strong financial growth during the first three years of operation by making a name for itself in the classic car restoration business. Mr. Jackson plans to work alone for the first six months and compensate his income with collision work.

Racing Stripes has a three-year plan for making a profit while transitioning into a custom-only shop. As the following charts show, Year 1 profits will be driven primarily by the volume of collision work while building custom and restoration clientele. Years 2 and 3 show a gradual transition in the source of profits from collision to restoration.

Percent Profits Three- Year Projection

Year 1

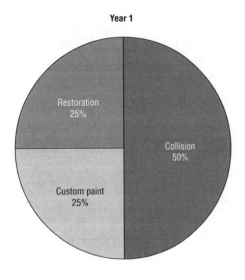

Year 2

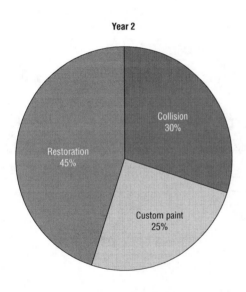

Year 3

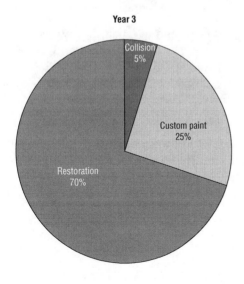

Sales and Marketing

According to the Small Business Development Center, word-of-mouth and referrals have served as the main advertising method for paint and body shops specializing in collision work. Referrals have been Mr. Jackson's marketing strategy in the past. However, now that the business is taking a new direction, Mr. Jackson has identified key advertising avenues and tactics to support Racing Stripes' growth strategy.

Racing Stripes will market the fact that it is the only paint and body shop in the area that uses waterborne paint. Using waterborne paint is not only environmentally friendly due to decreased volatile organic carbon emissions, but also provides a better color match since the auto industry uses this method on the production line.

Advertising

Classic car restoration

- Running ads in industry publications such as Hot Rod Magazine and Classic Driver.

- Attending/entering classic car shows to show off workmanship.

- His personal 1971 Dodge Challenger completely restored with custom paint job will be parked in view of the roadway to attract attention.

Custom Paint/ Collision

- Running regular newspaper ads in the Douglas Enterprise and the Douglas Shopper.

- Using social media such as Face Book to showcase workmanship.

- Racing Stripes decals will be placed on cars and trucks that are used for competition i.e. Southern Pullers Association

In addition to conventional advertising, the company will rely on quality work, great customer service, and fair prices to generate customers by word of mouth.

FINANCIAL ANALYSIS

Start-up costs

Estimated Start-up Costs

Land (1.5 acres)	$ 50,000
Metal building	$ 25,000
Chain link fence	$ 10,000
Spray booth	$ 15,000
Paint mixing system	$ 10,000
Frame machine	$ 3,500
Rotisserie	$ 3,000
Supplies/tools	$ 5,000
Parking lot	$ 5,000
Business license	$ 250
Website design	$ 1,000
Initial advertising/grand opening	$ 1,500
Parts estimator software	$ 2,000
Total	**$123,250**

Estimated Monthly Income

Mr. Jackson expects to repair at least two collisions per week. The average payout for a collision is $2,000, with body shop profits being $1,000. At a minimum, Mr. Jackson expects to make $8,000 profit per month from collision work. The cost of custom paint jobs will vary depending on the complexity of the job. The price of classic car restorations will also vary depending on the condition of the vehicle.

Prices for Custom Services

Real fire	$4,000
Graphics	$3,000
Show quality finish	$5,000
Murals	$ 250/hour
Frame up restoration	$ 50/hour plus materials

Estimated Monthly Expenses

Wages for Mr. Jackson and for an autobody technician/painter will be paid by the number of body and/or paint hours, which is determined by the insurance estimate. Mr. Jackson plans to work alone for the first six months, and then hire a full time technician. This will increase monthly expenses from $5,400 to $8,600.

Estimated Monthly Expenses

Waste disposal	$ 200
Bank loan	$ 400
Electricity	$ 250
Water	$ 50
Phone/Internet	$ 100
Advertising	$ 300
Insurance	$ 100
Wages for Mr. Jackson (est.)	$4,000
Wages for technician (est.)	$3,200
Total	**$5,400**
Total with technician	**$8,600**

Profit/Loss

Mr. Jackson takes a conservative approach and estimates $2,600 profit each month for the first six months. In Month 7, Mr. Jackson will hire a full time technician, which increases monthly expenses by $3,200. Mr. Jackson will hire a full time technician only after he has a restoration project, which pays $50 per hour. Mr. Jackson will spend approximately 30 hours per week on restorations, so monthly income will increase by $6,000.

Estimated profit months 1–6

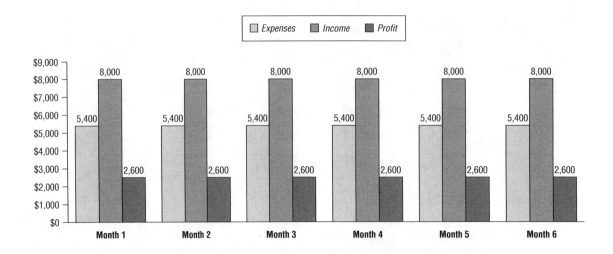

Estimated profit months 7–12

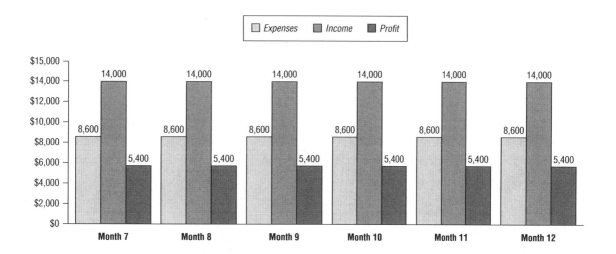

Estimated profit year 1

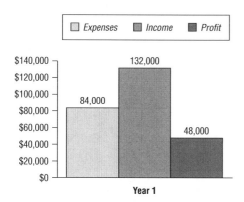

Financing

Mr. Jackson would like to take out a business line of credit for the amount needed to cover the start-up costs and the first month operating expenses. This loan would be in the amount of $128,650. Mr. Jackson hopes to use the land and building as collateral for the line of credit and plans to repay the line of credit in the third year of operation.

Dance Studio
Dancing Divas

7889 Washington St.
Jacksonville, FL 32202

Fran Fletcher

Dancing Divas is a dance studio located in Jacksonville, Florida co-owned by Farah Jones and Madelyn Johnson. Ms. Jones and Ms. Johnson want to share their passion for all things dance with Jacksonville area students ages 2 and older. Dancing Divas will offer multiple levels of instruction in ballet, jazz, tap, modern, ballroom, and hip hop.

BUSINESS SUMMARY

Dancing Divas is a dance studio located in Jacksonville, Florida co-owned by Farah Jones and Madelyn Johnson. Ms. Jones and Ms. Johnson want to share their passion for all things dance with Jacksonville area students ages 2 and older. Dancing Divas will offer multiple levels of instruction in ballet, jazz, tap, modern, ballroom, and hip hop.

Dancing Divas are excited about the opportunity to provide area dance students with a convenient location and class schedule. It is the mission of Dancing Divas to help students of all ages gain self-confidence and poise through dance in a structured but fun environment.

The owners of Dancing Divas are currently seeking financing for this venture. They have secured a location to rent that is highly visible and conveniently located to three schools. However, some renovations are needed to utilize the space for a dance studio. The owners are confident that classes will fill quickly and profits will follow.

COMPANY DESCRIPTION

Location
Dancing Divas is located in the Five Points shopping plaza, which also is home to Publix, Anytime Fitness, and Quiznos Subs. It is conveniently located near Hendricks Avenue Elementary School, Julia Landon Middle School, and Douglas Anderson School of the Arts, which have a combined student enrollment of 2,500 students. The retail space needs modifying in order to accommodate a dance studio. The owners would like to divide the space into two large studios, two restrooms, two changing rooms, office, storage area, reception area, and apparel/accessory area.

Hours of Operation

Dancing Divas will operate as follows:

> Monday-Thursday 12 PM—7 PM
>
> Friday 2 PM—5 PM

Summer Hours include:

> Tuesday-Thursday 10 AM—4 PM

Personnel

Farah Jones (co-owner/instructor)

Ms. Jones received her B.A. in performing arts from the University of Florida and an M.B.A. from Florida State University. She danced with the Atlanta Ballet Company for two years. She has 20 years of dance experience and three years of experience as a dance instructor at Dainty's School of Dance in Gainesville, FL.

Madelyn Johnson (co-owner/instructor)

Ms. Johnson received a bachelor's degree in business administration from Valdosta State University and a B.A. in performing arts from the University of Miami. She has 18 years of dance experience and two years of experience as a teaching assistant at Regina's Dance Studio in Valdosta, GA.

Student assistants

Two student assistants will be hired to assist with instruction. More may be added as needed.

Products and Services

Products

- Dance apparel
- Dance shoes
- Dance supplies

Services

- Dance Instruction for preschoolers
- Dance Instruction for children and teens
- Dance Instruction for adults
- Private Instruction

Class Schedule

Regular classes will start in September and end in May of each year. A summer schedule will also be offered, with limited spaces available, for students wishing to continue instruction during the summer.

Class Schedule—Monday

Studio	Class	Time	Student age	Max # students
A	Mommy and Me	1:00 p.m.	2 years	8
A	Baby Ballet	2:15 p.m.	3 years	8
A	Hip Hop for Kids	3:30 p.m.	5–7 years	12
A	Twinkle Toes	4:30 p.m.	4 years	12
A	Totally Tweens	5:45 p.m.	8–10 years	12
B	Modern Dance	3:00 p.m.	13+ years	12
B	Intermediate Ballet	4:00 p.m.	12+ years	12
B	Ballroom	6:00 p.m.	Adults	12

Class Schedule—Tuesday

Studio	Class	Time	Student age	Max # students
A	Mommy and Me	1:00 p.m.	2 years	8
A	Baby Ballet	2:15 p.m.	3 years	8
A	Totally Tweens	3:30 p.m.	11–12 years	12
A	Twinkle Toes	4:30 p.m.	4 years	12
A	Baby Ballet	5:45 p.m.	3 years	8
B	Twinkle Toes	4:00 p.m.	4 years	12
B	Hip Hop for Kids	5:30 p.m.	8–10 years	12

Class Schedule—Wednesday

Studio	Class	Time	Student age	Max # students
A	Mommy and Me	1:00 p.m.	2 years	8
A	Baby Ballet	2:15 p.m.	3 years	8
A	Intermediate Tap	3:30 p.m.	10+ years	12
A	Intermediate Jazz	4:30 p.m.	10+ years	12
A	Totally Tweens	6:00 p.m.	11–12 years	12
B	Modern Dance	4:00 p.m.	13+ years	12
B	Ballroom	5:30 p.m.	13+ years	12

Class Schedule—Thursday

Studio	Class	Time	Student age	Max # students
A	Intermediate Ballet	3:30 p.m.	12+ years	12
A	Intermediate Tap	4:30 p.m.	10+ years	12
A	Intermediate Jazz	5:45 p.m.	10+ years	12
A	Intermediate Hip Hop	6:45 p.m.	10+ years	12
B	Totally Tweens	6:00 p.m.	8–10 years	12
B	Advanced Ballet	4:00 p.m.	15+ years	12
B	Advanced Hip Hop	5:30 p.m.	13+ years	12

Class Schedule—Friday

Studio	Class	Time	Student age	Max # students
A	Private Instruction	3:00 p.m.	Any	2
A	Private Instruction	4:00 p.m.	Any	2
B	Private Instruction	3:00 p.m.	Any	2
B	Private Instruction	4:00 p.m.	Any	2

Summer Schedule (each class is limited to 12 students)

	Tuesday	Wednesday	Thursday
10:00 a.m.	Mommy and Me	Baby Ballet	Twinkle Toes
11:00 a.m.	Totally Tweens	Hip Hop for Kids	Ballroom
1:00 p.m.	Hip Hop for Kids	Totally Tweens	Mommy and Me
2:00 p.m.	Intermediate Ballet	Modern Dance	Advanced Ballet
3:00 p.m.	Private Instruction	Private Instruction	Private Instruction

MARKET ANALYSIS

Industry Overview

According to the Bureau of Labor Statistics, the job outlook for self-enrichment teachers is expected to increase by 21% from 2010 to 2020. Dance is a popular extracurricular activity that provides children of all ages with a fun form of exercise. Added benefits of dance are learning rhythm, increasing coordination, and boosting self-confidence.

Target Market

In the beginning, the target market for Dancing Divas will be preschoolers in surrounding neighborhoods and students attending Hendricks Avenue Elementary School, Julia Landon Middle School, and Douglas Anderson School of the Arts, which are in close proximity to the studio.

Eventually, children between the ages of 2 and 18 in the southeastern Jacksonville area will be the future target market for the dance studio. According to CLRSearch.com, in 2010, Jacksonville's youth population consisted of:

- Age 0-5: 75,982

- Age 6-11: 68,237

- Age 12-17: 70,874

Dance studios are generally limited in the number of students that can be accepted due to the fact that most children are enrolled in school and are unable to attend classes before 3:00 p.m. and after 7:00 p.m. The owners have plans to open an additional studio in a few years and would be able to accommodate more of Jacksonville's youth.

Competition

Dancing Divas wants to give its students the opportunity to experience a variety of dance types in order to present them with the opportunity to find a type in which they excel. There are currently three dance studios within ten miles of Dancing Divas. All three studios specialize in a specific area of dance.

- Just Dance—Specializes in hip hop

- Bunheads—Specializes in ballet

- Stella's Dance Academy—Specializes in dance competition

GROWTH STRATEGY

The overall strategy of Dancing Divas is to offer an environment where students feel free to express themselves through dance and music. The owners know that if students enjoy their classes that the studio will grow through referrals. The owners have created a conservative class schedule and expect classes to fill up quickly; however, more classes can be scheduled in Studio B if necessary. If Dancing Divas has a full class load, it will achieve financial independence during the first two years of operation.

Dancing Divas will have enough square footage to add a third studio so that additional classes and instructors can be added as needed. After funding is repaid and the owners have saved additional cash, Dancing Divas would like to open a second location to accommodate additional students in approximately four years.

Sales and Marketing

The company has identified key tactics to support the company's growth strategy.

Initial advertising will include:

- Running newspaper ads in the Florida Times Union

- Giving Dancing Diva pencils to students at area schools

- Mailing postcards to area neighborhoods

Ongoing marketing strategies:

- Using social media such as Face Book.

- Dancing Divas website

- Offering merchandise discounts for referrals

FINANCIAL ANALYSIS

Start-up Costs

Ms. Jones and Ms. Johnson have secured a space to rent; however, it needs some renovations. The owners have spoken to a contractor who estimates that the renovations will cost $38,000 and will take four to six weeks to complete.

Estimated Start-up Costs

Building renovations	$38,000
Legal fees	$ 5,000
Apparel/shoe inventory	$10,000
Office furniture	$ 7,000
Business license	$ 250
Website design	$ 500
Initial advertising	$ 500
Insurance	$ 2,000
Total	**$63,250**

Estimated Monthly Expenses

Monthly expenses are expected to remain constant each month.

Monthly Expenses

Rent	$ 1,500.00
Phone/Internet	$ 150.00
Advertising	$ 100.00
Insurance	$ 200.00
Wages instructors	$ 8,000.00
Wages student assistants	$ 800.00
Total	**$10,750.00**

Estimated Monthly Income

Estimated Tuition (September to May)

Class	Monthly tuition	Max students	Max revenue
Mommy and Me	50	24	$ 1,200.00
Baby Ballet	55	32	$ 1,760.00
Hip Hop for Kids	55	24	$ 1,320.00
Twinkle Toes	55	36	$ 1,980.00
Totally Tweens	60	48	$ 2,880.00
Intermediate Tap	55	24	$ 1,320.00
Intermediate Ballet	55	24	$ 1,320.00
Intermediate Jazz	55	24	$ 1,320.00
Intermediate Hip Hop	55	12	$ 660.00
Ballroom	65	12	$ 780.00
Advanced Ballet	65	12	$ 780.00
Modern Dance	60	24	$ 1,440.00
Advanced Hip Hop	60	12	$ 720.00
Private Instruction (appt only)	50/hr	4	$ 800.00
Total tuition (Sept–May)			**$18,280.00**

Estimated Tuition (July - August)

Class	Monthly tuition	Max students	Max revenue
Mommy and Me	50	24	$1,200.00
Baby Ballet	55	12	$ 660.00
Twinkle Toes	55	12	$ 660.00
Totally Tweens	60	24	$1,440.00
Hip Hop for Kids	55	24	$1,320.00
Intermediate Ballet	55	12	$ 660.00
Advanced Ballet	65	12	$ 780.00
Modern Dance	60	12	$ 720.00
Ballroom	65	12	$ 780.00
Private Instruction	50/hr	3	$ 600.00
Total tuition			**$8,820.00**

Profit/Loss

According to estimated expenses and income data, the summer months show some profit loss, the greatest loss in June when no classes are in session. The estimated profits for the rest of the year are enough to make up for this loss as shown in the "Annual Profit/Loss"chart.

Monthly profit/loss

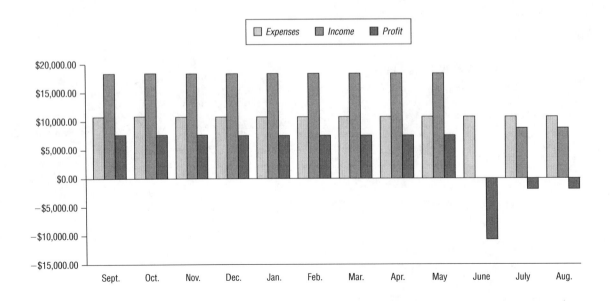

Annual profit/loss

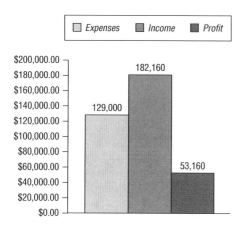

Financing

Dancing Divas is currently seeking financing in the amount of $85,000. This would cover start-up and operating expenses for two months. Ms. Jones and Ms. Johnson are confident that they will be able to repay this loan in the second year of operation and have approximately $21,320 in cash at the end of the second year as illustrated in the "Repayment Plan" chart.

Repayment plan

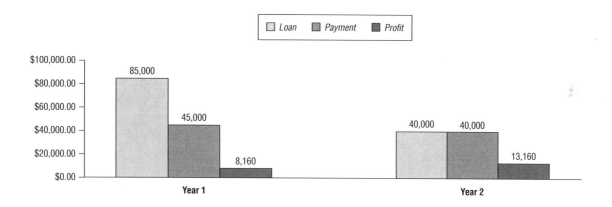

Dollar Store

Dollar Daze

3535 Lincoln Plaza Drive
Dayton, Ohio 45402

Dollar Daze is a business specializing in general merchandise. The store has access to the purchasing power of buying centers offering merchandise at prices 10 to 30 percent below wholesale with immediate delivery and low to no minimum orders. These centers are well-stocked and prepared to meet the increased demands of the peak selling seasons. Our mission is to provide the Dayton area with a wide variety of quality general merchandise generally priced at one dollar, in a clean and friendly atmosphere.

This business plan appeared in Business Plans Handbook, Volume 9. It has been updated for this volume.

1.0 EXECUTIVE SUMMARY

Dollar Daze is a business specializing in general merchandise. It will be located in the brand-new Town Square Plaza, which is in a high traffic area. The space will be next to Nicky's, a café and bakery. The space is easily accessible and provides ample parking for its customers. The space is visible from all points within the center itself as well as the traffic from Martin and Washington Streets. The business is a retail establishment selling current dollar variety merchandise. The majority of the merchandise is priced within a one-dollar price range, thus attracting the widest possible range of customers.

Dollar Daze has access to the purchasing power of buying centers offering merchandise at prices 10 to 30 percent below wholesale with immediate delivery and low to no minimum orders. These centers are well stocked and prepared to meet the increased demands of the peak selling seasons such as Seasonal Changes, Back-to-School, and Holiday Needs. Since delivery from these centers to the business takes only five to ten days, Dollar Daze is assured of a well-stocked store regardless of seasonal demands. Also, since these buying centers are able to deliver in such a short time, there is not a necessity to carry an extremely large inventory in advance of peak selling periods.

Dollar Daze attracts its customers through the use of specialized advertisements, handbills, news releases in newspapers as well as the traffic flow the area itself generates.

Proposed hours of operation are from 9:00 a.m. to 7:00 p.m. Monday through Saturday and 12:00 p.m. to 6:00 p.m. Sunday. Dollar Daze will also maintain extended Holiday hours. The business will be closed Christmas Day as well as three other national holidays yet to be decided.

A Grand Opening will commence after Dollar Daze has been in business for six to eight weeks. This event will be held on a Saturday. Dollar Daze's owner Melinda Parker will coordinate the Grand Opening. It will include a local political official, ribbon cutting ceremony, pictures, speaking, etc. Professional news releases will be submitted to the local and market area newspapers, and possibly radio and television.

The storeowner of Dollar Daze has access to over 250 of the best buying centers in the country. The buying centers provide inventory and fixtures. Melinda Parker will take a buying trip for initial inventory with her close friend and a professional buyer, Lucy Adams. All staff will be provided with in-store training.

According to the information contained in this business plan, we feel that Dollar Daze is a sound business investment for the financial institution to consider for a loan in the amount of $77,000.

1.1 Key to Success

The key to our successful retail business is our flexibility. The buying habits of customers change and vary. The availability of equally varied merchandise gives us the freedom to change with our customers.

1.2 Mission

Our mission is to provide the Dayton area with a wide variety of quality general merchandise largely priced at one dollar in a clean and friendly atmosphere.

2.0 COMPANY SUMMARY

Dollar Daze will rent a 1,300-square-foot space, having 1,000 square feet of selling space from Noel Sparks. Located in the brand-new Town Square Plaza, it is a high traffic area. The space will be next to Nicky's, a café and bakery. The space is easily accessible and provides ample parking for its customers. The space is visible from all points within the center itself as well as the traffic from Martin and Washington Streets.

Proposed hours of operation are from 9:00 A.M. to 7:00 P.M., Monday through Saturday and 12:00 P.M. to 6:00 P.M. on Sunday. Dollar Daze will also maintain extended holiday hours. The business will be closed Christmas Day as well as three other national holidays yet to be decided.

Since the selected location is in the heart of one of the busiest retail corridors in the area, we feel that this space is the best possible location in Dayton and surrounding areas.

2.1 Company Ownership

Dollar Daze is a sole-proprietorship and is registered to the owner, Melinda Parker.

2.2 Start-up Summary

Start-up costs will be financed through a combination of owner investment and a short-term loan. The start-up chart shows the distribution of financing.

Those expenses include:

- Inventory, fixtures, and supply fees of $53,680

- Marketing/advertising fees of $1,320 for our grand opening

- Build-out fees of $6,600 for our location including our sign

- Deposits on location, utilities, telephone, and insurance

Start-up plan

Start-up expenses

Deposit on location	$ 5,500
Rent (2 months)	$ 4,400
Build out of location (including sign)	$ 6,600
Telephone desposits/2 months payments	$ 1,650
Credit card machine	$ 330
License and permits	$ 220
Insurance (6 months)	$ 660
Advertising (2 months)	$ 1,320
Miscellaneous	$ 440
Total start-up expense	**$ 21,120**

Start-up assets needed

Cash requirements	$ 13,200
Start-up inventory	$ 53,680
Other short-term assets	$ 0
Total short-term assets	**$ 66,880**
Long-term assets	$ 0
Total assets	**$ 66,880**
Total start-up requirements:	**$ 88,000**
Left to finance:	$ 0

Start-up funding plan

Investment

Melinda Parker	$ 11,000
Investor 2	$ 0
Other	$ 0
Total investment	**$ 11,000**

Short-term liabilities

Unpaid expenses	$ 0
Short-term loans	$ 77,000
Interest-free short-term loans	$ 0
Subtotal short-term liabilities	**$ 77,000**
Long-term liabilities	$ 0
Total liabilities	**$ 77,000**
Loss at start-up	($21,120)
Total capital	**($10,120)**
Total capital and liabilities	**$ 66,880**

2.2.1 Equipment and Supplies

Listed below is our equipment and supplies list:

- Inventory at cost
- Gondolas
- Shelving
- Pegboard & Slatwall
- Pegboard & Slatwall Hooks
- Cash Register (Multi-Department)
- 2 Rolls Register Tape
- 2000 Plastic Bags
- 12 Shopping Baskets
- 1 2-Line Labeler
- 6 Rolls for Labeler

- Tissue Paper
- Weekly Bookkeeping & Record System
- Inventory Control System
- Supplier/Order System
- Advertising Manual
- Training Manual
- Promotional Idea Manual
- Custom Designed Handbills
- Customer Register Cards
- Pre-opening Guide
- Store Merchandise Guide
- Store Manual
- Buyers Guide
- Newsletter Service

3.0 PRODUCTS

Our product line will include items from the following categories:

- Hardware
- Toys
- Gift Items
- Office Supplies
- Schools Supplies
- Baby Products
- Bath Products
- Cleaning Products
- Pet Supplies
- Safety & Security Items
- Kitchen Items

We will always have an abundant selection of items available from which to choose.

4.0 MARKET ANALYSIS SUMMARY

The Dayton market faces the economic challenges of poverty, single parenthood, and public assistance, plus the generational squeeze of caring for the young and elderly at the same time. The majority of their budget goes to basics, such as rent and groceries. They are top-ranked for buying major household appliances and baby products and they tend to purchase fast food and takeout food.

General Statistics for 2010 in the Dayton area are as follows:

Total Population —161,696

Number of Households —67,467

Population by Race

- White - 50.5%
- Black - 42.6%
- Hispanic - 3%
- Asian Pacific Islander - .8%
- Other - 3.1%

Population by Gender

- Male - 48.7%
- Female - 51.3%

Income Figures

- Median Household Income - $27,423
- HH Income Under $50K - 75.3%
- HH Income $50K-$100 K - 20.8%
- HH Income Over $100K - 4.0%

2010 Housing Figures

- Average Home Value - $74,200
- Average Rent - $584

4.1 Market Segmentation

Dollar Daze will provide high quality merchandise at a discount price range to its customers. Since the majority of its items offered will be in the one-dollar price range, Dollar Daze will be able to maintain its competitiveness.

The target female market is in a growing community that has a population in excess of 161,696 people, well over 67,000 households, of which approximately 51.2 percent are female. The median family income for Dayton is $27,423.

4.2 Target Market Segment Strategy

The approaches to be used to attract these customers will be a website, radio and print advertising, signs in the store windows which are located in a busy area, and word-of-mouth advertising from our satisfied customers.

4.3 Industry Analysis

In 2011, retail sales amounted to $4.7 trillion dollars, up 1.8% from 2010. General merchandise and apparel grew to $1.11 trillion. According to the Department of Commerce, Internet shopping reached $188 billion or 13.7 percent of U.S. retail sales in 2010. The growth of traditional U.S. retailing should not be robust due to a dearth of economically favorable store locations. Many companies have responded by using their capital for other purposes such as reducing long-term debt and repurchasing their common stock.

Some companies can continue to grow their store count where they have a very specific demographic group to serve and locations can be developed in sparse locations at minimal costs. Keys to their success are convenient locations, relatively small stores, and the ability to provide most nonfood merchandise to their lower-income customer bases.

The retailing industry is mature and slow growing. These factors mean companies will have to do a better job of managing their operations. Specifically, retailers must close unprofitable stores, locate in regions with faster growth, and manage their inventory better. Retailers must also invest in automated processes to keep their costs down. Some companies have taken steps to reduce their exposure to economic cycles and consumer trends.

Traditional retailers may have finally recognized the potential of Internet commerce and its impact on their business. Initially, retailers had just a website that was more for informational purposes than e-commerce transactional purposes. However, it is now rare for a retailer to not have an online presence as a major aspect of their business.

4.3.1 Industry Trends
Consumers are more value conscious than they've been in the past. Their shopping habits have shifted from department stores to discounters and mass merchandisers. Many consumers can find the same items at a mass merchandiser that they can find at a department store at a substantially lower price.

4.3.2 Competition and Buying Patterns
There is currently no other store of this kind in the area, which ensures its success!

Dollar Daze will offer a wide selection of general merchandise priced at only one dollar. Having over 25,000 different items to choose from for its inventory selection insures that Dollar Daze will be able to maintain a full and diverse inventory for its customers. It will have suppliers that can deliver these items within 5-10 working days, so the shelves and walls will remain full and well-stocked.

The Christmas season has traditionally been important to retailers but there has been little to no growth in the past few years because of the lackluster economy. Part of the problem is shifting demographics. Older people tend to buy fewer items as they age. Since the baby boom generation is approaching their fifties, they will have less need for more items. So the target market of these stores leans towards men and women ages 18-49.

Some retailers have responded by offering theme promotions during other parts of the year, such as Valentine's Day, Independence Day, and Easter. Retailers are also requiring their suppliers to develop unique and exclusive merchandise and product assortments for their stores to avoid competition with another store for the same product.

Consumers are much more value-oriented which has contributed to the growth of mass merchandise stores. Another indication is the growth of the wholesale club and dollar store concept over the past two decades. These stores allow consumers to buy products in bulk and get more products for their money. These stores mostly carry fast-moving merchandise brands which are number one or two in their respective product categories.

The Dayton area continues to expand, offering the retail establishments an ever-growing opportunity for success.

5.0 STRATEGY AND IMPLEMENTATION SUMMARY

Melinda Parker has chosen three strategies for implementation of Dollar Daze and they are:

1. to build sales volume

2. to create a customer database

3. to develop an effective product line and pricing strategy

During the first few years, the store's sales, she hopes, will grow through the use of promotional campaigns, magazine advertisements, and website sales. Trisha will develop the customer database through careful selection and screening of mailing lists. She plans to select an inventory she feels is affordable and unique when compared to the other dollar store products. For her pricing strategy, she will establish an ongoing campaign to purchase products at pennies less than her competitors, whereas sometimes she can sell items at $.99 instead of $1.00.

5.1 Competitive Edge

Dollar Daze will be locally owned and operated, insuring that the needs and desires of the local community are met. It will also be able to provide special ordering of items for its customers and offer a personal and friendly atmosphere that you cannot find in larger chain variety stores.

5.2 Sales Strategy

Our sales strategy is to:

- develop a website for e-commerce sales within the next year

- provide quality customer service

- have a "no cash refund/exchanges only" policy

- accept all major credit cards

- survey our customers regarding products they would like to see added to our store

- sponsor school and other community events

- automate our sales process, such as using bar codes and a Point-of-Purchase cash register to track inventory and sales

5.2.1 Sales Forecast

Revenues of stores of this nature, using the available demographics, average between $176 to $177 in sales per square foot of selling space during their first year of business. This business projected its first year at 90 percent of low average.

Each year reflects an increase of 5 percent per year in fixed expenses to more than keep up with the current consumer price index (CPI).

Year 2 reflects a conservative growth rate of 15 percent. Year 3 reflects a growth rate of 10 percent. The information in the chart below is based on a 1,300-square-foot unit with 1,000 square feet of actual selling space.

Sales forecast

Sales	FY2012	FY2013	FY2014
Row 1	$348,480	$400,752	$440,827
Other	$ 0	$ 0	$ 0
Total sales	**$348,480**	**$400,752**	**$440,827**

Direct cost of sales	FY2012	FY2013	FY2014
Row 1	$200,376	$234,432	$234,432
Other	$ 0	$ 0	$ 0
Subtotal cost of sales	**$200,376**	**$234,432**	**$234,432**

6.0 MANAGEMENT SUMMARY

Melinda Parker, owner of Dollar Daze, has a B.A. degree in Marketing. For two years she has managed a dollar store similar to Dollar Daze. She has a full understanding of how to operate and manage a dollar store and its employees.

6.1 Personnel Plan

The personnel plan is included in the following table. It shows the owner's salary (Other) and two full-time salaries for cashiers. There will be no benefits offered at this time. Cashiers will have other duties as assigned.

Personnel plan

Personnel	FY2012	FY2013	FY2014
Cashier (1)	$13,200	$13,200	$13,200
Cashier (2)	$13,200	$13,200	$13,200
Other	$39,600	$39,600	$39,600
Total payroll	**$66,000**	**$66,000**	**$66,000**
Total headcount	**3**	**3**	**3**
Payroll burden	$ 9,900	$ 9,900	$ 9,900
Total payroll expenditures	**$75,900**	**$75,900**	**$75,900**

7.0 FINANCIAL PLAN

Our financial plan includes:

- moderate growth with a steady cash flow

- investing residual profits into company expansion

- repayment of our loan calculated at a high A.P.R. of 10 percent and at a 10-yearpayback on our $77,000 loan

7.1 Important Assumptions

We do not sell anything on credit. The personnel burden is low because benefits are not paid to our staff. We will continue to work on a short-term interest rate that is lower. We are also assuming the economy will continue to grow and there will continue to be a need for stores such as Dollar Daze.

General assumptions

	FY2012	FY2013	FY2014
Short-term interest rate %	10.00%	10.00%	10.00%
Long-term interest rate %	10.00%	10.00%	10.00%
Payment days estimator	30	30	30
Collection days estimator	45	45	45
Inventory turnover estimator	6.00	6.00	6.00
Tax rate %	25.00%	25.00%	25.00%
Expenses in cash %	10.00%	10.00%	10.00%
Sales on credit %	0.00%	0.00%	0.00%
Personnel burden %	15.00%	15.00%	15.00%

7.2 Break-even Analysis

A break-even analysis label has been completed on the basis of average costs/prices. With fixed costs averaging $5,979 and $176 to $177 in sales per square foot, we need $7,972 in sales per month to break-even.

Break-even analysis:

Monthly units break-even	17,538
Monthly sales break-even	$17,538

Assumptions:

Average per-unit revenue	$ 1.00
Average per-unit variable cost	$ 0.25
Estimated monthly fixed cost	$13,154

7.3 Projected Profit and Loss

We predict advertising costs will go down in the next three years as word of our store gets out to the public. Our net profit/sales ratio will be low the first year. We expect this ratio to rise at least 12 percent the second year and at least 3 percent in our third year. Normally, a startup concern will operate with negative profits through the first two years. We will avoid that kind of operating loss on our second year by knowing our competitors and having a full understanding of our target markets.

Profit and loss (income statement)

	FY2012	FY2013	FY2014
Sales	$348,480	$400,752	$ 440,827
Direct cost of sales	$200,376	$230,432	$ 253,475
Other	$ 13,200	$ 0	$ 0
Total cost of sales	**$213,576**	**$230,432**	**$253,4756**
Gross margin	$134,904	$170,320	$ 187,352
Gross margin %	38.71%	42.50%	42.50%
operating expenses:			
Rent	$ 22,000	$ 26,400	$ 26,400
Repairs and maintenance	$ 1,210	$ 1,320	$ 1,320
Insurance	$ 660	$ 1,320	$ 1,320
Professional fees	$ 1,320	$ 1,320	$ 1,320
Interest and bank charges	$ 660	$ 660	$ 660
Advertising	$ 6,600	$ 4,400	$ 2,200
Telephone	$ 1,650	$ 1,980	$ 1,980
Utilities	$ 6,600	$ 6,600	$ 6,600
Operating supplies	$ 2,640	$ 2,640	$ 2,640
Loan payment	$ 14,060	$ 15,338	$ 15,338
Capital purchases	$ 6,600	$ 6,600	$ 6,600
Travel	$ 0	$ 0	$ 0
Miscellaneous	$ 31,680	$ 2,640	$ 2,640
Payroll expense	$ 66,000	$ 66,000	$ 66,000
Payroll burden	$ 9,900	$ 9,900	$ 9,900
Depreciation	$ 0	$ 0	$ 0
Other	$ 0	$ 0	$ 0
Other	$ 0	$ 0	$ 0
Total operating expenses	**$169,380**	**$144,918**	**$ 142,718**
Profit before interest and taxes	($ 34,476)	$ 25,401	$ 44,634
Interest expense short-term	$ 7,700	$ 7,700	$ 7,700
Interest expense long-term	$ 0	$ 0	$ 0
Taxes incurred	($ 10,545)	$ 4,426	$ 9,233
Extraordinary items	$ 0	$ 0	$ 0
Net profit	**($ 31,632)**	**$ 13,277**	**$ 27,700**
Net profit/sales	**−9.08%**	**3.31%**	**6.28%**

7.4 Projected Cash Flow

We are positioning ourselves in the market as a medium risk concern with steady cash flows.

Pro-forma cash flow

	FY2012	FY2013	FY2014
Net profit	($ 31,632)	$13,277	$27,700
Plus:			
Depreciation	$ 0	$ 0	$ 0
Change in accounts payable	$ 6,582	$18,062	$ 700
Current borrowing (repayment)	$ 0	$ 0	$ 0
Increase (decrease) other liabilities	$ 0	$ 0	$ 0
Long-term borrowing (repayment)	$ 0	$ 0	$ 0
Capital input	$ 0	$ 0	$ 0
Subtotal	**($25,051)**	**$31,339**	**$28,400**
Less:	FY2012	FY2013	FY2014
Change in accounts receivable	$ 0	$ 0	$ 0
Change in inventory	($ 21,615)	$ 2,530	$ 3,461
Change in other short-term assets	$ 0	$ 0	$ 0
Capital expenditure	$ 0	$ 0	$ 0
Dividends	$ 0	$ 0	$ 0
Subtotal	**($ 21,615)**	**$ 2,530**	**$ 3,461**
Net cash flow	**($ 3,436)**	**$28,807**	**$24,941**
Cash balance	$ 9,764	$38,570	$63,512

7.5 Projected Balance Sheet

All of our tables will be updated monthly to reflect past performance and future assumptions. Future assumptions will not be based on past performance but rather on economic cycle activity, regional industry strength, and future cash flow possibilities. We expect a solid growth in net worth by the year 2015.

Pro-forma balance sheet

Assets

Short-term assets	FY2012	FY2013	FY2014
Cash	$ 9,764	$ 38,570	$ 63,512
Accounts receivable	$ 0	$ 0	$ 0
Inventory	$32,065	$ 34,595	$ 38,056
Other short-term assets	$ 0	$ 0	$ 0
Total short-term assets	**$41,829**	**$ 73,168**	**$101,568**
Long-term assets			
Capital assets	$ 0	$ 0	$ 0
Accumulated depreciation	$ 0	$ 0	$ 0
Total long-term assets	**$ 0**	**$ 0**	**$ 0**
Total assets	**$41,829**	**$ 73,168**	**$101,568**

Liabilities and capital	FY2012	FY2013	FY2014
Accounts payable	$ 6,582	$ 24,642	$ 25,344
Short-term notes	$77,000	$ 77,000	$ 77,000
Other short-term liabilities	$ 0	$ 0	$ 0
Subtotal short-term liabilities	**$83,582**	**$101,642**	**$102,344**
Long-term liabilities	$ 0	$ 0	$ 0
Total liabilities	**$83,582**	**$101,642**	**$102,344**
Paid in capital	$11,000	$ 11,000	$ 11,000
Retained earnings	($21,120)	($ 52,752)	($39,477)
Earnings	($31,632)	$ 13,277	$ 27,700
Total capital	**($41,752)**	**($28,477)**	**($ 777)**
Total liabilities and capital	**$41,829**	**$73,168**	**$101,567**
Net worth	($41,752)	($28,477)	($ 770)

7.6 Sales Forecast

Sales	Mar	Apr	May	Jun	Jul	Aug	Sep	Oct
	$27,878	$31,363	$26,136	$24,394	$24,394	$20,900	$31,363	$31,363
	Nov	**Dec**	**Jan**	**Feb**	**FY2012**	**FY2013**	**FY2014**	
	$34,848	$50,938	$20,909	$24,394	$348,880	$400,752	$440,827	

Direct cost of sales	Mar	Apr	May	Jun	Jul	Aug	Sep	Oct
	$16,029	$18,033	$15,028	$14,027	$14,027	$12,019	$18,033	$18,033
	Nov	**Dec**	**Jan**	**Feb**	**FY2012**	**FY2013**	**FY2014**	
	$20,038	$29,058	$12,023	$14,027	$200,376	$230,432	$253,475	

7.7 Personnel Plan

	Mar	Apr	May	Jun	Jul	Aug	Sep	Oct	Nov
Payroll	$ 0	$ 0	$ 0	$ 0	$ 0	$ 0	$ 0	$ 0	$ 0
Personnel simple									
Personnel plan									
Personnel	**Mar**	**Apr**	**May**	**Jun**	**Jul**	**Aug**	**Sep**	**Oct**	**Nov**
Cashier (1)	$1,100	$1,100	$1,100	$1,100	$1,100	$1,100	$1,100	$1,100	$1,100
Cashier (2)	$1,100	$1,100	$1,100	$1,100	$1,100	$1,100	$1,100	$1,100	$1,100
Other	$3,300	$3,300	$3,300	$3,300	$3,300	$3,300	$3,300	$3,300	$3,300
Total payroll	**$5,500**	**$5,500**	**$5,500**	**$5,500**	$5,500	**$5,500**	**$5,500**	**$5,500**	**$5,500**
Total headcount	3	3	3	3	3	3	3	3	3
Payroll burden	$ 825	$ 825	$ 825	$ 825	$ 825	$ 825	$ 825	$ 825	$ 825
Total payroll expenditures	**$6,325**	**$6,325**	**$6,325**	**$6,325**	**$6,325**	**$6,325**	**$6,325**	**$6,325**	**$6,325**

	Dec	Jan	Feb	FY2012	FY2013	FY2014	FY2015	FY2016
Payroll	$ 0	$ 0	$ 0	$ 0	$ 0	$ 0	$ 0	$ 0
Personnel simple								
Personnel plan								
Personnel	**Dec**	**Jan**	**Feb**	**FY2012**	**FY2013**	**FY2014**	**FY2015**	**FY2016**
Cashier (1)	$1,100	$1,100	$1,100	$13,200	$13,200	$13,200	$13,200	$13,200
Cashier (2)	$1,100	$1,100	$1,100	$13,200	$13,200	$13,200	$13,200	$13,200
Other	$3,300	$3,300	$3,300	$39,600	$39,600	$39,600	$39,600	$39,600
Total payroll	**$5,500**	**$5,500**	**$5,500**	**$66,000**	**$66,000**	**$66,000**	**$66,000**	**$66,000**
Total headcount	3	3	3	3	3	3	3	3
Payroll burden	$ 825	$ 825	$ 825	$ 9,900	$ 9,900	$ 9,900	$ 9,900	$ 9,900
Total payroll expenditures	**$6,325**	**$6,325**	**$6,325**	**$75,900**	**$75,900**	**$75,900**	**$75,900**	**$75,900**

7.8 General Assumptions

	Mar	Apr	May	Jun	Jul	Aug	Sep	Oct	Nov
Short-term interest rate %	10.00%	10.00%	10.00%	10.00%	10.00%	10.00%	10.00%	10.00%	10.00%
Long-term interest rate %	10.00%	10.00%	10.00%	10.00%	10.00%	10.00%	10.00%	10.00%	10.00%
Payment days estimator	30	30	30	30	30	30	30	30	30
Collection days estimator	45	45	45	45	45	45	45	45	45
Inventory turnover estimator	6.00	6.00	6.00	6.00	6.00	6.00	6.00	6.00	6.00
Tax rate %	25.00%	25.00%	25.00%	25.00%	25.00%	25.00%	25.00%	25.00%	25.00%
Expenses in cash %	10.00%	10.00%	10.00%	10.00%	10.00%	10.00%	10.00%	10.00%	10.00%
Sales on credit %	0.00%	0.00%	0.00%	0.00%	0.00%	0.00%	0.00%	0.00%	0.00%
Personnel burden %	15.00%	15.00%	15.00%	15.00%	15.00%	15.00%	15.00%	15.00%	15.00%

	Dec	Jan	Feb	FY2012	FY2013	FY2014	FY2015	FY2016
Short-term interest rate %	10.00%	10.00%	10.00%	10.00%	10.00%	10.00%	10.00%	10.00%
Long-term interest rate %	10.00%	10.00%	10.00%	10.00%	10.00%	10.00%	10.00%	10.00%
Payment days estimator	30	30	30	30	30	30	30	30
Collection days estimator	45	45	45	45	45	45	45	45
Inventory turnover estimator	6.00	6.00	6.00	6.00	6.00	6.00	6.00	6.00
Tax rate %	25.00%	25.00%	25.00%	25.00%	25.00%	25.00%	25.00%	25.00%
Expenses in cash %	10.00%	10.00%	10.00%	10.00%	10.00%	10.00%	10.00%	10.00%
Sales on credit %	0.00%	0.00%	0.00%	0.00%	0.00%	0.00%	0.00%	0.00%
Personnel burden %	15.00%	15.00%	15.00%	15.00%	15.00%	15.00%	15.00%	15.00%

7.9 Profit and Loss (Income Statement)

	Mar	Apr	May	Jun	Jul	Aug	Sep	Oct
Sales	$27,878	$31,363	$26,136	$24,394	$24,394	$20,900	$ 31,363	$31,363
Direct cost of sales	$16,029	$18,033	$15,028	$14,027	$14,027	$12,019	$ 18,033	$18,033
Production payroll	$ 0	$ 0	$ 0	$ 0	$ 0	$ 0	$ 0	$ 0
Other	$13,200	$ 0	$ 0	$ 0	$ 0	$ 0	$ 0	$ 0
Total cost of sales	**$ 29,229**	**$18,033**	**$15,028**	**$14,027**	**$14,027**	**$12,019**	**$ 18,033**	**$18,033**
Gross margin	($ 1,351)	$13,330	$11,108	$10,366	$10,366	$ 8,881	$ 13,330	$13,330
Gross margin %	−4.85%	42.50%	42.50%	42.50%	42.50%	42.49%	42.50%	42.50%
Operating expenses:								
Sales and marketing expenses								
Sales and marketing payroll	$ 0	$ 0	$ 0	$ 0	$ 0	$ 0	$ 0	$ 0
Rent	$ 0	$ 0	$ 2,200	$ 2,200	$ 2,200	$ 2,200	$ 2,200	$ 2,200
Repairs and maintenance	$ 0	$ 110	$ 110	$ 110	$ 110	$ 110	$ 110	$ 110
Insurance	$ 0	$ 0	$ 0	$ 0	$ 0	$ 0	$ 110	$ 110
Professional fees	$ 110	$ 110	$ 110	$ 110	$ 110	$ 110	$ 110	$ 110
Interest and bank charges	$ 55	$ 55	$ 55	$ 55	$ 55	$ 55	$ 55	$ 55
Advertising	$ 0	$ 0	$ 660	$ 660	$ 660	$ 660	$ 660	$ 660
Telephone	$ 0	$ 0	$ 165	$ 165	$ 165	$ 165	$ 165	$ 165
Utilities	$ 550	$ 550	$ 550	$ 550	$ 550	$ 550	$ 550	$ 550
Operating supplies	$ 220	$ 220	$ 220	$ 220	$ 220	$ 220	$ 220	$ 220
Loan payment	$ 0	$ 1,278	$ 1,278	$ 1 278	$ 1,278	$ 1,278	$ 1,278	$ 1,278
Capital purchases	$ 0	$ 0	$ 0	$ 0	$ 0	$ 0	$ 0	$ 0
Travel	$ 0	$ 0	$ 0	$ 0	$ 0	$ 0	$ 0	$ 0
Miscellaneous	$ 2,640	$ 2,640	$ 2,640	$ 2,640	$ 2,640	$ 2,640	$ 2,640	$ 2,640
Total sales and marketing expenses	**$ 0**	**$ 0**	**$ 0**	**$ 0**	**$ 0**	**$ 0**	**$ 0**	**$ 0**
Sales and marketing %	**0.00%**	**0.00%**	**0.00%**	**0.00%**	**0.00%**	**0.00%**	**0.00%**	**0.00%**
General and administrative expenses								
General and administrative payroll	$ 0	$ 0	$ 0	$ 0	$ 0	$ 0	$ 0	$ 0
Payroll expense	$ 5,500	$ 5,500	$ 5,500	$ 5,500	$ 5,500	$ 5,500	$ 5,500	$ 5,500
Payroll burden	$ 825	$ 825	$ 825	$ 825	$ 825	$ 825	$ 825	$ 825
Depreciation	$ 0	$ 0	$ 0	$ 0	$ 0	$ 0	$ 0	$ 0
Other	$ 0	$ 0	$ 0	$ 0	$ 0	$ 0	$ 0	$ 0
Total general and administrative expenses	**$ 0**	**$ 0**	**$ 0**	**$ 0**	**$ 0**	**$ 0**	**$ 0**	**$ 0**
General and administrative %	**0.00%**	**0.00%**	**0.00%**	**0.00%**	**0.00%**	**0.00%**	**0.00%**	**0.00%**
Other expenses								
Other payroll	$ 0	$ 0	$ 0	$ 0	$ 0	$ 0	$ 0	$ 0
Other	$ 0	$ 0	$ 0	$ 0	$ 0	$ 0	$ 0	$ 0
Total other expenses	**$ 0**	**$ 0**	**$ 0**	**$ 0**	**$ 0**	**$ 0**	**$ 0**	**$ 0**
Other %	0.00%	0.00%	0.00%	0.00%	0.00%	0.00%	0.00%	0.00%
Total operating expenses	**$ 9,900**	**$11,288**	**$14,313**	**$14,313**	**$14,313**	**$14,313**	**$ 14,423**	**$14,423**
Profit before interest and taxes	($ 11,251)	$ 2,042	($ 3,205)	($ 3,947)	($ 3,947)	($ 5,432)	($ 1,093)	($ 1,093)
Interest expense short-term	$ 642	$ 642	$ 642	$ 642	$ 642	$ 642	$ 642	$ 642
Interest expense long-term	$ 0	$ 0	$ 0	$ 0	$ 0	$ 0	$ 0	$ 0
Taxes incurred	($ 2,972)	$ 350	($ 961)	($ 1,146)	($ 1,146)	($ 1,518)	($ 433)	($ 433)
Extraordinary items	$ 0	$ 0	$ 0	$ 0	$ 0	$ 0	$ 0	$ 0
Net profit	**($ 8,919)**	**$ 1,049**	**($ 2,886)**	**($ 3,441)**	**($ 3,441)**	**($ 4,556)**	**($ 1,302)**	**($ 1,302)**
Net profit/sales	**−31.99%**	**3.35%**	**−11.04%**	**−14.11%**	**−14.11%**	**−21.79%**	**−4.15%**	**−4.15%**

7.9 Profit and Loss (Income Statement)cont.

	Nov	Dec	Jan	Feb	FY2012	FY2013	FY2014
Sales	$34,848	$50,938	$20,909	$24,394	$348,880	$400,752	$440,827
Direct cost of sales	$20,038	$29,058	$12,023	$14,027	$200,376	$230,432	$253,475
Production payroll	$ 0	$ 0	$ 0	$ 0	$ 0	$ 0	$ 0
Other	$ 0	$ 0	$ 0	$ 0	$ 13,200	$ 0	$ 0
Total cost of sales	**$20,038**	**$29,058**	**$12,023**	**$14,027**	**$213,576**	**$230,432**	**$253,475**
Gross margin	$14,810	$21,481	$ 8,886	$10,366	$134,904	$170,320	$187,352
Gross margin %	42.50%	42.50%	42.50%	42.50%	38.71%	42.50%	42.50%
Operating expenses:							
Sales and marketing expenses							
Sales and marketing payroll	$ 0	$ 0	$ 0	$ 0	$ 0	$ 0	$ 0
Rent	$ 2,200	$ 2,200	$ 2,200	$ 2,200	$ 22,000	$ 26,400	$ 26,400
Repairs and maintenance	$ 110	$ 110	$ 110	$ 110	$ 1,210	$ 1,320	$ 1,320
Insurance	$ 110	$ 110	$ 110	$ 110	$ 660	$ 1,320	$ 1,320
Professional fees	$ 110	$ 110	$ 110	$ 110	$ 1,320	$ 1,320	$ 1,320
Interest and bank charges	$ 55	$ 55	$ 55	$ 55	$ 660	$ 660	$ 660
Advertising	$ 660	$ 660	$ 660	$ 660	$ 6,600	$ 4,400	$ 2,200
Telephone	$ 165	$ 165	$ 165	$ 165	$ 1,650	$ 1,980	$ 1,980
Utilities	$ 550	$ 550	$ 550	$ 550	$ 6,600	$ 6,600	$ 6,600
Operating supplies	$ 220	$ 220	$ 220	$ 220	$ 2,640	$ 2,640	$ 2,640
Loan payment	$ 1,278	$ 1,278	$ 1,278	$ 1,278	$ 14,060	$ 15,338	$ 15,338
Capital purchases	$ 2,200	$ 2,200	$ 0	$ 0	$ 4,400	$ 4,400	$ 4,400
Travel	$ 0	$ 0	$ 0	$ 0	$ 0	$ 0	$ 0
Miscellaneous	$ 2,640	$ 2,640	$ 2,640	$ 2,640	$ 31,680	$ 31,680	$ 31,680
Total sales and marketing expenses	**$ 0**	**$ 0**	**$ 0**	**$ 0**	**$ 0**	**$ 0**	**$ 0**
Sales and marketing %	**0.00%**	**0.00%**	**0.00%**	**0.00%**	**0.00%**	**0.00%**	**0.00%**
General and administrative expenses							
General and administrative payroll	$ 0	$ 0	$ 0	$ 0	$ 0	$ 0	$ 0
Payroll expense	$ 5,500	$ 5,500	$ 5,500	$ 5,500	$ 66,000	$ 66,000	$ 66,000
Payroll burden	$ 825	$ 825	$ 825	$ 825	$ 9,900	$ 9,900	$ 9,900
Depreciation	$ 0	$ 0	$ 0	$ 0	$ 0	$ 0	$ 0
Other	$ 0	$ 0	$ 0	$ 0	$ 0	$ 0	$ 0
Total general and administrative expenses	**$ 0**	**$ 0**	**$ 0**	**$ 0**	**$ 0**	**$ 0**	**$ 0**
General and administrative %	**0.00%**	**0.00%**	**0.00%**	**0.00%**	**0.00%**	**0.00%**	**0.00%**
Other expenses							
Other payroll	$ 0	$ 0	$ 0	$ 0	$ 0	$ 0	$ 0
Other	$ 0	$ 0	$ 0	$ 0	$ 0	$ 0	$ 0
Total other expenses	**$ 0**	**$ 0**	**$ 0**	**$ 0**	**$ 0**	**$ 0**	**$ 0**
Other %	0.00%	0.00%	0.00%	0.00%	0.00%	0.00%	0.00%
Total operating expenses	**$16,623**	**$16,623**	**$14,423**	**$14,423**	**$169,380**	**$144,918**	**$142,718**
Profit before interest and taxes	($ 1,813)	$ 4,858	($ 5,537)	($ 4,057)	($ 34,476)	$ 25,401	$ 44,634
Interest expense short-term	$ 642	$ 642	$ 642	$ 642	$ 7,700	$ 7,700	$ 7,700
Interest expense long-term	$ 0	$ 0	$ 0	$ 0	$ 0	$ 0	$ 0
Taxes incurred	($ 614)	$ 1,054	($ 1,544)	($ 1,175)	($ 10,545)	$ 4,426	$ 9,233
Extraordinary items	$ 0	$ 0	$ 0	$ 0	$ 0	$ 0	$ 0
Net profit	**($ 1,841)**	**$ 3,161**	**($ 4,635)**	**($ 3,524)**	**($ 31,632)**	**$ 13,277**	**$ 27,700**
Net profit/sales	**−5.28%**	**6.26%**	**−22.16%**	**−14.45%**	**−9.08%**	**3.31%**	**6.28%**

7.10 Projected Cash Flow

	Mar	Apr	May	Jun	Jul	Aug	Sep	Oct
Net profit	($ 8,919)	$ 1,049	($ 2,886)	($ 3,441)	($ 3,441)	($ 4,556)	($ 1,302)	($ 1,302)
Plus:								
Depreciation	$ 0	$ 0	$ 0	$ 0	$ 0	$ 0	$ 0	$ 0
Change in accounts payable	$12,566	$ 6,926	($ 4,974)	$ 2,455	$ 1,742	($5,566)	$20,233	($10,465)
Current borrowing (repayment)	$ 0	$ 0	$ 0	$ 0	$ 0	$ 0	$ 0	$ 0
Increase (decrease) other liabilities	$ 0	$ 0	$ 0	$ 0	$ 0	$ 0	$ 0	$ 0
Long-term borrowing (repayment)	$ 0	$ 0	$ 0	$ 0	$ 0	$ 0	$ 0	$ 0
Capital input	$ 0	$ 0	$ 0	$ 0	$ 0	$ 0	$ 0	$ 0
Subtotal	$ 3,648	$ 7,975	($ 7,861)	($ 986)	($ 1,701)	($10,120)	$18,931	($11,767)
Less:								
Change in accounts receivable	$ 0	$ 0	$ 0	$ 0	$ 0	$ 0	$ 0	$ 0
Change in inventory	($16,029)	($ 1,584)	($ 6,010)	($ 2,002)	$ 0	($ 4,017)	$12,030	$ 0
Change in other short-term assets	$ 0	$ 0	$ 0	$ 0	$ 0	$ 0	$ 0	$ 0
Capital expenditure	$ 0	$ 0	$ 0	$ 0	$ 0	$ 0	$ 0	$ 0
Dividends	$ 0	$ 0	$ 0	$ 0	$ 0	$ 0	$ 0	$ 0
Subtotal	($16,029)	($ 1,584)	($ 6,010)	($ 2,002)	$ 0	($ 4,017)	$12,030	$ 0
Net cash flow	$19,677	$ 9,559	($ 1,850)	$ 1,016	($ 1,701)	($ 6,103)	$ 6,901	($11,768)
Cash balance	$32,877	$42,436	$40,586	$41,602	$39,901	$33,799	$40,700	$28,934

	Nov	Dec	Jan	Feb	FY2012	FY2013	FY2014
Net profit	($1,841)	$ 3,161	($ 4,635)	($ 3,524)	($31,632)	$13,277	$ 27,700
Plus:							
Depreciation	$ 0	$ 0	$ 0	$ 0	$ 0	$ 0	$ 0
Change in accounts payable	$ 6,989	$21,505	($45,151)	$ 321	$ 6,582	$18,062	$ 670
Current borrowing (repayment)	$ 0	$ 0	$ 0	$ 0	$ 0	$ 0	$ 0
Increase (decrease) other liabilities	$ 0	$ 0	$ 0	$ 0	$ 0	$ 0	$ 0
Long-term borrowing (repayment)	$ 0	$ 0	$ 0	$ 0	$ 0	$ 0	$ 0
Capital input	$ 0	$ 0	$ 0	$ 0	$ 0	$ 0	$ 0
Subtotal	$ 5,148	$24,669	($49,784)	($ 3,201)	($25,051)	$31,337	$ 28,400
Less:							
Change in accounts receivable	$ 0	$ 0	$ 0	$ 0	$ 0	$ 0	$ 0
Change in inventory	$ 4,008	$18,040	($12,023)	($14,027)	($21,615)	$ 2,530	$ 3,460
Change in other short-term assets	$ 0	$ 0	$ 0	$ 0	$ 0	$ 0	$ 0
Capital expenditure	$ 0	$ 0	$ 0	$ 0	$ 0	$ 0	$ 0
Dividends	$ 0	$ 0	$ 0	$ 0	$ 0	$ 0	$ 0
Subtotal	$ 4,008	$18,040	($12,023)	($14,027)	($21,615)	$ 2,530	$ 3,460
Net cash flow	$ 1,140	$ 6,629	($37,761)	$10,826	($ 3,436)	$28,807	$ 24,941
Cash balance	$30,072	$36,700	($ 1,060)	$ 9,764	$ 9,764	$38,570	$ 63,512

7.11 Projected Balance Sheet

Assets

Short-term assets	Mar	Apr	May	Jun	Jul	Aug	Sep	Oct
Cash	$32,877	$42,436	$40,586	$41,602	$39,901	$33,799	$ 40,700	$28,934
Accounts receivable	$ 0	$ 0	$ 0	$ 0	$ 0	$ 0	$ 0	$ 0
Inventory	$37,651	$36,067	$30,056	$28,054	$28,054	$24,037	$ 36,067	$36,067
Other short-term assets	$ 0	$ 0	$ 0	$ 0	$ 0	$ 0	$ 0	$ 0
Total short-term assets	**$70,528**	**$78,503**	**$70,642**	**$69,656**	**$67,956**	**$57,836**	**$ 76,767**	**$65,001**
Long-term assets	$ 0	$ 0	$ 0	$ 0	$ 0	$ 0	$ 0	$ 0
Capital assets	$ 0	$ 0	$ 0	$ 0	$ 0	$ 0	$ 0	$ 0
Accumulated depreciation	$ 0	$ 0	$ 0	$ 0	$ 0	$ 0	$ 0	$ 0
Total long-term assets	**$ 0**	**$ 0**	**$ 0**	**$ 0**	**$ 0**	**$ 0**	**$ 0**	**$ 0**
Total assets	**$70,528**	**$78,503**	**$70,642**	**$69,656**	**$67,956**	**$57,836**	**$ 76,767**	**$65,001**
Liabilities and capital								
Accounts payable	$12,566	$19,492	$14,518	$16,973	$18,713	$13,147	$ 33,381	$22,915
Short-term notes	$77,000	$77,000	$77,000	$77,000	$77,000	$77,000	$ 77,000	$77,000
Other short-term liabilities	$ 0	$ 0	$ 0	$ 0	$ 0	$ 0	$ 0	$ 0
Subtotal short-term liabilities	$89,566	$96,492	$91,518	$93,973	$95,713	$90,147	$110,381	$99,915
	$ 0	$ 0	$ 0	$ 0	$ 0	$ 0	$ 0	$ 0
Long-term liabilities	$ 0	$ 0	$ 0	$ 0	$ 0	$ 0	$ 0	$ 0
Total liabilities	**$89,566**	**$96,492**	**$91,518**	**$93,973**	**$95,713**	**$90,147**	**$110,381**	**$99,915**
	$ 0	$ 0	$ 0	$ 0	$ 0	$ 0	$ 0	$ 0
Paid in capital	$11,000	$11,000	$11,000	$11,000	$11,000	$11,000	$ 11,000	$11,000
Retained earnings	($21,120)	($21,120)	($21,120)	($21,120)	($21,120)	($21,120)	($ 21,120)	($21,120)
Earnings	($ 8,919)	($ 7,869)	($10,756)	($14,197)	($17,637)	($22,194)	($ 23,494)	($24,796)
Total capital	**($19,039)**	**($17,989)**	**($20,876)**	**($24,317)**	**($27,757)**	**($32,314)**	**($ 33,614)**	**($34,916)**
Total liabilities and capital	**$70,528**	**$78,503**	**$70,642**	**$69,656**	**$67,956**	**$57,836**	**$ 76,767**	**$65,001**
Net worth	**($19,039)**	**($17,989)**	**($20,876)**	**($24,317)**	**($27,757)**	**($32,314)**	**($ 33,614)**	**($34,916)**

Short-term assets	Nov	Dec	Jan	Feb	FY2012	FY2013	FY2014
Cash	$ 30,072	$ 36,700	($ 1,060)	$ 9,764	$ 9,764	$ 38,570	$ 63,512
Accounts receivable	$ 0	$ 0	$ 0	$ 0	$ 0	$ 0	$ 0
Inventory	$ 40,075	$ 58,115	$46,092	$32,065	$32,065	$ 34,595	$ 38,056
Other short-term assets	$ 0	$ 0	$ 0	$ 0	$ 0	$ 0	$ 0
Total short-term assets	**$ 70,147**	**$ 94,816**	**$45,032**	**$41,829**	**$41,829**	**$ 73,168**	**$101,567**
Long-term assets	$ 0	$ 0	$ 0	$ 0	$ 0	$ 0	$ 0
Capital assets	$ 0	$ 0	$ 0	$ 0	$ 0	$ 0	$ 0
Accumulated depreciation	$ 0	$ 0	$ 0	$ 0	$ 0	$ 0	$ 0
Total long-term assets	**$ 0**	**$ 0**	**$ 0**	**$ 0**	**$ 0**	**$ 0**	**$ 0**
Total assets	**$ 70,147**	**$ 94,816**	**$45,032**	**$41,829**	**$41,829**	**$ 73,168**	**$101,567**
Liabilities and capital							
Accounts payable	$ 29,905	$ 51,410	$ 6,259	$ 6,582	$ 6,582	$ 24,642	$ 25,344
Short-term notes	$ 77,000	$ 77,000	$77,000	$77,000	$77,000	$ 77,000	$ 77,000
Other short-term liabilities	$ 0	$ 0	$ 0	$ 0	$ 0	$ 0	$ 0
Subtotal short-term liabilities	$106,905	$128,410	$83,259	$83,582	$83,582	$101,642	$102,344
	$ 0	$ 0	$ 0	$ 0	$ 0	$ 0	$ 0
Long-term liabilities	$ 0	$ 0	$ 0	$ 0	$ 0	$ 0	$ 0
Total liabilities	**$106,905**	**$128,410**	**$83,259**	**$83,582**	**$83,582**	**$101,642**	**$102,344**
	$ 0	$ 0	$ 0	$ 0	$ 0	$ 0	$ 0
Paid in capital	$ 11,000	$ 11,000	$11,000	$11,000	$11,000	$ 11,000	$ 11,000
Retained earnings	($ 21,120)	($ 21,120)	($21,120)	($21,120)	($21,120)	($ 52,752)	($ 39,477)
Earnings	($ 26,635)	($ 23,474)	($28,109)	($31,632)	($31,632)	$ 13,277	$ 27,700
Total capital	**($ 36,755)**	**($ 33,594)**	**($38,229)**	**($41,752)**	**($41,752)**	**($ 28,477)**	**($ 777)**
Total liabilities and capital	**$ 70,147**	**$ 94,816**	**$45,032**	**$41,829**	**$41,829**	**$ 73,168**	**$101,567**
Net worth	**($ 36,755)**	**($ 33,594)**	**($38,229)**	**($41,752)**	**($41,752)**	**($ 28,477)**	**($ 777)**

Food Truck
Suerte Cuban Cuisine

PO Box 23145
Miami, Florida 33101

Kari Lucke

Suerte Cuban Cuisine aims to bring affordable, authentic, and delicious Cuban food to people living and working in the Miami area. This food truck business is owned and operated by Julio Nunez.

1.0 INTRODUCTION

1.1 Mission Statement

Suerte Cuban Cuisine aims to bring affordable, authentic, and delicious Cuban food to people living and working in the Miami area.

1.2 Executive Summary

Suerte Cuban Cuisine will be a locally owned and operated food truck located in Miami, Florida. This business will be owned and operated by Julio Nunez, and his business will serve busy working people, college students, and others who need a quick solution for lunch and/or dinner.

The primary target will be young professionals working in the city, who are often rushed and don't have time for a long meal. Targeting these young professionals will be fairly uncomplicated, as Suerte Cuban Cuisine will be parked conveniently in downtown Miami and will offer filling food at reasonable prices. There is room for growth for this business, as the base of customers is steady and reliable, and these customers will likely tell others about Suerte Cuban Cuisine.

1.3 Business Philosophy

At Suerte Cuban Cuisine, the customers come first. Julio wants to share his knowledge of traditional Cuban food with busy people who often don't have the time to enjoy a nice meal. Suerte Cuban Cuisine offers the taste and variety of more expensive establishments at a fraction of the cost and time. Time is money for these customers, and Suerte Cuban Cuisine works within their schedule to fuel them through a tough day at work.

1.4 Goals and Objectives

- Build a solid, reliable customer base within the first five months of operation

- Hire three additional employees after becoming more established

- Obtain attention through social media, blogging, and local press

- Earn $40,000 net profit in first year

1.5 Organization Structure

Suerte Cuban Cuisine will be run exclusively by Julio and his two college-aged sons in the first months. After gaining new customers and expanding hours, Julio will hire one part-time and one full-time employee. Julio will handle accounting, payroll, hiring, scheduling, and taxes.

1.6 Company History

Julio has a Cuban heritage, which has informed his knowledge and enthusiasm for Cuban cuisine. He has worked in food service for 20 years as a cook, server, bus boy, and caterer.

2.0 INDUSTRY AND MARKET

2.1 Industry Analysis

Food trucks have been growing in popularity since approximately 2008. In 2011, Zagat, the restaurant rating guide, added "Food Truck Reviews" to its publication categories, signally a wider acceptance—and celebration—of an industry that has become trendy. According to IBISWorld's Street Market Vendors in the US: Market Research Report (www.ibisworld.com, August 2012), food truck revenue for the food truck business is $1 billion annually, and annual growth from 2007 to 2012 was 8.4 percent. According to the Census Bureau, there are 1,930 licensed food trucks in the country, and a total of 6,708 employees. There has been a rise in the demand for food trucks because of their relative cost to the consumer, and social media such as Facebook and Twitter has given food trucks a platform on which to advertise their day-to-day locations.

2.2 Competition

There are 134 food trucks in the state of Florida, with 523 employees for those trucks. According to the South Florida Food Trucks Association (SFFTA), a trade association for the industry in Florida, there are approximately 30 other food trucks operating in Miami, which sell hot dogs, Vietnamese cuisine, Mexican food, seafood, gelato, gourmet grilled cheese, crepes, ice cream, barbecue, wings, shaved ice, and sandwiches, all of which are positively reviewed on Yelp and Google.

There are several locations and events hosted by the SFFTA such as the Miami Street Food Court and Food Truck Invasion that brings together all the currently operating food trucks in the Miami area and draws large crowds. Suerte Cuban Cuisine will participate in these round-ups, in part to compete with other vendors and in part to gain public exposure and market to new customers. Joining SFFTA will allow Julio to advertise his location and business summary on the website, also opening up opportunities for new customers. To compete with the other food trucks in the Miami area, Suerte Cuban Cuisine will offer authentic, delicious, affordable Cuban food, which is not currently being offered by other food truck vendors in the area. Other competitors would include brick-and-mortar restaurants, but their lack of mobility and convenience points them to a different market.

3.0 PERSONNEL

3.1 Management

Julio Nunez will handle the day-to-day business of Suerte Cuban Cuisine, such as interviewing prospective employees, hiring, scheduling, ordering supplies and materials, as well as working in the truck preparing and serving food. Julio has worked food service jobs in the Miami area for 20 years and has both serving and management experience. Most recently, he was assistant manager for a local Jimmy Johns restaurant. He has the experience to manage his own small business. His two sons, Esteban and Jesus, are recent college graduates and will be working part-time in the truck preparing and serving food. They both have food service experience. If Julio is incapacitated for any reason, Jesus can take over all business operations, as he has management experience as well.

3.2 Staffing

Besides Julio, Esteban, and Jesus, Suerte Cuban Cuisine will employ two part-time employees to work in the truck 25 hours a week each. Julio will post job openings in the student newspapers at the universities in the metro area and on Internet job sites such as Craigslist and Monster.

Miami and the surrounding area are home to six universities and one college, so demand for part-time jobs is high, and Julio should have no issues with finding applicants. Although finding applicants will not be a problem, finding enthusiastic, hard-working, and motivated individuals will of course prove more challenging but is key to Julio and his business. Experience in food service is not required but preferred, since Suerte Cuban Cuisine is anticipated to be high-volume and fast-paced.

Julio will interview all eligible applicants, and, if hired, employees will undergo a background check and must obtain a food handler's permit, in compliance with Florida state law. Each new employee will be trained with Julio for 20 hours before being allowed to work without supervision. Each employee will work with one other employee in the truck during each lunch and dinner shift.

A turnover rate of every school year is expected due to the likelihood that part-time employees will be university students.

3.3 Professional and Advisory Support

Julio will take care of all accounting and money management, so the only professional and advisory support will be an attorney, Senen Garcia of Senen Garcia Law Group, and an insurance agent, Manny Morin of State Farm, who are both located in Miami.

4.0 STRATEGIES

4.1 Business Strategy

The strategy for conducting business is as follows: Julio will contact businesses a month in advance in order to obtain permission to park in their lots to operate, making a monthly schedule for the locations. When SFFTA organizes food truck events, Julio will take part. The association hosts the Food Truck Invasion at the fairgrounds every Thursday, so Thursday's location is set every month. Julio will prepare rice, beans, chilled desserts such as dulce de leche, and tortillas before the start of the business day. Meat, including pork, chicken, and beef, will be cooked by employees as it is ordered. Vegetables will be cut before each business day but prepared on sight. There will be refrigerated facilities on the truck, and food will be prepared between lunch and dinner shifts as needed. Julio will keep track of hours, pay taxes, and record other information with Quicken Books software.

4.2 Growth Strategy

Word-of-mouth will be key to growing the business, and Julio will rely on his target audience's use of social media to get the word out. He hopes to reach new customers through Facebook and Twitter, as well as through advertising strategies offered through membership in SFFTA.

5.0 PRODUCTS AND SERVICES

5.1 Description

Suerte Cuban Cuisine will provide fast, affordable, authentic Cuban food to Miami area residents, specifically targeting those working in downtown Miami. Although locations will change, the truck will always be accessible to those working in downtown Miami. Suerte Cuban Cuisine will let followers of its Twitter and Facebook page know where the truck will be on any given day. Foods included will be empanadas, fried plantains, rice, black beans, coconut chicken, pot roast, squid, oysters, shredded beef, and Cuban sandwiches. This offers affordable, fast food to those with a tight schedule. Bottled drinks such as water and soda will also be available.

5.2 Pricing

Suerte Cuban Cuisine's pricing will be very competitive and based on use of quality products. Prices will range from $5 to $10 and will vary depending on the complexity of the food being ordered. For a basic beef empanada, customers can expect to pay $5. A Cuban sandwich of roast beef, pickles, mustard, and Swiss cheese on Cuban bread will also run $5. A platter plate of beans, plantains, rice, meat, and a drink is the most expensive item at $10. These prices are competitive with area food trucks and, while more expensive than fast food, is less expensive than a sit-down restaurant. Suerte Cuban Cuisine will accept cash and credit cards; Julio will use his smartphone to collect payments from customers.

6.0 MARKETING AND SALES

6.1 Advertising and Promotion

Suerte Cuban Cuisine will use the Internet, flyers, and newspaper advertisements as its main form of advertising. The website will feature the menu, a biography of Julio, links to the Twitter and Facebook page, promotions and coupons, and that month's locations calendar.

Quarter sheet flyers will be handed out on university campuses, posted on community boards, stuck under car windshield wipers, and otherwise distributed. Flyers will include website information and promotional offers. The side of the truck out of which the business operates also serve as advertisement, as the name, website, and phone number will be displayed prominently. Julio will also take out ads in the local universities' newspapers.

6.2 Costs

Ongoing costs are expected to be $100 a year for the website, $2,000 for painting the truck, and $300 a year for promotional flyers.

6.3 Image

Julio is concerned with providing quality food and offering friendly service. Often, restaurant customers find that customer service is poor and enthusiasm is low. Julio wants to give all his customers a memorable meal and an enjoyable experience, so the friendliness and enthusiasm of the staff and the quality of the food served is of utmost importance. To set it apart from other street vendors, food trucks, and food service establishments, Suerte Cuban Cuisine will focus on quality in experience, service, and product. Julio wants people to see his business as fun and friendly.

7.0 OPERATIONS

7.1 Customers

Miami is a city with a large downtown area, including the business district, historic Brickell, and Park West, providing a large customer base from those that live and work in this area. Suerte Cuban Cuisine will target the 20 to 35-year-old age range of these office workers looking for a quick lunch solution. This area is densely populated and busy, and the area is growing with addition of new office buildings, bars, and restaurants and thus the area attracts new people to work and live there. Targeted customers will be young adults who make $50,000 a year on average. According to the Miami Downtown Development Authority (www.miamidda.com, 2009), "The total current downtown area population is estimated at approximately 68,900 persons and is projected to increase to 85,000 by 2014." These new people moving to the downtown Miami area will fit the mold of those Julio wants to serve—the younger working people of downtown Miami. In addition, on weekends these young professionals are often out late and looking for a quick bite, so Suerte Cuban Cuisine will be open late on weekend nights.

7.2 Equipment

Julio will buy the food truck, which will feature a four-door refrigerator, flat grills, a four-burner stove top, and dry storage. He will also purchase supplies such as pots, pans, kitchen utensils, plastic silverware, takeout boxes, and paper bags. Initial food stock will include dry goods such as tortillas, bread, fruits, beans, rice, sauces, and spices as well as refrigerated items such as vegetables and meat.

7.3 Hours

Suerte Cuban Cuisine will be open for lunch and dinner, from 11 AM to 2 PM and 5 PM to 9 PM Sunday through Thursday, expanding these hours to 12 AM on Friday and Saturday nights.

7.4 Suppliers

The truck from which Suerte Cuban Cuisine will operate will come from Miami Trailer, a local Miami food truck supplier. Julio will buy some specialty products such as pimentos, cooking wines, sauces, and spices from Mejor De Cuba, an online Cuban grocery provider. The meat will be purchased from Miami wholesale provider Meats Supermarket. For bulk items such as rice and beans, Julio will use bulk supplier F. Garcia Wholesale and Export, located in Miami.

7.5 Facility and Location

The business will be operated out of a mobile kitchen purchased from Miami Trailers and will its change location every day throughout downtown Miami.

7.6 Production

Julio will prepare the day's food and refrigerate it on the truck for use throughout the day. In between lunch and dinner shifts, food will be prepared as needed. Julio will prepare the food at his house to keep on the truck for the day.

7.7 Legal Environment

All employees will have a food handler's card and will be licensed and bonded. All employees must wear gloves to handle food. The truck can park on private property with permission.

8.0 FINANCIAL ANALYSIS

Start-up costs are as follows:

Start-up expenses	Cost
Customized truck	$120,000
Uniforms	$ 100
Website	$ 100
Flyers	$ 300
Newspaper ads	$ 500
Insurance	$ 200
License	$ 100
Total	**$121,200**

Julio might be able to find a less expensive used truck for as little as $50,000. Start-up costs will be funded by money from Julio's saving account and a small business loan from a local Miami bank.

Monthly expenses	Cost
Food	$1,000
Salaries	$2,000
Insurance	$ 100
Incidentals	$ 200
Total	**$3,300**

Income will vary, but, on average, Julio estimates he will bring in $230 a day ($6,900 a month) during the first year, which, after subtracting expenses, leaves a profit margin of $3,600 a month ($43,200 for the first year).

General Staffing Company

G E N R X L L C

7641 Highway 141
Saskatoon, Saskatchewan S7N 1M7

Gerald Rekve

GENRX LLC's mission is to be the best staffing firm in our region. Our focus will be to secure clients who may require our services on an ongoing basis.

This business plan appeared in Business Plans Handbook, Volume 12. It has been updated for this volume.

EXECUTIVE SUMMARY

Business Strategy

GENRX LLC is opening a new general staffing company in 2012. Our area of focus is to be the best staffing firm in our region.

To begin, GENRX LLC will have six full-time staff, including the owner and five support staff to handle payroll, scheduling, and clients.

GENRX LLC will focus on the business sectors listed below. Other business sectors will be added as GENRX LLC matures and revenue potential for new sectors is increased.

- General labor

- Secretarial

- Specialized labor

- Manual labor

- Hourly or one day at a time

- Drop-in labor force

- Accounting staff

- Human Resource staff

- Technical staff

- Equipment operators

MARKET ANALYSIS

Saskatoon, Saskatchewan is a small market with only 260,600 people living in the city and one million living in the Province. There is another city 200 miles to the south named Regina with a population of 210,556. GENRX LLC will have an office in both locations.

There are more than 39,000 businesses that operate in the Province that are registered with the Government. Our focus will be to offer these business clients temporary staff as they require. While GENRX LLC will only focus our markets in Saskatoon and Regina, requests from clients outside these two markets will be reviewed to see if there is potential to make profits on an ongoing basis.

Marketing & Demographic Data

All information is provided by the Saskatchewan Economic Development Authority.

Leading growth industries, Saskatoon, 2012

	Count	% of total
Business & professional services	190	27.09%
Personal & household services	109	16.01%
Traditional retail	77	11.31%
Building & construction related services	74	10.87%
Commercial service sector	65	9.43%
Health, wellness & education services	57	8.37%
Repair & maintenance services	39	5.73%
Automotive sales & service	27	3.96%
Manufacturing	18	2.64%
Services related to manufacturing, wholesale & transportation	17	2.50%
Wholesale industries	8	1.17%
Total	**681**	**100.00%**

Competition

Our direct competitors in the market are Kelly Services, Labor Ready, Adecco, and Quest Staffing Services. Listed below are the areas where each one of these companies operate and the prices they charge.

Kelly Services

- Office & Administrative: $18—$22 per hour

- Customer Service: $15—$17 per hour

- Light Industrial: $16—$19 per hour

- Information Technology: $24—$40 per hour

- Scientific personnel: $29—$44 per hour

Labour Ready

- Construction: $18—$24 per hour

- Manufacturing: $16—$20 per hour

- Maintenance: $15—$18 per hour

- Farming: $18—$22 per hour

- Retail: $14—$16 per hour

- Transport: $20—$23 per hour

- Warehouse: $15—$17 per hour

- Hospitality: $14—$16 per hour

- Landscaping: $14—$16 per hour

- Horticulture: $14—$126per hour

Adecco
- Temporary Staffing: $14—$16 per hour

- Accounting & Finance:$16—$20 per hour

- Office & Administrative: $14—$16 per hour

- Engineering: $20—$24 per hour

- Hospitality: $14—$16 per hour

- Industrial: $16—$20 per hour

- Medical: $16—$20 per hour

- Transport: $18—$20 per hour

- Payroll services: Rate quote on request

- Call center: Rate quote on request

- Contract employment: Rate quote on request

- Permanent Staff Recruiting Service

Quest Staffing Services
- Construction: $17—$22 per hour

- Manufacturing: $19—$22 per hour

- Maintenance: $16—$17 per hour

- Farming: $15—$17 per hour

- Retail: $15—$17 per hour

- Transport: $15—$17 per hour

- Warehouse: $17—$18 per hour

- Hospitality: $15—$17 per hour

- Landscaping: $15—$18 per hour

Our Services & Pricing
- Construction: $14—$18 per hour

- Manufacturing: $14—$18 per hour

- Maintenance: $13.50—$15 per hour

- Farming: $15—$18 per hour

- Retail: $14—$15 per hour

- Transport: $18—$20 per hour

- Warehouse: $14—$16 per hour

- Hospitality: $14—$16 per hour

- Landscaping: $14—$16 per hour

- Horticulture: $14—$16 per hour

- Medical: $14—$16 per hour

- Accounting & Finance:$14—$18 per hour

- Office & Administrative: $12—$14 per hour

- Engineering: $18—$22 per hour

Growth Strategy

Our goal is to have a steady stream of staff to offer our clients. Our pricing strategy for the first 3 years is to make smaller margins for similar services that competitors offer. While doing this GENRX LLC will be able to win more contracts and build a steady revenue stream.

Our temporary staff will be paid above average wages and benefits. GENRX LLC will also go above the norm in the industry and offer medical and dental benefits to all temp staff who work 25 hours per week or more. While doing this will add to the bottom line cost of our company, it will help us achieve our long -term goal of attracting top-of-the-line workers and therefore offering our clients the best talent.

Marketing our business will take the traditional approach. In addition, we will employ new marketing strategies to build and grow our business. GENRX LLC will place small ads in the yellow pages of both cities in which we operate. Additionally, we will place sustaining business-card-size ads in local newspapers. Most importantly, we will create a state-of-the-art website with online account access for both the businesses that we serve as well as individuals looking for work.

Local Newspapers

Saskatoon Star Phoenix
- Annual Advertising budget of $12,000

- 56,000 paid circulation

- Daily newspaper

- MOPE Nadbank data reflects high business owner/manager readership

- A division of Postmedia Network Inc.

Regina Leader Post
- Annual Advertising budget of $9,000

- 51,000 paid circulation

- Daily newspaper

Prairie Dog Newspaper
- Annual Advertising budget of $8,000

- 32,000 paid circulation

- Weekly newspaper

Planet S
- Annual Advertising budget of $8,000

- 31,500 paid circulation

- Weekly newspaper

Radio Stations
- C95—Annual Advertising budget of $9,000

- CJME—Annual Advertising budget of $9,000

Building our new business will require spending on advertising and marketing. Over the course of the business start-up, however, we are confident that going into years three and four, our advertising spending will be reduced because we will have built our number of clients and will not be required to continue to spend money to get awareness.

Business name recognition will be important to our business. We will use a variety of methods to get this awareness in addition to word of mouth and media events like charity sponsorships.

Charity sponsorships will be easy to find; all we need to do is offer free staffing in exchange for name coverage via the radio, newspaper or television. This will allow us to get more exposure for less than the cost of traditional advertising.

CUSTOMERS

Our focus will be to secure clients who may require our services on an ongoing basis. This will mean GENRX LLC will ask specific questions once a client calls our firm. These questions will gather key market research information that will help us identify the client's present needs and future needs. GENRX LLC will place all this information in the client's file for assessment.

List of Potential Sectors
- Accounting & Finance
- Construction
- Engineering
- Farming
- Horticulture
- Hospitality
- Landscaping
- Maintenance
- Manufacturing
- Medical
- Office & Administrative
- Retailing
- Sales & Marketing
- Transport
- Trucking (both long and short haul)
- Warehouse

The industry norm is to charge a minimum of 25 percent for all work required to be done on the site by our staff. What this means is that if a client charged $10.00 per hour, then the worker gets $7.50 per hour and the staffing firm will get $2.50 per hour.

We do not feel this is fair for the worker or the client. Therefore, GENRX LLC will only charge 15 percent. This then will mean that for every $10.00 hour we charge a client, the staff person filling the position will make $8.50 per hour and $1.50 per hour will go to us.

This rate structure will also benefit the client, because we will be able to offer our clients the services of better staff than our competitors.

RISK FACTORS

There are risks in any business that starts from scratch, but having a solid business plan will be key to preparing for these risks.

One of our main risk factors is our competition. They are not likely to sit back and allow us to enter the market; in fact, we are confident that they will match our pricing once it becomes apparent to them that they are losing business. Based on our review of the market, if we can win 5% of the market in the first year of business and then maintain it, we will be well positioned for future success.

We are very confident that there is enough business for all of our competitors and us.

FINANCIAL ANALYSIS

Start-Up Expenses

Saskatoon Office

- Office Rental—$1,400 month
- Yellow pages—$250 month
- Telephone line & equipment—$400 month
- Internet—$75 month
- Office supplies—$1,000 (startup)
- Office supplies—$250 month
- Advertising—$15,000 (startup)
- Advertising—$1,000 month
- Office equipment—Computers, fax, copier, printers, etc.—$7,500
- Desks, file cabinets etc.—$3,000
- Utilities—included in rent
- Parking—included in rent
- Leasehold improvements—included in rent
- First 3 months rent—free with 3 year lease
- Payroll and other software—$2,500

Regina Office

- Office Rental—$1,200 month
- Yellow pages—$250 month
- Telephone line & equipment—$400 month
- Internet—$75 month
- Office supplies—$1,000 (startup)
- Office supplies—$250 month
- Advertising—$15,000 (startup)
- Advertising—$1,000 month

- Office equipment—Computers, fax, copier, printers, etc.—$7,500

- Desks, file cabinets etc.—$2,500

- Utilities—included in rent

- Parking—included in rent

- Leasehold improvements—included in rent

- First 3 months rent—free with 3 year lease

- Payroll and other software—$2,500

We were able to negotiate with the landlord for three free months of rent per year we are in business. Our total startup expenses will amount to $57,500 (not including wages and salaries to our full time staff).

Our ongoing monthly expense will be $6,550 for both locations (not including wages).

Our wages for our full time staff will be expensed at the following rate:

- Manager owner—Monthly salary of $6,000

- 5 staff persons—$2,400 per month for each staff person and 5% of bookings for each client they sign to contracts.

Therefore, our monthly staffing expense will be $18,000. Our total monthly company staff and office expense will be $24,550 per month.

Projected Income

We have determined that the in the first year we will set our goal to hire out an average of 60 staff per month for a total of 160 billable hours each at an average of $16.00 per hour.

Based on our estimates, we will average $23,040 per month in revenue. While this is less than our fixed costs, we have budgeted for the loss as a way to manage the risk.

Banking and Finance

Based on the required money to launch this business, the owner has invested $100,000 in cash.

Cash will be used to pay for all start-up expenses and monthly expenses as needed. Additionally this money will be used to secure an operating line of credit.

We have made an arrangement with the bank for an interest rate of six percent on the line of credit because we will maintain at least $50,000 in cash in the reserve.

The bank has also agreed to send us referrals if any of their business clients are in need of staff but cannot afford to hire full- or part-time staff by the traditional methods.

MANAGEMENT SUMMARY

Ben Worth—Owner/Manager

Ben has worked in the Human Resources sector for 20 years with four separate companies. These companies range from 40-employee firms all the way up to a 350-employee firm.

Over the course of the last seven years, Ben started putting aside money for the business start-up because he always wanted to own his own company. His experience in the HR area has given Ben the ability to understand staffing needs and requirements. Furthermore, his direct experience with the general staffing companies in the area has given him a good understanding of our competitors as well the market in general.

Gift Basket Service

Sunrise Gift Baskets

1555 Sunrise Blvd.
Sacramento, CA 95858

Claire Moore, MBA

This business plan for a gift basket service illustrates the importance of evaluating the target market and competition. A well thought out plan shows that the owner understands the challenges and potential pitfalls and has a plan for dealing with them in order to be successful. This plan is fictional and has not been used to secure funding from a bank or other lending institution.

EXECUTIVE SUMMARY

Sunrise Gift Baskets is a partnership that will provide theme and custom gift baskets to the greater Sacramento, California area and to customers across the country through its web site. The business will generate sales from both individual and corporate customers through its marketing efforts both within the local business community and online.

Sunrise Gift Baskets will be operated by partners Mary Flanagan and Sophie Merchant with the assistance of several outside consultants. Customers will purchase our products because they are affordable, high quality products from California producers and because we offer incredible customer service and the ability to customize baskets to meet customers' personal and financial needs. Customers will also appreciate the convenience of ordering baskets at any time, day or night, through our web site where they can choose products, customize their purchases and specify the delivery date.

Because Sunrise Gift Baskets will be located in the home of partner Mary Flanagan, costs will be kept to an absolute minimum. Both partners will share equally in running the business, purchasing product, marketing, and basket assembly and shipping. It is expected no additional staff will be required in the foreseeable future.

Company startup began in August 2012 and the web site is expected to go live by November 1, 2012, in time for the holiday buying season. In anticipation of holiday sales, a stock of supplies and product must be obtained so that deliveries are not delayed.

BUSINESS OVERVIEW

Objectives

Sunrise Gift Basket's objectives for the first three years of operation include:

- Establishing working relationships with several California growers and producers of specialty food items and the negotiation of the best possible purchasing terms.

- Establishing its brand identity as a provider of quality gift baskets that include unique offerings from California producers and growers.

- Establishing itself with corporate buyers and creating strong sales volume with the corporate market.

Mission

Sunrise Gift Basket's mission is to offer the best selection of theme and custom gift baskets coupled with the best quality products and customer service.

Keys to Success

The keys to Sunrise Gift Basket's success are:

- Quality affordable gift baskets filled with products that exemplify the best of California specialty food production.

- A variety of themed baskets at three price levels to appeal to customers' needs.

- The ability for customers to create their own baskets by choosing items from a menu of available products.

- Special services for corporate clients to help them customize their baskets to include marketing materials.

Risks

The risks involved with starting Sunrise Gift Baskets are:

- Intense competition from both local and established online gift basket services.

- Will customers be willing to shop online with a new company that has no track record?

COMPANY SUMMARY

Sunrise Gift Baskets (SGB) provides customers with theme and custom gift baskets for all occasions. Named for the well-known Sunrise Boulevard in Sacramento, California, Sunrise Gift Baskets will cater to customers through its web site at SunriseGiftBaskets.com.

Founded in August 2012 by owners Mary Flanagan and Sophie Merchant, Sunrise Gift Baskets was begun with a firm belief in supporting local businesses. As a result, our baskets are filled with the bounty from local California growers and producers. Our wine selections include the best that California's vineyards produce. SGB is structured as a partnership with both Mary Flanagan and Sophie Merchant as general partners with equal ownership.

Company Ownership

Sunrise Gift Baskets is structured as a partnership between Mary Flanagan and Sophie Merchant. Additional funding has been obtained from both Mary's and Sophie's parents, however these monies will be repaid over five years beginning in year three of the business.

When profits are to be dispensed by the business, profit share will be split 70/30 in Mary's favor to reimburse her for the use of her home as the principal facility for the business. The services of a local attorney have been engaged to create the partnership agreement that outlines ownership share in the business.

Company Location and Facilities

The business operations will be conducted in the home of Mary Flanagan and all sales will be generated through the company's web site and through contacts made with corporate buyers. Storage of supplies and product will be at Mary's home and if needed, a storage facility will be rented on a month-to-month basis.

Conducting operations from home will keep start-up costs low and prove more convenient for the owners to fill orders. The owners will consider moving operations to a storefront as soon as the business can support the added costs, however they do not anticipate a move for at least three years.

Facility Description

Mary's home is located in a rural area of Sacramento. In addition to her home, she houses a 40 foot single-wide trailer on her property in which storage and assembly of the gift baskets will be conducted. Mary's home office is a room within her home that is dedicated solely for SGB operations. It will house the computers, printers, and other office furniture and equipment. Business records will be stored in the home office.

Mary owns her home. Her mortgage, taxes, and insurance are paid from the income generated by her job and that of her husband.

Start-up Summary

SGB's start-up costs include: the creation of marketing materials, web site creation, social media setup, acquisition of inventory, supplies, and equipment.

Start-up Plan

Start-up costs

Legal	$ 1,500
Web site development	$ 2,000
Stationery, etc.	$ 350
Brochures	$ 300
Insurance (rider added to home & auto)	$ 200
Internet/phone service	$ 250
Computer	$ 750
Printer/fax/copier/scanner (2)	$ 500
Shelving	$ 250
Filing cabinets	$ 200
Work tables	$ 200
Craft tools/shrink wrapper/heat gun	$ 1,200
Computer desk with chair	$ 400
Retail supplies	$ 300
Packing/shipping equipment	$ 1,000
Packing/shipping supplies	$ 350
Misc.	$ 200
Total start-up costs	**$ 9,950**

Start-up assets needed

Cash requirements	$ 4,500
Start-up inventory	$ 3,000
Total short-term assets	**$ 7,500**
Long-term assets	$ 0
Capital assets	$ 0
Total assets needed	**$ 7,500**
Total start-up requirements:	**$17,450**

Start-up funding plan

Mary flanagan	$ 7,000
Sophie merchant	$ 7,000
Investor 1	$ 3,000
Investor 2	$ 3,000
Total start-up funding contributions	**$20,000**
Additional financing required for start-up	$ 0

PRODUCTS PLAN

Product Description Plan

Sunrise Gift Baskets will offer a variety of theme and custom gift baskets with three price options: small, medium, or large price point. Many of the baskets are centered around products from Northern California producers and growers.

Gift basket themes include: California Grown, The Corporate Collection, New Baby, and Spa. Custom baskets are also an option allowing the customer to choose from a list of products that varies by price range.

Theme Baskets: Customers will be able to choose from a variety of theme baskets. What distinguishes one price from another is the quantity and variety of items placed within the basket. All customers have the option to add a custom ribbon and card to their purchase. Custom ribbons can be embossed with a personal message. Seasonal theme baskets will be available for Christmas, Valentine's Day, Mother's Day, Father's Day, May Graduations, and Thanksgiving.

Custom Baskets: Customers can build their own basket by first choosing a price level and then choosing the basket contents from a list of available products. They can choose from a selection of baskets, color wrap, and ribbons. Custom ribbons can be embossed with a personal message.

Gift Cards: For those customers who desire the ultimate in convenience, giving a gift card not only makes giving easy, it assures recipients will receive exactly the products that they want.

Competitive Comparison Plan

Sunrise Gift Baskets will be joining a community of established gift basket services in Sacramento. It will be the unique, however, in placing an emphasis on stocking its baskets with the best of California specialty food products. It will also place an emphasis on serving the corporate market along with individual customers.

Sourcing Plan

Sunrise Gift Baskets is working to establish relationships with California vendors for as many of its supplies and inventory as possible. We have already located several California-based basket producers who produce quality unique baskets. SGB is currently completing negotiations with RAGUSA Trading Company in Santa Clara, California for its supply of baskets. Other supplies will be purchased through vendors such as ArtisticGiftBaskets.com and Creative Gift Packaging.com.

Arrangements have also been made to obtain products from California specialty food vendors including: Valley Fig Growers, California Garden Products, Inc., and Sacramento's own Bariani Olive Oil, LLC.

Service Expansion Plan

SGB plans to maintain operations within Mary Flanagan's home indefinitely. The advantage in the form of cost savings and convenience will help assure SGB's success. Future plans for expansion of sales include contacting local businesses and professionals such as realtors and flower shops. The owners plan to create working relationships that will generate sales to the mutual benefit of both parties through cross-selling.

MARKET ANALYSIS SUMMARY PLAN

Despite the lingering effects of the recession, 2012 figures show that consumers are more willing to open up their wallets and spend on gifts. In February the National Retail Federation (NRF) projected that consumers would spend an average of $126.03 for Valentine's Day. This is an increase of 8.5% from 2011. According to NRF's 2012 Father's Day spending survey conducted by BIGinsight, spending for

Father's Day gifts in 2012 would average $117.14 the **Monthly Consumer Survey May 2012** (Worthington: BIGinsight, 2012). An increase of 10% from 2011 but still not as much as the average spent on Mother's Day which this year hit an average of $152.

Corporate gift giving is up too from 2010 as reported by the Advertising Specialty Institute (ASI) in the**2011 Corporate Gift Giving Survey** (Trevose: ASI, 2011). Highlights of the 2011 corporate gift-giving survey include:

- Average spending on clients or prospect increased by 13.9% to $29.91

- 38% plan to give gift cards to employees

- The gifts given most often to clients and prospects were food and beverages.

- The hottest corporate gifts of 2011 included coffee-table books and customized wine and spirits

Sunrise Gift Baskets will achieve competitive advantage by emphasizing the unique quality of its products and its ability to customize baskets to meet the needs of both consumer and corporate markets.

Target Markets Plan

SGB serves two customer groups: individuals and corporate. Individuals will appreciate the convenience of choosing and sending a high-quality custom gift at any time of the day or night by shopping online. Corporate customers will appreciate the ability to customize their gift baskets by including their marketing materials and logo into any basket. Custom ribbons can be added for a more personal touch.

Individuals typically comprise at least 80% of customers for a gift basket business. However, individual purchases tend to have highs and lows because most purchases are related to a holiday. SGB will aim to develop its corporate customers to where this segment represents 80% of its sales. The advantage of this strategy is the high likelihood of repeat business and fewer seasonal spikes and dips in sales. Moreover, businesses, who are constantly working to develop their market, even in a depressed economy, are more likely than individuals to spend money on gift baskets.

Industry Analysis Plan

There is much competition from other gift basket companies in the Sacramento area, in California and online. However, few specialize in the products of California, especially the rich San Joaquin Valley with its varieties of healthy produce and the many specialty food producers who create breads, pastries, dried fruits, nuts, oils, candy, and body products.

Market Analysis Plan

Sunrise Gift Baskets aims to serve both individual consumers and corporate clients. Individuals typically purchase gift baskets during the holidays and for special occasions such as birthdays, weddings, get well and sympathy gifts. In contrast, corporate clients purchase gift baskets as part of their marketing efforts, for continued goodwill with clients and customers, and as thank you gifts for staff. As such, their purchases are not tied so much to seasonality.

By serving both classes of customer, Sunrise Gift Baskets expects to achieve a base level of revenues that can be expected on a monthly basis to counterbalance the seasonal highs and lows experienced in serving the general public.

Other Sacramento-area gift basket providers include Basket Works & Beyond and Cookie Connection, Inc. Sunrise Gift Baskets will distinguish itself from the competition by providing unique product combinations of fresh, locally produced products. By working with a select group of vendors Sunrise expects to keep costs in check by negotiating the best prices and terms for obtaining products.

Unique products combined with the option to customize basket contents will ensure success for Sunrise Gift Baskets as a premier provider of gift baskets.

STRATEGY AND IMPLEMENTATION SUMMARY PLAN

Competitive Edge Plan

Sunrise Gift Baskets will position itself as a provider of high-quality, locally grown and produced products that can be purchased in several price ranges. It will create quality gift baskets that are filled with the best of California agriculture and wine making. Due to competition from other local gift basket companies as well as the market reach of larger online competitors such as GourmetGiftBaskets.com and WineCountryGiftBaskets.com Sunrise will place an emphasis on working with local businesses both as vendors and as customers. It will stress the fact that most of its products are produced locally in California and that many of them are organic. Moreover, the baskets are created with green products with an eye toward sustainability.

Sales Strategy Plan

SGB serves two different groups of customers: individual consumers and corporate customers.

Individuals: When individuals purchase gift baskets, roughly 50% of purchases are made in connection with a holiday such as Valentine's Day, Mother's Day or Christmas. Gift baskets are also ideal presents to celebrate weddings, new births, birthdays, and house-warmings. According to research conducted in 2010 by market research publisher Packaged Facts in *Food Gifting in the U.S., 2nd Edition* (Rockville: 2010), specialty foods have become the foundation of the U.S. market for food gifting.

For example, in the 2010 survey, 53% of adults said that they are interested in high-quality foods and 30% said that they wanted healthy products. This suggests that there is a large market for healthy food gift items. The 2010 survey also showed that 74% of respondents liked the convenience of purchasing specialty food gifts online.

The two most commonly cited reasons for purchasing specialty foods as gifts were:

1. that the gift was likely to be used

2. it was something that the recipient would not normally buy

Corporate: When businesses purchase gift baskets it is either to reward employees and customers or to generate new sales leads. Corporate giving does not follow the same seasonality as of the individual consumers therefore the development of corporate customers will be a key strategy for SGB.

Pricing Plan

SGB uses a formula for pricing its baskets that begins with a base amount that consists of the cost for the basket, wrapping, ribbon, decorative filler material, and one hour of assembly time. The base cost of a basket will vary based on the size of the basket: small, medium, or large.

Then, the cost of the products is considered. The sales price of the basket will be twice the amount of the total basket cost or a 100% markup. This pricing strategy will result in a 50% profit margin. The pricing strategy is typical for gift basket services.

Charges for shipping are calculated separately based on the size of the basket, and the destination. The base shipping cost is estimated to be at least $6.95 for a small basket.

Basket Products Descriptions Plan

Sunrise Gift Baskets offers several baskets that are centered around products from Northern California producers and growers. Many of the baskets are available in small, medium, and large sizes and prices.

Wines are shipped only to states where its shipping is not prohibited. Recipients must be at least 21 years of age. Wine shipments cannot be delivered without an adult signature.

Gift basket themes include: California Grown, Gardeners Collection, New Baby, and Spa. Custom baskets are also an option allowing the customer to choose from a list of products that varies by price range.

California Grown theme choices include:

The Italian Collection Plan

An assortment of pastas and sauces, cold-pressed olive oil, pistachios, and pastries. Customers may choose from an assortment of California wines to complete this taste sensation.

Valley Harvest Plan

Just south of Sacramento lies the lush San Joaquin Valley where much of the nation's produce originates. This basket includes such delights as: chile peppers, tomato sauce, marinated artichokes, and a veggie medley of carrots, cauliflower and onion. Also included are cookies, crackers, cheese spread, and bottle of California Cabernet.

The Sweet Tooth Plan

This basket is filled with California's best dried fruits and nuts, toffee and buttery caramels along with Ghirardelli chocolates.

California Dreamin' Plan

California's bounty also includes an wide assortment of herbs and flowers. This basket includes fragrant products for the body, mind, and spirit. Enjoy bath salts scented with rose petals, lavender eye pillows, a hand-crafted soy candle, scented linen spray, loofah, massager, and olive oil soaps.

Financial Analysis Plan

The business will be funded by the owners with additional capital provided by their parents. As sales increase it is anticipated that the company will need to have an open credit line to purchase supplies and inventory. The owners plan to begin working with a local bank in order to develop a track record and establish a working relationship.

Owners Mary Flanagan and Sophie Merchant will continue to work at their current jobs with the expectation that as SGB grows, they will gradually decrease their hours spent at the job and increase the hours devoted to filling basket orders and running SGB.

The advantage of having a steady income is that there will be less need to seek outside funding or debt. The disadvantage is that the business will grow slower than it might if the owners could devote full time to the business. However, the existence of two owners means that together they can dedicate full-time hours to the establishing of their enterprise.

The following sales figures reflect the fact that the owners will be splitting their time between their jobs and the running of SGB. Because the owners do not depend on profits for their living expenses, they plan to reinvest profits into inventory, marketing, and continuing education for the first two years of the business.

	2012	2013	2014
Sales	$2,200	$22,000	$25,000
Direct cost of sales	$1,100	$11,000	$12,500
Other costs of sales	$ 0	$ 0	$ 0
Total cost of sales	**$1,100**	**$11,000**	**$12,500**
Gross margin	$1,100	$11,000	$12,500
Gross margin %	50.00%	50.00%	50.00%
Expenses			
Insurance	$ 34	$ 34	$ 34
Web site	$ 120	$ 120	$ 120
Advertising	$ 200	$ 200	$ 200
Other expenses	$ 200	$ 200	$ 200
Total operating expenses	**$ 554**	**$ 554**	**$ 554**
Net profit	**$ 546**	**$10,446**	**$11,946**
Net profit/sales	**24.82%**	**47.48%**	**47.78%**

Projected monthly sales first year

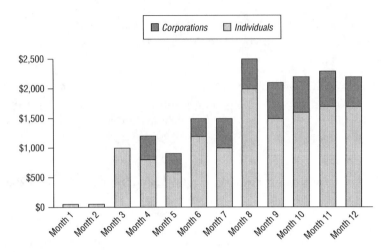

Milestones Plan

SGB anticipates that it will meet several milestones within its first six months of operation. This business plan is being created for internal use rather than to seek funding from outside sources. As such it will remain the guiding force in the startup phase and continued growth of the company.

·   Completion of the business plan.

·   Office setup.

·   Web site setup.

·   Production of marketing materials.

·   Social media setup.

·   Sales site goes live. First sale.

·   Hitting the 100th sale mark.

Milestones

Milestone	Start date	End date	Budget	Manager
Completion of business plan	8/1/2012	9/1/2012	$ 0	Mary
Office setup	8/2/2012	8/2/2012	$ 0	Sophie
Web site setup	8/1/2012	10/31/2012	$1,500	Sophie
Marketing materials creation	8/1/2012	9/30/2012	$ 500	Mary
Social media setup	8/1/2012	8/31/2012	$ 0	Sophie
Web site goes live	8/1/2012	11/1/2012	0	
First sale	11/11/2012	11/11/2012	$ 0	
100 baskets sold	2/28/2013	2/28/2013	$ 0	
Totals			**$2,000**	

Marketing and Sales Plan

Sunrise Gift Baskets will conduct its business through its web site hosted on GoDaddy.com. Purchase of a domain name and site setup run less than $100 because GoDaddy's design services will not be used. Instead, the services of a web designer have been contracted to create the site and to set up the catalog and shopping cart. The site will incorporate the BaskWeb eCommerce shopping cart software, Enterprise edition at $75 per month.

The BaskWeb shopping cart software will handle the task of showcasing basket products and taking orders online 24 hours a day, seven days a week, 365 days a year. The software allows for such custom options as:

- multiple recipients per order: a feature that allows the same basket to be shipped to multiple recipients

- customer address books: customers can save the names and addresses of recipients; a feature that encourages repeat purchases

- real time credit card processing: completion of customer payment through payment gateways such as Authorize.net and LinkPoint.

- gift certificate codes

Gaining an audience for the web site will be achieved through a variety of marketing activities including:

- networking with local business professionals at local meetings of business and professional groups

- advertisements in local business publications such as News and Review and Comstock

- advertising in the yellow pages

- direct mail advertising to local businesses

- presentations to local business groups showcasing the advantages of gift baskets as a marketing tool

- use of social media sites Facebook, Twitter, and Pinterest

MANAGEMENT SUMMARY PLAN

Management will be provided by owners Mary Flanagan and Sophie Merchant who have a combined 15 years of experience working in retail sales. Mary and Sophie have gathered a team of consultants who will be working with them during their first year in business to formulate their marketing strategy, web and social media presence, and in creating profitable relationships with suppliers.

SGB is a partnership between owners Mary Flanagan and Sophie Merchant who are currently the only staff. There is no need to incorporate at present, however the owners my consider incorporating as the business grows and takes on employees. The liability protection that incorporating or forming an LLC would provide is outweighed by the costs of incorporation and the $800 minimum annual franchise tax fee charged by the State of California. The owners will obtain a comprehensive liability insurance policy to cover any potential liability exposure.

Mary Flanagan holds a bachelor's degree in business from California State University, Sacramento. While a student, Mary worked part-time for a local florist where she learned to create floral arrangements and gift baskets. Mary learned her craft amid the pressures of holiday deadlines while balancing her school work. She gained valuable experience in working with customers and learning their needs and concerns.

Sophie Merchant graduated from Sacramento City College with an associate's degree in business and has worked as a bookkeeper for various businesses in the Sacramento area for the past ten years. For the past four years Sophie has performed bookkeeping services for Tyler's Market in Sacramento where she regularly interacted with the store's many suppliers of gourmet food and wine.

Both Mary and Sophie are members of the National Association for the Specialty Food Trade (NASFT), an industry group that provides training and resources for members of the specialty food sales community. SGB plans to network with several of the 96 NAFST members who are based in California in order to obtain products for its gift baskets.

Mary and Sophie will be relying on the services of several freelance consultants during the startup phase of the company.

- Amanda Burnley: web site developer; will create the company web site and set up the catalog and shopping cart operation for online sales.

- Coryon Raymond: will create the social media presence and advise on Internet marketing strategies.

- Ralph Newman: will use his years of experience as a buyer for Tyler's Market and other specialty food stores to assist in locating and negotiating contracts with vendors.

Personnel Plan Plan

The owners of SGB will contribute a combined total of 40 hours a week to management, sales, and marketing activities. As the business grows they expect to be able to devote even more time to the business. For this reason, and because the ecommerce software is so complete in its capabilities, the owners do not anticipate hiring additional staff within the next few years.

During holiday seasons, if more staffing is needed, it may be secured through the participation of family members or through the hiring of temporary workers. Temp workers present a viable option because they do not incur the addition costs of payroll taxes and employee benefits. Moreover, they can be released at any time without risk of penalty or incurring the costs of unemployment insurance.

Growth Strategy Plan

The business strengths lie in the experience of the owners and their team of consultants. Originality in the creation of themed baskets will help to set SGB apart from its competition. The company also plans to create a memorable brand identity based largely on its belief and support of California businesses. This identity will be enhance through the networking relationships developed with suppliers.

SGB also plans to place an emphasis on marketing its gift basket services to local corporations. By creating on-going relationships with a number of corporate customers, SGB will be able to enhance its market reach and maintain a steady income stream.

Weaknesses faced by SGB include limited working capital and the uphill fight to establish an identity in a saturated market. It is expected that business growth will be fairly slow the first year as SGB establishes its identity and differentiates itself within the marketplace.

Handmade Writing Instruments & Accessories Business

StanMark Gifts Inc.

2840 Central Ave.
Wakefield, MN 58623

Paul Greenland

StanMark Gifts Inc. makes heirloom-quality, custom, handmade writing instruments and accessories from a variety of exotic hardwoods and other materials.

EXECUTIVE SUMMARY

Business Overview

Stan Myers spent 23 years teaching industrial arts to high school students in Wakefield, Minnesota, specializing in woodworking courses. When budget cuts prompted the Wakefield Consolidated School District to eliminate its industrial arts program, Myers was faced with unemployment. However, the situation has presented him with an exciting opportunity to utilize his skills in a new endeavor.

Although he is highly skilled in many aspects of woodworking, Myers is well-known for his work with the lathe, a piece of equipment that is used to shape and sculpt wood. Although the lathe commonly is associated with wooden items like spindles, bowls, and baseball bats, over the last five years Myers began making smaller, highly specialized gifts for friends and family. In particular, Myers has developed a reputation for producing beautiful handmade pens, mechanical pencils, and letter openers.

Over the years, Myers has made custom items from a variety of exotic hardwoods, as well as different types of acrylic. Fine, custom-made writing instruments and accessories (e.g., letter openers, key chains, styluses, magnifiers, etc.) command premium market prices (sometimes hundreds of dollars). Already equipped with the tools and equipment needed for production backspace, Myers decided to test the market himself. He purchased enough supplies to produce 50 handcrafted pens and pencils and sold them at weekend art fairs and collectible shows.

The return on investment for Myers' initial batch of writing instruments was $1,025. In addition to selling all of the ready-made pens, he received 38 orders for custom-made items, resulting in an additional $1,834 in revenue. This success prompted Myers to turn his one-time hobby into Stan-Mark Gifts Inc., a business that leverages the power of the Internet to reach prospective buyers throughout the world. This business plan outlines Myers' strategy for establishing and growing his new enterprise.

INDUSTRY ANALYSIS

Although StanMark Gifts is a highly-specialized, home-based enterprise, it is part of the larger retail industry. According to data from the National Retail Federation, industry sales were expected to reach $2.53 trillion in 2012, an increase of 3.4 percent from the previous year. While dire economic conditions had negatively impacted retailers for several years, by early 2012 retail industry growth was outpacing that of other industries.

The Gift and Home Trade Association is a more specialized organization serving retailers like StanMark Gifts. The non-profit group "was designed to help and encourage vendors, sales agencies, industry affiliates and retailers to work together, improving relationships and making business better by providing members with the opportunity to exchange ideas and network with industry leaders." Each year, the organization hosts an annual conference. It also provides its members with a number of special benefits, including news and industry data.

MARKET ANALYSIS

StanMark Gifts will concentrate its promotional efforts on the consumer and business gift markets. Stan Myers believes that the greatest opportunity exists for customers seeking unique, high-quality gifts for birthdays, graduations, weddings, anniversaries, as well as promotions, employee recognition, and customer appreciation.

Even during difficult economic times, there always is a market for distinct, high-quality gifts. Stan Myers experienced this while "piloting" the sale of fine writing instruments at weekend art fairs and collectible shows. Sales of pre-made items were strong, and he received a surprising number of orders for custom-made items.

StanMark Gifts' primary competitors include other independent craftsman. While many potential competitors only sell their products locally or regionally, and not via the Internet, there are a number of competing craftsmen who have adopted the e-commerce model. However, Stan Myers believes that his products are superior, and will therefore adopt a "quality leader" marketing position. His products will be backed by a lifetime guarantee.

Other competition will come from big-box office supply stores like OfficeMax and Office Depot, as well as mall-based retailers such as Things Remembered, which custom engrave premium gift items. These competitors carry premium writing instruments and products from leading manufacturers such as Waterford and Cross.

PRODUCTS

Although approximately 80 percent of StanMark Gifts' production will pertain to writing instruments, the business will offer additional handcrafted items. These may be sold separately, or in combination as part of special gift sets. Following is a detailed breakdown of the types of products that will be offered:

Product Types
- Pens (ballpoint, rollerball & fountain)
- Mechanical Pencils
- Letter Openers
- Styluses (for use with tablet computers & mobile devices)

- Keychains

- Bottle Openers

- Bottle Stoppers

- Magnifiers

- Candlestick Holders

- Flash Memory

Styles

- Traditional

- Slimline

- Bullet

- Comfort

- Designer

- Executive

- Art Deco

- Sculpted

Hardware Plating & Finishes

- Chrome

- Gold Titanium

- Black Titanium

- Gunmetal

- Rhodium

- Gold

- Black Enamel

- Copper

- Silver

- Brushed Silver

Material Types

Wood:

StanMark Gifts will utilize the finest exotic hardwoods for its products, including:

- African Blackwood

- African Olivewood

- Argentine Lignum

- Beeswing Narra

- Australian Blackwood

- Bloodwood

- Buckeye Burl

- Black Palm
- Bolivian Rosewood
- Borneo Rosewood
- Burmese Rosewood
- Brazilian Rosewood
- Black & White Ebony
- Brazilian Tulipwood
- Biblical Woods
- Blue Mahoe
- Boxwood
- Box Elder
- Briar Burl
- Brazilian Kingwood
- Burma Blackwood
- Canarywood
- Desert Ironwood
- East Indian Rosewood
- Hawaiian Woods
- India Ironwood
- Lacewood
- Leadwood
- Macassar Ebony
- Marblewood
- Maple Burl
- Pink Ivory
- Red Palm
- Sandalwood
- Snakewood
- Striped Ebony
- Tambootie
- Zebrawood
- Ziricote
- Yew

In addition, pens, pencils, and other custom-made items can be produced from wood supplied by the customer. Examples might include wood from a tree, piece of furniture, or building that has special significance or sentimental value.

Acrylics:
Several different types of acrylic stocks are available, providing customers with interesting combinations of patterns and swirls.

Pricing

StanMark Gifts will create custom-made pens and accessories that range in price from $85-$140. Prices depend on the combination of materials used and customer specifications.

In addition to custom-made items, a selection of popular ready-made writing instruments and accessories also will be available for purchase at a lower cost. These typically will range in price from $60-$85.

All writing instruments (e.g., pens, pencils, and combination sets), come with a decorative wooden box at no additional cost and are backed by a lifetime guarantee.

OPERATIONS

Manufacturing Process

1. Material Selection: This involves choosing a specific type of wood or acrylic from which the body of the writing instrument or product will be produced. In addition, hardware specific to the product also is selected.

2. Production: Utilizing a lathe, material stock (blanks) are "turned." During this process, chisels are used to shape the blank until the desired shape is obtained. Then, sanding and finishing are performed.

3. Assembly: Finally, pen tubes or other hardware is inserted into the finished material. Products are then packaged appropriately for shipping.

Production Equipment

-   Lathe
-   Lathe Chisels
-   Pen Mandrel
-   Barrel Trimmer
-   Insertion Tool
-   Common Hand Tools

Realizing that commercial production levels will increase wear and tear on his equipment, Stan has budgeted money to purchase a new, commercial-grade lathe when needed.

Supplies

-   Finishes
-   Sandpaper
-   Glue
-   Pen Kits

Location and Facilities

StanMark Gifts will be a home-based business. The owner already has a dedicated workshop area that can be utilized for production purposes. In addition, a spare bedroom will be converted into a home office, providing space for customer service and administrative activities.

Major Suppliers

Lumber

Our business will use a variety of suppliers to purchase the exotic woods needed for production, including:

- Peterson Exotic Woods Inc., Waterloo, Iowa
- Remington Lumber Company Inc., Johnston, Minnesota
- American Lumber Company L.P., Hamburg, Illinois
- Brookside Lumber and Supply Co., Bethel Park, Oklahoma
- Graebers Lumber Co., Fairless Hills, Wisconsin
- GV Moore Lumber Company Inc., Ayer, Iowa
- Jackson Lumber and Millwork Co., Lawrence, Wisconsin
- Lakeville Lumber, Lakeville, Minnesota
- OC Cluss Lumber Co., Aliquippa, South Dakota

Hardware

Likewise, a number of different organizations supply the hardware needed to produce the writing instruments and other items manufactured by our company. Key suppliers will include:

- Webster International LLC, Richardson, New York
- Acme Pen Supply Corp., Phoenix, Arizona
- Johnson Manufacturing Inc., Los Angeles

Shipping

Unless other arrangements are made per the customer's request, StanMark Gifts will utilize U.S. Postal Service Priority Mail to ship all orders. Shipping and handling charges will apply. Shipping insurance will be available for an additional charge.

MANAGEMENT SUMMARY

Owner

Stan Myers spent 23 years teaching industrial arts to high school students in Wakefield, Minnesota, specializing in woodworking courses. When budget cuts prompted the Wakefield Consolidated School District to eliminate its industrial arts program, Myers was faced with unemployment. However, the situation presented him with an exciting opportunity to utilize his skills in a new endeavor.

Although he is highly skilled in many aspects of woodworking, Myers is well-known for his work with the lathe, a piece of equipment that is used to shape and sculpt wood. Although the lathe commonly is associated with wooden items like spindles, bowls, and baseball bats, over the last five years Myers began making smaller, highly specialized gifts for friends and family. In particular, Myers has developed a reputation for producing beautiful handmade pens, mechanical pencils, and letter openers.

Myers has made custom items from a variety of exotic hardwoods, as well as different types of acrylic. Because fine, custom-made writing instruments and accessories (e.g., keychains, styluses, letter openers, magnifiers, etc.) command premium market prices (sometimes hundreds of dollars), Myers has decided to turn his one-time hobby into StanMark Gifts Inc., which leverages the power of the Internet to reach prospective buyers throughout the world.

In addition to his educational background and woodworking skills, Stan has taken the initiative to make sure that he has the fundamental business management knowledge needed to make StanMark Gifts a success. He has attended several seminars hosted by SCORE, a nonprofit association that utilizes education and mentorship to help small businesses get started successfully and achieve their goals. SCORE is supported by the U.S. Small Business Administration. Stan also has taken a series of small business management classes from Wakefield Community College, providing him with basic knowledge about marketing, accounting, and more.

Professional & Advisory Support

StanMark Gifts has established a business banking account with Wakefield Community Bank, including a merchant account for accepting credit card payments. Tax advisement is provided by Accurate Accounting Advisors LLC. In addition, legal services are provided by the firm of Blankenship & Moore.

GROWTH STRATEGY

Stan Myers has spent the last six months developing a conservative, low-risk, three-year growth strategy for his new business.

He will begin operation of StanMark Gifts as a part-time enterprise. While substitute teaching during years one and two, Stan will devote a growing number of total hours to the business. The majority of his weekly work hours will be devoted to production, with administration and marketing accounting for the remainder, as demonstrated in the following table:

Year	Total	Production	Marketing	Administration
1	20	14	3	3
2	30	21	4.5	4.5
3	40	28	6	6

During year three, Stan will devote himself to the business on a full-time basis.

Based on estimated weekly production of 14 hours and a 50-week work year, Stan anticipates gross revenues of $144,200 during the first year (see Financial Analysis section of this plan). Revenues will increase 50 percent in year two, reaching $216,300. Revenues are projected to increase approximately 46 percent in year three, totaling $316,400. These substantial increases are attributed to additional production hours during the second and third years.

MARKETING & SALES

StanMark Gifts' heirloom quality products will be marketed as gift items for occasions such as:

- Weddings

- Anniversaries

- Promotions

- Employee Recognition

- Customer Appreciation

- Birthdays

- Graduations

The majority of the business' marketing dollars will be devoted to online advertising, social media promotion, and search-engine optimization strategies. Target Online LLC, an online marketing firm based in Minneapolis, has been hired to assist with the development and implementation of StanMark Gifts' online marketing program.

Target Online also will help to develop an e-commerce Web site, which will be hosted by a local provider in Minneapolis. The site will be built using proven, effective "off-the-shelf" e-commerce modules (e.g., features such as shopping cart, payment processing, product listing, etc.), in order to minimize development costs. In addition, a custom domain will be purchased, along with corresponding e-mail accounts.

SWOT ANALYSIS

Strengths: The level of craftsmanship and quality offered by StanMark Gifts is a key differential.

Weaknesses: At least initially, StanMark Gifts will be a lean enterprise. Because the owner will focus much of his time on production, customer service inquiries may be not as responsive as larger gift retailers that offer features such as 24/7 telephone and online chat support from customer service representatives.

Opportunities: There is ample demand and growth potential among individual and corporate customers seeking unique and distinctive gifts.

Threats: Because StanMark Gifts will be a one-man operation, the risk of injury or illness could jeopardize operations or the company's reputation, in the event that orders are delayed.

FINANCIAL ANALYSIS

Stan Myers estimates that he can produce two pre-made items and one custom item per hour, generating gross hourly revenue of $206. Based on this figure, estimated weekly production of 14 hours, and a 50-week work year, Stan anticipates gross revenues of $144,200 during the first year. Revenues will increase 50 percent in year two, reaching $216,300. Revenues are projected to increase about 46 percent in year three, totaling $316,400. The substantial increases will be attributed to additional production hours during the second and third years.

Initial startup costs (detailed breakdown available upon request) will be minimal, and will be covered by a $10,000 investment from the owner's personal savings.

Following is a pro-forma profit and loss statement for the business. Additional financial statements have been prepared by our accountants and are available upon request.

	Year 1	Year 2	Year 3
Gross sales	$144,200	$216,300	$316,400
Cost of goods sold	$ 17,850	$ 26,775	$ 35,700
Net sales	$126,350	$189,525	$280,700
Expenses			
Salary	$ 50,000	$ 75,000	$100,000
Equipment	$ 1,000	$ 2,500	$ 2,500
Marketing	$ 30,000	$ 30,000	$ 30,000
Licenses & fees	$ 500	$ 500	$ 500
Health insurance	$ 10,000	$ 12,000	$ 15,000
Business insurance	$ 1,250	$ 1,250	$ 1,250
Telecommunications	$ 1,000	$ 1,000	$ 1,000
Supplies	$ 1,050	$ 1,575	$ 2,100
Payroll taxes	$ 5,250	$ 7,500	$ 9,000
	$100,050	$131,325	$161,350
Net profit	**$ 26,300**	**$ 58,200**	**$119,350**

This business plan will be evaluated every six months during the first three years of operations, and annually thereafter.

Hedge Fund

Oxford Advisors

54446 Wall St.
New York, NY 10001

BizPlanDB.com

The purpose of this business plan is to raise $10,000,000 for the development of a hedge fund while showcasing the expected financials and operations over the next three years. Oxford Advisors Inc. is a New York based corporation that will provide investment management for its investors in its targeted market. The Company was founded in 2008 by John Shagena.

1.0 EXECUTIVE SUMMARY

The purpose of this business plan is to raise $10,000,000 for the development of a hedge fund while showcasing the expected financials and operations over the next three years. Oxford Advisors Inc. is a New York based corporation that will provide investment management for its investors in its targeted market. The Company was founded in 2008 by John Shagena.

1.1 The Services

Oxford Advisors will solicit capital from accredited investors (defined later) with the intent to use this capital to make investments marketable securities and other hedge funds. The Company expects to generate compounded annual returns of 25% to 35% per year on capital invested into Oxford Advisors' portfolio holdings.

The Management of Oxford Advisors will retain a 20% ownership interest in the firm. Details of the fee arrangements for Oxford Advisors can be found in the Company's private placement memorandum.

The third section of the business plan will further describe the investment management services offered by Oxford Advisors.

1.2 Financing

At this time, the Company is seeking to raise $10,000,000 for the development of operations. Mr. Shagena is seeking to sell an 80% ownership interest in the business in exchange for this capital. 95% of the invested capital will be used for direct investments into the firm's investments. Briefly, the capital will be used as follows:

- Acquisition of profitable investments and marketable securities.

- Development of the Company's office.

- General working capital.

1.3 Mission Statement

Management's mission is to develop Oxford Advisors into a large scale investment firm that will provide dividend income, capital appreciation, and interest income to the Company's investors and senior directors.

1.4 Management Team

The Company was founded by John Shagena. Mr. Shagena has more than 10 years of experience in the investment management industry. Through his expertise, he will be able to bring the operations of the business to profitability within its first year of operations.

1.5 Income Forecasts

Mr. Shagena expects a strong rate of growth at the start of operations. Below are the expected financials over the next three years.

Proforma profit and loss (yearly)

Year	1	2	3
Sales	$3,498,852	$4,198,622	$4,912,388
Operating costs	$1,154,265	$1,311,037	$1,585,869
EBITDA	$2,169,645	$2,677,654	$3,080,900
Taxes, interest, and depreciation	$ 859,715	$1,052,759	$1,205,992
Net profit	$1,309,930	$1,624,896	$1,874,908

Sales, operating costs, and profit forecast

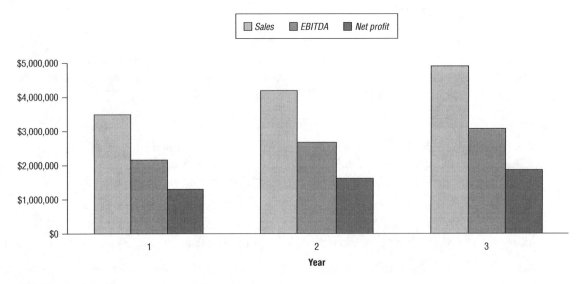

1.6 Expansion Plan

The Company will to undergo an aggressive expansion after the successful completion of the initial capital raising period. As Oxford Advisors is a multifaceted investment firm, Management will expand each segment of the business by developing limited partnerships that will attract additional capital for the Company's marketable securities and fund of funds portfolios.

2.0 COMPANY AND FINANCING SUMMARY

2.1 Registered Name and Corporate Structure

Oxford Advisors, Inc. is registered as a corporation in the State of New York.

2.2 Required Funds

At this time, Oxford Advisors requires $10,000,000 of equity funds. Below is a breakdown of how these funds will be used:

Projected startup costs

Initial lease payments and deposits	$ 50,000
Working capital	$ 1,000,000
FF&E	$ 125,000
Leasehold improvements	$ 100,000
Security deposits	$ 100,000
Insurance	$ 25,000
Investment capital	$ 8,500,000
Marketing budget	$ 75,000
Miscellaneous and unforeseen costs	$ 25,000
Total startup costs	**$10,000,000**

2.3 Investor Equity

At this time, Mr. Shagena is seeking to sell an 80% interest in Oxford Advisors in exchange for the capital sought in this business plan. Please reference the Company's private placement memorandum regarding more information regarding the Company's fee and ownership structure.

2.4 Management Equity

John Shagena currently owns 100% of Oxford Advisors, Inc.

2.5 Exit Strategies

The Management has planned for two possible exit strategies. The first strategy would be to sell the Company to a larger entity at a significant premium. Since, the financial management and hedge fund industry maintains a very low risk profile once the business is established; the Management feels that the Company could be sold for ten to fifteen times earnings.

The second exit scenario would entail selling a portion of the Company via an initial public offering (or "IPO"). After a detailed analysis, it was found that the Company could sell for twenty to thirty times earnings on the open market depending on the business's annual growth rate and strength of earnings. However, taking a company public involves significant legal red tape. Oxford Advisors, Inc. would be bound by the significant legal framework of the Sarbanes-Oxley Act in addition to the legal requirements set forth in form S1 of the Securities and Exchange Commission. The Company would also have to comply with the Securities Act of 1933 and the Exchange Act of 1934.

2.6 Investor Divesture

This will be discussed during negotiations.

3.0 INVESTMENT OPERATIONS

Below is a description of the investment management services offered by Oxford Advisors.

3.1 Marketable Securities

Management will make investments directly into marketable securities and other hedge funds that specialize in specific areas of trading. The Company intends to develop a number of trading strategies including options trading, LEAPs trading, long position/short position trading, and other methods of trading that will produce small but consistent gains on a weekly and monthly basis. Oxford Advisors may also engage a covered call strategy that would allow the fund to amply it return on investment for securities that are held for an extended period of time.

In regards to investing in other hedge funds, outsourcing trading activities is expensive as hedge funds charge large AUM fees and performance fees on their aggregate capital pools.

3.2 Mortgage Based Securities

As the Company expands, Oxford Advisors may become a syndicate and distributor of real estate limited partnerships based around prime mortgages. This would allow the Company to engage and extremely aggressive expansion.

In the event that the economy develops an unusually high prime interest rate, the Company may seek to act as a grantor of mortgages so that the Company can generate income on its unused cash. As such, in this event, Oxford Advisors can employ its cash reserves in the purchase of mortgages and associated debt instruments so that the business can earn additional streams of income from its monetary holdings. These mortgages can also be sold within the secondary market through the myriad of mortgage investment banks that have developed since the real estate boom. As the credit crisis has prompted a sharp drop off in the number of issued mortgages, Management sees a significant opportunity to acquire and trade distressed mortgage assets that could produce both capital appreciation and income for Oxford Advisors.

4.0 STRATEGIC AND MARKET ANALYSIS

4.1 Economic Outlook

This section of the analysis will detail the economic climate, the investment management industry, the customer profile, and the competition that the business will face as it progresses through its business operations.

Currently, the economic market condition in the United States is in sluggish. This slowdown in the economy has also greatly impacted real estate sales, which has halted to historical lows. Many economists expect that this sluggish growth will occur for three more years, at which point the economy will begin a prolonged recovery period with normal growth. However, Oxford Advisors has strategies that will allow the business to generate profits whether or not the market is going up or down.

4.2 Industry Analysis

The financial services sector has become one of the fastest growing business segments in the U.S. economy. Computerized technologies allow financial firms to operate advisory and brokerage services anywhere in the country. In previous decades, most financial firms needed to be within a close proximity to Wall Street in order to provide their clients the highest level of service. This is no longer the case as a firm can access almost every facet of the financial markets through Internet connections and specialized trading and investment management software. With these advances, several new firms have been created to address the needs of people in rural and suburban areas.

The Bureau of Labor Statistics estimates that there are approximately 94,000 investment advisors currently employed throughout the United States. The average annual income for an investment advisor is $62,700. Salaries are expected to increase at a rate of 2.1% a year as inflation increases.

In the last study conducted by the U.S. Economic Census, it was found that the revenues of the investment advisory industry increased from $14.8 billion dollars in 1992 to over $52.9 billion dollars by 2005. This represents a five year growth rate of 257%. The number of investment advisory establishments increased 61.5% over the same period. This trend is expected to continue as the 'baby boomer' generation begins to move into retirement age.

4.3 Customer Profile

Oxford Advisorss have a very limited scope of people to which they can market their investment portfolio. This is especially true as the Company will use marketable securities as its primary method of its day to day revenue generating activities.

Among people that the Company will solicit for investment, Management has identified the following demographic profile:

- Income of at least $500,000

- Average net worth of $3,000,000

- Is a bank, trust, or other private equity organization with at least $5,000,000 of assets.

Unfortunately, this business (for its investors) caters only to high net worth individuals that have an aggregate income of over $200,000 (if single) or $300,000 (if the client is married) or a net worth of at least one million dollars. Strict regulatory oversights prevent the Company from marketing the hedge fund to anyone that is not considered an accredited investor. These regulations may become more stringent as the Securities and Exchange Commission moves to have greater regulatory oversight over the hedge fund industry.

4.4 Competition

As the investment advisory and hedge fund industries have grown, so has the level of competition. One of the drawbacks to the industry is that there are very low barriers to entry. Any individual or business may register itself as an investment advisor after completing the proper examinations and filings. The expected costs to build an investment advisory are low as it is a service oriented business. There are more than 8,000 other private investment groups that operate in a similar capacity.

5.0 MARKETING PLAN

Oxford Advisors intends to maintain an extensive marketing campaign that will ensure maximum visibility for the business in its targeted market. Below is an overview of the marketing strategies and objectives of Oxford Advisors.

5.1 Marketing Objectives

- Establish relationships with other investment advisories within the United States in regards to referral relationships.

- Work closely with banks and other financial institutions that will make investments using their own funds.

5.2 Marketing Strategies

As the Company cannot directly market its services to the general public, Oxford Advisors will hire a capital introduction firm to showcase the operations of the business to potential investors. These firms, for a commission, will introduce potential investors and investment groups to Management. These companies maintain extensive lists of accredited investors and institutions that frequently make investments into private investment companies.

Oxford Advisors will also develop a website specifically for investors that have registered or have become clients with the Company. This website will showcase the strategies that the Company uses, relevant contact information, and for registered inventors - information specifically related to their account.

Mr. Shagena will also make presentations at popular hedge fund conventions while concurrently obtaining speaking engagements among other investment meetings so that his visibility and that of the firm increase over time.

5.3 Pricing

The business will receive an annual fee equal to 2% of the total funds under management. Oxford Advisors, Inc. (via Mr. Shagena) will also receive a fee equal to 20% of all profits generated.

6.0 ORGANIZATIONAL PLAN AND PERSONNEL SUMMARY

6.1 Corporate Organization

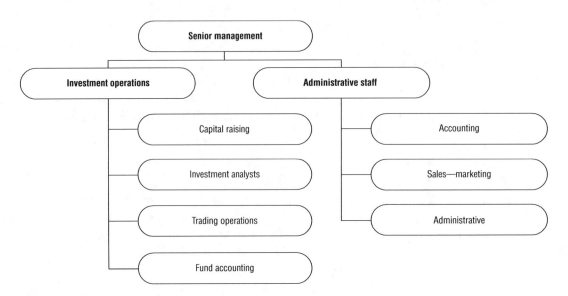

6.2 Organizational Budget

Personnel plan—yearly

Year	1	2	3
Senior management	$250,000	$257,500	$265,225
Investment analysts	$150,000	$154,500	$238,703
Accountants	$ 85,000	$175,100	$180,353
Traders	$100,000	$103,000	$212,180
Administrative	$ 90,000	$ 92,700	$ 95,481
Total	**$675,000**	**$782,800**	**$991,942**

Numbers of personnel

Senior management	2	2	2
Investment analysts	2	2	3
Accountants	1	2	2
Traders	1	1	2
Administrative	2	2	2
Totals	**8**	**9**	**11**

Personnel expense breakdown

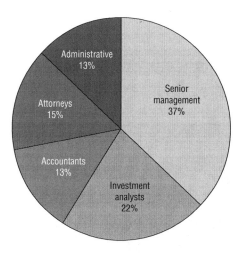

7.0 FINANCIAL PLAN

7.1 Underlying Assumptions

The Company has based its proforma financial statements on the following:

- Oxford Advisors will have an annual revenue growth rate of 15% per year.

- The Owner will acquire $10,000,000 of equity funds to develop the business.

- The Company will earn a compounded annual return of 30% on its investment portfolio.

7.2 Sensitivity Analysis

It is the goal of the Company to make investments in economically viable companies that will produce dividend income, interest income, and capital appreciation. During times of economic recession, the Company's portfolio may have issues with profit generation, which in turn, could lead to lower ROI's on Oxford Advisors' portfolio. However, the Company intends to use a number of investment strategies that will ensure that the firm will produce profits regardless of the general economic climate.

7.3 Source of Funds

Financing

Equity contributions	
Investor(s)	$ 10,000,000.00
Total equity financing	**$10,000,000.00**
Banks and lenders	
Total debt financing	**$ 0.00**
Total financing	**$10,000,000.00**

7.4 General Assumptions

General assumptions

Year	1	2	3
Short term interest rate	9.5%	9.5%	9.5%
Long term interest rate	10.0%	10.0%	10.0%
Federal tax rate	33.0%	33.0%	33.0%
State tax rate	5.0%	5.0%	5.0%
Personnel taxes	15.0%	15.0%	15.0%

7.5 Profit and Loss Statements

Proforma profit and loss (yearly)

Year	1	2	3
Sales	$3,498,852	$4,198,622	$4,912,388
Cost of goods sold	$ 174,943	$ 209,931	$ 245,619
Gross margin	95.00%	95.00%	95.00%
Operating income	$3,323,909	$3,988,691	$4,666,769
Expenses			
Payroll	$ 675,000	$ 782,800	$ 991,942
General and administrative	$ 41,988	$ 43,668	$ 45,414
Marketing expenses	$ 34,989	$ 41,986	$ 49,124
Professional fees and licensure	$ 55,219	$ 56,876	$ 58,582
Insurance costs	$ 61,987	$ 65,086	$ 68,341
Travel and vehicle costs	$ 77,596	$ 85,356	$ 93,891
Rent and utilities	$ 64,250	$ 67,463	$ 70,836
Miscellaneous costs	$ 41,986	$ 50,383	$ 58,949
Payroll taxes	$ 101,250	$ 117,420	$ 148,791
Total operating costs	$1,154,265	$1,311,037	$1,585,869
EBITDA	$2,169,645	$2,677,654	$3,080,900
Federal income tax	$ 715,983	$ 883,626	$1,016,697
State income tax	$ 108,482	$ 133,883	$ 154,045
Interest expense	$ 0	$ 0	$ 0
Depreciation expenses	$ 35,250	$ 35,250	$ 35,250
Net profit	$1,309,930	$1,624,896	$1,874,908
Profit margin	37.44%	38.70%	38.17%

Sales, operating costs, and profit forecast

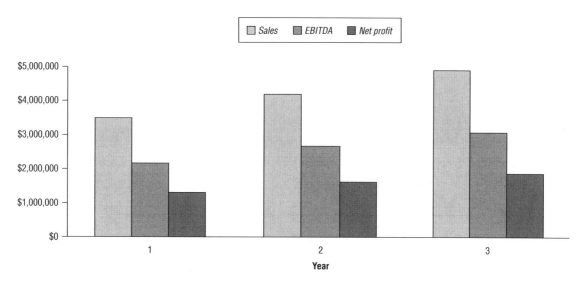

7.6 Cash Flow Analysis

Proforma cash flow analysis—yearly

Year	1	2	3
Cash from operations	$ 1,345,180	$1,660,146	$1,910,158
Cash from receivables	$ 0	$ 0	$ 0
Operating cash inflow	**$ 1,345,180**	**$1,660,146**	**$1,910,158**
Other cash inflows			
Equity investment	$10,000,000	$ 0	$ 0
Increased borrowings	$ 0	$ 0	$ 0
Sales of business assets	$ 0	$ 0	$ 0
A/P increases	$ 37,902	$ 43,587	$ 50,125
Total other cash inflows	**$10,037,902**	**$ 43,587**	**$ 50,125**
Total cash inflow	**$11,383,082**	**$1,703,733**	**$1,960,283**
Cash outflows			
Repayment of principal	$ 0	$ 0	$ 0
A/P decreases	$ 24,897	$ 29,876	$ 35,852
A/R increases	$ 0	$ 0	$ 0
Asset purchases	$ 8,875,000	$ 996,087	$1,146,095
Dividends	$ 0	$ 581,051	$ 668,555
Total cash outflows	**$ 8,899,897**	**$1,607,015**	**$1,850,502**
Net cash flow	**$ 2,483,185**	**$ 96,718**	**$ 109,782**
Cash balance	**$ 2,483,185**	**$2,579,903**	**$2,689,684**

Proforma cash flow (yearly)

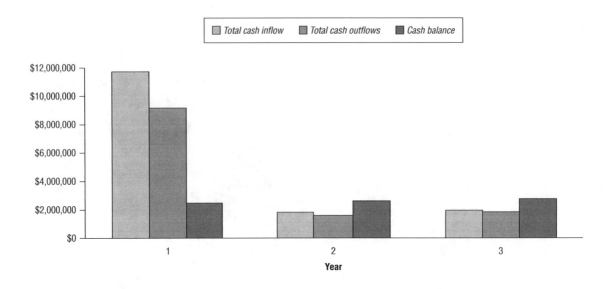

7.7 Balance Sheet

Proforma balance sheet—yearly

Year	1	2	3
Assets			
Cash	$ 2,483,185	$ 2,579,903	$ 2,689,684
Amortized development/expansion costs	$ 250,000	$ 349,609	$ 464,218
Investment portfolio	$ 10,200,000	$ 14,980,246	$ 21,615,837
FF&E	$ 125,000	$ 224,609	$ 339,218
Accumulated depreciation	($ 35,250)	($ 70,500)	($ 105,750)
Total assets	**$13,022,935**	**$18,063,866**	**$25,003,208**
Liabilities and equity			
Accounts payable	$ 13,005	$ 26,716	$ 40,990
Long term liabilities	$ 0	$ 0	$ 0
Other liabilities	$ 0	$ 0	$ 0
Total liabilities	**$ 13,005**	**$ 26,716**	**$ 40,990**
Net worth	**$13,009,930**	**$18,037,150**	**$24,962,219**
Total liabilities and equity	**$13,022,935**	**$18,063,866**	**$25,003,208**

Proforma balance sheet

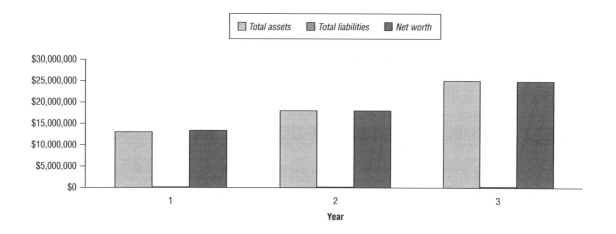

7.8 Breakeven Analysis

Monthly break even analysis

Year	1	2	3
Monthly revenue	$ 101,251	$ 115,003	$ 139,111
Yearly revenue	$1,215,016	$1,380,039	$1,669,336

Break even analysis

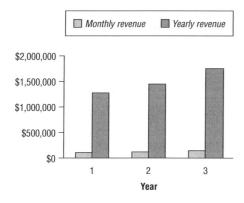

7.9 Business Ratios

Business ratios—yearly

Year	1	2	3
Sales			
Sales growth	0.00%	20.00%	17.00%
Gross margin	95.00%	95.00%	95.00%
Financials			
Profit margin	37.44%	38.70%	38.17%
Assets to liabilities	1001.38	676.15	609.99
Equity to liabilities	1000.38	675.15	608.99
Assets to equity	1.00	1.00	1.00
Liquidity			
Acid test	190.94	96.57	65.62
Cash to assets	0.19	0.14	0.11

7.10 Three Year Profit and Loss Statement

Profit and loss statement (first year)

Months	1	2	3	4	5	6	7
Sales	**$289,800**	**$290,122**	**$290,444**	**$290,766**	**$291,088**	**$291,410**	**$291,732**
Cost of goods sold	$ 14,490	$ 14,506	$ 14,522	$ 14,538	$ 14,554	$ 14,571	$ 14,587
Gross margin	95.00%	95.00%	95.00%	95.00%	95.00%	95.00%	95.00%
Operating income	**$275,310**	**$275,616**	**$275,922**	**$276,228**	**$276,534**	**$276,840**	**$277,145**
Expenses							
Payroll	$ 56,250	$ 56,250	$ 56,250	$ 56,250	$ 56,250	$ 56,250	$ 56,250
General and administrative	$ 3,499	$ 3,499	$ 3,499	$ 3,499	$ 3,499	$ 3,499	$ 3,499
Marketing expenses	$ 2,916	$ 2,916	$ 2,916	$ 2,916	$ 2,916	$ 2,916	$ 2,916
Professional fees and licensure	$ 4,602	$ 4,602	$ 4,602	$ 4,602	$ 4,602	$ 4,602	$ 4,602
Insurance costs	$ 5,166	$ 5,166	$ 5,166	$ 5,166	$ 5,166	$ 5,166	$ 5,166
Travel and vehicle costs	$ 6,466	$ 6,466	$ 6,466	$ 6,466	$ 6,466	$ 6,466	$ 6,466
Rent and utilities	$ 5,354	$ 5,354	$ 5,354	$ 5,354	$ 5,354	$ 5,354	$ 5,354
Miscellaneous costs	$ 3,499	$ 3,499	$ 3,499	$ 3,499	$ 3,499	$ 3,499	$ 3,499
Payroll taxes	$ 8,438	$ 8,438	$ 8,438	$ 8,438	$ 8,438	$ 8,438	$ 8,438
Total operating costs	**$ 96,189**	**$ 96,189**	**$ 96,189**	**$ 96,189**	**$ 96,189**	**$ 96,189**	**$ 96,189**
EBITDA	**$179,121**	**$179,427**	**$179,733**	**$180,039**	**$180,345**	**$180,651**	**$180,957**
Federal income tax	$ 59,303	$ 59,369	$ 59,435	$ 59,500	$ 59,566	$ 59,632	$ 59,698
State income tax	$ 8,985	$ 8,995	$ 9,005	$ 9,015	$ 9,025	$ 9,035	$ 9,045
Interest expense	$ 0	$ 0	$ 0	$ 0	$ 0	$ 0	$ 0
Depreciation expense	$ 2,938	$ 2,938	$ 2,938	$ 2,938	$ 2,938	$ 2,938	$ 2,938
Net profit	**$107,896**	**$108,126**	**$108,356**	**$108,586**	**$108,816**	**$109,046**	**$109,276**

Profit and loss statement (first year cont.)

Month	8	9	10	11	12	1
Sales	$292,054	$292,376	$292,698	$293,020	$293,342	$3,498,852
Cost of goods sold	$ 14,603	$ 14,619	$ 14,635	$ 14,651	$ 14,667	$ 174,943
Gross margin	95.00%	95.00%	95.00%	95.00%	95.00%	95.00%
Operating income	$277,451	$277,757	$278,063	$278,369	$278,675	$3,323,909
Expenses						
Payroll	$ 56,250	$ 56,250	$ 56,250	$ 56,250	$ 56,250	$ 675,000
General and administrative	$ 3,499	$ 3,499	$ 3,499	$ 3,499	$ 3,499	$ 41,988
Marketing expenses	$ 2,916	$ 2,916	$ 2,916	$ 2,916	$ 2,916	$ 34,989
Professional fees and licensure	$ 4,602	$ 4,602	$ 4,602	$ 4,602	$ 4,602	$ 55,219
Insurance costs	$ 5,166	$ 5,166	$ 5,166	$ 5,166	$ 5,166	$ 61,987
Travel and vehicle costs	$ 6,466	$ 6,466	$ 6,466	$ 6,466	$ 6,466	$ 77,596
Rent and utilities	$ 5,354	$ 5,354	$ 5,354	$ 5,354	$ 5,354	$ 64,250
Miscellaneous costs	$ 3,499	$ 3,499	$ 3,499	$ 3,499	$ 3,499	$ 41,986
Payroll taxes	$ 8,438	$ 8,438	$ 8,438	$ 8,438	$ 8,438	$ 101,250
Total operating costs	$ 96,189	$ 96,189	$ 96,189	$ 96,189	$ 96,189	$1,154,265
EBITDA	$181,263	$181,568	$181,874	$182,180	$182,486	$2,169,645
Federal income tax	$ 59,764	$ 59,830	$ 59,896	$ 59,962	$ 60,028	$ 715,983
State income tax	$ 9,055	$ 9,065	$ 9,075	$ 9,085	$ 9,095	$ 108,482
Interest expense	$ 0	$ 0	$ 0	$ 0	$ 0	$ 0
Depreciation expense	$ 2,938	$ 2,938	$ 2,938	$ 2,938	$ 2,938	$ 35,250
Net profit	$109,506	$109,736	$109,966	$110,196	$110,426	$1,309,930

Profit and loss statement (second year)

Quarter	Q1	2 Q2	Q3	Q4	2
Sales	$839,724	$1,049,656	$1,133,628	$1,175,614	$4,198,622
Cost of goods sold	$ 41,986	$ 52,483	$ 56,681	$ 58,781	$ 209,931
Gross margin	95.00%	95.00%	95.00%	95.00%	95.00%
Operating income	$797,738	$ 997,173	$1,076,947	$1,116,834	$3,988,691
Expenses					
Payroll	$156,560	$ 195,700	$ 211,356	$ 219,184	$ 782,800
General and administrative	$ 8,734	$ 10,917	$ 11,790	$ 12,227	$ 43,668
Marketing expenses	$ 8,397	$ 10,497	$ 11,336	$ 11,756	$ 41,986
Professional fees and licensure	$ 11,375	$ 14,219	$ 15,356	$ 15,925	$ 56,876
Insurance costs	$ 13,017	$ 16,272	$ 17,573	$ 18,224	$ 65,086
Travel and vehicle costs	$ 17,071	$ 21,339	$ 23,046	$ 23,900	$ 85,356
Rent and utilities	$ 13,493	$ 16,866	$ 18,215	$ 18,890	$ 67,463
Miscellaneous costs	$ 10,077	$ 12,596	$ 13,604	$ 14,107	$ 50,383
Payroll taxes	$ 23,484	$ 29,355	$ 31,703	$ 32,878	$ 117,420
Total operating costs	$262,207	$ 327,759	$ 353,980	$ 367,090	$1,311,037
EBITDA	$535,531	$ 669,414	$ 722,967	$ 749,743	$2,677,654
Federal income tax	$176,725	$ 220,906	$ 238,579	$ 247,415	$ 883,626
State income tax	$ 26,777	$ 33,471	$ 36,148	$ 37,487	$ 133,883
Interest expense	$ 0	$ 0	$ 0	$ 0	$ 0
Depreciation expense	$ 8,813	$ 8,813	$ 8,813	$ 8,813	$ 35,250
Net profit	$323,217	$ 406,224	$ 439,427	$ 456,028	$1,624,896

Profit and loss statement (third year)

Quarter	Q1	3 Q2	Q3	Q4	3
Sales	$982,478	$1,228,097	$1,326,345	$1,375,469	$4,912,388
Cost of goods sold	$ 49,124	$ 61,405	$ 66,317	$ 68,773	$ 245,619
Gross margin	95.00%	95.00%	95.00%	95.00%	95.00%
Operating income	$933,354	$1,166,692	$1,260,028	$1,306,695	$4,666,769
Expenses					
Payroll	$198,388	$ 247,985	$ 267,824	$ 277,744	$ 991,942
General and administrative	$ 9,083	$ 11,354	$ 12,262	$ 12,716	$ 45,414
Marketing expenses	$ 9,825	$ 12,281	$ 13,263	$ 13,755	$ 49,124
Professional fees and licensure	$ 11,716	$ 14,645	$ 15,817	$ 16,403	$ 58,582
Insurance costs	$ 13,668	$ 17,085	$ 18,452	$ 19,135	$ 68,341
Travel and vehicle costs	$ 18,778	$ 23,473	$ 25,351	$ 26,290	$ 93,891
Rent and utilities	$ 14,167	$ 17,709	$ 19,126	$ 19,834	$ 70,836
Miscellaneous costs	$ 11,790	$ 14,737	$ 15,916	$ 16,506	$ 58,949
Payroll taxes	$ 29,758	$ 37,198	$ 40,174	$ 41,662	$ 148,791
Total operating costs	$317,174	$ 396,467	$ 428,185	$ 444,043	$1,585,869
EBITDA	$616,180	$ 770,225	$ 831,843	$ 862,652	$3,080,900
Federal income tax	$203,339	$ 254,174	$ 274,508	$ 284,675	$1,016,697
State income tax	$ 30,809	$ 38,511	$ 41,592	$ 43,133	$ 154,045
Interest expense	$ 0	$ 0	$ 0	$ 0	$ 0
Depreciation expense	$ 8,813	$ 8,813	$ 8,813	$ 8,813	$ 35,250
Net profit	$373,219	$ 468,727	$ 506,930	$ 526,032	$1,874,908

7.11 Three Year Cash Flow Analysis

Cash flow analysis (first year)

Month	1	2	3	4	5	6	7
Cash from operations	$ 110,833	$ 111,063	$ 111,293	$ 111,523	$ 111,753	$ 111,983	$ 112,213
Cash from receivables	$ 0	$ 0	$ 0	$ 0	$ 0	$ 0	$ 0
Operating cash inflow	$ 110,833	$ 111,063	$ 111,293	$ 111,523	$ 111,753	$ 111,983	$ 112,213
Other cash inflows							
Equity investment	$10,000,000	$ 0	$ 0	$ 0	$ 0	$ 0	$ 0
Increased borrowings	$ 0	$ 0	$ 0	$ 0	$ 0	$ 0	$ 0
Sales of business assets	$ 0	$ 0	$ 0	$ 0	$ 0	$ 0	$ 0
A/P increases	$ 3,159	$ 3,159	$ 3,159	$ 3,159	$ 3,159	$ 3,159	$ 3,159
Total other cash inflows	$10,003,159	$ 3,159	$ 3,159	$ 3,159	$ 3,159	$ 3,159	$ 3,159
Total cash inflow	$10,113,992	$ 114,222	$ 114,452	$ 114,682	$ 114,912	$ 115,142	$ 115,372
Cash outflows							
Repayment of principal	$ 0	$ 0	$ 0	$ 0	$ 0	$ 0	$ 0
A/P decreases	$ 2,075	$ 2,075	$ 2,075	$ 2,075	$ 2,075	$ 2,075	$ 2,075
A/R increases	$ 0	$ 0	$ 0	$ 0	$ 0	$ 0	$ 0
Asset purchases	$ 8,875,000	$ 0	$ 0	$ 0	$ 0	$ 0	$ 0
Dividends	$ 0	$ 0	$ 0	$ 0	$ 0	$ 0	$ 0
Total cash outflows	$ 8,877,075	$ 2,075	$ 2,075	$ 2,075	$ 2,075	$ 2,075	$ 2,075
Net cash flow	$ 1,236,917	$ 112,147	$ 112,377	$ 112,607	$ 112,837	$ 113,067	$ 113,297
Cash balance	$ 1,236,917	$1,349,064	$1,461,441	$1,574,048	$1,686,885	$1,799,952	$1,913,249

Cash flow analysis (first year cont.)

Month	8	9	10	11	12	1
Cash from operations	$ 112,443	$ 112,673	$ 112,903	$ 113,133	$ 113,363	$ 1,345,180
Cash from receivables	$ 0	$ 0	$ 0	$ 0	$ 0	$ 0
Operating cash inflow	**$ 112,443**	**$ 112,673**	**$ 112,903**	**$ 113,133**	**$ 113,363**	**$ 1,345,180**
Other cash inflows						
Equity investment	$ 0	$ 0	$ 0	$ 0	$ 0	$10,000,000
Increased borrowings	$ 0	$ 0	$ 0	$ 0	$ 0	$ 0
Sales of business assets	$ 0	$ 0	$ 0	$ 0	$ 0	$ 0
A/P increases	$ 3,159	$ 3,159	$ 3,159	$ 3,159	$ 3,159	$ 37,902
Total other cash inflows	**$ 3,159**	**$ 3,159**	**$ 3,159**	**$ 3,159**	**$ 3,159**	**$10,037,902**
Total cash inflow	**$ 115,602**	**$ 115,832**	**$ 116,062**	**$ 116,292**	**$ 116,522**	**$11,383,082**
Cash outflows						
Repayment of principal	$ 0	$ 0	$ 0	$ 0	$ 0	$ 0
A/P decreases	$ 2,075	$ 2,075	$ 2,075	$ 2,075	$ 2,075	$ 24,897
A/R increases	$ 0	$ 0	$ 0	$ 0	$ 0	$ 0
Asset purchases	$ 0	$ 0	$ 0	$ 0	$ 0	$ 8,875,000
Dividends	$ 0	$ 0	$ 0	$ 0	$ 0	$ 0
Total cash outflows	**$ 2,075**	**$ 2,075**	**$ 2,075**	**$ 2,075**	**$ 2,075**	**$ 8,899,897**
Net cash flow	**$ 113,527**	**$ 113,757**	**$ 113,987**	**$ 114,217**	**$ 114,447**	**$ 2,483,185**
Cash balance	**$2,026,776**	**$2,140,533**	**$2,254,520**	**$2,368,737**	**$2,483,185**	**$ 2,483,185**

Cash flow analysis (second year)

Quarter	Q1	2			
		Q2	Q3	Q4	2
Cash from operations	$ 332,029	$ 415,036	$ 448,239	$ 464,841	$1,660,146
Cash from receivables	$ 0	$ 0	$ 0	$ 0	$ 0
Operating cash inflow	**$ 332,029**	**$ 415,036**	**$ 448,239**	**$ 464,841**	**$1,660,146**
Other cash inflows					
Equity investment	$ 0	$ 0	$ 0	$ 0	$ 0
Increased borrowings	$ 0	$ 0	$ 0	$ 0	$ 0
Sales of business assets	$ 0	$ 0	$ 0	$ 0	$ 0
A/P increases	$ 8,717	$ 10,897	$ 11,769	$ 12,204	$ 43,587
Total other cash inflows	**$ 8,717**	**$ 10,897**	**$ 11,769**	**$ 12,204**	**$ 43,587**
Total cash inflow	**$ 340,747**	**$ 425,933**	**$ 460,008**	**$ 477,045**	**$1,703,733**
Cash outflows					
Repayment of principal	$ 0	$ 0	$ 0	$ 0	$ 0
A/P decreases	$ 5,975	$ 7,469	$ 8,067	$ 8,365	$ 29,876
A/R increases	$ 0	$ 0	$ 0	$ 0	$ 0
Asset purchases	$ 199,217	$ 249,022	$ 268,944	$ 278,904	$ 996,087
Dividends	$ 116,210	$ 145,263	$ 156,884	$ 162,694	$ 581,051
Total cash outflows	**$ 321,403**	**$ 401,754**	**$ 433,894**	**$ 449,964**	**$1,607,015**
Net cash flow	**$ 19,344**	**$ 24,180**	**$ 26,114**	**$ 27,081**	**$ 96,718**
Cash balance	**$2,502,528**	**$2,526,708**	**$2,552,822**	**$2,579,903**	**$2,579,903**

Cash flow analysis (third year)

Quarter	Q1	Q2	Q3	Q4	3
Cash from operations	$ 382,032	$ 477,540	$ 515,743	$ 534,844	$1,910,158
Cash from receivables	$ 0	$ 0	$ 0	$ 0	$ 0
Operating cash inflow	**$ 382,032**	**$ 477,540**	**$ 515,743**	**$ 534,844**	**$1,910,158**
Other cash inflows					
Equity investment	$ 0	$ 0	$ 0	$ 0	$ 0
Increased borrowings	$ 0	$ 0	$ 0	$ 0	$ 0
Sales of business assets	$ 0	$ 0	$ 0	$ 0	$ 0
A/P increases	$ 10,025	$ 12,531	$ 13,534	$ 14,035	$ 50,125
Total other cash inflows	**$ 10,025**	**$ 12,531**	**$ 13,534**	**$ 14,035**	**$ 50,125**
Total cash inflow	**$ 392,057**	**$ 490,071**	**$ 529,277**	**$ 548,879**	**$1,960,283**
Cash outflows					
Repayment of principal	$ 0	$ 0	$ 0	$ 0	$ 0
A/P decreases	$ 7,170	$ 8,963	$ 9,680	$ 10,038	$ 35,852
A/R increases	$ 0	$ 0	$ 0	$ 0	$ 0
Asset purchases	$ 229,219	$ 286,524	$ 309,446	$ 320,907	$1,146,095
Dividends	$ 133,711	$ 167,139	$ 180,510	$ 187,195	$ 668,555
Total cash outflows	**$ 370,100**	**$ 462,625**	**$ 499,635**	**$ 518,141**	**$1,850,502**
Net cash flow	**$ 21,956**	**$ 27,445**	**$ 29,641**	**$ 30,739**	**$ 109,782**
Cash balance	**$2,601,859**	**$2,629,305**	**$2,658,946**	**$2,689,684**	**$2,689,684**

Home Accessibility Services Provider

AccessibilityWorx Inc.

2309 Rogers Ave.
Indianapolis, IN 32619

Paul Greenland

AccessibilityWorx Inc. provides home modification services, equipment, and supplies to help elderly and disabled individuals maximize their independence, comfort, and safety.

EXECUTIVE SUMMARY

Incorporated in Indiana, AccessibilityWorx Inc. provides home modification services, equipment, and supplies to help elderly and disabled individuals maximize their independence, comfort, and safety. The business is being established by brothers Brian and John Peterson.

Like many business ideas, the inspiration for AccessibilityWorx emerged from a personal experience. In 2012 the Peterson's 78-year-old father, Rex, suffered a stroke that left him partially paralyzed. Before this tragic event Rex was the picture of health and vitality, teaching water exercise courses at a local community center, serving as a Boy Scout leader, and volunteering many hours at his local VFW chapter. Following the stroke, which required a lengthy stay at a rehabilitation hospital, Rex's family realized that his life would be very different. Most of all, it was apparent that he would be unable to live at home without significant changes to his environment.

Although their father's stroke was a stressful event, Brian and John enjoyed helping their parents develop a plan to make their home safer and more accessible. During this experience the brothers realized that they each had unique skills and abilities that could be used to establish a business with significant market potential. Brian Peterson is the safety director for a large steel fabrication company. His responsibilities include 16,000 employees at 13 plants throughout the United States. Ready for a career change, and recognizing that he now needs to be closer to his parents during their older years (his current position requires frequent travel), Brian came up with the idea for AccessibilityWorx, which combines his safety expertise with John's knowledge of construction and remodeling.

MARKET ANALYSIS

Although AccessibilityWorx initially will serve the immediate Indianapolis area, the company has the potential for explosive regional and national growth.

According research from Paragon Report, the number of Americans over the age of 50 was expected to reach 100 million in 2012, fueled by the aging of the 77 million-member Baby Boomer population.

Between 2000 and 2030, the number of Americans over the age of 65 is projected to double, based on federal Administration on Aging figures.

These larger trends are evident in the Indianapolis area. According to an August 6, 2012, article in the **Indianapolis Business Journal**, research from Indiana University reveals that the state was home to approximately 840,000 individuals over the age of 65 in 2010. This figure is projected to reach 1.1 million in 2020, and 1.5 million by 2050. Although the average state population will increase approximately 6 percent, the 65-plus population segment will grow at a rate of about 30 percent.

PERSONNEL

Brian Peterson, CSP

With more than 15 years of experience, Brian Peterson is a Certified Safety Professional. He earned an undergraduate degree from Cunningham University in 1993, majoring in both business and industrial psychology. Peterson subsequently earned a Masters in Science degree in 1996. After working as the safety manager for a large manufacturing firm, Peterson secured a safety director position with a large steel fabrication company, where he has worked for the past seven years. His areas of expertise include Human Factors Industrial Engineering and Safety Management. Peterson is a member of the Human Factors and Ergonomics Society, as well as the American Society of Safety Engineers. Although his expertise has been focused on manufacturing environments, Peterson's safety skills and knowledge can easily be transferred to residential environments.

John Peterson, CAPS

For 12 years, John Peterson has owned and operated Peterson Construction Inc., a construction and remodeling company serving the greater Indianapolis area. In 2008 Peterson's construction business began to suffer. As economic conditions deteriorated, the number of remodeling and construction projects performed by his business declined. Although conditions have improved somewhat, Peterson has sought ways to specialize his business and gain a differential from his competitors. In this regard, he has obtained Certified Aging-in-Placed Specialist (CAPS) certification from the National Association of Homebuilders, providing him with the knowledge and skills needed to perform remodeling projects that meet the unique requirements of an aging population. As part of this process, Peterson completed courses in business management, design/build solutions for aging and accessibility, and more.

GROWTH STRATEGY

Year One: AccessibilityWorx will concentrate tremendous resources on establishing a reputation of trust in the Indianapolis market during its first year of operation. Unfortunately, many elderly individuals are the victims of fraud; especially when it comes to home remodeling contractors. In this regard, John Peterson's established reputation will be most helpful. Peterson Construction is a long-time member of the Indianapolis Chamber Of Commerce. Likewise, AccessibilityWorx will become a chamber member. In addition, AccessibilityWorx will pursue registration with the Better Business Bureau. The company's advertising will feature the Peterson brothers and their father, Rex, who is well-known in the community. By sharing their personal story, the owners are hopeful that they can quickly gain the trust of senior citizens in the Indianapolis area, as well as their adult children, who often are key decision-makers in their care. In addition to establishing a reputation of trust, AccessibilityWorx will establish a goal of generating first-year gross sales of $365,000 and net sales of $115,400.

Year Two: During its second year of operations, AccessibilityWorx will consider expanding its scope of products and services to include home monitoring systems. This will be accomplished via a reseller agreement with an established provider. This technology will enable seniors to push a button on a wearable lanyard, which is connected to a call center that will notify the appropriate resource in the event of an emergency. In addition to home monitoring, the business will consider expanding the products it sells to include telephone amplifiers, telephone ringers and flashers, amplification systems, vibrating watches, specialized alarm clocks, door sensors, and similar devices. During its second year, AccessibilityWorx will establish a goal of generating gross sales of $492,750 and net sales of $209,900.

Year Three: Based on growth during years one and two, AccessibilityWorx will consider expanding beyond the Indianapolis market during year three. This will involve adding additional personnel to the business, and also to Peterson Construction. The Peterson brothers will no longer be able to provide direct service to all of their customers. Therefore, at least one customer care coordinator will need to be hired and trained. In addition, formal job descriptions, as well as employment policies and procedures, will need to be created. Any expansion efforts would occur during year four and would be funded entirely with net revenues generated by the business during its first three years of operation. During its third year, AccessibilityWorx will establish a goal of generating gross sales of $591,300 and net sales of $256,650.

RODUCTS & SERVICES

Remodeling Services

Remodeling services will involve a consultation with the Peterson brothers, in order to develop a custom home modification plan. Then, actual construction work will be performed via a contract with Peterson construction. The Peterson brothers will personally supervise every project. Services will be performed in accordance to specifications of the Americans with Disabilities Act, as well as all local and state building codes and regulations.

Customers will be required to provide 50 percent of project funding in advance, with the remainder due upon completion. The Petersons have made arrangements to offer competitive financing plans (based on the customer's credit score) through BrilliantStar Financial Services.

Following are examples of the types of installations that will be performed by AccessibilityWorx:

Accessible Bathrooms
- Showers
- Bathtubs
- Grab Bars
- Shower Seats (Roll-in, Fold-up, Fold-away)
- Bathtub Chair Seat Lifts
- Transfer Benches & Chairs
- Shower Stools
- Nonslip Steps

Accessible Kitchens
- Specialized Shelving
- Adjustable Countertops
- Cabinet Lifts

Entry Modifications

- Wheelchair Ramps

- Doorways

- Railings

Lifts

- Battery-Powered Stair Lifts

- Electric-Powered Stair Lifts

- Cargo Stair Lifts (for transporting groceries or heavy items between floors)

- Outdoor Stair Lifts

- Wheelchair Stair-Climbers

- Dumbwaiters

Products & Accessories

AccessibilityWorx has established wholesale agreements with several reputable suppliers of accessibility products. These will be sold as enhanced offerings, at a mark-up, to customers for whom we are performing remodeling projects, allowing us to provide a comprehensive accessibility package. Although we will sell products to non-remodeling customers, this will not be our focus, since it will be difficult to compete with established providers such as online retailers, drugstores, and home medical equipment companies, who specialize in these types of items. Examples of the items we will sell include:

- Battery-operated Grill Brushes

- Package-openers

- Splatter Guards

- Wearable Heat-Resistance Cooking Tongs

- Pan Handlers & Holders

- Pot Stabilizers

- Jar Openers

- Can Openers

- Power Scissors

MARKETING & SALES

The Peterson brothers have identified several key tactics for establishing and growing AccessibilityWorx. These mainly focus on the target market of older adults, as well as the children of older adults who purchase services for their parents. These tactics include:

- A Web site with complete details about the services and products that we offer.

- A social media strategy involving popular social networking sites, such as Facebook.

- A public relations strategy that involves quarterly pitches to local newspapers, bloggers, radio stations, and television network affiliates (e.g., ABC, CBS, NBC, and FOX), allowing us to serve as thought leaders for the needs of the aging population. As part of the strategy, we will share powerful customer testimonials and stories.

- An attractive, four-color brochure will be developed to promote our business and the products and services we provide. The brochure will be ideal for direct marketing campaigns, and also can be provided to people requesting additional information about our business.

- AccessibilityWorx will run regular newspaper ads in *The Indianapolis Senior Times*, a local free newspaper serving the senior market. This publication offers affordable advertising rates and a substantial readership base.

- A sustained direct marketing program targeting individuals aged 45-55, who are likely to be making elder care decisions for their parents, as well as older individuals (e.g., 55-plus), who may have an interest in purchasing our products and services directly.

- A referral program that offers a 15 percent discount for friends and family.

- Magnetic signage that can be affixed to our vehicle in order to promote the business.

- Magnetic business cards that will double as advertising specialties.

- Active membership in the Indianapolis Chamber of Commerce.

- Presentations to special interest groups (e.g., Rotary, retiree groups, church groups, etc.).

- Trade show marketing at the annual Indianapolis Senior Expo.

OPERATIONS

Location

AccessibilityWorx will share office space with Peterson Construction, which owns a small warehouse that includes an office area and conference room. Although the facility is equipped for customer meetings, AccessibilityWorx typically will offer to meet with customers directly in their homes, or at an alternate location, for the sake of convenience. A dedicated phone number will be established for AccessibilityWorx, which the office staff for Peterson Construction will answer.

FINANCIAL ANALYSIS

AccessibilityWorx will require virtually no overhead. The majority of start-up costs will be marketing-related. The Peterson brothers will contribute $50,000 in personal savings to the business, which they expect to recoup during the first year.

Gross sales for AccessibilityWorx are expected to increase 35 percent during the second year and 20 percent during the third year, at which time the business will be at capacity. Additional personnel will then be needed in order to handle additional volume and/or expand into new geographic areas. Profits during the first three years of operation will be used to fund any additional expansion in year four. After recouping their $50,000 investment, the Peterson brothers anticipate that total net profits during the first three years will total $531,950.

Following is a pro-forma profit and loss statement for the business. Additional financial statements have been prepared by the Petersons' accountants and are available upon request.

Pro-forma profit and loss statement

	2013	2014	2015
Home modification*	$365,000	$492,750	$591,300
Gross product sales	$ 50,000	$ 60,000	$ 69,000
Cost of goods sold	$ 35,000	$ 42,000	$ 48,300
Net sales	$380,000	$510,750	$612,000
Expenses			
Salaries	$150,000	$200,000	$250,000
Equipment	$ 2,500	$ 3,000	$ 3,500
Marketing	$ 85,000	$ 65,000	$ 65,000
Transportation	$ 4,000	$ 5,000	$ 6,000
Licenses & fees	$ 1,250	$ 1,250	$ 1,250
Health insurance	$ 12,500	$ 15,000	$ 16,500
Business insurance	$ 2,150	$ 2,150	$ 2,150
Mobile telecommunications	$ 1,350	$ 1,350	$ 1,350
Office supplies	$ 600	$ 600	$ 600
Payroll taxes	$ 5,250	$ 7,500	$ 9,000
Total expenses	**$264,600**	**$300,850**	**$355,350**
Net profit	**$115,400**	**$209,900**	**$256,650**

*Consulting & project management

Paintball Store and Field

X-Treme Paintball

65757 N. Hubert
Woodmere, NY 11598

BizPlanDB.com

The purpose of this business plan is to raise $250,000 for the development of a paintball store and playing field facility while showcasing the expected financials and operations over the next three years. X-Treme Paintball, Inc. is a New York based corporation that will provide sales of paintball guns/supplies as well as a venue where customers can play paintball. The Company was founded by Todd Ferranti.

1.0 EXECUTIVE SUMMARY

The purpose of this business plan is to raise $250,000 for the development of a paintball store and playing field facility while showcasing the expected financials and operations over the next three years. X-Treme Paintball, Inc. is a New York based corporation that will provide sales of paintball guns/supplies as well as a venue where customers can play paintball. The Company was founded by Todd Ferranti.

1.1 The Services

The primary revenue center for the Company will be the sale of paintball guns and paintball supplies through its retail location, which will be located in a relatively rural area within the Company's targeted New York metropolitan market so that the Company can provide a place where paintball enthusiasts can play.

The facility will feature a 30 acre paintball playing arena where people can rent paintball guns, fatigues, and purchase paintball supplies. Management expects that this segment of the business will generate 35% of X-Treme Paintball, Inc.'s aggregate revenues.

The third section of the business plan will further describe the services offered by X-Treme Paintball, Inc.

1.2 Financing

Mr. Ferranti is seeking to raise $250,000 from as a bank loan. The interest rate and loan agreement are to be further discussed during negotiation. This business plan assumes that the business will receive a 10 year loan with a 9% fixed interest rate. The financing will be used for the following:

*   Development of the Company's X-Treme Paintball location.

*   Financing for the first six months of operation.

*   Capital to purchase the Company's inventory.

Mr. Ferranti will contribute $50,000 to the venture.

165

1.3 Mission Statement

X-Treme Paintball's mission is to become the recognized local (and possibly regional) leader in providing customers with an expansive line of paintball products coupled with an exciting facility from which paintball enthusiasts can play the sport.

1.4 Management Team

The Company was founded by Todd Ferranti. Mr. Ferranti has more than 10 years of experience in the retail management industry. Through his expertise, he will be able to bring the operations of the business to profitability within its first year of operations.

1.5 Sales Forecasts

Mr. Ferranti expects a strong rate of growth at the start of operations. Below are the expected financials over the next three years.

Proforma profit and loss (yearly)

Year	1	2	3
Sales	$731,952	$805,147	$885,662
Operating costs	$447,480	$463,770	$480,758
EBITDA	$ 89,749	$127,182	$169,289
Taxes, interest, and depreciation	$ 71,663	$ 76,647	$ 91,620
Net profit	$ 18,086	$ 50,535	$ 77,669

Sales, operating costs, and profit forecast

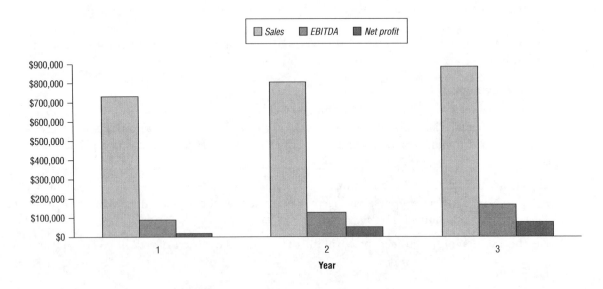

1.6 Expansion Plan

The Founder expects that the business will aggressively expand during the first three years of operation. Mr. Ferranti intends to implement marketing campaigns that will effectively target individuals (especially males between the ages of 16 and 35) within the target market.

2.0 COMPANY AND FINANCING SUMMARY

2.1 Registered Name and Corporate Structure

X-Treme Paintball, Inc. is registered as a corporation in the State of New York.

2.2 Required Funds

At this time, X-Treme Paintball, Inc. requires $250,000 of debt funds. Mr. Ferranti will place $50,000 into the venture. Below is a breakdown of how these funds will be used:

Projected startup costs

Initial lease payments and deposits	$ 25,000
Working capital	$ 60,000
FF&E	$ 50,000
Playing field development	$ 75,000
Security deposits	$ 15,000
Insurance	$ 10,000
Initial inventory	$ 40,000
Marketing budget	$ 20,000
Miscellaneous and unforeseen costs	$ 5,000
Total startup costs	**$300,000**

Use of funds

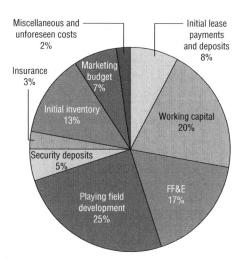

2.3 Investor Equity

Mr. Ferranti is not seeking an investment from a third party at this time.

2.4 Management Equity

Todd Ferranti owns 100% of X-Treme Paintball, Inc.

2.5 Exit Strategy

If the business is very successful, Mr. Ferranti may seek to sell the business to a third party for a significant earnings multiple. Most likely, the Company will hire a qualified business broker to sell the business on behalf of X-Treme Paintball. Based on historical numbers, the business could fetch a sales premium of up to 4 times earnings.

3.0 PRODUCTS AND SERVICES

Below is a description of the paintball products and field rental services offered by X-Treme Paintball, Inc.

3.1 Sales of Paintball Guns and Paintball Supplies

The Company will carry an extensive variety of pistols, large caliber paintball/air guns, and a number of accessories commonly used within amateur and professional paintball games. The paintball gun products offered by the Company are priced from $80 to $800, which allows paintball enthusiasts of any socioeconomic level the ability to purchase the Company's products. The business also offers an extensive collection of accessories, which includes:

- Paintballs
- Flashlights
- Helmets, Goggles, and Face Masks
- Pouches
- Body Armor
- Communication Devices

3.2 Rental of Paintball Equipment and Field Usage

The secondary revenue source for the business will come from the ongoing usage of the Company's paintball field coupled with the rental/sale of paintball equipment (guns, fatigues, CO2 canisters, and paintballs). Each person playing the sport will be given access to the field for six hours. Customers will pay a flat rate of $60 to $80 for renting gear and using the Company's paintball field facility. The sales of paintball ammunition will not be included in the rental fees. This is an extremely important source of revenue for the business as the contribution margins generated through this income center are extremely high. Additionally, it will allow the business to remain profitable despite any declines in sale of paintball guns.

4.0 STRATEGIC AND MARKET ANALYSIS

4.1 Economic Outlook

This section of the analysis will detail the economic climate, the paintball industry, the customer profile, and the competition that the business will face as it progresses through its business operations.

Currently, the economic market condition in the United States is moderate. The meltdown of the sub prime mortgage market coupled with increasing gas prices has led many people to believe that the US is on the cusp of a double dip economic recession. This slowdown in the economy has also greatly impacted real estate sales, which has halted to historical lows. However, the high gross margins generated from the usage of the X-Treme Paintball venue will allow the business to remain profitable and cash flow positive at all times.

4.2 Industry Analysis

Insurance statistics show that paintball is one of the safest sports in existence, even more so than golf. The sport requires a significant amount of equipment that can cost anywhere from a few hundred dollars to a few thousand dollars. Among paintball gun retailers and field providers, the aggregate revenues generated exceed $500 million dollars in 2007. Management expects that the ongoing growth rate of the industry will remain in step with the growth of the general economy. However, paintball is quickly becoming a popular sport among the industry's core demographic of young males, and Management foresees the possibility that the industry will grow at a higher than expected rate as more people become paintball enthusiasts.

4.3 Customer Profile

The National Shooting Sports Foundation estimates that there are approximately 8 million paintball enthusiasts within the United States. Males dominate the market with 88% of the market share. By age demographics, males between 12 and 24 comprise of more than 50% of the market. The remaining age demographics are primary among males 25 to 35. Men over the age of 40 consist of a very small portion of the aggregate market.

The average paintball enthusiast spends approximately $1,200 per year on equipment, rentals, and accessories related to the sport of paintball. Approximately $300 is spent per year on fees relating to the use of paintball facilities among enthusiasts. The NSSF defines a paintball enthusiast as a person that engages in paintball activities at a licensed facility more than 10 times per year.

Management is well aware of the statistics relating to the paintball industry and the Company's marketing messages, sales literature, and other marketing strategies are properly geared towards the market's core audience of males aged 16 to 35.

4.4 Competition

Competition among paintball fields is limited. Within the New York metropolitan area, there are only seven other locations. This is primarily due to the fact that paintball venues require a large portion of space. Mr. Ferranti has already found the parcel of land (which is slightly outside of the five boroughs of New York City) that is suitable for action packed paintball experiences. As such, the business should not have issues with generating top line income due to competitive threats.

5.0 MARKETING PLAN

X-Treme Paintball, Inc. intends to maintain an extensive marketing campaign that will ensure maximum visibility for the business in its targeted market. Below is an overview of the marketing strategies and objectives of the business.

5.1 Marketing Objectives

- Develop strong relationships with corporate event planners that will host team building events at the location.

- Implement a large scale website that showcases the field, inventory, and event hosting services offered by the business.

- Develop an online presence by placing advertisements on blogs/websites that focus on paintball and paintball clubs.

5.2 Marketing Strategies

Initially, Management intends to implement a traditional marketing campaign within the New York metropolitan area so that individuals that are interested in paintball will become aware of the Company's brand name. This will be accomplished by taking out advertisements among local periodicals that focus on paintball as well as on internet websites that are geared towards paintball clubs. This is the most cost effective way of reaching the Company's targeted audience of younger men that are interested in the sport.

On a secondary level, once paintball enthusiasts are aware of the location, the business will actively seek to develop relationships with corporate event planners. In many instances, these planners have used opportunities to use the sport of paintball as a team building exercise. If Management is able to effectively develop these ongoing relationships then the revenues of the business may substantially increase.

In the future, in order to reduce internal marketing and sales costs, the business may hire a New York based small business advertising agency to handle this aspect of the Company's operations.

5.3 Pricing

Mr. Ferranti expects that each visit to X-Treme Paintball will result in approximately $60 $200 of revenue depending on whether or not an individual purchases a paintball gun from the business. The business anticipates revenues of $1,000 to $2,000 for hosting team building corporate events.

6.0 ORGANIZATIONAL PLAN AND PERSONNEL SUMMARY

6.1 Corporate Organization

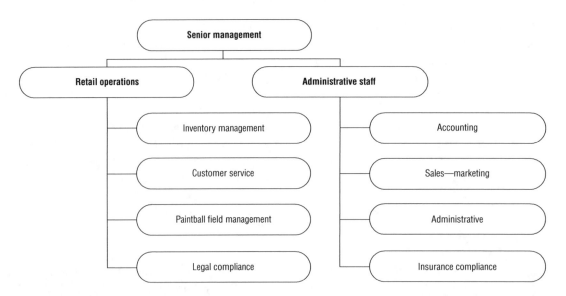

6.2 Organizational Budget

Personnel plan—yearly

Year	1	2	3
Owner	$ 45,000	$ 46,350	$ 47,741
Store manager	$ 35,000	$ 36,050	$ 37,132
Field manager	$ 65,000	$ 66,950	$ 68,959
Customer service employees	$ 85,000	$ 87,550	$ 90,177
Administrative	$ 44,000	$ 45,320	$ 46,680
Total	**$274,000**	**$282,220**	**$290,687**

Numbers of personnel

Owner	1	1	1
Store manager	1	1	1
Field manager	2	2	2
Customer service employees	5	5	5
Administrative	2	2	2
Totals	**11**	**11**	**11**

Personnel expense breakdown

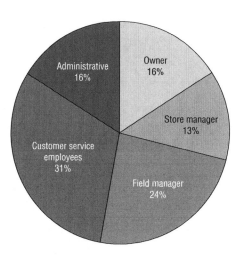

7.0 FINANCIAL PLAN

7.1 Underlying Assumptions

The Company has based its proforma financial statements on the following:

• X-Treme Paintball, Inc. will have an annual revenue growth rate of 10% per year.

• The Owner will acquire $250,000 of debt funds to develop the business.

• The loan will have a 10 year term with a 9% interest rate.

7.2 Sensitivity Analysis

In the event of an economic downturn, the business may have a decline in its revenues. However, the sport of paintball is a relatively low cost activity, and the Company will continue to generate very high margin streams of income from the rental and usage of its equipment and playing field, which will ensure the continued profitability of the business despite potential declines in sales of paintball equipment.

7.3 Source of Funds

Financing

Equity contributions	
Management investment	$ 50,000.00
Total equity financing	**$ 50,000.00**
Banks and lenders	
Banks and lenders	$ 250,000.00
Total debt financing	**$250,000.00**
Total financing	**$300,000.00**

7.4 General Assumptions

General assumptions

Year	1	2	3
Short term interest rate	9.5%	9.5%	9.5%
Long term interest rate	10.0%	10.0%	10.0%
Federal tax rate	33.0%	33.0%	33.0%
State tax rate	5.0%	5.0%	5.0%
Personnel taxes	15.0%	15.0%	15.0%

7.5 Profit and Loss Statements

Proforma profit and loss (yearly)

Year	1	2	3
Sales	**$731,952**	**$805,147**	**$885,662**
Cost of goods sold	$194,723	$214,195	$235,615
Gross margin	73.40%	73.40%	73.40%
Operating income	**$537,229**	**$590,952**	**$650,047**
Expenses			
Payroll	$274,000	$282,220	$290,687
General and administrative	$ 25,200	$ 26,208	$ 27,256
Marketing expenses	$ 25,200	$ 26,208	$ 27,256
Professional fees and licensure	$ 15,219	$ 15,676	$ 16,146
Insurance costs	$ 21,987	$ 23,086	$ 24,241
Travel and vehicle costs	$ 17,596	$ 19,356	$ 21,291
Rent and utilities	$ 24,250	$ 25,463	$ 26,736
Miscellaneous costs	$ 2,928	$ 3,221	$ 3,543
Payroll taxes	$ 41,100	$ 42,333	$ 43,603
Total operating costs	**$447,480**	**$463,770**	**$480,758**
EBITDA	**$ 89,749**	**$127,182**	**$169,289**
Federal income tax	$ 29,617	$ 35,262	$ 49,704
State income tax	$ 4,487	$ 5,343	$ 7,531
Interest expense	$ 21,844	$ 20,328	$ 18,671
Depreciation expenses	$ 15,714	$ 15,714	$ 15,714
Net profit	**$ 18,086**	**$ 50,535**	**$ 77,669**
Profit margin	**2.47%**	**6.28%**	**8.77%**

Sales, operating costs, and profit forecast

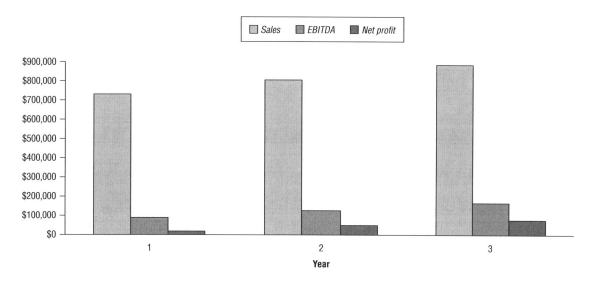

7.6 Cash Flow Analysis

Proforma cash flow analysis—yearly

Year	1	2	3
Cash from operations	$ 33,800	$ 66,249	$ 93,383
Cash from receivables	$ 0	$ 0	$ 0
Operating cash inflow	**$ 33,800**	**$ 66,249**	**$ 93,383**
Other cash inflows			
Equity investment	$ 50,000	$ 0	$ 0
Increased borrowings	$250,000	$ 0	$ 0
Sales of business assets	$ 0	$ 0	$ 0
A/P increases	$ 37,902	$ 43,587	$ 50,125
Total other cash inflows	**$337,902**	**$ 43,587**	**$ 50,125**
Total cash inflow	**$371,702**	**$109,837**	**$143,509**
Cash outflows			
Repayment of principal	$ 16,158	$ 17,674	$ 19,332
A/P decreases	$ 24,897	$ 29,876	$ 35,852
A/R increases	$ 0	$ 0	$ 0
Asset purchases	$220,000	$ 16,562	$ 23,346
Dividends	$ 20,280	$ 39,750	$ 56,030
Total cash outflows	**$281,336**	**$103,863**	**$134,560**
Net cash flow	**$ 90,367**	**$ 5,974**	**$ 8,949**
Cash balance	**$ 90,367**	**$ 96,341**	**$105,290**

Proforma cash flow (yearly)

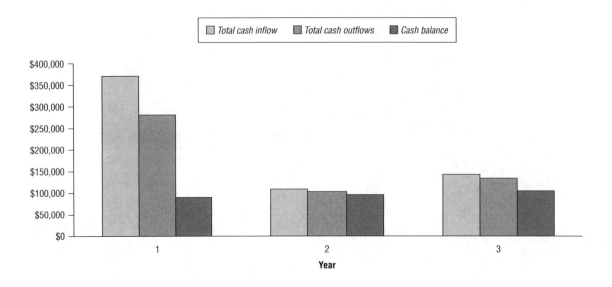

7.7 Balance Sheet

Proforma balance sheet—yearly

Year	1	2	3
Assets			
Cash	$ 90,367	$ 96,341	$105,290
Amortized development/expansion costs	$130,000	$131,656	$133,991
Inventory	$ 40,000	$ 51,594	$ 67,936
FF&E	$ 50,000	$ 53,312	$ 57,982
Accumulated depreciation	($ 15,714)	($ 31,429)	($ 47,143)
Total assets	**$294,652**	**$301,474**	**$318,055**
Liabilities and equity			
Accounts payable	$ 13,005	$ 26,716	$ 40,990
Long term liabilities	$233,842	$216,167	$198,493
Other liabilities	$ 0	$ 0	$ 0
Total liabilities	**$246,847**	**$242,883**	**$239,483**
Net worth	**$ 47,806**	**$ 58,591**	**$ 78,572**
Total liabilities and equity	**$294,652**	**$301,474**	**$318,055**

Proforma balance sheet

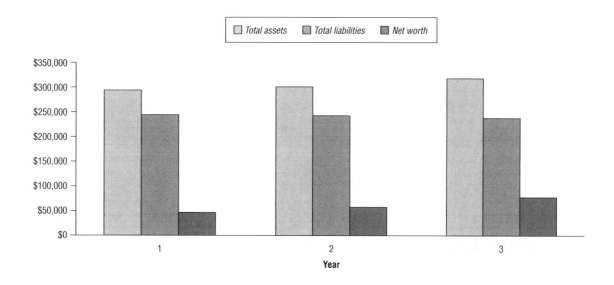

7.8 Breakeven Analysis

Monthly break even analysis

Year	1	2	3
Monthly revenue	$ 50,806	$ 52,656	$ 54,584
Yearly revenue	$609,673	$631,867	$655,013

Break even analysis

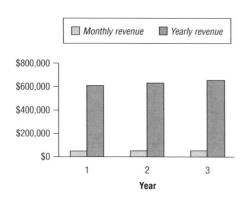

7.9 Business Ratios

Business ratios—yearly

Year	1	2	3
Sales			
Sales growth	0.00%	10.00%	10.00%
Gross margin	73.40%	73.40%	73.40%
Financials			
Profit margin	2.47%	6.28%	8.77%
Assets to liabilities	1.19	1.24	1.33
Equity to liabilities	0.19	0.24	0.33
Assets to equity	6.16	5.15	4.05
Liquidity			
Acid test	0.37	0.40	0.44
Cash to assets	0.31	0.32	0.33

7.10 Three Year Profit and Loss Statement

Profit and loss statement (first year)

Months	1	2	3	4	5	6	7
Sales	$59,984	$60,168	$60,352	$60,536	$60,720	$60,904	$61,088
Cost of goods sold	$15,958	$16,007	$16,056	$16,105	$16,154	$16,202	$16,251
Gross margin	73.4%	73.4%	73.4%	73.4%	73.4%	73.4%	73.4%
Operating income	$44,026	$44,161	$44,296	$44,431	$44,567	$44,702	$44,837
Expenses							
Payroll	$22,833	$22,833	$22,833	$22,833	$22,833	$22,833	$22,833
General and administrative	$ 2,100	$ 2,100	$ 2,100	$ 2,100	$ 2,100	$ 2,100	$ 2,100
Marketing expenses	$ 2,100	$ 2,100	$ 2,100	$ 2,100	$ 2,100	$ 2,100	$ 2,100
Professional fees and licensure	$ 1,268	$ 1,268	$ 1,268	$ 1,268	$ 1,268	$ 1,268	$ 1,268
Insurance costs	$ 1,832	$ 1,832	$ 1,832	$ 1,832	$ 1,832	$ 1,832	$ 1,832
Travel and vehicle costs	$ 1,466	$ 1,466	$ 1,466	$ 1,466	$ 1,466	$ 1,466	$ 1,466
Rent and utilities	$ 2,021	$ 2,021	$ 2,021	$ 2,021	$ 2,021	$ 2,021	$ 2,021
Miscellaneous costs	$ 244	$ 244	$ 244	$ 244	$ 244	$ 244	$ 244
Payroll taxes	$ 3,425	$ 3,425	$ 3,425	$ 3,425	$ 3,425	$ 3,425	$ 3,425
Total operating costs	$37,290	$37,290	$37,290	$37,290	$37,290	$37,290	$37,290
EBITDA	$ 6,736	$ 6,871	$ 7,006	$ 7,141	$ 7,277	$ 7,412	$ 7,547
Federal income tax	$ 2,427	$ 2,435	$ 2,442	$ 2,449	$ 2,457	$ 2,464	$ 2,472
State income tax	$ 368	$ 369	$ 370	$ 371	$ 372	$ 373	$ 375
Interest expense	$ 1,875	$ 1,865	$ 1,856	$ 1,846	$ 1,836	$ 1,826	$ 1,816
Depreciation expense	$ 1,310	$ 1,310	$ 1,310	$ 1,310	$ 1,310	$ 1,310	$ 1,310
Net profit	$ 757	$ 893	$ 1,029	$ 1,166	$ 1,302	$ 1,438	$ 1,575

Profit and loss statement (first year cont.)

Month	8	9	10	11	12	1
Sales	$61,272	$61,456	$61,640	$61,824	$62,008	$731,952
Cost of goods sold	$16,300	$16,349	$16,398	$16,447	$16,496	$194,723
Gross margin	73.4%	73.4%	73.4%	73.4%	73.4%	73.4%
Operating income	$44,972	$45,107	$45,242	$45,377	$45,512	$537,229
Expenses						
Payroll	$22,833	$22,833	$22,833	$22,833	$22,833	$274,000
General and administrative	$ 2,100	$ 2,100	$ 2,100	$ 2,100	$ 2,100	$ 25,200
Marketing expenses	$ 2,100	$ 2,100	$ 2,100	$ 2,100	$ 2,100	$ 25,200
Professional fees and licensure	$ 1,268	$ 1,268	$ 1,268	$ 1,268	$ 1,268	$ 15,219
Insurance costs	$ 1,832	$ 1,832	$ 1,832	$ 1,832	$ 1,832	$ 21,987
Travel and vehicle costs	$ 1,466	$ 1,466	$ 1,466	$ 1,466	$ 1,466	$ 17,596
Rent and utilities	$ 2,021	$ 2,021	$ 2,021	$ 2,021	$ 2,021	$ 24,250
Miscellaneous costs	$ 244	$ 244	$ 244	$ 244	$ 244	$ 2,928
Payroll taxes	$ 3,425	$ 3,425	$ 3,425	$ 3,425	$ 3,425	$ 41,100
Total operating costs	$37,290	$37,290	$37,290	$37,290	$37,290	$447,480
EBITDA	$ 7,682	$ 7,817	$ 7,952	$ 8,087	$ 8,222	$ 89,749
Federal income tax	$ 2,479	$ 2,487	$ 2,494	$ 2,502	$ 2,509	$ 29,617
State income tax	$ 376	$ 377	$ 378	$ 379	$ 380	$ 4,487
Interest expense	$ 1,806	$ 1,795	$ 1,785	$ 1,775	$ 1,764	$ 21,844
Depreciation expense	$ 1,310	$ 1,310	$ 1,310	$ 1,310	$ 1,310	$ 15,714
Net profit	$ 1,712	$ 1,848	$ 1,985	$ 2,122	$ 2,259	$ 18,086

Profit and loss statement (second year)

Quarter	Q1	2 Q2	Q3	Q4	2
Sales	$161,029	$201,287	$217,390	$225,441	$805,147
Cost of goods sold	$ 42,839	$ 53,549	$ 57,833	$ 59,975	$214,195
Gross margin	73.40%	73.40%	73.40%	73.40%	73.40%
Operating income	$118,190	$147,738	$159,557	$165,467	$590,952
Expenses					
Payroll	$ 56,444	$ 70,555	$ 76,199	$ 79,022	$282,220
General and administrative	$ 5,242	$ 6,552	$ 7,076	$ 7,338	$ 26,208
Marketing expenses	$ 5,242	$ 6,552	$ 7,076	$ 7,338	$ 26,208
Professional fees and licensure	$ 3,135	$ 3,919	$ 4,232	$ 4,389	$ 15,676
Insurance costs	$ 4,617	$ 5,772	$ 6,233	$ 6,464	$ 23,086
Travel and vehicle costs	$ 3,871	$ 4,839	$ 5,226	$ 5,420	$ 19,356
Rent and utilities	$ 5,093	$ 6,366	$ 6,875	$ 7,130	$ 25,463
Miscellaneous costs	$ 644	$ 805	$ 870	$ 902	$ 3,221
Payroll taxes	$ 8,467	$ 10,583	$ 11,430	$ 11,853	$ 42,333
Total operating costs	$ 92,754	$115,942	$125,218	$129,855	$463,770
EBITDA	$ 25,436	$ 31,796	$ 34,339	$ 35,611	$127,182
Federal income tax	$ 7,052	$ 8,815	$ 9,521	$ 9,873	$ 35,262
State income tax	$ 1,069	$ 1,336	$ 1,443	$ 1,496	$ 5,343
Interest expense	$ 5,230	$ 5,133	$ 5,034	$ 4,932	$ 20,328
Depreciation expense	$ 3,929	$ 3,929	$ 3,929	$ 3,929	$ 15,714
Net profit	$ 8,157	$ 12,583	$ 14,414	$ 15,381	$ 50,535

Profit and loss statement (third year)

Quarter	Q1	3 Q2	Q3	Q4	3
Sales	$177,132	$221,415	$239,129	$247,985	$885,662
Cost of goods sold	$ 47,123	$ 58,904	$ 63,616	$ 65,972	$235,615
Gross margin	73.40%	73.40%	73.40%	73.40%	73.40%
Operating income	$130,009	$162,512	$175,513	$182,013	$650,047
Expenses					
Payroll	$ 58,137	$ 72,672	$ 78,485	$ 81,392	$290,687
General and administrative	$ 5,451	$ 6,814	$ 7,359	$ 7,632	$ 27,256
Marketing expenses	$ 5,451	$ 6,814	$ 7,359	$ 7,632	$ 27,256
Professional fees and licensure	$ 3,229	$ 4,036	$ 4,359	$ 4,521	$ 16,146
Insurance costs	$ 4,848	$ 6,060	$ 6,545	$ 6,787	$ 24,241
Travel and vehicle costs	$ 4,258	$ 5,323	$ 5,749	$ 5,962	$ 21,291
Rent and utilities	$ 5,347	$ 6,684	$ 7,219	$ 7,486	$ 26,736
Miscellaneous costs	$ 709	$ 886	$ 957	$ 992	$ 3,543
Payroll taxes	$ 8,721	$ 10,901	$ 11,773	$ 12,209	$ 43,603
Total operating costs	$ 96,152	$120,190	$129,805	$134,612	$480,758
EBITDA	$ 33,858	$ 42,322	$ 45,708	$ 47,401	$169,289
Federal income tax	$ 9,941	$ 12,426	$ 13,420	$ 13,917	$ 49,704
State income tax	$ 1,506	$ 1,883	$ 2,033	$ 2,109	$ 7,531
Interest expense	$ 4,829	$ 4,723	$ 4,615	$ 4,504	$ 18,671
Depreciation expense	$ 3,929	$ 3,929	$ 3,929	$ 3,929	$ 15,714
Net profit	$ 13,653	$ 19,362	$ 21,711	$ 22,943	$ 77,669

7.11 Three Year Cash Flow Analysis

Cash flow analysis (first year)

Month	1	2	3	4	5	6	7
Cash from operations	$ 2,066	$ 2,203	$ 2,339	$ 2,475	$ 2,612	$ 2,748	$ 2,885
Cash from receivables	$ 0	$ 0	$ 0	$ 0	$ 0	$ 0	$ 0
Operating cash inflow	$ 2,066	$ 2,203	$ 2,339	$ 2,475	$ 2,612	$ 2,748	$ 2,885
Other cash inflows							
Equity investment	$ 50,000	$ 0	$ 0	$ 0	$ 0	$ 0	$ 0
Increased borrowings	$250,000	$ 0	$ 0	$ 0	$ 0	$ 0	$ 0
Sales of business assets	$ 0	$ 0	$ 0	$ 0	$ 0	$ 0	$ 0
A/P increases	$ 3,159	$ 3,159	$ 3,159	$ 3,159	$ 3,159	$ 3,159	$ 3,159
Total other cash inflows	$303,159	$ 3,159	$ 3,159	$ 3,159	$ 3,159	$ 3,159	$ 3,159
Total cash inflow	$305,225	$ 5,361	$ 5,497	$ 5,634	$ 5,770	$ 5,906	$ 6,043
Cash outflows							
Repayment of principal	$ 1,292	$ 1,302	$ 1,311	$ 1,321	$ 1,331	$ 1,341	$ 1,351
A/P decreases	$ 2,075	$ 2,075	$ 2,075	$ 2,075	$ 2,075	$ 2,075	$ 2,075
A/R increases	$ 0	$ 0	$ 0	$ 0	$ 0	$ 0	$ 0
Asset purchases	$220,000	$ 0	$ 0	$ 0	$ 0	$ 0	$ 0
Dividends	$ 0	$ 0	$ 0	$ 0	$ 0	$ 0	$ 0
Total cash outflows	$223,367	$ 3,376	$ 3,386	$ 3,396	$ 3,406	$ 3,416	$ 3,426
Net cash flow	$ 81,858	$ 1,985	$ 2,111	$ 2,238	$ 2,364	$ 2,491	$ 2,617
Cash balance	$ 81,858	$83,843	$85,954	$88,192	$90,556	$93,047	$95,664

Cash flow analysis (first year cont.)

Month	8	9	10	11	12	1
Cash from operations	$ 3,021	$ 3,158	$ 3,295	$ 3,431	$ 3,568	$ 33,800
Cash from receivables	$ 0	$ 0	$ 0	$ 0	$ 0	$ 0
Operating cash inflow	**$ 3,021**	**$ 3,158**	**$ 3,295**	**$ 3,431**	**$ 3,568**	**$ 33,800**
Other cash inflows						
Equity investment	$ 0	$ 0	$ 0	$ 0	$ 0	$ 50,000
Increased borrowings	$ 0	$ 0	$ 0	$ 0	$ 0	$250,000
Sales of business assets	$ 0	$ 0	$ 0	$ 0	$ 0	$ 0
A/P increases	$ 3,159	$ 3,159	$ 3,159	$ 3,159	$ 3,159	$ 37,902
Total other cash inflows	**$ 3,159**	**$ 3,159**	**$ 3,159**	**$ 3,159**	**$ 3,159**	**$337,902**
Total cash inflow	**$ 6,180**	**$ 6,316**	**$ 6,453**	**$ 6,590**	**$ 6,727**	**$371,702**
Cash outflows						
Repayment of principal	$ 1,361	$ 1,371	$ 1,382	$ 1,392	$ 1,403	$ 16,158
A/P decreases	$ 2,075	$ 2,075	$ 2,075	$ 2,075	$ 2,075	$ 24,897
A/R increases	$ 0	$ 0	$ 0	$ 0	$ 0	$ 0
Asset purchases	$ 0	$ 0	$ 0	$ 0	$ 0	$220,000
Dividends	$ 0	$ 0	$ 0	$ 0	$20,280	$ 20,280
Total cash outflows	**$ 3,436**	**$ 3,446**	**$ 3,457**	**$ 3,467**	**$23,757**	**$281,336**
Net cash flow	**$ 2,744**	**$ 2,870**	**$ 2,997**	**$ 3,123**	**−$17,030**	**$ 90,367**
Cash balance	**$98,408**	**$101,278**	**$104,274**	**$107,397**	**$90,367**	**$ 90,367**

Cash flow analysis (second year)

Quarter	Q1	2 Q2	Q3	Q4	2
Cash from operations	$13,250	$16,562	$17,887	$18,550	$ 66,249
Cash from receivables	$ 0	$ 0	$ 0	$ 0	$ 0
Operating cash inflow	**$13,250**	**$16,562**	**$17,887**	**$18,550**	**$ 66,249**
Other cash inflows					
Equity investment	$ 0	$ 0	$ 0	$ 0	$ 0
Increased borrowings	$ 0	$ 0	$ 0	$ 0	$ 0
Sales of business assets	$ 0	$ 0	$ 0	$ 0	$ 0
A/P increases	$ 8,717	$10,897	$11,769	$12,204	$ 43,587
Total other cash inflows	**$ 8,717**	**$10,897**	**$11,769**	**$12,204**	**$ 43,587**
Total cash inflow	**$21,967**	**$27,459**	**$29,656**	**$30,754**	**$109,837**
Cash outflows					
Repayment of principal	$ 4,271	$ 4,368	$ 4,467	$ 4,568	$ 17,674
A/P decreases	$ 5,975	$ 7,469	$ 8,067	$ 8,365	$ 29,876
A/R increases	$ 0	$ 0	$ 0	$ 0	$ 0
Asset purchases	$ 3,312	$ 4,141	$ 4,472	$ 4,637	$ 16,562
Dividends	$ 7,950	$ 9,937	$10,732	$11,130	$ 39,750
Total cash outflows	**$21,509**	**$25,915**	**$27,738**	**$28,701**	**$103,863**
Net cash flow	**$ 459**	**$ 1,544**	**$ 1,918**	**$ 2,053**	**$ 5,974**
Cash balance	**$90,825**	**$92,369**	**$94,287**	**$96,341**	**$ 96,341**

Cash flow analysis (third year)

Quarter	Q1	3 Q2	Q3	Q4	3
Cash from operations	$18,677	$23,346	$ 25,214	$ 26,147	$ 93,383
Cash from receivables	$ 0	$ 0	$ 0	$ 0	$ 0
Operating cash inflow	**$18,677**	**$23,346**	**$ 25,214**	**$ 26,147**	**$ 93,383**
Other cash inflows					
Equity investment	$ 0	$ 0	$ 0	$ 0	$ 0
Increased borrowings	$ 0	$ 0	$ 0	$ 0	$ 0
Sales of business assets	$ 0	$ 0	$ 0	$ 0	$ 0
A/P increases	$10,025	$12,531	$ 13,534	$ 14,035	$ 50,125
Total other cash inflows	**$10,025**	**$12,531**	**$ 13,534**	**$ 14,035**	**$ 50,125**
Total cash inflow	**$28,702**	**$35,877**	**$ 38,747**	**$ 40,182**	**$143,509**
Cash outflows					
Repayment of principal	$ 4,672	$ 4,778	$ 4,886	$ 4,997	$ 19,332
A/P decreases	$ 7,170	$ 8,963	$ 9,680	$ 10,038	$ 35,852
A/R increases	$ 0	$ 0	$ 0	$ 0	$ 0
Asset purchases	$ 4,669	$ 5,836	$ 6,303	$ 6,537	$ 23,346
Dividends	$11,206	$14,008	$ 15,128	$ 15,688	$ 56,030
Total cash outflows	**$27,717**	**$33,585**	**$ 35,997**	**$ 37,260**	**$134,560**
Net cash flow	**$ 984**	**$ 2,293**	**$ 2,750**	**$ 2,922**	**$ 8,949**
Cash balance	**$97,325**	**$99,618**	**$102,368**	**$105,290**	**$105,290**

Real Estate Investment Company

Schroeder Real Estate

44445 E. 98th St.
New York, NY 10001

BizPlanDB.com

The purpose of this business plan is to raise $7,500,000 for the development of a real estate investment firm that specializes in the rental and sale of residential properties while showcasing the expected financials and operations over the next three years. Schroeder Real Estate, Inc. is a New York based corporation that will provide real estate acquisition rental services to customers in its targeted market. The Company was founded by Tom Schroeder.

1.0 EXECUTIVE SUMMARY

The purpose of this business plan is to raise $7,500,000 for the development of a real estate investment firm that specializes in the rental and sale of residential properties while showcasing the expected financials and operations over the next three years. Schroeder Real Estate, Inc. is a New York based corporation that will provide real estate acquisition rental services to customers in its targeted market. The Company was founded by Tom Schroeder.

1.1 The Services

The primary revenue center for the business is acquiring properties with the intent to rent the properties to the general public. The business will generate profits from the ongoing rental income paid to Schroeder Real Estate while also generating capital appreciation from the long term holding of these properties. Now that the real estate market has hit come to its bottom or near bottom, Management expects that the market will have a future growth rate of 3% to 5% per year starting in 2013.

The third section of the business plan will further document the residential rental services offered by the business.

1.2 Financing

Mr. Schroeder is seeking to raise $7,500,000 from an investor. The terms, dividend payouts, and aspects of the deal are to be determined at negotiation. This business plan assumes that an investor will receive 85% of the Company's stock, a regular stream of dividends, and a seat on the board of directors. The financing will be used for the following:

- Financing to acquire the initial properties.

- Financing for the first six months of operation.

- Capital to purchase a company vehicle.

1.3 Mission Statement

Mr. Schroeder's mission is to develop Schroeder Real Estate into a premier regional real estate investment firm that will acquire and rent properties profitably.

1.4 Management Team

The Company was founded by Tom Schroeder. Mr. Schroeder has more than 10 years of experience in the real estate industry. Through his expertise, he will be able to bring the operations of the business to profitability within its first year of operations.

1.5 Sales Forecasts

Mr. Schroeder expects a strong rate of growth at the start of operations. Below are the expected financials over the next three years.

Proforma profit and loss (yearly)

Year	1	2	3
Sales	$990,000	$1,188,000	$1,389,960
Operating costs	$329,652	$ 342,013	$ 354,790
EBITDA	$400,848	$ 534,587	$ 670,832
Taxes, interest, and depreciation	$349,309	$ 400,130	$ 451,903
Net profit	$ 51,539	$ 134,457	$ 218,929

Sales, operating costs, and profit forecast

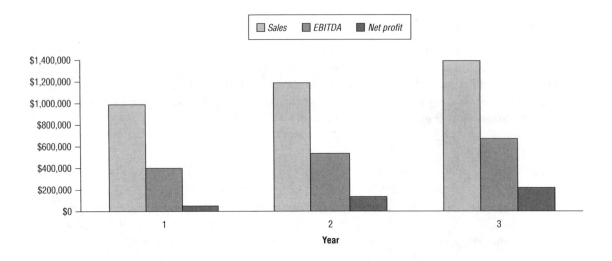

1.6 Expansion Plan

The Founder expects that the business will aggressively expand during the first three years of operation. As the real estate market returns to normal conditions, Schroeder Real Estate will be an excellent position to recognize profits from the sale of properties. In the future, the business may seek to acquire additional capital for the acquisition of additional properties.

2.0 COMPANY AND FINANCING SUMMARY

2.1 Registered Name and Corporate Structure

Schroeder Real Estate, Inc. is registered as a corporation in the State of New York.

2.2 Required Funds

At this time, Schroeder Real Estate requires $7,500,000 of investor funds. Below is a breakdown of how these funds will be used:

Projected startup costs

Working capital	$ 150,000
FF&E	$ 100,000
Leasehold improvements	$ 50,000
Security deposits	$ 50,000
Insurance	$ 25,000
Property acquisitions	$ 7,000,000
Marketing budget	$ 75,000
Miscellaneous and unforeseen costs	$ 50,000
Total startup costs	**$7,500,000**

2.3 Investor Equity

Tom Schroeder intends to sell 85% of Schroeder Real Estate in exchange for the capital.

2.4 Management Equity

Tom Schroeder will retain 15% of the business once the capital is raised.

2.5 Exit Strategy

If the business is very successful, Mr. Schroeder may seek to sell the business to a third party for a significant earnings multiple or divest the properties individually. Most likely, the Company will hire a qualified real estate broker to sell the properties on behalf of Schroeder Real Estate.

2.6 Investor Divestiture

This will be discussed during negotiations.

3.0 REAL ESTATE SERVICES

Below is a description of the real estate services offered by Schroeder Real Estate.

3.1 Rental of Acquired Properties

The direct finance and purchase of residential property is the primary business of Schroeder Real Estate. Residential real estate will provide a continuous stream of rental income that the Management will use for reinvestment and profit stability for the Company.

Management is developing a complex economic pricing strategy that will determine the fair market rate of a property based on its capitalization rate in conjunction with the market values of residential property. Residential real estate is the least risky form of real estate investing because the service offered is a necessity.

4.0 STRATEGIC AND MARKET ANALYSIS

4.1 Economic Outlook

Management is developing a very complex pricing method to ensure that the Company can continue to provide its units at profit despite possible drawbacks in the overall economic market. The Company's two prong approach to real estate will allow the business to grow successfully in the rapidly changing real estate market.

More importantly, this strategy will allow the Company to offset the risks from each unit so that there is a diversified balance in the Company's real estate portfolio. This is especially important as the business uses leverage to finance the acquisition of its properties.

4.2 Real Estate Strategies

Schroeder Real Estate plans to actively pursue a real estate acquisition program that will focus on the purchase of multiunit apartment buildings with the intent of creating a recurring stream of income. Management will use reasonable leverage to purchase these properties so that a positive cash flow is generated after debt service has been paid.

The recurring streams of revenue generated from the rental of multi-unit residential property will allow the Company to continually recognize revenue despite drawbacks in the real estate market. As these properties increase in value through capital appreciation, the Company will divest of these properties to reap its capital gain profits.

The Company will divest its properties once Management feels that its real estate holdings have become overvalued. Mr. Schroeder has worked diligently to create a pricing model that will allow the business to understand when the properties have become overvalued. This model will examine the capitalization rates of the income producing properties for a determination of true asset value.

There are tremendous tax benefits for the Company as it engages its real estate investments. As the business makes its real estate divestitures, The Company will recognize capital gain income rather than income on its properties. These windfall gains will be taxed at a rate that is significantly lower than the federal regular income tax levels. This assumes that the business will divest its properties after one year's time

4.3 Customer Profile

As the Company intends to operate among several different investment and operating units, it is hard to characterize any specific tenant that will occupy the Company's properties. However, Management will enact strict tenant quality and credit review procedures to ensure the Company's revenues will not be interrupted by tenant default.

4.4 Competition

Since real estate is effectually one of the most free market oriented businesses in the country, competition can not be accurately categorized. The Company anticipates that there will be a sizable amount of competition from both single owner investment firms to large construction companies that are seeking to gain from the unusually high real estate prices throughout the New York metropolitan area.

5.0 MARKETING PLAN

Schroeder Real Estate intends to maintain an extensive marketing campaign that will ensure maximum visibility for the acquired units in its targeted market. Below is an overview of the marketing strategies and objectives of the Company.

5.1 Marketing Objectives

- Develop an online presence by acquiring accounts for major online real estate portals.

- Implement a local campaign with the Company's targeted market via the use of flyers, local newspaper advertisements, and word of mouth.

- Establish relationships with other real estate brokers and agents within the targeted market.

5.2 Marketing Strategies

Property and renter buyer marketing will be the most difficult portion of the marketing strategy. This task will be accomplished through the business's broad marketing campaign throughout its targeted market. Primarily, Mr. Schroeder intends to use local real estate brokerage firms to place tenants (and attract buyers during property sales) with the Company's residential properties. In addition to using a real estate broker, Mr. Schroeder intends to develop his own marketing strategies that will further increase the visibility of the business's units. This is especially important with the current real estate market environment.

Schroeder Real Estate will also use an internet based strategy. This is very important as many people seeking real estate for purchase or rent use the Internet to conduct their preliminary searches. Mr. Schroeder will register Company and its properties with these online portals such as Loopnet.com and the MLS system so that potential buyers/renters can easily reach the business. The Company will also develop its own online website showcasing available properties for rent or for sale.

5.3 Pricing

Management expects that each rental unit will produce $600 to $1,000 per month of income. Mr. Schroeder further anticipates that the business will recognize $500,000 of revenue from the sale of each property.

6.0 ORGANIZATIONAL PLAN AND PERSONNEL SUMMARY

6.1 Corporate Organization

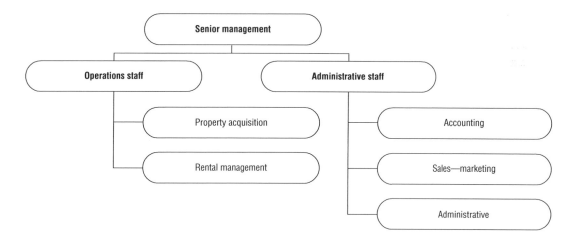

6.2 Organizational Budget

Personnel plan—yearly

Year	1	2	3
Senior management	$125,000	$128,750	$132,613
Property manager	$ 50,000	$ 51,500	$ 53,045
Marketing staff	$ 25,000	$ 25,750	$ 26,523
Sales and placement staff	$ 22,500	$ 23,175	$ 23,870
Administrative staff	$ 27,500	$ 28,325	$ 29,175
Total	**$250,000**	**$257,500**	**$265,225**

Numbers of personnel

Senior management	1	1	1
Property manager	1	1	1
Marketing staff	1	1	1
Sales and placement staff	1	1	1
Administrative staff	1	1	1
Totals	**5**	**5**	**5**

Personnel expense breakdown

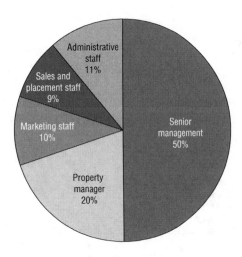

7.0 FINANCIAL PLAN

7.1 Underlying Assumptions

The Company has based its proforma financial statements on the following:

- Schroeder Real Estate will have an annual revenue growth rate of 15.4% per year.

- The Owner will acquire $7,500,000 of investor funds to develop the business.

- The Company will not seek debt financing in the first three years of operations.

7.2 Sensitivity Analysis

The Company's revenues can change depending on the general economic climate of the real estate industry. In times of economic recession, the Company may have issues with its top line income as fewer sales will be made and rental income may decrease. However, the Company will generate income from its rental business, which will reduce the risks associated with this business.

7.3 Source of Funds

Financing

Equity contributions

Investor(s)	$ 7,500,000.00
Total equity financing	**$7,500,000.00**
Banks and lenders	
Total debt financing	**$ 0.00**
Total financing	**$7,500,000.00**

7.4 General Assumptions

General assumptions

Year	1	2	3
Short term interest rate	9.5%	9.5%	9.5%
Long term interest rate	10.0%	10.0%	10.0%
Federal tax rate	33.0%	33.0%	33.0%
State tax rate	5.0%	5.0%	5.0%
Personnel taxes	15.0%	15.0%	15.0%

Proforma profit and loss (yearly)

Year	1	2	3
Sales	**$990,000**	**$1,188,000**	**$1,389,960**
Cost of goods sold	$259,500	$ 311,400	$ 364,338
Gross margin	73.79%	73.79%	73.79%
Operating income	**$730,500**	**$ 876,600**	**$1,025,622**
Expenses			
Payroll	$250,000	$ 257,500	$ 265,225
General and administrative	$ 13,200	$ 13,728	$ 14,277
Marketing expenses	$ 4,950	$ 5,940	$ 6,950
Professional fees and licensure	$ 5,219	$ 5,376	$ 5,537
Insurance costs	$ 1,987	$ 2,086	$ 2,191
Travel and vehicle costs	$ 7,596	$ 8,356	$ 9,191
Rent and utilities	$ 4,250	$ 4,463	$ 4,686
Miscellaneous costs	$ 4,950	$ 5,940	$ 6,950
Payroll taxes	$ 37,500	$ 38,625	$ 39,784
Total operating costs	**$329,652**	**$ 342,013**	**$ 354,790**
EBITDA	**$400,848**	**$ 534,587**	**$ 670,832**
Federal income tax	$132,280	$ 176,414	$ 221,375
State income tax	$ 20,042	$ 26,729	$ 33,542
Interest expense	$ 0	$ 0	$ 0
Depreciation expenses	$196,987	$ 196,987	$ 196,987
Net profit	**$ 51,539**	**$ 134,457**	**$ 218,929**
Profit margin	**5.21%**	**11.32%**	**15.75%**

7.5 Profit and Loss Statements

Sales, operating costs, and profit forecast

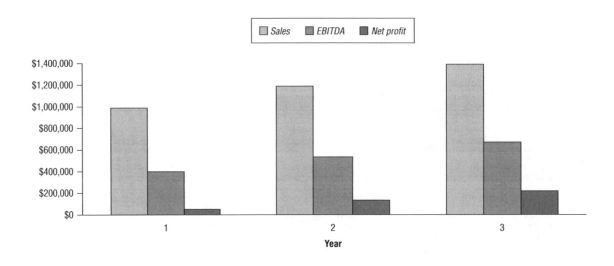

Proforma cash flow analysis—yearly

Year	1	2	3
Cash from operations	$ 248,526	$331,444	$415,916
Cash from receivables	$ 0	$ 0	$ 0
Operating cash inflow	**$ 248,526**	**$331,444**	**$415,916**
Other cash inflows			
Equity investment	$7,500,000	$ 0	$ 0
Increased borrowings	$ 0	$ 0	$ 0
Sales of business assets	$ 0	$ 0	$ 0
A/P increases	$ 37,902	$ 43,587	$ 50,125
Total other cash inflows	**$7,537,902**	**$ 43,587**	**$ 50,125**
Total cash inflow	**$7,786,428**	**$375,031**	**$466,041**
Cash outflows			
Repayment of principal	$ 0	$ 0	$ 0
A/P decreases	$ 24,897	$ 29,876	$ 35,852
A/R increases	$ 0	$ 0	$ 0
Asset purchases	$7,262,500	$ 82,861	$103,979
Dividends	$ 173,968	$232,011	$291,141
Total cash outflows	**$7,461,365**	**$344,748**	**$430,972**
Net cash flow	**$ 325,063**	**$ 30,283**	**$ 35,070**
Cash balance	**$ 325,063**	**$355,346**	**$390,415**

7.6 Cash Flow Analysis

Proforma cash flow (yearly)

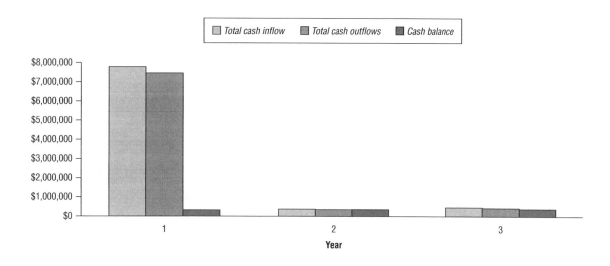

Proforma balance sheet—yearly

Year	1	2	3
Assets			
Cash	$ 325,063	$ 355,346	$ 390,415
Amortized development/expansion costs	$ 112,500	$ 120,786	$ 131,184
Property	$ 7,420,000	$ 7,931,074	$ 8,489,602
FF&E	$ 150,000	$ 162,429	$ 178,026
Accumulated depreciation	($ 196,987)	($ 393,974)	($ 590,962)
Total assets	**$7,810,576**	**$8,175,661**	**$8,598,266**
Liabilities and equity			
Accounts payable	$ 13,005	$ 26,716	$ 40,990
Long term liabilities	$ 0	$ 0	$ 0
Other liabilities	$ 0	$ 0	$ 0
Total liabilities	**$ 13,005**	**$ 26,716**	**$ 40,990**
Net worth	**$7,797,571**	**$8,148,945**	**$8,557,276**
Total liabilities and equity	**$7,810,576**	**$8,175,661**	**$8,598,266**

7.7 Balance Sheet

Proforma balance sheet

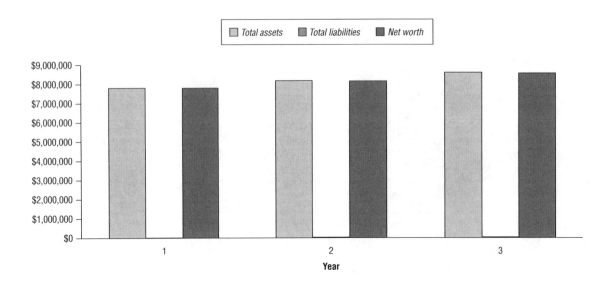

Monthly break even analysis

Year	1	2	3
Monthly revenue	$ 37,230	$ 38,626	$ 40,069
Yearly revenue	$446,756	$463,508	$480,824

7.8 Breakeven Analysis

Break even analysis

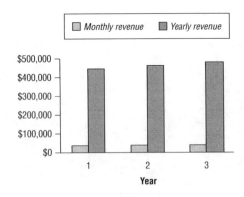

Business ratios—yearly

Year	1	2	3
Sales			
Sales growth	0.00%	20.00%	17.00%
Gross margin	73.80%	73.80%	73.80%
Financials			
Profit margin	5.21%	11.32%	15.75%
Assets to liabilities	600.58	306.02	209.77
Equity to liabilities	599.58	305.02	208.77
Assets to equity	1.00	1.00	1.00
Liquidity			
Acid test	25.00	13.30	9.52
Cash to assets	0.04	0.04	0.05

7.9 Business Ratios

Profit and loss statement (first year)

Months	1	2	3	4	5	6	7
Sales	$132,500	$32,500	$32,500	$32,500	$32,500	$132,500	$232,500
Cost of goods sold	$ 41,625	$ 1,625	$ 1,625	$ 1,625	$ 1,625	$ 41,625	$ 81,625
Gross margin	68.60%	95.00%	95.00%	95.00%	95.00%	68.60%	64.90%
Operating income	$ 90,875	$30,875	$30,875	$30,875	$30,875	$ 90,875	$150,875
Expenses							
Payroll	$ 20,833	$20,833	$20,833	$20,833	$20,833	$ 20,833	$ 20,833
General and administrative	$ 1,100	$ 1,100	$ 1,100	$ 1,100	$ 1,100	$ 1,100	$ 1,100
Marketing expenses	$ 413	$ 413	$ 413	$ 413	$ 413	$ 413	$ 413
Professional fees and licensure	$ 435	$ 435	$ 435	$ 435	$ 435	$ 435	$ 435
Insurance costs	$ 166	$ 166	$ 166	$ 166	$ 166	$ 166	$ 166
Travel and vehicle costs	$ 633	$ 633	$ 633	$ 633	$ 633	$ 633	$ 633
Rent and utilities	$ 354	$ 354	$ 354	$ 354	$ 354	$ 354	$ 354
Miscellaneous costs	$ 413	$ 413	$ 413	$ 413	$ 413	$ 413	$ 413
Payroll taxes	$ 3,125	$ 3,125	$ 3,125	$ 3,125	$ 3,125	$ 3,125	$ 3,125
Total operating costs	$ 27,471	$27,471	$27,471	$27,471	$27,471	$ 27,471	$ 27,471
EBITDA	$ 63,404	$ 3,404	$ 3,404	$ 3,404	$ 3,404	$ 63,404	$123,404
Federal income tax	$ 17,704	$ 4,343	$ 4,343	$ 4,343	$ 4,343	$ 17,704	$ 31,066
State income tax	$ 2,682	$ 658	$ 658	$ 658	$ 658	$ 2,682	$ 4,707
Interest expense	$ 0	$ 0	$ 0	$ 0	$ 0	$ 0	$ 0
Depreciation expense	$ 16,416	$16,416	$16,416	$16,416	$16,416	$ 16,416	$ 16,416
Net profit	$ 26,602	−$18,012	−$18,012	−$18,012	−$18,012	$ 26,602	$ 71,216

7.10 Three Year Profit and Loss Statement

Profit and loss statement (first year cont.)

Month	8	9	10	11	12	1
Sales	$32,500	$32,500	$32,500	$32,500	$232,500	$990,000
Cost of goods sold	$ 1,625	$ 1,625	$ 1,625	$ 1,625	$ 81,625	$259,500
Gross margin	95.00%	95.00%	95.00%	95.00%	64.90%	73.80%
Operating income	**$30,875**	**$30,875**	**$30,875**	**$30,875**	**$150,875**	**$730,500**
Expenses						
Payroll	$20,833	$20,833	$20,833	$20,833	$ 20,833	$250,000
General and administrative	$ 1,100	$ 1,100	$ 1,100	$ 1,100	$ 1,100	$ 13,200
Marketing expenses	$ 413	$ 413	$ 413	$ 413	$ 413	$ 4,950
Professional fees and licensure	$ 435	$ 435	$ 435	$ 435	$ 435	$ 5,219
Insurance costs	$ 166	$ 166	$ 166	$ 166	$ 166	$ 1,987
Travel and vehicle costs	$ 633	$ 633	$ 633	$ 633	$ 633	$ 7,596
Rent and utilities	$ 354	$ 354	$ 354	$ 354	$ 354	$ 4,250
Miscellaneous costs	$ 413	$ 413	$ 413	$ 413	$ 413	$ 4,950
Payroll taxes	$ 3,125	$ 3,125	$ 3,125	$ 3,125	$ 3,125	$ 37,500
Total operating costs	**$27,471**	**$27,471**	**$27,471**	**$27,471**	**$ 27,471**	**$329,652**
EBITDA	**$ 3,404**	**$ 3,404**	**$ 3,404**	**$ 3,404**	**$123,404**	**$400,848**
Federal income tax	$ 4,343	$ 4,343	$ 4,343	$ 4,343	$ 31,066	$132,280
State income tax	$ 658	$ 658	$ 658	$ 658	$ 4,707	$ 20,042
Interest expense	$ 0	$ 0	$ 0	$ 0	$ 0	$ 0
Depreciation expense	$16,416	$16,416	$16,416	$16,416	$ 16,416	$196,987
Net profit	**−$18,012**	**−$18,012**	**−$18,012**	**−$18,012**	**$ 71,216**	**$ 51,539**

Profit and loss statement (second year)

		2			
Quarter	Q1	Q2	Q3	Q4	2
Sales	$237,600	$297,000	$320,760	$332,640	$1,188,000
Cost of goods sold	$ 62,280	$ 77,850	$ 84,078	$ 87,192	$ 311,400
Gross margin	73.80%	73.80%	73.80%	73.80%	73.80%
Operating income	**$175,320**	**$219,150**	**$236,682**	**$245,448**	**$ 876,600**
Expenses					
Payroll	$ 51,500	$ 64,375	$ 69,525	$ 72,100	$ 257,500
General and administrative	$ 2,746	$ 3,432	$ 3,707	$ 3,844	$ 13,728
Marketing expenses	$ 1,188	$ 1,485	$ 1,604	$ 1,663	$ 5,940
Professional fees and licensure	$ 1,075	$ 1,344	$ 1,451	$ 1,505	$ 5,376
Insurance costs	$ 417	$ 522	$ 563	$ 584	$ 2,086
Travel and vehicle costs	$ 1,671	$ 2,089	$ 2,256	$ 2,340	$ 8,356
Rent and utilities	$ 893	$ 1,116	$ 1,205	$ 1,250	$ 4,463
Miscellaneous costs	$ 1,188	$ 1,485	$ 1,604	$ 1,663	$ 5,940
Payroll taxes	$ 7,725	$ 9,656	$ 10,429	$ 10,815	$ 38,625
Total operating costs	**$ 68,403**	**$ 85,503**	**$ 92,344**	**$ 95,764**	**$ 342,013**
EBITDA	**$106,917**	**$133,647**	**$144,338**	**$149,684**	**$ 534,587**
Federal income tax	$ 35,283	$ 44,103	$ 47,632	$ 49,396	$ 176,414
State income tax	$ 5,346	$ 6,682	$ 7,217	$ 7,484	$ 26,729
Interest expense	$ 0	$ 0	$ 0	$ 0	$ 0
Depreciation expense	$ 49,247	$ 49,247	$ 49,247	$ 49,247	$ 196,987
Net profit	**$ 17,042**	**$ 33,614**	**$ 40,243**	**$ 43,558**	**$ 134,457**

Profit and loss statement (third year)

Quarter	Q1	Q2	Q3	Q4	3
Sales	$277,992	$347,490	$375,289	$389,189	$1,389,960
Cost of goods sold	$ 72,868	$ 91,085	$ 98,371	$102,015	$ 364,338
Gross margin	73.80%	73.80%	73.80%	73.80%	73.80%
Operating income	$205,124	$256,406	$276,918	$287,174	$1,025,622
Expenses					
Payroll	$ 53,045	$ 66,306	$ 71,611	$ 74,263	$ 265,225
General and administrative	$ 2,855	$ 3,569	$ 3,855	$ 3,998	$ 14,277
Marketing expenses	$ 1,390	$ 1,737	$ 1,876	$ 1,946	$ 6,950
Professional fees and licensure	$ 1,107	$ 1,384	$ 1,495	$ 1,550	$ 5,537
Insurance costs	$ 438	$ 548	$ 591	$ 613	$ 2,191
Travel and vehicle costs	$ 1,838	$ 2,298	$ 2,482	$ 2,574	$ 9,191
Rent and utilities	$ 937	$ 1,171	$ 1,265	$ 1,312	$ 4,686
Miscellaneous costs	$ 1,390	$ 1,737	$ 1,876	$ 1,946	$ 6,950
Payroll taxes	$ 7,957	$ 9,946	$ 10,742	$ 11,139	$ 39,784
Total operating costs	$ 70,958	$ 88,697	$ 95,793	$ 99,341	$ 354,790
EBITDA	$134,166	$167,708	$181,125	$187,833	$ 670,832
Federal income tax	$ 44,275	$ 55,344	$ 59,771	$ 61,985	$ 221,375
State income tax	$ 6,708	$ 8,385	$ 9,056	$ 9,392	$ 33,542
Interest expense	$ 0	$ 0	$ 0	$ 0	$ 0
Depreciation expense	$ 49,247	$ 49,247	$ 49,247	$ 49,247	$ 196,987
Net profit	$ 33,936	$ 54,732	$ 63,051	$ 67,210	$ 218,929

Cash flow analysis (first year)

Month	1	2	3	4	5	6	7
Cash from operations	$ 43,017	−$ 1,596	−$ 1,596	−$ 1,596	−$ 1,596	$ 43,017	$ 87,631
Cash from receivables	$ 0	$ 0	$ 0	$ 0	$ 0	$ 0	$ 0
Operating cash inflow	$ 43,017	−$ 1,596	−$ 1,596	−$ 1,596	−$ 1,596	$ 43,017	$ 87,631
Other cash inflows							
Equity investment	$7,500,000	$ 0	$ 0	$ 0	$ 0	$ 0	$ 0
Increased borrowings	$ 0	$ 0	$ 0	$ 0	$ 0	$ 0	$ 0
Sales of business assets	$ 0	$ 0	$ 0	$ 0	$ 0	$ 0	$ 0
A/P increases	$ 3,159	$ 3,159	$ 3,159	$ 3,159	$ 3,159	$ 3,159	$ 3,159
Total other cash inflows	$7,503,159	$ 3,159	$ 3,159	$ 3,159	$ 3,159	$ 3,159	$ 3,159
Total cash inflow	$7,546,176	$ 1,562	$ 1,562	$ 1,562	$ 1,562	$ 46,176	$ 90,790
Cash outflows							
Repayment of principal	$ 0	$ 0	$ 0	$ 0	$ 0	$ 0	$ 0
A/P decreases	$ 2,075	$ 2,075	$ 2,075	$ 2,075	$ 2,075	$ 2,075	$ 2,075
A/R increases	$ 0	$ 0	$ 0	$ 0	$ 0	$ 0	$ 0
Asset purchases	$7,262,500	$ 0	$ 0	$ 0	$ 0	$ 0	$ 0
Dividends	$ 0	$ 0	$ 0	$ 0	$ 0	$ 0	$ 0
Total cash outflows	$7,264,575	$ 2,075	$ 2,075	$ 2,075	$ 2,075	$ 2,075	$ 2,075
Net cash flow	$ 281,601	−$ 513	−$ 513	−$ 513	−$ 513	$ 44,101	$ 88,715
Cash balance	$ 281,601	$281,088	$280,576	$280,063	$279,550	$323,651	$412,367

7.11 Three Year Cash Flow Analysis

Cash flow analysis (first year cont.)

Month	8	9	10	11	12	1
Cash from operations	−$ 1,596	−$ 1,595	−$ 1,596	−$ 1,596	$ 87,630	$ 248,526
Cash from receivables	$ 0	$ 0	$ 0	$ 0	$ 0	$ 0
Operating cash inflow	**−$ 1,596**	**−$ 1,595**	**−$ 1,596**	**−$ 1,596**	**$ 87,630**	**$ 248,526**
Other cash inflows						
Equity investment	$ 0	$ 0	$ 0	$ 0	$ 0	$7,500,000
Increased borrowings	$ 0	$ 0	$ 0	$ 0	$ 0	$ 0
Sales of business assets	$ 0	$ 0	$ 0	$ 0	$ 0	$ 0
A/P increases	$ 3,159	$ 3,159	$ 3,159	$ 3,159	$ 3,159	$ 37,902
Total other cash inflows	**$ 3,159**	**$ 3,159**	**$ 3,159**	**$ 3,159**	**$ 3,159**	**$7,537,902**
Total cash inflow	**$ 1,562**	**$ 1,563**	**$ 1,562**	**$ 1,562**	**$ 90,789**	**$7,786,428**
Cash outflows						
Repayment of principal	$ 0	$ 0	$ 0	$ 0	$ 0	$ 0
A/P decreases	$ 2,075	$ 2,075	$ 2,075	$ 2,075	$ 2,075	$ 24,897
A/R increases	$ 0	$ 0	$ 0	$ 0	$ 0	$ 0
Asset purchases	$ 0	$ 0	$ 0	$ 0	$ 0	$7,262,500
Dividends	$ 0	$ 0	$ 0	$ 0	$173,968	$ 173,968
Total cash outflows	**$ 2,075**	**$ 2,075**	**$ 2,075**	**$ 2,075**	**$176,043**	**$7,461,365**
Net cash flow	**−$ 513**	**−$ 512**	**−$ 513**	**−$ 513**	**−$ 85,254**	**$ 325,063**
Cash balance	**$411,854**	**$411,342**	**$410,829**	**$410,317**	**$325,063**	**$ 325,063**

Cash flow analysis (second year)

Quarter	Q1	2 Q2	Q3	Q4	2
Cash from operations	$ 66,289	$ 82,861	$ 89,490	$ 92,804	$331,444
Cash from receivables	$ 0	$ 0	$ 0	$ 0	$ 0
Operating cash inflow	**$ 66,289**	**$ 82,861**	**$ 89,490**	**$ 92,804**	**$331,444**
Other cash inflows					
Equity investment	$ 0	$ 0	$ 0	$ 0	$ 0
Increased borrowings	$ 0	$ 0	$ 0	$ 0	$ 0
Sales of business assets	$ 0	$ 0	$ 0	$ 0	$ 0
A/P increases	$ 8,717	$ 10,897	$ 11,769	$ 12,204	$ 43,587
Total other cash inflows	**$ 8,717**	**$ 10,897**	**$ 11,769**	**$ 12,204**	**$ 43,587**
Total cash inflow	**$ 75,006**	**$ 93,758**	**$101,258**	**$105,009**	**$375,031**
Cash outflows					
Repayment of principal	$ 0	$ 0	$ 0	$ 0	$ 0
A/P decreases	$ 5,975	$ 7,469	$ 8,067	$ 8,365	$ 29,876
A/R increases	$ 0	$ 0	$ 0	$ 0	$ 0
Asset purchases	$ 16,572	$ 20,715	$ 22,372	$ 23,201	$ 82,861
Dividends	$ 46,402	$ 58,003	$ 62,643	$ 64,963	$232,011
Total cash outflows	**$ 68,950**	**$ 86,187**	**$ 93,082**	**$ 96,529**	**$344,748**
Net cash flow	**$ 6,057**	**$ 7,571**	**$ 8,176**	**$ 8,479**	**$ 30,283**
Cash balance	**$331,119**	**$338,690**	**$346,867**	**$355,346**	**$355,346**

Cash flow analysis (third year)

Quarter	Q1	3 Q2	Q3	Q4	3
Cash from operations	$ 83,183	$103,979	$112,297	$116,456	$415,916
Cash from receivables	$ 0	$ 0	$ 0	$ 0	$ 0
Operating cash inflow	**$ 83,183**	**$103,979**	**$112,297**	**$116,456**	**$415,916**
Other cash inflows					
Equity investment	$ 0	$ 0	$ 0	$ 0	$ 0
Increased borrowings	$ 0	$ 0	$ 0	$ 0	$ 0
Sales of business assets	$ 0	$ 0	$ 0	$ 0	$ 0
A/P increases	$ 10,025	$ 12,531	$ 13,534	$ 14,035	$ 50,125
Total other cash inflows	**$ 10,025**	**$ 12,531**	**$ 13,534**	**$ 14,035**	**$ 50,125**
Total cash inflow	**$ 93,208**	**$116,510**	**$125,831**	**$130,492**	**$466,041**
Cash outflows					
Repayment of principal	$ 0	$ 0	$ 0	$ 0	$ 0
A/P decreases	$ 7,170	$ 8,963	$ 9,680	$ 10,038	$ 35,852
A/R increases	$ 0	$ 0	$ 0	$ 0	$ 0
Asset purchases	$ 20,796	$ 25,995	$ 28,074	$ 29,114	$103,979
Dividends	$ 58,228	$ 72,785	$ 78,608	$ 81,520	$291,141
Total cash outflows	**$ 86,194**	**$107,743**	**$116,362**	**$120,672**	**$430,972**
Net cash flow	**$ 7,014**	**$ 8,767**	**$ 9,469**	**$ 9,819**	**$ 35,070**
Cash balance	**$362,360**	**$371,127**	**$380,596**	**$390,415**	**$390,415**

Resume Writing Business

Nieberger Career Consulting, LLC

19978 East Main Street
Elmhurst, IL 60126

Kim Nylander Herrera

This plan provides an overview of a start-up organization that delivers resume writing and career coaching services to professionals undergoing career transition. Services are specifically geared to mid- to senior-level professionals within the private sector job market.

EXECUTIVE SUMMARY

Established in 2012, Nieberger Career Consulting, LLC is a professional services company that offers resume writing services specifically designed to meet the needs of the mid- to senior-level professional. The company was founded by Karen Nieberger, a Chicago native who has 15 years of human resources and executive recruiting experience. Having identified, led and developed top talent within Fortune 100 and 500 companies, Nieberger is well positioned to understand the needs of the executive in career transition. She utilizes her HR knowledge to assist clients to strategically identify and achieve their career goals—including promotions, career changes, or new employment opportunities due to layoffs or other displacements.

In addition to professionally written resumes, to maximize client success in the job market the company offers additional career collateral services including: professionally written cover letters, thank you letters, professional biographies, LinkedIn profiles, along with basic interview and salary negotiation coaching services.

The company is located in the metro Chicago area, but serves clients on a national basis through the use of web and mobile technology including phone, webcast, and Skype.

BUSINESS DESCRIPTION & MISSION

Company Mission

Nieberger Career Consulting helps individuals get jobs, grow as professionals, and succeed in their careers. The company puts its human resources expertise to use, providing each client with the HR insider tools necessary to succeed in today's highly competitive marketplace.

In order to achieve this mission, the organization commits to:

1. Develop lasting relationships with satisfied clients.

2. Follow through on commitments.

3. Develop a lasting presence in the local community.

4. Be a recognized national subject matter expert in job search solutions and career development.

5. Provide unparralled service and results based on a thorough understanding of each individual's unique needs.

6. Drive individual performance through breaking down barriers to success—by optimizing client talent and productivity.

Company Goals

In support of the organization's mission, the business operates under the following goals:

1. To become a leading provider of career solutions to the mid- and executive-level professional marketplace.

2. To be a nationally recognized and trusted provider of effective, results-oriented personal coaching and career collateral.

3. To exist as a referral-based organization whose reputation for results is based on exceptional customer service.

4. To consistently demonstrate value through quantifiable success measures directly aligned to client revenue and/or career goals.

Customer Service Philosophy

To reach its goals and distinguish itself from its competitors, the company operates under the following customer service philosophy:

1. Customer Intimacy: The company begins every engagement by taking the time to understand the unique needs of each client and creates a plan specifically designed to meet that individual's needs.

2. If for any reason the company is unable to provide the best services possible to a particular client, company leadership will do what it can to get the individual referred to a colleague who can provide the subject matter expertise or 'fit' that is required to get the client's goals obtained.

3. The company values diversity and works proactively to incorporate new ideas and perspectives into the business.

4. The company will respect its client's time and budget. Company leadership will implement the most cost effective plans that are designed to remove barriers to client success and help clients focus on their business/career goals.

Success Measures:

Coaching clients will report that through the services offered they are able to meet their personal and professional goals including: securing new employment, reaching promotional goals, and expanding their leadership competencies (the latter as defined by personal and/or employer established goals and objectives).

DEFINITION OF THE MARKET

Industry Outlook

As the U.S. continues to work through recovery efforts of the economic recession, there will be a need for qualified professionals who have the skills to strategically help displaced workers secure new employment opportunities. In addition, as the economy improves and new jobs are created, there will be a need for professionals who can assist clients with securing new job opportunities outside of their current employer as well as assist them with applying for promotional positions within their current organization. These opportunities will exist not only with individual clients, but will exist within the corporate sector, in which organizations will require assistance with outplacement programs, as well as coaching and development of identified personnel in order to retain key leaders, thereby reducing recruiting costs within organizations.

In support of these market assumptions, in years one through five Nieberger will implement strategies to penetrate the individual client market. During year five (which is outside the scope of this plan) the company will expand its services offerings and will implement strategies for entering the corporate career services marketplace.

Current Target Market

While there are a number of niche markets within the individual client resume writing/career services industry (including: high school and college students, recent college graduates, military veterans, public sector employees, and board-level executives) Nieberger Career Consulting will focus its efforts on providing services to the mid- and executive-level professional within the private sector. This decision is based on the experience of the company owner and her background in recruiting, placing, and developing leaders at this level.

For the purpose of this plan, mid-level professionals are defined as individuals who have at least seven to 10 years of progressive leadership experience within a corporate or nonprofit setting. Executive-level professionals are defined as individuals who have at least 10 years of leadership experience at the vice president or above level within a corporate or nonprofit environment.

While Nieberger's clients may come from a variety of industries and professions within corporate or nonprofit, the following industries/professions will be considered out of scope for the purposes of the company's target market:

- Legal

- Medical

- Academia

- Military

- Public sector

Potential clients from these disciplines will be referred to qualified coaches/writers who specialize in these markets/professions.

Critical Needs of Target Market:

Mid-professional to executive clients have unique needs with the following attributes common across both groups:

- Intense competition with a narrowed field of job availability, especially when relocation, either domestically or abroad, is not an option.

- Individuals may possess a high degree of tenure, be well compensated, and may have a stable work history with little experience developing resumes or interviewing.

- Biographies and other collateral are often necessary due to speaking engagements and other presentation opportunities.

- When employed, the individuals at this career level will have little time to meet with the writer/ coach, therefore, effective communication and delivery methods are critical.

- Career change is more likely at this time and more extensive work may be required to help identify and create documents that communicate the professional's ability to make an effective and successful move into a new role/position.

All company deliverables (as defined in the Products and Services section of this plan) are designed to meet these needs.

Competition

In order to effectively penetrate the resume writing market and secure a successful degree of market share, Nieberger Career Consulting will implement aggressive advertising and marketing strategies to compete with the largest competitive threat—currently identified as large-scale executive online resume services as well as local and national boutique executive placement firms. The latter of which, on average, generate client portfolios as part of their service offering.

To beat the competition from these competitors, Nieberger Career Consulting will implement strategic marketing initiatives that provide differentiation of its company's services based on Nieberger's extensive background working inside executive placement and corporate HR, as well as the personal attention and customized deliverables the company provides to each client—the latter of which is not offered through online competitors or most placement firms. Partnerships with professional membership organizations, as well as extensive use of social media and the creation of e-books and subject matter expert (SME) status will be used to further differentiate the company and establish the competitiveness of the brand.

DESCRIPTION OF PRODUCTS & SERVICES

The company's product offerings will include the following:

Resume and Career Collateral Preparation

Resume Consultation & Feedback Session

A one hour meeting to review client's existing resume. Tips, strategies, and feedback are provided. A solution for professionals looking to update a current resume or for individuals who want a professional second opinion as they write their own document.

Professional Resume Stand Alone Package

A one hour phone consultation coupled with extensive follow-up client interviews that results in a professionally written, customized resume targeted to the client's industry/profession.

Total Resume Package

A professionally written resume along with customized cover letter and thank you letter templates that the client can easily update when applying for jobs.

LinkedIn Profile

A professionally written LinkedIn profile that incorporates client online branding with SEO techniques to help increase client visibility.

Professional Bio

A memorably crafted bio suitable for use across both print and electronic media.

Total Career Package

All of the above career collateral products including: resume, LinkedIn profile, customized cover letter and thank you letter templates, and professional bio.

Interview Coaching/Preparation

2 Hour Mock Interview:
A personalized 45 minute mock interview, followed by a 75 minute feedback session. Designed for the client who has been out of the job market for an extended period of time or who has other limited interview experience.

45 Minute Interview Prep Session:
A review of the three basic types of interview questions (standard, situational, and behavioral) and tips for how to address each question type, along with a review of what questions to ask during the interview, and a mini interview practice session that provides real-time coaching and feedback on interview performance.

1/2 Hour Job Offer Negotiation Coaching
A personalized half hour phone consultation that provides clients with tips and strategies for finalizing a job offer.

Price List for Services:

To fit client needs and offer a competitive differentiator from other resume writing services, Nieberger Career Consulting clients will be offered a choice of an a la carte or package rate for all services. On average package pricing will save clients 10-15% off a la carte services.

Resume Consultation & Feedback Session—$150

Professional Resume Stand Alone—$500

Total Resume Package—$550

LinkedIn Profile—$150

Professional Bio—$300

Total Career Package—$900

1/2 Hour Job Offer Negotiation Coaching—$75

2 Hour Mock Interview—$300

45 Minute Interview Prep Session—$100

All services will come with complementary email and phone support for those times when clients have a quick question between sessions. Nieberger will also offer a complementary half hour initial confidential phone consultation to determine the best approach to meet client need.

ORGANIZATION & MANAGEMENT

Company Structure

The company will function as a single member LLC organized in the state of Illinois.

Staff

During years one through three, Nieberger will be the sole writer and coach for the organization and will be responsible for all operations of the business. During year three, when projected company growth measures are met, Nieberger will add two additional resume writers to the organization. Writers will work during years 3—5 as independent contractors of the business in order to save on payroll and other associated benefit costs. All writers hired will be certified in resume writing by an official accrediting body and will have at least five to seven years of human resources or full-time recruiting experience.

Owner Biography

Karen Nieberger, the sole proprietor of the business has a background in executive recruiting and human resources management. She has 15 years of HR experience working most recently as the vice president of human resources for the North American division of a global Fortune 100 company. After successfully building and supporting leadership teams within the corporate sector, Nieberger accepted a role as a senior partner with for one of the top three executive search firms placing mid-career to senior management in Fortune 100 to Fortune 500 companies. She received her undergraduate degree in human resources from Loyola University in Chicago, and she received her MBA from the University of Chicago. Nieberger is also a Certified Professional Resume Writer (CPRW), maintains her certification as a Senior Professional in Human Resources (SPHR), and effective third quarter of 2013 will be a Certified Career Professional (CCP).

MARKETING & SALES STRATEGY

To meet company goals and objectives, as well as increase market share, the company will implement the following sales and marketing techniques:

1. Provide pro-bono services to local, regional, and national charities and non-profits in order to increase visibility within the community and expand its contact/referral base.

2. Use effective branding techniques across all print and electronic media.

3. Utilize social media tools such as Twitter/Twitter chats, LinkedIn, Facebook groups, and blogging to expand visibility and credibility to potential clients and strategic partners.

4. Build strategic partnerships with established/creditable career coaches, resume writers, and HR service providers in order to share referrals and other networking opportunities.

5. Developing partnerships with career centers at local universities and alumni centers.

6. Attend trade shows and career fairs. Offer special promotions for attendees through take away cards and consumer reward programs.

7. Offer a range of options for clients to purchase services, including a la carte and bundled packaging.

8. Implement post-engagement surveys to solicit client feedback for continuous improvement and communication.

9. Offer discounts on future services to clients to make a referral.

10. Participate in professional speaking engagements.

11. Increase networking within professional associations and across personal contacts.

12. Work with the PR and journalism community to be a SME for career-based articles and media events.

FINANCIAL MANAGEMENT

Investment/Funding Information

Start-up capital of $8,398 will be required with all funding coming from Nieberger's personal savings. She will be the sole investor and will contribute seed money comprised of $10,000.

Sources of capital

Owners' investment
(name and percent ownership)

Nieberger, 100% ownership	$10,000
Other investor	—
Total investment	**$10,000**

Startup expenses

Buildings/real estate	A home office will be used
Total buildings/real estate	—

Capital equipment list

Furniture	$	200
Equipment		—
Fixtures		—
Machinery—all in one printer/scanner/fax/ copier	$	150
External hard drive	$	75
Total capital equipment	**$**	**425**

Location and admin expenses

Rental—mailbox	$	360
Utility deposits		—
Legal and accounting fees	$	500
Prepaid insurance		—
Pre-opening salaries		—
Phone line	$	360
Total location and admin expenses	**$**	**1,220**

Opening inventory

Resume paper	$	121
Resume envelopes	$	111
CD ROMs for client copies of resumes	$	57
Presentation folders for client collateral	$	49
Office supplies, including printer ink, pens, paper, stapler, etc.	$	250
Total inventory	**$**	**588**

Advertising and promotional expenses

Website development & hosting	$	1,500
Signage	$	250
Printing	$	75
Travel/entertainment—industry conferences	$	1,200
Business cards	$	50
Total advertising/promotional expenses	**$**	**3,075**

Other expenses

Professional certification	$	250
LLC filing fees	$	500
Professional memberships	$	340
Total other expenses	**$**	**1,090**
Reserve for contingencies	**$**	**2,000**

Summary statement

Sources of capital

Owners' and other investments	$10,000
Bank loans	—
Other loans	—
Total source of funds	**$10,000**

Startup expenses

Buildings/real estate		—
Capital equipment	$	425
Location/administration expenses	$	1,220
Opening inventory	$	588
Advertising/promotional expenses	$	3,075
Other expenses	$	1,090
Contingency fund	$	2,000
Total startup expenses	**$**	**8,398**

Notes on funding

1. The organization's initial capital costs have been accounted for and acquired, however, updated equipment and tools will need to be budgeted for going forward due to depreciation and need to upgrade to new technology as it becomes available.

2. Dollars available to invest in an outsourced payroll vendor to manage quarterly tax filings as well as issuance of payroll to self and contractors will need to be budgeted beginning in year three.

Cash management and planning

1. The company will be managed using a cash accounting system.

2. Financial targets are set on an annual basis for a fiscal year beginning in Jan.

3. Results against target will be measured informally on a monthly basis with full analysis conducted on a quarterly basis.

4. Adjustments to plan that do not have a direct impact on staff/contractors will be made on a rolling basis. Adjustments to plan that have a direct impact on staff/contractors—such as reduction in force or pay/benefits, will be more formally handled on a month-end basis.

APPENDIX:

Includes:

- Nieberger Resume
- Company brochure
- Press releases

Solar Panel Installation Service

Living Green Energy Services

989981 W. 101st St.
New York, NY 10001

BizPlanDB.com

The purpose of this business plan is to raise $200,000 for the development of a solar panel installation company while showcasing the expected financials and operations over the next three years. Living Green Energy Services, Inc. is a New York based corporation that will provide installation and sale of solar panels to commercial and residential customers in its targeted market. The Company was founded by Charlie Militello.

1.0 EXECUTIVE SUMMARY

The purpose of this business plan is to raise $200,000 for the development of a solar panel installation company while showcasing the expected financials and operations over the next three years. Living Green Energy Services, Inc. is a New York based corporation that will provide installation and sale of solar panels to commercial and residential customers in its targeted market. The Company was founded by Charlie Militello.

1.1 The Products and Services

As mentioned above, the Company will provide for the installation of solar panels (both heat absorbing and photovoltaic) to residences and commercial building owners throughout the target market. Living Green Energy Services, Inc. will generate substantial gross margins from the labor fees associated with these product installations.

The Company will also generate substantial income from the direct sale of the solar panels that will be provided to customers as part of the installation service. The Company anticipates that it will earn gross margins of 50% on sale of solar panels to residential and commercial customers.

With the recent rapid increase in the price of energy products, the Company sees a substantial opportunity to capitalize on the demand for energy saving measures, such as the installation of solar panels. While expensive, the return on investment for a homeowner/building owner is substantial.

The third section of the business plan will further describe the services offered by Living Green Energy Services.

1.2 Financing

Mr. Militello is seeking to raise $200,000 from as a bank loan. The interest rate and loan agreement are to be further discussed during negotiation. This business plan assumes that the business will receive a 10 year loan with a 9% fixed interest rate. The financing will be used for the following:

- Development of the Company's office location.

- Financing for the first six months of operation.

- Capital to purchase a company vehicle.

- Capital for inventory purchases.

Mr. Militello will contribute $50,000 to the venture.

1.3 Mission Statement

The Company's mission is to become the recognized leader in its targeted market for solar panel installation and sales.

1.4 Management Team

The Company was founded by Charlie Militello. Mr. Militello has more than 10 years of experience in the construction industry. Through his expertise, he will be able to bring the operations of the business to profitability within its first year of operations.

1.5 Sales Forecasts

Mr. Militello expects a strong rate of growth at the start of operations. Below are the expected financials over the next three years.

Proforma profit and loss (yearly)

Year	1	2	3
Sales	$887,502	$1,065,002	$1,246,053
Operating costs	$440,440	$ 516,751	$ 536,186
EBITDA	$145,691	$ 186,606	$ 286,742
Taxes, interest, and depreciation	$ 83,731	$ 91,886	$ 129,115
Net profit	$ 61,960	$ 94,720	$ 157,626

Sales, operating costs, and profit forecast

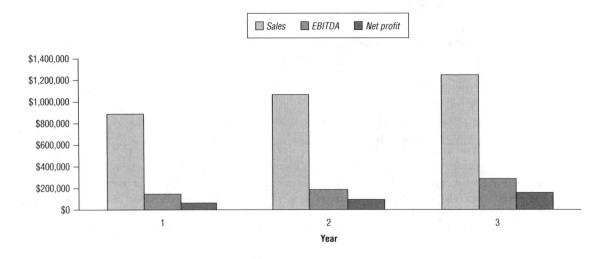

1.6 Expansion Plan

The Founder expects that the business will aggressively expand during the first three years of operation. Mr. Militello intends to implement marketing campaigns that will effectively target individuals, building owners, and contractors, within the target market.

2.0 COMPANY AND FINANCING SUMMARY

2.1 Registered Name and Corporate Structure

Living Green Energy Services, Inc. is registered as a corporation in the State of New York.

2.2 Required Funds

At this time, Living Green Energy Services, Inc. requires $200,000 of debt funds. Mr. Militello will provide a capital injection of $50,000 into the business. Below is a breakdown of how these funds will be used:

Projected startup costs

Initial lease payments and deposits	$ 25,000
Working capital	$ 70,000
FF&E	$ 20,000
Leasehold improvements	$ 5,000
Security deposits	$ 7,500
Company vehicle	$ 35,000
Solar panel inventory	$ 75,000
Marketing budget	$ 7,500
Miscellaneous and unforeseen costs	$ 5,000
Total startup costs	**$250,000**

Use of funds

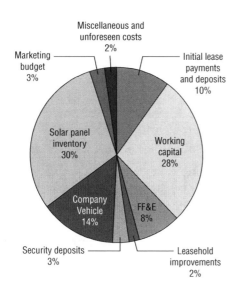

2.3 Investor Equity

Mr. Militello is not seeking an investment from a third party at this time.

2.4 Management Equity

Charlie Militello owns 100% of Living Green Energy Services, Inc.

2.5 Exit Strategy

If the business is very successful, Mr. Militello may seek to sell the business to a third party for a significant earnings multiple. Most likely, the Company will hire a qualified business broker to sell the business on behalf of Living Green Energy Services, Inc. Based on historical numbers, the business could fetch a sales premium of up to 4 times earnings.

3.0 PRODUCTS AND SERVICES

Below is a description of the solar panel product and installation services offered by Living Green Energy Services.

3.1 Solar Panel Product Installation

The primary source of revenue for the business will come from the instillation of heat absorbing and photovoltaic panel installations for consumers and residences throughout the Company's targeted market. As stated in the executive summary, while these installations are expensive, they almost always completely eliminate a client's heating and electric bills. As such, the return on investment for consumers is extremely high as they will not have any future heating or energy expenditures, but they will also add a significant amount of value to their properties. Additionally, if property installed, some houses and buildings can actually receive income from their solar panels by selling excess energy back into the local power-grid (for photovoltaic cells only).

Mr. Militello and his staff will be properly certified to install solar panels and related products for their customers. In most jurisdictions, solar panel installation companies have the same licensure requirements as HVAC contractors.

3.2 Sales of Solar Panels

The secondary stream of revenue for the business will come from the direct sale of the solar panels to be used in conjunction with the installation services offered by the Company. Mr. Militello expects that the business will generate margins of 50% on each dollar of revenue generated through the sale of standard heat absorbing and photovoltaic panel products.

4.0 STRATEGIC AND MARKET ANALYSIS

4.1 Economic Outlook

This section of the analysis will detail the economic climate, the solar panel industry, the customer profile, and the competition that the business will face as it progresses through its business operations.

Currently, the economic market condition in the United States is moderate. The meltdown of the sub prime mortgage market coupled with increasing gas prices has led many people to believe that the US is on the cusp of a double dip economic recession. This slowdown in the economy has also greatly impacted real estate sales, which has halted to historical lows. However, with these rising energy costs, homeowners and building owners are looking to make investments into their properties that will not only reduce (or eliminate) their utility bills, but also provide less impact on the environment. As such, and despite the current housing situation, Management expects that the business will be relatively immune from change in the general economy.

4.2 Industry Analysis

Currently, the installation and sale of solar panels to the general public is a $10 billion dollar per year industry. Aggregately, there are approximately 4,000 companies that specialize in this segment of the HVAC industry (as discussed earlier, solar paneling contractors are part of the HVAC market). The industry employs approximately 50,000 people while providing payrolls of approximately $2 billion per year.

The growth rate of this industry is expected to expand much faster than that of the general economy as people continue to look for ways to remove their impact on the environment while concurrently saving money on high utility costs. Based on information provided by the Federal Government, Management anticipates that the industry will grow at an annual rate of 7% to 8% over the next 10 years.

4.3 Customer Profile

The Company's average client will be a residential property owner or commercial property within in the Company's target market. Common traits among clients will include:

- Annual household income exceeding $200,000

- Will spend $7,500 to $10,000 on solar panel installations (residential)

- Will spend $15,000 to $25,000 on solar panel installations (commercial)

- Is seeking to substantial reduce month to month utility costs while concurrently increasing the value of their properties

- Is seeking to reduce their environmental impact.

4.4 Competition

As the pricing for electricity and energy have fluctuated substantially over the past five years, the demand among consumers and businesses to reduce/normalize these costs have increased significantly. As such, many HVAC contracts (as well as electricians) have entered the market with solar panel projects. The primary way that Mr. Militello intends to differentiate this business from other companies is that the business will offer a broad range of photovoltaic cells, rooftop solar heating systems, and related products. Additionally, all installation employees will be licensed journeyman or apprentices that know how to properly install and maintain solar panel systems.

5.0 MARKETING PLAN

Living Green Energy Services, Inc. intends to maintain an extensive marketing campaign that will ensure maximum visibility for the business in its targeted market. Below is an overview of the marketing strategies and objectives of the Company.

5.1 Marketing Objectives

- Establish relationships with HVAC/general contractors and real estate developers.

- Establish relationships with municipal agencies that are seeking to capitalize on federal funding that provides for the installation of solar panels.

- Develop relationships with real estate developers that are using solar panels in conjunction with their new constructions.

5.2 Marketing Strategies

Mr. Militello intends on using a number of marketing strategies that will allow Living Green Energy Services, Inc. to easily residential and commercial property owners within the target market. These strategies include trade journals advertisements and ads placed on search engines on the Internet. Foremost, the Company intends to develop relationships with real estate developers, municipal agencies, and HVAC/general contractors and real estate developers that will outsource the installation and sale of solar panel products in conjunction with their development projects.

The business, at the onset of operations, intends to hire a third party independent sales team in order market the Company's products to consumers and business customers. A commission ranging from 5% to 15% of the sale will be paid to the third party independent sales agent. Although this may contribute to higher operating costs during early operations, Mr. Militello feels that this strategy will more rapidly increase the brand name of Living Green Energy Services, Inc.

5.3 Pricing

Management anticipates that each installation will generate $7,500 to $10,000 among residential buyers and approximately $20,000 among commercial property owners. The Company's gross margin will be 66 cents on each dollar of revenue.

6.0 ORGANIZATIONAL PLAN AND PERSONNEL SUMMARY

6.1 Corporate Organization

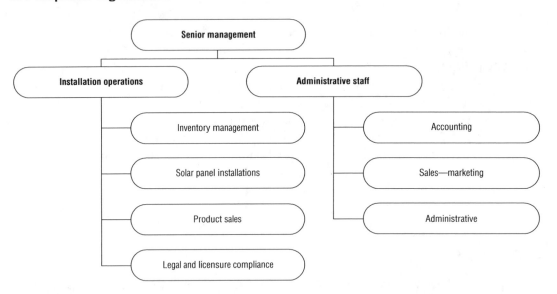

6.2 Organizational Budget

Personnel plan—yearly

Year	1	2	3
Owner	$ 40,000	$ 41,200	$ 42,436
Foreman	$ 75,000	$ 77,250	$ 79,568
Installation employees	$168,000	$201,880	$207,936
Bookkeeper (P/T)	$ 9,000	$ 9,270	$ 9,548
Administrative	$ 22,000	$ 45,320	$ 46,680
Total	**$314,000**	**$374,920**	**$386,168**

Numbers of personnel

Owner	1	1	1
Foreman	2	2	2
Installation employees	6	7	7
Bookkeeper (P/T)	1	1	1
Administrative	1	2	2
Totals	**11**	**13**	**13**

Personnel expense breakdown

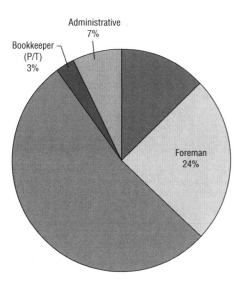

7.0 FINANCIAL PLAN

7.1 Underlying Assumptions

The Company has based its proforma financial statements on the following:

- Living Green Energy Services will have an annual revenue growth rate of 14.9% per year.

- The Owner will acquire $200,000 of debt funds to develop the business.

- The loan will have a 10 year term with a 9% interest rate.

7.2 Sensitivity Analysis

In the event of an economic downturn, the business may have a decline in its revenues. However, solar panel installation companies are in high demand with the current state of the energy markets. The business will also be able to capitalize on federal funding that allows for grants/tax breaks to companies and municipal agencies that install solar panels. As such, Management does not anticipate that the business will have any trouble generating revenues from the onset of operations.

7.3 Source of Funds

Financing

Equity contributions	
Management investment	$ 50,000.00
Total equity financing	**$ 50,000.00**
Banks and lenders	
Banks and lenders	$ 200,000.00
Total debt financing	**$200,000.00**
Total financing	**$250,000.00**

7.4 General Assumptions

General assumptions

Year	1	2	3
Short term interest rate	9.5%	9.5%	9.5%
Long term interest rate	10.0%	10.0%	10.0%
Federal tax rate	33.0%	33.0%	33.0%
State tax rate	5.0%	5.0%	5.0%
Personnel taxes	15.0%	15.0%	15.0%

7.5 Profit and Loss Statements

Proforma profit and loss (yearly)

Year	1	2	3
Sales	**$887,502**	**$1,065,002**	**$1,246,053**
Cost of goods sold	$301,371	$ 361,645	$ 423,125
Gross margin	66.04%	66.04%	66.04%
Operating income	**$586,131**	**$ 703,357**	**$ 822,928**
Expenses			
Payroll	$314,000	$ 374,920	$ 386,168
General and administrative	$ 25,200	$ 26,208	$ 27,256
Marketing expenses	$ 4,438	$ 5,325	$ 6,230
Professional fees and licensure	$ 5,219	$ 5,376	$ 5,537
Insurance costs	$ 11,987	$ 12,586	$ 13,216
Travel and vehicle costs	$ 7,596	$ 8,356	$ 9,191
Rent and utilities	$ 14,250	$ 14,963	$ 15,711
Miscellaneous costs	$ 10,650	$ 12,780	$ 14,953
Payroll taxes	$ 47,100	$ 56,238	$ 57,925
Total operating costs	**$440,440**	**$ 516,751**	**$ 536,186**
EBITDA	**$145,691**	**$ 186,606**	**$ 286,742**
Federal income tax	$ 48,078	$ 56,213	$ 89,696
State income tax	$ 7,285	$ 8,517	$ 13,590
Interest expense	$ 17,475	$ 16,263	$ 14,936
Depreciation expenses	$ 10,893	$ 10,893	$ 10,893
Net profit	**$ 61,960**	**$ 94,720**	**$ 157,626**
Profit margin	**6.98%**	**8.89%**	**12.65%**

Sales, operating costs, and profit forecast

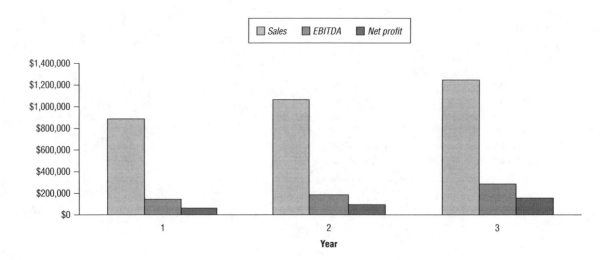

7.6 Cash Flow Analysis

Proforma cash flow analysis—yearly

Year	1	2	3
Cash from operations	$ 72,853	$105,613	$168,519
Cash from receivables	$ 0	$ 0	$ 0
Operating cash inflow	**$ 72,853**	**$105,613**	**$168,519**
Other cash inflows			
Equity investment	$ 50,000	$ 0	$ 0
Increased borrowings	$200,000	$ 0	$ 0
Sales of business assets	$ 0	$ 0	$ 0
A/P increases	$ 37,902	$ 43,587	$ 50,125
Total other cash inflows	**$287,902**	**$ 43,587**	**$ 50,125**
Total cash inflow	**$360,755**	**$149,200**	**$218,645**
Cash outflows			
Repayment of principal	$ 12,927	$ 14,139	$ 15,466
A/P decreases	$ 24,897	$ 29,876	$ 35,852
A/R increases	$ 0	$ 0	$ 0
Asset purchases	$152,500	$ 26,403	$ 42,130
Dividends	$ 50,997	$ 73,929	$117,963
Total cash outflows	**$241,321**	**$144,348**	**$211,411**
Net cash flow	**$119,434**	**$ 4,852**	**$ 7,234**
Cash balance	**$119,434**	**$124,286**	**$131,520**

Proforma cash flow (yearly)

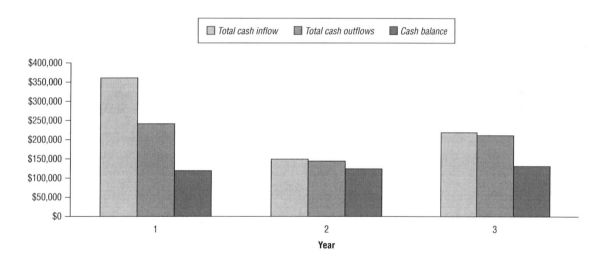

7.7 Balance Sheet

Proforma balance sheet—yearly

Year	1	2	3
Assets			
Cash	$119,434	$124,286	$131,520
Amortized development/expansion costs	$ 22,500	$ 29,101	$ 39,633
Inventory	$ 75,000	$ 88,202	$109,267
Vehicles	$ 35,000	$ 37,640	$ 43,960
FF&E	$ 20,000	$ 23,960	$ 30,280
Accumulated depreciation	($ 10,893)	($ 21,786)	($ 32,679)
Total assets	**$261,041**	**$281,404**	**$321,981**
Liabilities and equity			
Accounts payable	$ 13,005	$ 26,716	$ 40,990
Long term liabilities	$187,073	$172,934	$158,794
Other liabilities	$ 0	$ 0	$ 0
Total liabilities	**$200,078**	**$199,650**	**$199,784**
Net worth	**$ 60,963**	**$ 81,754**	**$122,197**
Total liabilities and equity	**$261,041**	**$281,404**	**$321,981**

Proforma balance sheet

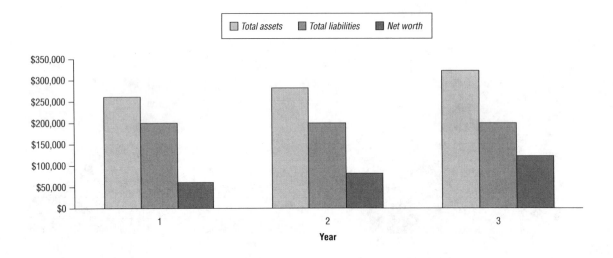

7.8 Breakeven Analysis

Monthly break even analysis

Year	1	2	3
Monthly revenue	$ 55,575	$ 65,204	$ 67,656
Yearly revenue	$666,900	$782,449	$811,877

Break even analysis

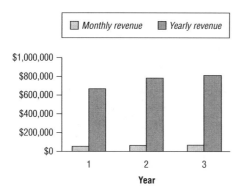

7.9 Business Ratios

Business ratios—yearly

Year	1	2	3
Sales			
Sales growth	0.00%	20.00%	17.00%
Gross margin	66.00%	66.00%	66.00%
Financials			
Profit margin	6.98%	8.89%	12.65%
Assets to liabilities	1.30	1.41	1.61
Equity to liabilities	0.30	0.41	0.61
Assets to equity	4.28	3.44	2.63
Liquidity			
Acid test	0.60	0.62	0.66
Cash to assets	0.46	0.44	0.41

7.10 Three Year Profit and Loss Statement

Profit and loss statement (first year)

Months	1	2	3	4	5	6	7
Sales	$72,930	$73,117	$73,304	$73,491	$73,678	$73,865	$74,052
Cost of goods sold	$24,765	$24,829	$24,892	$24,956	$25,019	$25,083	$25,146
Gross margin	66.00%	66.00%	66.00%	66.00%	66.00%	66.00%	66.00%
Operating income	$48,165	$48,289	$48,412	$48,536	$48,659	$48,783	$48,906
Expenses							
Payroll	$26,167	$26,167	$26,167	$26,167	$26,167	$26,167	$26,167
General and administrative	$2,100	$2,100	$2,100	$2,100	$2,100	$2,100	$2,100
Marketing expenses	$370	$370	$370	$370	$370	$370	$370
Professional fees and licensure	$435	$435	$435	$435	$435	$435	$435
Insurance costs	$999	$999	$999	$999	$999	$999	$999
Travel and vehicle costs	$633	$633	$633	$633	$633	$633	$633
Rent and utilities	$1,188	$1,188	$1,188	$1,188	$1,188	$1,188	$1,188
Miscellaneous costs	$888	$888	$888	$888	$888	$888	$888
Payroll taxes	$3,925	$3,925	$3,925	$3,925	$3,925	$3,925	$3,925
Total operating costs	$36,703	$36,703	$36,703	$36,703	$36,703	$36,703	$36,703
EBITDA	$11,462	$11,585	$11,709	$11,832	$11,956	$12,079	$12,203
Federal income tax	$3,951	$3,961	$3,971	$3,981	$3,991	$4,001	$4,012
State income tax	$599	$600	$602	$603	$605	$606	$608
Interest expense	$1,500	$1,492	$1,484	$1,477	$1,469	$1,461	$1,453
Depreciation expense	$908	$908	$908	$908	$908	$908	$908
Net profit	$4,505	$4,624	$4,744	$4,863	$4,983	$5,103	$5,223

Profit and loss statement (first year cont.)

Month	8	9	10	11	12	1
Sales	$74,239	$74,426	$74,613	$74,800	$74,987	$887,502
Cost of goods sold	$25,210	$25,273	$25,337	$25,400	$25,464	$301,371
Gross margin	66.00%	66.00%	66.00%	66.00%	66.00%	66.00%
Operating income	$49,030	$49,153	$49,277	$49,400	$49,524	$586,131
Expenses						
Payroll	$26,167	$26,167	$26,167	$26,167	$26,167	$314,000
General and administrative	$2,100	$2,100	$2,100	$2,100	$2,100	$25,200
Marketing expenses	$370	$370	$370	$370	$370	$4,438
Professional fees and licensure	$435	$435	$435	$435	$435	$5,219
Insurance costs	$999	$999	$999	$999	$999	$11,987
Travel and vehicle costs	$633	$633	$633	$633	$633	$7,596
Rent and utilities	$1,188	$1,188	$1,188	$1,188	$1,188	$14,250
Miscellaneous costs	$888	$888	$888	$888	$888	$10,650
Payroll taxes	$3,925	$3,925	$3,925	$3,925	$3,925	$47,100
Total operating costs	$36,703	$36,703	$36,703	$36,703	$36,703	$440,440
EBITDA	$12,326	$12,450	$12,573	$12,697	$12,820	$145,691
Federal income tax	$4,022	$4,032	$4,042	$4,052	$4,062	$48,078
State income tax	$609	$611	$612	$614	$615	$7,285
Interest expense	$1,445	$1,436	$1,428	$1,420	$1,411	$17,475
Depreciation expense	$908	$908	$908	$908	$908	$10,893
Net profit	$5,343	$5,463	$5,583	$5,703	$5,823	$61,960

Profit and loss statement (second year)

Quarter	Q1	2 Q2	Q3	Q4	2
Sales	$213,000	$266,251	$287,551	$298,201	$1,065,002
Cost of goods sold	$ 72,329	$ 90,411	$ 97,644	$101,261	$ 361,645
Gross margin	66.00%	66.00%	66.00%	66.00%	66.00%
Operating income	$140,671	$175,839	$189,906	$196,940	$ 703,357
Expenses					
Payroll	$ 74,984	$ 93,730	$101,228	$104,978	$ 374,920
General and administrative	$ 5,242	$ 6,552	$ 7,076	$ 7,338	$ 26,208
Marketing expenses	$ 1,065	$ 1,331	$ 1,438	$ 1,491	$ 5,325
Professional fees and licensure	$ 1,075	$ 1,344	$ 1,451	$ 1,505	$ 5,376
Insurance costs	$ 2,517	$ 3,147	$ 3,398	$ 3,524	$ 12,586
Travel and vehicle costs	$ 1,671	$ 2,089	$ 2,256	$ 2,340	$ 8,356
Rent and utilities	$ 2,993	$ 3,741	$ 4,040	$ 4,190	$ 14,963
Miscellaneous costs	$ 2,556	$ 3,195	$ 3,451	$ 3,578	$ 12,780
Payroll taxes	$ 11,248	$ 14,060	$ 15,184	$ 15,747	$ 56,238
Total operating costs	$103,350	$129,188	$139,523	$144,690	$ 516,751
EBITDA	$ 37,321	$ 46,652	$ 50,384	$ 52,250	$ 186,606
Federal income tax	$ 11,243	$ 14,053	$ 15,178	$ 15,740	$ 56,213
State income tax	$ 1,703	$ 2,129	$ 2,300	$ 2,385	$ 8,517
Interest expense	$ 4,184	$ 4,106	$ 4,027	$ 3,946	$ 16,263
Depreciation expense	$ 2,723	$ 2,723	$ 2,723	$ 2,723	$ 10,893
Net profit	$ 17,468	$ 23,640	$ 26,156	$ 27,456	$ 94,720

Profit and loss statement (third year)

Quarter	Q1	3 Q2	Q3	Q4	3
Sales	$249,211	$311,513	$336,434	$348,895	$1,246,053
Cost of goods sold	$ 84,625	$105,781	$114,244	$118,475	$ 423,125
Gross margin	66.00%	66.00%	66.00%	66.00%	66.00%
Operating income	$164,586	$205,732	$222,191	$230,420	$ 822,928
Expenses					
Payroll	$ 77,234	$ 96,542	$104,265	$108,127	$ 386,168
General and administrative	$ 5,451	$ 6,814	$ 7,359	$ 7,632	$ 27,256
Marketing expenses	$ 1,246	$ 1,558	$ 1,682	$ 1,744	$ 6,230
Professional fees and licensure	$ 1,107	$ 1,384	$ 1,495	$ 1,550	$ 5,537
Insurance costs	$ 2,643	$ 3,304	$ 3,568	$ 3,700	$ 13,216
Travel and vehicle costs	$ 1,838	$ 2,298	$ 2,482	$ 2,574	$ 9,191
Rent and utilities	$ 3,142	$ 3,928	$ 4,242	$ 4,399	$ 15,711
Miscellaneous costs	$ 2,991	$ 3,738	$ 4,037	$ 4,187	$ 14,953
Payroll taxes	$ 11,585	$ 14,481	$ 15,640	$ 16,219	$ 57,925
Total operating costs	$107,237	$134,047	$144,770	$150,132	$ 536,186
EBITDA	$ 57,348	$ 71,685	$ 77,420	$ 80,288	$ 286,742
Federal income tax	$ 17,939	$ 22,424	$ 24,218	$ 25,115	$ 89,696
State income tax	$ 2,718	$ 3,398	$ 3,669	$ 3,805	$ 13,590
Interest expense	$ 3,863	$ 3,778	$ 3,692	$ 3,603	$ 14,936
Depreciation expense	$ 2,723	$ 2,723	$ 2,723	$ 2,723	$ 10,893
Net profit	$ 30,105	$ 39,362	$ 43,118	$ 45,041	$ 157,626

7.11 Three Year Cash Flow Analysis

Cash flow analysis (first year)

Month	1	2	3	4	5	6	7
Cash from operations	$ 5,412	$ 5,532	$ 5,652	$ 5,771	$ 5,891	$ 6,011	$ 6,131
Cash from receivables	$ 0	$ 0	$ 0	$ 0	$ 0	$ 0	$ 0
Operating cash inflow	**$ 5,412**	**$ 5,532**	**$ 5,652**	**$ 5,771**	**$ 5,891**	**$ 6,011**	**$ 6,131**
Other cash inflows							
Equity investment	$ 50,000	$ 0	$ 0	$ 0	$ 0	$ 0	$ 0
Increased borrowings	$200,000	$ 0	$ 0	$ 0	$ 0	$ 0	$ 0
Sales of business assets	$ 0	$ 0	$ 0	$ 0	$ 0	$ 0	$ 0
A/P increases	$ 3,159	$ 3,159	$ 3,159	$ 3,159	$ 3,159	$ 3,159	$ 3,159
Total other cash inflows	**$253,159**	**$ 3,159**	**$ 3,159**	**$ 3,159**	**$ 3,159**	**$ 3,159**	**$ 3,159**
Total cash inflow	**$258,571**	**$ 8,690**	**$ 8,810**	**$ 8,930**	**$ 9,049**	**$ 9,169**	**$ 9,289**
Cash outflows							
Repayment of principal	$ 1,034	$ 1,041	$ 1,049	$ 1,057	$ 1,065	$ 1,073	$ 1,081
A/P decreases	$ 2,075	$ 2,075	$ 2,075	$ 2,075	$ 2,075	$ 2,075	$ 2,075
A/R increases	$ 0	$ 0	$ 0	$ 0	$ 0	$ 0	$ 0
Asset purchases	$152,500	$ 0	$ 0	$ 0	$ 0	$ 0	$ 0
Dividends	$ 0	$ 0	$ 0	$ 0	$ 0	$ 0	$ 0
Total cash outflows	**$155,608**	**$ 3,116**	**$ 3,124**	**$ 3,132**	**$ 3,140**	**$ 3,148**	**$ 3,156**
Net cash flow	**$102,963**	**$ 5,574**	**$ 5,686**	**$ 5,798**	**$ 5,910**	**$ 6,022**	**$ 6,134**
Cash balance	**$102,963**	**$108,537**	**$114,223**	**$120,021**	**$125,931**	**$131,953**	**$138,086**

Cash flow analysis (first year cont.)

Month	8	9	10	11	12	1
Cash from operations	$ 6,251	$ 6,371	$ 6,491	$ 6,611	$ 6,730	$ 72,853
Cash from receivables	$ 0	$ 0	$ 0	$ 0	$ 0	$ 0
Operating cash inflow	**$ 6,251**	**$ 6,371**	**$ 6,491**	**$ 6,611**	**$ 6,730**	**$ 72,853**
Other cash inflows						
Equity investment	$ 0	$ 0	$ 0	$ 0	$ 0	$ 50,000
Increased borrowings	$ 0	$ 0	$ 0	$ 0	$ 0	$200,000
Sales of business assets	$ 0	$ 0	$ 0	$ 0	$ 0	$ 0
A/P increases	$ 3,159	$ 3,159	$ 3,159	$ 3,159	$ 3,159	$ 37,902
Total other cash inflows	**$ 3,159**	**$ 3,159**	**$ 3,159**	**$ 3,159**	**$ 3,159**	**$287,902**
Total cash inflow	**$ 9,409**	**$ 9,529**	**$ 9,649**	**$ 9,769**	**$ 9,889**	**$360,755**
Cash outflows						
Repayment of principal	$ 1,089	$ 1,097	$ 1,105	$ 1,114	$ 1,122	$ 12,927
A/P decreases	$ 2,075	$ 2,075	$ 2,075	$ 2,075	$ 2,075	$ 24,897
A/R increases	$ 0	$ 0	$ 0	$ 0	$ 0	$ 0
Asset purchases	$ 0	$ 0	$ 0	$ 0	$ 0	$152,500
Dividends	$ 0	$ 0	$ 0	$ 0	$ 50,997	$ 50,997
Total cash outflows	**$ 3,164**	**$ 3,172**	**$ 3,180**	**$ 3,188**	**$ 54,194**	**$241,321**
Net cash flow	**$ 6,245**	**$ 6,357**	**$ 6,469**	**$ 6,581**	**−$ 44,305**	**$119,434**
Cash balance	**$144,332**	**$150,689**	**$157,158**	**$163,739**	**$119,434**	**$119,434**

Cash flow analysis (second year)

Quarter	Q1	2 Q2	Q3	Q4	2
Cash from operations	$ 21,123	$ 26,403	$ 28,515	$ 29,572	$105,613
Cash from receivables	$ 0	$ 0	$ 0	$ 0	$ 0
Operating cash inflow	**$ 21,123**	**$ 26,403**	**$ 28,515**	**$ 29,572**	**$105,613**
Other cash inflows					
Equity investment	$ 0	$ 0	$ 0	$ 0	$ 0
Increased borrowings	$ 0	$ 0	$ 0	$ 0	$ 0
Sales of business assets	$ 0	$ 0	$ 0	$ 0	$ 0
A/P increases	$ 8,717	$ 10,897	$ 11,769	$ 12,204	$ 43,587
Total other cash inflows	**$ 8,717**	**$ 10,897**	**$ 11,769**	**$ 12,204**	**$ 43,587**
Total cash inflow	**$ 29,840**	**$ 37,300**	**$ 40,284**	**$ 41,776**	**$149,200**
Cash outflows					
Repayment of principal	$ 3,417	$ 3,494	$ 3,574	$ 3,655	$ 14,139
A/P decreases	$ 5,975	$ 7,469	$ 8,067	$ 8,365	$ 29,876
A/R increases	$ 0	$ 0	$ 0	$ 0	$ 0
Asset purchases	$ 5,281	$ 6,601	$ 7,129	$ 7,393	$ 26,403
Dividends	$ 14,786	$ 18,482	$ 19,961	$ 20,700	$ 73,929
Total cash outflows	**$ 29,459**	**$ 36,047**	**$ 38,730**	**$ 40,113**	**$144,348**
Net cash flow	**$ 381**	**$ 1,254**	**$ 1,554**	**$ 1,663**	**$ 4,852**
Cash balance	**$119,816**	**$121,069**	**$122,623**	**$124,286**	**$124,286**

Cash flow analysis (third year)

Quarter	Q1	3 Q2	Q3	Q4	3
Cash from operations	$ 33,704	$ 42,130	$ 45,500	$ 47,185	$168,519
Cash from receivables	$ 0	$ 0	$ 0	$ 0	$ 0
Operating cash inflow	**$ 33,704**	**$ 42,130**	**$ 45,500**	**$ 47,185**	**$168,519**
Other cash inflows					
Equity investment	$ 0	$ 0	$ 0	$ 0	$ 0
Increased borrowings	$ 0	$ 0	$ 0	$ 0	$ 0
Sales of business assets	$ 0	$ 0	$ 0	$ 0	$ 0
A/P increases	$ 10,025	$ 12,531	$ 13,534	$ 14,035	$ 50,125
Total other cash inflows	**$ 10,025**	**$ 12,531**	**$ 13,534**	**$ 14,035**	**$ 50,125**
Total cash inflow	**$ 43,729**	**$ 54,661**	**$ 59,034**	**$ 61,221**	**$218,645**
Cash outflows					
Repayment of principal	$ 3,737	$ 3,822	$ 3,909	$ 3,997	$ 15,466
A/P decreases	$ 7,170	$ 8,963	$ 9,680	$ 10,038	$ 35,852
A/R increases	$ 0	$ 0	$ 0	$ 0	$ 0
Asset purchases	$ 8,426	$ 10,532	$ 11,375	$ 11,796	$ 42,130
Dividends	$ 23,593	$ 29,491	$ 31,850	$ 33,030	$117,963
Total cash outflows	**$ 42,926**	**$ 52,808**	**$ 56,814**	**$ 58,862**	**$211,411**
Net cash flow	**$ 803**	**$ 1,853**	**$ 2,220**	**$ 2,359**	**$ 7,234**
Cash balance	**$125,089**	**$126,942**	**$129,162**	**$131,520**	**$131,520**

BUSINESS PLAN TEMPLATE

USING THIS TEMPLATE

A business plan carefully spells out a company's projected course of action over a period of time, usually the first two to three years after the start-up. In addition, banks, lenders, and other investors examine the information and financial documentation before deciding whether or not to finance a new business venture. Therefore, a business plan is an essential tool in obtaining financing and should describe the business itself in detail as well as all important factors influencing the company, including the market, industry, competition, operations and management policies, problem solving strategies, financial resources and needs, and other vital information. The plan enables the business owner to anticipate costs, plan for difficulties, and take advantage of opportunities, as well as design and implement strategies that keep the company running as smoothly as possible.

This template has been provided as a model to help you construct your own business plan. Please keep in mind that there is no single acceptable format for a business plan, and that this template is in no way comprehensive, but serves as an example.

The business plans provided in this section are fictional and have been used by small business agencies as models for clients to use in compiling their own business plans.

GENERIC BUSINESS PLAN

Main headings included below are topics that should be covered in a comprehensive business plan. They include:

Business Summary

Purpose
Provides a brief overview of your business, succinctly highlighting the main ideas of your plan.

Includes

- Name and Type of Business
- Description of Product/Service
- Business History and Development
- Location
- Market
- Competition
- Management
- Financial Information
- Business Strengths and Weaknesses
- Business Growth

Table of Contents

Purpose
Organized in an Outline Format, the Table of Contents illustrates the selection and arrangement of information contained in your plan.

Includes

- Topic Headings and Subheadings
- Page Number References

Business History and Industry Outlook

Purpose

Examines the conception and subsequent development of your business within an industry specific context.

Includes

- Start-up Information
- Owner/Key Personnel Experience
- Location
- Development Problems and Solutions
- Investment/Funding Information
- Future Plans and Goals
- Market Trends and Statistics
- Major Competitors
- Product/Service Advantages
- National, Regional, and Local Economic Impact

Product/Service

Purpose

Introduces, defines, and details the product and/or service that inspired the information of your business.

Includes

- Unique Features
- Niche Served
- Market Comparison
- Stage of Product/Service Development
- Production
- Facilities, Equipment, and Labor
- Financial Requirements
- Product/Service Life Cycle
- Future Growth

Market Examination

Purpose

Assessment of product/service applications in relation to consumer buying cycles.

Includes

- Target Market
- Consumer Buying Habits
- Product/Service Applications
- Consumer Reactions
- Market Factors and Trends
- Penetration of the Market
- Market Share
- Research and Studies
- Cost
- Sales Volume and Goals

Competition

Purpose

Analysis of Competitors in the Marketplace.

Includes

- Competitor Information
- Product/Service Comparison
- Market Niche
- Product/Service Strengths and Weaknesses
- Future Product/Service Development

Marketing

Purpose

Identifies promotion and sales strategies for your product/service.

Includes

- Product/Service Sales Appeal
- Special and Unique Features
- Identification of Customers
- Sales and Marketing Staff
- Sales Cycles

- Type of Advertising/ Promotion
- Pricing
- Competition
- Customer Services

Operations

Purpose

Traces product/service development from production/inception to the market environment.

Includes

- Cost Effective Production Methods
- Facility
- Location

- Equipment
- Labor
- Future Expansion

Administration and Management

Purpose

Offers a statement of your management philosophy with an in-depth focus on processes and procedures.

Includes

- Management Philosophy
- Structure of Organization
- Reporting System
- Methods of Communication
- Employee Skills and Training

- Employee Needs and Compensation
- Work Environment
- Management Policies and Procedures
- Roles and Responsibilities

Key Personnel

Purpose

Describes the unique backgrounds of principle employees involved in business.

Includes

- Owner(s)/Employee Education and Experience
- Positions and Roles

- Benefits and Salary
- Duties and Responsibilities
- Objectives and Goals

Potential Problems and Solutions

Purpose

Discussion of problem solving strategies that change issues into opportunities.

Includes

- Risks
- Litigation
- Future Competition

- Economic Impact
- Problem Solving Skills

Financial Information

Purpose

Secures needed funding and assistance through worksheets and projections detailing financial plans, methods of repayment, and future growth opportunities.

Includes

- Financial Statements
- Bank Loans
- Methods of Repayment
- Tax Returns
- Start-up Costs
- Projected Income (3 years)
- Projected Cash Flow (3 Years)
- Projected Balance Statements (3 years)

Appendices

Purpose

Supporting documents used to enhance your business proposal.

Includes

- Photographs of product, equipment, facilities, etc.
- Copyright/Trademark Documents
- Legal Agreements
- Marketing Materials
- Research and or Studies
- Operation Schedules
- Organizational Charts
- Job Descriptions
- Resumes
- Additional Financial Documentation

Fictional Food Distributor

Commercial Foods, Inc.

3003 Avondale Ave.
Knoxville, TN 37920

This plan demonstrates how a partnership can have a positive impact on a new business. It demonstrates how two individuals can carve a niche in the specialty foods market by offering gourmet foods to upscale restaurants and fine hotels. This plan is fictional and has not been used to gain funding from a bank or other lending institution.

STATEMENT OF PURPOSE

Commercial Foods, Inc. seeks a loan of $75,000 to establish a new business. This sum, together with $5,000 equity investment by the principals, will be used as follows:

- Merchandise inventory $25,000

- Office fixture/equipment $12,000

- Warehouse equipment $14,000

- One delivery truck $10,000

- Working capital $39,000

- Total $100,000

DESCRIPTION OF THE BUSINESS

Commercial Foods, Inc. will be a distributor of specialty food service products to hotels and upscale restaurants in the geographical area of a 50 mile radius of Knoxville. Richard Roberts will direct the sales effort and John Williams will manage the warehouse operation and the office. One delivery truck will be used initially with a second truck added in the third year. We expect to begin operation of the business within 30 days after securing the requested financing.

MANAGEMENT

A. Richard Roberts is a native of Memphis, Tennessee. He is a graduate of Memphis State University with a Bachelor's degree from the School of Business. After graduation, he worked for a major manufacturer of specialty food service products as a detail sales person for five years, and, for the past three years, he has served as a product sales manager for this firm.

B. John Williams is a native of Nashville, Tennessee. He holds a B.S. Degree in Food Technology from the University of Tennessee. His career includes five years as a product development chemist in gourmet food products and five years as operations manager for a food service distributor.

Both men are healthy and energetic. Their backgrounds complement each other, which will ensure the success of Commercial Foods, Inc. They will set policies together and personnel decisions will be made jointly. Initial salaries for the owners will be $1,000 per month for the first few years. The spouses of both principals are successful in the business world and earn enough to support the families.

They have engaged the services of Foster Jones, CPA, and William Hale, Attorney, to assist them in an advisory capacity.

PERSONNEL

The firm will employ one delivery truck driver at a wage of $8.00 per hour. One office worker will be employed at $7.50 per hour. One part-time employee will be used in the office at $5.00 per hour. The driver will load and unload his own trucks. Mr. Williams will assist in the warehouse operation as needed to assist one stock person at $7.00 per hour. An additional delivery truck and driver will be added the third year.

LOCATION

The firm will lease a 20,000 square foot building at 3003 Avondale Ave., in Knoxville, which contains warehouse and office areas equipped with two-door truck docks. The annual rental is $9,000. The building was previously used as a food service warehouse and very little modification to the building will be required.

PRODUCTS AND SERVICES

The firm will offer specialty food service products such as soup bases, dessert mixes, sauce bases, pastry mixes, spices, and flavors, normally used by upscale restaurants and nice hotels. We are going after a niche in the market with high quality gourmet products. There is much less competition in this market than in standard run of the mill food service products. Through their work experiences, the principals have contacts with supply sources and with local chefs.

THE MARKET

We know from our market survey that there are over 200 hotels and upscale restaurants in the area we plan to serve. Customers will be attracted by a direct sales approach. We will offer samples of our products and product application data on use of our products in the finished prepared foods. We will cultivate the chefs in these establishments. The technical background of John Williams will be especially useful here.

COMPETITION

We find that we will be only distributor in the area offering a full line of gourmet food service products. Other foodservice distributors offer only a few such items in conjunction with their standard product line. Our survey shows that many of the chefs are ordering products from Atlanta and Memphis because of a lack of adequate local supply.

SUMMARY

Commercial Foods, Inc. will be established as a foodservice distributor of specialty food in Knoxville. The principals, with excellent experience in the industry, are seeking a $75,000 loan to establish the business. The principals are investing $25,000 as equity capital.

The business will be set up as an S Corporation with each principal owning 50% of the common stock in the corporation.

FICTIONAL HARDWARE STORE

OSHKOSH HARDWARE, Inc.

123 Main St.
Oshkosh, WI 54901

The following plan outlines how a small hardware store can survive competition from large discount chains by offering products and providing expert advice in the use of any product it sells. This plan is fictional and has not been used to gain funding from a bank or other lending institution.

EXECUTIVE SUMMARY

Oshkosh Hardware, Inc. is a new corporation that is going to establish a retail hardware store in a strip mall in Oshkosh, Wisconsin. The store will sell hardware of all kinds, quality tools, paint, and housewares. The business will make revenue and a profit by servicing its customers not only with needed hardware but also with expert advice in the use of any product it sells.

Oshkosh Hardware, Inc. will be operated by its sole shareholder, James Smith. The company will have a total of four employees. It will sell its products in the local market. Customers will buy our products because we will provide free advice on the use of all of our products and will also furnish a full refund warranty.

Oshkosh Hardware, Inc. will sell its products in the Oshkosh store staffed by three sales representatives. No additional employees will be needed to achieve its short and long range goals. The primary short range goal is to open the store by October 1, 1994. In order to achieve this goal a lease must be signed by July 1, 1994 and the complete inventory ordered by August 1, 1994.

Mr. James Smith will invest $30,000 in the business. In addition, the company will have to borrow $150,000 during the first year to cover the investment in inventory, accounts receivable, and furniture and equipment. The company will be profitable after six months of operation and should be able to start repayment of the loan in the second year.

THE BUSINESS

The business will sell hardware of all kinds, quality tools, paint, and housewares. We will purchase our products from three large wholesale buying groups.

In general our customers are homeowners who do their own repair and maintenance, hobbyists, and housewives. Our business is unique in that we will have a complete line of all hardware items and will be able to get special orders by overnight delivery. The business makes revenue and profits by servicing our customers not only with needed hardware but also with expert advice in the use of any product we sell. Our major costs for bringing our products to market are cost of merchandise of 36%, salaries of $45,000, and occupancy costs of $60,000.

Oshkosh Hardware, Inc.'s retail outlet will be located at 1524 Frontage Road, which is in a newly developed retail center of Oshkosh. Our location helps facilitate accessibility from all parts of town and reduces our delivery costs. The store will occupy 7500 square feet of space. The major equipment involved in our business is counters and shelving, a computer, a paint mixing machine, and a truck.

THE MARKET

Oshkosh Hardware, Inc. will operate in the local market. There are 15,000 potential customers in this market area. We have three competitors who control approximately 98% of the market at present. We feel we can capture 25% of the market within the next four years. Our major reason for believing this is that our staff is technically competent to advise our customers in the correct use of all products we sell.

After a careful market analysis, we have determined that approximately 60% of our customers are men and 40% are women. The percentage of customers that fall into the following age categories are:

Under 16: 0%
17-21: 5%
22-30: 30%
31-40: 30%
41-50: 20%
51-60: 10%
61-70: 5%
Over 70: 0%

The reasons our customers prefer our products is our complete knowledge of their use and our full refund warranty.

We get our information about what products our customers want by talking to existing customers. There seems to be an increasing demand for our product. The demand for our product is increasing in size based on the change in population characteristics.

SALES

At Oshkosh Hardware, Inc. we will employ three sales people and will not need any additional personnel to achieve our sales goals. These salespeople will need several years experience in home repair and power tool usage. We expect to attract 30% of our customers from newspaper ads, 5% of our customers from local directories, 5% of our customers from the yellow pages, 10% of our customers from family and friends, and 50% of our customers from current customers. The most cost effect source will be current customers. In general our industry is growing.

MANAGEMENT

We would evaluate the quality of our management staff as being excellent. Our manager is experienced and very motivated to achieve the various sales and quality assurance objectives we have set. We will use a management information system that produces key inventory, quality assurance, and sales data on a weekly basis. All data is compared to previously established goals for that week, and deviations are the primary focus of the management staff.

GOALS IMPLEMENTATION

The short term goals of our business are:

1. Open the store by October 1, 1994
2. Reach our breakeven point in two months
3. Have sales of $100,000 in the first six months

In order to achieve our first short term goal we must:

1. Sign the lease by July 1, 1994
2. Order a complete inventory by August 1, 1994

In order to achieve our second short term goal we must:

1. Advertise extensively in Sept. and Oct.
2. Keep expenses to a minimum

In order to achieve our third short term goal we must:

1. Promote power tool sales for the Christmas season
2. Keep good customer traffic in Jan. and Feb.

The long term goals for our business are:

1. Obtain sales volume of $600,000 in three years
2. Become the largest hardware dealer in the city
3. Open a second store in Fond du Lac

The most important thing we must do in order to achieve the long term goals for our business is to develop a highly profitable business with excellent cash flow.

FINANCE

Oshkosh Hardware, Inc. Faces some potential threats or risks to our business. They are discount house competition. We believe we can avoid or compensate for this by providing quality products complimented by quality advice on the use of every product we sell. The financial projections we have prepared are located at the end of this document.

JOB DESCRIPTION-GENERAL MANAGER

The General Manager of the business of the corporation will be the president of the corporation. He will be responsible for the complete operation of the retail hardware store which is owned by the corporation. A detailed description of his duties and responsibilities is as follows.

Sales

Train and supervise the three sales people. Develop programs to motivate and compensate these employees. Coordinate advertising and sales promotion effects to achieve sales totals as outlined in budget. Oversee purchasing function and inventory control procedures to insure adequate merchandise at all times at a reasonable cost.

Finance
Prepare monthly and annual budgets. Secure adequate line of credit from local banks. Supervise office personnel to insure timely preparation of records, statements, all government reports, control of receivables and payables, and monthly financial statements.

Administration
Perform duties as required in the areas of personnel, building leasing and maintenance, licenses and permits, and public relations.

Organizations, Agencies, & Consultants

A listing of Associations and Consultants of interest to entrepreneurs, followed by the ten Small Business Administration Regional Offices, Small Business Development Centers, Service Corps of Retired Executives offices, and Venture Capital and Finance Companies.

Associations

This section contains a listing of associations and other agencies of interest to the small business owner. Entries are listed alphabetically by organization name.

American Business Women's Association
9100 Ward Pkwy.
PO Box 8728
Kansas City, MO 64114-0728
(800)228-0007
E-mail: abwa@abwa.org
Website: http://www.abwa.org
Jeanne Banks, National President

American Franchisee Association
53 W Jackson Blvd., Ste. 1157
Chicago, IL 60604
(312)431-0545
E-mail: info@franchisee.org
Website: http://www.franchisee.org
Susan P. Kezios, President

American Independent Business Alliance
222 S Black Ave.
Bozeman, MT 59715
(406)582-1255
E-mail: info@amiba.net
Website: http://www.amiba.net
Jennifer Rockne, Director

American Small Businesses Association
206 E College St., Ste. 201
Grapevine, TX 76051
800-942-2722
E-mail: info@asbaonline.org
Website: http://www.asbaonline.org/

American Women's Economic Development Corporation
216 East 45th St., 10th Floor
New York, NY 10017
(917)368-6100

Fax: (212)986-7114
E-mail: info@awed.org
Website: http://www.awed.org
Roseanne Antonucci, Exec. Dir.

Association for Enterprise Opportunity
1601 N Kent St., Ste. 1101
Arlington, VA 22209
(703)841-7760
Fax: (703)841-7748
E-mail: aeo@assoceo.org
Website: http://www.micro enterpriseworks.org
Bill Edwards, Exec.Dir.

Association of Small Business Development Centers
c/o Don Wilson
8990 Burke Lake Rd.
Burke, VA 22015
(703)764-9850
Fax: (703)764-1234
E-mail: info@asbdc-us.org
Website: http://www.asbdc-us.org
Don Wilson, Pres./CEO

BEST Employers Association
2505 McCabe Way
Irvine, CA 92614
(949)253-4080
800-433-0088
Fax: (714)553-0883
E-mail: info@bestlife.com
Website: http://www.bestlife.com
Donald R. Lawrenz, CEO

Center for Family Business
PO Box 24219
Cleveland, OH 44124
(440)460-5409
E-mail: grummi@aol.com
Dr. Leon A. Danco, Chm.

Coalition for Government Procurement
1990 M St. NW, Ste. 400
Washington, DC 20036
(202)331-0975
E-mail: info@thecgp.org
Website: http://www.coalgovpro.org
Paul Caggiano, Pres.

Employers of America
PO Box 1874
Mason City, IA 50402-1874
(641)424-3187
800-728-3187
Fax: (641)424-1673
E-mail: employer@employerhelp.org
Website: http://www.employerhelp.org
Jim Collison, Pres.

Family Firm Institute
200 Lincoln St., Ste. 201
Boston, MA 02111
(617)482-3045
Fax: (617)482-3049
E-mail: ffi@ffi.org
Website: http://www.ffi.org
Judy L. Green, Ph.D., Exec.Dir.

Independent Visually Impaired Enterprisers
500 S 3rd St., Apt. H
Burbank, CA 91502
(818)238-9321
E-mail: abazyn@bazyn communications.com
http://www.acb.org/affiliates
Adris Bazyn, Pres.

International Association for Business Organizations
3 Woodthorn Ct., Ste. 12
Owings Mills, MD 21117
(410)581-1373
E-mail: nahbb@msn.com
Rudolph Lewis, Exec. Officer

International Council for Small Business
The George Washington University School of Business and Public Management
2115 G St. NW, Ste. 403
Washington, DC 20052
(202)994-0704
Fax: (202)994-4930
E-mail: icsb@gwu.edu
Website: http://www.icsb.org
Susan G. Duffy. Admin.

International Small Business Consortium
3309 Windjammer St.
Norman, OK 73072
E-mail: sb@isbc.com
Website: http://www.isbc.com

Kauffman Center for Entrepreneurial Leadership
4801 Rockhill Rd.
Kansas City, MO 64110-2046
(816)932-1000
E-mail: info@kauffman.org
Website: http://www.entreworld.org

National Alliance for Fair Competition
3 Bethesda Metro Center, Ste. 1100
Bethesda, MD 20814
(410)235-7116
Fax: (410)235-7116
E-mail: ampesq@aol.com
Tony Ponticelli, Exec.Dir.

National Association for the Self-Employed
PO Box 612067
DFW Airport
Dallas, TX 75261-2067
(800)232-6273
E-mail: mpetron@nase.org
Website: http://www.nase.org
Robert Hughes, Pres.

National Association of Business Leaders
4132 Shoreline Dr., Ste. J & H
Earth City, MO 63045
Fax: (314)298-9110
E-mail: nabl@nabl.com
Website: http://www.nabl.com/
Gene Blumenthal, Contact

National Association of Private Enterprise
PO Box 15550
Long Beach, CA 90815
888-224-0953

Fax: (714)844-4942
Website: http://www.napeonline.net
Laura Squiers, Exec.Dir.

National Association of Small Business Investment Companies
666 11th St. NW, Ste. 750
Washington, DC 20001
(202)628-5055
Fax: (202)628-5080
E-mail: nasbic@nasbic.org
Website: http://www.nasbic.org
Lee W. Mercer, Pres.

National Business Association
PO Box 700728
5151 Beltline Rd., Ste. 1150
Dallas, TX 75370
(972)458-0900
800-456-0440
Fax: (972)960-9149
E-mail: info@nationalbusiness.org
Website: http://www.national business.org
Raj Nisankarao, Pres.

National Business Owners Association
PO Box 111
Stuart, VA 24171
(276)251-7500
(866)251-7505
Fax: (276)251-2217
E-mail: membershipservices@nboa.org
Website: http://www.rvmdb.com.nboa
Paul LaBarr, Pres.

National Center for Fair Competition
PO Box 220
Annandale, VA 22003
(703)280-4622
Fax: (703)280-0942
E-mail: kentonp1@aol.com
Kenton Pattie, Pres.

National Family Business Council
1640 W. Kennedy Rd.
Lake Forest, IL 60045
(847)295-1040
Fax: (847)295-1898
E-mail: lmsnfbc@email.msn.com
Jogn E. Messervey, Pres.

National Federation of Independent Business
53 Century Blvd., Ste. 250
Nashville, TN 37214
(615)872-5800
800-NFIBNOW
Fax: (615)872-5353
Website: http://www.nfib.org
Jack Faris, Pres. and CEO

National Small Business Association
1156 15th St. NW, Ste. 1100
Washington, DC 20005
(202)293-8830
800-345-6728
Fax: (202)872-8543
E-mail: press@nsba.biz
Website: http://www.nsba.biz
Rob Yunich, Dir. of Communications

PUSH Commercial Division
930 E 50th St.
Chicago, IL 60615-2702
(773)373-3366
Fax: (773)373-3571
E-mail: info@rainbowpush.org
Website: http://www.rainbowpush.org
Rev. Willie T. Barrow, Co-Chm.

Research Institute for Small and Emerging Business
722 12th St. NW
Washington, DC 20005
(202)628-8382
Fax: (202)628-8392
E-mail: info@riseb.org
Website: http://www.riseb.org
Allan Neece, Jr., Chm.

Sales Professionals USA
PO Box 149
Arvada, CO 80001
(303)534-4937
888-736-7767
E-mail: salespro@salesprofessionals-usa.com
Website: http://www.salesprofessionals-usa.com
Sharon Herbert, Natl. Pres.

Score Association - Service Corps of Retired Executives
409 3rd St. SW, 6th Fl.
Washington, DC 20024
(202)205-6762
800-634-0245
Fax: (202)205-7636
E-mail: media@score.org
Website: http://www.score.org
W. Kenneth Yancey, Jr., CEO

Small Business and Entrepreneurship Council
1920 L St. NW, Ste. 200
Washington, DC 20036
(202)785-0238
Fax: (202)822-8118
E-mail: membership@sbec.org
Website: http://www.sbecouncil.org
Karen Kerrigan, Pres./CEO

Small Business in Telecommunications
1331 H St. NW, Ste. 500
Washington, DC 20005
(202)347-4511
Fax: (202)347-8607
E-mail: sbt@sbthome.org
Website: http://www.sbthome.org
Lonnie Danchik, Chm.

Small Business Legislative Council
1010 Massachusetts Ave. NW, Ste. 540
Washington, DC 20005
(202)639-8500
Fax: (202)296-5333
E-mail: email@sblc.org
Website: http://www.sblc.org
John Satagaj, Pres.

Small Business Service Bureau
554 Main St.
PO Box 15014
Worcester, MA 01615-0014
(508)756-3513
800-343-0939
Fax: (508)770-0528
E-mail: membership@sbsb.com
Website: http://www.sbsb.com
Francis R. Carroll, Pres.

Small Publishers Association
of North America
1618 W Colorado Ave.
Colorado Springs, CO 80904
(719)475-1726
Fax: (719)471-2182
E-mail: span@spannet.org
Website: http://www.spannet.org
Scott Flora, Exec. Dir.

SOHO America
PO Box 941
Hurst, TX 76053-0941
800-495-SOHO
E-mail: soho@1sas.com
Website: http://www.soho.org

Structured Employment Economic
Development Corporation
915 Broadway, 17th Fl.
New York, NY 10010
(212)473-0255
Fax: (212)473-0357
E-mail: info@seedco.org
Website: http://www.seedco.org
William Grinker, CEO

Support Services Alliance
107 Prospect St.
Schoharie, NY 12157
800-836-4772

E-mail: info@ssamembers.com
Website: http://www.ssainfo.com
Steve COle, Pres.

United States Association for Small
Business and Entrepreneurship
975 University Ave., No. 3260
Madison, WI 53706
(608)262-9982
Fax: (608)263-0818
E-mail: jgillman@wisc.edu
Website: http://www.ususbe.org
Joan Gillman, Exec. Dir.

Consultants

This section contains a listing of consultants specializing in small business development. It is arranged alphabetically by country, then by state or province, then by city, then by firm name.

Canada

Alberta

Common Sense Solutions
3405 16A Ave.
Edmonton, AB, Canada
(403)465-7330
Fax: (403)465-7380
E-mail: gcoulson@comsense
solutions.com
Website: http://www.comsense
solutions.com

Varsity Consulting Group
School of Business
University of Alberta
Edmonton, AB, Canada T6G 2R6
(780)492-2994
Fax: (780)492-5400
Website: http://www.bus.ualberta.ca/vcg

Viro Hospital Consulting
42 Commonwealth Bldg., 9912-106
St. NW
Edmonton, AB, Canada T5K 1C5
(403)425-3871
Fax: (403)425-3871
E-mail: rpb@freenet.edmonton.ab.ca

British Columbia

SRI Strategic Resources Inc.
4330 Kingsway, Ste. 1600
Burnaby, BC, Canada V5H 4G7
(604)435-0627
Fax: (604)435-2782

E-mail: inquiry@sri.bc.ca
Website: http://www.sri.com

Andrew R. De Boda Consulting
1523 Milford Ave.
Coquitlam, BC, Canada V3J 2V9
(604)936-4527
Fax: (604)936-4527
E-mail: deboda@intergate.bc.ca
Website: http://www.ourworld.
compuserve.com/homepages/deboda

The Sage Group Ltd.
980 - 355 Burrard St.
744 W Haistings, Ste. 410
Vancouver, BC, Canada V6C 1A5
(604)669-9269
Fax: (604)669-6622

Tikkanen-Bradley
1345 Nelson St., Ste. 202
Vancouver, BC, Canada V6E 1J8
(604)669-0583
E-mail: webmaster@tikkanen
bradley.com
Website: http://www.tikkanenbradley.com

Ontario

The Cynton Co.
17 Massey St.
Brampton, ON, Canada L6S 2V6
(905)792-7769
Fax: (905)792-8116
E-mail: cynton@home.com
Website: http://www.cynton.com

Begley & Associates
RR 6
Cambridge, ON, Canada N1R 5S7
(519)740-3629
Fax: (519)740-3629
E-mail: begley@in.on.ca
Website: http://www.in.on.ca/~begley/
index.htm

CRO Engineering Ltd.
1895 William Hodgins Ln.
Carp, ON, Canada K0A 1L0
(613)839-1108
Fax: (613)839-1406
E-mail: J.Grefford@ieee.ca
Website: http://www.geocities.com/
WallStreet/District/7401/

Task Enterprises
Box 69, RR 2 Hamilton
Flamborough, ON, Canada L8N 2Z7
(905)659-0153
Fax: (905)659-0861

HST Group Ltd.
430 Gilmour St.
Ottawa, ON, Canada K2P 0R8
(613)236-7303
Fax: (613)236-9893

Harrison Associates
BCE Pl.
181 Bay St., Ste. 3740
PO Box 798
Toronto, ON, Canada M5J 2T3
(416)364-5441
Fax: (416)364-2875

TCI Convergence Ltd. Management Consultants
99 Crown's Ln.
Toronto, ON, Canada M5R 3P4
(416)515-4146
Fax: (416)515-2097
E-mail: tci@inforamp.net
Website: http://tciconverge.com/index.1.html

Ken Wyman & Associates Inc.
64B Shuter St., Ste. 200
Toronto, ON, Canada M5B 1B1
(416)362-2926
Fax: (416)362-3039
E-mail: kenwyman@compuserve.com

JPL Business Consultants
82705 Metter Rd.
Wellandport, ON, Canada L0R 2J0
(905)386-7450
Fax: (905)386-7450
E-mail: plamarch@freenet.npiec.on.ca

Quebec

The Zimmar Consulting Partnership Inc.
Westmount
PO Box 98
Montreal, QC, Canada H3Z 2T1
(514)484-1459
Fax: (514)484-3063

Saskatchewan

Trimension Group
No. 104-110 Research Dr.
Innovation Place, SK, Canada S7N 3R3
(306)668-2560
Fax: (306)975-1156
E-mail: trimension@trimension.ca
Website: http://www.trimension.ca

Corporate Management Consultants
40 Government Road - PO Box 185
Prud Homme, SK, Canada, S0K 3K0
(306)654-4569
Fax: (650)618-2742

E-mail: cmccorporatemanagement@shaw.ca
Website: http://www.Corporate managementconsultants.com
Gerald Rekve

United States

Alabama

Business Planning Inc.
300 Office Park Dr.
Birmingham, AL 35223-2474
(205)870-7090
Fax: (205)870-7103

Tradebank of Eastern Alabama
546 Broad St., Ste. 3
Gadsden, AL 35901
(205)547-8700
Fax: (205)547-8718
E-mail: mansion@webex.com
Website: http://www.webex.com/~tea

Alaska

AK Business Development Center
3335 Arctic Blvd., Ste. 203
Anchorage, AK 99503
(907)562-0335
Free: 800-478-3474
Fax: (907)562-6988
E-mail: abdc@gci.net
Website: http://www.abdc.org

Business Matters
PO Box 287
Fairbanks, AK 99707
(907)452-5650

Arizona

Carefree Direct Marketing Corp.
8001 E Serene St.
PO Box 3737
Carefree, AZ 85377-3737
(480)488-4227
Fax: (480)488-2841

Trans Energy Corp.
1739 W 7th Ave.
Mesa, AZ 85202
(480)827-7915
Fax: (480)967-6601
E-mail: aha@clean-air.org
Website: http://www.clean-air.org

CMAS
5125 N 16th St.
Phoenix, AZ 85016

(602)395-1001
Fax: (602)604-8180

Comgate Telemanagement Ltd.
706 E Bell Rd., Ste. 105
Phoenix, AZ 85022
(602)485-5708
Fax: (602)485-5709
E-mail: comgate@netzone.com
Website: http://www.comgate.com

Moneysoft Inc.
1 E Camelback Rd. #550
Phoenix, AZ 85012
Free: 800-966-7797
E-mail: mbray@moneysoft.com

Harvey C. Skoog
PO Box 26439
Prescott Valley, AZ 86312
(520)772-1714
Fax: (520)772-2814

LMC Services
8711 E Pinnacle Peak Rd., No. 340
Scottsdale, AZ 85255-3555
(602)585-7177
Fax: (602)585-5880
E-mail: louws@earthlink.com

Sauerbrun Technology Group Ltd.
7979 E Princess Dr., Ste. 5
Scottsdale, AZ 85255-5878
(602)502-4950
Fax: (602)502-4292
E-mail: info@sauerbrun.com
Website: http://www.sauerbrun.com

Gary L. McLeod
PO Box 230
Sonoita, AZ 85637
Fax: (602)455-5661

Van Cleve Associates
6932 E 2nd St.
Tucson, AZ 85710
(520)296-2587
Fax: (520)296-3358

California

Acumen Group Inc.
(650)949-9349
Fax: (650)949-4845
E-mail: acumen-g@ix.netcom.com
Website: http://pw2.netcom.com/~janed/acumen.html

On-line Career and Management Consulting
420 Central Ave., No. 314
Alameda, CA 94501

(510)864-0336
Fax: (510)864-0336
E-mail: career@dnai.com
Website: http://www.dnai.com/~career

**Career Paths-Thomas E. Church
& Associates Inc.**
PO Box 2439
Aptos, CA 95001
(408)662-7950
Fax: (408)662-7955
E-mail: church@ix.netcom.com
Website: http://www.careerpaths-tom.com

Keck & Co. Business Consultants
410 Walsh Rd.
Atherton, CA 94027
(650)854-9588
Fax: (650)854-7240
E-mail: info@keckco.com
Website: http://www.keckco.com

Ben W. Laverty III, PhD, REA, CEI
4909 Stockdale Hwy., Ste. 132
Bakersfield, CA 93309
(661)283-8300
Free: 800-833-0373
Fax: (661)283-8313
E-mail: cstc@cstcsafety.com
Website: http://www.cstcsafety.com/cstc

**Lindquist Consultants-Venture
Planning**
225 Arlington Ave.
Berkeley, CA 94707
(510)524-6685
Fax: (510)527-6604

Larson Associates
PO Box 9005
Brea, CA 92822
(714)529-4121
Fax: (714)572-3606
E-mail: ray@consultlarson.com
Website: http://www.consultlarson.com

Kremer Management Consulting
PO Box 500
Carmel, CA 93921
(408)626-8311
Fax: (408)624-2663
E-mail: ddkremer@aol.com

W and J PARTNERSHIP
PO Box 2499
18876 Edwin Markham Dr.
Castro Valley, CA 94546
(510)583-7751
Fax: (510)583-7645
E-mail: wamorgan@wjpartnership.com
Website: http://www.wjpartnership.com

JB Associates
21118 Gardena Dr.
Cupertino, CA 95014
(408)257-0214
Fax: (408)257-0216
E-mail: semarang@sirius.com

House Agricultural Consultants
PO Box 1615
Davis, CA 95617-1615
(916)753-3361
Fax: (916)753-0464
E-mail: infoag@houseag.com
Website: http://www.houseag.com/

3C Systems Co.
16161 Ventura Blvd., Ste. 815
Encino, CA 91436
(818)907-1302
Fax: (818)907-1357
E-mail: mark@3CSysCo.com
Website: http://www.3CSysCo.com

**Technical Management
Consultants**
3624 Westfall Dr.
Encino, CA 91436-4154
(818)784-0626
Fax: (818)501-5575
E-mail: tmcrs@aol.com

**RAINWATER-GISH & Associates,
Business Finance & Development**
317 3rd St., Ste. 3
Eureka, CA 95501
(707)443-0030
Fax: (707)443-5683

Global Tradelinks
451 Pebble Beach Pl.
Fullerton, CA 92835
(714)441-2280
Fax: (714)441-2281
E-mail: info@globaltradelinks.com
Website: http://www.globaltradelinks.com

Strategic Business Group
800 Cienaga Dr.
Fullerton, CA 92835-1248
(714)449-1040
Fax: (714)525-1631

Burnes Consulting
20537 Wolf Creek Rd.
Grass Valley, CA 95949
(530)346-8188
Free: 800-949-9021
Fax: (530)346-7704
E-mail: kent@burnesconsulting.com
Website: http://www.burnesconsulting.com

Pioneer Business Consultants
9042 Garfield Ave., Ste. 312
Huntington Beach, CA 92646
(714)964-7600

Beblie, Brandt & Jacobs Inc.
16 Technology, Ste. 164
Irvine, CA 92618
(714)450-8790
Fax: (714)450-8799
E-mail: darcy@bbjinc.com
Website: http://198.147.90.26

Fluor Daniel Inc.
3353 Michelson Dr.
Irvine, CA 92612-0650
(949)975-2000
Fax: (949)975-5271
E-mail: sales.consulting@fluordaniel.com
Website: http://www.fluordaniel
consulting.com

MCS Associates
18300 Von Karman, Ste. 710
Irvine, CA 92612
(949)263-8700
Fax: (949)263-0770
E-mail: info@mcsassociates.com
Website: http://www.mcsassociates.com

Inspired Arts Inc.
4225 Executive Sq., Ste. 1160
La Jolla, CA 92037
(619)623-3525
Free: 800-851-4394
Fax: (619)623-3534
E-mail: info@inspiredarts.com
Website: http://www.inspiredarts.com

The Laresis Companies
PO Box 3284
La Jolla, CA 92038
(619)452-2720
Fax: (619)452-8744

RCL & Co.
PO Box 1143
737 Pearl St., Ste. 201
La Jolla, CA 92038
(619)454-8883
Fax: (619)454-8880

Comprehensive Business Services
3201 Lucas Cir.
Lafayette, CA 94549
(925)283-8272
Fax: (925)283-8272

The Ribble Group
27601 Forbes Rd., Ste. 52
Laguna Niguel, CA 92677

(714)582-1085
Fax: (714)582-6420
E-mail: ribble@deltanet.com

Norris Bernstein, CMC
9309 Marina Pacifica Dr. N
Long Beach, CA 90803
(562)493-5458
Fax: (562)493-5459
E-mail: norris@ctecomputer.com
Website: http://foodconsultants.com/
bernstein/

Horizon Consulting Services
1315 Garthwick Dr.
Los Altos, CA 94024
(415)967-0906
Fax: (415)967-0906

Brincko Associates Inc.
1801 Avenue of the Stars, Ste. 1054
Los Angeles, CA 90067
(310)553-4523
Fax: (310)553-6782

Rubenstein/Justman Management Consultants
2049 Century Park E, 24th Fl.
Los Angeles, CA 90067
(310)282-0800
Fax: (310)282-0400
E-mail: info@rjmc.net
Website: http://www.rjmc.net

F.J. Schroeder & Associates
1926 Westholme Ave.
Los Angeles, CA 90025
(310)470-2655
Fax: (310)470-6378
E-mail: fjsacons@aol.com
Website: http://www.mcninet.com/
GlobalLook/Fjschroe.html

Western Management Associates
5959 W Century Blvd., Ste. 565
Los Angeles, CA 90045-6506
(310)645-1091
Free: (888)788-6534
Fax: (310)645-1092
E-mail: gene@cfoforrent.com
Website: http://www.cfoforrent.com

Darrell Sell and Associates
Los Gatos, CA 95030
(408)354-7794
E-mail: darrell@netcom.com

Leslie J. Zambo
3355 Michael Dr.
Marina, CA 93933
(408)384-7086

Fax: (408)647-4199
E-mail: 104776.1552@compuserve.com

Marketing Services Management
PO Box 1377
Martinez, CA 94553
(510)370-8527
Fax: (510)370-8527
E-mail: markserve@biotechnet.com

William M. Shine Consulting Service
PO Box 127
Moraga, CA 94556-0127
(510)376-6516

Palo Alto Management Group Inc.
2672 Bayshore Pky., Ste. 701
Mountain View, CA 94043
(415)968-4374
Fax: (415)968-4245
E-mail: mburwen@pamg.com

BizplanSource
1048 Irvine Ave., Ste. 621
Newport Beach, CA 92660
Free: 888-253-0974
Fax: 800-859-8254
E-mail: info@bizplansource.com
Website: http://www.bizplansource.com
Adam Greengrass, President

The Market Connection
4020 Birch St., Ste. 203
Newport Beach, CA 92660
(714)731-6273
Fax: (714)833-0253

Muller Associates
PO Box 7264
Newport Beach, CA 92658
(714)646-1169
Fax: (714)646-1169

International Health Resources
PO Box 329
North San Juan, CA 95960-0329
(530)292-1266
Fax: (530)292-1243
Website: http://www.futureof
healthcare.com

NEXUS - Consultants to Management
PO Box 1531
Novato, CA 94948
(415)897-4400
Fax: (415)898-2252
E-mail: jimnexus@aol.com

Aerospcace.Org
PO Box 28831
Oakland, CA 94604-8831

(510)530-9169
Fax: (510)530-3411
Website: http://www.aerospace.org

Intelequest Corp.
722 Gailen Ave.
Palo Alto, CA 94303
(415)968-3443
Fax: (415)493-6954
E-mail: frits@iqix.com

McLaughlin & Associates
66 San Marino Cir.
Rancho Mirage, CA 92270
(760)321-2932
Fax: (760)328-2474
E-mail: jackmcla@msn.com

Carrera Consulting Group, a division of Maximus
2110 21st St., Ste. 400
Sacramento, CA 95818
(916)456-3300
Fax: (916)456-3306
E-mail: central@carreraconsulting.com
Website: http://www.carreraconsulting.com

Bay Area Tax Consultants and Bayhill Financial Consultants
1150 Bayhill Dr., Ste. 1150
San Bruno, CA 94066-3004
(415)952-8786
Fax: (415)588-4524
E-mail: baytax@compuserve.com
Website: http://www.baytax.com/

AdCon Services, LLC
8871 Hillery Dr.
Dan Diego, CA 92126
(858)433-1411
E-mail: adam@adconservices.com
Website: http://www.adconservices.com
Adam Greengrass

California Business Incubation Network
101 W Broadway, No. 480
San Diego, CA 92101
(619)237-0559
Fax: (619)237-0521

G.R. Gordetsky Consultants Inc.
11414 Windy Summit Pl.
San Diego, CA 92127
(619)487-4939
Fax: (619)487-5587
E-mail: gordet@pacbell.net

Freeman, Sullivan & Co.
131 Steuart St., Ste. 500
San Francisco, CA 94105
(415)777-0707

Free: 800-777-0737
Fax: (415)777-2420
Website: http://www.fsc-research.com

Ideas Unlimited
2151 California St., Ste. 7
San Francisco, CA 94115
(415)931-0641
Fax: (415)931-0880

Russell Miller Inc.
300 Montgomery St., Ste. 900
San Francisco, CA 94104
(415)956-7474
Fax: (415)398-0620
E-mail: rmi@pacbell.net
Website: http://www.rmisf.com

PKF Consulting
425 California St., Ste. 1650
San Francisco, CA 94104
(415)421-5378
Fax: (415)956-7708
E-mail: callahan@pkfc.com
Website: http://www.pkfonline.com

Welling & Woodard Inc.
1067 Broadway
San Francisco, CA 94133
(415)776-4500
Fax: (415)776-5067

Highland Associates
16174 Highland Dr.
San Jose, CA 95127
(408)272-7008
Fax: (408)272-4040

ORDIS Inc.
6815 Trinidad Dr.
San Jose, CA 95120-2056
(408)268-3321
Free: 800-446-7347
Fax: (408)268-3582
E-mail: ordis@ordis.com
Website: http://www.ordis.com

Stanford Resources Inc.
20 Great Oaks Blvd., Ste. 200
San Jose, CA 95119
(408)360-8400
Fax: (408)360-8410
E-mail: sales@stanfordsources.com
Website: http://www.stanfordresources.com

Technology Properties Ltd. Inc.
PO Box 20250
San Jose, CA 95160
(408)243-9898
Fax: (408)296-6637
E-mail: sanjose@tplnet.com

Helfert Associates
1777 Borel Pl., Ste. 508
San Mateo, CA 94402-3514
(650)377-0540
Fax: (650)377-0472

Mykytyn Consulting Group Inc.
185 N Redwood Dr., Ste. 200
San Rafael, CA 94903
(415)491-1770
Fax: (415)491-1251
E-mail: info@mcgi.com
Website: http://www.mcgi.com

Omega Management Systems Inc.
3 Mount Darwin Ct.
San Rafael, CA 94903-1109
(415)499-1300
Fax: (415)492-9490
E-mail: omegamgt@ix.netcom.com

The Information Group Inc.
4675 Stevens Creek Blvd., Ste. 100
Santa Clara, CA 95051
(408)985-7877
Fax: (408)985-2945
E-mail: dvincent@tig-usa.com
Website: http://www.tig-usa.com

Cast Management Consultants
1620 26th St., Ste. 2040N
Santa Monica, CA 90404
(310)828-7511
Fax: (310)453-6831

Cuma Consulting Management
Box 724
Santa Rosa, CA 95402
(707)785-2477
Fax: (707)785-2478

The E-Myth Academy
131B Stony Cir., Ste. 2000
Santa Rosa, CA 95401
(707)569-5600
Free: 800-221-0266
Fax: (707)569-5700
E-mail: info@e-myth.com
Website: http://www.e-myth.com

Reilly, Connors & Ray
1743 Canyon Rd.
Spring Valley, CA 91977
(619)698-4808
Fax: (619)460-3892
E-mail: davidray@adnc.com

Management Consultants
Sunnyvale, CA 94087-4700
(408)773-0321

RJR Associates
1639 Lewiston Dr.
Sunnyvale, CA 94087
(408)737-7720
E-mail: bobroy@rjrassoc.com
Website: http://www.rjrassoc.com

Schwafel Associates
333 Cobalt Way, Ste. 21
Sunnyvale, CA 94085
(408)720-0649
Fax: (408)720-1796
E-mail: schwafel@ricochet.net
Website: http://www.patca.org

Staubs Business Services
23320 S Vermont Ave.
Torrance, CA 90502-2940
(310)830-9128
Fax: (310)830-9128
E-mail: Harry_L_Staubs@Lamg.com

Out of Your Mind...and Into the Marketplace
13381 White Sands Dr.
Tustin, CA 92780-4565
(714)544-0248
Free: 800-419-1513
Fax: (714)730-1414
E-mail: lpinson@aol.com
Website: http://www.business-plan.com

Independent Research Services
PO Box 2426
Van Nuys, CA 91404-2426
(818)993-3622

Ingman Company Inc.
7949 Woodley Ave., Ste. 120
Van Nuys, CA 91406-1232
(818)375-5027
Fax: (818)894-5001

Innovative Technology Associates
3639 E Harbor Blvd., Ste. 203E
Ventura, CA 93001
(805)650-9353

Grid Technology Associates
20404 Tufts Cir.
Walnut, CA 91789
(909)444-0922
Fax: (909)444-0922
E-mail: grid_technology@msn.com

Ridge Consultants Inc.
100 Pringle Ave., Ste. 580
Walnut Creek, CA 94596
(925)274-1990
Fax: (510)274-1956
E-mail: info@ridgecon.com
Website: http://www.ridgecon.com

Bell Springs Publishing
PO Box 1240
Willits, CA 95490
(707)459-6372
E-mail: bellsprings@sabernet
Website: http://www.bellsprings.com

Hutchinson Consulting and Appraisal
23245 Sylvan St., Ste. 103
Woodland Hills, CA 91367
(818)888-8175
Free: 800-977-7548
Fax: (818)888-8220
E-mail: r.f.hutchinson-cpa@worldnet.
att.net

Colorado

Sam Boyer & Associates
4255 S Buckley Rd., No. 136
Aurora, CO 80013
Free: 800-785-0485
Fax: (303)766-8740
E-mail: samboyer@samboyer.com
Website: http://www.samboyer.com/

Ameriwest Business Consultants Inc.
PO Box 26266
Colorado Springs, CO 80936
(719)380-7096
Fax: (719)380-7096
E-mail: email@abchelp.com
Website: http://www.abchelp.com

GVNW Consulting Inc.
2270 La Montana Way
Colorado Springs, CO 80936
(719)594-5800
Fax: (719)594-5803
Website: http://www.gvnw.com

M-Squared Inc.
755 San Gabriel Pl.
Colorado Springs, CO 80906
(719)576-2554
Fax: (719)576-2554

Thornton Financial FNIC
1024 Centre Ave., Bldg. E
Fort Collins, CO 80526-1849
(970)221-2089
Fax: (970)484-5206

TenEyck Associates
1760 Cherryville Rd.
Greenwood Village, CO 80121-1503
(303)758-6129
Fax: (303)761-8286

Associated Enterprises Ltd.
13050 W Ceder Dr., Unit 11
Lakewood, CO 80228

(303)988-6695
Fax: (303)988-6739
E-mail: ael1@classic.msn.com

The Vincent Company Inc.
200 Union Blvd., Ste. 210
Lakewood, CO 80228
(303)989-7271
Free: 800-274-0733
Fax: (303)989-7570
E-mail: vincent@vincentco.com
Website: http://www.vincentco.com

Johnson & West Management Consultants Inc.
7612 S Logan Dr.
Littleton, CO 80122
(303)730-2810
Fax: (303)730-3219

Western Capital Holdings Inc.
10050 E Applwood Dr.
Parker, CO 80138
(303)841-1022
Fax: (303)770-1945

Connecticut

Stratman Group Inc.
40 Tower Ln.
Avon, CT 06001-4222
(860)677-2898
Free: 800-551-0499
Fax: (860)677-8210

Cowherd Consulting Group Inc.
106 Stephen Mather Rd.
Darien, CT 06820
(203)655-2150
Fax: (203)655-6427

Greenwich Associates
8 Greenwich Office Park
Greenwich, CT 06831-5149
(203)629-1200
Fax: (203)629-1229
E-mail: lisa@greenwich.com
Website: http://www.greenwich.com

Follow-up News
185 Pine St., Ste. 818
Manchester, CT 06040
(860)647-7542
Free: 800-708-0696
Fax: (860)646-6544
E-mail: Followupnews@aol.com

Lovins & Associates Consulting
309 Edwards St.
New Haven, CT 06511
(203)787-3367

Fax: (203)624-7599
E-mail: Alovinsphd@aol.com
Website: http://www.lovinsgroup.com

JC Ventures Inc.
4 Arnold St.
Old Greenwich, CT 06870-1203
(203)698-1990
Free: 800-698-1997
Fax: (203)698-2638

Charles L. Hornung Associates
52 Ned's Mountain Rd.
Ridgefield, CT 06877
(203)431-0297

Manus
100 Prospect St., S Tower
Stamford, CT 06901
(203)326-3880
Free: 800-445-0942
Fax: (203)326-3890
E-mail: manus1@aol.com
Website: http://www.RightManus.com

RealBusinessPlans.com
156 Westport Rd.
Wilton, CT 06897
(914)837-2886
E-mail: ct@realbusinessplans.com
Website: http://www.RealBusinessPlans.com
Tony Tecce

Delaware

Focus Marketing
61-7 Habor Dr.
Claymont, DE 19703
(302)793-3064

Daedalus Ventures Ltd.
PO Box 1474
Hockessin, DE 19707
(302)239-6758
Fax: (302)239-9991
E-mail: daedalus@mail.del.net

The Formula Group
PO Box 866
Hockessin, DE 19707
(302)456-0952
Fax: (302)456-1354
E-mail: formula@netaxs.com

Selden Enterprises Inc.
2502 Silverside Rd., Ste. 1
Wilmington, DE 19810-3740
(302)529-7113
Fax: (302)529-7442
E-mail: selden2@bellatlantic.net
Website: http://www.seldenenterprises.com

District of Columbia

Bruce W. McGee and Associates
7826 Eastern Ave. NW, Ste. 30
Washington, DC 20012
(202)726-7272
Fax: (202)726-2946

McManis Associates Inc.
1900 K St. NW, Ste. 700
Washington, DC 20006
(202)466-7680
Fax: (202)872-1898
Website: http://www.mcmanis-mmi.com

Smith, Dawson & Andrews Inc.
1000 Connecticut Ave., Ste. 302
Washington, DC 20036
(202)835-0740
Fax: (202)775-8526
E-mail: webmaster@sda-inc.com
Website: http://www.sda-inc.com

Florida

BackBone, Inc.
20404 Hacienda Court
Boca Raton, FL 33498
(561)470-0965
Fax: 516-908-4038
E-mail: BPlans@backboneinc.com
Website: http://www.backboneinc.com
Charles Epstein, President

Whalen & Associates Inc.
4255 Northwest 26 Ct.
Boca Raton, FL 33434
(561)241-5950
Fax: (561)241-7414
E-mail: drwhalen@ix.netcom.com

E.N. Rysso & Associates
180 Bermuda Petrel Ct.
Daytona Beach, FL 32119
(386)760-3028
E-mail: erysso@aol.com

Virtual Technocrats LLC
560 Lavers Circle, #146
Delray Beach, FL 33444
(561)265-3509
E-mail: josh@virtualtechnocrats.com;
info@virtualtechnocrats.com
Website: http://www.virtualtechno
crats.com
Josh Eikov, Managing Director

Eric Sands Consulting Services
6193 Rock Island Rd., Ste. 412
Fort Lauderdale, FL 33319
(954)721-4767

Fax: (954)720-2815
E-mail: easands@aol.com
Website: http://www.ericsandsconsultig.com

Professional Planning Associates, Inc.
1975 E. Sunrise Blvd. Suite 607
Fort Lauderdale, FL 33304
(954)764-5204
Fax: 954-463-4172
E-mail: Mgoldstein@proplana.com
Website: http://proplana.com
Michael Goldstein, President

Host Media Corp.
3948 S 3rd St., Ste. 191
Jacksonville Beach, FL 32250
(904)285-3239
Fax: (904)285-5618
E-mail: msconsulting@compuserve.com
Website: http://www.media
servicesgroup.com

William V. Hall
1925 Brickell, Ste. D-701
Miami, FL 33129
(305)856-9622
Fax: (305)856-4113
E-mail: williamvhall@compuserve.com

F.A. McGee Inc.
800 Claughton Island Dr., Ste. 401
Miami, FL 33131
(305)377-9123

Taxplan Inc.
Mirasol International Ctr.
2699 Collins Ave.
Miami Beach, FL 33140
(305)538-3303

T.C. Brown & Associates
8415 Excalibur Cir., Apt. B1
Naples, FL 34108
(941)594-1949
Fax: (941)594-0611
E-mail: tcater@naples.net.com

RLA International Consulting
713 Lagoon Dr.
North Palm Beach, FL 33408
(407)626-4258
Fax: (407)626-5772

Comprehensive Franchising Inc.
2465 Ridgecrest Ave.
Orange Park, FL 32065
(904)272-6567
Free: 800-321-6567
Fax: (904)272-6750
E-mail: theimp@cris.com
Website: http://www.franchise411.com

Hunter G. Jackson Jr. - Consulting Environmental Physicist
PO Box 618272
Orlando, FL 32861-8272
(407)295-4188
E-mail: hunterjackson@juno.com

F. Newton Parks
210 El Brillo Way
Palm Beach, FL 33480
(561)833-1727
Fax: (561)833-4541

Avery Business Development Services
2506 St. Michel Ct.
Ponte Vedra Beach, FL 32082
(904)285-6033
Fax: (904)285-6033

Strategic Business Planning Co.
PO Box 821006
South Florida, FL 33082-1006
(954)704-9100
Fax: (954)438-7333
E-mail: info@bizplan.com
Website: http://www.bizplan.com

Dufresne Consulting Group Inc.
10014 N Dale Mabry, Ste. 101
Tampa, FL 33618-4426
(813)264-4775
Fax: (813)264-9300
Website: http://www.dcgconsult.com

Agrippa Enterprises Inc.
PO Box 175
Venice, FL 34284-0175
(941)355-7876
E-mail: webservices@agrippa.com
Website: http://www.agrippa.com

Center for Simplified Strategic Planning Inc.
PO Box 3324
Vero Beach, FL 32964-3324
(561)231-3636
Fax: (561)231-1099
Website: http://www.cssp.com

Georgia

Marketing Spectrum Inc.
115 Perimeter Pl., Ste. 440
Atlanta, GA 30346
(770)395-7244
Fax: (770)393-4071

Business Ventures Corp.
1650 Oakbrook Dr., Ste. 405
Norcross, GA 30093
(770)729-8000
Fax: (770)729-8028

Informed Decisions Inc.
100 Falling Cheek
Sautee Nacoochee, GA 30571
(706)878-1905
Fax: (706)878-1802
E-mail: skylake@compuserve.com

Tom C. Davis & Associates, P.C.
3189 Perimeter Rd.
Valdosta, GA 31602
(912)247-9801
Fax: (912)244-7704
E-mail: mail@tcdcpa.com
Website: http://www.tcdcpa.com/

Illinois

TWD and Associates
431 S Patton
Arlington Heights, IL 60005
(847)398-6410
Fax: (847)255-5095
E-mail: tdoo@aol.com

Management Planning Associates Inc.
2275 Half Day Rd., Ste. 350
Bannockburn, IL 60015-1277
(847)945-2421
Fax: (847)945-2425

Phil Faris Associates
86 Old Mill Ct.
Barrington, IL 60010
(847)382-4888
Fax: (847)382-4890
E-mail: pfaris@meginsnet.net

Seven Continents Technology
787 Stonebridge
Buffalo Grove, IL 60089
(708)577-9653
Fax: (708)870-1220

Grubb & Blue Inc.
2404 Windsor Pl.
Champaign, IL 61820
(217)366-0052
Fax: (217)356-0117

ACE Accounting Service Inc.
3128 N Bernard St.
Chicago, IL 60618
(773)463-7854
Fax: (773)463-7854

AON Consulting Worldwide
200 E Randolph St., 10th Fl.
Chicago, IL 60601
(312)381-4800
Free: 800-438-6487
Fax: (312)381-0240
Website: http://www.aon.com

FMS Consultants
5801 N Sheridan Rd., Ste. 3D
Chicago, IL 60660
(773)561-7362
Fax: (773)561-6274

Grant Thornton
800 1 Prudential Plz.
130 E Randolph St.
Chicago, IL 60601
(312)856-0001
Fax: (312)861-1340
E-mail: gtinfo@gt.com
Website: http://www.grantthornton.com

Kingsbury International Ltd.
5341 N Glenwood Ave.
Chicago, IL 60640
(773)271-3030
Fax: (773)728-7080
E-mail: jetlag@mcs.com
Website: http://www.kingbiz.com

MacDougall & Blake Inc.
1414 N Wells St., Ste. 311
Chicago, IL 60610-1306
(312)587-3330
Fax: (312)587-3699
E-mail: jblake@compuserve.com

James C. Osburn Ltd.
6445 N. Western Ave., Ste. 304
Chicago, IL 60645
(773)262-4428
Fax: (773)262-6755
E-mail: osburnltd@aol.com

Tarifero & Tazewell Inc.
211 S Clark
Chicago, IL 60690
(312)665-9714
Fax: (312)665-9716

Human Energy Design Systems
620 Roosevelt Dr.
Edwardsville, IL 62025
(618)692-0258
Fax: (618)692-0819

China Business Consultants Group
931 Dakota Cir.
Naperville, IL 60563
(630)778-7992
Fax: (630)778-7915
E-mail: cbcq@aol.com

Center for Workforce Effectiveness
500 Skokie Blvd., Ste. 222
Northbrook, IL 60062
(847)559-8777
Fax: (847)559-8778

E-mail: office@cwelink.com
Website: http://www.cwelink.com

Smith Associates
1320 White Mountain Dr.
Northbrook, IL 60062
(847)480-7200
Fax: (847)480-9828

Francorp Inc.
20200 Governors Dr.
Olympia Fields, IL 60461
(708)481-2900
Free: 800-372-6244
Fax: (708)481-5885
E-mail: francorp@aol.com
Website: http://www.francorpinc.com

Camber Business Strategy Consultants
1010 S Plum Tree Ct
Palatine, IL 60078-0986
(847)202-0101
Fax: (847)705-7510
E-mail: camber@ameritech.net

Partec Enterprise Group
5202 Keith Dr.
Richton Park, IL 60471
(708)503-4047
Fax: (708)503-9468

Rockford Consulting Group Ltd.
Century Plz., Ste. 206
7210 E State St.
Rockford, IL 61108
(815)229-2900
Free: 800-667-7495
Fax: (815)229-2612
E-mail: rligus@RockfordConsulting.com
Website: http://www.Rockford
Consulting.com

RSM McGladrey Inc.
1699 E Woodfield Rd., Ste. 300
Schaumburg, IL 60173-4969
(847)413-6900
Fax: (847)517-7067
Website: http://www.rsmmcgladrey.com

A.D. Star Consulting
320 Euclid
Winnetka, IL 60093
(847)446-7827
Fax: (847)446-7827
E-mail: startwo@worldnet.att.net

Indiana

Modular Consultants Inc.
3109 Crabtree Ln.
Elkhart, IN 46514

(219)264-5761
Fax: (219)264-5761
E-mail: sasabo5313@aol.com

Midwest Marketing Research
PO Box 1077
Goshen, IN 46527
(219)533-0548
Fax: (219)533-0540
E-mail: 103365.654@compuserve

Ketchum Consulting Group
8021 Knue Rd., Ste. 112
Indianapolis, IN 46250
(317)845-5411
Fax: (317)842-9941

**MDI Management
Consulting**
1519 Park Dr.
Munster, IN 46321
(219)838-7909
Fax: (219)838-7909

Iowa

McCord Consulting Group Inc.
4533 Pine View Dr. NE
PO Box 11024
Cedar Rapids, IA 52410
(319)378-0077
Fax: (319)378-1577
E-mail: smmccord@hom.com
Website: http://www.mccordgroup.com

Management Solutions L.C.
3815 Lincoln Pl. Dr.
Des Moines, IA 50312
(515)277-6408
Fax: (515)277-3506
E-mail: wasunimers@uswest.net

Grandview Marketing
15 Red Bridge Dr.
Sioux City, IA 51104
(712)239-3122
Fax: (712)258-7578
E-mail: eandrews@pionet.net

Kansas

Assessments in Action
513A N Mur-Len
Olathe, KS 66062
(913)764-6270
Free: (888)548-1504
Fax: (913)764-6495
E-mail: lowdene@qni.com
Website: http://www.assessments-
in-action.com

Maine

Edgemont Enterprises
PO Box 8354
Portland, ME 04104
(207)871-8964
Fax: (207)871-8964

Pan Atlantic Consultants
5 Milk St.
Portland, ME 04101
(207)871-8622
Fax: (207)772-4842
E-mail: pmurphy@maine.rr.com
Website: http://www.panatlantic.net

Maryland

Clemons & Associates Inc.
5024-R Campbell Blvd.
Baltimore, MD 21236
(410)931-8100
Fax: (410)931-8111
E-mail: info@clemonsmgmt.com
Website: http://www.clemonsmgmt.com

Imperial Group Ltd.
305 Washington Ave., Ste. 204
Baltimore, MD 21204-6009
(410)337-8500
Fax: (410)337-7641

Leadership Institute
3831 Yolando Rd.
Baltimore, MD 21218
(410)366-9111
Fax: (410)243-8478
E-mail: behconsult@aol.com

Burdeshaw Associates Ltd.
4701 Sangamore Rd.
Bethesda, MD 20816-2508
(301)229-5800
Fax: (301)229-5045
E-mail: jstacy@burdeshaw.com
Website: http://www.burdeshaw.com

Michael E. Cohen
5225 Pooks Hill Rd., Ste. 1119 S
Bethesda, MD 20814
(301)530-5738
Fax: (301)530-2988
E-mail: mecohen@crosslink.net

World Development Group Inc.
5272 River Rd., Ste. 650
Bethesda, MD 20816-1405
(301)652-1818
Fax: (301)652-1250
E-mail: wdg@has.com
Website: http://www.worlddg.com

Swartz Consulting
PO Box 4301
Crofton, MD 21114-4301
(301)262-6728

Software Solutions International Inc.
9633 Duffer Way
Gaithersburg, MD 20886
(301)330-4136
Fax: (301)330-4136

Strategies Inc.
8 Park Center Ct., Ste. 200
Owings Mills, MD 21117
(410)363-6669
Fax: (410)363-1231
E-mail: strategies@strat1.com
Website: http://www.strat1.com

Hammer Marketing Resources
179 Inverness Rd.
Severna Park, MD 21146
(410)544-9191
Fax: (305)675-3277
E-mail: info@gohammer.com
Website: http://www.gohammer.com

Andrew Sussman & Associates
13731 Kretsinger
Smithsburg, MD 21783
(301)824-2943
Fax: (301)824-2943

Massachusetts

Geibel Marketing and Public Relations
PO Box 611
Belmont, MA 02478-0005
(617)484-8285
Fax: (617)489-3567
E-mail: jgeibel@geibelpr.com
Website: http://www.geibelpr.com

Bain & Co.
2 Copley Pl.
Boston, MA 02116
(617)572-2000
Fax: (617)572-2427
E-mail: corporate.inquiries@bain.com
Website: http://www.bain.com

Mehr & Co.
62 Kinnaird St.
Cambridge, MA 02139
(617)876-3311
Fax: (617)876-3023
E-mail: mehrco@aol.com

Monitor Company Inc.
2 Canal Park
Cambridge, MA 02141

(617)252-2000
Fax: (617)252-2100
Website: http://www.monitor.com

Information & Research Associates
PO Box 3121
Framingham, MA 01701
(508)788-0784

Walden Consultants Ltd.
252 Pond St.
Hopkinton, MA 01748
(508)435-4882
Fax: (508)435-3971
Website: http://www.waldencon
sultants.com

Jeffrey D. Marshall
102 Mitchell Rd.
Ipswich, MA 01938-1219
(508)356-1113
Fax: (508)356-2989

Consulting Resources Corp.
6 Northbrook Park
Lexington, MA 02420
(781)863-1222
Fax: (781)863-1441
E-mail: res@consultingresources.net
Website: http://www.consulting
resources.net

Planning Technologies Group L.L.C.
92 Hayden Ave.
Lexington, MA 02421
(781)778-4678
Fax: (781)861-1099
E-mail: ptg@plantech.com
Website: http://www.plantech.com

Kalba International Inc.
23 Sandy Pond Rd.
Lincoln, MA 01773
(781)259-9589
Fax: (781)259-1460
E-mail: info@kalbainternational.com
Website: http://www.kalbainter
national.com

VMB Associates Inc.
115 Ashland St.
Melrose, MA 02176
(781)665-0623
Fax: (425)732-7142
E-mail: vmbinc@aol.com

The Company Doctor
14 Pudding Stone Ln.
Mendon, MA 01756
(508)478-1747
Fax: (508)478-0520

Data and Strategies Group Inc.
190 N Main St.
Natick, MA 01760
(508)653-9990
Fax: (508)653-7799
E-mail: dsginc@dsggroup.com
Website: http://www.dsggroup.com

The Enterprise Group
73 Parker Rd.
Needham, MA 02494
(617)444-6631
Fax: (617)433-9991
E-mail: lsacco@world.std.com
Website: http://www.enterprise-group.com

PSMJ Resources Inc.
10 Midland Ave.
Newton, MA 02458
(617)965-0055
Free: 800-537-7765
Fax: (617)965-5152
E-mail: psmj@tiac.net
Website: http://www.psmj.com

Scheur Management Group Inc.
255 Washington St., Ste. 100
Newton, MA 02458-1611
(617)969-7500
Fax: (617)969-7508
E-mail: smgnow@scheur.com
Website: http://www.scheur.com

I.E.E.E., Boston Section
240 Bear Hill Rd., 202B
Waltham, MA 02451-1017
(781)890-5294
Fax: (781)890-5290

Business Planning and Consulting Services
20 Beechwood Ter.
Wellesley, MA 02482
(617)237-9151
Fax: (617)237-9151

Michigan

Walter Frederick Consulting
1719 South Blvd.
Ann Arbor, MI 48104
(313)662-4336
Fax: (313)769-7505

Fox Enterprises
6220 W Freeland Rd.
Freeland, MI 48623
(517)695-9170
Fax: (517)695-9174
E-mail: foxjw@concentric.net
Website: http://www.cris.com/~foxjw

G.G.W. and Associates
1213 Hampton
Jackson, MI 49203
(517)782-2255
Fax: (517)782-2255

Altamar Group Ltd.
6810 S Cedar, Ste. 2-B
Lansing, MI 48911
(517)694-0910
Free: 800-443-2627
Fax: (517)694-1377

Sheffieck Consultants Inc.
23610 Greening Dr.
Novi, MI 48375-3130
(248)347-3545
Fax: (248)347-3530
E-mail: cfsheff@concentric.net

Rehmann, Robson PC
5800 Gratiot
Saginaw, MI 48605
(517)799-9580
Fax: (517)799-0227
Website: http://www.rrpc.com

Francis & Co.
17200 W 10 Mile Rd., Ste. 207
Southfield, MI 48075
(248)559-7600
Fax: (248)559-5249

Private Ventures Inc.
16000 W 9 Mile Rd., Ste. 504
Southfield, MI 48075
(248)569-1977
Free: 800-448-7614
Fax: (248)569-1838
E-mail: pventuresi@aol.com

JGK Associates
14464 Kerner Dr.
Sterling Heights, MI 48313
(810)247-9055
Fax: (248)822-4977
E-mail: kozlowski@home.com

Minnesota

Health Fitness Corp.
3500 W 80th St., Ste. 130
Bloomington, MN 55431
(612)831-6830
Fax: (612)831-7264

Consatech Inc.
PO Box 1047
Burnsville, MN 55337
(612)953-1088
Fax: (612)435-2966

Robert F. Knotek
14960 Ironwood Ct.
Eden Prairie, MN 55346
(612)949-2875

DRI Consulting
7715 Stonewood Ct.
Edina, MN 55439
(612)941-9656
Fax: (612)941-2693
E-mail: dric@dric.com
Website: http://www.dric.com

Markin Consulting
12072 87th Pl. N
Maple Grove, MN 55369
(612)493-3568
Fax: (612)493-5744
E-mail: markin@markinconsulting.com
Website: http://www.markin
consulting.com

Minnesota Cooperation Office for Small Business & Job Creation Inc.
5001 W 80th St., Ste. 825
Minneapolis, MN 55437
(612)830-1230
Fax: (612)830-1232
E-mail: mncoop@msn.com
Website: http://www.mnco.org

Enterprise Consulting Inc.
PO Box 1111
Minnetonka, MN 55345
(612)949-5909
Fax: (612)906-3965

Amdahl International
724 1st Ave. SW
Rochester, MN 55902
(507)252-0402
Fax: (507)252-0402
E-mail: amdahl@best-service.com
Website: http://www.wp.com/amdahl_int

Power Systems Research
1365 Corporate Center Curve, 2nd Fl.
St. Paul, MN 55121
(612)905-8400
Free: (888)625-8612
Fax: (612)454-0760
E-mail: Barb@Powersys.com
Website: http://www.powersys.com

Missouri

Business Planning and Development Corp.
4030 Charlotte St.
Kansas City, MO 64110
(816)753-0495

E-mail: humph@bpdev.demon.co.uk
Website: http://www.bpdev.demon.co.uk

CFO Service
10336 Donoho
St. Louis, MO 63131
(314)750-2940
E-mail: jskae@cfoservice.com
Website: http://www.cfoservice.com

Nebraska

International Management Consulting Group Inc.
1309 Harlan Dr., Ste. 205
Bellevue, NE 68005
(402)291-4545
Free: 800-665-IMCG
Fax: (402)291-4343
E-mail: imcg@neonramp.com
Website: http://www.mgtcon
sulting.com

Heartland Management Consulting Group
1904 Barrington Pky.
Papillion, NE 68046
(402)339-2387
Fax: (402)339-1319

Nevada

The DuBois Group
865 Tahoe Blvd., Ste. 108
Incline Village, NV 89451
(775)832-0550
Free: 800-375-2935
Fax: (775)832-0556
E-mail: DuBoisGrp@aol.com

New Hampshire

Wolff Consultants
10 Buck Rd.
Hanover, NH 03755
(603)643-6015

BPT Consulting Associates Ltd.
12 Parmenter Rd., Ste. B-6
Londonderry, NH 03053
(603)437-8484
Free: (888)278-0030
Fax: (603)434-5388
E-mail: bptcons@tiac.net
Website: http://www.bptconsulting.com

New Jersey

Bedminster Group Inc.
1170 Rte. 22 E
Bridgewater, NJ 08807

(908)500-4155
Fax: (908)766-0780
E-mail: info@bedminstergroup.com
Website: http://www.bedminster
group.com
Fax: (202)806-1777
Terry Strong, Acting Regional Dir.

Delta Planning Inc.
PO Box 425
Denville, NJ 07834
(913)625-1742
Free: 800-672-0762
Fax: (973)625-3531
E-mail: DeltaP@worldnet.att.net
Website: http://deltaplanning.com

Kumar Associates Inc.
1004 Cumbermeade Rd.
Fort Lee, NJ 07024
(201)224-9480
Fax: (201)585-2343
E-mail: mail@kumarassociates.com
Website: http://kumarassociates.com

John Hall & Company Inc.
PO Box 187
Glen Ridge, NJ 07028
(973)680-4449
Fax: (973)680-4581
E-mail: jhcompany@aol.com

Market Focus
PO Box 402
Maplewood, NJ 07040
(973)378-2470
Fax: (973)378-2470
E-mail: mcss66@marketfocus.com

Vanguard Communications Corp.
100 American Rd.
Morris Plains, NJ 07950
(973)605-8000
Fax: (973)605-8329
Website: http://www.vanguard.net/

ConMar International Ltd.
1901 US Hwy. 130
North Brunswick, NJ 08902
(732)940-8347
Fax: (732)274-1199

KLW New Products
156 Cedar Dr.
Old Tappan, NJ 07675
(201)358-1300
Fax: (201)664-2594
E-mail: lrlarsen@usa.net
Website: http://www.klwnew
products.com

PA Consulting Group
315A Enterprise Dr.
Plainsboro, NJ 08536
(609)936-8300
Fax: (609)936-8811
E-mail: info@paconsulting.com
Website: http://www.pa-consulting.com

Aurora Marketing Management Inc.
66 Witherspoon St., Ste. 600
Princeton, NJ 08542
(908)904-1125
Fax: (908)359-1108
E-mail: aurora2@voicenet.com
Website: http://www.auroramarketing.net

Smart Business Supersite
88 Orchard Rd., CN-5219
Princeton, NJ 08543
(908)321-1924
Fax: (908)321-5156
E-mail: irv@smartbiz.com
Website: http://www.smartbiz.com

Tracelin Associates
1171 Main St., Ste. 6K
Rahway, NJ 07065
(732)381-3288

Schkeeper Inc.
130-6 Bodman Pl.
Red Bank, NJ 07701
(732)219-1965
Fax: (732)530-3703

Henry Branch Associates
2502 Harmon Cove Twr.
Secaucus, NJ 07094
(201)866-2008
Fax: (201)601-0101
E-mail: hbranch161@home.com

Robert Gibbons & Company Inc.
46 Knoll Rd.
Tenafly, NJ 07670-1050
(201)871-3933
Fax: (201)871-2173
E-mail: crisisbob@aol.com

PMC Management Consultants Inc.
6 Thistle Ln.
Three Bridges, NJ 08887-0332
(908)788-1014
Free: 800-PMC-0250
Fax: (908)806-7287
E-mail: int@pmc-management.com
Website: http://www.pmc-management.com

R.W. Bankart & Associates
20 Valley Ave., Ste. D-2
Westwood, NJ 07675-3607
(201)664-7672

New Mexico

Vondle & Associates Inc.
4926 Calle de Tierra, NE
Albuquerque, NM 87111
(505)292-8961
Fax: (505)296-2790
E-mail: vondle@aol.com

InfoNewMexico
2207 Black Hills Rd., NE
Rio Rancho, NM 87124
(505)891-2462
Fax: (505)896-8971

New York

Powers Research and Training Institute
PO Box 78
Bayville, NY 11709
(516)628-2250
Fax: (516)628-2252
E-mail: powercocch@compuserve.com
Website: http://www.nancypowers.com

Consortium House
296 Wittenberg Rd.
Bearsville, NY 12409
(845)679-8867
Fax: (845)679-9248
E-mail: eugenegs@aol.com
Website: http://www.chpub.com

Progressive Finance Corp.
3549 Tiemann Ave.
Bronx, NY 10469
(718)405-9029
Free: 800-225-8381
Fax: (718)405-1170

Wave Hill Associates Inc.
2621 Palisade Ave., Ste. 15-C
Bronx, NY 10463
(718)549-7368
Fax: (718)601-9670
E-mail: pepper@compuserve.com

Management Insight
96 Arlington Rd.
Buffalo, NY 14221
(716)631-3319
Fax: (716)631-0203
E-mail: michalski@foodservice
insight.com
Website: http://www.foodservice
insight.com

Samani International Enterprises, Marions Panyaught Consultancy
2028 Parsons
Flushing, NY 11357-3436
(917)287-8087
Fax: 800-873-8939
E-mail: vjp2@biostrategist.com
Website: http://www.biostrategist.com

Marketing Resources Group
71-58 Austin St.
Forest Hills, NY 11375
(718)261-8882

Mangabay Business Plans & Development Subsidiary of Innis Asset Allocation
125-10 Queens Blvd., Ste. 2202
Kew Gardens, NY 11415
(905)527-1947
Fax: 509-472-1935
E-mail: mangabay@mangabay.com
Website: http://www.mangabay.com
Lee Toh, Managing Partner

ComputerEase Co.
1301 Monmouth Ave.
Lakewood, NY 08701
(212)406-9464
Fax: (914)277-5317
E-mail: crawfordc@juno.com

Boice Dunham Group
30 W 13th St.
New York, NY 10011
(212)924-2200
Fax: (212)924-1108

Elizabeth Capen
27 E 95th St.
New York, NY 10128
(212)427-7654
Fax: (212)876-3190

Haver Analytics
60 E 42nd St., Ste. 2424
New York, NY 10017
(212)986-9300
Fax: (212)986-5857
E-mail: data@haver.com
Website: http://www.haver.com

The Jordan, Edmiston Group Inc.
150 E 52nd Ave., 18th Fl.
New York, NY 10022
(212)754-0710
Fax: (212)754-0337

KPMG International
345 Park Ave.
New York, NY 10154-0102
(212)758-9700

Fax: (212)758-9819
Website: http://www.kpmg.com

Mahoney Cohen Consulting Corp.
111 W 40th St., 12th Fl.
New York, NY 10018
(212)490-8000
Fax: (212)790-5913

Management Practice Inc.
342 Madison Ave.
New York, NY 10173-1230
(212)867-7948
Fax: (212)972-5188
Website: http://www.mpiweb.com

Moseley Associates Inc.
342 Madison Ave., Ste. 1414
New York, NY 10016
(212)213-6673
Fax: (212)687-1520

Practice Development Counsel
60 Sutton Pl. S
New York, NY 10022
(212)593-1549
Fax: (212)980-7940
E-mail: pwhaserot@pdcounsel.com
Website: http://www.pdcounsel.com

Unique Value International Inc.
575 Madison Ave., 10th Fl.
New York, NY 10022-1304
(212)605-0590
Fax: (212)605-0589

The Van Tulleken Co.
126 E 56th St.
New York, NY 10022
(212)355-1390
Fax: (212)755-3061
E-mail: newyork@vantulleken.com

Vencon Management Inc.
301 W 53rd St.
New York, NY 10019
(212)581-8787
Fax: (212)397-4126
Website: http://www.venconinc.com

Werner International Inc.
55 E 52nd, 29th Fl.
New York, NY 10055
(212)909-1260
Fax: (212)909-1273
E-mail: richard.downing@rgh.com
Website: http://www.wernertex.com

Zimmerman Business Consulting Inc.
44 E 92nd St., Ste. 5-B
New York, NY 10128

(212)860-3107
Fax: (212)860-7730
E-mail: ljzzbci@aol.com
Website: http://www.zbcinc.com

Overton Financial
7 Allen Rd.
Peekskill, NY 10566
(914)737-4649
Fax: (914)737-4696

Stromberg Consulting
2500 Westchester Ave.
Purchase, NY 10577
(914)251-1515
Fax: (914)251-1562
E-mail: strategy@stromberg_consul
ting.com
Website: http://www.stromberg_
consulting.com

Innovation Management Consulting Inc.
209 Dewitt Rd.
Syracuse, NY 13214-2006
(315)425-5144
Fax: (315)445-8989
E-mail: missonneb@axess.net

M. Clifford Agress
891 Fulton St.
Valley Stream, NY 11580
(516)825-8955
Fax: (516)825-8955

Destiny Kinal Marketing Consultancy
105 Chemung St.
Waverly, NY 14892
(607)565-8317
Fax: (607)565-4083

Valutis Consulting Inc.
5350 Main St., Ste. 7
Williamsville, NY 14221-5338
(716)634-2553
Fax: (716)634-2554
E-mail: valutis@localnet.com
Website: http://www.valutisconsulting.com

North Carolina

Best Practices L.L.C.
6320 Quadrangle Dr., Ste. 200
Chapel Hill, NC 27514
(919)403-0251
Fax: (919)403-0144
E-mail: best@best:in/class
Website: http://www.best-in-class.com

Norelli & Co.
Bank of America Corporate Ctr.
100 N Tyron St., Ste. 5160

Charlotte, NC 28202-4000
(704)376-5484
Fax: (704)376-5485
E-mail: consult@norelli.com
Website: http://www.norelli.com

North Dakota

Center for Innovation
4300 Dartmouth Dr.
PO Box 8372
Grand Forks, ND 58202
(701)777-3132
Fax: (701)777-2339
E-mail: bruce@innovators.net
Website: http://www.innovators.net

Ohio

Transportation Technology Services
208 Harmon Rd.
Aurora, OH 44202
(330)562-3596

Empro Systems Inc.
4777 Red Bank Expy., Ste. 1
Cincinnati, OH 45227-1542
(513)271-2042
Fax: (513)271-2042

Alliance Management International Ltd.
1440 Windrow Ln.
Cleveland, OH 44147-3200
(440)838-1922
Fax: (440)838-0979
E-mail: bgruss@amiltd.com
Website: http://www.amiltd.com

Bozell Kamstra Public Relations
1301 E 9th St., Ste. 3400
Cleveland, OH 44114
(216)623-1511
Fax: (216)623-1501
E-mail: jfeniger@cleveland.bozellk
amstra.com
Website: http://www.bozellk
amstra.com

Cory Dillon Associates
111 Schreyer Pl. E
Columbus, OH 43214
(614)262-8211
Fax: (614)262-3806

Holcomb Gallagher Adams
300 Marconi, Ste. 303
Columbus, OH 43215
(614)221-3343
Fax: (614)221-3367
E-mail: riadams@acme.freenet.oh.us

Young & Associates
PO Box 711
Kent, OH 44240
(330)678-0524
Free: 800-525-9775
Fax: (330)678-6219
E-mail: online@younginc.com
Website: http://www.younginc.com

Robert A. Westman & Associates
8981 Inversary Dr. SE
Warren, OH 44484-2551
(330)856-4149
Fax: (330)856-2564

Oklahoma

Innovative Partners L.L.C.
4900 Richmond Sq., Ste. 100
Oklahoma City, OK 73118
(405)840-0033
Fax: (405)843-8359
E-mail: ipartners@juno.com

Oregon

INTERCON - The International Converting Institute
5200 Badger Rd.
Crooked River Ranch, OR 97760
(541)548-1447
Fax: (541)548-1618
E-mail: johnbowler@
crookedriverranch.com

Talbott ARM
HC 60, Box 5620
Lakeview, OR 97630
(541)635-8587
Fax: (503)947-3482

Management Technology Associates Ltd.
2768 SW Sherwood Dr, Ste. 105
Portland, OR 97201-2251
(503)224-5220
Fax: (503)224-5334
E-mail: lcuster@mta-ltd.com
Website: http://www.mgmt-tech.com

Pennsylvania

Healthscope Inc.
400 Lancaster Ave.
Devon, PA 19333
(610)687-6199
Fax: (610)687-6376
E-mail: health@voicenet.com
Website: http://www.healthscope.net/

Elayne Howard & Associates Inc.
3501 Masons Mill Rd., Ste. 501

Huntingdon Valley, PA 19006-3509
(215)657-9550

GRA Inc.
115 West Ave., Ste. 201
Jenkintown, PA 19046
(215)884-7500
Fax: (215)884-1385
E-mail: gramail@gra-inc.com
Website: http://www.gra-inc.com

Mifflin County Industrial Development Corp.
Mifflin County Industrial Plz.
6395 SR 103 N
Bldg. 50
Lewistown, PA 17044
(717)242-0393
Fax: (717)242-1842
E-mail: mcide@acsworld.net

Autech Products
1289 Revere Rd.
Morrisville, PA 19067
(215)493-3759
Fax: (215)493-9791
E-mail: autech4@yahoo.com

Advantage Associates
434 Avon Dr.
Pittsburgh, PA 15228
(412)343-1558
Fax: (412)362-1684
E-mail: ecocba1@aol.com

Regis J. Sheehan & Associates
Pittsburgh, PA 15220
(412)279-1207

James W. Davidson Company Inc.
23 Forest View Rd.
Wallingford, PA 19086
(610)566-1462

Puerto Rico

Diego Chevere & Co.
Metro Parque 7, Ste. 204
Metro Office
Caparra Heights, PR 00920
(787)774-9595
Fax: (787)774-9566
E-mail: dcco@coqui.net

Manuel L. Porrata and Associates
898 Munoz Rivera Ave., Ste. 201
San Juan, PR 00927
(787)765-2140
Fax: (787)754-3285
E-mail: m_porrata@manuelporrata.com
Website: http://manualporrata.com

South Carolina

Aquafood Business Associates
PO Box 13267
Charleston, SC 29422
(843)795-9506
Fax: (843)795-9477
E-mail: rraba@aol.com

Profit Associates Inc.
PO Box 38026
Charleston, SC 29414
(803)763-5718
Fax: (803)763-5719
E-mail: bobrog@awod.com
Website: http://www.awod.com/gallery/
business/proasc

Strategic Innovations International
12 Executive Ct.
Lake Wylie, SC 29710
(803)831-1225
Fax: (803)831-1177
E-mail: stratinnov@aol.com
Website: http://www.
strategicinnovations.com

Minus Stage
Box 4436
Rock Hill, SC 29731
(803)328-0705
Fax: (803)329-9948

Tennessee

Daniel Petchers & Associates
8820 Fernwood CV
Germantown, TN 38138
(901)755-9896

Business Choices
1114 Forest Harbor, Ste. 300
Hendersonville, TN 37075-9646
(615)822-8692
Free: 800-737-8382
Fax: (615)822-8692
E-mail: bz-ch@juno.com

RCFA Healthcare Management Services L.L.C.
9648 Kingston Pke., Ste. 8
Knoxville, TN 37922
(865)531-0176
Free: 800-635-4040
Fax: (865)531-0722
E-mail: info@rcfa.com
Website: http://www.rcfa.com

Growth Consultants of America
3917 Trimble Rd.
Nashville, TN 37215

(615)383-0550
Fax: (615)269-8940
E-mail: 70244.451@compuserve.com

Texas

Integrated Cost Management Systems Inc.
2261 Brookhollow Plz. Dr., Ste. 104
Arlington, TX 76006
(817)633-2873
Fax: (817)633-3781
E-mail: abm@icms.net
Website: http://www.icms.net

Lori Williams
1000 Leslie Ct.
Arlington, TX 76012
(817)459-3934
Fax: (817)459-3934

Business Resource Software Inc.
2013 Wells Branch Pky., Ste. 305
Austin, TX 78728
Free: 800-423-1228
Fax: (512)251-4401
E-mail: info@brs-inc.com
Website: http://www.brs-inc.com

Erisa Adminstrative Services Inc.
12325 Hymeadow Dr., Bldg. 4
Austin, TX 78750-1847
(512)250-9020
Fax: (512)250-9487
Website: http://www.cserisa.com

R. Miller Hicks & Co.
1011 W 11th St.
Austin, TX 78703
(512)477-7000
Fax: (512)477-9697
E-mail: millerhicks@rmhicks.com
Website: http://www.rmhicks.com

Pragmatic Tactics Inc.
3303 Westchester Ave.
College Station, TX 77845
(409)696-5294
Free: 800-570-5294
Fax: (409)696-4994
E-mail: ptactics@aol.com
Website: http://www.ptatics.com

Perot Systems
12404 Park Central Dr.
Dallas, TX 75251
(972)340-5000
Free: 800-688-4333
Fax: (972)455-4100
E-mail: corp.comm@ps.net
Website: http://www.perotsystems.com

ReGENERATION Partners
3838 Oak Lawn Ave.
Dallas, TX 75219
(214)559-3999
Free: 800-406-1112
E-mail: info@regeneration-partner.com
Website: http://www.regeneration-partners.com

High Technology Associates - Division of Global Technologies Inc.
1775 St. James Pl., Ste. 105
Houston, TX 77056
(713)963-9300
Fax: (713)963-8341
E-mail: hta@infohwy.com

MasterCOM
103 Thunder Rd.
Kerrville, TX 78028
(830)895-7990
Fax: (830)443-3428
E-mail: jmstubblefield@master training.com
Website: http://www.mastertraining.com

PROTEC
4607 Linden Pl.
Pearland, TX 77584
(281)997-9872
Fax: (281)997-9895
E-mail: p.oman@ix.netcom.com

Alpha Quadrant Inc.
10618 Auldine
San Antonio, TX 78230
(210)344-3330
Fax: (210)344-8151
E-mail: mbussone@sbcglobal.net
Website:http://www.a-quadrant.com
Michele Bussone

Bastian Public Relations
614 San Dizier
San Antonio, TX 78232
(210)404-1839
E-mail: lisa@bastianpr.com
Website: http://www.bastianpr.com
Lisa Bastian CBC

Business Strategy Development Consultants
PO Box 690365
San Antonio, TX 78269
(210)696-8000
Free: 800-927-BSDC
Fax: (210)696-8000

Tom Welch, CPC
6900 San Pedro Ave., Ste. 147
San Antonio, TX 78216-6207

(210)737-7022
Fax: (210)737-7022
E-mail: bplan@iamerica.net
Website: http://www.moneywords.com

Utah

Business Management Resource
PO Box 521125
Salt Lake City, UT 84152-1125
(801)272-4668
Fax: (801)277-3290
E-mail: pingfong@worldnet.att.net

Virginia

Tindell Associates
209 Oxford Ave.
Alexandria, VA 22301
(703)683-0109
Fax: 703-783-0219
E-mail: scott@tindell.net
Website: http://www.tindell.net
Scott Lockett, President

Elliott B. Jaffa
2530-B S Walter Reed Dr.
Arlington, VA 22206
(703)931-0040
E-mail: thetrainingdoctor@excite.com
Website: http://www.tregistry.com/jaffa.htm

Koach Enterprises - USA
5529 N 18th St.
Arlington, VA 22205
(703)241-8361
Fax: (703)241-8623

Federal Market Development
5650 Chapel Run Ct.
Centreville, VA 20120-3601
(703)502-8930
Free: 800-821-5003
Fax: (703)502-8929

Huff, Stuart & Carlton
2107 Graves Mills Rd., Ste. C
Forest, VA 24551
(804)316-9356
Free: (888)316-9356
Fax: (804)316-9357
Website: http://www.wealthmgt.net

AMX International Inc.
1420 Spring Hill Rd. , Ste. 600
McLean, VA 22102-3006
(703)690-4100
Fax: (703)643-1279
E-mail: amxmail@amxi.com
Website: http://www.amxi.com

Charles Scott Pugh (Investor)
4101 Pittaway Dr.
Richmond, VA 23235-1022
(804)560-0979
Fax: (804)560-4670

John C. Randall and Associates Inc.
PO Box 15127
Richmond, VA 23227
(804)746-4450
Fax: (804)730-8933
E-mail: randalljcx@aol.com
Website: http://www.johncrandall.com

McLeod & Co.
410 1st St.
Roanoke, VA 24011
(540)342-6911
Fax: (540)344-6367
Website: http://www.mcleodco.com/

Salzinger & Company Inc.
8000 Towers Crescent Dr., Ste. 1350
Vienna, VA 22182
(703)442-5200
Fax: (703)442-5205
E-mail: info@salzinger.com
Website: http://www.salzinger.com

The Small Business Counselor
12423 Hedges Run Dr., Ste. 153
Woodbridge, VA 22192
(703)490-6755
Fax: (703)490-1356

Washington

Burlington Consultants
10900 NE 8th St., Ste. 900
Bellevue, WA 98004
(425)688-3060
Fax: (425)454-4383
E-mail: partners@burlington
consultants.com
Website: http://www.burlington
consultants.com

Perry L. Smith Consulting
800 Bellevue Way NE, Ste. 400
Bellevue, WA 98004-4208
(425)462-2072
Fax: (425)462-5638

St. Charles Consulting Group
1420 NW Gilman Blvd.
Issaquah, WA 98027
(425)557-8708
Fax: (425)557-8731
E-mail: info@stcharlesconsulting.com
Website: http://www.stcharlescon
sulting.com

Independent Automotive Training Services
PO Box 334
Kirkland, WA 98083
(425)822-5715
E-mail: ltunney@autosvccon.com
Website: http://www.autosvccon.com

Kahle Associate Inc.
6203 204th Dr. NE
Redmond, WA 98053
(425)836-8763
Fax: (425)868-3770
E-mail: randykahle@kahleassociates.com
Website: http://www.kahleassociates.com

Dan Collin
3419 Wallingord Ave N, No. 2
Seattle, WA 98103
(206)634-9469
E-mail: dc@dancollin.com
Website: http://members.home.net/
dcollin/

ECG Management Consultants Inc.
1111 3rd Ave., Ste. 2700
Seattle, WA 98101-3201
(206)689-2200
Fax: (206)689-2209
E-mail: ecg@ecgmc.com
Website: http://www.ecgmc.com

Northwest Trade Adjustment Assistance Center
900 4th Ave., Ste. 2430
Seattle, WA 98164-1001
(206)622-2730
Free: 800-667-8087
Fax: (206)622-1105
E-mail: matchingfunds@nwtaac.org
Website: http://www.taacenters.org

Business Planning Consultants
S 3510 Ridgeview Dr.
Spokane, WA 99206
(509)928-0332
Fax: (509)921-0842
E-mail: bpci@nextdim.com

West Virginia

**Stanley & Associates Inc./
BusinessandMarketingPlans.com**
1687 Robert C. Byrd Dr.
Beckley, WV 25801
(304)252-0324
Free: 888-752-6720
Fax: (304)252-0470
E-mail: cclay@charterinternet.com

Website: http://www.Businessand
MarketingPlans.com
Christopher Clay

Wisconsin

White & Associates Inc.
5349 Somerset Ln. S
Greenfield, WI 53221
(414)281-7373
Fax: (414)281-7006
E-mail: wnaconsult@aol.com

Small business administration regional offices

This section contains a listing of Small Business Administration offices arranged numerically by region. Service areas are provided. Contact the appropriate office for a referral to the nearest field office, or visit the Small Business Administration online at www.sba.gov.

Region 1

U.S. Small Business Administration
Region I Office
10 Causeway St., Ste. 812
Boston, MA 02222-1093
Phone: (617)565-8415
Fax: (617)565-8420
Serves Connecticut, Maine, Massachusetts, New Hampshire, Rhode Island, and Vermont.

Region 2

U.S. Small Business Administration
Region II Office
26 Federal Plaza, Ste. 3108
New York, NY 10278
Phone: (212)264-1450
Fax: (212)264-0038
Serves New Jersey, New York, Puerto Rico, and the Virgin Islands.

Region 3

U.S. Small Business Administration
Region III Office
Robert N C Nix Sr. Federal Building
900 Market St., 5th Fl.
Philadelphia, PA 19107
(215)580-2807
Serves Delaware, the District of Columbia, Maryland, Pennsylvania, Virginia, and West Virginia.

Region 4

U.S. Small Business Administration
Region IV Office
233 Peachtree St. NE
Harris Tower 1800
Atlanta, GA 30303
Phone: (404)331-4999
Fax: (404)331-2354
Serves Alabama, Florida, Georgia, Kentucky, Mississippi, North Carolina, South Carolina, and Tennessee.

Region 5

U.S. Small Business Administration
Region V Office
500 W. Madison St.
Citicorp Center, Ste. 1240
Chicago, IL 60661-2511
Phone: (312)353-0357
Fax: (312)353-3426
Serves Illinois, Indiana, Michigan, Minnesota, Ohio, and Wisconsin.

Region 6

U.S. Small Business Administration
Region VI Office
4300 Amon Carter Blvd., Ste. 108
Fort Worth, TX 76155
Phone: (817)684-5581
Fax: (817)684-5588
Serves Arkansas, Louisiana, New Mexico, Oklahoma, and Texas.

Region 7

U.S. Small Business Administration
Region VII Office
323 W. 8th St., Ste. 307
Kansas City, MO 64105-1500
Phone: (816)374-6380
Fax: (816)374-6339
Serves Iowa, Kansas, Missouri, and Nebraska.

Region 8

U.S. Small Business Administration
Region VIII Office
721 19th St., Ste. 400
Denver, CO 80202
Phone: (303)844-0500
Fax: (303)844-0506
Serves Colorado, Montana, North Dakota, South Dakota, Utah, and Wyoming.

Region 9

U.S. Small Business Administration
Region IX Office
330 N Brand Blvd., Ste. 1270
Glendale, CA 91203-2304
Phone: (818)552-3434
Fax: (818)552-3440
Serves American Samoa, Arizona, California, Guam, Hawaii, Nevada, and the Trust Territory of the Pacific Islands.

Region 10

U.S. Small Business Administration
Region X Office
2401 Fourth Ave., Ste. 400
Seattle, WA 98121
Phone: (206)553-5676
Fax: (206)553-4155
Serves Alaska, Idaho, Oregon, and Washington.

Small business development centers

This section contains a listing of all Small Business Development Centers, organized alphabetically by state/U.S. territory, then by city, then by agency name.

Alabama

Alabama SBDC
UNIVERSITY OF ALABAMA
2800 Milan Court Suite 124
Birmingham, AL 35211-6908
Phone: 205-943-6750
Fax: 205-943-6752
E-Mail: wcampbell@provost.uab.edu
Website: http://www.asbdc.org
Mr. William Campbell Jr, State Director

Alaska

Alaska SBDC
UNIVERSITY OF ALASKA - ANCHORAGE
430 West Seventh Avenue, Suite 110
Anchorage, AK 99501
Phone: 907-274 -7232
Fax: 907-274-9524
E-Mail: anerw@uaa.alaska.edu
Website: http://www.aksbdc.org
Ms. Jean R. Wall, State Director

American Samoa

American Samoa SBDC
AMERICAN SAMOA COMMUNITY COLLEGE
P.O. Box 2609
Pago Pago, American Samoa 96799
Phone: 011-684-699-4830
Fax: 011-684-699-6132
E-Mail: htalex@att.net
Mr. Herbert Thweatt, Director

Arizona

Arizona SBDC
MARICOPA COUNTY COMMUNITY COLLEGE
2411 West 14th Street, Suite 132
Tempe, AZ 85281
Phone: 480-731-8720
Fax: 480-731-8729
E-Mail: mike.york@domail.maricopa.edu
Website: http://www.dist.maricopa.edu.sbdc
Mr. Michael York, State Director

Arkansas

Arkansas SBDC
UNIVERSITY OF ARKANSAS
2801 South University Avenue
Little Rock, AR 72204
Phone: 501-324-9043
Fax: 501-324-9049
E-Mail: jmroderick@ualr.edu
Website: http://asbdc.ualr.edu
Ms. Janet M. Roderick, State Director

California

California - San Francisco SBDC
Northern California SBDC Lead Center
HUMBOLDT STATE UNIVERSITY
Office of Economic Development
1 Harpst Street 2006A, Siemens Hall
Arcata, CA, 95521
Phone: 707-826-3922
Fax: 707-826-3206
E-Mail: gainer@humboldt.edu
Ms. Margaret A. Gainer, Regional Director

California - Sacramento SBDC
CALIFORNIA STATE UNIVERSITY - CHICO
Chico, CA 95929-0765
Phone: 530-898-4598
Fax: 530-898-4734

E-Mail: dripke@csuchico.edu
Website: http://gsbdc.csuchico.edu
Mr. Dan Ripke, Interim Regional Director

California - San Diego SBDC
SOUTHWESTERN COMMUNITY
COLLEGE DISTRICT
900 Otey Lakes Road
Chula Vista, CA 91910
Phone: 619-482-6388
Fax: 619-482-6402
E-Mail: dtrujillo@swc.cc.ca.us
Website: http://www.sbditc.org
Ms. Debbie P. Trujillo, Regional Director

California - Fresno SBDC
UC Merced Lead Center
UNIVERSITY OF CALIFORNIA -
MERCED
550 East Shaw, Suite 105A
Fresno, CA 93710
Phone: 559-241-6590
Fax: 559-241-7422
E-Mail: crosander@ucmerced.edu
Website: http://sbdc.ucmerced.edu
Mr. Chris Rosander, State Director

California - Santa Ana SBDC
Tri-County Lead SBDC
CALIFORNIA STATE UNIVERSITY -
FULLERTON
800 North State College Boulevard, LH640
Fullerton, CA 92834
Phone: 714-278-2719
Fax: 714-278-7858
E-Mail: vpham@fullerton.edu
Website: http://www.leadsbdc.org
Ms. Vi Pham, Lead Center Director

California - Los Angeles Region SBDC
LONG BEACH COMMUNITY
COLLEGE DISTRICT
3950 Paramount Boulevard, Ste 101
Lakewood, CA 90712
Phone: 562-938-5004
Fax: 562-938-5030
E-Mail: ssloan@lbcc.edu
Ms. Sheneui Sloan, Interim Lead Center
Director

Colorado

Colorado SBDC
OFFICE OF ECONOMIC
DEVELOPMENT
1625 Broadway, Suite 170
Denver, CO 80202
Phone: 303-892-3864
Fax: 303-892-3848
E-Mail: Kelly.Manning@state.co.us

Website: http://www.state.co.us/oed/sbdc
Ms. Kelly Manning, State Director

Connecticut

Connecticut SBDC
UNIVERSITY OF CONNECTICUT
1376 Storrs Road, Unit 4094
Storrs, CT 06269-1094
Phone: 860-870-6370
Fax: 860-870-6374
E-Mail: richard.cheney@uconn.edu
Website: http://www.sbdc.uconn.edu
Mr. Richard Cheney, Interim State Director

Delaware

Delaware SBDC
DELAWARE TECHNOLOGY PARK
1 Innovation Way, Suite 301
Newark, DE 19711
Phone: 302-831-2747
Fax: 302-831-1423
E-Mail: Clinton.tymes@mvs.udel.edu
Website: http://www.delawaresbdc.org
Mr. Clinton Tymes, State Director

District of Columbia

District of Columbia SBDC
HOWARD UNIVERSITY
2600 6th Street, NW Room 128
Washington, DC 20059
Phone: 202-806-1550
Fax: 202-806-1777
E-Mail: hturner@howard.edu
Website: http://www.dcsbdc.com/
Mr. Henry Turner, Executive Director

Florida

Florida SBDC
UNIVERSITY OF WEST FLORIDA
401 East Chase Street, Suite 100
Pensacola, FL 32502
Phone: 850-473-7800
Fax: 850-473-7813
E-Mail: jcartwri@uwf.edu
Website: http://www.floridasbdc.com
Mr. Jerry Cartwright, State Director

Georgia

Georgia SBDC
UNIVERSITY OF GEORGIA
1180 East Broad Street
Athens, GA 30602
Phone: 706-542-6762
Fax: 706-542-6776
E-mail: aadams@sbdc.uga.edu

Website: http://www.sbdc.uga.edu
Mr. Allan Adams, Interim State Director

Guam

Guam Small Business Development
Center
UNIVERSITY OF GUAM
Pacific Islands SBDC
P.O. Box 5014 - U.O.G. Station
Mangilao, GU 96923
Phone: 671-735-2590
Fax: 671-734-2002
E-mail: casey@pacificsbdc.com
Website: http://www.uog.edu/sbdc
Mr. Casey Jeszenka, Director

Hawaii

Hawaii SBDC
UNIVERSITY OF HAWAII - HILO
308 Kamehameha Avenue, Suite 201
Hilo, HI 96720
Phone: 808-974-7515
Fax: 808-974-7683
E-Mail: darrylm@interpac.net
Website: http://www.hawaii-sbdc.org
Mr. Darryl Mleynek, State Director

Idaho

Idaho SBDC
BOISE STATE UNIVERSITY
1910 University Drive
Boise, ID 83725
Phone: 208-426-3799
Fax: 208-426-3877
E-mail: jhogge@boisestate.edu
Website: http://www.idahosbdc.org
Mr. Jim Hogge, State Director

Illinois

Illinois SBDC
DEPARTMENT OF COMMERCE
AND ECONOMIC OPPORTUNITY
620 E. Adams, S-4
Springfield, IL 62701
Phone: 217-524-5700
Fax: 217-524-0171
E-mail: mpatrilli@ildceo.net
Website: http://www.ilsbdc.biz
Mr. Mark Petrilli, State Director

Indiana

Indiana SBDC
INDIANA ECONOMIC
DEVELOPMENT CORPORATION
One North Capitol, Suite 900
Indianapolis, IN 46204

Phone: 317-234-8872
Fax: 317-232-8874
E-mail: dtrocha@isbdc.org
Website: http://www.isbdc.org
Ms. Debbie Bishop Trocha, State
Director

Iowa

Iowa SBDC
IOWA STATE UNIVERSITY
340 Gerdin Business Bldg.
Ames, IA 50011-1350
Phone: 515-294-2037
Fax: 515-294-6522
E-mail: jonryan@iastate.edu
Website: http://www.iabusnet.org
Mr. Jon Ryan, State Director

Kansas

Kansas SBDC
FORT HAYS STATE UNIVERSITY
214 SW Sixth Street, Suite 301
Topeka, KS 66603
Phone: 785-296-6514
Fax: 785-291-3261
E-mail: ksbdc.wkearns@fhsu.edu
Website: http://www.fhsu.edu/ksbdc
Mr. Wally Kearns, State Director

Kentucky

Kentucky SBDC
UNIVERSITY OF KENTUCKY
225 Gatton College of Business
Economics Building
Lexington, KY 40506-0034
Phone: 859-257-7668
Fax: 859-323-1907
E-mail: lrnaug0@pop.uky.edu
Website: http://www.ksbdc.org
Ms. Becky Naugle, State Director

Louisiana

Louisiana SBDC
**UNIVERSITY OF LOUISIANA -
MONROE**
College of Business Administration
700 University Avenue
Monroe, LA 71209
Phone: 318-342-5506
Fax: 318-342-5510
E-mail: wilkerson@ulm.edu
Website: http://www.lsbdc.org
Ms. Mary Lynn Wilkerson, State
Director

Maine

Maine SBDC
**UNIVERSITY OF SOUTHERN
MAINE**
96 Falmouth Street P.O. Box 9300
Portland, ME 04103
Phone: 207-780-4420
Fax: 207-780-4810
E-mail: jrmassaua@maine.edu
Website: http://www.mainesbdc.org
Mr. John Massaua, State Director

Maryland

Maryland SBDC
UNIVERSITY OF MARYLAND
7100 Baltimore Avenue, Suite 401
College Park, MD 20742
Phone: 301-403-8300
Fax: 301-403-8303
E-mail: rsprow@mdsbdc.umd.edu
Website: http://www.mdsbdc.umd.edu
Ms. Renee Sprow, State Director

Massachusetts

Massachusetts SBDC
UNIVERSITY OF MASSACHUSETTS
School of Management, Room 205
Amherst, MA 01003-4935
Phone: 413-545-6301
Fax: 413-545-1273
E-mail: gep@msbdc.umass.edu
Website: http://msbdc.som.umass.edu
Ms. Georgianna Parkin, State Director

Michigan

Michigan SBTDC
**GRAND VALLEY STATE
UNIVERSITY**
510 West Fulton Avenue
Grand Rapids, MI 49504
Phone: 616-331-7485
Fax: 616-331-7389
E-mail: lopuckic@gvsu.edu
Website: http://www.misbtdc.org
Ms. Carol Lopucki, State Director

Minnesota

Minnesota SBDC
**MINNESOTA SMALL BUSINESS
DEVELOPMENT CENTER**
1st National Bank Building
332 Minnesota Street, Suite E200
St. Paul, MN 55101-1351
Phone: 651-297-5773
Fax: 651-296-5287

E-mail: michael.myhre@state.mn.us
Website: http://www.mnsbdc.com
Mr. Michael Myhre, State Director

Mississippi

Mississippi SBDC
UNIVERSITY OF MISSISSIPPI
B-19 Jeanette Phillips Drive
P.O. Box 1848
University, MS 38677
Phone: 662-915-5001
Fax: 662-915-5650
E-mail: wgurley@olemiss.edu
Website: http://www.olemiss.edu/depts/
mssbdc
Mr. Doug Gurley, Jr., State Director

Missouri

Missouri SBDC
UNIVERSITY OF MISSOURI
1205 University Avenue, Suite 300
Columbia, MO 65211
Phone: 573-882-1348
Fax: 573-884-4297
E-mail: summersm@missouri.edu
Website: http://www.mo-sbdc.org/
index.shtml
Mr. Max Summers, State Director

Montana

Montana SBDC
DEPARTMENT OF COMMERCE
301 South Park Avenue, Room 114 /
P.O. Box 200505
Helena, MT 59620
Phone: 406-841-2746
Fax: 406-444-1872
E-mail: adesch@state.mt.us
Website: http://commerce.state.mt.us/
brd/BRD_SBDC.html
Ms. Ann Desch, State Director

Nebraska

Nebraska SBDC
**UNIVERSITY OF NEBRASKA -
OMAHA**
60th & Dodge Street, CBA Room 407
Omaha, NE 68182
Phone: 402-554-2521
Fax: 402-554-3473
E-mail: rbernier@unomaha.edu
Website: http://nbdc.unomaha.edu
Mr. Robert Bernier, State Director

Nevada

Nevada SBDC
UNIVERSITY OF NEVADA - RENO
Reno College of Business
Administration, Room 411
Reno, NV 89557-0100
Phone: 775-784-1717
Fax: 775-784-4337
E-mail: males@unr.edu
Website: http://www.nsbdc.org
Mr. Sam Males, State Director

New Hampshire

New Hampshire SBDC
UNIVERSITY OF NEW HAMPSHIRE
108 McConnell Hall
Durham, NH 03824-3593
Phone: 603-862-4879
Fax: 603-862-4876
E-mail: Mary.Collins@unh.edu
Website: http://www.nhsbdc.org
Ms. Mary Collins, State Director

New Jersey

New Jersey SBDC
RUTGERS UNIVERSITY
49 Bleeker Street
Newark, NJ 07102-1993
Phone: 973-353-5950
Fax: 973-353-1110
E-mail: bhopper@njsbdc.com
Website: http://www.njsbdc.com/home
Ms. Brenda Hopper, State Director

New Mexico

New Mexico SBDC
SANTA FE COMMUNITY COLLEGE
6401 Richards Avenue
Santa Fe, NM 87505
Phone: 505-428-1362
Fax: 505-471-9469
E-mail: rmiller@santa-fe.cc.nm.us
Website: http://www.nmsbdc.org
Mr. Roy Miller, State Director

New York

New York SBDC
STATE UNIVERSITY OF NEW YORK
SUNY Plaza, S-523
Albany, NY 12246
Phone: 518-443-5398
Fax: 518-443-5275
E-mail: j.king@nyssbdc.org
Website: http://www.nyssbdc.org
Mr. Jim King, State Director

North Carolina

North Carolina SBDTC
UNIVERSITY OF NORTH CAROLINA
5 West Hargett Street, Suite 600
Raleigh, NC 27601
Phone: 919-715-7272
Fax: 919-715-7777
E-mail: sdaugherty@sbtdc.org
Website: http://www.sbtdc.org
Mr. Scott Daugherty, State Director

North Dakota

North Dakota SBDC
UNIVERSITY OF NORTH DAKOTA
1600 E. Century Avenue, Suite 2
Bismarck, ND 58503
Phone: 701-328-5375
Fax: 701-328-5320
E-mail: christine.martin@und.nodak.edu
Website: http://www.ndsbdc.org
Ms. Christine Martin-Goldman, State
Director

Ohio

Ohio SBDC
OHIO DEPARTMENT
OF DEVELOPMENT
77 South High Street
Columbus, OH 43216
Phone: 614-466-5102
Fax: 614-466-0829
E-mail: mabraham@odod.state.oh.us
Website: http://www.ohiosbdc.org
Ms. Michele Abraham, State Director

Oklahoma

Oklahoma SBDC
SOUTHEAST OKLAHOMA STATE
UNIVERSITY
517 University, Box 2584, Station A
Durant, OK 74701
Phone: 580-745-7577
Fax: 580-745-7471
E-mail: gpennington@sosu.edu
Website: http://www.osbdc.org
Mr. Grady Pennington, State Director

Oregon

Oregon SBDC
LANE COMMUNITY COLLEGE
99 West Tenth Avenue, Suite 390
Eugene, OR 97401-3021
Phone: 541-463-5250
Fax: 541-345-6006
E-mail: carterb@lanecc.edu

Website: http://www.bizcenter.org
Mr. William Carter, State Director

Pennsylvania

Pennsylvania SBDC
UNIVERSITY OF PENNSYLVANIA
The Wharton School
3733 Spruce Street
Philadelphia, PA 19104-6374
Phone: 215-898-1219
Fax: 215-573-2135
E-mail: ghiggins@wharton.upenn.edu
Website: http://pasbdc.org
Mr. Gregory Higgins, State Director

Puerto Rico

Puerto Rico SBDC
INTER-AMERICAN UNIVERSITY
OF PUERTO RICO
416 Ponce de Leon Avenue, Union Plaza,
Seventh Floor
Hato Rey, PR 00918
Phone: 787-763-6811
Fax: 787-763-4629
E-mail: cmarti@prsbdc.org
Website: http://www.prsbdc.org
Ms. Carmen Marti, Executive Director

Rhode Island

Rhode Island SBDC
BRYANT UNIVERSITY
1150 Douglas Pike
Smithfield, RI 02917
Phone: 401-232-6923
Fax: 401-232-6933
E-mail: adawson@bryant.edu
Website: http://www.risbdc.org
Ms. Diane Fournaris, Interim State Director

South Carolina

South Carolina SBDC
UNIVERSITY OF SOUTH CAROLINA
College of Business Administration
1710 College Street
Columbia, SC 29208
Phone: 803-777-4907
Fax: 803-777-4403
E-mail: lenti@moore.sc.edu
Website: http://scsbdc.moore.sc.edu
Mr. John Lenti, State Director

South Dakota

South Dakota SBDC
UNIVERSITY OF SOUTH DAKOTA
414 East Clark Street, Patterson Hall
Vermillion, SD 57069

Phone: 605-677-6256
Fax: 605-677-5427
E-mail: jshemmin@usd.edu
Website: http://www.sdsbdc.org
Mr. John S. Hemmingstad, State
Director

Tennessee

Tennessee SBDC
TENNESSEE BOARD OF REGENTS
1415 Murfressboro Road, Suite 540
Nashville, TN 37217-2833
Phone: 615-898-2745
Fax: 615-893-7089
E-mail: pgeho@mail.tsbdc.org
Website: http://www.tsbdc.org
Mr. Patrick Geho, State Director

Texas

Texas-North SBDC
**DALLAS COUNTY COMMUNITY
COLLEGE**
1402 Corinth Street
Dallas, TX 75215
Phone: 214-860-5835
Fax: 214-860-5813
E-mail: emk9402@dcccd.edu
Website: http://www.ntsbdc.org
Ms. Liz Klimback, Region Director

Texas-Houston SBDC
UNIVERSITY OF HOUSTON
2302 Fannin, Suite 200
Houston, TX 77002
Phone: 713-752-8425
Fax: 713-756-1500
E-mail: fyoung@uh.edu
Website: http://sbdcnetwork.uh.edu
Mr. Mike Young, Executive Director

Texas-NW SBDC
TEXAS TECH UNIVERSITY
2579 South Loop 289, Suite 114
Lubbock, TX 79423
Phone: 806-745-3973
Fax: 806-745-6207
E-mail: c.bean@nwtsbdc.org
Website: http://www.nwtsbdc.org
Mr. Craig Bean, Executive Director

Texas-South-West Texas Border
Region SBDC
**UNIVERSITY OF TEXAS -
SAN ANTONIO**
501 West Durango Boulevard
San Antonio, TX 78207-4415
Phone: 210-458-2742
Fax: 210-458-2464

E-mail: albert.salgado@utsa.edu
Website: http://www.iedtexas.org
Mr. Alberto Salgado, Region Director

Utah

Utah SBDC
SALT LAKE COMMUNITY COLLEGE
9750 South 300 West
Sandy, UT 84070
Phone: 801-957-3493
Fax: 801-957-3488
E-mail: Greg.Panichello@slcc.edu
Website: http://www.slcc.edu/sbdc
Mr. Greg Panichello, State Director

Vermont

Vermont SBDC
VERMONT TECHNICAL COLLEGE
PO Box 188, 1 Main Street
Randolph Center, VT 05061-0188
Phone: 802-728-9101
Fax: 802-728-3026
E-mail: lquillen@vtc.edu
Website: http://www.vtsbdc.org
Ms. Lenae Quillen-Blume, State Director

Virgin Islands

Virgin Islands SBDC
**UNIVERSITY OF THE VIRGIN
ISLANDS**
8000 Nisky Center, Suite 720
St. Thomas, VI 00802-5804
Phone: 340-776-3206
Fax: 340-775-3756
E-mail: wbush@webmail.uvi.edu
Website: http://rps.uvi.edu/SBDC
Mr. Warren Bush, State Director

Virginia

Virginia SBDC
GEORGE MASON UNIVERSITY
4031 University Drive, Suite 200
Fairfax, VA 22030-3409
Phone: 703-277-7727
Fax: 703-352-8515
E-mail: jkeenan@gmu.edu
Website: http://www.virginiasbdc.org
Ms. Jody Keenan, Director

Washington

Washington SBDC
WASHINGTON STATE UNIVERSITY
534 E. Trent Avenue
P.O. Box 1495
Spokane, WA 99210-1495

Phone: 509-358-7765
Fax: 509-358-7764
E-mail: barogers@wsu.edu
Website: http://www.wsbdc.org
Mr. Brett Rogers, State Director

West Virginia

West Virginia SBDC
**WEST VIRGINIA DEVELOPMENT
OFFICE**
Capital Complex, Building 6, Room 652
Charleston, WV 25301
Phone: 304-558-2960
Fax: 304-558-0127
E-mail: csalyer@wvsbdc.org
Website: http://www.wvsbdc.org
Mr. Conley Salyor, State Director

Wisconsin

Wisconsin SBDC
UNIVERSITY OF WISCONSIN
432 North Lake Street, Room 423
Madison, WI 53706
Phone: 608-263-7794
Fax: 608-263-7830
E-mail: erica.kauten@uwex.edu
Website: http://www.wisconsinsbdc.org
Ms. Erica Kauten, State Director

Wyoming

Wyoming SBDC
UNIVERSITY OF WYOMING
P.O. Box 3922
Laramie, WY 82071-3922
Phone: 307-766-3505
Fax: 307-766-3406
E-mail: DDW@uwyo.edu
Website: http://www.uwyo.edu/sbdc
Ms. Debbie Popp, Acting State Director

Service corps of retired executives (score) offices

*This section contains a listing of all
SCORE offices organized alphabetically by
state/U.S. territory, then by city, then by
agency name.*

Alabama

SCORE Office (Northeast Alabama)
1330 Quintard Ave.
Anniston, AL 36202
(256)237-3536

SCORE Office (North Alabama)
901 South 15th St, Rm. 201
Birmingham, AL 35294-2060
(205)934-6868
Fax: (205)934-0538

SCORE Office (Baldwin County)
29750 Larry Dee Cawyer Dr.
Daphne, AL 36526
(334)928-5838

SCORE Office (Shoals)
612 S. COurt
Florence, AL 35630
(256)764-4661
Fax: (256)766-9017
E-mail: shoals@shoalschamber.com

SCORE Office (Mobile)
600 S Court St.
Mobile, AL 36104
(334)240-6868
Fax: (334)240-6869

SCORE Office (Alabama Capitol City)
600 S. Court St.
Montgomery, AL 36104
(334)240-6868
Fax: (334)240-6869

SCORE Office (East Alabama)
601 Ave. A
Opelika, AL 36801
(334)745-4861
E-mail: score636@hotmail.com
Website: http://www.angelfire.com/sc/
score636/

SCORE Office (Tuscaloosa)
2200 University Blvd.
Tuscaloosa, AL 35402
(205)758-7588

Alaska

SCORE Office (Anchorage)
510 L St., Ste. 310
Anchorage, AK 99501
(907)271-4022
Fax: (907)271-4545

Arizona

SCORE Office (Lake Havasu)
10 S. Acoma Blvd.
Lake Havasu City, AZ 86403
(520)453-5951
E-mail: SCORE@ctaz.com
Website: http://www.scorearizona.org/
lake_havasu/

SCORE Office (East Valley)
Federal Bldg., Rm. 104
26 N. MacDonald St.
Mesa, AZ 85201
(602)379-3100
Fax: (602)379-3143
E-mail: 402@aol.com
Website: http://www.scorearizona.
org/mesa/

SCORE Office (Phoenix)
2828 N. Central Ave., Ste. 800
Central & One Thomas
Phoenix, AZ 85004
(602)640-2329
Fax: (602)640-2360
E-mail: e-mail@SCORE-phoenix.org
Website: http://www.score-phoenix.org/

SCORE Office (Prescott Arizona)
1228 Willow Creek Rd., Ste. 2
Prescott, AZ 86301
(520)778-7438
Fax: (520)778-0812
E-mail: score@northlink.com
Website: http://www.scorearizona.org/
prescott/

SCORE Office (Tucson)
110 E. Pennington St.
Tucson, AZ 85702
(520)670-5008
Fax: (520)670-5011
E-mail: score@azstarnet.com
Website: http://www.scorearizona.org/
tucson/

SCORE Office (Yuma)
281 W. 24th St., Ste. 116
Yuma, AZ 85364
(520)314-0480
E-mail: score@C2i2.com
Website: http://www.scorearizona.org/
yuma

Arkansas

SCORE Office (South Central)
201 N. Jackson Ave.
El Dorado, AR 71730-5803
(870)863-6113
Fax: (870)863-6115

SCORE Office (Ozark)
Fayetteville, AR 72701
(501)442-7619

SCORE Office (Northwest Arkansas)
Glenn Haven Dr., No. 4
Ft. Smith, AR 72901
(501)783-3556

SCORE Office (Garland County)
Grand & Ouachita
PO Box 6012
Hot Springs Village, AR 71902
(501)321-1700

SCORE Office (Little Rock)
2120 Riverfront Dr., Rm. 100
Little Rock, AR 72202-1747
(501)324-5893
Fax: (501)324-5199

SCORE Office (Southeast Arkansas)
121 W. 6th
Pine Bluff, AR 71601
(870)535-7189
Fax: (870)535-1643

California

SCORE Office (Golden Empire)
1706 Chester Ave., No. 200
Bakersfield, CA 93301
(805)322-5881
Fax: (805)322-5663

SCORE Office (Greater Chico Area)
1324 Mangrove St., Ste. 114
Chico, CA 95926
(916)342-8932
Fax: (916)342-8932

SCORE Office (Concord)
2151-A Salvio St., Ste. B
Concord, CA 94520
(510)685-1181
Fax: (510)685-5623

SCORE Office (Covina)
935 W. Badillo St.
Covina, CA 91723
(818)967-4191
Fax: (818)966-9660

SCORE Office (Rancho Cucamonga)
8280 Utica, Ste. 160
Cucamonga, CA 91730
(909)987-1012
Fax: (909)987-5917

SCORE Office (Culver City)
PO Box 707
Culver City, CA 90232-0707
(310)287-3850
Fax: (310)287-1350

SCORE Office (Danville)
380 Diablo Rd., Ste. 103
Danville, CA 94526
(510)837-4400

SCORE Office (Downey)
11131 Brookshire Ave.
Downey, CA 90241
(310)923-2191
Fax: (310)864-0461

SCORE Office (El Cajon)
109 Rea Ave.
El Cajon, CA 92020
(619)444-1327
Fax: (619)440-6164

SCORE Office (El Centro)
1100 Main St.
El Centro, CA 92243
(619)352-3681
Fax: (619)352-3246

SCORE Office (Escondido)
720 N. Broadway
Escondido, CA 92025
(619)745-2125
Fax: (619)745-1183

SCORE Office (Fairfield)
1111 Webster St.
Fairfield, CA 94533
(707)425-4625
Fax: (707)425-0826

SCORE Office (Fontana)
17009 Valley Blvd., Ste. B
Fontana, CA 92335
(909)822-4433
Fax: (909)822-6238

SCORE Office (Foster City)
1125 E. Hillsdale Blvd.
Foster City, CA 94404
(415)573-7600
Fax: (415)573-5201

SCORE Office (Fremont)
2201 Walnut Ave., Ste. 110
Fremont, CA 94538
(510)795-2244
Fax: (510)795-2240

SCORE Office (Central California)
2719 N. Air Fresno Dr., Ste. 200
Fresno, CA 93727-1547
(559)487-5605
Fax: (559)487-5636

SCORE Office (Gardena)
1204 W. Gardena Blvd.
Gardena, CA 90247
(310)532-9905
Fax: (310)515-4893

SCORE Office (Lompoc)
330 N. Brand Blvd., Ste. 190
Glendale, CA 91203-2304

(818)552-3206
Fax: (818)552-3323

SCORE Office (Los Angeles)
330 N. Brand Blvd., Ste. 190
Glendale, CA 91203-2304
(818)552-3206
Fax: (818)552-3323

SCORE Office (Glendora)
131 E. Foothill Blvd.
Glendora, CA 91740
(818)963-4128
Fax: (818)914-4822

SCORE Office (Grover Beach)
177 S. 8th St.
Grover Beach, CA 93433
(805)489-9091
Fax: (805)489-9091

SCORE Office (Hawthorne)
12477 Hawthorne Blvd.
Hawthorne, CA 90250
(310)676-1163
Fax: (310)676-7661

SCORE Office (Hayward)
22300 Foothill Blvd., Ste. 303
Hayward, CA 94541
(510)537-2424

SCORE Office (Hemet)
1700 E. Florida Ave.
Hemet, CA 92544-4679
(909)652-4390
Fax: (909)929-8543

SCORE Office (Hesperia)
16367 Main St.
PO Box 403656
Hesperia, CA 92340
(619)244-2135

SCORE Office (Holloster)
321 San Felipe Rd., No. 11
Hollister, CA 95023

SCORE Office (Hollywood)
7018 Hollywood Blvd.
Hollywood, CA 90028
(213)469-8311
Fax: (213)469-2805

SCORE Office (Indio)
82503 Hwy. 111
PO Drawer TTT
Indio, CA 92202
(619)347-0676

SCORE Office (Inglewood)
330 Queen St.

Inglewood, CA 90301
(818)552-3206

SCORE Office (La Puente)
218 N. Grendanda St. D.
La Puente, CA 91744
(818)330-3216
Fax: (818)330-9524

SCORE Office (La Verne)
2078 Bonita Ave.
La Verne, CA 91750
(909)593-5265
Fax: (714)929-8475

SCORE Office (Lake Elsinore)
132 W. Graham Ave.
Lake Elsinore, CA 92530
(909)674-2577

SCORE Office (Lakeport)
PO Box 295
Lakeport, CA 95453
(707)263-5092

SCORE Office (Lakewood)
5445 E. Del Amo Blvd., Ste. 2
Lakewood, CA 90714
(213)920-7737

SCORE Office (Long Beach)
1 World Trade Center
Long Beach, CA 90831

SCORE Office (Los Alamitos)
901 W. Civic Center Dr., Ste. 160
Los Alamitos, CA 90720

SCORE Office (Los Altos)
321 University Ave.
Los Altos, CA 94022
(415)948-1455

SCORE Office (Manhattan Beach)
PO Box 3007
Manhattan Beach, CA 90266
(310)545-5313
Fax: (310)545-7203

SCORE Office (Merced)
1632 N. St.
Merced, CA 95340
(209)725-3800
Fax: (209)383-4959

SCORE Office (Milpitas)
75 S. Milpitas Blvd., Ste. 205
Milpitas, CA 95035
(408)262-2613
Fax: (408)262-2823

SCORE Office (Yosemite)
1012 11th St., Ste. 300
Modesto, CA 95354
(209)521-9333

SCORE Office (Montclair)
5220 Benito Ave.
Montclair, CA 91763

SCORE Office (Monterey Bay)
380 Alvarado St.
PO Box 1770
Monterey, CA 93940-1770
(408)649-1770

SCORE Office (Moreno Valley)
25480 Alessandro
Moreno Valley, CA 92553

SCORE Office (Morgan Hill)
25 W. 1st St.
PO Box 786
Morgan Hill, CA 95038
(408)779-9444
Fax: (408)778-1786

SCORE Office (Morro Bay)
880 Main St.
Morro Bay, CA 93442
(805)772-4467

SCORE Office (Mountain View)
580 Castro St.
Mountain View, CA 94041
(415)968-8378
Fax: (415)968-5668

SCORE Office (Napa)
1556 1st St.
Napa, CA 94559
(707)226-7455
Fax: (707)226-1171

SCORE Office (North Hollywood)
5019 Lankershim Blvd.
North Hollywood, CA 91601
(818)552-3206

SCORE Office (Northridge)
8801 Reseda Blvd.
Northridge, CA 91324
(818)349-5676

SCORE Office (Novato)
807 De Long Ave.
Novato, CA 94945
(415)897-1164
Fax: (415)898-9097

SCORE Office (East Bay)
519 17th St.
Oakland, CA 94612

(510)273-6611
Fax: (510)273-6015
E-mail: webmaster@eastbayscore.org
Website: http://www.eastbayscore.org

SCORE Office (Oceanside)
928 N. Coast Hwy.
Oceanside, CA 92054
(619)722-1534

SCORE Office (Ontario)
121 West B. St.
Ontario, CA 91762
Fax: (714)984-6439

SCORE Office (Oxnard)
PO Box 867
Oxnard, CA 93032
(805)385-8860
Fax: (805)487-1763

SCORE Office (Pacifica)
450 Dundee Way, Ste. 2
Pacifica, CA 94044
(415)355-4122

SCORE Office (Palm Desert)
72990 Hwy. 111
Palm Desert, CA 92260
(619)346-6111
Fax: (619)346-3463

SCORE Office (Palm Springs)
650 E. Tahquitz Canyon Way Ste. D
Palm Springs, CA 92262-6706
(760)320-6682
Fax: (760)323-9426

SCORE Office (Lakeside)
2150 Low Tree
Palmdale, CA 93551
(805)948-4518
Fax: (805)949-1212

SCORE Office (Palo Alto)
325 Forest Ave.
Palo Alto, CA 94301
(415)324-3121
Fax: (415)324-1215

SCORE Office (Pasadena)
117 E. Colorado Blvd., Ste. 100
Pasadena, CA 91105
(818)795-3355
Fax: (818)795-5663

SCORE Office (Paso Robles)
1225 Park St.
Paso Robles, CA 93446-2234
(805)238-0506
Fax: (805)238-0527

SCORE Office (Petaluma)
799 Baywood Dr., Ste. 3
Petaluma, CA 94954
(707)762-2785
Fax: (707)762-4721

SCORE Office (Pico Rivera)
9122 E. Washington Blvd.
Pico Rivera, CA 90660

SCORE Office (Pittsburg)
2700 E. Leland Rd.
Pittsburg, CA 94565
(510)439-2181
Fax: (510)427-1599

SCORE Office (Pleasanton)
777 Peters Ave.
Pleasanton, CA 94566
(510)846-9697

SCORE Office (Monterey Park)
485 N. Garey
Pomona, CA 91769

SCORE Office (Pomona)
485 N. Garey Ave.
Pomona, CA 91766
(909)622-1256

SCORE Office (Antelope Valley)
4511 West Ave. M-4
Quartz Hill, CA 93536
(805)272-0087
E-mail: avscore@ptw.com
Website: http://www.score.av.org/

SCORE Office (Shasta)
737 Auditorium Dr.
Redding, CA 96099
(916)225-2770

SCORE Office (Redwood City)
1675 Broadway
Redwood City, CA 94063
(415)364-1722
Fax: (415)364-1729

SCORE Office (Richmond)
3925 MacDonald Ave.
Richmond, CA 94805

SCORE Office (Ridgecrest)
PO Box 771
Ridgecrest, CA 93555
(619)375-8331
Fax: (619)375-0365

SCORE Office (Riverside)
3685 Main St., Ste. 350
Riverside, CA 92501
(909)683-7100

SCORE Office (Sacramento)
9845 Horn Rd., 260-B
Sacramento, CA 95827
(916)361-2322
Fax: (916)361-2164
E-mail: sacchapter@directcon.net

SCORE Office (Salinas)
PO Box 1170
Salinas, CA 93902
(408)424-7611
Fax: (408)424-8639

SCORE Office (Inland Empire)
777 E. Rialto Ave.
Purchasing
San Bernardino, CA 92415-0760
(909)386-8278

SCORE Office (San Carlos)
San Carlos Chamber of Commerce
PO Box 1086
San Carlos, CA 94070
(415)593-1068
Fax: (415)593-9108

SCORE Office (Encinitas)
550 W. C St., Ste. 550
San Diego, CA 92101-3540
(619)557-7272
Fax: (619)557-5894

SCORE Office (San Diego)
550 West C. St., Ste. 550
San Diego, CA 92101-3540
(619)557-7272
Fax: (619)557-5894
Website: http://www.score-sandiego.org

SCORE Office (Menlo Park)
1100 Merrill St.
San Francisco, CA 94105
(415)325-2818
Fax: (415)325-0920

SCORE Office (San Francisco)
455 Market St., 6th Fl.
San Francisco, CA 94105
(415)744-6827
Fax: (415)744-6750
E-mail: sfscore@sfscore.
Website: http://www.sfscore.com

SCORE Office (San Gabriel)
401 W. Las Tunas Dr.
San Gabriel, CA 91776
(818)576-2525
Fax: (818)289-2901

SCORE Office (San Jose)
Deanza College
208 S. 1st. St., Ste. 137
San Jose, CA 95113
(408)288-8479
Fax: (408)535-5541

SCORE Office (Silicon Valley)
84 W. Santa Clara St., Ste. 100
San Jose, CA 95113
(408)288-8479
Fax: (408)535-5541
E-mail: info@svscore.org
Website: http://www.svscore.org

SCORE Office (San Luis Obispo)
3566 S. Hiquera, No. 104
San Luis Obispo, CA 93401
(805)547-0779

SCORE Office (San Mateo)
1021 S. El Camino, 2nd Fl.
San Mateo, CA 94402
(415)341-5679

SCORE Office (San Pedro)
390 W. 7th St.
San Pedro, CA 90731
(310)832-7272

SCORE Office (Orange County)
200 W. Santa Anna Blvd., Ste. 700
Santa Ana, CA 92701
(714)550-7369
Fax: (714)550-0191
Website: http://www.score114.org

SCORE Office (Santa Barbara)
3227 State St.
Santa Barbara, CA 93130
(805)563-0084

SCORE Office (Central Coast)
509 W. Morrison Ave.
Santa Maria, CA 93454
(805)347-7755

SCORE Office (Santa Maria)
614 S. Broadway
Santa Maria, CA 93454-5111
(805)925-2403
Fax: (805)928-7559

SCORE Office (Santa Monica)
501 Colorado, Ste. 150
Santa Monica, CA 90401
(310)393-9825
Fax: (310)394-1868

SCORE Office (Santa Rosa)
777 Sonoma Ave., Rm. 115E
Santa Rosa, CA 95404

(707)571-8342
Fax: (707)541-0331
Website: http://www.pressdemo.com/community/score/score.html

SCORE Office (Scotts Valley)
4 Camp Evers Ln.
Scotts Valley, CA 95066
(408)438-1010
Fax: (408)438-6544

SCORE Office (Simi Valley)
40 W. Cochran St., Ste. 100
Simi Valley, CA 93065
(805)526-3900
Fax: (805)526-6234

SCORE Office (Sonoma)
453 1st St. E
Sonoma, CA 95476
(707)996-1033

SCORE Office (Los Banos)
222 S. Shepard St.
Sonora, CA 95370
(209)532-4212

SCORE Office (Tuolumne County)
39 North Washington St.
Sonora, CA 95370
(209)588-0128
E-mail: score@mlode.com

SCORE Office (South San Francisco)
445 Market St., Ste. 6th Fl.
South San Francisco, CA 94105
(415)744-6827
Fax: (415)744-6812

SCORE Office (Stockton)
401 N. San Joaquin St., Rm. 215
Stockton, CA 95202
(209)946-6293

SCORE Office (Taft)
314 4th St.
Taft, CA 93268
(805)765-2165
Fax: (805)765-6639

SCORE Office (Conejo Valley)
625 W. Hillcrest Dr.
Thousand Oaks, CA 91360
(805)499-1993
Fax: (805)498-7264

SCORE Office (Torrance)
3400 Torrance Blvd., Ste. 100
Torrance, CA 90503
(310)540-5858
Fax: (310)540-7662

SCORE Office (Truckee)
PO Box 2757
Truckee, CA 96160
(916)587-2757
Fax: (916)587-2439

SCORE Office (Visalia)
113 S. M St,
Tulare, CA 93274
(209)627-0766
Fax: (209)627-8149

SCORE Office (Upland)
433 N. 2nd Ave.
Upland, CA 91786
(909)931-4108

SCORE Office (Vallejo)
2 Florida St.
Vallejo, CA 94590
(707)644-5551
Fax: (707)644-5590

SCORE Office (Van Nuys)
14540 Victory Blvd.
Van Nuys, CA 91411
(818)989-0300
Fax: (818)989-3836

SCORE Office (Ventura)
5700 Ralston St., Ste. 310
Ventura, CA 93001
(805)658-2688
Fax: (805)658-2252
E-mail: scoreven@jps.net
Website: http://www.jps.net/scoreven

SCORE Office (Vista)
201 E. Washington St.
Vista, CA 92084
(619)726-1122
Fax: (619)226-8654

SCORE Office (Watsonville)
PO Box 1748
Watsonville, CA 95077
(408)724-3849
Fax: (408)728-5300

SCORE Office (West Covina)
811 S. Sunset Ave.
West Covina, CA 91790
(818)338-8496
Fax: (818)960-0511

SCORE Office (Westlake)
30893 Thousand Oaks Blvd.
Westlake Village, CA 91362
(805)496-5630
Fax: (818)991-1754

Colorado

SCORE Office (Colorado Springs)
2 N. Cascade Ave., Ste. 110
Colorado Springs, CO 80903
(719)636-3074
Website: http://www.cscc.org/score02/
index.html

SCORE Office (Denver)
US Custom's House, 4th Fl.
721 19th St.
Denver, CO 80201-0660
(303)844-3985
Fax: (303)844-6490
E-mail: score62@csn.net
Website: http://www.sni.net/score62

SCORE Office (Tri-River)
1102 Grand Ave.
Glenwood Springs, CO 81601
(970)945-6589

SCORE Office (Grand Junction)
2591 B & 3/4 Rd.
Grand Junction, CO 81503
(970)243-5242

SCORE Office (Gunnison)
608 N. 11th
Gunnison, CO 81230
(303)641-4422

SCORE Office (Montrose)
1214 Peppertree Dr.
Montrose, CO 81401
(970)249-6080

SCORE Office (Pagosa Springs)
PO Box 4381
Pagosa Springs, CO 81157
(970)731-4890

SCORE Office (Rifle)
0854 W. Battlement Pky., Apt. C106
Parachute, CO 81635
(970)285-9390

SCORE Office (Pueblo)
302 N. Santa Fe
Pueblo, CO 81003
(719)542-1704
Fax: (719)542-1624
E-mail: mackey@iex.net
Website: http://www.pueblo.org/score

SCORE Office (Ridgway)
143 Poplar Pl.
Ridgway, CO 81432

SCORE Office (Silverton)
PO Box 480

Silverton, CO 81433
(303)387-5430

SCORE Office (Minturn)
PO Box 2066
Vail, CO 81658
(970)476-1224

Connecticut

SCORE Office (Greater Bridgeport)
230 Park Ave.
Bridgeport, CT 06601-0999
(203)576-4369
Fax: (203)576-4388

SCORE Office (Bristol)
10 Main St. 1st. Fl.
Bristol, CT 06010
(203)584-4718
Fax: (203)584-4722

SCORE office (Greater Danbury)
246 Federal Rd.
Unit LL2, Ste. 7
Brookfield, CT 06804
(203)775-1151

SCORE Office (Greater Danbury)
246 Federal Rd., Unit LL2, Ste. 7
Brookfield, CT 06804
(203)775-1151

SCORE Office (Eastern Connecticut)
Administration Bldg., Rm. 313
PO 625
61 Main St. (Chapter 579)
Groton, CT 06475
(203)388-9508

SCORE Office (Greater Hartford County)
330 Main St.
Hartford, CT 06106
(860)548-1749
Fax: (860)240-4659
Website: http://www.score56.org

SCORE Office (Manchester)
20 Hartford Rd.
Manchester, CT 06040
(203)646-2223
Fax: (203)646-5871

SCORE Office (New Britain)
185 Main St., Ste. 431
New Britain, CT 06051
(203)827-4492
Fax: (203)827-4480

SCORE Office (New Haven)
25 Science Pk., Bldg. 25, Rm. 366

New Haven, CT 06511
(203)865-7645

SCORE Office (Fairfield County)
24 Beldon Ave., 5th Fl.
Norwalk, CT 06850
(203)847-7348
Fax: (203)849-9308

SCORE Office (Old Saybrook)
146 Main St.
Old Saybrook, CT 06475
(860)388-9508

SCORE Office (Simsbury)
Box 244
Simsbury, CT 06070
(203)651-7307
Fax: (203)651-1933

SCORE Office (Torrington)
23 North Rd.
Torrington, CT 06791
(203)482-6586

Delaware

SCORE Office (Dover)
Treadway Towers
PO Box 576
Dover, DE 19903
(302)678-0892
Fax: (302)678-0189

SCORE Office (Lewes)
PO Box 1
Lewes, DE 19958
(302)645-8073
Fax: (302)645-8412

SCORE Office (Milford)
204 NE Front St.
Milford, DE 19963
(302)422-3301

SCORE Office (Wilmington)
824 Market St., Ste. 610
Wilmington, DE 19801
(302)573-6652
Fax: (302)573-6092
Website: http://www.scoredelaware.com

District of Columbia

SCORE Office (George Mason University)
409 3rd St. SW, 4th Fl.
Washington, DC 20024
800-634-0245

SCORE Office (Washington DC)
1110 Vermont Ave. NW, 9th Fl.

Washington, DC 20043
(202)606-4000
Fax: (202)606-4225
E-mail: dcscore@hotmail.com
Website: http://www.scoredc.org/

Florida

SCORE Office (Desota County Chamber of Commerce)
16 South Velucia Ave.
Arcadia, FL 34266
(941)494-4033

SCORE Office (Suncoast/Pinellas)
Airport Business Ctr.
4707 - 140th Ave. N, No. 311
Clearwater, FL 33755
(813)532-6800
Fax: (813)532-6800

SCORE Office (DeLand)
336 N. Woodland Blvd.
DeLand, FL 32720
(904)734-4331
Fax: (904)734-4333

SCORE Office (South Palm Beach)
1050 S. Federal Hwy., Ste. 132
Delray Beach, FL 33483
(561)278-7752
Fax: (561)278-0288

SCORE Office (Ft. Lauderdale)
Federal Bldg., Ste. 123
299 E. Broward Blvd.
Ft. Lauderdale, FL 33301
(954)356-7263
Fax: (954)356-7145

SCORE Office (Southwest Florida)
The Renaissance
8695 College Pky., Ste. 345 & 346
Ft. Myers, FL 33919
(941)489-2935
Fax: (941)489-1170

SCORE Office (Treasure Coast)
Professional Center, Ste. 2
3220 S. US, No. 1
Ft. Pierce, FL 34982
(561)489-0548

SCORE Office (Gainesville)
101 SE 2nd Pl., Ste. 104
Gainesville, FL 32601
(904)375-8278

SCORE Office (Hialeah Dade Chamber)
59 W. 5th St.
Hialeah, FL 33010

(305)887-1515
Fax: (305)887-2453

SCORE Office (Daytona Beach)
921 Nova Rd., Ste. A
Holly Hills, FL 32117
(904)255-6889
Fax: (904)255-0229
E-mail: score87@dbeach.com

SCORE Office (South Broward)
3475 Sheridian St., Ste. 203
Hollywood, FL 33021
(305)966-8415

SCORE Office (Citrus County)
5 Poplar Ct.
Homosassa, FL 34446
(352)382-1037

SCORE Office (Jacksonville)
7825 Baymeadows Way, Ste. 100-B
Jacksonville, FL 32256
(904)443-1911
Fax: (904)443-1980
E-mail: scorejax@juno.com
Website: http://www.scorejax.org/

SCORE Office (Jacksonville Satellite)
3 Independent Dr.
Jacksonville, FL 32256
(904)366-6600
Fax: (904)632-0617

SCORE Office (Central Florida)
5410 S. Florida Ave., No. 3
Lakeland, FL 33801
(941)687-5783
Fax: (941)687-6225

SCORE Office (Lakeland)
100 Lake Morton Dr.
Lakeland, FL 33801
(941)686-2168

SCORE Office (St. Petersburg)
800 W. Bay Dr., Ste. 505
Largo, FL 33712
(813)585-4571

SCORE Office (Leesburg)
9501 US Hwy. 441
Leesburg, FL 34788-8751
(352)365-3556
Fax: (352)365-3501

SCORE Office (Cocoa)
1600 Farno Rd., Unit 205
Melbourne, FL 32935
(407)254-2288

SCORE Office (Melbourne)
Melbourne Professional Complex
1600 Sarno, Ste. 205
Melbourne, FL 32935
(407)254-2288
Fax: (407)245-2288

SCORE Office (Merritt Island)
1600 Sarno Rd., Ste. 205
Melbourne, FL 32935
(407)254-2288
Fax: (407)254-2288

SCORE Office (Space Coast)
Melbourn Professional Complex
1600 Sarno, Ste. 205
Melbourne, FL 32935
(407)254-2288
Fax: (407)254-2288

SCORE Office (Dade)
49 NW 5th St.
Miami, FL 33128
(305)371-6889
Fax: (305)374-1882
E-mail: score@netrox.net
Website: http://www.netrox.net/~score/

SCORE Office (Naples of Collier)
International College
2654 Tamiami Trl. E
Naples, FL 34112
(941)417-1280
Fax: (941)417-1281
E-mail: score@naples.net
Website: http://www.naples.net/clubs/
score/index.htm

SCORE Office (Pasco County)
6014 US Hwy. 19, Ste. 302
New Port Richey, FL 34652
(813)842-4638

SCORE Office (Southeast Volusia)
115 Canal St.
New Smyrna Beach, FL 32168
(904)428-2449
Fax: (904)423-3512

SCORE Office (Ocala)
110 E. Silver Springs Blvd.
Ocala, FL 34470
(352)629-5959

Clay County SCORE Office
Clay County Chamber of Commerce
1734 Kingsdey Ave.
PO Box 1441
Orange Park, FL 32073
(904)264-2651
Fax: (904)269-0363

SCORE Office (Orlando)
80 N. Hughey Ave.
Rm. 445 Federal Bldg.
Orlando, FL 32801
(407)648-6476
Fax: (407)648-6425

SCORE Office (Emerald Coast)
19 W. Garden St., No. 325
Pensacola, FL 32501
(904)444-2060
Fax: (904)444-2070

SCORE Office (Charlotte County)
201 W. Marion Ave., Ste. 211
Punta Gorda, FL 33950
(941)575-1818
E-mail: score@gls3c.com
Website: http://www.charlotte-
florida.com/business/scorepg01.htm

SCORE Office (St. Augustine)
1 Riberia St.
St. Augustine, FL 32084
(904)829-5681
Fax: (904)829-6477

SCORE Office (Bradenton)
2801 Fruitville, Ste. 280
Sarasota, FL 34237
(813)955-1029

SCORE Office (Manasota)
2801 Fruitville Rd., Ste. 280
Sarasota, FL 34237
(941)955-1029
Fax: (941)955-5581
E-mail: score116@gte.net
Website: http://www.score-suncoast.org/

SCORE Office (Tallahassee)
200 W. Park Ave.
Tallahassee, FL 32302
(850)487-2665

SCORE Office (Hillsborough)
4732 Dale Mabry Hwy. N, Ste. 400
Tampa, FL 33614-6509
(813)870-0125

SCORE Office (Lake Sumter)
122 E. Main St.
Tavares, FL 32778-3810
(352)365-3556

SCORE Office (Titusville)
2000 S. Washington Ave.
Titusville, FL 32780
(407)267-3036
Fax: (407)264-0127

SCORE Office (Venice)
257 N. Tamiami Trl.
Venice, FL 34285
(941)488-2236
Fax: (941)484-5903

SCORE Office (Palm Beach)
500 Australian Ave. S, Ste. 100
West Palm Beach, FL 33401
(561)833-1672
Fax: (561)833-1712

SCORE Office (Wildwood)
103 N. Webster St.
Wildwood, FL 34785

Georgia

SCORE Office (Atlanta)
Harris Tower, Suite 1900
233 Peachtree Rd., NE
Atlanta, GA 30309
(404)347-2442
Fax: (404)347-1227

SCORE Office (Augusta)
3126 Oxford Rd.
Augusta, GA 30909
(706)869-9100

SCORE Office (Columbus)
School Bldg.
PO Box 40
Columbus, GA 31901
(706)327-3654

SCORE Office (Dalton-Whitfield)
305 S. Thorton Ave.
Dalton, GA 30720
(706)279-3383

SCORE Office (Gainesville)
PO Box 374
Gainesville, GA 30503
(770)532-6206
Fax: (770)535-8419

SCORE Office (Macon)
711 Grand Bldg.
Macon, GA 31201
(912)751-6160

SCORE Office (Brunswick)
4 Glen Ave.
St. Simons Island, GA 31520
(912)265-0620
Fax: (912)265-0629

SCORE Office (Savannah)
111 E. Liberty St., Ste. 103
Savannah, GA 31401
(912)652-4335

Fax: (912)652-4184
E-mail: info@scoresav.org
Website: http://www.coastalempire.com/
score/index.htm

Guam

SCORE Office (Guam)
Pacific News Bldg., Rm. 103
238 Archbishop Flores St.
Agana, GU 96910-5100
(671)472-7308

Hawaii

SCORE Office (Hawaii, Inc.)
1111 Bishop St., Ste. 204
PO Box 50207
Honolulu, HI 96813
(808)522-8132
Fax: (808)522-8135
E-mail: hnlscore@juno.com

SCORE Office (Kahului)
250 Alamaha, Unit N16A
Kahului, HI 96732
(808)871-7711

SCORE Office (Maui, Inc.)
590 E. Lipoa Pkwy., Ste. 227
Kihei, HI 96753
(808)875-2380

Idaho

SCORE Office (Treasure Valley)
1020 Main St., No. 290
Boise, ID 83702
(208)334-1696
Fax: (208)334-9353

SCORE Office (Eastern Idaho)
2300 N. Yellowstone, Ste. 119
Idaho Falls, ID 83401
(208)523-1022
Fax: (208)528-7127

Illinois

SCORE Office (Fox Valley)
40 W. Downer Pl.
PO Box 277
Aurora, IL 60506
(630)897-9214
Fax: (630)897-7002

SCORE Office (Greater Belvidere)
419 S. State St.
Belvidere, IL 61008
(815)544-4357
Fax: (815)547-7654

SCORE Office (Bensenville)
1050 Busse Hwy. Suite 100
Bensenville, IL 60106
(708)350-2944
Fax: (708)350-2979

SCORE Office (Central Illinois)
402 N. Hershey Rd.
Bloomington, IL 61704
(309)644-0549
Fax: (309)663-8270
E-mail: webmaster@central-illinois-
score.org
Website: http://www.central-illinois-
score.org/

SCORE Office (Southern Illinois)
150 E. Pleasant Hill Rd.
Box 1
Carbondale, IL 62901
(618)453-6654
Fax: (618)453-5040

SCORE Office (Chicago)
Northwest Atrium Ctr.
500 W. Madison St., No. 1250
Chicago, IL 60661
(312)353-7724
Fax: (312)886-5688
Website: http://www.mcs.net/~bic/

SCORE Office (Chicago–Oliver Harvey College)
Pullman Bldg.
1000 E. 11th St., 7th Fl.
Chicago, IL 60628
Fax: (312)468-8086

SCORE Office (Danville)
28 W. N. Street
Danville, IL 61832
(217)442-7232
Fax: (217)442-6228

SCORE Office (Decatur)
Milliken University
1184 W. Main St.
Decatur, IL 62522
(217)424-6297
Fax: (217)424-3993
E-mail: charding@mail.millikin.edu
Website: http://www.millikin.edu/
academics/Tabor/score.html

SCORE Office (Downers Grove)
925 Curtis
Downers Grove, IL 60515
(708)968-4050
Fax: (708)968-8368

SCORE Office (Elgin)
24 E. Chicago, 3rd Fl.
PO Box 648
Elgin, IL 60120
(847)741-5660
Fax: (847)741-5677

SCORE Office (Freeport Area)
26 S. Galena Ave.
Freeport, IL 61032
(815)233-1350
Fax: (815)235-4038

SCORE Office (Galesburg)
292 E. Simmons St.
PO Box 749
Galesburg, IL 61401
(309)343-1194
Fax: (309)343-1195

SCORE Office (Glen Ellyn)
500 Pennsylvania
Glen Ellyn, IL 60137
(708)469-0907
Fax: (708)469-0426

SCORE Office (Greater Alton)
Alden Hall
5800 Godfrey Rd.
Godfrey, IL 62035-2466
(618)467-2280
Fax: (618)466-8289
Website: http://www.altonweb.com/
score/

SCORE Office (Grayslake)
19351 W. Washington St.
Grayslake, IL 60030
(708)223-3633
Fax: (708)223-9371

SCORE Office (Harrisburg)
303 S. Commercial
Harrisburg, IL 62946-1528
(618)252-8528
Fax: (618)252-0210

SCORE Office (Joliet)
100 N. Chicago
Joliet, IL 60432
(815)727-5371
Fax: (815)727-5374

SCORE Office (Kankakee)
101 S. Schuyler Ave.
Kankakee, IL 60901
(815)933-0376
Fax: (815)933-0380

SCORE Office (Macomb)
216 Seal Hall, Rm. 214

Macomb, IL 61455
(309)298-1128
Fax: (309)298-2520

SCORE Office (Matteson)
210 Lincoln Mall
Matteson, IL 60443
(708)709-3750
Fax: (708)503-9322

SCORE Office (Mattoon)
1701 Wabash Ave.
Mattoon, IL 61938
(217)235-5661
Fax: (217)234-6544

SCORE Office (Quad Cities)
622 19th St.
Moline, IL 61265
(309)797-0082
Fax: (309)757-5435
E-mail: score@qconline.com
Website: http://www.qconline.com/
business/score/

SCORE Office (Naperville)
131 W. Jefferson Ave.
Naperville, IL 60540
(708)355-4141
Fax: (708)355-8355

SCORE Office (Northbrook)
2002 Walters Ave.
Northbrook, IL 60062
(847)498-5555
Fax: (847)498-5510

SCORE Office (Palos Hills)
10900 S. 88th Ave.
Palos Hills, IL 60465
(847)974-5468
Fax: (847)974-0078

SCORE Office (Peoria)
124 SW Adams, Ste. 300
Peoria, IL 61602
(309)676-0755
Fax: (309)676-7534

SCORE Office (Prospect Heights)
1375 Wolf Rd.
Prospect Heights, IL 60070
(847)537-8660
Fax: (847)537-7138

SCORE Office (Quincy Tri-State)
300 Civic Center Plz., Ste. 245
Quincy, IL 62301
(217)222-8093
Fax: (217)222-3033

SCORE Office (River Grove)
2000 5th Ave.
River Grove, IL 60171
(708)456-0300
Fax: (708)583-3121

SCORE Office (Northern Illinois)
515 N. Court St.
Rockford, IL 61103
(815)962-0122
Fax: (815)962-0122

SCORE Office (St. Charles)
103 N. 1st Ave.
St. Charles, IL 60174-1982
(847)584-8384
Fax: (847)584-6065

SCORE Office (Springfield)
511 W. Capitol Ave., Ste. 302
Springfield, IL 62704
(217)492-4416
Fax: (217)492-4867

SCORE Office (Sycamore)
112 Somunak St.
Sycamore, IL 60178
(815)895-3456
Fax: (815)895-0125

SCORE Office (University)
Hwy. 50 & Stuenkel Rd. Ste. C3305
University Park, IL 60466
(708)534-5000
Fax: (708)534-8457

Indiana

SCORE Office (Anderson)
205 W. 11th St.
Anderson, IN 46015
(317)642-0264

SCORE Office (Bloomington)
Star Center
216 W. Allen
Bloomington, IN 47403
(812)335-7334
E-mail: wtfische@indiana.edu
Website: http://www.brainfreezemedia.
com/score527/

SCORE Office (South East Indiana)
500 Franklin St.
Box 29
Columbus, IN 47201
(812)379-4457

SCORE Office (Corydon)
310 N. Elm St.
Corydon, IN 47112

(812)738-2137
Fax: (812)738-6438

SCORE Office (Crown Point)
Old Courthouse Sq. Ste. 206
PO Box 43
Crown Point, IN 46307
(219)663-1800

SCORE Office (Elkhart)
418 S. Main St.
Elkhart, IN 46515
(219)293-1531
Fax: (219)294-1859

SCORE Office (Evansville)
1100 W. Lloyd Expy., Ste. 105
Evansville, IN 47708
(812)426-6144

SCORE Office (Fort Wayne)
1300 S. Harrison St.
Ft. Wayne, IN 46802
(219)422-2601
Fax: (219)422-2601

SCORE Office (Gary)
973 W. 6th Ave., Rm. 326
Gary, IN 46402
(219)882-3918

SCORE Office (Hammond)
7034 Indianapolis Blvd.
Hammond, IN 46324
(219)931-1000
Fax: (219)845-9548

SCORE Office (Indianapolis)
429 N. Pennsylvania St., Ste. 100
Indianapolis, IN 46204-1873
(317)226-7264
Fax: (317)226-7259
E-mail: inscore@indy.net
Website: http://www.score-
indianapolis.org/

SCORE Office (Jasper)
PO Box 307
Jasper, IN 47547-0307
(812)482-6866

**SCORE Office (Kokomo/Howard
Counties)**
106 N. Washington St.
Kokomo, IN 46901
(765)457-5301
Fax: (765)452-4564

SCORE Office (Logansport)
300 E. Broadway, Ste. 103
Logansport, IN 46947
(219)753-6388

SCORE Office (Madison)
301 E. Main St.
Madison, IN 47250
(812)265-3135
Fax: (812)265-2923

SCORE Office (Marengo)
Rt. 1 Box 224D
Marengo, IN 47140
Fax: (812)365-2793

SCORE Office (Marion/Grant Counties)
215 S. Adams
Marion, IN 46952
(765)664-5107

SCORE Office (Merrillville)
255 W. 80th Pl.
Merrillville, IN 46410
(219)769-8180
Fax: (219)736-6223

SCORE Office (Michigan City)
200 E. Michigan Blvd.
Michigan City, IN 46360
(219)874-6221
Fax: (219)873-1204

SCORE Office (South Central Indiana)
4100 Charleston Rd.
New Albany, IN 47150-9538
(812)945-0066

SCORE Office (Rensselaer)
104 W. Washington
Rensselaer, IN 47978

SCORE Office (Salem)
210 N. Main St.
Salem, IN 47167
(812)883-4303
Fax: (812)883-1467

SCORE Office (South Bend)
300 N. Michigan St.
South Bend, IN 46601
(219)282-4350
E-mail: chair@southbend-score.org
Website: http://www.southbend-score.org/

SCORE Office (Valparaiso)
150 Lincolnway
Valparaiso, IN 46383
(219)462-1105
Fax: (219)469-5710

SCORE Office (Vincennes)
27 N. 3rd
PO Box 553
Vincennes, IN 47591
(812)882-6440
Fax: (812)882-6441

SCORE Office (Wabash)
PO Box 371
Wabash, IN 46992
(219)563-1168
Fax: (219)563-6920

Iowa

SCORE Office (Burlington)
Federal Bldg.
300 N. Main St.
Burlington, IA 52601
(319)752-2967

SCORE Office (Cedar Rapids)
2750 1st Ave. NE, Ste 350
Cedar Rapids, IA 52401-1806
(319)362-6405
Fax: (319)362-7861
E:mail: score@scorecr.org
Website: http://www.scorecr.org

SCORE Office (Illowa)
333 4th Ave. S
Clinton, IA 52732
(319)242-5702

SCORE Office (Council Bluffs)
7 N. 6th St.
Council Bluffs, IA 51502
(712)325-1000

SCORE Office (Northeast Iowa)
3404 285th St.
Cresco, IA 52136
(319)547-3377

SCORE Office (Des Moines)
Federal Bldg., Rm. 749
210 Walnut St.
Des Moines, IA 50309-2186
(515)284-4760

SCORE Office (Ft. Dodge)
Federal Bldg., Rm. 436
205 S. 8th St.
Ft. Dodge, IA 50501
(515)955-2622

SCORE Office (Independence)
110 1st. St. east
Independence, IA 50644
(319)334-7178
Fax: (319)334-7179

SCORE Office (Iowa City)
210 Federal Bldg.
PO Box 1853
Iowa City, IA 52240-1853
(319)338-1662

SCORE Office (Keokuk)
401 Main St.
Pierce Bldg., No. 1
Keokuk, IA 52632
(319)524-5055

SCORE Office (Central Iowa)
Fisher Community College
709 S. Center
Marshalltown, IA 50158
(515)753-6645

SCORE Office (River City)
15 West State St.
Mason City, IA 50401
(515)423-5724

SCORE Office (South Central)
SBDC, Indian Hills Community College
525 Grandview Ave.
Ottumwa, IA 52501
(515)683-5127
Fax: (515)683-5263

SCORE Office (Dubuque)
10250 Sundown Rd.
Peosta, IA 52068
(319)556-5110

SCORE Office (Southwest Iowa)
614 W. Sheridan
Shenandoah, IA 51601
(712)246-3260

SCORE Office (Sioux City)
Federal Bldg.
320 6th St.
Sioux City, IA 51101
(712)277-2324
Fax: (712)277-2325

SCORE Office (Iowa Lakes)
122 W. 5th St.
Spencer, IA 51301
(712)262-3059

SCORE Office (Vista)
119 W. 6th St.
Storm Lake, IA 50588
(712)732-3780

SCORE Office (Waterloo)
215 E. 4th
Waterloo, IA 50703
(319)233-8431

Kansas

SCORE Office (Southwest Kansas)
501 W. Spruce
Dodge City, KS 67801
(316)227-3119

SCORE Office (Emporia)
811 Homewood
Emporia, KS 66801
(316)342-1600

SCORE Office (Golden Belt)
1307 Williams
Great Bend, KS 67530
(316)792-2401

SCORE Office (Hays)
PO Box 400
Hays, KS 67601
(913)625-6595

SCORE Office (Hutchinson)
1 E. 9th St.
Hutchinson, KS 67501
(316)665-8468
Fax: (316)665-7619

SCORE Office (Southeast Kansas)
404 Westminster Pl.
PO Box 886
Independence, KS 67301
(316)331-4741

SCORE Office (McPherson)
306 N. Main
PO Box 616
McPherson, KS 67460
(316)241-3303

SCORE Office (Salina)
120 Ash St.
Salina, KS 67401
(785)243-4290
Fax: (785)243-1833

SCORE Office (Topeka)
1700 College
Topeka, KS 66621
(785)231-1010

SCORE Office (Wichita)
100 E. English, Ste. 510
Wichita, KS 67202
(316)269-6273
Fax: (316)269-6499

SCORE Office (Ark Valley)
205 E. 9th St.
Winfield, KS 67156
(316)221-1617

Kentucky

SCORE Office (Ashland)
PO Box 830
Ashland, KY 41105
(606)329-8011
Fax: (606)325-4607

SCORE Office (Bowling Green)
812 State St.
PO Box 51
Bowling Green, KY 42101
(502)781-3200
Fax: (502)843-0458

SCORE Office (Tri-Lakes)
508 Barbee Way
Danville, KY 40422-1548
(606)231-9902

SCORE Office (Glasgow)
301 W. Main St.
Glasgow, KY 42141
(502)651-3161
Fax: (502)651-3122

SCORE Office (Hazard)
B & I Technical Center
100 Airport Gardens Rd.
Hazard, KY 41701
(606)439-5856
Fax: (606)439-1808

SCORE Office (Lexington)
410 W. Vine St., Ste. 290, Civic C
Lexington, KY 40507
(606)231-9902
Fax: (606)253-3190
E-mail: scorelex@uky.campus.mci.net

SCORE Office (Louisville)
188 Federal Office Bldg.
600 Dr. Martin L. King Jr. Pl.
Louisville, KY 40202
(502)582-5976

SCORE Office (Madisonville)
257 N. Main
Madisonville, KY 42431
(502)825-1399
Fax: (502)825-1396

SCORE Office (Paducah)
Federal Office Bldg.
501 Broadway, Rm. B-36
Paducah, KY 42001
(502)442-5685

Louisiana

SCORE Office (Central Louisiana)
802 3rd St.
Alexandria, LA 71309
(318)442-6671

SCORE Office (Baton Rouge)
564 Laurel St.
PO Box 3217
Baton Rouge, LA 70801

(504)381-7130
Fax: (504)336-4306

SCORE Office (North Shore)
2 W. Thomas
Hammond, LA 70401
(504)345-4457
Fax: (504)345-4749

SCORE Office (Lafayette)
804 St. Mary Blvd.
Lafayette, LA 70505-1307
(318)233-2705
Fax: (318)234-8671
E-mail: score302@aol.com

SCORE Office (Lake Charles)
120 W. Pujo St.
Lake Charles, LA 70601
(318)433-3632

SCORE Office (New Orleans)
365 Canal St., Ste. 3100
New Orleans, LA 70130
(504)589-2356
Fax: (504)589-2339

SCORE Office (Shreveport)
400 Edwards St.
Shreveport, LA 71101
(318)677-2536
Fax: (318)677-2541

Maine

SCORE Office (Augusta)
40 Western Ave.
Augusta, ME 04330
(207)622-8509

SCORE Office (Bangor)
Peabody Hall, Rm. 229
One College Cir.
Bangor, ME 04401
(207)941-9707

SCORE Office (Central & Northern Arroostock)
111 High St.
Caribou, ME 04736
(207)492-8010
Fax: (207)492-8010

SCORE Office (Penquis)
South St.
Dover Foxcroft, ME 04426
(207)564-7021

SCORE Office (Maine Coastal)
Mill Mall
Box 1105
Ellsworth, ME 04605-1105

(207)667-5800
E-mail: score@arcadia.net

SCORE Office (Lewiston-Auburn)
BIC of Maine-Bates Mill Complex
35 Canal St.
Lewiston, ME 04240-7764
(207)782-3708
Fax: (207)783-7745

SCORE Office (Portland)
66 Pearl St., Rm. 210
Portland, ME 04101
(207)772-1147
Fax: (207)772-5581
E-mail: Score53@score.maine.org
Website: http://www.score.maine.org/
chapter53/

SCORE Office (Western Mountains)
255 River St.
PO Box 252
Rumford, ME 04257-0252
(207)369-9976

SCORE Office (Oxford Hills)
166 Main St.
South Paris, ME 04281
(207)743-0499

Maryland

SCORE Office (Southern Maryland)
2525 Riva Rd., Ste. 110
Annapolis, MD 21401
(410)266-9553
Fax: (410)573-0981
E-mail: score390@aol.com
Website: http://members.aol.com/
score390/index.htm

SCORE Office (Baltimore)
The City Crescent Bldg., 6th Fl.
10 S. Howard St.
Baltimore, MD 21201
(410)962-2233
Fax: (410)962-1805

SCORE Office (Bel Air)
108 S. Bond St.
Bel Air, MD 21014
(410)838-2020
Fax: (410)893-4715

SCORE Office (Bethesda)
7910 Woodmont Ave., Ste. 1204
Bethesda, MD 20814
(301)652-4900
Fax: (301)657-1973

SCORE Office (Bowie)
6670 Race Track Rd.
Bowie, MD 20715
(301)262-0920
Fax: (301)262-0921

SCORE Office (Dorchester County)
203 Sunburst Hwy.
Cambridge, MD 21613
(410)228-3575

SCORE Office (Upper Shore)
210 Marlboro Ave.
Easton, MD 21601
(410)822-4606
Fax: (410)822-7922

SCORE Office (Frederick County)
43A S. Market St.
Frederick, MD 21701
(301)662-8723
Fax: (301)846-4427

SCORE Office (Gaithersburg)
9 Park Ave.
Gaithersburg, MD 20877
(301)840-1400
Fax: (301)963-3918

SCORE Office (Glen Burnie)
103 Crain Hwy. SE
Glen Burnie, MD 21061
(410)766-8282
Fax: (410)766-9722

SCORE Office (Hagerstown)
111 W. Washington St.
Hagerstown, MD 21740
(301)739-2015
Fax: (301)739-1278

SCORE Office (Laurel)
7901 Sandy Spring Rd. Ste. 501
Laurel, MD 20707
(301)725-4000
Fax: (301)725-0776

SCORE Office (Salisbury)
300 E. Main St.
Salisbury, MD 21801
(410)749-0185
Fax: (410)860-9925

Massachusetts

SCORE Office (NE Massachusetts)
100 Cummings Ctr., Ste. 101 K
Beverly, MA 01923
(978)922-9441
Website: http://www1.shore.net/~score/

SCORE Office (Boston)
10 Causeway St., Rm. 265
Boston, MA 02222-1093
(617)565-5591
Fax: (617)565-5598
E-mail: boston-score-20@worldnet.att.net
Website: http://www.scoreboston.org/

SCORE office (Bristol/Plymouth County)
53 N. 6th St., Federal Bldg.
Bristol, MA 02740
(508)994-5093

SCORE Office (SE Massachusetts)
60 School St.
Brockton, MA 02401
(508)587-2673
Fax: (508)587-1340
Website: http://www.metrosouth
chamber.com/score.html

SCORE Office (North Adams)
820 N. State Rd.
Cheshire, MA 01225
(413)743-5100

SCORE Office (Clinton Satellite)
1 Green St.
Clinton, MA 01510
Fax: (508)368-7689

SCORE Office (Greenfield)
PO Box 898
Greenfield, MA 01302
(413)773-5463
Fax: (413)773-7008

SCORE Office (Haverhill)
87 Winter St.
Haverhill, MA 01830
(508)373-5663
Fax: (508)373-8060

SCORE Office (Hudson Satellite)
PO Box 578
Hudson, MA 01749
(508)568-0360
Fax: (508)568-0360

SCORE Office (Cape Cod)
Independence Pk., Ste. 5B
270 Communications Way
Hyannis, MA 02601
(508)775-4884
Fax: (508)790-2540

SCORE Office (Lawrence)
264 Essex St.
Lawrence, MA 01840
(508)686-0900
Fax: (508)794-9953

SCORE Office (Leominster Satellite)
110 Erdman Way
Leominster, MA 01453
(508)840-4300
Fax: (508)840-4896

SCORE Office (Bristol/Plymouth Counties)
53 N. 6th St., Federal Bldg.
New Bedford, MA 02740
(508)994-5093

SCORE Office (Newburyport)
29 State St.
Newburyport, MA 01950
(617)462-6680

SCORE Office (Pittsfield)
66 West St.
Pittsfield, MA 01201
(413)499-2485

SCORE Office (Haverhill-Salem)
32 Derby Sq.
Salem, MA 01970
(508)745-0330
Fax: (508)745-3855

SCORE Office (Springfield)
1350 Main St.
Federal Bldg.
Springfield, MA 01103
(413)785-0314

SCORE Office (Carver)
12 Taunton Green, Ste. 201
Taunton, MA 02780
(508)824-4068
Fax: (508)824-4069

SCORE Office (Worcester)
33 Waldo St.
Worcester, MA 01608
(508)753-2929
Fax: (508)754-8560

Michigan

SCORE Office (Allegan)
PO Box 338
Allegan, MI 49010
(616)673-2479

SCORE Office (Ann Arbor)
425 S. Main St., Ste. 103
Ann Arbor, MI 48104
(313)665-4433

SCORE Office (Battle Creek)
34 W. Jackson Ste. 4A
Battle Creek, MI 49017-3505

(616)962-4076
Fax: (616)962-6309

SCORE Office (Cadillac)
222 Lake St.
Cadillac, MI 49601
(616)775-9776
Fax: (616)768-4255

SCORE Office (Detroit)
477 Michigan Ave., Rm. 515
Detroit, MI 48226
(313)226-7947
Fax: (313)226-3448

SCORE Office (Flint)
708 Root Rd., Rm. 308
Flint, MI 48503
(810)233-6846

SCORE Office (Grand Rapids)
111 Pearl St. NW
Grand Rapids, MI 49503-2831
(616)771-0305
Fax: (616)771-0328
E-mail: scoreone@iserv.net
Website: http://www.iserv.net/
~scoreone/

SCORE Office (Holland)
480 State St.
Holland, MI 49423
(616)396-9472

SCORE Office (Jackson)
209 East Washington
PO Box 80
Jackson, MI 49204
(517)782-8221
Fax: (517)782-0061

SCORE Office (Kalamazoo)
345 W. Michigan Ave.
Kalamazoo, MI 49007
(616)381-5382
Fax: (616)384-0096
E-mail: score@nucleus.net

SCORE Office (Lansing)
117 E. Allegan
PO Box 14030
Lansing, MI 48901
(517)487-6340
Fax: (517)484-6910

SCORE Office (Livonia)
15401 Farmington Rd.
Livonia, MI 48154
(313)427-2122
Fax: (313)427-6055

SCORE Office (Madison Heights)
26345 John R
Madison Heights, MI 48071
(810)542-5010
Fax: (810)542-6821

SCORE Office (Monroe)
111 E. 1st
Monroe, MI 48161
(313)242-3366
Fax: (313)242-7253

SCORE Office (Mt. Clemens)
58 S/B Gratiot
Mt. Clemens, MI 48043
(810)463-1528
Fax: (810)463-6541

SCORE Office (Muskegon)
PO Box 1087
230 Terrace Plz.
Muskegon, MI 49443
(616)722-3751
Fax: (616)728-7251

SCORE Office (Petoskey)
401 E. Mitchell St.
Petoskey, MI 49770
(616)347-4150

SCORE Office (Pontiac)
Executive Office Bldg.
1200 N. Telegraph Rd.
Pontiac, MI 48341
(810)975-9555

SCORE Office (Pontiac)
PO Box 430025
Pontiac, MI 48343
(810)335-9600

SCORE Office (Port Huron)
920 Pinegrove Ave.
Port Huron, MI 48060
(810)985-7101

SCORE Office (Rochester)
71 Walnut Ste. 110
Rochester, MI 48307
(810)651-6700
Fax: (810)651-5270

SCORE Office (Saginaw)
901 S. Washington Ave.
Saginaw, MI 48601
(517)752-7161
Fax: (517)752-9055

SCORE Office (Upper Peninsula)
2581 I-75 Business Spur
Sault Ste. Marie, MI 49783
(906)632-3301

SCORE Office (Southfield)

21000 W. 10 Mile Rd.

Southfield, MI 48075

(810)204-3050

Fax: (810)204-3099

SCORE Office (Traverse City)

202 E. Grandview Pkwy.

PO Box 387

Traverse City, MI 49685

(616)947-5075

Fax: (616)946-2565

SCORE Office (Warren)

30500 Van Dyke, Ste. 118

Warren, MI 48093

(810)751-3939

Minnesota

SCORE Office (Aitkin)

Aitkin, MN 56431

(218)741-3906

SCORE Office (Albert Lea)

202 N. Broadway Ave.

Albert Lea, MN 56007

(507)373-7487

SCORE Office (Austin)

PO Box 864

Austin, MN 55912

(507)437-4561

Fax: (507)437-4869

SCORE Office (South Metro)

Ames Business Ctr.

2500 W. County Rd., No. 42

Burnsville, MN 55337

(612)898-5645

Fax: (612)435-6972

E-mail: southmetro@scoreminn.org

Website: http://www.scoreminn.org/

southmetro/

SCORE Office (Duluth)

1717 Minnesota Ave.

Duluth, MN 55802

(218)727-8286

Fax: (218)727-3113

E-mail: duluth@scoreminn.org

Website: http://www.scoreminn.org

SCORE Office (Fairmont)

PO Box 826

Fairmont, MN 56031

(507)235-5547

Fax: (507)235-8411

SCORE Office (Southwest Minnesota)

112 Riverfront St.

Box 999

Mankato, MN 56001

(507)345-4519

Fax: (507)345-4451

Website: http://www.scoreminn.org/

SCORE Office (Minneapolis)

North Plaza Bldg., Ste. 51

5217 Wayzata Blvd.

Minneapolis, MN 55416

(612)591-0539

Fax: (612)544-0436

Website: http://www.scoreminn.org/

SCORE Office (Owatonna)

PO Box 331

Owatonna, MN 55060

(507)451-7970

Fax: (507)451-7972

SCORE Office (Red Wing)

2000 W. Main St., Ste. 324

Red Wing, MN 55066

(612)388-4079

SCORE Office (Southeastern Minnesota)

220 S. Broadway, Ste. 100

Rochester, MN 55901

(507)288-1122

Fax: (507)282-8960

Website: http://www.scoreminn.org/

SCORE Office (Brainerd)

St. Cloud, MN 56301

SCORE Office (Central Area)

1527 Northway Dr.

St. Cloud, MN 56301

(320)240-1332

Fax: (320)255-9050

Website: http://www.scoreminn.org/

SCORE Office (St. Paul)

350 St. Peter St., No. 295

Lowry Professional Bldg.

St. Paul, MN 55102

(651)223-5010

Fax: (651)223-5048

Website: http://www.scoreminn.org/

SCORE Office (Winona)

Box 870

Winona, MN 55987

(507)452-2272

Fax: (507)454-8814

SCORE Office (Worthington)

1121 3rd Ave.

Worthington, MN 56187

(507)372-2919

Fax: (507)372-2827

Mississippi

SCORE Office (Delta)

915 Washington Ave.

PO Box 933

Greenville, MS 38701

(601)378-3141

SCORE Office (Gulfcoast)

1 Government Plaza

2909 13th St., Ste. 203

Gulfport, MS 39501

(228)863-0054

SCORE Office (Jackson)

1st Jackson Center, Ste. 400

101 W. Capitol St.

Jackson, MS 39201

(601)965-5533

SCORE Office (Meridian)

5220 16th Ave.

Meridian, MS 39305

(601)482-4412

Missouri

SCORE Office (Lake of the Ozark)

University Extension

113 Kansas St.

PO Box 1405

Camdenton, MO 65020

(573)346-2644

Fax: (573)346-2694

E-mail: score@cdoc.net

Website: http://sites.cdoc.net/score/

Chamber of Commerce (Cape Girardeau)

PO Box 98

Cape Girardeau, MO 63702-0098

(314)335-3312

SCORE Office (Mid-Missouri)

1705 Halstead Ct.

Columbia, MO 65203

(573)874-1132

SCORE Office (Ozark-Gateway)

1486 Glassy Rd.

Cuba, MO 65453-1640

(573)885-4954

SCORE Office (Kansas City)

323 W. 8th St., Ste. 104

Kansas City, MO 64105

(816)374-6675

Fax: (816)374-6692

E-mail: SCOREBIC@AOL.COM

Website: http://www.crn.org/score/

SCORE Office (Sedalia)
Lucas Place
323 W. 8th St., Ste.104
Kansas City, MO 64105
(816)374-6675

SCORE office (Tri-Lakes)
PO Box 1148
Kimberling, MO 65686
(417)739-3041

SCORE Office (Tri-Lakes)
HCRI Box 85
Lampe, MO 65681
(417)858-6798

SCORE Office (Mexico)
111 N. Washington St.
Mexico, MO 65265
(314)581-2765

SCORE Office (Southeast Missouri)
Rte. 1, Box 280
Neelyville, MO 63954
(573)989-3577

SCORE office (Poplar Bluff Area)
806 Emma St.
Poplar Bluff, MO 63901
(573)686-8892

SCORE Office (St. Joseph)
3003 Frederick Ave.
St. Joseph, MO 64506
(816)232-4461

SCORE Office (St. Louis)
815 Olive St., Rm. 242
St. Louis, MO 63101-1569
(314)539-6970
Fax: (314)539-3785
E-mail: info@stlscore.org
Website: http://www.stlscore.org/

SCORE Office (Lewis & Clark)
425 Spencer Rd.
St. Peters, MO 63376
(314)928-2900
Fax: (314)928-2900
E-mail: score01@mail.win.org

SCORE Office (Springfield)
620 S. Glenstone, Ste. 110
Springfield, MO 65802-3200
(417)864-7670
Fax: (417)864-4108

SCORE office (Southeast Kansas)
1206 W. First St.
Webb City, MO 64870
(417)673-3984

Montana

SCORE Office (Billings)
815 S. 27th St.
Billings, MT 59101
(406)245-4111

SCORE Office (Bozeman)
1205 E. Main St.
Bozeman, MT 59715
(406)586-5421

SCORE Office (Butte)
1000 George St.
Butte, MT 59701
(406)723-3177

SCORE Office (Great Falls)
710 First Ave. N
Great Falls, MT 59401
(406)761-4434
E-mail: scoregtf@in.tch.com

SCORE Office (Havre, Montana)
518 First St.
Havre, MT 59501
(406)265-4383

SCORE Office (Helena)
Federal Bldg.
301 S. Park
Helena, MT 59626-0054
(406)441-1081

SCORE Office (Kalispell)
2 Main St.
Kalispell, MT 59901
(406)756-5271
Fax: (406)752-6665

SCORE Office (Missoula)
723 Ronan
Missoula, MT 59806
(406)327-8806
E-mail: score@safeshop.com
Website: http://missoula.bigsky.net/score/

Nebraska

SCORE Office (Columbus)
Columbus, NE 68601
(402)564-2769

SCORE Office (Fremont)
92 W. 5th St.
Fremont, NE 68025
(402)721-2641

SCORE Office (Hastings)
Hastings, NE 68901
(402)463-3447

SCORE Office (Lincoln)
8800 O St.
Lincoln, NE 68520
(402)437-2409

SCORE Office (Panhandle)
150549 CR 30
Minatare, NE 69356
(308)632-2133
Website: http://www.tandt.com/SCORE

SCORE Office (Norfolk)
3209 S. 48th Ave.
Norfolk, NE 68106
(402)564-2769

SCORE Office (North Platte)
3301 W. 2nd St.
North Platte, NE 69101
(308)532-4466

SCORE Office (Omaha)
11145 Mill Valley Rd.
Omaha, NE 68154
(402)221-3606
Fax: (402)221-3680
E-mail: infoctr@ne.uswest.net
Website: http://www.tandt.com/score/

Nevada

SCORE Office (Incline Village)
969 Tahoe Blvd.
Incline Village, NV 89451
(702)831-7327
Fax: (702)832-1605

SCORE Office (Carson City)
301 E. Stewart
PO Box 7527
Las Vegas, NV 89125
(702)388-6104

SCORE Office (Las Vegas)
300 Las Vegas Blvd. S, Ste. 1100
Las Vegas, NV 89101
(702)388-6104

SCORE Office (Northern Nevada)
SBDC, College of Business
Administration
Univ. of Nevada
Reno, NV 89557-0100
(702)784-4436
Fax: (702)784-4337

New Hampshire

SCORE Office (North Country)
PO Box 34

Berlin, NH 03570
(603)752-1090

SCORE Office (Concord)
143 N. Main St., Rm. 202A
PO Box 1258
Concord, NH 03301
(603)225-1400
Fax: (603)225-1409

SCORE Office (Dover)
299 Central Ave.
Dover, NH 03820
(603)742-2218
Fax: (603)749-6317

SCORE Office (Monadnock)
34 Mechanic St.
Keene, NH 03431-3421
(603)352-0320

SCORE Office (Lakes Region)
67 Water St., Ste. 105
Laconia, NH 03246
(603)524-9168

SCORE Office (Upper Valley)
Citizens Bank Bldg., Rm. 310
20 W. Park St.
Lebanon, NH 03766
(603)448-3491
Fax: (603)448-1908
E-mail: billt@valley.net
Website: http://www.valley.net/~score/

SCORE Office (Merrimack Valley)
275 Chestnut St., Rm. 618
Manchester, NH 03103
(603)666-7561
Fax: (603)666-7925

SCORE Office (Mt. Washington Valley)
PO Box 1066
North Conway, NH 03818
(603)383-0800

SCORE Office (Seacoast)
195 Commerce Way, Unit-A
Portsmouth, NH 03801-3251
(603)433-0575

New Jersey

SCORE Office (Somerset)
Paritan Valley Community College,
Rte. 28
Branchburg, NJ 08807
(908)218-8874
E-mail: nj-score@grizbiz.com.
Website: http://www.nj-score.org/

SCORE Office (Chester)
5 Old Mill Rd.
Chester, NJ 07930
(908)879-7080

**SCORE Office
(Greater Princeton)**
4 A George Washington Dr.
Cranbury, NJ 08512
(609)520-1776

SCORE Office (Freehold)
36 W. Main St.
Freehold, NJ 07728
(908)462-3030
Fax: (908)462-2123

SCORE Office (North West)
Picantinny Innovation Ctr.
3159 Schrader Rd.
Hamburg, NJ 07419
(973)209-8525
Fax: (973)209-7252
E-mail: nj-score@grizbiz.com
Website: http://www.nj-score.org/

SCORE Office (Monmouth)
765 Newman Springs Rd.
Lincroft, NJ 07738
(908)224-2573
E-mail: nj-score@grizbiz.com
Website: http://www.nj-score.org/

SCORE Office (Manalapan)
125 Symmes Dr.
Manalapan, NJ 07726
(908)431-7220

SCORE Office (Jersey City)
2 Gateway Ctr., 4th Fl.
Newark, NJ 07102
(973)645-3982
Fax: (973)645-2375

SCORE Office (Newark)
2 Gateway Center, 15th Fl.
Newark, NJ 07102-5553
(973)645-3982
Fax: (973)645-2375
E-mail: nj-score@grizbiz.com
Website: http://www.nj-score.org

SCORE Office (Bergen County)
327 E. Ridgewood Ave.
Paramus, NJ 07652
(201)599-6090
E-mail: nj-score@grizbiz.com
Website: http://www.nj-score.org/

SCORE Office (Pennsauken)
4900 Rte. 70

Pennsauken, NJ 08109
(609)486-3421

SCORE Office (Southern New Jersey)
4900 Rte. 70
Pennsauken, NJ 08109
(609)486-3421
E-mail: nj-score@grizbiz.com
Website: http://www.nj-score.org/

SCORE Office (Greater Princeton)
216 Rockingham Row
Princeton Forrestal Village
Princeton, NJ 08540
(609)520-1776
Fax: (609)520-9107
E-mail: nj-score@grizbiz.com
Website: http://www.nj-score.org/

SCORE Office (Shrewsbury)
Hwy. 35
Shrewsbury, NJ 07702
(908)842-5995
Fax: (908)219-6140

SCORE Office (Ocean County)
33 Washington St.
Toms River, NJ 08754
(732)505-6033
E-mail: nj-score@grizbiz.com
Website: http://www.nj-score.org/

SCORE Office (Wall)
2700 Allaire Rd.
Wall, NJ 07719
(908)449-8877

SCORE Office (Wayne)
2055 Hamburg Tpke.
Wayne, NJ 07470
(201)831-7788
Fax: (201)831-9112

New Mexico

SCORE Office (Albuquerque)
525 Buena Vista, SE
Albuquerque, NM 87106
(505)272-7999
Fax: (505)272-7963

SCORE Office (Las Cruces)
Loretto Towne Center
505 S. Main St., Ste. 125
Las Cruces, NM 88001
(505)523-5627
Fax: (505)524-2101
E-mail: score.397@zianet.com

SCORE Office (Roswell)
Federal Bldg., Rm. 237

Roswell, NM 88201
(505)625-2112
Fax: (505)623-2545

SCORE Office (Santa Fe)
Montoya Federal Bldg.
120 Federal Place, Rm. 307
Santa Fe, NM 87501
(505)988-6302
Fax: (505)988-6300

New York

SCORE Office (Northeast)
1 Computer Dr. S
Albany, NY 12205
(518)446-1118
Fax: (518)446-1228

SCORE Office (Auburn)
30 South St.
PO Box 675
Auburn, NY 13021
(315)252-7291

SCORE Office (South Tier Binghamton)
Metro Center, 2nd Fl.
49 Court St.
PO Box 995
Binghamton, NY 13902
(607)772-8860

SCORE Office (Queens County City)
12055 Queens Blvd., Rm. 333
Borough Hall, NY 11424
(718)263-8961

SCORE Office (Buffalo)
Federal Bldg., Rm. 1311
111 W. Huron St.
Buffalo, NY 14202
(716)551-4301
Website: http://www2.pcom.net/score/
buf45.html

SCORE Office (Canandaigua)
Chamber of Commerce Bldg.
113 S. Main St.
Canandaigua, NY 14424
(716)394-4400
Fax: (716)394-4546

SCORE Office (Chemung)
333 E. Water St., 4th Fl.
Elmira, NY 14901
(607)734-3358

SCORE Office (Geneva)
Chamber of Commerce Bldg.
PO Box 587

Geneva, NY 14456
(315)789-1776
Fax: (315)789-3993

SCORE Office (Glens Falls)
84 Broad St.
Glens Falls, NY 12801
(518)798-8463
Fax: (518)745-1433

SCORE Office (Orange County)
40 Matthews St.
Goshen, NY 10924
(914)294-8080
Fax: (914)294-6121

SCORE Office (Huntington Area)
151 W. Carver St.
Huntington, NY 11743
(516)423-6100

SCORE Office (Tompkins County)
904 E. Shore Dr.
Ithaca, NY 14850
(607)273-7080

SCORE Office (Long Island City)
120-55 Queens Blvd.
Jamaica, NY 11424
(718)263-8961
Fax: (718)263-9032

SCORE Office (Chatauqua)
101 W. 5th St.
Jamestown, NY 14701
(716)484-1103

SCORE Office (Westchester)
2 Caradon Ln.
Katonah, NY 10536
(914)948-3907
Fax: (914)948-4645
E-mail: score@w-w-w.com
Website: http://w-w-w.com/score/

SCORE Office (Queens County)
Queens Borough Hall
120-55 Queens Blvd. Rm. 333
Kew Gardens, NY 11424
(718)263-8961
Fax: (718)263-9032

SCORE Office (Brookhaven)
3233 Rte. 112
Medford, NY 11763
(516)451-6563
Fax: (516)451-6925

SCORE Office (Melville)
35 Pinelawn Rd., Rm. 207-W
Melville, NY 11747
(516)454-0771

SCORE Office (Nassau County)
400 County Seat Dr., No. 140
Mineola, NY 11501
(516)571-3303
E-mail: Counse1998@aol.com
Website: http://members.aol.com/
Counse1998/Default.htm

SCORE Office (Mt. Vernon)
4 N. 7th Ave.
Mt. Vernon, NY 10550
(914)667-7500

SCORE Office (New York)
26 Federal Plz., Rm. 3100
New York, NY 10278
(212)264-4507
Fax: (212)264-4963
E-mail: score1000@erols.com
Website: http://users.erols.com/
score-nyc/

SCORE Office (Newburgh)
47 Grand St.
Newburgh, NY 12550
(914)562-5100

SCORE Office (Owego)
188 Front St.
Owego, NY 13827
(607)687-2020

SCORE Office (Peekskill)
1 S. Division St.
Peekskill, NY 10566
(914)737-3600
Fax: (914)737-0541

SCORE Office (Penn Yan)
2375 Rte. 14A
Penn Yan, NY 14527
(315)536-3111

SCORE Office (Dutchess)
110 Main St.
Poughkeepsie, NY 12601
(914)454-1700

SCORE Office (Rochester)
601 Keating Federal Bldg., Rm. 410
100 State St.
Rochester, NY 14614
(716)263-6473
Fax: (716)263-3146
Website: http://www.ggw.org/score/

SCORE Office (Saranac Lake)
30 Main St.
Saranac Lake, NY 12983
(315)448-0415

SCORE Office (Suffolk)
286 Main St.
Setauket, NY 11733
(516)751-3886

SCORE Office (Staten Island)
130 Bay St.
Staten Island, NY 10301
(718)727-1221

SCORE Office (Ulster)
Clinton Bldg., Rm. 107
Stone Ridge, NY 12484
(914)687-5035
Fax: (914)687-5015
Website: http://www.scoreulster.org/

SCORE Office (Syracuse)
401 S. Salina, 5th Fl.
Syracuse, NY 13202
(315)471-9393

SCORE Office (Utica)
SUNY Institute of Technology, Route 12
Utica, NY 13504-3050
(315)792-7553

SCORE Office (Watertown)
518 Davidson St.
Watertown, NY 13601
(315)788-1200
Fax: (315)788-8251

North Carolina

SCORE office (Asheboro)
317 E. Dixie Dr.
Asheboro, NC 27203
(336)626-2626
Fax: (336)626-7077

SCORE Office (Asheville)
Federal Bldg., Rm. 259
151 Patton
Asheville, NC 28801-5770
(828)271-4786
Fax: (828)271-4009

SCORE Office (Chapel Hill)
104 S. Estes Dr.
PO Box 2897
Chapel Hill, NC 27514
(919)967-7075

SCORE Office (Coastal Plains)
PO Box 2897
Chapel Hill, NC 27515
(919)967-7075
Fax: (919)968-6874

SCORE Office (Charlotte)
200 N. College St., Ste. A-2015

Charlotte, NC 28202
(704)344-6576
Fax: (704)344-6769
E-mail: CharlotteSCORE47@AOL.com
Website: http://www.charweb.org/
business/score/

SCORE Office (Durham)
411 W. Chapel Hill St.
Durham, NC 27707
(919)541-2171

SCORE Office (Gastonia)
PO Box 2168
Gastonia, NC 28053
(704)864-2621
Fax: (704)854-8723

SCORE Office (Greensboro)
400 W. Market St., Ste. 103
Greensboro, NC 27401-2241
(910)333-5399

SCORE Office (Henderson)
PO Box 917
Henderson, NC 27536
(919)492-2061
Fax: (919)430-0460

SCORE Office (Hendersonville)
Federal Bldg., Rm. 108
W. 4th Ave. & Church St.
Hendersonville, NC 28792
(828)693-8702
E-mail: score@circle.net
Website: http://www.wncguide.com/
score/Welcome.html

SCORE Office (Unifour)
PO Box 1828
Hickory, NC 28603
(704)328-6111

SCORE Office (High Point)
1101 N. Main St.
High Point, NC 27262
(336)882-8625
Fax: (336)889-9499

SCORE Office (Outer Banks)
Collington Rd. and Mustain
Kill Devil Hills, NC 27948
(252)441-8144

SCORE Office (Down East)
312 S. Front St., Ste. 6
New Bern, NC 28560
(252)633-6688
Fax: (252)633-9608

SCORE Office (Kinston)
PO Box 95

New Bern, NC 28561
(919)633-6688

SCORE Office (Raleigh)
Century Post Office Bldg., Ste. 306
300 Federal St. Mall
Raleigh, NC 27601
(919)856-4739
E-mail: jendres@ibm.net
Website: http://www.intrex.net/score96/
score96.htm

SCORE Office (Sanford)
1801 Nash St.
Sanford, NC 27330
(919)774-6442
Fax: (919)776-8739

SCORE Office (Sandhills Area)
1480 Hwy. 15-501
PO Box 458
Southern Pines, NC 28387
(910)692-3926

SCORE Office (Wilmington)
Corps of Engineers Bldg.
96 Darlington Ave., Ste. 207
Wilmington, NC 28403
(910)815-4576
Fax: (910)815-4658

North Dakota

**SCORE Office
(Bismarck-Mandan)**
700 E. Main Ave., 2nd Fl.
PO Box 5509
Bismarck, ND 58506-5509
(701)250-4303

SCORE Office (Fargo)
657 2nd Ave., Rm. 225
Fargo, ND 58108-3083
(701)239-5677

SCORE Office (Upper Red River)
4275 Technology Dr., Rm. 156
Grand Forks, ND 58202-8372
(701)777-3051

SCORE Office (Minot)
100 1st St. SW
Minot, ND 58701-3846
(701)852-6883
Fax: (701)852-6905

Ohio

SCORE Office (Akron)
1 Cascade Plz., 7th Fl.
Akron, OH 44308

(330)379-3163
Fax: (330)379-3164

SCORE Office (Ashland)
Gill Center
47 W. Main St.
Ashland, OH 44805
(419)281-4584

SCORE Office (Canton)
116 Cleveland Ave. NW, Ste. 601
Canton, OH 44702-1720
(330)453-6047

SCORE Office (Chillicothe)
165 S. Paint St.
Chillicothe, OH 45601
(614)772-4530

SCORE Office (Cincinnati)
Ameritrust Bldg., Rm. 850
525 Vine St.
Cincinnati, OH 45202
(513)684-2812
Fax: (513)684-3251
Website: http://www.score.
chapter34.org/

SCORE Office (Cleveland)
Eaton Center, Ste. 620
1100 Superior Ave.
Cleveland, OH 44114-2507
(216)522-4194
Fax: (216)522-4844

SCORE Office (Columbus)
2 Nationwide Plz., Ste. 1400
Columbus, OH 43215-2542
(614)469-2357
Fax: (614)469-2391
E-mail: info@scorecolumbus.org
Website: http://www.scorecolumbus.org/

SCORE Office (Dayton)
Dayton Federal Bldg., Rm. 505
200 W. Second St.
Dayton, OH 45402-1430
(513)225-2887
Fax: (513)225-7667

SCORE Office (Defiance)
615 W. 3rd St.
PO Box 130
Defiance, OH 43512
(419)782-7946

SCORE Office (Findlay)
123 E. Main Cross St.
PO Box 923
Findlay, OH 45840
(419)422-3314

SCORE Office (Lima)
147 N. Main St.
Lima, OH 45801
(419)222-6045
Fax: (419)229-0266

SCORE Office (Mansfield)
55 N. Mulberry St.
Mansfield, OH 44902
(419)522-3211

SCORE Office (Marietta)
Thomas Hall
Marietta, OH 45750
(614)373-0268

SCORE Office (Medina)
County Administrative Bldg.
144 N. Broadway
Medina, OH 44256
(216)764-8650

SCORE Office (Licking County)
50 W. Locust St.
Newark, OH 43055
(614)345-7458

SCORE Office (Salem)
2491 State Rte. 45 S
Salem, OH 44460
(216)332-0361

SCORE Office (Tiffin)
62 S. Washington St.
Tiffin, OH 44883
(419)447-4141
Fax: (419)447-5141

SCORE Office (Toledo)
608 Madison Ave, Ste. 910
Toledo, OH 43624
(419)259-7598
Fax: (419)259-6460

SCORE Office (Heart of Ohio)
377 W. Liberty St.
Wooster, OH 44691
(330)262-5735
Fax: (330)262-5745

SCORE Office (Youngstown)
306 Williamson Hall
Youngstown, OH 44555
(330)746-2687

Oklahoma

SCORE Office (Anadarko)
PO Box 366
Anadarko, OK 73005
(405)247-6651

SCORE Office (Ardmore)
410 W. Main
Ardmore, OK 73401
(580)226-2620

SCORE Office (Northeast Oklahoma)
210 S. Main
Grove, OK 74344
(918)787-2796
Fax: (918)787-2796
E-mail: Score595@greencis.net

SCORE Office (Lawton)
4500 W. Lee Blvd., Bldg. 100, Ste. 107
Lawton, OK 73505
(580)353-8727
Fax: (580)250-5677

SCORE Office (Oklahoma City)
210 Park Ave., No. 1300
Oklahoma City, OK 73102
(405)231-5163
Fax: (405)231-4876
E-mail: score212@usa.net

SCORE Office (Stillwater)
439 S. Main
Stillwater, OK 74074
(405)372-5573
Fax: (405)372-4316

SCORE Office (Tulsa)
616 S. Boston, Ste. 406
Tulsa, OK 74119
(918)581-7462
Fax: (918)581-6908
Website: http://www.ionet.net/~tulscore/

Oregon

SCORE Office (Bend)
63085 N. Hwy. 97
Bend, OR 97701
(541)923-2849
Fax: (541)330-6900

SCORE Office (Willamette)
1401 Willamette St.
PO Box 1107
Eugene, OR 97401-4003
(541)465-6600
Fax: (541)484-4942

SCORE Office (Florence)
3149 Oak St.
Florence, OR 97439
(503)997-8444
Fax: (503)997-8448

SCORE Office (Southern Oregon)
33 N. Central Ave., Ste. 216

Medford, OR 97501
(541)776-4220
E-mail: pgr134f@prodigy.com

SCORE Office (Portland)
1515 SW 5th Ave., Ste. 1050
Portland, OR 97201
(503)326-3441
Fax: (503)326-2808
E-mail: gr134@prodigy.com

SCORE Office (Salem)
416 State St. (corner of Liberty)
Salem, OR 97301
(503)370-2896

Pennsylvania

SCORE Office (Altoona-Blair)
1212 12th Ave.
Altoona, PA 16601-3493
(814)943-8151

SCORE Office (Lehigh Valley)
Rauch Bldg. 37
Lehigh University
621 Taylor St.
Bethlehem, PA 18015
(610)758-4496
Fax: (610)758-5205

SCORE Office (Butler County)
100 N. Main St.
PO Box 1082
Butler, PA 16003
(412)283-2222
Fax: (412)283-0224

SCORE Office (Harrisburg)
4211 Trindle Rd.
Camp Hill, PA 17011
(717)761-4304
Fax: (717)761-4315

SCORE Office (Cumberland Valley)
75 S. 2nd St.
Chambersburg, PA 17201
(717)264-2935

SCORE Office (Monroe County-Stroudsburg)
556 Main St.
East Stroudsburg, PA 18301
(717)421-4433

SCORE Office (Erie)
120 W. 9th St.
Erie, PA 16501
(814)871-5650
Fax: (814)871-7530

SCORE Office (Bucks County)
409 Hood Blvd.
Fairless Hills, PA 19030
(215)943-8850
Fax: (215)943-7404

SCORE Office (Hanover)
146 Broadway
Hanover, PA 17331
(717)637-6130
Fax: (717)637-9127

SCORE Office (Harrisburg)
100 Chestnut, Ste. 309
Harrisburg, PA 17101
(717)782-3874

SCORE Office (East Montgomery County)
Baederwood Shopping Center
1653 The Fairways, Ste. 204
Jenkintown, PA 19046
(215)885-3027

SCORE Office (Kittanning)
2 Butler Rd.
Kittanning, PA 16201
(412)543-1305
Fax: (412)543-6206

SCORE Office (Lancaster)
118 W. Chestnut St.
Lancaster, PA 17603
(717)397-3092

SCORE Office (Westmoreland County)
300 Fraser Purchase Rd.
Latrobe, PA 15650-2690
(412)539-7505
Fax: (412)539-1850

SCORE Office (Lebanon)
252 N. 8th St.
PO Box 899
Lebanon, PA 17042-0899
(717)273-3727
Fax: (717)273-7940

SCORE Office (Lewistown)
3 W. Monument Sq., Ste. 204
Lewistown, PA 17044
(717)248-6713
Fax: (717)248-6714

SCORE Office (Delaware County)
602 E. Baltimore Pike
Media, PA 19063
(610)565-3677
Fax: (610)565-1606

SCORE Office (Milton Area)
112 S. Front St.
Milton, PA 17847

(717)742-7341
Fax: (717)792-2008

SCORE Office (Mon-Valley)
435 Donner Ave.
Monessen, PA 15062
(412)684-4277
Fax: (412)684-7688

SCORE Office (Monroeville)
William Penn Plaza
2790 Mosside Blvd., Ste. 295
Monroeville, PA 15146
(412)856-0622
Fax: (412)856-1030

SCORE Office (Airport Area)
986 Brodhead Rd.
Moon Township, PA 15108-2398
(412)264-6270
Fax: (412)264-1575

SCORE Office (Northeast)
8601 E. Roosevelt Blvd.
Philadelphia, PA 19152
(215)332-3400
Fax: (215)332-6050

SCORE Office (Philadelphia)
1315 Walnut St., Ste. 500
Philadelphia, PA 19107
(215)790-5050
Fax: (215)790-5057
E-mail: score46@bellatlantic.net
Website: http://www.pgweb.net/score46/

SCORE Office (Pittsburgh)
1000 Liberty Ave., Rm. 1122
Pittsburgh, PA 15222
(412)395-6560
Fax: (412)395-6562

SCORE Office (Tri-County)
801 N. Charlotte St.
Pottstown, PA 19464
(610)327-2673

SCORE Office (Reading)
601 Penn St.
Reading, PA 19601
(610)376-3497

SCORE Office (Scranton)
Oppenheim Bldg.
116 N. Washington Ave., Ste. 650
Scranton, PA 18503
(717)347-4611
Fax: (717)347-4611

SCORE Office (Central Pennsylvania)
200 Innovation Blvd., Ste. 242-B
State College, PA 16803

(814)234-9415
Fax: (814)238-9686
Website: http://countrystore.org/
business/score.htm

SCORE Office (Monroe-Stroudsburg)
556 Main St.
Stroudsburg, PA 18360
(717)421-4433

SCORE Office (Uniontown)
Federal Bldg.
Pittsburg St.
PO Box 2065 DTS
Uniontown, PA 15401
(412)437-4222
E-mail: uniontownscore@lcsys.net

SCORE Office (Warren County)
315 2nd Ave.
Warren, PA 16365
(814)723-9017

SCORE Office (Waynesboro)
323 E. Main St.
Waynesboro, PA 17268
(717)762-7123
Fax: (717)962-7124

SCORE Office (Chester County)
Government Service Center, Ste. 281
601 Westtown Rd.
West Chester, PA 19382-4538
(610)344-6910
Fax: (610)344-6919
E-mail: score@locke.ccil.org

SCORE Office (Wilkes-Barre)
7 N. Wilkes-Barre Blvd.
Wilkes Barre, PA 18702-5241
(717)826-6502
Fax: (717)826-6287

SCORE Office (North Central Pennsylvania)
240 W. 3rd St., Rm. 227
PO Box 725
Williamsport, PA 17703
(717)322-3720
Fax: (717)322-1607
E-mail: score234@mail.csrlink.net
Website: http://www.lycoming.org/
score/

SCORE Office (York)
Cyber Center
2101 Pennsylvania Ave.
York, PA 17404
(717)845-8830
Fax: (717)854-9333

Puerto Rico

SCORE Office (Puerto Rico & Virgin Islands)
PO Box 12383-96
San Juan, PR 00914-0383
(787)726-8040
Fax: (787)726-8135

Rhode Island

SCORE Office (Barrington)
281 County Rd.
Barrington, RI 02806
(401)247-1920
Fax: (401)247-3763

SCORE Office (Woonsocket)
640 Washington Hwy.
Lincoln, RI 02865
(401)334-1000
Fax: (401)334-1009

SCORE Office (Wickford)
8045 Post Rd.
North Kingstown, RI 02852
(401)295-5566
Fax: (401)295-8987

SCORE Office (J.G.E. Knight)
380 Westminster St.
Providence, RI 02903
(401)528-4571
Fax: (401)528-4539
Website: http://www.riscore.org

SCORE Office (Warwick)
3288 Post Rd.
Warwick, RI 02886
(401)732-1100
Fax: (401)732-1101

SCORE Office (Westerly)
74 Post Rd.
Westerly, RI 02891
(401)596-7761
800-732-7636
Fax: (401)596-2190

South Carolina

SCORE Office (Aiken)
PO Box 892
Aiken, SC 29802
(803)641-1111
800-542-4536
Fax: (803)641-4174

SCORE Office (Anderson)
Anderson Mall
3130 N. Main St.

Anderson, SC 29621
(864)224-0453

SCORE Office (Coastal)
284 King St.
Charleston, SC 29401
(803)727-4778
Fax: (803)853-2529

SCORE Office (Midlands)
Strom Thurmond Bldg., Rm. 358
1835 Assembly St., Rm 358
Columbia, SC 29201
(803)765-5131
Fax: (803)765-5962
Website: http://www.scoremid
lands.org/

SCORE Office (Piedmont)
Federal Bldg., Rm. B-02
300 E. Washington St.
Greenville, SC 29601
(864)271-3638

SCORE Office (Greenwood)
PO Drawer 1467
Greenwood, SC 29648
(864)223-8357

SCORE Office (Hilton Head Island)
52 Savannah Trail
Hilton Head, SC 29926
(803)785-7107
Fax: (803)785-7110

SCORE Office (Grand Strand)
937 Broadway
Myrtle Beach, SC 29577
(803)918-1079
Fax: (803)918-1083
E-mail: score381@aol.com

SCORE Office (Spartanburg)
PO Box 1636
Spartanburg, SC 29304
(864)594-5000
Fax: (864)594-5055

South Dakota

SCORE Office (West River)
Rushmore Plz. Civic Ctr.
444 Mount Rushmore Rd., No. 209
Rapid City, SD 57701
(605)394-5311
E-mail: score@gwtc.net

SCORE Office (Sioux Falls)
First Financial Center
110 S. Phillips Ave., Ste. 200
Sioux Falls, SD 57104-6727

(605)330-4231
Fax: (605)330-4231

Tennessee

SCORE Office (Chattanooga)
Federal Bldg., Rm. 26
900 Georgia Ave.
Chattanooga, TN 37402
(423)752-5190
Fax: (423)752-5335

SCORE Office (Cleveland)
PO Box 2275
Cleveland, TN 37320
(423)472-6587
Fax: (423)472-2019

SCORE Office (Upper Cumberland Center)
1225 S. Willow Ave.
Cookeville, TN 38501
(615)432-4111
Fax: (615)432-6010

SCORE Office (Unicoi County)
PO Box 713
Erwin, TN 37650
(423)743-3000
Fax: (423)743-0942

SCORE Office (Greeneville)
115 Academy St.
Greeneville, TN 37743
(423)638-4111
Fax: (423)638-5345

SCORE Office (Jackson)
194 Auditorium St.
Jackson, TN 38301
(901)423-2200

SCORE Office (Northeast Tennessee)
1st Tennessee Bank Bldg.
2710 S. Roan St., Ste. 584
Johnson City, TN 37601
(423)929-7686
Fax: (423)461-8052

SCORE Office (Kingsport)
151 E. Main St.
Kingsport, TN 37662
(423)392-8805

SCORE Office (Greater Knoxville)
Farragot Bldg., Ste. 224
530 S. Gay St.
Knoxville, TN 37902
(423)545-4203
E-mail: scoreknox@ntown.com
Website: http://www.scoreknox.org/

SCORE Office (Maryville)
201 S. Washington St.
Maryville, TN 37804-5728
(423)983-2241
800-525-6834
Fax: (423)984-1386

SCORE Office (Memphis)
Federal Bldg., Ste. 390
167 N. Main St.
Memphis, TN 38103
(901)544-3588

SCORE Office (Nashville)
50 Vantage Way, Ste. 201
Nashville, TN 37228-1500
(615)736-7621

Texas

SCORE Office (Abilene)
2106 Federal Post Office and Court Bldg.
Abilene, TX 79601
(915)677-1857

SCORE Office (Austin)
2501 S. Congress
Austin, TX 78701
(512)442-7235
Fax: (512)442-7528

SCORE Office (Golden Triangle)
450 Boyd St.
Beaumont, TX 77704
(409)838-6581
Fax: (409)833-6718

SCORE Office (Brownsville)
3505 Boca Chica Blvd., Ste. 305
Brownsville, TX 78521
(210)541-4508

SCORE Office (Brazos Valley)
3000 Briarcrest, Ste. 302
Bryan, TX 77802
(409)776-8876
E-mail: 102633.2612@compuserve.com

SCORE Office (Cleburne)
Watergarden Pl., 9th Fl., Ste. 400
Cleburne, TX 76031
(817)871-6002

SCORE Office (Corpus Christi)
651 Upper North Broadway, Ste. 654
Corpus Christi, TX 78477
(512)888-4322
Fax: (512)888-3418

SCORE Office (Dallas)
6260 E. Mockingbird
Dallas, TX 75214-2619

(214)828-2471
Fax: (214)821-8033

SCORE Office (El Paso)
10 Civic Center Plaza
El Paso, TX 79901
(915)534-0541
Fax: (915)534-0513

SCORE Office (Bedford)
100 E. 15th St., Ste. 400
Ft. Worth, TX 76102
(817)871-6002

SCORE Office (Ft. Worth)
100 E. 15th St., No. 24
Ft. Worth, TX 76102
(817)871-6002
Fax: (817)871-6031
E-mail: fwbac@onramp.net

SCORE Office (Garland)
2734 W. Kingsley Rd.
Garland, TX 75041
(214)271-9224

SCORE Office (Granbury Chamber of Commerce)
416 S. Morgan
Granbury, TX 76048
(817)573-1622
Fax: (817)573-0805

SCORE Office (Lower Rio Grande Valley)
222 E. Van Buren, Ste. 500
Harlingen, TX 78550
(956)427-8533
Fax: (956)427-8537

SCORE Office (Houston)
9301 Southwest Fwy., Ste. 550
Houston, TX 77074
(713)773-6565
Fax: (713)773-6550

SCORE Office (Irving)
3333 N. MacArthur Blvd., Ste. 100
Irving, TX 75062
(214)252-8484
Fax: (214)252-6710

SCORE Office (Lubbock)
1205 Texas Ave., Rm. 411D
Lubbock, TX 79401
(806)472-7462
Fax: (806)472-7487

SCORE Office (Midland)
Post Office Annex
200 E. Wall St., Rm. P121
Midland, TX 79701
(915)687-2649

SCORE Office (Orange)
1012 Green Ave.
Orange, TX 77630-5620
(409)883-3536
800-528-4906
Fax: (409)886-3247

SCORE Office (Plano)
1200 E. 15th St.
PO Drawer 940287
Plano, TX 75094-0287
(214)424-7547
Fax: (214)422-5182

SCORE Office (Port Arthur)
4749 Twin City Hwy., Ste. 300
Port Arthur, TX 77642
(409)963-1107
Fax: (409)963-3322

SCORE Office (Richardson)
411 Belle Grove
Richardson, TX 75080
(214)234-4141
800-777-8001
Fax: (214)680-9103

SCORE Office (San Antonio)
Federal Bldg., Rm. A527
727 E. Durango
San Antonio, TX 78206
(210)472-5931
Fax: (210)472-5935

SCORE Office (Texarkana State College)
819 State Line Ave.
Texarkana, TX 75501
(903)792-7191
Fax: (903)793-4304

SCORE Office (East Texas)
RTDC
1530 SSW Loop 323, Ste. 100
Tyler, TX 75701
(903)510-2975
Fax: (903)510-2978

SCORE Office (Waco)
401 Franklin Ave.
Waco, TX 76701
(817)754-8898
Fax: (817)756-0776
Website: http://www.brc-waco.com/

SCORE Office (Wichita Falls)
Hamilton Bldg.
900 8th St.
Wichita Falls, TX 76307
(940)723-2741
Fax: (940)723-8773

Utah

SCORE Office (Northern Utah)
160 N. Main
Logan, UT 84321
(435)746-2269

SCORE Office (Ogden)
1701 E. Windsor Dr.
Ogden, UT 84604
(801)629-8613
E-mail: score158@netscape.net

SCORE Office (Central Utah)
1071 E. Windsor Dr.
Provo, UT 84604
(801)373-8660

SCORE Office (Southern Utah)
225 South 700 East
St. George, UT 84770
(435)652-7751

SCORE Office (Salt Lake)
310 S Main St.
Salt Lake City, UT 84101
(801)746-2269
Fax: (801)746-2273

Vermont

SCORE Office (Champlain Valley)
Winston Prouty Federal Bldg.
11 Lincoln St., Rm. 106
Essex Junction, VT 05452
(802)951-6762

SCORE Office (Montpelier)
87 State St., Rm. 205
PO Box 605
Montpelier, VT 05601
(802)828-4422
Fax: (802)828-4485

SCORE Office (Marble Valley)
256 N. Main St.
Rutland, VT 05701-2413
(802)773-9147

SCORE Office (Northeast Kingdom)
20 Main St.
PO Box 904
St. Johnsbury, VT 05819
(802)748-5101

Virgin Islands

SCORE Office (St. Croix)
United Plaza Shopping Center
PO Box 4010, Christiansted
St. Croix, VI 00822
(809)778-5380

SCORE Office (St. Thomas-St. John)
Federal Bldg., Rm. 21
Veterans Dr.
St. Thomas, VI 00801
(809)774-8530

Virginia

SCORE Office (Arlington)
2009 N. 14th St., Ste. 111
Arlington, VA 22201
(703)525-2400

SCORE Office (Blacksburg)
141 Jackson St.
Blacksburg, VA 24060
(540)552-4061

SCORE Office (Bristol)
20 Volunteer Pkwy.
Bristol, VA 24203
(540)989-4850

SCORE Office (Central Virginia)
1001 E. Market St., Ste. 101
Charlottesville, VA 22902
(804)295-6712
Fax: (804)295-7066

SCORE Office (Alleghany Satellite)
241 W. Main St.
Covington, VA 24426
(540)962-2178
Fax: (540)962-2179

SCORE Office (Central Fairfax)
3975 University Dr., Ste. 350
Fairfax, VA 22030
(703)591-2450

SCORE Office (Falls Church)
PO Box 491
Falls Church, VA 22040
(703)532-1050
Fax: (703)237-7904

SCORE Office (Glenns)
Glenns Campus
Box 287
Glenns, VA 23149
(804)693-9650

SCORE Office (Peninsula)
6 Manhattan Sq.
PO Box 7269
Hampton, VA 23666
(757)766-2000
Fax: (757)865-0339
E-mail: score100@seva.net

SCORE Office (Tri-Cities)
108 N. Main St.

Hopewell, VA 23860
(804)458-5536

SCORE Office (Lynchburg)
Federal Bldg.
1100 Main St.
Lynchburg, VA 24504-1714
(804)846-3235

SCORE Office (Greater Prince William)
8963 Center St
Manassas, VA 20110
(703)368-4813
Fax: (703)368-4733

SCORE Office (Martinsville)
115 Broad St.
Martinsville, VA 24112-0709
(540)632-6401
Fax: (540)632-5059

SCORE Office (Hampton Roads)
Federal Bldg., Rm. 737
200 Grandby St.
Norfolk, VA 23510
(757)441-3733
Fax: (757)441-3733
E-mail: scorehr60@juno.com

SCORE Office (Norfolk)
Federal Bldg., Rm. 737
200 Granby St.
Norfolk, VA 23510
(757)441-3733
Fax: (757)441-3733

SCORE Office (Virginia Beach)
Chamber of Commerce
200 Grandby St., Rm 737
Norfolk, VA 23510
(804)441-3733

SCORE Office (Radford)
1126 Norwood St.
Radford, VA 24141
(540)639-2202

SCORE Office (Richmond)
Federal Bldg.
400 N. 8th St., Ste. 1150
PO Box 10126
Richmond, VA 23240-0126
(804)771-2400
Fax: (804)771-8018
E-mail: scorechapter12@yahoo.com
Website: http://www.cvco.org/score/

SCORE Office (Roanoke)
Federal Bldg., Rm. 716
250 Franklin Rd.
Roanoke, VA 24011

(540)857-2834
Fax: (540)857-2043
E-mail: scorerva@juno.com
Website: http://hometown.aol.com/
scorerv/Index.html

SCORE Office (Fairfax)
8391 Old Courthouse Rd., Ste. 300
Vienna, VA 22182
(703)749-0400

SCORE Office (Greater Vienna)
513 Maple Ave. West
Vienna, VA 22180
(703)281-1333
Fax: (703)242-1482

SCORE Office (Shenandoah Valley)
301 W. Main St.
Waynesboro, VA 22980
(540)949-8203
Fax: (540)949-7740
E-mail: score427@intelos.net

SCORE Office (Williamsburg)
201 Penniman Rd.
Williamsburg, VA 23185
(757)229-6511
E-mail: wacc@williamsburgcc.com

SCORE Office (Northern Virginia)
1360 S. Pleasant Valley Rd.
Winchester, VA 22601
(540)662-4118

Washington

SCORE Office (Gray's Harbor)
506 Duffy St.
Aberdeen, WA 98520
(360)532-1924
Fax: (360)533-7945

SCORE Office (Bellingham)
101 E. Holly St.
Bellingham, WA 98225
(360)676-3307

SCORE Office (Everett)
2702 Hoyt Ave.
Everett, WA 98201-3556
(206)259-8000

SCORE Office (Gig Harbor)
3125 Judson St.
Gig Harbor, WA 98335
(206)851-6865

SCORE Office (Kennewick)
PO Box 6986
Kennewick, WA 99336
(509)736-0510

SCORE Office (Puyallup)
322 2nd St. SW
PO Box 1298
Puyallup, WA 98371
(206)845-6755
Fax: (206)848-6164

SCORE Office (Seattle)
1200 6th Ave., Ste. 1700
Seattle, WA 98101
(206)553-7320
Fax: (206)553-7044
E-mail: score55@aol.com
Website: http://www.scn.org/civic/score-online/index55.html

SCORE Office (Spokane)
801 W. Riverside Ave., No. 240
Spokane, WA 99201
(509)353-2820
Fax: (509)353-2600
E-mail: score@dmi.net
Website: http://www.dmi.net/score/

SCORE Office (Clover Park)
PO Box 1933
Tacoma, WA 98401-1933
(206)627-2175

SCORE Office (Tacoma)
1101 Pacific Ave.
Tacoma, WA 98402
(253)274-1288
Fax: (253)274-1289

SCORE Office (Fort Vancouver)
1701 Broadway, S-1
Vancouver, WA 98663
(360)699-1079

SCORE Office (Walla Walla)
500 Tausick Way
Walla Walla, WA 99362
(509)527-4681

SCORE Office (Mid-Columbia)
1113 S. 14th Ave.
Yakima, WA 98907
(509)574-4944
Fax: (509)574-2943
Website: http://www.ellensburg.com/
~score/

West Virginia

SCORE Office (Charleston)
1116 Smith St.
Charleston, WV 25301
(304)347-5463
E-mail: score256@juno.com

Organizations, Agencies, & Consultants

SCORE Office (Virginia Street)
1116 Smith St., Ste. 302
Charleston, WV 25301
(304)347-5463

SCORE Office (Marion County)
PO Box 208
Fairmont, WV 26555-0208
(304)363-0486

SCORE Office (Upper Monongahela Valley)
1000 Technology Dr., Ste. 1111
Fairmont, WV 26555
(304)363-0486
E-mail: score537@hotmail.com

SCORE Office (Huntington)
1101 6th Ave., Ste. 220
Huntington, WV 25701-2309
(304)523-4092

SCORE Office (Wheeling)
1310 Market St.
Wheeling, WV 26003
(304)233-2575
Fax: (304)233-1320

Wisconsin

SCORE Office (Fox Cities)
227 S. Walnut St.
Appleton, WI 54913
(920)734-7101
Fax: (920)734-7161

SCORE Office (Beloit)
136 W. Grand Ave., Ste. 100
PO Box 717
Beloit, WI 53511
(608)365-8835
Fax: (608)365-9170

SCORE Office (Eau Claire)
Federal Bldg., Rm. B11
510 S. Barstow St.
Eau Claire, WI 54701
(715)834-1573
E-mail: score@ecol.net
Website: http://www.ecol.net/~score/

SCORE Office (Fond du Lac)
207 N. Main St.
Fond du Lac, WI 54935
(414)921-9500
Fax: (414)921-9559

SCORE Office (Green Bay)
835 Potts Ave.
Green Bay, WI 54304
(414)496-8930
Fax: (414)496-6009

SCORE Office (Janesville)
20 S. Main St., Ste. 11
PO Box 8008
Janesville, WI 53547
(608)757-3160
Fax: (608)757-3170

SCORE Office (La Crosse)
712 Main St.
La Crosse, WI 54602-0219
(608)784-4880

SCORE Office (Madison)
505 S. Rosa Rd.
Madison, WI 53719
(608)441-2820

SCORE Office (Manitowoc)
1515 Memorial Dr.
PO Box 903
Manitowoc, WI 54221-0903
(414)684-5575
Fax: (414)684-1915

SCORE Office (Milwaukee)
310 W. Wisconsin Ave., Ste. 425
Milwaukee, WI 53203
(414)297-3942
Fax: (414)297-1377

SCORE Office (Central Wisconsin)
1224 Lindbergh Ave.
Stevens Point, WI 54481
(715)344-7729

SCORE Office (Superior)
Superior Business Center Inc.
1423 N. 8th St.
Superior, WI 54880
(715)394-7388
Fax: (715)393-7414

SCORE Office (Waukesha)
223 Wisconsin Ave.
Waukesha, WI 53186-4926
(414)542-4249

SCORE Office (Wausau)
300 3rd St., Ste. 200
Wausau, WI 54402-6190
(715)845-6231

SCORE Office (Wisconsin Rapids)
2240 Kingston Rd.
Wisconsin Rapids, WI 54494
(715)423-1830

Wyoming

SCORE Office (Casper)
Federal Bldg., No. 2215
100 East B St.

Casper, WY 82602
(307)261-6529
Fax: (307)261-6530

Venture capital & financing companies

This section contains a listing of financing and loan companies in the United States and Canada. These listing are arranged alphabetically by country, then by state or province, then by city, then by organization name.

Canada

Alberta

Launchworks Inc.
1902J 11th St., S.E.
Calgary, AB, Canada T2G 3G2
(403)269-1119
Fax: (403)269-1141
Website: http://www.launchworks.com

Native Venture Capital Company, Inc.
21 Artist View Point, Box 7
Site 25, RR 12
Calgary, AB, Canada T3E 6W3
(903)208-5380

Miralta Capital Inc.
4445 Calgary Trail South
888 Terrace Plaza Alberta
Edmonton, AB, Canada T6H 5R7
(780)438-3535
Fax: (780)438-3129

Vencap Equities Alberta Ltd.
10180-101st St., Ste. 1980
Edmonton, AB, Canada T5J 3S4
(403)420-1171
Fax: (403)429-2541

British Columbia

Discovery Capital
5th Fl., 1199 West Hastings
Vancouver, BC, Canada V6E 3T5
(604)683-3000
Fax: (604)662-3457
E-mail: info@discoverycapital.com
Website: http://www.discoverycapital.com

Greenstone Venture Partners
1177 West Hastings St.
Ste. 400
Vancouver, BC, Canada V6E 2K3
(604)717-1977
Fax: (604)717-1976
Website: http://www.greenstonevc.com

Growthworks Capital
2600-1055 West Georgia St.
Box 11170 Royal Centre
Vancouver, BC, Canada V6E 3R5
(604)895-7259
Fax: (604)669-7605
Website: http://www.wofund.com

MDS Discovery Venture Management, Inc.
555 W. Eighth Ave., Ste. 305
Vancouver, BC, Canada V5Z 1C6
(604)872-8464
Fax: (604)872-2977
E-mail: info@mds-ventures.com

Ventures West Management Inc.
1285 W. Pender St., Ste. 280
Vancouver, BC, Canada V6E 4B1
(604)688-9495
Fax: (604)687-2145
Website: http://www.ventureswest.com

Nova Scotia

ACF Equity Atlantic Inc.
Purdy's Wharf Tower II
Ste. 2106
Halifax, NS, Canada B3J 3R7
(902)421-1965
Fax: (902)421-1808

Montgomerie, Huck & Co.
146 Bluenose Dr.
PO Box 538
Lunenburg, NS, Canada B0J 2C0
(902)634-7125
Fax: (902)634-7130

Ontario

IPS Industrial Promotion Services Ltd.
60 Columbia Way, Ste. 720
Markham, ON, Canada L3R 0C9
(905)475-9400
Fax: (905)475-5003

Betwin Investments Inc.
Box 23110
Sault Ste. Marie, ON, Canada P6A 6W6
(705)253-0744
Fax: (705)253-0744

Bailey & Company, Inc.
594 Spadina Ave.
Toronto, ON, Canada M5S 2H4
(416)921-6930
Fax: (416)925-4670

BCE Capital
200 Bay St.

South Tower, Ste. 3120
Toronto, ON, Canada M5J 2J2
(416)815-0078
Fax: (416)941-1073
Website: http://www.bcecapital.com

Castlehill Ventures
55 University Ave., Ste. 500
Toronto, ON, Canada M5J 2H7
(416)862-8574
Fax: (416)862-8875

CCFL Mezzanine Partners of Canada
70 University Ave.
Ste. 1450
Toronto, ON, Canada M5J 2M4
(416)977-1450
Fax: (416)977-6764
E-mail: info@ccfl.com
Website: http://www.ccfl.com

Celtic House International
100 Simcoe St., Ste. 100
Toronto, ON, Canada M5H 3G2
(416)542-2436
Fax: (416)542-2435
Website: http://www.celtic-house.com

Clairvest Group Inc.
22 St. Clair Ave. East
Ste. 1700
Toronto, ON, Canada M4T 2S3
(416)925-9270
Fax: (416)925-5753

Crosbie & Co., Inc.
One First Canadian Place
9th Fl.
PO Box 116
Toronto, ON, Canada M5X 1A4
(416)362-7726
Fax: (416)362-3447
E-mail: info@crosbieco.com
Website: http://www.crosbieco.com

Drug Royalty Corp.
Eight King St. East
Ste. 202
Toronto, ON, Canada M5C 1B5
(416)863-1865
Fax: (416)863-5161

Grieve, Horner, Brown & Asculai
8 King St. E, Ste. 1704
Toronto, ON, Canada M5C 1B5
(416)362-7668
Fax: (416)362-7660

Jefferson Partners
77 King St. West
Ste. 4010

PO Box 136
Toronto, ON, Canada M5K 1H1
(416)367-1533
Fax: (416)367-5827
Website: http://www.jefferson.com

J.L. Albright Venture Partners
Canada Trust Tower, 161 Bay St.
Ste. 4440
PO Box 215
Toronto, ON, Canada M5J 2S1
(416)367-2440
Fax: (416)367-4604
Website: http://www.jlaventures.com

McLean Watson Capital Inc.
One First Canadian Place
Ste. 1410
PO Box 129
Toronto, ON, Canada M5X 1A4
(416)363-2000
Fax: (416)363-2010
Website: http://www.mcleanwatson.com

Middlefield Capital Fund
One First Canadian Place
85th Fl.
PO Box 192
Toronto, ON, Canada M5X 1A6
(416)362-0714
Fax: (416)362-7925
Website: http://www.middlefield.com

Mosaic Venture Partners
24 Duncan St.
Ste. 300
Toronto, ON, Canada M5V 3M6
(416)597-8889
Fax: (416)597-2345

Onex Corp.
161 Bay St.
PO Box 700
Toronto, ON, Canada M5J 2S1
(416)362-7711
Fax: (416)362-5765

Penfund Partners Inc.
145 King St. West
Ste. 1920
Toronto, ON, Canada M5H 1J8
(416)865-0300
Fax: (416)364-6912
Website: http://www.penfund.com

Primaxis Technology Ventures Inc.
1 Richmond St. West, 8th Fl.
Toronto, ON, Canada M5H 3W4
(416)313-5210
Fax: (416)313-5218
Website: http://www.primaxis.com

Priveq Capital Funds
240 Duncan Mill Rd., Ste. 602
Toronto, ON, Canada M3B 3P1
(416)447-3330
Fax: (416)447-3331
E-mail: priveq@sympatico.ca

Roynat Ventures
40 King St. West, 26th Fl.
Toronto, ON, Canada M5H 1H1
(416)933-2667
Fax: (416)933-2783
Website: http://www.roynatcapital.com

Tera Capital Corp.
366 Adelaide St. East, Ste. 337
Toronto, ON, Canada M5A 3X9
(416)368-1024
Fax: (416)368-1427

Working Ventures Canadian Fund Inc.
250 Bloor St. East, Ste. 1600
Toronto, ON, Canada M4W 1E6
(416)934-7718
Fax: (416)929-0901
Website: http://www.workingventures.ca

Quebec

Altamira Capital Corp.
202 University
Niveau de Maisoneuve, Bur. 201
Montreal, QC, Canada H3A 2A5
(514)499-1656
Fax: (514)499-9570

Federal Business Development Bank
Venture Capital Division
Five Place Ville Marie, Ste. 600
Montreal, QC, Canada H3B 5E7
(514)283-1896
Fax: (514)283-5455

Hydro-Quebec Capitech Inc.
75 Boul, Rene Levesque Quest
Montreal, QC, Canada H2Z 1A4
(514)289-4783
Fax: (514)289-5420
Website: http://www.hqcapitech.com

Investissement Desjardins
2 complexe Desjardins
C.P. 760
Montreal, QC, Canada H5B 1B8
(514)281-7131
Fax: (514)281-7808
Website: http://www.desjardins.com/id

Marleau Lemire Inc.
One Place Ville-Marie, Ste. 3601
Montreal, QC, Canada H3B 3P2

(514)877-3800
Fax: (514)875-6415

Speirs Consultants Inc.
365 Stanstead
Montreal, QC, Canada H3R 1X5
(514)342-3858
Fax: (514)342-1977

Tecnocap Inc.
4028 Marlowe
Montreal, QC, Canada H4A 3M2
(514)483-6009
Fax: (514)483-6045
Website: http://www.technocap.com

Telsoft Ventures
1000, Rue de la Gauchetiere
Quest, 25eme Etage
Montreal, QC, Canada H3B 4W5
(514)397-8450
Fax: (514)397-8451

Saskatchewan

Saskatchewan Government Growth Fund
1801 Hamilton St., Ste. 1210
Canada Trust Tower
Regina, SK, Canada S4P 4B4
(306)787-2994
Fax: (306)787-2086

United states

Alabama

FHL Capital Corp.
600 20th Street North
Suite 350
Birmingham, AL 35203
(205)328-3098
Fax: (205)323-0001

Harbert Management Corp.
One Riverchase Pkwy. South
Birmingham, AL 35244
(205)987-5500
Fax: (205)987-5707
Website: http://www.harbert.net

Jefferson Capital Fund
PO Box 13129
Birmingham, AL 35213
(205)324-7709

Private Capital Corp.
100 Brookwood Pl., 4th Fl.
Birmingham, AL 35209
(205)879-2722
Fax: (205)879-5121

21st Century Health Ventures
One Health South Pkwy.
Birmingham, AL 35243
(256)268-6250
Fax: (256)970-8928

FJC Growth Capital Corp.
200 W. Side Sq., Ste. 340
Huntsville, AL 35801
(256)922-2918
Fax: (256)922-2909

Hickory Venture Capital Corp.
301 Washington St. NW
Suite 301
Huntsville, AL 35801
(256)539-1931
Fax: (256)539-5130
E-mail: hvcc@hvcc.com
Website: http://www.hvcc.com

Southeastern Technology Fund
7910 South Memorial Pkwy., Ste. F
Huntsville, AL 35802
(256)883-8711
Fax: (256)883-8558

Cordova Ventures
4121 Carmichael Rd., Ste. 301
Montgomery, AL 36106
(334)271-6011
Fax: (334)260-0120
Website: http://www.cordova
ventures.com

**Small Business Clinic of Alabama/AG
Bartholomew & Associates**
PO Box 231074
Montgomery, AL 36123-1074
(334)284-3640

Arizona

Miller Capital Corp.
4909 E. McDowell Rd.
Phoenix, AZ 85008
(602)225-0504
Fax: (602)225-9024
Website: http://www.themiller
group.com

The Columbine Venture Funds
9449 North 90th St., Ste. 200
Scottsdale, AZ 85258
(602)661-9222
Fax: (602)661-6262

Koch Ventures
17767 N. Perimeter Dr., Ste. 101
Scottsdale, AZ 85255
(480)419-3600

Fax: (480)419-3606
Website: http://www.kochventures.com

McKee & Co.
7702 E. Doubletree Ranch Rd.
Suite 230
Scottsdale, AZ 85258
(480)368-0333
Fax: (480)607-7446

Merita Capital Ltd.
7350 E. Stetson Dr., Ste. 108-A
Scottsdale, AZ 85251
(480)947-8700
Fax: (480)947-8766

Valley Ventures / Arizona Growth Partners L.P.
6720 N. Scottsdale Rd., Ste. 208
Scottsdale, AZ 85253
(480)661-6600
Fax: (480)661-6262

Estreetcapital.com
660 South Mill Ave., Ste. 315
Tempe, AZ 85281
(480)968-8400
Fax: (480)968-8480
Website: http://www.estreetcapital.com

Coronado Venture Fund
PO Box 65420
Tucson, AZ 85728-5420
(520)577-3764
Fax: (520)299-8491

Arkansas

Arkansas Capital Corp.
225 South Pulaski St.
Little Rock, AR 72201
(501)374-9247
Fax: (501)374-9425
Website: http://www.arcapital.com

California

Sundance Venture Partners, L.P.
100 Clocktower Place, Ste. 130
Carmel, CA 93923
(831)625-6500
Fax: (831)625-6590

Westar Capital (Costa Mesa)
949 South Coast Dr., Ste. 650
Costa Mesa, CA 92626
(714)481-5160
Fax: (714)481-5166
E-mail: mailbox@westarcapital.com
Website: http://www.westarcapital.com

Alpine Technology Ventures
20300 Stevens Creek Boulevard, Ste. 495
Cupertino, CA 95014
(408)725-1810
Fax: (408)725-1207
Website: http://www.alpineventures.com

Bay Partners
10600 N. De Anza Blvd.
Cupertino, CA 95014-2031
(408)725-2444
Fax: (408)446-4502
Website: http://www.baypartners.com

Novus Ventures
20111 Stevens Creek Blvd., Ste. 130
Cupertino, CA 95014
(408)252-3900
Fax: (408)252-1713
Website: http://www.novusventures.com

Triune Capital
19925 Stevens Creek Blvd., Ste. 200
Cupertino, CA 95014
(310)284-6800
Fax: (310)284-3290

Acorn Ventures
268 Bush St., Ste. 2829
Daly City, CA 94014
(650)994-7801
Fax: (650)994-3305
Website: http://www.acornventures.com

Digital Media Campus
2221 Park Place
El Segundo, CA 90245
(310)426-8000
Fax: (310)426-8010
E-mail: info@thecampus.com
Website: http://www.digital
mediacampus.com

BankAmerica Ventures / BA Venture Partners
950 Tower Ln., Ste. 700
Foster City, CA 94404
(650)378-6000
Fax: (650)378-6040
Website: http://
www.baventurepartners.com

Starting Point Partners
666 Portofino Lane
Foster City, CA 94404
(650)722-1035
Website: http://www.startingpoint
partners.com

Opportunity Capital Partners
2201 Walnut Ave., Ste. 210

Fremont, CA 94538
(510)795-7000
Fax: (510)494-5439
Website: http://www.ocpcapital.com

Imperial Ventures Inc.
9920 S. La Cienega Boulevar, 14th Fl.
Inglewood, CA 90301
(310)417-5409
Fax: (310)338-6115

Ventana Global (Irvine)
18881 Von Karman Ave., Ste. 1150
Irvine, CA 92612
(949)476-2204
Fax: (949)752-0223
Website: http://www.ventanaglobal.com

Integrated Consortium Inc.
50 Ridgecrest Rd.
Kentfield, CA 94904
(415)925-0386
Fax: (415)461-2726

Enterprise Partners
979 Ivanhoe Ave., Ste. 550
La Jolla, CA 92037
(858)454-8833
Fax: (858)454-2489
Website: http://www.epvc.com

Domain Associates
28202 Cabot Rd., Ste. 200
Laguna Niguel, CA 92677
(949)347-2446
Fax: (949)347-9720
Website: http://www.domainvc.com

Cascade Communications Ventures
60 E. Sir Francis Drake Blvd., Ste. 300
Larkspur, CA 94939
(415)925-6500
Fax: (415)925-6501

Allegis Capital
One First St., Ste. Two
Los Altos, CA 94022
(650)917-5900
Fax: (650)917-5901
Website: http://www.allegiscapital.com

Aspen Ventures
1000 Fremont Ave., Ste. 200
Los Altos, CA 94024
(650)917-5670
Fax: (650)917-5677
Website: http://www.aspenventures.com

AVI Capital L.P.
1 First St., Ste. 2
Los Altos, CA 94022

(650)949-9862
Fax: (650)949-8510
Website: http://www.avicapital.com

Bastion Capital Corp.
1999 Avenue of the Stars, Ste. 2960
Los Angeles, CA 90067
(310)788-5700
Fax: (310)277-7582
E-mail: ga@bastioncapital.com
Website: http://www.bastioncapital.com

Davis Group
PO Box 69953
Los Angeles, CA 90069-0953
(310)659-6327
Fax: (310)659-6337

Developers Equity Corp.
1880 Century Park East, Ste. 211
Los Angeles, CA 90067
(213)277-0300

Far East Capital Corp.
350 S. Grand Ave., Ste. 4100
Los Angeles, CA 90071
(213)687-1361
Fax: (213)617-7939
E-mail: free@fareastnationalbank.com

Kline Hawkes & Co.
11726 San Vicente Blvd., Ste. 300
Los Angeles, CA 90049
(310)442-4700
Fax: (310)442-4707
Website: http://www.klinehawkes.com

Lawrence Financial Group
701 Teakwood
PO Box 491773
Los Angeles, CA 90049
(310)471-4060
Fax: (310)472-3155

Riordan Lewis & Haden
300 S. Grand Ave., 29th Fl.
Los Angeles, CA 90071
(213)229-8500
Fax: (213)229-8597

Union Venture Corp.
445 S. Figueroa St., 9th Fl.
Los Angeles, CA 90071
(213)236-4092
Fax: (213)236-6329

Wedbush Capital Partners
1000 Wilshire Blvd.
Los Angeles, CA 90017
(213)688-4545
Fax: (213)688-6642
Website: http://www.wedbush.com

Advent International Corp.
2180 Sand Hill Rd., Ste. 420
Menlo Park, CA 94025
(650)233-7500
Fax: (650)233-7515
Website: http://www.adventinter
national.com

Altos Ventures
2882 Sand Hill Rd., Ste. 100
Menlo Park, CA 94025
(650)234-9771
Fax: (650)233-9821
Website: http://www.altosvc.com

Applied Technology
1010 El Camino Real, Ste. 300
Menlo Park, CA 94025
(415)326-8622
Fax: (415)326-8163

APV Technology Partners
535 Middlefield, Ste. 150
Menlo Park, CA 94025
(650)327-7871
Fax: (650)327-7631
Website: http://www.apvtp.com

August Capital Management
2480 Sand Hill Rd., Ste. 101
Menlo Park, CA 94025
(650)234-9900
Fax: (650)234-9910
Website: http://www.augustcap.com

Baccharis Capital Inc.
2420 Sand Hill Rd., Ste. 100
Menlo Park, CA 94025
(650)324-6844
Fax: (650)854-3025

Benchmark Capital
2480 Sand Hill Rd., Ste. 200
Menlo Park, CA 94025
(650)854-8180
Fax: (650)854-8183
E-mail: info@benchmark.com
Website: http://www.benchmark.com

Bessemer Venture Partners (Menlo Park)
535 Middlefield Rd., Ste. 245
Menlo Park, CA 94025
(650)853-7000
Fax: (650)853-7001
Website: http://www.bvp.com

The Cambria Group
1600 El Camino Real Rd., Ste. 155
Menlo Park, CA 94025
(650)329-8600

Fax: (650)329-8601
Website: http://www.cambriagroup.com

Canaan Partners
2884 Sand Hill Rd., Ste. 115
Menlo Park, CA 94025
(650)854-8092
Fax: (650)854-8127
Website: http://www.canaan.com

Capstone Ventures
3000 Sand Hill Rd., Bldg. One, Ste. 290
Menlo Park, CA 94025
(650)854-2523
Fax: (650)854-9010
Website: http://www.capstonevc.com

Comdisco Venture Group (Silicon Valley)
3000 Sand Hill Rd., Bldg. 1, Ste. 155
Menlo Park, CA 94025
(650)854-9484
Fax: (650)854-4026

Commtech International
535 Middlefield Rd., Ste. 200
Menlo Park, CA 94025
(650)328-0190
Fax: (650)328-6442

Compass Technology Partners
1550 El Camino Real, Ste. 275
Menlo Park, CA 94025-4111
(650)322-7595
Fax: (650)322-0588
Website: http://www.compass
techpartners.com

Convergence Partners
3000 Sand Hill Rd., Ste. 235
Menlo Park, CA 94025
(650)854-3010
Fax: (650)854-3015
Website: http://www.conver
gencepartners.com

The Dakota Group
PO Box 1025
Menlo Park, CA 94025
(650)853-0600
Fax: (650)851-4899
E-mail: info@dakota.com

Delphi Ventures
3000 Sand Hill Rd.
Bldg. One, Ste. 135
Menlo Park, CA 94025
(650)854-9650
Fax: (650)854-2961
Website: http://www.delphiventures.com

El Dorado Ventures
2884 Sand Hill Rd., Ste. 121
Menlo Park, CA 94025
(650)854-1200
Fax: (650)854-1202
Website: http://www.eldorado
ventures.com

Glynn Ventures
3000 Sand Hill Rd., Bldg. 4, Ste. 235
Menlo Park, CA 94025
(650)854-2215

Indosuez Ventures
2180 Sand Hill Rd., Ste. 450
Menlo Park, CA 94025
(650)854-0587
Fax: (650)323-5561
Website: http://www.indosuez
ventures.com

Institutional Venture Partners
3000 Sand Hill Rd., Bldg. 2, Ste. 290
Menlo Park, CA 94025
(650)854-0132
Fax: (650)854-5762
Website: http://www.ivp.com

Interwest Partners (Menlo Park)
3000 Sand Hill Rd., Bldg. 3, Ste. 255
Menlo Park, CA 94025-7112
(650)854-8585
Fax: (650)854-4706
Website: http://www.interwest.com

**Kleiner Perkins Caufield & Byers
(Menlo Park)**
2750 Sand Hill Rd.
Menlo Park, CA 94025
(650)233-2750
Fax: (650)233-0300
Website: http://www.kpcb.com

Magic Venture Capital LLC
1010 El Camino Real, Ste. 300
Menlo Park, CA 94025
(650)325-4149

Matrix Partners
2500 Sand Hill Rd., Ste. 113
Menlo Park, CA 94025
(650)854-3131
Fax: (650)854-3296
Website: http://www.matrixpartners.com

Mayfield Fund
2800 Sand Hill Rd.
Menlo Park, CA 94025
(650)854-5560
Fax: (650)854-5712
Website: http://www.mayfield.com

**McCown De Leeuw and Co. (Menlo
Park)**
3000 Sand Hill Rd., Bldg. 3, Ste. 290
Menlo Park, CA 94025-7111
(650)854-6000
Fax: (650)854-0853
Website: http://www.mdcpartners.com

Menlo Ventures
3000 Sand Hill Rd., Bldg. 4, Ste. 100
Menlo Park, CA 94025
(650)854-8540
Fax: (650)854-7059
Website: http://www.menloventures.com

Merrill Pickard Anderson & Eyre
2480 Sand Hill Rd., Ste. 200
Menlo Park, CA 94025
(650)854-8600
Fax: (650)854-0345

**New Enterprise Associates (Menlo
Park)**
2490 Sand Hill Rd.
Menlo Park, CA 94025
(650)854-9499
Fax: (650)854-9397
Website: http://www.nea.com

Onset Ventures
2400 Sand Hill Rd., Ste. 150
Menlo Park, CA 94025
(650)529-0700
Fax: (650)529-0777
Website: http://www.onset.com

Paragon Venture Partners
3000 Sand Hill Rd., Bldg. 1, Ste. 275
Menlo Park, CA 94025
(650)854-8000
Fax: (650)854-7260

**Pathfinder Venture Capital Funds
(Menlo Park)**
3000 Sand Hill Rd., Bldg. 3, Ste. 255
Menlo Park, CA 94025
(650)854-0650
Fax: (650)854-4706

Rocket Ventures
3000 Sandhill Rd., Bldg. 1, Ste. 170
Menlo Park, CA 94025
(650)561-9100
Fax: (650)561-9183
Website: http://www.rocketventures.com

Sequoia Capital
3000 Sand Hill Rd., Bldg. 4, Ste. 280
Menlo Park, CA 94025
(650)854-3927
Fax: (650)854-2977

E-mail: sequoia@sequoiacap.com
Website: http://www.sequoiacap.com

Sierra Ventures
3000 Sand Hill Rd., Bldg. 4, Ste. 210
Menlo Park, CA 94025
(650)854-1000
Fax: (650)854-5593
Website: http://www.sierraventures.com

Sigma Partners
2884 Sand Hill Rd., Ste. 121
Menlo Park, CA 94025-7022
(650)853-1700
Fax: (650)853-1717
E-mail: info@sigmapartners.com
Website: http://www.sigmapartners.com

Sprout Group (Menlo Park)
3000 Sand Hill Rd.
Bldg. 3, Ste. 170
Menlo Park, CA 94025
(650)234-2700
Fax: (650)234-2779
Website: http://www.sproutgroup.com

TA Associates (Menlo Park)
70 Willow Rd., Ste. 100
Menlo Park, CA 94025
(650)328-1210
Fax: (650)326-4933
Website: http://www.ta.com

Thompson Clive & Partners Ltd.
3000 Sand Hill Rd., Bldg. 1, Ste. 185
Menlo Park, CA 94025-7102
(650)854-0314
Fax: (650)854-0670
E-mail: mail@tcvc.com
Website: http://www.tcvc.com

Trinity Ventures Ltd.
3000 Sand Hill Rd., Bldg. 1, Ste. 240
Menlo Park, CA 94025
(650)854-9500
Fax: (650)854-9501
Website: http://www.trinityventures.com

U.S. Venture Partners
2180 Sand Hill Rd., Ste. 300
Menlo Park, CA 94025
(650)854-9080
Fax: (650)854-3018
Website: http://www.usvp.com

USVP-Schlein Marketing Fund
2180 Sand Hill Rd., Ste. 300
Menlo Park, CA 94025
(415)854-9080
Fax: (415)854-3018
Website: http://www.usvp.com

Venrock Associates
2494 Sand Hill Rd., Ste. 200
Menlo Park, CA 94025
(650)561-9580
Fax: (650)561-9180
Website: http://www.venrock.com

Brad Peery Capital Inc.
145 Chapel Pkwy.
Mill Valley, CA 94941
(415)389-0625
Fax: (415)389-1336

Dot Edu Ventures
650 Castro St., Ste. 270
Mountain View, CA 94041
(650)575-5638
Fax: (650)325-5247
Website: http://www.dotedu
ventures.com

Forrest, Binkley & Brown
840 Newport Ctr. Dr., Ste. 480
Newport Beach, CA 92660
(949)729-3222
Fax: (949)729-3226
Website: http://www.fbbvc.com

Marwit Capital LLC
180 Newport Center Dr., Ste. 200
Newport Beach, CA 92660
(949)640-6234
Fax: (949)720-8077
Website: http://www.marwit.com

Kaiser Permanente / National Venture Development
1800 Harrison St., 22nd Fl.
Oakland, CA 94612
(510)267-4010
Fax: (510)267-4036
Website: http://www.kpventures.com

Nu Capital Access Group, Ltd.
7677 Oakport St., Ste. 105
Oakland, CA 94621
(510)635-7345
Fax: (510)635-7068

Inman and Bowman
4 Orinda Way, Bldg. D, Ste. 150
Orinda, CA 94563
(510)253-1611
Fax: (510)253-9037

Accel Partners (San Francisco)
428 University Ave.
Palo Alto, CA 94301
(650)614-4800
Fax: (650)614-4880
Website: http://www.accel.com

Advanced Technology Ventures
485 Ramona St., Ste. 200
Palo Alto, CA 94301
(650)321-8601
Fax: (650)321-0934
Website: http://www.atvcapital.com

Anila Fund
400 Channing Ave.
Palo Alto, CA 94301
(650)833-5790
Fax: (650)833-0590
Website: http://www.anila.com

Asset Management Company Venture Capital
2275 E. Bayshore, Ste. 150
Palo Alto, CA 94303
(650)494-7400
Fax: (650)856-1826
E-mail: postmaster@assetman.com
Website: http://www.assetman.com

BancBoston Capital / BancBoston Ventures
435 Tasso St., Ste. 250
Palo Alto, CA 94305
(650)470-4100
Fax: (650)853-1425
Website: http://www.bancboston
capital.com

Charter Ventures
525 University Ave., Ste. 1400
Palo Alto, CA 94301
(650)325-6953
Fax: (650)325-4762
Website: http://www.charterventures.com

Communications Ventures
505 Hamilton Avenue, Ste. 305
Palo Alto, CA 94301
(650)325-9600
Fax: (650)325-9608
Website: http://www.comven.com

HMS Group
2468 Embarcadero Way
Palo Alto, CA 94303-3313
(650)856-9862
Fax: (650)856-9864

Jafco America Ventures, Inc.
505 Hamilton Ste. 310
Palto Alto, CA 94301
(650)463-8800
Fax: (650)463-8801
Website: http://www.jafco.com

New Vista Capital
540 Cowper St., Ste. 200

Palo Alto, CA 94301
(650)329-9333
Fax: (650)328-9434
E-mail: fgreene@nvcap.com
Website: http://www.nvcap.com

Norwest Equity Partners (Palo Alto)
245 Lytton Ave., Ste. 250
Palo Alto, CA 94301-1426
(650)321-8000
Fax: (650)321-8010
Website: http://www.norwestvp.com

Oak Investment Partners
525 University Ave., Ste. 1300
Palo Alto, CA 94301
(650)614-3700
Fax: (650)328-6345
Website: http://www.oakinv.com

Patricof & Co. Ventures, Inc. (Palo Alto)
2100 Geng Rd., Ste. 150
Palo Alto, CA 94303
(650)494-9944
Fax: (650)494-6751
Website: http://www.patricof.com

RWI Group
835 Page Mill Rd.
Palo Alto, CA 94304
(650)251-1800
Fax: (650)213-8660
Website: http://www.rwigroup.com

Summit Partners (Palo Alto)
499 Hamilton Ave., Ste. 200
Palo Alto, CA 94301
(650)321-1166
Fax: (650)321-1188
Website: http://www.summit
partners.com

Sutter Hill Ventures
755 Page Mill Rd., Ste. A-200
Palo Alto, CA 94304
(650)493-5600
Fax: (650)858-1854
E-mail: shv@shv.com

Vanguard Venture Partners
525 University Ave., Ste. 600
Palo Alto, CA 94301
(650)321-2900
Fax: (650)321-2902
Website: http://www.vanguard
ventures.com

Venture Growth Associates
2479 East Bayshore St., Ste. 710
Palo Alto, CA 94303

(650)855-9100
Fax: (650)855-9104

Worldview Technology Partners
435 Tasso St., Ste. 120
Palo Alto, CA 94301
(650)322-3800
Fax: (650)322-3880
Website: http://www.worldview.com

Draper, Fisher, Jurvetson / Draper Associates
400 Seaport Ct., Ste.250
Redwood City, CA 94063
(415)599-9000
Fax: (415)599-9726
Website: http://www.dfj.com

Gabriel Venture Partners
350 Marine Pkwy., Ste. 200
Redwood Shores, CA 94065
(650)551-5000
Fax: (650)551-5001
Website: http://www.gabrielvp.com

Hallador Venture Partners, L.L.C.
740 University Ave., Ste. 110
Sacramento, CA 95825-6710
(916)920-0191
Fax: (916)920-5188
E-mail: chris@hallador.com

Emerald Venture Group
12396 World Trade Dr., Ste. 116
San Diego, CA 92128
(858)451-1001
Fax: (858)451-1003
Website: http://www.emerald
venture.com

Forward Ventures
9255 Towne Centre Dr.
San Diego, CA 92121
(858)677-6077
Fax: (858)452-8799
E-mail: info@forwardventure.com
Website: http://www.forward
venture.com

Idanta Partners Ltd.
4660 La Jolla Village Dr., Ste. 850
San Diego, CA 92122
(619)452-9690
Fax: (619)452-2013
Website: http://www.idanta.com

Kingsbury Associates
3655 Nobel Dr., Ste. 490
San Diego, CA 92122
(858)677-0600
Fax: (858)677-0800

Kyocera International Inc.
Corporate Development
8611 Balboa Ave.
San Diego, CA 92123
(858)576-2600
Fax: (858)492-1456

Sorrento Associates, Inc.
4370 LaJolla Village Dr., Ste. 1040
San Diego, CA 92122
(619)452-3100
Fax: (619)452-7607
Website: http://www.sorrento
ventures.com

Western States Investment Group
9191 Towne Ctr. Dr., Ste. 310
San Diego, CA 92122
(619)678-0800
Fax: (619)678-0900

Aberdare Ventures
One Embarcadero Center, Ste. 4000
San Francisco, CA 94111
(415)392-7442
Fax: (415)392-4264
Website: http://www.aberdare.com

Acacia Venture Partners
101 California St., Ste. 3160
San Francisco, CA 94111
(415)433-4200
Fax: (415)433-4250
Website: http://www.acaciavp.com

Access Venture Partners
319 Laidley St.
San Francisco, CA 94131
(415)586-0132
Fax: (415)392-6310
Website: http://www.access
venturepartners.com

Alta Partners
One Embarcadero Center, Ste. 4050
San Francisco, CA 94111
(415)362-4022
Fax: (415)362-6178
E-mail: alta@altapartners.com
Website: http://www.altapartners.com

Bangert Dawes Reade Davis & Thom
220 Montgomery St., Ste. 424
San Francisco, CA 94104
(415)954-9900
Fax: (415)954-9901
E-mail: bdrdt@pacbell.net

Berkeley International Capital Corp.
650 California St., Ste. 2800
San Francisco, CA 94108-2609

(415)249-0450
Fax: (415)392-3929
Website: http://www.berkeleyvc.com

Blueprint Ventures LLC
456 Montgomery St., 22nd Fl.
San Francisco, CA 94104
(415)901-4000
Fax: (415)901-4035
Website: http://www.blue
printventures.com

Blumberg Capital Ventures
580 Howard St., Ste. 401
San Francisco, CA 94105
(415)905-5007
Fax: (415)357-5027
Website: http://www.blumberg-
capital.com

Burr, Egan, Deleage, and Co. (San Francisco)
1 Embarcadero Center, Ste. 4050
San Francisco, CA 94111
(415)362-4022
Fax: (415)362-6178

Burrill & Company
120 Montgomery St., Ste. 1370
San Francisco, CA 94104
(415)743-3160
Fax: (415)743-3161
Website: http://www.burrillandco.com

CMEA Ventures
235 Montgomery St., Ste. 920
San Francisco, CA 94401
(415)352-1520
Fax: (415)352-1524
Website: http://www.cmeaventures.com

Crocker Capital
1 Post St., Ste. 2500
San Francisco, CA 94101
(415)956-5250
Fax: (415)959-5710

Dominion Ventures, Inc.
44 Montgomery St., Ste. 4200
San Francisco, CA 94104
(415)362-4890
Fax: (415)394-9245

Dorset Capital
Pier 1
Bay 2
San Francisco, CA 94111
(415)398-7101
Fax: (415)398-7141
Website: http://www.dorsetcapital.com

Gatx Capital
Four Embarcadero Center, Ste. 2200
San Francisco, CA 94904
(415)955-3200
Fax: (415)955-3449

IMinds
135 Main St., Ste. 1350
San Francisco, CA 94105
(415)547-0000
Fax: (415)227-0300
Website: http://www.iminds.com

LF International Inc.
360 Post St., Ste. 705
San Francisco, CA 94108
(415)399-0110
Fax: (415)399-9222
Website: http://www.lfvc.com

Newbury Ventures
535 Pacific Ave., 2nd Fl.
San Francisco, CA 94133
(415)296-7408
Fax: (415)296-7416
Website: http://www.newburyven.com

Quest Ventures (San Francisco)
333 Bush St., Ste. 1750
San Francisco, CA 94104
(415)782-1414
Fax: (415)782-1415

Robertson-Stephens Co.
555 California St., Ste. 2600
San Francisco, CA 94104
(415)781-9700
Fax: (415)781-2556
Website: http://www.omegaad
ventures.com

Rosewood Capital, L.P.
One Maritime Plaza, Ste. 1330
San Francisco, CA 94111-3503
(415)362-5526
Fax: (415)362-1192
Website: http://www.rosewoodvc.com

Ticonderoga Capital Inc.
555 California St., No. 4950
San Francisco, CA 94104
(415)296-7900
Fax: (415)296-8956

21st Century Internet Venture Partners
Two South Park
2nd Floor
San Francisco, CA 94107
(415)512-1221
Fax: (415)512-2650
Website: http://www.21vc.com

VK Ventures
600 California St., Ste.1700
San Francisco, CA 94111
(415)391-5600
Fax: (415)397-2744

Walden Group of Venture Capital Funds
750 Battery St., Seventh Floor
San Francisco, CA 94111
(415)391-7225
Fax: (415)391-7262

Acer Technology Ventures
2641 Orchard Pkwy.
San Jose, CA 95134
(408)433-4945
Fax: (408)433-5230

Authosis
226 Airport Pkwy., Ste. 405
San Jose, CA 95110
(650)814-3603
Website: http://www.authosis.com

Western Technology Investment
2010 N. First St., Ste. 310
San Jose, CA 95131
(408)436-8577
Fax: (408)436-8625
E-mail: mktg@westerntech.com

Drysdale Enterprises
177 Bovet Rd., Ste. 600
San Mateo, CA 94402
(650)341-6336
Fax: (650)341-1329
E-mail: drysdale@aol.com

Greylock
2929 Campus Dr., Ste. 400
San Mateo, CA 94401
(650)493-5525
Fax: (650)493-5575
Website: http://www.greylock.com

Technology Funding
2000 Alameda de las Pulgas, Ste. 250
San Mateo, CA 94403
(415)345-2200
Fax: (415)345-1797

2M Invest Inc.
1875 S. Grant St.
Suite 750
San Mateo, CA 94402
(650)655-3765
Fax: (650)372-9107
E-mail: 2minfo@2minvest.com
Website: http://www.2minvest.com

Phoenix Growth Capital Corp.
2401 Kerner Blvd.
San Rafael, CA 94901
(415)485-4569
Fax: (415)485-4663

NextGen Partners LLC
1705 East Valley Rd.
Santa Barbara, CA 93108
(805)969-8540
Fax: (805)969-8542
Website: http://www.nextgen
partners.com

Denali Venture Capital
1925 Woodland Ave.
Santa Clara, CA 95050
(408)690-4838
Fax: (408)247-6979
E-mail: wael@denaliventurecapital.com
Website: http://www.denali
venturecapital.com

Dotcom Ventures LP
3945 Freedom Circle, Ste. 740
Santa Clara, CA 95045
(408)919-9855
Fax: (408)919-9857
Website: http://www.dotcom
venturesatl.com

Silicon Valley Bank
3003 Tasman
Santa Clara, CA 95054
(408)654-7400
Fax: (408)727-8728

Al Shugart International
920 41st Ave.
Santa Cruz, CA 95062
(831)479-7852
Fax: (831)479-7852
Website: http://www.alshugart.com

Leonard Mautner Associates
1434 Sixth St.
Santa Monica, CA 90401
(213)393-9788
Fax: (310)459-9918

Palomar Ventures
100 Wilshire Blvd., Ste. 450
Santa Monica, CA 90401
(310)260-6050
Fax: (310)656-4150
Website: http://www.palomar
ventures.com

Medicus Venture Partners
12930 Saratoga Ave., Ste. D8
Saratoga, CA 95070

(408)447-8600
Fax: (408)447-8599
Website: http://www.medicusvc.com

Redleaf Venture Management
14395 Saratoga Ave., Ste. 130
Saratoga, CA 95070
(408)868-0800
Fax: (408)868-0810
E-mail: nancy@redleaf.com
Website: http://www.redleaf.com

Artemis Ventures
207 Second St., Ste. E
3rd Fl.
Sausalito, CA 94965
(415)289-2500
Fax: (415)289-1789
Website: http://www.artemisventures.com

Deucalion Venture Partners
19501 Brooklime
Sonoma, CA 95476
(707)938-4974
Fax: (707)938-8921

Windward Ventures
PO Box 7688
Thousand Oaks, CA 91359-7688
(805)497-3332
Fax: (805)497-9331

National Investment Management, Inc.
2601 Airport Dr., Ste.210
Torrance, CA 90505
(310)784-7600
Fax: (310)784-7605

Southern California Ventures
406 Amapola Ave. Ste. 125
Torrance, CA 90501
(310)787-4381
Fax: (310)787-4382

Sandton Financial Group
21550 Oxnard St., Ste. 300
Woodland Hills, CA 91367
(818)702-9283

Woodside Fund
850 Woodside Dr.
Woodside, CA 94062
(650)368-5545
Fax: (650)368-2416
Website: http://www.woodsidefund.com

Colorado

Colorado Venture Management
Ste. 300
Boulder, CO 80301

(303)440-4055
Fax: (303)440-4636

Dean & Associates
4362 Apple Way
Boulder, CO 80301
Fax: (303)473-9900

Roser Ventures LLC
1105 Spruce St.
Boulder, CO 80302
(303)443-6436
Fax: (303)443-1885
Website: http://www.roserventures.com

Sequel Venture Partners
4430 Arapahoe Ave., Ste. 220
Boulder, CO 80303
(303)546-0400
Fax: (303)546-9728
E-mail: tom@sequelvc.com
Website: http://www.sequelvc.com

New Venture Resources
445C E. Cheyenne Mtn. Blvd.
Colorado Springs, CO 80906-4570
(719)598-9272
Fax: (719)598-9272

The Centennial Funds
1428 15th St.
Denver, CO 80202-1318
(303)405-7500
Fax: (303)405-7575
Website: http://www.centennial.com

Rocky Mountain Capital Partners
1125 17th St., Ste. 2260
Denver, CO 80202
(303)291-5200
Fax: (303)291-5327

Sandlot Capital LLC
600 South Cherry St., Ste. 525
Denver, CO 80246
(303)893-3400
Fax: (303)893-3403
Website: http://www.sandlotcapital.com

Wolf Ventures
50 South Steele St., Ste. 777
Denver, CO 80209
(303)321-4800
Fax: (303)321-4848
E-mail: businessplan@wolf
ventures.com
Website: http://www.wolfventures.com

The Columbine Venture Funds
5460 S. Quebec St., Ste. 270
Englewood, CO 80111

(303)694-3222
Fax: (303)694-9007

Investment Securities of Colorado, Inc.
4605 Denice Dr.
Englewood, CO 80111
(303)796-9192

Kinship Partners
6300 S. Syracuse Way, Ste. 484
Englewood, CO 80111
(303)694-0268
Fax: (303)694-1707
E-mail: block@vailsys.com

Boranco Management, L.L.C.
1528 Hillside Dr.
Fort Collins, CO 80524-1969
(970)221-2297
Fax: (970)221-4787

Aweida Ventures
890 West Cherry St., Ste. 220
Louisville, CO 80027
(303)664-9520
Fax: (303)664-9530
Website: http://www.aweida.com

Access Venture Partners
8787 Turnpike Dr., Ste. 260
Westminster, CO 80030
(303)426-8899
Fax: (303)426-8828

Medmax Ventures LP
1 Northwestern Dr., Ste. 203
Bloomfield, CT 06002
(860)286-2960
Fax: (860)286-9960

James B. Kobak & Co.
Four Mansfield Place
Darien, CT 06820
(203)656-3471
Fax: (203)655-2905

Orien Ventures
1 Post Rd.
Fairfield, CT 06430
(203)259-9933
Fax: (203)259-5288

ABP Acquisition Corporation
115 Maple Ave.
Greenwich, CT 06830
(203)625-8287
Fax: (203)447-6187

Catterton Partners
9 Greenwich Office Park
Greenwich, CT 06830
(203)629-4901

Fax: (203)629-4903
Website: http://www.cpequity.com

Consumer Venture Partners
3 Pickwick Plz.
Greenwich, CT 06830
(203)629-8800
Fax: (203)629-2019

Insurance Venture Partners
31 Brookside Dr., Ste. 211
Greenwich, CT 06830
(203)861-0030
Fax: (203)861-2745

The NTC Group
Three Pickwick Plaza
Ste. 200
Greenwich, CT 06830
(203)862-2800
Fax: (203)622-6538

Regulus International Capital Co., Inc.
140 Greenwich Ave.
Greenwich, CT 06830
(203)625-9700
Fax: (203)625-9706

Axiom Venture Partners
City Place II
185 Asylum St., 17th Fl.
Hartford, CT 06103
(860)548-7799
Fax: (860)548-7797
Website: http://www.axiomventures.com

Conning Capital Partners
City Place II
185 Asylum St.
Hartford, CT 06103-4105
(860)520-1289
Fax: (860)520-1299
E-mail: pe@conning.com
Website: http://www.conning.com

First New England Capital L.P.
100 Pearl St.
Hartford, CT 06103
(860)293-3333
Fax: (860)293-3338
E-mail: info@firstnewenglandcapital.com
Website: http://www.firstnewengland capital.com

Northeast Ventures
One State St., Ste. 1720
Hartford, CT 06103
(860)547-1414
Fax: (860)246-8755

Windward Holdings
38 Sylvan Rd.
Madison, CT 06443
(203)245-6870
Fax: (203)245-6865

Advanced Materials Partners, Inc.
45 Pine St.
PO Box 1022
New Canaan, CT 06840
(203)966-6415
Fax: (203)966-8448
E-mail: wkb@amplink.com

RFE Investment Partners
36 Grove St.
New Canaan, CT 06840
(203)966-2800
Fax: (203)966-3109
Website: http://www.rfeip.com

Connecticut Innovations, Inc.
999 West St.
Rocky Hill, CT 06067
(860)563-5851
Fax: (860)563-4877
E-mail: pamela.hartley@ctin novations.com
Website: http://www.ctinnovations.com

Canaan Partners
105 Rowayton Ave.
Rowayton, CT 06853
(203)855-0400
Fax: (203)854-9117
Website: http://www.canaan.com

Landmark Partners, Inc.
10 Mill Pond Ln.
Simsbury, CT 06070
(860)651-9760
Fax: (860)651-8890
Website: http:// www.landmarkpartners.com

Sweeney & Company
PO Box 567
Southport, CT 06490
(203)255-0220
Fax: (203)255-0220
E-mail: sweeney@connix.com

Baxter Associates, Inc.
PO Box 1333
Stamford, CT 06904
(203)323-3143
Fax: (203)348-0622

Beacon Partners Inc.
6 Landmark Sq., 4th Fl.
Stamford, CT 06901-2792

(203)359-5776
Fax: (203)359-5876

Collinson, Howe, and Lennox, LLC
1055 Washington Blvd., 5th Fl.
Stamford, CT 06901
(203)324-7700
Fax: (203)324-3636
E-mail: info@chlmedical.com
Website: http://www.chlmedical.com

Prime Capital Management Co.
550 West Ave.
Stamford, CT 06902
(203)964-0642
Fax: (203)964-0862

Saugatuck Capital Co.
1 Canterbury Green
Stamford, CT 06901
(203)348-6669
Fax: (203)324-6995
Website: http://www.sauga tuckcapital.com

Soundview Financial Group Inc.
22 Gatehouse Rd.
Stamford, CT 06902
(203)462-7200
Fax: (203)462-7350
Website: http://www.sndv.com

TSG Ventures, L.L.C.
177 Broad St., 12th Fl.
Stamford, CT 06901
(203)406-1500
Fax: (203)406-1590

Whitney & Company
177 Broad St.
Stamford, CT 06901
(203)973-1400
Fax: (203)973-1422
Website: http://www.jhwhitney.com

Cullinane & Donnelly Venture Partners L.P.
970 Farmington Ave.
West Hartford, CT 06107
(860)521-7811

The Crestview Investment and Financial Group
431 Post Rd. E, Ste. 1
Westport, CT 06880-4403
(203)222-0333
Fax: (203)222-0000

Marketcorp Venture Associates, L.P. (MCV)
274 Riverside Ave.
Westport, CT 06880

(203)222-3030
Fax: (203)222-3033

Oak Investment Partners (Westport)
1 Gorham Island
Westport, CT 06880
(203)226-8346
Fax: (203)227-0372
Website: http://www.oakinv.com

Oxford Bioscience Partners
315 Post Rd. W
Westport, CT 06880-5200
(203)341-3300
Fax: (203)341-3309
Website: http://www.oxbio.com

Prince Ventures (Westport)
25 Ford Rd.
Westport, CT 06880
(203)227-8332
Fax: (203)226-5302

LTI Venture Leasing Corp.
221 Danbury Rd.
Wilton, CT 06897
(203)563-1100
Fax: (203)563-1111
Website: http://www.ltileasing.com

Delaware

Blue Rock Capital
5803 Kennett Pike, Ste. A
Wilmington, DE 19807
(302)426-0981
Fax: (302)426-0982
Website: http://www.bluerockcapital.com

District of Columbia

Allied Capital Corp.
1919 Pennsylvania Ave. NW
Washington, DC 20006-3434
(202)331-2444
Fax: (202)659-2053
Website: http://www.alliedcapital.com

Atlantic Coastal Ventures, L.P.
3101 South St. NW
Washington, DC 20007
(202)293-1166
Fax: (202)293-1181
Website: http://www.atlanticcv.com

Columbia Capital Group, Inc.
1660 L St. NW, Ste. 308
Washington, DC 20036
(202)775-8815
Fax: (202)223-0544

Core Capital Partners
901 15th St., NW
9th Fl.
Washington, DC 20005
(202)589-0090
Fax: (202)589-0091
Website: http://www.core-capital.com

Next Point Partners
701 Pennsylvania Ave. NW, Ste. 900
Washington, DC 20004
(202)661-8703
Fax: (202)434-7400
E-mail: mf@nextpoint.vc
Website: http://www.nextpointvc.com

Telecommunications Development Fund
2020 K. St. NW
Ste. 375
Washington, DC 20006
(202)293-8840
Fax: (202)293-8850
Website: http://www.tdfund.com

Wachtel & Co., Inc.
1101 4th St. NW
Washington, DC 20005-5680
(202)898-1144

Winslow Partners LLC
1300 Connecticut Ave. NW
Washington, DC 20036-1703
(202)530-5000
Fax: (202)530-5010
E-mail: winslow@winslowpartners.com

Women's Growth Capital Fund
1054 31st St., NW
Ste. 110
Washington, DC 20007
(202)342-1431
Fax: (202)341-1203
Website: http://www.wgcf.com

Sigma Capital Corp.
22668 Caravelle Circle
Boca Raton, FL 33433
(561)368-9783

North American Business Development Co., L.L.C.
111 East Las Olas Blvd.
Ft. Lauderdale, FL 33301
(305)463-0681
Fax: (305)527-0904
Website: http://www.northamericanfund.com

Chartwell Capital Management Co. Inc.
1 Independent Dr., Ste. 3120

Jacksonville, FL 32202
(904)355-3519
Fax: (904)353-5833
E-mail: info@chartwellcap.com

CEO Advisors
1061 Maitland Center Commons
Ste. 209
Maitland, FL 32751
(407)660-9327
Fax: (407)660-2109

Henry & Co.
8201 Peters Rd., Ste. 1000
Plantation, FL 33324
(954)797-7400

Avery Business Development Services
2506 St. Michel Ct.
Ponte Vedra, FL 32082
(904)285-6033

New South Ventures
5053 Ocean Blvd.
Sarasota, FL 34242
(941)358-6000
Fax: (941)358-6078
Website: http://www.newsouthventures.com

Venture Capital Management Corp.
PO Box 2626
Satellite Beach, FL 32937
(407)777-1969

Florida Capital Venture Ltd.
325 Florida Bank Plaza
100 W. Kennedy Blvd.
Tampa, FL 33602
(813)229-2294
Fax: (813)229-2028

Quantum Capital Partners
339 South Plant Ave.
Tampa, FL 33606
(813)250-1999
Fax: (813)250-1998
Website: http://www.quantumcapitalpartners.com

South Atlantic Venture Fund
614 W. Bay St.
Tampa, FL 33606-2704
(813)253-2500
Fax: (813)253-2360
E-mail: venture@southatlantic.com
Website: http://www.southatlantic.com

LM Capital Corp.
120 S. Olive, Ste. 400
West Palm Beach, FL 33401

(561)833-9700
Fax: (561)655-6587
Website: http://www.lmcapital
securities.com

Georgia

Venture First Associates
4811 Thornwood Dr.
Acworth, GA 30102
(770)928-3733
Fax: (770)928-6455

Alliance Technology Ventures
8995 Westside Pkwy., Ste. 200
Alpharetta, GA 30004
(678)336-2000
Fax: (678)336-2001
E-mail: info@atv.com
Website: http://www.atv.com

Cordova Ventures
2500 North Winds Pkwy., Ste. 475
Alpharetta, GA 30004
(678)942-0300
Fax: (678)942-0301
Website: http://www.cordovaventures.
com

Advanced Technology Development Fund
1000 Abernathy, Ste. 1420
Atlanta, GA 30328-5614
(404)668-2333
Fax: (404)668-2333

CGW Southeast Partners
12 Piedmont Center, Ste. 210
Atlanta, GA 30305
(404)816-3255
Fax: (404)816-3258
Website: http://www.cgwlp.com

Cyberstarts
1900 Emery St., NW
3rd Fl.
Atlanta, GA 30318
(404)267-5000
Fax: (404)267-5200
Website: http://www.cyberstarts.com

EGL Holdings, Inc.
10 Piedmont Center, Ste. 412
Atlanta, GA 30305
(404)949-8300
Fax: (404)949-8311

Equity South
1790 The Lenox Bldg.
3399 Peachtree Rd. NE
Atlanta, GA 30326

(404)237-6222
Fax: (404)261-1578

Five Paces
3400 Peachtree Rd., Ste. 200
Atlanta, GA 30326
(404)439-8300
Fax: (404)439-8301
Website: http://www.fivepaces.com

Frontline Capital, Inc.
3475 Lenox Rd., Ste. 400
Atlanta, GA 30326
(404)240-7280
Fax: (404)240-7281

Fuqua Ventures LLC
1201 W. Peachtree St. NW, Ste. 5000
Atlanta, GA 30309
(404)815-4500
Fax: (404)815-4528
Website: http://www.fuquaventures.com

Noro-Moseley Partners
4200 Northside Pkwy., Bldg. 9
Atlanta, GA 30327
(404)233-1966
Fax: (404)239-9280
Website: http://www.noro-moseley.com

Renaissance Capital Corp.
34 Peachtree St. NW, Ste. 2230
Atlanta, GA 30303
(404)658-9061
Fax: (404)658-9064

River Capital, Inc.
Two Midtown Plaza
1360 Peachtree St. NE, Ste. 1430
Atlanta, GA 30309
(404)873-2166
Fax: (404)873-2158

State Street Bank & Trust Co.
3414 Peachtree Rd. NE, Ste. 1010
Atlanta, GA 30326
(404)364-9500
Fax: (404)261-4469

UPS Strategic Enterprise Fund
55 Glenlake Pkwy. NE
Atlanta, GA 30328
(404)828-8814
Fax: (404)828-8088
E-mail: jcacyce@ups.com
Website: http://www.ups.com/sef/
sef_home

Wachovia
191 Peachtree St. NE, 26th Fl.
Atlanta, GA 30303

(404)332-1000
Fax: (404)332-1392
Website: http://www.wachovia.com/wca

Brainworks Ventures
4243 Dunwoody Club Dr.
Chamblee, GA 30341
(770)239-7447

First Growth Capital Inc.
Best Western Plaza, Ste. 105
PO Box 815
Forsyth, GA 31029
(912)781-7131

Financial Capital Resources, Inc.
21 Eastbrook Bend, Ste. 116
Peachtree City, GA 30269
(404)487-6650

Hawaii

HMS Hawaii Management Partners
Davies Pacific Center
841 Bishop St., Ste. 860
Honolulu, HI 96813
(808)545-3755
Fax: (808)531-2611

Idaho

Sun Valley Ventures
160 Second St.
Ketchum, ID 83340
(208)726-5005
Fax: (208)726-5094

Illinois

Open Prairie Ventures
115 N. Neil St., Ste. 209
Champaign, IL 61820
(217)351-7000
Fax: (217)351-7051
E-mail: inquire@openprairie.com
Website: http://www.openprairie.com

ABN AMRO Private Equity
208 S. La Salle St., 10th Fl.
Chicago, IL 60604
(312)855-7079
Fax: (312)553-6648
Website: http://www.abnequity.com

Alpha Capital Partners, Ltd.
122 S. Michigan Ave., Ste. 1700
Chicago, IL 60603
(312)322-9800
Fax: (312)322-9808
E-mail: acp@alphacapital.com

Ameritech Development Corp.
30 S. Wacker Dr., 37th Fl.
Chicago, IL 60606
(312)750-5083
Fax: (312)609-0244

Apex Investment Partners
225 W. Washington, Ste. 1450
Chicago, IL 60606
(312)857-2800
Fax: (312)857-1800
E-mail: apex@apexvc.com
Website: http://www.apexvc.com

Arch Venture Partners
8725 W. Higgins Rd., Ste. 290
Chicago, IL 60631
(773)380-6600
Fax: (773)380-6606
Website: http://www.archventure.com

The Bank Funds
208 South LaSalle St., Ste. 1680
Chicago, IL 60604
(312)855-6020
Fax: (312)855-8910

Batterson Venture Partners
303 W. Madison St., Ste. 1110
Chicago, IL 60606-3309
(312)269-0300
Fax: (312)269-0021
Website: http://www.battersonvp.com

William Blair Capital Partners, L.L.C.
222 W. Adams St., Ste. 1300
Chicago, IL 60606
(312)364-8250
Fax: (312)236-1042
E-mail: privateequity@wmblair.com
Website: http://www.wmblair.com

Bluestar Ventures
208 South LaSalle St., Ste. 1020
Chicago, IL 60604
(312)384-5000
Fax: (312)384-5005
Website: http://www.bluestarventures.com

The Capital Strategy Management Co.
233 S. Wacker Dr.
Box 06334
Chicago, IL 60606
(312)444-1170

DN Partners
77 West Wacker Dr., Ste. 4550
Chicago, IL 60601
(312)332-7960
Fax: (312)332-7979

Dresner Capital Inc.
29 South LaSalle St., Ste. 310
Chicago, IL 60603
(312)726-3600
Fax: (312)726-7448

Eblast Ventures LLC
11 South LaSalle St., 5th Fl.
Chicago, IL 60603
(312)372-2600
Fax: (312)372-5621
Website: http://www.eblastventures.com

Essex Woodlands Health Ventures, L.P.
190 S. LaSalle St., Ste. 2800
Chicago, IL 60603
(312)444-6040
Fax: (312)444-6034
Website: http://www.essexwood
lands.com

First Analysis Venture Capital
233 S. Wacker Dr., Ste. 9500
Chicago, IL 60606
(312)258-1400
Fax: (312)258-0334
Website: http://www.firstanalysis.com

Frontenac Co.
135 S. LaSalle St., Ste.3800
Chicago, IL 60603
(312)368-0044
Fax: (312)368-9520
Website: http://www.frontenac.com

GTCR Golder Rauner, LLC
6100 Sears Tower
Chicago, IL 60606
(312)382-2200
Fax: (312)382-2201
Website: http://www.gtcr.com

High Street Capital LLC
311 South Wacker Dr., Ste. 4550
Chicago, IL 60606
(312)697-4990
Fax: (312)697-4994
Website: http://www.highstr.com

IEG Venture Management, Inc.
70 West Madison
Chicago, IL 60602
(312)644-0890
Fax: (312)454-0369
Website: http://www.iegventure.com

JK&B Capital
180 North Stetson, Ste. 4500
Chicago, IL 60601
(312)946-1200
Fax: (312)946-1103

E-mail: gspencer@jkbcapital.com
Website: http://www.jkbcapital.com

Kettle Partners L.P.
350 W. Hubbard, Ste. 350
Chicago, IL 60610
(312)329-9300
Fax: (312)527-4519
Website: http://www.kettlevc.com

Lake Shore Capital Partners
20 N. Wacker Dr., Ste. 2807
Chicago, IL 60606
(312)803-3536
Fax: (312)803-3534

LaSalle Capital Group Inc.
70 W. Madison St., Ste. 5710
Chicago, IL 60602
(312)236-7041
Fax: (312)236-0720

Linc Capital, Inc.
303 E. Wacker Pkwy., Ste. 1000
Chicago, IL 60601
(312)946-2670
Fax: (312)938-4290
E-mail: bdemars@linccap.com

Madison Dearborn Partners, Inc.
3 First National Plz., Ste. 3800
Chicago, IL 60602
(312)895-1000
Fax: (312)895-1001
E-mail: invest@mdcp.com
Website: http://www.mdcp.com

Mesirow Private Equity Investments Inc.
350 N. Clark St.
Chicago, IL 60610
(312)595-6950
Fax: (312)595-6211
Website: http://www.meisrow
financial.com

Mosaix Ventures LLC
1822 North Mohawk
Chicago, IL 60614
(312)274-0988
Fax: (312)274-0989
Website: http://www.mosaix
ventures.com

Nesbitt Burns
111 West Monroe St.
Chicago, IL 60603
(312)416-3855
Fax: (312)765-8000
Website: http://www.harrisbank.com

Polestar Capital, Inc.
180 N. Michigan Ave., Ste. 1905
Chicago, IL 60601
(312)984-9090
Fax: (312)984-9877
E-mail: wl@polestarvc.com
Website: http://www.polestarvc.com

Prince Ventures (Chicago)
10 S. Wacker Dr., Ste. 2575
Chicago, IL 60606-7407
(312)454-1408
Fax: (312)454-9125

Prism Capital
444 N. Michigan Ave.
Chicago, IL 60611
(312)464-7900
Fax: (312)464-7915
Website: http://www.prismfund.com

Third Coast Capital
900 N. Franklin St., Ste. 700
Chicago, IL 60610
(312)337-3303
Fax: (312)337-2567
E-mail: manic@earthlink.com
Website: http://www.third
coastcapital.com

Thoma Cressey Equity Partners
4460 Sears Tower, 92nd Fl.
233 S. Wacker Dr.
Chicago, IL 60606
(312)777-4444
Fax: (312)777-4445
Website: http://www.thomacressey.com

Tribune Ventures
435 N. Michigan Ave., Ste. 600
Chicago, IL 60611
(312)527-8797
Fax: (312)222-5993
Website: http://www.tribuneventures.com

Wind Point Partners (Chicago)
676 N. Michigan Ave., Ste. 330
Chicago, IL 60611
(312)649-4000
Website: http://www.wppartners.com

Marquette Venture Partners
520 Lake Cook Rd., Ste. 450
Deerfield, IL 60015
(847)940-1700
Fax: (847)940-1724
Website: http://www.marquette
ventures.com

Duchossois Investments Limited, LLC
845 Larch Ave.
Elmhurst, IL 60126

(630)530-6105
Fax: (630)993-8644
Website: http://www.duchtec.com

Evanston Business Investment Corp.
1840 Oak Ave.
Evanston, IL 60201
(847)866-1840
Fax: (847)866-1808
E-mail: t-parkinson@nwu.com
Website: http://www.ebic.com

Inroads Capital Partners L.P.
1603 Orrington Ave., Ste. 2050
Evanston, IL 60201-3841
(847)864-2000
Fax: (847)864-9692

The Cerulean Fund/WGC Enterprises
1701 E. Lake Ave., Ste. 170
Glenview, IL 60025
(847)657-8002
Fax: (847)657-8168

Ventana Financial Resources, Inc.
249 Market Sq.
Lake Forest, IL 60045
(847)234-3434

Beecken, Petty & Co.
901 Warrenville Rd., Ste. 205
Lisle, IL 60532
(630)435-0300
Fax: (630)435-0370
E-mail: hep@bpcompany.com
Website: http://www.bpcompany.com

Allstate Private Equity
3075 Sanders Rd., Ste. G5D
Northbrook, IL 60062-7127
(847)402-8247
Fax: (847)402-0880

KB Partners
1101 Skokie Blvd., Ste. 260
Northbrook, IL 60062-2856
(847)714-0444
Fax: (847)714-0445
E-mail: keith@kbpartners.com
Website: http://www.kbpartners.com

Transcap Associates Inc.
900 Skokie Blvd., Ste. 210
Northbrook, IL 60062
(847)753-9600
Fax: (847)753-9090

Graystone Venture Partners, L.L.C. / Portage Venture Partners
One Northfield Plaza, Ste. 530
Northfield, IL 60093

(847)446-9460
Fax: (847)446-9470
Website: http://www.portage
ventures.com

Motorola Inc.
1303 E. Algonquin Rd.
Schaumburg, IL 60196-1065
(847)576-4929
Fax: (847)538-2250
Website: http://www.mot.com/mne

Indiana

Irwin Ventures LLC
500 Washington St.
Columbus, IN 47202
(812)373-1434
Fax: (812)376-1709
Website: http://www.irwinventures.com

Cambridge Venture Partners
4181 East 96th St., Ste. 200
Indianapolis, IN 46240
(317)814-6192
Fax: (317)944-9815

CID Equity Partners
One American Square, Ste. 2850
Box 82074
Indianapolis, IN 46282
(317)269-2350
Fax: (317)269-2355
Website: http://www.cidequity.com

Gazelle Techventures
6325 Digital Way, Ste. 460
Indianapolis, IN 46278
(317)275-6800
Fax: (317)275-1101
Website: http://www.gazellevc.com

Monument Advisors Inc.
Bank One Center/Circle
111 Monument Circle, Ste. 600
Indianapolis, IN 46204-5172
(317)656-5065
Fax: (317)656-5060
Website: http://www.monumentadv.com

MWV Capital Partners
201 N. Illinois St., Ste. 300
Indianapolis, IN 46204
(317)237-2323
Fax: (317)237-2325
Website: http://www.mwvcapital.com

First Source Capital Corp.
100 North Michigan St.
PO Box 1602
South Bend, IN 46601

(219)235-2180
Fax: (219)235-2227

Iowa

Allsop Venture Partners
118 Third Ave. SE, Ste. 837
Cedar Rapids, IA 52401
(319)368-6675
Fax: (319)363-9515

InvestAmerica Investment Advisors, Inc.
101 2nd St. SE, Ste. 800
Cedar Rapids, IA 52401
(319)363-8249
Fax: (319)363-9683

Pappajohn Capital Resources
2116 Financial Center
Des Moines, IA 50309
(515)244-5746
Fax: (515)244-2346
Website: http://www.pappajohn.com

Berthel Fisher & Company Planning Inc.
701 Tama St.
PO Box 609
Marion, IA 52302
(319)497-5700
Fax: (319)497-4244

Kansas

Enterprise Merchant Bank
7400 West 110th St., Ste. 560
Overland Park, KS 66210
(913)327-8500
Fax: (913)327-8505

Kansas Venture Capital, Inc. (Overland Park)
6700 Antioch Plz., Ste. 460
Overland Park, KS 66204
(913)262-7117
Fax: (913)262-3509
E-mail: jdalton@kvci.com

Child Health Investment Corp.
6803 W. 64th St., Ste. 208
Shawnee Mission, KS 66202
(913)262-1436
Fax: (913)262-1575
Website: http://www.chca.com

Kansas Technology Enterprise Corp.
214 SW 6th, 1st Fl.
Topeka, KS 66603-3719
(785)296-5272
Fax: (785)296-1160

E-mail: ktec@ktec.com
Website: http://www.ktec.com

Kentucky

Kentucky Highlands Investment Corp.
362 Old Whitley Rd.
London, KY 40741
(606)864-5175
Fax: (606)864-5194
Website: http://www.khic.org

Chrysalis Ventures, L.L.C.
1850 National City Tower
Louisville, KY 40202
(502)583-7644
Fax: (502)583-7648
E-mail: bobsany@chrysalisventures.com
Website: http://www.chrysalis
ventures.com

Humana Venture Capital
500 West Main St.
Louisville, KY 40202
(502)580-3922
Fax: (502)580-2051
E-mail: gemont@humana.com
George Emont, Director

Summit Capital Group, Inc.
6510 Glenridge Park Pl., Ste. 8
Louisville, KY 40222
(502)332-2700

Louisiana

Bank One Equity Investors, Inc.
451 Florida St.
Baton Rouge, LA 70801
(504)332-4421
Fax: (504)332-7377

Advantage Capital Partners
LLE Tower
909 Poydras St., Ste. 2230
New Orleans, LA 70112
(504)522-4850
Fax: (504)522-4950
Website: http://www.advantagecap.com

Maine

CEI Ventures / Coastal Ventures LP
2 Portland Fish Pier, Ste. 201
Portland, ME 04101
(207)772-5356
Fax: (207)772-5503
Website: http://www.ceiventures.com

Commwealth Bioventures, Inc.
4 Milk St.
Portland, ME 04101

(207)780-0904
Fax: (207)780-0913

Maryland

Annapolis Ventures LLC
151 West St., Ste. 302
Annapolis, MD 21401
(443)482-9555
Fax: (443)482-9565
Website: http://www.annapolis
ventures.com

Delmag Ventures
220 Wardour Dr.
Annapolis, MD 21401
(410)267-8196
Fax: (410)267-8017
Website: http://www.delmag
ventures.com

Abell Venture Fund
111 S. Calvert St., Ste. 2300
Baltimore, MD 21202
(410)547-1300
Fax: (410)539-6579
Website: http://www.abell.org

ABS Ventures (Baltimore)
1 South St., Ste. 2150
Baltimore, MD 21202
(410)895-3895
Fax: (410)895-3899
Website: http://www.absventures.com

Anthem Capital, L.P.
16 S. Calvert St., Ste. 800
Baltimore, MD 21202-1305
(410)625-1510
Fax: (410)625-1735
Website: http://www.anthemcapital.com

Catalyst Ventures
1119 St. Paul St.
Baltimore, MD 21202
(410)244-0123
Fax: (410)752-7721

Maryland Venture Capital Trust
217 E. Redwood St., Ste. 2200
Baltimore, MD 21202
(410)767-6361
Fax: (410)333-6931

New Enterprise Associates (Baltimore)
1119 St. Paul St.
Baltimore, MD 21202
(410)244-0115
Fax: (410)752-7721
Website: http://www.nea.com

T. Rowe Price Threshold Partnerships
100 E. Pratt St., 8th Fl.
Baltimore, MD 21202
(410)345-2000
Fax: (410)345-2800

Spring Capital Partners
16 W. Madison St.
Baltimore, MD 21201
(410)685-8000
Fax: (410)727-1436
E-mail: mailbox@springcap.com

Arete Corporation
3 Bethesda Metro Ctr., Ste. 770
Bethesda, MD 20814
(301)657-6268
Fax: (301)657-6254
Website: http://www.arete-microgen.com

Embryon Capital
7903 Sleaford Place
Bethesda, MD 20814
(301)656-6837
Fax: (301)656-8056

Potomac Ventures
7920 Norfolk Ave., Ste. 1100
Bethesda, MD 20814
(301)215-9240
Website: http://www.potomac
ventures.com

Toucan Capital Corp.
3 Bethesda Metro Center, Ste. 700
Bethesda, MD 20814
(301)961-1970
Fax: (301)961-1969
Website: http://www.toucancapital.com

Kinetic Ventures LLC
2 Wisconsin Cir., Ste. 620
Chevy Chase, MD 20815
(301)652-8066
Fax: (301)652-8310
Website: http://www.kineticventures.com

Boulder Ventures Ltd.
4750 Owings Mills Blvd.
Owings Mills, MD 21117
(410)998-3114
Fax: (410)356-5492
Website: http://www.boulderventures.com

Grotech Capital Group
9690 Deereco Rd., Ste. 800
Timonium, MD 21093
(410)560-2000
Fax: (410)560-1910
Website: http://www.grotech.com

Massachusetts

Adams, Harkness & Hill, Inc.
60 State St.
Boston, MA 02109
(617)371-3900

Advent International
75 State St., 29th Fl.
Boston, MA 02109
(617)951-9400
Fax: (617)951-0566
Website: http://www.adventiner
national.com

American Research and Development
30 Federal St.
Boston, MA 02110-2508
(617)423-7500
Fax: (617)423-9655

Ascent Venture Partners
255 State St., 5th Fl.
Boston, MA 02109
(617)270-9400
Fax: (617)270-9401
E-mail: info@ascentvp.com
Website: http://www.ascentvp.com

Atlas Venture
222 Berkeley St.
Boston, MA 02116
(617)488-2200
Fax: (617)859-9292
Website: http://www.atlasventure.com

Axxon Capital
28 State St., 37th Fl.
Boston, MA 02109
(617)722-0980
Fax: (617)557-6014
Website: http://www.axxoncapital.com

**BancBoston Capital/BancBoston
Ventures**
175 Federal St., 10th Fl.
Boston, MA 02110
(617)434-2509
Fax: (617)434-6175
Website: http://
www.bancbostoncapital.com

Boston Capital Ventures
Old City Hall
45 School St.
Boston, MA 02108
(617)227-6550
Fax: (617)227-3847
E-mail: info@bcv.com
Website: http://www.bcv.com

Boston Financial & Equity Corp.
20 Overland St.
PO Box 15071
Boston, MA 02215
(617)267-2900
Fax: (617)437-7601
E-mail: debbie@bfec.com

Boston Millennia Partners
30 Rowes Wharf
Boston, MA 02110
(617)428-5150
Fax: (617)428-5160
Website: http://www.millennia
partners.com

Bristol Investment Trust
842A Beacon St.
Boston, MA 02215-3199
(617)566-5212
Fax: (617)267-0932

Brook Venture Management LLC
50 Federal St., 5th Fl.
Boston, MA 02110
(617)451-8989
Fax: (617)451-2369
Website: http://www.brookventure.com

Burr, Egan, Deleage, and Co. (Boston)
200 Clarendon St., Ste. 3800
Boston, MA 02116
(617)262-7770
Fax: (617)262-9779

Cambridge/Samsung Partners
One Exeter Plaza
Ninth Fl.
Boston, MA 02116
(617)262-4440
Fax: (617)262-5562

Chestnut Street Partners, Inc.
75 State St., Ste. 2500
Boston, MA 02109
(617)345-7220
Fax: (617)345-7201
E-mail: chestnut@chestnutp.com

Claflin Capital Management, Inc.
10 Liberty Sq., Ste. 300
Boston, MA 02109
(617)426-6505
Fax: (617)482-0016
Website: http://www.claflincapital.com

Copley Venture Partners
99 Summer St., Ste. 1720
Boston, MA 02110
(617)737-1253
Fax: (617)439-0699

Corning Capital / Corning Technology Ventures
121 High Street, Ste. 400
Boston, MA 02110
(617)338-2656
Fax: (617)261-3864
Website: http://www.corningventures.com

Downer & Co.
211 Congress St.
Boston, MA 02110
(617)482-6200
Fax: (617)482-6201
E-mail: cdowner@downer.com
Website: http://www.downer.com

Fidelity Ventures
82 Devonshire St.
Boston, MA 02109
(617)563-6370
Fax: (617)476-9023
Website: http://www.fidelityventures.com

Greylock Management Corp. (Boston)
1 Federal St.
Boston, MA 02110-2065
(617)423-5525
Fax: (617)482-0059

Gryphon Ventures
222 Berkeley St., Ste.1600
Boston, MA 02116
(617)267-9191
Fax: (617)267-4293
E-mail: all@gryphoninc.com

Halpern, Denny & Co.
500 Boylston St.
Boston, MA 02116
(617)536-6602
Fax: (617)536-8535

Harbourvest Partners, LLC
1 Financial Center, 44th Fl.
Boston, MA 02111
(617)348-3707
Fax: (617)350-0305
Website: http://www.hvpllc.com

Highland Capital Partners
2 International Pl.
Boston, MA 02110
(617)981-1500
Fax: (617)531-1550
E-mail: info@hcp.com
Website: http://www.hcp.com

Lee Munder Venture Partners
John Hancock Tower T-53
200 Clarendon St.
Boston, MA 02103

(617)380-5600
Fax: (617)380-5601
Website: http://www.leemunder.com

M/C Venture Partners
75 State St., Ste. 2500
Boston, MA 02109
(617)345-7200
Fax: (617)345-7201
Website: http://www.mcventure
partners.com

Massachusetts Capital Resources Co.
420 Boylston St.
Boston, MA 02116
(617)536-3900
Fax: (617)536-7930

Massachusetts Technology Development Corp. (MTDC)
148 State St.
Boston, MA 02109
(617)723-4920
Fax: (617)723-5983
E-mail: jhodgman@mtdc.com
Website: http://www.mtdc.com

New England Partners
One Boston Place, Ste. 2100
Boston, MA 02108
(617)624-8400
Fax: (617)624-8999
Website: http://www.nepartners.com

North Hill Ventures
Ten Post Office Square
11th Fl.
Boston, MA 02109
(617)788-2112
Fax: (617)788-2152
Website: http://www.northhill
ventures.com

OneLiberty Ventures
150 Cambridge Park Dr.
Boston, MA 02140
(617)492-7280
Fax: (617)492-7290
Website: http://www.oneliberty.com

Schroder Ventures
Life Sciences
60 State St., Ste. 3650
Boston, MA 02109
(617)367-8100
Fax: (617)367-1590
Website: http://www.shroderventures.com

Shawmut Capital Partners
75 Federal St., 18th Fl.
Boston, MA 02110

(617)368-4900
Fax: (617)368-4910
Website: http://www.shawmutcapital.com

Solstice Capital LLC
15 Broad St., 3rd Fl.
Boston, MA 02109
(617)523-7733
Fax: (617)523-5827
E-mail: solticecapital@solcap.com

Spectrum Equity Investors
One International Pl., 29th Fl.
Boston, MA 02110
(617)464-4600
Fax: (617)464-4601
Website: http://www.spectrumequity.com

Spray Venture Partners
One Walnut St.
Boston, MA 02108
(617)305-4140
Fax: (617)305-4144
Website: http://www.sprayventure.com

The Still River Fund
100 Federal St., 29th Fl.
Boston, MA 02110
(617)348-2327
Fax: (617)348-2371
Website: http://www.stillriverfund.com

Summit Partners
600 Atlantic Ave., Ste. 2800
Boston, MA 02210-2227
(617)824-1000
Fax: (617)824-1159
Website: http://www.summitpartners.com

TA Associates, Inc. (Boston)
High Street Tower
125 High St., Ste. 2500
Boston, MA 02110
(617)574-6700
Fax: (617)574-6728
Website: http://www.ta.com

TVM Techno Venture Management
101 Arch St., Ste. 1950
Boston, MA 02110
(617)345-9320
Fax: (617)345-9377
E-mail: info@tvmvc.com
Website: http://www.tvmvc.com

UNC Ventures
64 Burough St.
Boston, MA 02130-4017
(617)482-7070
Fax: (617)522-2176

Venture Investment Management Company (VIMAC)
177 Milk St.
Boston, MA 02190-3410
(617)292-3300
Fax: (617)292-7979
E-mail: bzeisig@vimac.com
Website: http://www.vimac.com

MDT Advisers, Inc.
125 Cambridge Park Dr.
Cambridge, MA 02140-2314
(617)234-2200
Fax: (617)234-2210
Website: http://www.mdtai.com

TTC Ventures
One Main St., 6th Fl.
Cambridge, MA 02142
(617)528-3137
Fax: (617)577-1715
E-mail: info@ttcventures.com

Zero Stage Capital Co. Inc.
101 Main St., 17th Fl.
Cambridge, MA 02142
(617)876-5355
Fax: (617)876-1248
Website: http://www.zerostage.com

Atlantic Capital
164 Cushing Hwy.
Cohasset, MA 02025
(617)383-9449
Fax: (617)383-6040
E-mail: info@atlanticcap.com
Website: http://www.atlanticcap.com

Seacoast Capital Partners
55 Ferncroft Rd.
Danvers, MA 01923
(978)750-1300
Fax: (978)750-1301
E-mail: gdeli@seacoastcapital.com
Website: http://www.seacoast
capital.com

Sage Management Group
44 South Street
PO Box 2026
East Dennis, MA 02641
(508)385-7172
Fax: (508)385-7272
E-mail: sagemgt@capecod.net

Applied Technology
1 Cranberry Hill
Lexington, MA 02421-7397
(617)862-8622
Fax: (617)862-8367

Royalty Capital Management
5 Downing Rd.
Lexington, MA 02421-6918
(781)861-8490

Argo Global Capital
210 Broadway, Ste. 101
Lynnfield, MA 01940
(781)592-5250
Fax: (781)592-5230
Website: http://www.gsmcapital.com

Industry Ventures
6 Bayne Lane
Newburyport, MA 01950
(978)499-7606
Fax: (978)499-0686
Website: http://
www.industryventures.com

Softbank Capital Partners
10 Langley Rd., Ste. 202
Newton Center, MA 02459
(617)928-9300
Fax: (617)928-9305
E-mail: clax@bvc.com

Advanced Technology Ventures (Boston)
281 Winter St., Ste. 350
Waltham, MA 02451
(781)290-0707
Fax: (781)684-0045
E-mail: info@atvcapital.com
Website: http://www.atvcapital.com

Castile Ventures
890 Winter St., Ste. 140
Waltham, MA 02451
(781)890-0060
Fax: (781)890-0065
Website: http://www.castileventures.com

Charles River Ventures
1000 Winter St., Ste. 3300
Waltham, MA 02451
(781)487-7060
Fax: (781)487-7065
Website: http://www.crv.com

Comdisco Venture Group (Waltham)
Totton Pond Office Center
400-1 Totten Pond Rd.
Waltham, MA 02451
(617)672-0250
Fax: (617)398-8099

Marconi Ventures
890 Winter St., Ste. 310
Waltham, MA 02451
(781)839-7177

Fax: (781)522-7477
Website: http://www.marconi.com

Matrix Partners
Bay Colony Corporate Center
1000 Winter St., Ste.4500
Waltham, MA 02451
(781)890-2244
Fax: (781)890-2288
Website: http://www.matrix
partners.com

North Bridge Venture Partners
950 Winter St. Ste. 4600
Waltham, MA 02451
(781)290-0004
Fax: (781)290-0999
E-mail: eta@nbvp.com

Polaris Venture Partners
Bay Colony Corporate Ctr.
1000 Winter St., Ste. 3500
Waltham, MA 02451
(781)290-0770
Fax: (781)290-0880
E-mail: partners@polarisventures.com
Website: http://www.polar
isventures.com

Seaflower Ventures
Bay Colony Corporate Ctr.
1000 Winter St. Ste. 1000
Waltham, MA 02451
(781)466-9552
Fax: (781)466-9553
E-mail: moot@seaflower.com
Website: http://www.seaflower.com

Ampersand Ventures
55 William St., Ste. 240
Wellesley, MA 02481
(617)239-0700
Fax: (617)239-0824
E-mail: info@ampersandventures.com
Website: http://www.ampersand
ventures.com

Battery Ventures (Boston)
20 William St., Ste. 200
Wellesley, MA 02481
(781)577-1000
Fax: (781)577-1001
Website: http://www.battery.com

Commonwealth Capital Ventures, L.P.
20 William St., Ste.225
Wellesley, MA 02481
(781)237-7373
Fax: (781)235-8627
Website: http://www.ccvlp.com

Fowler, Anthony & Company
20 Walnut St.
Wellesley, MA 02481
(781)237-4201
Fax: (781)237-7718

Gemini Investors
20 William St.
Wellesley, MA 02481
(781)237-7001
Fax: (781)237-7233

Grove Street Advisors Inc.
20 William St., Ste. 230
Wellesley, MA 02481
(781)263-6100
Fax: (781)263-6101
Website: http://www.groves
treetadvisors.com

Mees Pierson Investeringsmaat B.V.
20 William St., Ste. 210
Wellesley, MA 02482
(781)239-7600
Fax: (781)239-0377

Norwest Equity Partners
40 William St., Ste. 305
Wellesley, MA 02481-3902
(781)237-5870
Fax: (781)237-6270
Website: http://www.norwestvp.com

Bessemer Venture Partners (Wellesley Hills)
83 Walnut St.
Wellesley Hills, MA 02481
(781)237-6050
Fax: (781)235-7576
E-mail: travis@bvpny.com
Website: http://www.bvp.com

Venture Capital Fund of New England
20 Walnut St., Ste. 120
Wellesley Hills, MA 02481-2175
(781)239-8262
Fax: (781)239-8263

Prism Venture Partners
100 Lowder Brook Dr., Ste. 2500
Westwood, MA 02090
(781)302-4000
Fax: (781)302-4040
E-mail: dwbaum@prismventure.com

Palmer Partners LP
200 Unicorn Park Dr.
Woburn, MA 01801
(781)933-5445
Fax: (781)933-0698

Michigan

Arbor Partners, L.L.C.
130 South First St.
Ann Arbor, MI 48104
(734)668-9000
Fax: (734)669-4195
Website: http://www.arborpartners.com

EDF Ventures
425 N. Main St.
Ann Arbor, MI 48104
(734)663-3213
Fax: (734)663-7358
E-mail: edf@edfvc.com
Website: http://www.edfvc.com

White Pines Management, L.L.C.
2401 Plymouth Rd., Ste. B
Ann Arbor, MI 48105
(734)747-9401
Fax: (734)747-9704
E-mail: ibund@whitepines.com
Website: http://www.whitepines.com

Wellmax, Inc.
3541 Bendway Blvd., Ste. 100
Bloomfield Hills, MI 48301
(248)646-3554
Fax: (248)646-6220

Venture Funding, Ltd.
Fisher Bldg.
3011 West Grand Blvd., Ste. 321
Detroit, MI 48202
(313)871-3606
Fax: (313)873-4935

Investcare Partners L.P. / GMA Capital LLC
32330 W. Twelve Mile Rd.
Farmington Hills, MI 48334
(248)489-9000
Fax: (248)489-8819
E-mail: gma@gmacapital.com
Website: http://www.gmacapital.com

Liberty Bidco Investment Corp.
30833 Northwestern Highway, Ste. 211
Farmington Hills, MI 48334
(248)626-6070
Fax: (248)626-6072

Seaflower Ventures
5170 Nicholson Rd.
PO Box 474
Fowlerville, MI 48836
(517)223-3335
Fax: (517)223-3337
E-mail: gibbons@seaflower.com
Website: http://www.seaflower.com

Ralph Wilson Equity Fund LLC
15400 E. Jefferson Ave.
Gross Pointe Park, MI 48230
(313)821-9122
Fax: (313)821-9101
Website: http://www.Ralph
WilsonEquityFund.com
J. Skip Simms, President

Minnesota

Development Corp. of Austin
1900 Eighth Ave., NW
Austin, MN 55912
(507)433-0346
Fax: (507)433-0361
E-mail: dca@smig.net
Website: http://www.spamtownusa.com

Northeast Ventures Corp.
802 Alworth Bldg.
Duluth, MN 55802
(218)722-9915
Fax: (218)722-9871

Medical Innovation Partners, Inc.
6450 City West Pkwy.
Eden Prairie, MN 55344-3245
(612)828-9616
Fax: (612)828-9596

St. Paul Venture Capital, Inc.
10400 Vicking Dr., Ste. 550
Eden Prairie, MN 55344
(612)995-7474
Fax: (612)995-7475
Website: http://www.stpaulvc.com

Cherry Tree Investments, Inc.
7601 France Ave. S, Ste. 150
Edina, MN 55435
(612)893-9012
Fax: (612)893-9036
Website: http://www.cherrytree.com

Shared Ventures, Inc.
6550 York Ave. S
Edina, MN 55435
(612)925-3411

Sherpa Partners LLC
5050 Lincoln Dr., Ste. 490
Edina, MN 55436
(952)942-1070
Fax: (952)942-1071
Website: http://www.sherpapartners.com

Affinity Capital Management
901 Marquette Ave., Ste. 1810
Minneapolis, MN 55402
(612)252-9900

Fax: (612)252-9911
Website: http://www.affinitycapital.com

Artesian Capital
1700 Foshay Tower
821 Marquette Ave.
Minneapolis, MN 55402
(612)334-5600
Fax: (612)334-5601
E-mail: artesian@artesian.com

Coral Ventures
60 S. 6th St., Ste. 3510
Minneapolis, MN 55402
(612)335-8666
Fax: (612)335-8668
Website: http://www.coralventures.com

Crescendo Venture Management, L.L.C.
800 LaSalle Ave., Ste. 2250
Minneapolis, MN 55402
(612)607-2800
Fax: (612)607-2801
Website: http://www.crescendo
ventures.com

Gideon Hixon Venture
1900 Foshay Tower
821 Marquette Ave.
Minneapolis, MN 55402
(612)904-2314
Fax: (612)204-0913

Norwest Equity Partners
3600 IDS Center
80 S. 8th St.
Minneapolis, MN 55402
(612)215-1600
Fax: (612)215-1601
Website: http://www.norwestvp.com

Oak Investment Partners (Minneapolis)
4550 Norwest Center
90 S. 7th St.
Minneapolis, MN 55402
(612)339-9322
Fax: (612)337-8017
Website: http://www.oakinv.com

Pathfinder Venture Capital Funds (Minneapolis)
7300 Metro Blvd., Ste. 585
Minneapolis, MN 55439
(612)835-1121
Fax: (612)835-8389
E-mail: jahrens620@aol.com

U.S. Bancorp Piper Jaffray Ventures, Inc.
800 Nicollet Mall, Ste. 800
Minneapolis, MN 55402

(612)303-5686
Fax: (612)303-1350
Website: http://www.paperjaffrey
ventures.com

The Food Fund, Ltd. Partnership
5720 Smatana Dr., Ste. 300
Minnetonka, MN 55343
(612)939-3950
Fax: (612)939-8106

Mayo Medical Ventures
200 First St. SW
Rochester, MN 55905
(507)266-4586
Fax: (507)284-5410
Website: http://www.mayo.edu

Missouri

Bankers Capital Corp.
3100 Gillham Rd.
Kansas City, MO 64109
(816)531-1600
Fax: (816)531-1334

Capital for Business, Inc. (Kansas City)
1000 Walnut St., 18th Fl.
Kansas City, MO 64106
(816)234-2357
Fax: (816)234-2952
Website: http://
www.capitalforbusiness.com

De Vries & Co. Inc.
800 West 47th St.
Kansas City, MO 64112
(816)756-0055
Fax: (816)756-0061

InvestAmerica Venture Group Inc. (Kansas City)
Commerce Tower
911 Main St., Ste. 2424
Kansas City, MO 64105
(816)842-0114
Fax: (816)471-7339

Kansas City Equity Partners
233 W. 47th St.
Kansas City, MO 64112
(816)960-1771
Fax: (816)960-1777
Website: http://www.kcep.com

Bome Investors, Inc.
8000 Maryland Ave., Ste. 1190
St. Louis, MO 63105
(314)721-5707
Fax: (314)721-5135

Website: http://www.gateway
ventures.com

Capital for Business, Inc. (St. Louis)
11 S. Meramac St., Ste. 1430
St. Louis, MO 63105
(314)746-7427
Fax: (314)746-8739
Website: http://www.capitalfor
business.com

Crown Capital Corp.
540 Maryville Centre Dr., Ste. 120
Saint Louis, MO 63141
(314)576-1201
Fax: (314)576-1525
Website: http://www.crown-
cap.com

Gateway Associates L.P.
8000 Maryland Ave., Ste. 1190
St. Louis, MO 63105
(314)721-5707
Fax: (314)721-5135

Harbison Corp.
8112 Maryland Ave., Ste. 250
Saint Louis, MO 63105
(314)727-8200
Fax: (314)727-0249

Heartland Capital Fund, Ltd.
PO Box 642117
Omaha, NE 68154
(402)778-5124
Fax: (402)445-2370
Website: http://www.heartland
capitalfund.com

Odin Capital Group
1625 Farnam St., Ste. 700
Omaha, NE 68102
(402)346-6200
Fax: (402)342-9311
Website: http://www.odincapital.com

Nevada

Edge Capital Investment Co. LLC
1350 E. Flamingo Rd., Ste. 3000
Las Vegas, NV 89119
(702)438-3343
E-mail: info@edgecapital.net
Website: http://www.edgecapital.net

The Benefit Capital Companies Inc.
PO Box 542
Logandale, NV 89021
(702)398-3222
Fax: (702)398-3700

Millennium Three Venture Group LLC
6880 South McCarran Blvd., Ste. A-11
Reno, NV 89509
(775)954-2020
Fax: (775)954-2023
Website: http://www.m3vg.com

New Jersey

Alan I. Goldman & Associates
497 Ridgewood Ave.
Glen Ridge, NJ 07028
(973)857-5680
Fax: (973)509-8856

CS Capital Partners LLC
328 Second St., Ste. 200
Lakewood, NJ 08701
(732)901-1111
Fax: (212)202-5071
Website: http://www.cs-capital.com

Edison Venture Fund
1009 Lenox Dr., Ste. 4
Lawrenceville, NJ 08648
(609)896-1900
Fax: (609)896-0066
E-mail: info@edisonventure.com
Website: http://www.edisonventure.com

Tappan Zee Capital Corp. (New Jersey)
201 Lower Notch Rd.
PO Box 416
Little Falls, NJ 07424
(973)256-8280
Fax: (973)256-2841

The CIT Group/Venture Capital, Inc.
650 CIT Dr.
Livingston, NJ 07039
(973)740-5429
Fax: (973)740-5555
Website: http://www.cit.com

Capital Express, L.L.C.
1100 Valleybrook Ave.
Lyndhurst, NJ 07071
(201)438-8228
Fax: (201)438-5131
E-mail: niles@capitalexpress.com
Website: http://www.capitalexpress.com

Westford Technology Ventures, L.P.
17 Academy St.
Newark, NJ 07102
(973)624-2131
Fax: (973)624-2008

Accel Partners
1 Palmer Sq.
Princeton, NJ 08542

(609)683-4500
Fax: (609)683-4880
Website: http://www.accel.com

Cardinal Partners
221 Nassau St.
Princeton, NJ 08542
(609)924-6452
Fax: (609)683-0174
Website: http://www.cardinal
healthpartners.com

Domain Associates L.L.C.
One Palmer Sq., Ste. 515
Princeton, NJ 08542
(609)683-5656
Fax: (609)683-9789
Website: http://www.domainvc.com

Johnston Associates, Inc.
181 Cherry Valley Rd.
Princeton, NJ 08540
(609)924-3131
Fax: (609)683-7524
E-mail: jaincorp@aol.com

Kemper Ventures
Princeton Forrestal Village
155 Village Blvd.
Princeton, NJ 08540
(609)936-3035
Fax: (609)936-3051

Penny Lane Parnters
One Palmer Sq., Ste. 309
Princeton, NJ 08542
(609)497-4646
Fax: (609)497-0611

Early Stage Enterprises L.P.
995 Route 518
Skillman, NJ 08558
(609)921-8896
Fax: (609)921-8703
Website: http://www.esevc.com

MBW Management Inc.
1 Springfield Ave.
Summit, NJ 07901
(908)273-4060
Fax: (908)273-4430

BCI Advisors, Inc.
Glenpointe Center W.
Teaneck, NJ 07666
(201)836-3900
Fax: (201)836-6368
E-mail: info@bciadvisors.com
Website: http://www.bci
partners.com

Demuth, Folger & Wetherill / DFW Capital Partners
Glenpointe Center E., 5th Fl.
300 Frank W. Burr Blvd.
Teaneck, NJ 07666
(201)836-2233
Fax: (201)836-5666
Website: http://www.dfwcapital.com

First Princeton Capital Corp.
189 Berdan Ave., No. 131
Wayne, NJ 07470-3233
(973)278-3233
Fax: (973)278-4290
Website: http://www.lytellcatt.net

Edelson Technology Partners
300 Tice Blvd.
Woodcliff Lake, NJ 07675
(201)930-9898
Fax: (201)930-8899
Website: http://www.edelsontech.com

New Mexico

Bruce F. Glaspell & Associates
10400 Academy Rd. NE, Ste. 313
Albuquerque, NM 87111
(505)292-4505
Fax: (505)292-4258

High Desert Ventures, Inc.
6101 Imparata St. NE, Ste. 1721
Albuquerque, NM 87111
(505)797-3330
Fax: (505)338-5147

New Business Capital Fund, Ltd.
5805 Torreon NE
Albuquerque, NM 87109
(505)822-8445

SBC Ventures
10400 Academy Rd. NE, Ste. 313
Albuquerque, NM 87111
(505)292-4505
Fax: (505)292-4528

Technology Ventures Corp.
1155 University Blvd. SE
Albuquerque, NM 87106
(505)246-2882
Fax: (505)246-2891

New York

New York State Science & Technology Foundation
Small Business Technology Investment Fund
99 Washington Ave., Ste. 1731
Albany, NY 12210

(518)473-9741
Fax: (518)473-6876

Rand Capital Corp.
2200 Rand Bldg.
Buffalo, NY 14203
(716)853-0802
Fax: (716)854-8480
Website: http://www.randcapital.com

Seed Capital Partners
620 Main St.
Buffalo, NY 14202
(716)845-7520
Fax: (716)845-7539
Website: http://www.seedcp.com

Coleman Venture Group
5909 Northern Blvd.
PO Box 224
East Norwich, NY 11732
(516)626-3642
Fax: (516)626-9722

Vega Capital Corp.
45 Knollwood Rd.
Elmsford, NY 10523
(914)345-9500
Fax: (914)345-9505

Herbert Young Securities, Inc.
98 Cuttermill Rd.
Great Neck, NY 11021
(516)487-8300
Fax: (516)487-8319

Sterling/Carl Marks Capital, Inc.
175 Great Neck Rd., Ste. 408
Great Neck, NY 11021
(516)482-7374
Fax: (516)487-0781
E-mail: stercrlmar@aol.com
Website: http://www.serling
carlmarks.com

Impex Venture Management Co.
PO Box 1570
Green Island, NY 12183
(518)271-8008
Fax: (518)271-9101

Corporate Venture Partners L.P.
200 Sunset Park
Ithaca, NY 14850
(607)257-6323
Fax: (607)257-6128

Arthur P. Gould & Co.
One Wilshire Dr.
Lake Success, NY 11020
(516)773-3000
Fax: (516)773-3289

Dauphin Capital Partners
108 Forest Ave.
Locust Valley, NY 11560
(516)759-3339
Fax: (516)759-3322
Website: http://www.dauphincapital.com

550 Digital Media Ventures
555 Madison Ave., 10th Fl.
New York, NY 10022
Website: http://www.550dmv.com

Aberlyn Capital Management Co., Inc.
500 Fifth Ave.
New York, NY 10110
(212)391-7750
Fax: (212)391-7762

Adler & Company
342 Madison Ave., Ste. 807
New York, NY 10173
(212)599-2535
Fax: (212)599-2526

Alimansky Capital Group, Inc.
605 Madison Ave., Ste. 300
New York, NY 10022-1901
(212)832-7300
Fax: (212)832-7338

Allegra Partners
515 Madison Ave., 29th Fl.
New York, NY 10022
(212)826-9080
Fax: (212)759-2561

The Argentum Group
The Chyrsler Bldg.
405 Lexington Ave.
New York, NY 10174
(212)949-6262
Fax: (212)949-8294
Website: http://www.argentum
group.com

Axavision Inc.
14 Wall St., 26th Fl.
New York, NY 10005
(212)619-4000
Fax: (212)619-7202

Bedford Capital Corp.
18 East 48th St., Ste. 1800
New York, NY 10017
(212)688-5700
Fax: (212)754-4699
E-mail: info@bedfordnyc.com
Website: http://www.bedfordnyc.com

Bloom & Co.
950 Third Ave.

New York, NY 10022
(212)838-1858
Fax: (212)838-1843

Bristol Capital Management
300 Park Ave., 17th Fl.
New York, NY 10022
(212)572-6306
Fax: (212)705-4292

**Citicorp Venture Capital Ltd.
(New York City)**
399 Park Ave., 14th Fl.
Zone 4
New York, NY 10043
(212)559-1127
Fax: (212)888-2940

CM Equity Partners
135 E. 57th St.
New York, NY 10022
(212)909-8428
Fax: (212)980-2630

Cohen & Co., L.L.C.
800 Third Ave.
New York, NY 10022
(212)317-2250
Fax: (212)317-2255
E-mail: nlcohen@aol.com

Cornerstone Equity Investors, L.L.C.
717 5th Ave., Ste. 1100
New York, NY 10022
(212)753-0901
Fax: (212)826-6798
Website: http://www.cornerstone-
equity.com

CW Group, Inc.
1041 3rd Ave., 2nd fl.
New York, NY 10021
(212)308-5266
Fax: (212)644-0354
Website: http://www.cwventures.com

DH Blair Investment Banking Corp.
44 Wall St., 2nd Fl.
New York, NY 10005
(212)495-5000
Fax: (212)269-1438

Dresdner Kleinwort Capital
75 Wall St.
New York, NY 10005
(212)429-3131
Fax: (212)429-3139
Website: http://www.dresdnerkb.com

East River Ventures, L.P.
645 Madison Ave., 22nd Fl.

New York, NY 10022
(212)644-2322
Fax: (212)644-5498

Easton Hunt Capital Partners
641 Lexington Ave., 21st Fl.
New York, NY 10017
(212)702-0950
Fax: (212)702-0952
Website: http://www.eastoncapital.com

Elk Associates Funding Corp.
747 3rd Ave., Ste. 4C
New York, NY 10017
(212)355-2449
Fax: (212)759-3338

EOS Partners, L.P.
320 Park Ave., 22nd Fl.
New York, NY 10022
(212)832-5800
Fax: (212)832-5815
E-mail: mfirst@eospartners.com
Website: http://www.eospartners.com

Euclid Partners
45 Rockefeller Plaza, Ste. 3240
New York, NY 10111
(212)218-6880
Fax: (212)218-6877
E-mail: graham@euclidpartners.com
Website: http://www.euclidpartners.com

Evergreen Capital Partners, Inc.
150 East 58th St.
New York, NY 10155
(212)813-0758
Fax: (212)813-0754

Exeter Capital L.P.
10 E. 53rd St.
New York, NY 10022
(212)872-1172
Fax: (212)872-1198
E-mail: exeter@usa.net

Financial Technology Research Corp.
518 Broadway
Penthouse
New York, NY 10012
(212)625-9100
Fax: (212)431-0300
E-mail: fintek@financier.com

4C Ventures
237 Park Ave., Ste. 801
New York, NY 10017
(212)692-3680
Fax: (212)692-3685
Website: http://www.4cventures.com

Fusient Ventures
99 Park Ave., 20th Fl.
New York, NY 10016
(212)972-8999
Fax: (212)972-9876
E-mail: info@fusient.com
Website: http://www.fusient.com

Generation Capital Partners
551 Fifth Ave., Ste. 3100
New York, NY 10176
(212)450-8507
Fax: (212)450-8550
Website: http://www.genpartners.com

Golub Associates, Inc.
555 Madison Ave.
New York, NY 10022
(212)750-6060
Fax: (212)750-5505

Hambro America Biosciences Inc.
650 Madison Ave., 21st Floor
New York, NY 10022
(212)223-7400
Fax: (212)223-0305

Hanover Capital Corp.
505 Park Ave., 15th Fl.
New York, NY 10022
(212)755-1222
Fax: (212)935-1787

Harvest Partners, Inc.
280 Park Ave, 33rd Fl.
New York, NY 10017
(212)559-6300
Fax: (212)812-0100
Website: http://www.harvpart.com

Holding Capital Group, Inc.
10 E. 53rd St., 30th Fl.
New York, NY 10022
(212)486-6670
Fax: (212)486-0843

Hudson Venture Partners
660 Madison Ave., 14th Fl.
New York, NY 10021-8405
(212)644-9797
Fax: (212)644-7430
Website: http://www.hudsonptr.com

IBJS Capital Corp.
1 State St., 9th Fl.
New York, NY 10004
(212)858-2018
Fax: (212)858-2768

InterEquity Capital Partners, L.P.
220 5th Ave.
New York, NY 10001

(212)779-2022
Fax: (212)779-2103
Website: http://www.interequity-capital.com

The Jordan Edmiston Group Inc.
150 East 52nd St., 18th Fl.
New York, NY 10022
(212)754-0710
Fax: (212)754-0337

Josephberg, Grosz and Co., Inc.
633 3rd Ave., 13th Fl.
New York, NY 10017
(212)974-9926
Fax: (212)397-5832

J.P. Morgan Capital Corp.
60 Wall St.
New York, NY 10260-0060
(212)648-9000
Fax: (212)648-5002
Website: http://www.jpmorgan.com

The Lambda Funds
380 Lexington Ave., 54th Fl.
New York, NY 10168
(212)682-3454
Fax: (212)682-9231

Lepercq Capital Management Inc.
1675 Broadway
New York, NY 10019
(212)698-0795
Fax: (212)262-0155

Loeb Partners Corp.
61 Broadway, Ste. 2400
New York, NY 10006
(212)483-7000
Fax: (212)574-2001

Madison Investment Partners
660 Madison Ave.
New York, NY 10021
(212)223-2600
Fax: (212)223-8208

MC Capital Inc.
520 Madison Ave., 16th Fl.
New York, NY 10022
(212)644-0841
Fax: (212)644-2926

**McCown, De Leeuw and Co.
(New York)**
65 E. 55th St., 36th Fl.
New York, NY 10022
(212)355-5500
Fax: (212)355-6283
Website: http://www.mdcpartners.com

Morgan Stanley Venture Partners
1221 Avenue of the Americas, 33rd Fl.
New York, NY 10020
(212)762-7900
Fax: (212)762-8424
E-mail: msventures@ms.com
Website: http://www.msvp.com

Nazem and Co.
645 Madison Ave., 12th Fl.
New York, NY 10022
(212)371-7900
Fax: (212)371-2150

Needham Capital Management, L.L.C.
445 Park Ave.
New York, NY 10022
(212)371-8300
Fax: (212)705-0299
Website: http://www.needhamco.com

Norwood Venture Corp.
1430 Broadway, Ste. 1607
New York, NY 10018
(212)869-5075
Fax: (212)869-5331
E-mail: nvc@mail.idt.net
Website: http://www.norven.com

Noveltek Venture Corp.
521 Fifth Ave., Ste. 1700
New York, NY 10175
(212)286-1963

Paribas Principal, Inc.
787 7th Ave.
New York, NY 10019
(212)841-2005
Fax: (212)841-3558

Patricof & Co. Ventures, Inc.
(New York)
445 Park Ave.
New York, NY 10022
(212)753-6300
Fax: (212)319-6155
Website: http://www.patricof.com

The Platinum Group, Inc.
350 Fifth Ave, Ste. 7113
New York, NY 10118
(212)736-4300
Fax: (212)736-6086
Website: http://www.platinumgroup.com

Pomona Capital
780 Third Ave., 28th Fl.
New York, NY 10017
(212)593-3639
Fax: (212)593-3987
Website: http://www.pomonacapital.com

Prospect Street Ventures
10 East 40th St., 44th Fl.
New York, NY 10016
(212)448-0702
Fax: (212)448-9652
E-mail: wkohler@prospectstreet.com
Website: http://www.prospectstreet.com

Regent Capital Management
505 Park Ave., Ste. 1700
New York, NY 10022
(212)735-9900
Fax: (212)735-9908

Rothschild Ventures, Inc.
1251 Avenue of the Americas, 51st Fl.
New York, NY 10020
(212)403-3500
Fax: (212)403-3652
Website: http://www.nmrothschild.com

Sandler Capital Management
767 Fifth Ave., 45th Fl.
New York, NY 10153
(212)754-8100
Fax: (212)826-0280

Siguler Guff & Company
630 Fifth Ave., 16th Fl.
New York, NY 10111
(212)332-5100
Fax: (212)332-5120

Spencer Trask Ventures Inc.
535 Madison Ave.
New York, NY 10022
(212)355-5565
Fax: (212)751-3362
Website: http://www.spencertrask.com

Sprout Group (New York City)
277 Park Ave.
New York, NY 10172
(212)892-3600
Fax: (212)892-3444
E-mail: info@sproutgroup.com
Website: http://www.sproutgroup.com

US Trust Private Equity
114 W.47th St.
New York, NY 10036
(212)852-3949
Fax: (212)852-3759
Website: http://www.ustrust.com/
privateequity

Vencon Management Inc.
301 West 53rd St., Ste. 10F
New York, NY 10019
(212)581-8787
Fax: (212)397-4126
Website: http://www.venconinc.com

Venrock Associates
30 Rockefeller Plaza, Ste. 5508
New York, NY 10112
(212)649-5600
Fax: (212)649-5788
Website: http://www.venrock.com

Venture Capital Fund of America, Inc.
509 Madison Ave., Ste. 812
New York, NY 10022
(212)838-5577
Fax: (212)838-7614
E-mail: mail@vcfa.com
Website: http://www.vcfa.com

Venture Opportunities Corp.
150 E. 58th St.
New York, NY 10155
(212)832-3737
Fax: (212)980-6603

Warburg Pincus Ventures, Inc.
466 Lexington Ave., 11th Fl.
New York, NY 10017
(212)878-9309
Fax: (212)878-9200
Website: http://www.warburgpincus.com

Wasserstein, Perella & Co. Inc.
31 W. 52nd St., 27th Fl.
New York, NY 10019
(212)702-5691
Fax: (212)969-7879

Welsh, Carson, Anderson, & Stowe
320 Park Ave., Ste. 2500
New York, NY 10022-6815
(212)893-9500
Fax: (212)893-9575

Whitney and Co. (New York)
630 Fifth Ave. Ste. 3225
New York, NY 10111
(212)332-2400
Fax: (212)332-2422
Website: http://www.jhwitney.com

Winthrop Ventures
74 Trinity Place, Ste. 600
New York, NY 10006
(212)422-0100

The Pittsford Group
8 Lodge Pole Rd.
Pittsford, NY 14534
(716)223-3523

Genesee Funding
70 Linden Oaks, 3rd Fl.
Rochester, NY 14625
(716)383-5550
Fax: (716)383-5305

Gabelli Multimedia Partners
One Corporate Center
Rye, NY 10580
(914)921-5395
Fax: (914)921-5031

Stamford Financial
108 Main St.
Stamford, NY 12167
(607)652-3311
Fax: (607)652-6301
Website: http://www.stamford
financial.com

Northwood Ventures LLC
485 Underhill Blvd., Ste. 205
Syosset, NY 11791
(516)364-5544
Fax: (516)364-0879
E-mail: northwood@northwood.com
Website: http://www.north
woodventures.com

Exponential Business Development Co.
216 Walton St.
Syracuse, NY 13202-1227
(315)474-4500
Fax: (315)474-4682
E-mail: dirksonn@aol.com
Website: http://www.exponential-ny.com

Onondaga Venture Capital Fund Inc.
714 State Tower Bldg.
Syracuse, NY 13202
(315)478-0157
Fax: (315)478-0158

Bessemer Venture Partners (Westbury)
1400 Old Country Rd., Ste. 109
Westbury, NY 11590
(516)997-2300
Fax: (516)997-2371
E-mail: bob@bvpny.com
Website: http://www.bvp.com

Ovation Capital Partners
120 Bloomingdale Rd., 4th Fl.
White Plains, NY 10605
(914)258-0011
Fax: (914)684-0848
Website: http://www.ovation
capital.com

North Carolina

Carolinas Capital Investment Corp.
1408 Biltmore Dr.
Charlotte, NC 28207
(704)375-3888
Fax: (704)375-6226

First Union Capital Partners
1st Union Center, 12th Fl.
301 S. College St.
Charlotte, NC 28288-0732
(704)383-0000
Fax: (704)374-6711
Website: http://www.fucp.com

Frontier Capital LLC
525 North Tryon St., Ste. 1700
Charlotte, NC 28202
(704)414-2880
Fax: (704)414-2881
Website: http://www.frontierfunds.com

Kitty Hawk Capital
2700 Coltsgate Rd., Ste. 202
Charlotte, NC 28211
(704)362-3909
Fax: (704)362-2774
Website: http://www.kittyhawk
capital.com

Piedmont Venture Partners
One Morrocroft Centre
6805 Morisson Blvd., Ste. 380
Charlotte, NC 28211
(704)731-5200
Fax: (704)365-9733
Website: http://www.piedmontvp.com

Ruddick Investment Co.
1800 Two First Union Center
Charlotte, NC 28282
(704)372-5404
Fax: (704)372-6409

The Shelton Companies Inc.
3600 One First Union Center
301 S. College St.
Charlotte, NC 28202
(704)348-2200
Fax: (704)348-2260

Wakefield Group
1110 E. Morehead St.
PO Box 36329
Charlotte, NC 28236
(704)372-0355
Fax: (704)372-8216
Website: http://www.wakefiel
dgroup.com

Aurora Funds, Inc.
2525 Meridian Pkwy., Ste. 220
Durham, NC 27713
(919)484-0400
Fax: (919)484-0444
Website: http://www.aurora
funds.com

Intersouth Partners
3211 Shannon Rd., Ste. 610
Durham, NC 27707
(919)493-6640
Fax: (919)493-6649
E-mail: info@intersouth.com
Website: http://www.intersouth.com

Geneva Merchant Banking Partners
PO Box 21962
Greensboro, NC 27420
(336)275-7002
Fax: (336)275-9155
Website: http://www.geneva
merchantbank.com

The North Carolina Enterprise Fund, L.P.
3600 Glenwood Ave., Ste. 107
Raleigh, NC 27612
(919)781-2691
Fax: (919)783-9195
Website: http://www.ncef.com

Ohio

Senmend Medical Ventures
4445 Lake Forest Dr., Ste. 600
Cincinnati, OH 45242
(513)563-3264
Fax: (513)563-3261

The Walnut Group
312 Walnut St., Ste. 1151
Cincinnati, OH 45202
(513)651-3300
Fax: (513)929-4441
Website: http://www.thewal
nutgroup.com

Brantley Venture Partners
20600 Chagrin Blvd., Ste. 1150
Cleveland, OH 44122
(216)283-4800
Fax: (216)283-5324

Clarion Capital Corp.
1801 E. 9th St., Ste. 1120
Cleveland, OH 44114
(216)687-1096
Fax: (216)694-3545

Crystal Internet Venture Fund, L.P.
1120 Chester Ave., Ste. 418
Cleveland, OH 44114
(216)263-5515
Fax: (216)263-5518
E-mail: jf@crystalventure.com
Website: http://www.crystal
venture.com

Key Equity Capital Corp.
127 Public Sq., 28th Fl.
Cleveland, OH 44114
(216)689-3000
Fax: (216)689-3204
Website: http://www.keybank.com

Morgenthaler Ventures
Terminal Tower
50 Public Square, Ste. 2700
Cleveland, OH 44113
(216)416-7500
Fax: (216)416-7501
Website: http://www.morgenthaler.com

National City Equity Partners Inc.
1965 E. 6th St.
Cleveland, OH 44114
(216)575-2491
Fax: (216)575-9965
E-mail: nccap@aol.com
Website: http://www.nccapital.com

Primus Venture Partners, Inc.
5900 LanderBrook Dr., Ste. 2000
Cleveland, OH 44124-4020
(440)684-7300
Fax: (440)684-7342
E-mail: info@primusventure.com
Website: http://www.primusventure.com

Banc One Capital Partners (Columbus)
150 East Gay St., 24th Fl.
Columbus, OH 43215
(614)217-1100
Fax: (614)217-1217

Battelle Venture Partners
505 King Ave.
Columbus, OH 43201
(614)424-7005
Fax: (614)424-4874

Ohio Partners
62 E. Board St., 3rd Fl.
Columbus, OH 43215
(614)621-1210
Fax: (614)621-1240

Capital Technology Group, L.L.C.
400 Metro Place North, Ste. 300
Dublin, OH 43017
(614)792-6066
Fax: (614)792-6036
E-mail: info@capitaltech.com
Website: http://www.capitaltech.com

Northwest Ohio Venture Fund
4159 Holland-Sylvania R., Ste. 202
Toledo, OH 43623
(419)824-8144

Fax: (419)882-2035
E-mail: bwalsh@novf.com

Oklahoma

Moore & Associates
1000 W. Wilshire Blvd., Ste. 370
Oklahoma City, OK 73116
(405)842-3660
Fax: (405)842-3763

Chisholm Private Capital Partners
100 West 5th St., Ste. 805
Tulsa, OK 74103
(918)584-0440
Fax: (918)584-0441
Website: http://www.chisholmvc.com

Davis, Tuttle Venture Partners (Tulsa)
320 S. Boston, Ste. 1000
Tulsa, OK 74103-3703
(918)584-7272
Fax: (918)582-3404
Website: http://www.davistuttle.com

RBC Ventures
2627 E. 21st St.
Tulsa, OK 74114
(918)744-5607
Fax: (918)743-8630

Oregon

Utah Ventures II LP
10700 SW Beaverton-Hillsdale Hwy.,
Ste. 548
Beaverton, OR 97005
(503)574-4125
E-mail: adishlip@uven.com
Website: http://www.uven.com

Orien Ventures
14523 SW Westlake Dr.
Lake Oswego, OR 97035
(503)699-1680
Fax: (503)699-1681

OVP Venture Partners (Lake Oswego)
340 Oswego Pointe Dr., Ste. 200
Lake Oswego, OR 97034
(503)697-8766
Fax: (503)697-8863
E-mail: info@ovp.com
Website: http://www.ovp.com

Oregon Resource and Technology Development Fund
4370 NE Halsey St., Ste. 233
Portland, OR 97213-1566
(503)282-4462
Fax: (503)282-2976

Shaw Venture Partners
400 SW 6th Ave., Ste. 1100
Portland, OR 97204-1636
(503)228-4884
Fax: (503)227-2471
Website: http://www.shawventures.com

Pennsylvania

Mid-Atlantic Venture Funds
125 Goodman Dr.
Bethlehem, PA 18015
(610)865-6550
Fax: (610)865-6427
Website: http://www.mavf.com

Newspring Ventures
100 W. Elm St., Ste. 101
Conshohocken, PA 19428
(610)567-2380
Fax: (610)567-2388
Website: http://www.news
printventures.com

Patricof & Co. Ventures, Inc.
455 S. Gulph Rd., Ste. 410
King of Prussia, PA 19406
(610)265-0286
Fax: (610)265-4959
Website: http://www.patricof.com

Loyalhanna Venture Fund
527 Cedar Way, Ste. 104
Oakmont, PA 15139
(412)820-7035
Fax: (412)820-7036

Innovest Group Inc.
2000 Market St., Ste. 1400
Philadelphia, PA 19103
(215)564-3960
Fax: (215)569-3272

Keystone Venture Capital Management Co.
1601 Market St., Ste. 2500
Philadelphia, PA 19103
(215)241-1200
Fax: (215)241-1211
Website: http://www.keystonevc.com

Liberty Venture Partners
2005 Market St., Ste. 200
Philadelphia, PA 19103
(215)282-4484
Fax: (215)282-4485
E-mail: info@libertyvp.com
Website: http://www.libertyvp.com

Penn Janney Fund, Inc.
1801 Market St., 11th Fl.
Philadelphia, PA 19103

(215)665-4447
Fax: (215)557-0820

Philadelphia Ventures, Inc.
The Bellevue
200 S. Broad St.
Philadelphia, PA 19102
(215)732-4445
Fax: (215)732-4644

Birchmere Ventures Inc.
2000 Technology Dr.
Pittsburgh, PA 15219-3109
(412)803-8000
Fax: (412)687-8139
Website: http://www.birchmerevc.com

CEO Venture Fund
2000 Technology Dr., Ste. 160
Pittsburgh, PA 15219-3109
(412)687-3451
Fax: (412)687-8139
E-mail: ceofund@aol.com
Website: http://www.ceoventure
fund.com

Innovation Works Inc.
2000 Technology Dr., Ste. 250
Pittsburgh, PA 15219
(412)681-1520
Fax: (412)681-2625
Website: http://www.innovation
works.org

Keystone Minority Capital Fund L.P.
1801 Centre Ave., Ste. 201
Williams Sq.
Pittsburgh, PA 15219
(412)338-2230
Fax: (412)338-2224

Mellon Ventures, Inc.
One Mellon Bank Ctr., Rm. 3500
Pittsburgh, PA 15258
(412)236-3594
Fax: (412)236-3593
Website: http://www.mellon
ventures.com

Pennsylvania Growth Fund
5850 Ellsworth Ave., Ste. 303
Pittsburgh, PA 15232
(412)661-1000
Fax: (412)361-0676

Point Venture Partners
The Century Bldg.
130 Seventh St., 7th Fl.
Pittsburgh, PA 15222
(412)261-1966
Fax: (412)261-1718

Cross Atlantic Capital Partners
5 Radnor Corporate Center, Ste. 555
Radnor, PA 19087
(610)995-2650
Fax: (610)971-2062
Website: http://www.xacp.com

Meridian Venture Partners (Radnor)
The Radnor Court Bldg., Ste. 140
259 Radnor-Chester Rd.
Radnor, PA 19087
(610)254-2999
Fax: (610)254-2996
E-mail: mvpart@ix.netcom.com

TDH
919 Conestoga Rd., Bldg. 1, Ste. 301
Rosemont, PA 19010
(610)526-9970
Fax: (610)526-9971

Adams Capital Management
500 Blackburn Ave.
Sewickley, PA 15143
(412)749-9454
Fax: (412)749-9459
Website: http://www.acm.com

S.R. One, Ltd.
Four Tower Bridge
200 Barr Harbor Dr., Ste. 250
W. Conshohocken, PA 19428
(610)567-1000
Fax: (610)567-1039

Greater Philadelphia Venture Capital Corp.
351 East Conestoga Rd.
Wayne, PA 19087
(610)688-6829
Fax: (610)254-8958

PA Early Stage
435 Devon Park Dr., Bldg. 500, Ste. 510
Wayne, PA 19087
(610)293-4075
Fax: (610)254-4240
Website: http://www.paearlystage.com

The Sandhurst Venture Fund, L.P.
351 E. Constoga Rd.
Wayne, PA 19087
(610)254-8900
Fax: (610)254-8958

TL Ventures
700 Bldg.
435 Devon Park Dr.
Wayne, PA 19087-1990
(610)975-3765
Fax: (610)254-4210
Website: http://www.tlventures.com

Rockhill Ventures, Inc.
100 Front St., Ste. 1350
West Conshohocken, PA 19428
(610)940-0300
Fax: (610)940-0301

Puerto Rico

Advent-Morro Equity Partners
Banco Popular Bldg.
206 Tetuan St., Ste. 903
San Juan, PR 00902
(787)725-5285
Fax: (787)721-1735

North America Investment Corp.
Mercantil Plaza, Ste. 813
PO Box 191831
San Juan, PR 00919
(787)754-6178
Fax: (787)754-6181

Rhode Island

Manchester Humphreys, Inc.
40 Westminster St., Ste. 900
Providence, RI 02903
(401)454-0400
Fax: (401)454-0403

Navis Partners
50 Kennedy Plaza, 12th Fl.
Providence, RI 02903
(401)278-6770
Fax: (401)278-6387
Website: http://www.navis
partners.com

South Carolina

Capital Insights, L.L.C.
PO Box 27162
Greenville, SC 29616-2162
(864)242-6832
Fax: (864)242-6755
E-mail: jwarner@capitalinsights.com
Website: http://www.capitalin
sights.com

Transamerica Mezzanine Financing
7 N. Laurens St., Ste. 603
Greenville, SC 29601
(864)232-6198
Fax: (864)241-4444

Tennessee

Valley Capital Corp.
Krystal Bldg.
100 W. Martin Luther King Blvd.,
Ste. 212

Chattanooga, TN 37402
(423)265-1557
Fax: (423)265-1588

Coleman Swenson Booth Inc.
237 2nd Ave. S
Franklin, TN 37064-2649
(615)791-9462
Fax: (615)791-9636
Website: http://
www.colemanswenson.com

Capital Services & Resources, Inc.
5159 Wheelis Dr., Ste. 106
Memphis, TN 38117
(901)761-2156
Fax: (907)767-0060

Paradigm Capital Partners LLC
6410 Poplar Ave., Ste. 395
Memphis, TN 38119
(901)682-6060
Fax: (901)328-3061

SSM Ventures
845 Crossover Ln., Ste. 140
Memphis, TN 38117
(901)767-1131
Fax: (901)767-1135
Website: http://www.ssm
ventures.com

Capital Across America L.P.
501 Union St., Ste. 201
Nashville, TN 37219
(615)254-1414
Fax: (615)254-1856
Website: http://
www.capitalacrossamerica.com

Equitas L.P.
2000 Glen Echo Rd., Ste. 101
PO Box 158838
Nashville, TN 37215-8838
(615)383-8673
Fax: (615)383-8693

Massey Burch Capital Corp.
One Burton Hills Blvd., Ste. 350
Nashville, TN 37215
(615)665-3221
Fax: (615)665-3240
E-mail: tcalton@masseyburch.com
Website: http://www.masseyburch.com

Nelson Capital Corp.
3401 West End Ave., Ste. 300
Nashville, TN 37203
(615)292-8787
Fax: (615)385-3150

Texas

Phillips-Smith Specialty Retail Group
5080 Spectrum Dr., Ste. 805 W
Addison, TX 75001
(972)387-0725
Fax: (972)458-2560
E-mail: pssrg@aol.com
Website: http://www.phillips-smith.com

Austin Ventures, L.P.
701 Brazos St., Ste. 1400
Austin, TX 78701
(512)485-1900
Fax: (512)476-3952
E-mail: info@ausven.com
Website: http://www.austinventures.com

The Capital Network
3925 West Braker Lane, Ste. 406
Austin, TX 78759-5321
(512)305-0826
Fax: (512)305-0836

Techxas Ventures LLC
5000 Plaza on the Lake
Austin, TX 78746
(512)343-0118
Fax: (512)343-1879
E-mail: bruce@techxas.com
Website: http://www.techxas.com

Alliance Financial of Houston
218 Heather Ln.
Conroe, TX 77385-9013
(936)447-3300
Fax: (936)447-4222

Amerimark Capital Corp.
1111 W. Mockingbird, Ste. 1111
Dallas, TX 75247
(214)638-7878
Fax: (214)638-7612
E-mail: amerimark@amcapital.com
Website: http://www.amcapital.com

AMT Venture Partners / AMT Capital Ltd.
5220 Spring Valley Rd., Ste. 600
Dallas, TX 75240
(214)905-9757
Fax: (214)905-9761
Website: http://www.amtcapital.com

Arkoma Venture Partners
5950 Berkshire Lane, Ste. 1400
Dallas, TX 75225
(214)739-3515
Fax: (214)739-3572
E-mail: joelf@arkomavp.com

Capital Southwest Corp.
12900 Preston Rd., Ste. 700
Dallas, TX 75230
(972)233-8242
Fax: (972)233-7362
Website: http://
www.capitalsouthwest.com

Dali, Hook Partners
One Lincoln Center, Ste. 1550
5400 LBJ Freeway
Dallas, TX 75240
(972)991-5457
Fax: (972)991-5458
E-mail: dhook@hookpartners.com
Website: http://www.hookpartners.com

HO2 Partners
Two Galleria Tower
13455 Noel Rd., Ste. 1670
Dallas, TX 75240
(972)702-1144
Fax: (972)702-8234
Website: http://www.ho2.com

Interwest Partners (Dallas)
2 Galleria Tower
13455 Noel Rd., Ste. 1670
Dallas, TX 75240
(972)392-7279
Fax: (972)490-6348
Website: http://www.interwest.com

Kahala Investments, Inc.
8214 Westchester Dr., Ste. 715
Dallas, TX 75225
(214)987-0077
Fax: (214)987-2332

MESBIC Ventures Holding Co.
2435 North Central Expressway, Ste. 200
Dallas, TX 75080
(972)991-1597
Fax: (972)991-4770
Website: http://www.mvhc.com

North Texas MESBIC, Inc.
9500 Forest Lane, Ste. 430
Dallas, TX 75243
(214)221-3565
Fax: (214)221-3566

Richard Jaffe & Company, Inc,
7318 Royal Cir.
Dallas, TX 75230
(214)265-9397
Fax: (214)739-1845

Sevin Rosen Management Co.
13455 Noel Rd., Ste. 1670
Dallas, TX 75240

(972)702-1100
Fax: (972)702-1103
E-mail: info@srfunds.com
Website: http://www.srfunds.com

Stratford Capital Partners, L.P.
300 Crescent Ct., Ste. 500
Dallas, TX 75201
(214)740-7377
Fax: (214)720-7393
E-mail: stratcap@hmtf.com

Sunwestern Investment Group
12221 Merit Dr., Ste. 935
Dallas, TX 75251
(972)239-5650
Fax: (972)701-0024

Wingate Partners
750 N. St. Paul St., Ste. 1200
Dallas, TX 75201
(214)720-1313
Fax: (214)871-8799

Buena Venture Associates
201 Main St., 32nd Fl.
Fort Worth, TX 76102
(817)339-7400
Fax: (817)390-8408
Website: http://www.buenaventure.com

The Catalyst Group
3 Riverway, Ste. 770
Houston, TX 77056
(713)623-8133
Fax: (713)623-0473
E-mail: herman@thecatalystgroup.net
Website: http://www.thecatalyst
group.net

Cureton & Co., Inc.
1100 Louisiana, Ste. 3250
Houston, TX 77002
(713)658-9806
Fax: (713)658-0476

Davis, Tuttle Venture Partners (Dallas)
8 Greenway Plaza, Ste. 1020
Houston, TX 77046
(713)993-0440
Fax: (713)621-2297
Website: http://www.davistuttle.com

Houston Partners
401 Louisiana, 8th Fl.
Houston, TX 77002
(713)222-8600
Fax: (713)222-8932

Southwest Venture Group
10878 Westheimer, Ste. 178

Houston, TX 77042
(713)827-8947
(713)461-1470

AM Fund
4600 Post Oak Place, Ste. 100
Houston, TX 77027
(713)627-9111
Fax: (713)627-9119

Ventex Management, Inc.
3417 Milam St.
Houston, TX 77002-9531
(713)659-7870
Fax: (713)659-7855

MBA Venture Group
1004 Olde Town Rd., Ste. 102
Irving, TX 75061
(972)986-6703

First Capital Group Management Co.
750 East Mulberry St., Ste. 305
PO Box 15616
San Antonio, TX 78212
(210)736-4233
Fax: (210)736-5449

The Southwest Venture Partnerships
16414 San Pedro, Ste. 345
San Antonio, TX 78232
(210)402-1200
Fax: (210)402-1221
E-mail: swvp@aol.com

Medtech International Inc.
1742 Carriageway
Sugarland, TX 77478
(713)980-8474
Fax: (713)980-6343

Utah

First Security Business Investment Corp.
15 East 100 South, Ste. 100
Salt Lake City, UT 84111
(801)246-5737
Fax: (801)246-5740

Utah Ventures II, L.P.
423 Wakara Way, Ste. 206
Salt Lake City, UT 84108
(801)583-5922
Fax: (801)583-4105
Website: http://www.uven.com

Wasatch Venture Corp.
1 S. Main St., Ste. 1400
Salt Lake City, UT 84133
(801)524-8939

Fax: (801)524-8941
E-mail: mail@wasatchvc.com

Vermont

North Atlantic Capital Corp.
76 Saint Paul St., Ste. 600
Burlington, VT 05401
(802)658-7820
Fax: (802)658-5757
Website: http://www.north
atlanticcapital.com

Green Mountain Advisors Inc.
PO Box 1230
Quechee, VT 05059
(802)296-7800
Fax: (802)296-6012
Website: http://www.gmtcap.com

Virginia

Oxford Financial Services Corp.
Alexandria, VA 22314
(703)519-4900
Fax: (703)519-4910
E-mail: oxford133@aol.com

Continental SBIC
4141 N. Henderson Rd.
Arlington, VA 22203
(703)527-5200
Fax: (703)527-3700

Novak Biddle Venture Partners
1750 Tysons Blvd., Ste. 1190
McLean, VA 22102
(703)847-3770
Fax: (703)847-3771
E-mail: roger@novakbiddle.com
Website: http://www.novakbiddle.com

Spacevest
11911 Freedom Dr., Ste. 500
Reston, VA 20190
(703)904-9800
Fax: (703)904-0571
E-mail: spacevest@spacevest.com
Website: http://www.spacevest.com

Virginia Capital
1801 Libbie Ave., Ste. 201
Richmond, VA 23226
(804)648-4802
Fax: (804)648-4809
E-mail: webmaster@vacapital.com
Website: http://www.vacapital.com

Calvert Social Venture Partners
402 Maple Ave. W
Vienna, VA 22180

(703)255-4930
Fax: (703)255-4931
E-mail: calven2000@aol.com

Fairfax Partners
8000 Towers Crescent Dr., Ste. 940
Vienna, VA 22182
(703)847-9486
Fax: (703)847-0911

Global Internet Ventures
8150 Leesburg Pike, Ste. 1210
Vienna, VA 22182
(703)442-3300
Fax: (703)442-3388
Website: http://www.givinc.com

Walnut Capital Corp. (Vienna)
8000 Towers Crescent Dr., Ste. 1070
Vienna, VA 22182
(703)448-3771
Fax: (703)448-7751

Washington

Encompass Ventures
777 108th Ave. NE, Ste. 2300
Bellevue, WA 98004
(425)486-3900
Fax: (425)486-3901
E-mail: info@evpartners.com
Website: http://www.encom
passventures.com

Fluke Venture Partners
11400 SE Sixth St., Ste. 230
Bellevue, WA 98004
(425)453-4590
Fax: (425)453-4675
E-mail: gabelein@flukeventures.com
Website: http://www.flukeventures.com

Pacific Northwest Partners SBIC, L.P.
15352 SE 53rd St.
Bellevue, WA 98006
(425)455-9967
Fax: (425)455-9404

Materia Venture Associates, L.P.
3435 Carillon Pointe
Kirkland, WA 98033-7354
(425)822-4100
Fax: (425)827-4086

OVP Venture Partners (Kirkland)
2420 Carillon Pt.
Kirkland, WA 98033
(425)889-9192
Fax: (425)889-0152
E-mail: info@ovp.com
Website: http://www.ovp.com

Digital Partners
999 3rd Ave., Ste. 1610
Seattle, WA 98104
(206)405-3607
Fax: (206)405-3617
Website: http://www.digitalpartners.com

Frazier & Company
601 Union St., Ste. 3300
Seattle, WA 98101
(206)621-7200
Fax: (206)621-1848
E-mail: jon@frazierco.com

Kirlan Venture Capital, Inc.
221 First Ave. W, Ste. 108
Seattle, WA 98119-4223
(206)281-8610
Fax: (206)285-3451
Website: http://www.kirlanventure.com

Phoenix Partners
1000 2nd Ave., Ste. 3600
Seattle, WA 98104
(206)624-8968
Fax: (206)624-1907

Voyager Capital
800 5th St., Ste. 4100
Seattle, WA 98103
(206)470-1180
Fax: (206)470-1185
E-mail: info@voyagercap.com
Website: http://www.voyagercap.com

Northwest Venture Associates
221 N. Wall St., Ste. 628
Spokane, WA 99201
(509)747-0728
Fax: (509)747-0758
Website: http://www.nwva.com

Wisconsin

Venture Investors Management, L.L.C.
University Research Park
505 S. Rosa Rd.
Madison, WI 53719
(608)441-2700
Fax: (608)441-2727
E-mail: roger@ventureinvestors.com
Website: http://www.venture
investers.com

Capital Investments, Inc.
1009 West Glen Oaks Lane, Ste. 103
Mequon, WI 53092
(414)241-0303
Fax: (414)241-8451
Website: http://
www.capitalinvestmentsinc.com

Future Value Venture, Inc.
2745 N. Martin Luther King
Dr., Ste. 204
Milwaukee, WI 53212-2300
(414)264-2252
Fax: (414)264-2253
E-mail: fvvventures@aol.com
William Beckett, President

Lubar and Co., Inc.
700 N. Water St., Ste. 1200
Milwaukee, WI 53202
(414)291-9000
Fax: (414)291-9061

GCI
20875 Crossroads Cir., Ste. 100
Waukesha, WI 53186
(262)798-5080
Fax: (262)798-5087

Glossary of Small Business Terms

Absolute liability
Liability that is incurred due to product defects or negligent actions. Manufacturers or retail establishments are held responsible, even though the defect or action may not have been intentional or negligent.

ACE
See Active Corps of Executives

Accident and health benefits
Benefits offered to employees and their families in order to offset the costs associated with accidental death, accidental injury, or sickness.

Account statement
A record of transactions, including payments, new debt, and deposits, incurred during a defined period of time.

Accounting system
System capturing the costs of all employees and/or machinery included in business expenses.

Accounts payable
See Trade credit

Accounts receivable
Unpaid accounts which arise from unsettled claims and transactions from the sale of a company's products or services to its customers.

Active Corps of Executives (ACE)
A group of volunteers for a management assistance program of the U.S. Small Business Administration; volunteers provide one-on-one counseling and teach workshops and seminars for small firms.

ADA
See Americans with Disabilities Act

Adaptation
The process whereby an invention is modified to meet the needs of users.

Adaptive engineering
The process whereby an invention is modified to meet the manufacturing and commercial requirements of a targeted market.

Adverse selection
The tendency for higher-risk individuals to purchase health care and more comprehensive plans, resulting in increased costs.

Advertising
A marketing tool used to capture public attention and influence purchasing decisions for a product or service. Utilizes various forms of media to generate consumer response, such as flyers, magazines, newspapers, radio, and television.

Age discrimination
The denial of the rights and privileges of employment based solely on the age of an individual.

Agency costs
Costs incurred to insure that the lender or investor maintains control over assets while allowing the borrower or entrepreneur to use them. Monitoring and information costs are the two major types of agency costs.

Agribusiness
The production and sale of commodities and products from the commercial farming industry.

America Online
An online service which is accessible by computer modem. The service features Internet access, bulletin boards, online periodicals, electronic mail, and other services for subscribers.

Americans with Disabilities Act (ADA)
Law designed to ensure equal access and opportunity to handicapped persons.

311

Annual report
Yearly financial report prepared by a business that adheres to the requirements set forth by the Securities and Exchange Commission (SEC).

Antitrust immunity
Exemption from prosecution under antitrust laws. In the transportation industry, firms with antitrust immunity are permitted under certain conditions to set schedules and sometimes prices for the public benefit.

Applied research
Scientific study targeted for use in a product or process.

Asians
A minority category used by the U.S. Bureau of the Census to represent a diverse group that includes Aleuts, Eskimos, American Indians, Asian Indians, Chinese, Japanese, Koreans, Vietnamese, Filipinos, Hawaiians, and other Pacific Islanders.

Assets
Anything of value owned by a company.

Audit
The verification of accounting records and business procedures conducted by an outside accounting service.

Average cost
Total production costs divided by the quantity produced.

Balance Sheet
A financial statement listing the total assets and liabilities of a company at a given time.

Bankruptcy
The condition in which a business cannot meet its debt obligations and petitions a federal district court either for reorganization of its debts (Chapter 11) or for liquidation of its assets (Chapter 7).

Basic research
Theoretical scientific exploration not targeted to application.

Basket clause
A provision specifying the amount of public pension funds that may be placed in investments not included on a state's legal list (see separate citation).

BBS
See Bulletin Board Service

BDC
See Business development corporation

Benefit
Various services, such as health care, flextime, day care, insurance, and vacation, offered to employees as part of a hiring package. Typically subsidized in whole or in part by the business.

BIDCO
See Business and industrial development company

Billing cycle
A system designed to evenly distribute customer billing throughout the month, preventing clerical backlogs.

Birth
See Business birth

Blue chip security
A low-risk, low-yield security representing an interest in a very stable company.

Blue sky laws
A general term that denotes various states' laws regulating securities.

Bond
A written instrument executed by a bidder or contractor (the principal) and a second party (the surety or sureties) to assure fulfillment of the principal's obligations to a third party (the obligee or government) identified in the bond. If the principal's obligations are not met, the bond assures payment to the extent stipulated of any loss sustained by the obligee.

Bonding requirements
Terms contained in a bond (see separate citation).

Bonus
An amount of money paid to an employee as a reward for achieving certain business goals or objectives.

Brainstorming
A group session where employees contribute their ideas for solving a problem or meeting a company objective without fear of retribution or ridicule.

Brand name
The part of a brand, trademark, or service mark that can be spoken. It can be a word, letter, or group of words or letters.

Bridge financing
A short-term loan made in expectation of intermediateterm or long-term financing. Can be used when a company plans to go public in the near future.

Broker
One who matches resources available for innovation with those who need them.

Budget
An estimate of the spending necessary to complete a project or offer a service in comparison to cash-on-hand and expected earnings for the coming year, with an emphasis on cost control.

Bulletin Board Service (BBS)
An online service enabling users to communicate with each other about specific topics.

Business and industrial development company (BIDCO)
A private, for-profit financing corporation chartered by the state to provide both equity and long-term debt capital to small business owners (see separate citations for equity and debt capital).

Business birth
The formation of a new establishment or enterprise. The appearance of a new establishment or enterprise in the Small Business Data Base (see separate citation).

Business conditions
Outside factors that can affect the financial performance of a business.

Business contractions
The number of establishments that have decreased in employment during a specified time.

Business cycle
A period of economic recession and recovery. These cycles vary in duration.

Business death
The voluntary or involuntary closure of a firm or establishment. The disappearance of an establishment or enterprise from the Small Business Data Base (see separate citation).

Business development corporation (BDC)
A business financing agency, usually composed of the financial institutions in an area or state, organized to assist in financing businesses unable to obtain assistance through normal channels; the risk is spread among various members of the business development corporation, and interest rates may vary somewhat from those charged by member institutions. A venture capital firm in which shares of ownership are publicly held and to which the Investment Act of 1940 applies.

Business dissolution
For enumeration purposes, the absence of a business that was present in the prior time period from any current record.

Business entry
See Business birth

Business ethics
Moral values and principles espoused by members of the business community as a guide to fair and honest business practices.

Business exit
See Business death

Business expansions
The number of establishments that added employees during a specified time.

Business failure
Closure of a business causing a loss to at least one creditor.

Business format franchising
The purchase of the name, trademark, and an ongoing business plan of the parent corporation or franchisor by the franchisee.

Business license
A legal authorization issued by municipal and state governments and required for business operations.

Business name
Enterprises must register their business names with local governments usually on a "doing business as" (DBA) form. (This name is sometimes referred to as a

"fictional name.") The procedure is part of the business licensing process and prevents any other business from using that same name for a similar business in the same locality.

Business norms
See Financial ratios

Business permit
See Business license

Business plan
A document that spells out a company's expected course of action for a specified period, usually including a detailed listing and analysis of risks and uncertainties. For the small business, it should examine the proposed products, the market, the industry, the management policies, the marketing policies, production needs, and financial needs. Frequently, it is used as a prospectus for potential investors and lenders.

Business proposal
See Business plan

Business service firm
An establishment primarily engaged in rendering services to other business organizations on a fee or contract basis.

Business start
For enumeration purposes, a business with a name or similar designation that did not exist in a prior time period.

Cafeteria plan
See Flexible benefit plan

Capacity
Level of a firm's, industry's, or nation's output corresponding to full practical utilization of available resources.

Capital
Assets less liabilities, representing the ownership interest in a business. A stock of accumulated goods, especially at a specified time and in contrast to income received during a specified time period. Accumulated goods devoted to production. Accumulated possessions calculated to bring income.

Capital expenditure
Expenses incurred by a business for improvements that will depreciate over time.

Capital gain
The monetary difference between the purchase price and the selling price of capital. Capital gains are taxed at a rate of 28% by the federal government.

Capital intensity
The relative importance of capital in the production process, usually expressed as the ratio of capital to labor but also sometimes as the ratio of capital to output.

Capital resource
The equipment, facilities and labor used to create products and services.

Caribbean Basin Initiative
An interdisciplinary program to support commerce among the businesses in the nations of the Caribbean Basin and the United States. Agencies involved include: the Agency for International Development, the U.S. Small Business Administration, the International Trade Administration of the U.S. Department of Commerce, and various private sector groups.

Catastrophic care
Medical and other services for acute and long-term illnesses that cost more than insurance coverage limits or that cost the amount most families may be expected to pay with their own resources.

CDC
See Certified development corporation

CD-ROM
Compact disc with read-only memory used to store large amounts of digitized data.

Certified development corporation (CDC)
A local area or statewide corporation or authority (for profit or nonprofit) that packages U.S. Small Business Administration (SBA), bank, state, and/or private money into financial assistance for existing business capital improvements. The SBA holds the second lien on its maximum share of 40 percent involvement. Each state has at least one certified development

corporation. This program is called the SBA 504 Program.

Certified lenders

Banks that participate in the SBA guaranteed loan program (see separate citation). Such banks must have a good track record with the U.S. Small Business Administration (SBA) and must agree to certain conditions set forth by the agency. In return, the SBA agrees to process any guaranteed loan application within three business days.

Champion

An advocate for the development of an innovation.

Channel of distribution

The means used to transport merchandise from the manufacturer to the consumer.

Chapter 7 of the 1978 Bankruptcy Act

Provides for a court-appointed trustee who is responsible for liquidating a company's assets in order to settle outstanding debts.

Chapter 11 of the 1978 Bankruptcy Act

Allows the business owners to retain control of the company while working with their creditors to reorganize their finances and establish better business practices to prevent liquidation of assets.

Closely held corporation

A corporation in which the shares are held by a few persons, usually officers, employees, or others close to the management; these shares are rarely offered to the public.

Code of Federal Regulations

Codification of general and permanent rules of the federal government published in the Federal Register.

Code sharing

See Computer code sharing

Coinsurance

Upon meeting the deductible payment, health insurance participants may be required to make additional health care cost-sharing payments. Coinsurance is a payment of a fixed percentage of the cost of each service; copayment is usually a fixed amount to be paid with each service.

Collateral

Securities, evidence of deposit, or other property pledged by a borrower to secure repayment of a loan.

Collective ratemaking

The establishment of uniform charges for services by a group of businesses in the same industry.

Commercial insurance plan

See Underwriting

Commercial loans

Short-term renewable loans used to finance specific capital needs of a business.

Commercialization

The final stage of the innovation process, including production and distribution.

Common stock

The most frequently used instrument for purchasing ownership in private or public companies. Common stock generally carries the right to vote on certain corporate actions and may pay dividends, although it rarely does in venture investments. In liquidation, common stockholders are the last to share in the proceeds from the sale of a corporation's assets; bondholders and preferred shareholders have priority. Common stock is often used in firstround start-up financing.

Community development corporation

A corporation established to develop economic programs for a community and, in most cases, to provide financial support for such development.

Competitor

A business whose product or service is marketed for the same purpose/use and to the same consumer group as the product or service of another.

Computer code sharing

An arrangement whereby flights of a regional airline are identified by the two-letter code of a major carrier in the computer reservation system to help direct passengers to new regional carriers.

Consignment

A merchandising agreement, usually referring to secondhand shops, where the dealer pays the owner of an item a percentage of the profit when the item is sold.

Consortium
A coalition of organizations such as banks and corporations for ventures requiring large capital resources.

Consultant
An individual that is paid by a business to provide advice and expertise in a particular area.

Consumer price index
A measure of the fluctuation in prices between two points in time.

Consumer research
Research conducted by a business to obtain information about existing or potential consumer markets.

Continuation coverage
Health coverage offered for a specified period of time to employees who leave their jobs and to their widows, divorced spouses, or dependents.

Contractions
See Business contractions

Convertible preferred stock
A class of stock that pays a reasonable dividend and is convertible into common stock (see separate citation). Generally the convertible feature may only be exercised after being held for a stated period of time. This arrangement is usually considered second-round financing when a company needs equity to maintain its cash flow.

Convertible securities
A feature of certain bonds, debentures, or preferred stocks that allows them to be exchanged by the owner for another class of securities at a future date and in accordance with any other terms of the issue.

Copayment
See Coinsurance

Copyright
A legal form of protection available to creators and authors to safeguard their works from unlawful use or claim of ownership by others. Copyrights may be acquired for works of art, sculpture, music, and published or unpublished manuscripts. All copyrights should be registered at the Copyright Office of the Library of Congress.

Corporate financial ratios
The relationship between key figures found in a company's financial statement expressed as a numeric value. Used to evaluate risk and company performance. Also known as Financial averages, Operating ratios, and Business ratios.

Corporation
A legal entity, chartered by a state or the federal government, recognized as a separate entity having its own rights, privileges, and liabilities distinct from those of its members.

Cost containment
Actions taken by employers and insurers to curtail rising health care costs; for example, increasing employee cost sharing (see separate citation), requiring second opinions, or preadmission screening.

Cost sharing
The requirement that health care consumers contribute to their own medical care costs through deductibles and coinsurance (see separate citations). Cost sharing does not include the amounts paid in premiums. It is used to control utilization of services; for example, requiring a fixed amount to be paid with each health care service.

Cottage industry
Businesses based in the home in which the family members are the labor force and family-owned equipment is used to process the goods.

Credit Rating
A letter or number calculated by an organization (such as Dun & Bradstreet) to represent the ability and disposition of a business to meet its financial obligations.

Customer service
Various techniques used to ensure the satisfaction of a customer.

Cyclical peak
The upper turning point in a business cycle.

Cyclical trough
The lower turning point in a business cycle.

DBA
See Business name

Death
See Business death

Debenture
A certificate given as acknowledgment of a debt (see separate citation) secured by the general credit of the issuing corporation. A bond, usually without security, issued by a corporation and sometimes convertible to common stock.

Debt
Something owed by one person to another. Financing in which a company receives capital that must be repaid; no ownership is transferred.

Debt capital
Business financing that normally requires periodic interest payments and repayment of the principal within a specified time.

Debt financing
See Debt capital

Debt securities
Loans such as bonds and notes that provide a specified rate of return for a specified period of time.

Deductible
A set amount that an individual must pay before any benefits are received.

Demand shock absorbers
A term used to describe the role that some small firms play by expanding their output levels to accommodate a transient surge in demand.

Demographics
Statistics on various markets, including age, income, and education, used to target specific products or services to appropriate consumer groups.

Demonstration
Showing that a product or process has been modified sufficiently to meet the needs of users.

Deregulation
The lifting of government restrictions; for example, the lifting of government restrictions on the entry of new businesses, the expansion of services, and the setting of prices in particular industries.

Desktop Publishing
Using personal computers and specialized software to produce camera-ready copy for publications.

Disaster loans
Various types of physical and economic assistance available to individuals and businesses through the U.S. Small Business Administration (SBA). This is the only SBA loan program available for residential purposes.

Discrimination
The denial of the rights and privileges of employment based on factors such as age, race, religion, or gender.

Diseconomies of scale
The condition in which the costs of production increase faster than the volume of production.

Dissolution
See Business dissolution

Distribution
Delivering a product or process to the user.

Distributor
One who delivers merchandise to the user.

Diversified company
A company whose products and services are used by several different markets.

Doing business as (DBA)
See Business name

Dow Jones
An information services company that publishes the Wall Street Journal and other sources of financial information.

Dow Jones Industrial Average
An indicator of stock market performance.

Earned income
A tax term that refers to wages and salaries earned by the recipient, as opposed to monies earned through interest and dividends.

Economic efficiency
The use of productive resources to the fullest practical extent in the provision of the set of goods and services that is most preferred by purchasers in the economy.

Economic indicators
Statistics used to express the state of the economy. These include the length of the average work week, the rate of unemployment, and stock prices.

Economically disadvantaged
See Socially and economically disadvantaged

Economies of scale
See Scale economies

EEOC
See Equal Employment Opportunity Commission

8(a) Program
A program authorized by the Small Business Act that directs federal contracts to small businesses owned and operated by socially and economically disadvantaged individuals.

Electronic mail (e-mail)
The electronic transmission of mail via phone lines.

E-mail
See Electronic mail

Employee leasing
A contract by which employers arrange to have their workers hired by a leasing company and then leased back to them for a management fee. The leasing company typically assumes the administrative burden of payroll and provides a benefit package to the workers.

Employee tenure
The length of time an employee works for a particular employer.

Employer identification number
The business equivalent of a social security number. Assigned by the U.S. Internal Revenue Service.

Enterprise
An aggregation of all establishments owned by a parent company. An enterprise may consist of a single, independent establishment or include subsidiaries and other branches under the same ownership and control.

Enterprise zone
A designated area, usually found in inner cities and other areas with significant unemployment, where businesses receive tax credits and other incentives to entice them to establish operations there.

Entrepreneur
A person who takes the risk of organizing and operating a new business venture.

Entry
See Business entry

Equal Employment Opportunity Commission (EEOC)
A federal agency that ensures nondiscrimination in the hiring and firing practices of a business.

Equal opportunity employer
An employer who adheres to the standards set by the Equal Employment Opportunity Commission (see separate citation).

Equity
The ownership interest. Financing in which partial or total ownership of a company is surrendered in exchange for capital. An investor's financial return comes from dividend payments and from growth in the net worth of the business.

Equity capital
See Equity; Equity midrisk venture capital

Equity financing
See Equity; Equity midrisk venture capital

Equity midrisk venture capital
An unsecured investment in a company. Usually a purchase of ownership interest in a company that occurs in the later stages of a company's development.

Equity partnership
A limited partnership arrangement for providing start-up and seed capital to businesses.

Equity securities
See Equity

Equity-type
Debt financing subordinated to conventional debt.

Establishment
A single-location business unit that may be independent (a single-establishment enterprise) or owned by a parent enterprise.

Establishment and Enterprise Microdata File
See U.S. Establishment and Enterprise Microdata File

Establishment birth
See Business birth

Establishment Longitudinal Microdata File
See U.S. Establishment Longitudinal Microdata File

Ethics
See Business ethics

Evaluation
Determining the potential success of translating an invention into a product or process.

Exit
See Business exit

Experience rating
See Underwriting

Export
A product sold outside of the country.

Export license
A general or specific license granted by the U.S. Department of Commerce required of anyone wishing to export goods. Some restricted articles need approval from the U.S. Departments of State, Defense, or Energy.

Failure
See Business failure

Fair share agreement
An agreement reached between a franchisor and a minority business organization to extend business ownership to minorities by either reducing the amount of capital required or by setting aside certain marketing areas for minority business owners.

Feasibility study
A study to determine the likelihood that a proposed product or development will fulfill the objectives of a particular investor.

Federal Trade Commission (FTC)
Federal agency that promotes free enterprise and competition within the U.S.

Federal Trade Mark Act of 1946
See Lanham Act

Fictional name
See Business name

Fiduciary
An individual or group that hold assets in trust for a beneficiary.

Financial analysis
The techniques used to determine money needs in a business. Techniques include ratio analysis, calculation of return on investment, guides for measuring profitability, and break-even analysis to determine ultimate success.

Financial intermediary
A financial institution that acts as the intermediary between borrowers and lenders. Banks, savings and loan associations, finance companies, and venture capital companies are major financial intermediaries in the United States.

Financial ratios
See Corporate financial ratios; Industry financial ratios

Financial statement
A written record of business finances, including balance sheets and profit and loss statements.

Financing
See First-stage financing; Second-stage financing; Thirdstage financing

First-stage financing
Financing provided to companies that have expended their initial capital, and require funds to start full-scale manufacturing and sales. Also known as First-round financing.

Fiscal year
Any twelve-month period used by businesses for accounting purposes.

504 Program
See Certified development corporation

Flexible benefit plan
A plan that offers a choice among cash and/or qualified benefits such as group term life insurance, accident and health insurance, group legal services, dependent care assistance, and vacations.

FOB
See Free on board

Format franchising
See Business format franchising; Franchising

401(k) plan
A financial plan where employees contribute a percentage of their earnings to a fund that is invested in stocks, bonds, or money markets for the purpose of saving money for retirement.

Four Ps
Marketing terms referring to Product, Price, Place, and Promotion.

Franchising
A form of licensing by which the owner-the franchisor- distributes or markets a product, method, or service through affiliated dealers called franchisees. The product, method, or service being marketed is identified by a brand name, and the franchisor maintains control over the marketing methods employed. The franchisee is often given exclusive access to a defined geographic area.

Free on board (FOB)
A pricing term indicating that the quoted price includes the cost of loading goods into transport vessels at a specified place.

Frictional unemployment
See Unemployment

FTC
See Federal Trade Commission

Fulfillment
The systems necessary for accurate delivery of an ordered item, including subscriptions and direct marketing.

Full-time workers
Generally, those who work a regular schedule of more than 35 hours per week.

Garment registration number
A number that must appear on every garment sold in the U.S. to indicate the manufacturer of the garment, which may or may not be the same as the label under which the garment is sold. The U.S. Federal Trade Commission assigns and regulates garment registration numbers.

Gatekeeper
A key contact point for entry into a network.

GDP
See Gross domestic product

General obligation bond
A municipal bond secured by the taxing power of the municipality. The Tax Reform Act of 1986 limits the purposes for which such bonds may be issued and establishes volume limits on the extent of their issuance.

GNP
See Gross national product

Good Housekeeping Seal
Seal appearing on products that signifies the fulfillment of the standards set by the Good Housekeeping Institute to protect consumer interests.

Goods sector
All businesses producing tangible goods, including agriculture, mining, construction, and manufacturing businesses.

GPO
See Gross product originating

Gross domestic product (GDP)
The part of the nation's gross national product (see separate citation) generated by private business using resources from within the country.

Gross national product (GNP)
The most comprehensive single measure of aggregate economic output. Represents the market value of the total output of goods and services produced by a nation's economy.

Gross product originating (GPO)
A measure of business output estimated from the income or production side using employee compensation, profit income, net interest, capital consumption, and indirect business taxes.

HAL
See Handicapped assistance loan program

Handicapped assistance loan program (HAL)
Low-interest direct loan program through the U.S. Small Business Administration (SBA) for handicapped persons. The SBA requires that these persons demonstrate that their disability is such that it is

impossible for them to secure employment, thus making it necessary to go into their own business to make a living.

Health maintenance organization (HMO)
Organization of physicians and other health care professionals that provides health services to subscribers and their dependents on a prepaid basis.

Health provider
An individual or institution that gives medical care. Under Medicare, an institutional provider is a hospital, skilled nursing facility, home health agency, or provider of certain physical therapy services.

Hispanic
A person of Cuban, Mexican, Puerto Rican, Latin American (Central or South American), European Spanish, or other Spanish-speaking origin or ancestry.

HMO
See Health maintenance organization

Home-based business
A business with an operating address that is also a residential address (usually the residential address of the proprietor).

Hub-and-spoke system
A system in which flights of an airline from many different cities (the spokes) converge at a single airport (the hub). After allowing passengers sufficient time to make connections, planes then depart for different cities.

Human Resources Management
A business program designed to oversee recruiting, pay, benefits, and other issues related to the company's work force, including planning to determine the optimal use of labor to increase production, thereby increasing profit.

Idea
An original concept for a new product or process.

Import
Products produced outside the country in which they are consumed.

Income
Money or its equivalent, earned or accrued, resulting from the sale of goods and services.

Income statement
A financial statement that lists the profits and losses of a company at a given time.

Incorporation
The filing of a certificate of incorporation with a state's secretary of state, thereby limiting the business owner's liability.

Incubator
A facility designed to encourage entrepreneurship and minimize obstacles to new business formation and growth, particularly for high-technology firms, by housing a number of fledgling enterprises that share an array of services, such as meeting areas, secretarial services, accounting, research library, on-site financial and management counseling, and word processing facilities.

Independent contractor
An individual considered self-employed (see separate citation) and responsible for paying Social Security taxes and income taxes on earnings.

Indirect health coverage
Health insurance obtained through another individual's health care plan; for example, a spouse's employersponsored plan.

Industrial development authority
The financial arm of a state or other political subdivision established for the purpose of financing economic development in an area, usually through loans to nonprofit organizations, which in turn provide facilities for manufacturing and other industrial operations.

Industry financial ratios
Corporate financial ratios averaged for a specified industry. These are used for comparison purposes and reveal industry trends and identify differences between the performance of a specific company and the performance of its industry. Also known as Industrial averages, Industry ratios, Financial averages, and Business or Industrial norms.

Inflation
Increases in volume of currency and credit, generally resulting in a sharp and continuing rise in price levels.

Glossary

Informal capital
Financing from informal, unorganized sources; includes informal debt capital such as trade credit or loans from friends and relatives and equity capital from informal investors.

Initial public offering (IPO)
A corporation's first offering of stock to the public.

Innovation
The introduction of a new idea into the marketplace in the form of a new product or service or an improvement in organization or process.

Intellectual property
Any idea or work that can be considered proprietary in nature and is thus protected from infringement by others.

Internal capital
Debt or equity financing obtained from the owner or through retained business earnings.

Internet
A government-designed computer network that contains large amounts of information and is accessible through various vendors for a fee.

Intrapreneurship
The state of employing entrepreneurial principles to nonentrepreneurial situations.

Invention
The tangible form of a technological idea, which could include a laboratory prototype, drawings, formulas, etc.

IPO
See Initial public offering

Job description
The duties and responsibilities required in a particular position.

Job tenure
A period of time during which an individual is continuously employed in the same job.

Joint marketing agreements
Agreements between regional and major airlines, often involving the coordination of flight schedules, fares, and baggage transfer. These agreements help regional carriers operate at lower cost.

Joint venture
Venture in which two or more people combine efforts in a particular business enterprise, usually a single transaction or a limited activity, and agree to share the profits and losses jointly or in proportion to their contributions.

Keogh plan
Designed for self-employed persons and unincorporated businesses as a tax-deferred pension account.

Labor force
Civilians considered eligible for employment who are also willing and able to work.

Labor force participation rate
The civilian labor force as a percentage of the civilian population.

Labor intensity
The relative importance of labor in the production process, usually measured as the capital-labor ratio; i.e., the ratio of units of capital (typically, dollars of tangible assets) to the number of employees. The higher the capital-labor ratio exhibited by a firm or industry, the lower the capital intensity of that firm or industry is said to be.

Labor surplus area
An area in which there exists a high unemployment rate. In procurement (see separate citation), extra points are given to firms in counties that are designated a labor surplus area; this information is requested on procurement bid sheets.

Labor union
An organization of similarly-skilled workers who collectively bargain with management over the conditions of employment.

Laboratory prototype
See Prototype

LAN
See Local Area Network

Lanham Act
Refers to the Federal Trade Mark Act of 1946. Protects registered trademarks, trade names, and other service marks used in commerce.

Large business-dominated industry
Industry in which a minimum of 60 percent of employment or sales is in firms with more than 500 workers.

LBO
See Leveraged buy-out

Leader pricing
A reduction in the price of a good or service in order to generate more sales of that good or service.

Legal list
A list of securities selected by a state in which certain institutions and fiduciaries (such as pension funds, insurance companies, and banks) may invest. Securities not on the list are not eligible for investment. Legal lists typically restrict investments to high quality securities meeting certain specifications. Generally, investment is limited to U.S. securities and investment-grade blue chip securities (see separate citation).

Leveraged buy-out (LBO)
The purchase of a business or a division of a corporation through a highly leveraged financing package.

Liability
An obligation or duty to perform a service or an act. Also defined as money owed.

License
A legal agreement granting to another the right to use a technological innovation.

Limited partnerships
See Venture capital limited partnerships

Liquidity
The ability to convert a security into cash promptly.

Loans
See Commercial loans; Disaster loans; SBA direct loans; SBA guaranteed loans; SBA special lending institution categories Local Area Network (LAN) Computer networks contained within a single building or small area; used to facilitate the sharing of information.

Local development corporation
An organization, usually made up of local citizens of a community, designed to improve the economy of the area by inducing business and industry to locate and expand there. A local development corporation establishes a capability to finance local growth.

Long-haul rates
Rates charged by a transporter in which the distance traveled is more than 800 miles.

Long-term debt
An obligation that matures in a period that exceeds five years.

Low-grade bond
A corporate bond that is rated below investment grade by the major rating agencies (Standard and Poor's, Moody's).

Macro-efficiency
Efficiency as it pertains to the operation of markets and market systems.

Managed care
A cost-effective health care program initiated by employers whereby low-cost health care is made available to the employees in return for exclusive patronage to program doctors.

Management Assistance Programs
See SBA Management Assistance Programs

Management and technical assistance
A term used by many programs to mean business (as opposed to technological) assistance.

Mandated benefits
Specific treatments, providers, or individuals required by law to be included in commercial health plans.

Market evaluation
The use of market information to determine the sales potential of a specific product or process.

Market failure
The situation in which the workings of a competitive market do not produce the best results from the point of view of the entire society.

Market information
Data of any type that can be used for market evaluation, which could include demographic data, technology forecasting, regulatory changes, etc.

Market research
A systematic collection, analysis, and reporting of data about the market and its preferences, opinions, trends, and plans; used for corporate decision-making.

Market share
In a particular market, the percentage of sales of a specific product.

Marketing
Promotion of goods or services through various media.

Master Establishment List (MEL)
A list of firms in the United States developed by the U.S. Small Business Administration; firms can be selected by industry, region, state, standard metropolitan statistical area (see separate citation), county, and zip code.

Maturity
The date upon which the principal or stated value of a bond or other indebtedness becomes due and payable.

Medicaid (Title XIX)
A federally aided, state-operated and administered program that provides medical benefits for certain low income persons in need of health and medical care who are eligible for one of the government's welfare cash payment programs, including the aged, the blind, the disabled, and members of families with dependent children where one parent is absent, incapacitated, or unemployed.

Medicare (Title XVIII)
A nationwide health insurance program for disabled and aged persons. Health insurance is available to insured persons without regard to income. Monies from payroll taxes cover hospital insurance and monies from general revenues and beneficiary premiums pay for supplementary medical insurance.

MEL
See Master Establishment List

MESBIC
See Minority enterprise small business investment corporation

MET
See Multiple employer trust

Metropolitan statistical area (MSA)
A means used by the government to define large population centers that may transverse different governmental jurisdictions. For example, the Washington, D.C. MSA includes the District of Columbia and contiguous parts of Maryland and Virginia because all of these geopolitical areas comprise one population and economic operating unit.

Mezzanine financing
See Third-stage financing

Micro-efficiency
Efficiency as it pertains to the operation of individual firms.

Microdata
Information on the characteristics of an individual business firm.

Mid-term debt
An obligation that matures within one to five years.

Midrisk venture capital
See Equity midrisk venture capital

Minimum premium plan
A combination approach to funding an insurance plan aimed primarily at premium tax savings. The employer self-funds a fixed percentage of estimated monthly claims and the insurance company insures the excess.

Minimum wage
The lowest hourly wage allowed by the federal government.

Minority Business Development Agency
Contracts with private firms throughout the nation to sponsor Minority Business Development Centers which provide minority firms with advice and technical assistance on a fee basis.

Minority Enterprise Small Business Investment Corporation (MESBIC)
A federally funded private venture capital firm licensed by the U.S. Small Business Administration to provide capital to minority-owned businesses (see separate citation).

Minority-owned business
Businesses owned by those who are socially or economically disadvantaged (see separate citation).

Mom and Pop business
A small store or enterprise having limited capital, principally employing family members.

Moonlighter
A wage-and-salary worker with a side business.

MSA
See Metropolitan statistical area

Multi-employer plan
A health plan to which more than one employer is required to contribute and that may be maintained through a collective bargaining agreement and required to meet standards prescribed by the U.S. Department of Labor.

Multi-level marketing
A system of selling in which you sign up other people to assist you and they, in turn, recruit others to help them. Some entrepreneurs have built successful companies on this concept because the main focus of their activities is their product and product sales.

Multimedia
The use of several types of media to promote a product or service. Also, refers to the use of several different types of media (sight, sound, pictures, text) in a CD-ROM (see separate citation) product.

Multiple employer trust (MET)
A self-funded benefit plan generally geared toward small employers sharing a common interest.

NAFTA
See North American Free Trade Agreement

NASDAQ
See National Association of Securities Dealers Automated Quotations

National Association of Securities Dealers Automated Quotations
Provides price quotes on over-the-counter securities as well as securities listed on the New York Stock Exchange.

National income
Aggregate earnings of labor and property arising from the production of goods and services in a nation's economy.

Net assets
See Net worth

Net income
The amount remaining from earnings and profits after all expenses and costs have been met or deducted. Also known as Net earnings.

Net profit
Money earned after production and overhead expenses (see separate citations) have been deducted.

Net worth
The difference between a company's total assets and its total liabilities.

Network
A chain of interconnected individuals or organizations sharing information and/or services.

New York Stock Exchange (NYSE)
The oldest stock exchange in the U.S. Allows for trading in stocks, bonds, warrants, options, and rights that meet listing requirements.

Niche
A career or business for which a person is well-suited. Also, a product which fulfills one need of a particular market segment, often with little or no competition.

Nodes
One workstation in a network, either local area or wide area (see separate citations).

Nonbank bank
A bank that either accepts deposits or makes loans, but not both. Used to create many new branch banks.

Noncompetitive awards
A method of contracting whereby the federal government negotiates with only one contractor to supply a product or service.

Nonmember bank
A state-regulated bank that does not belong to the federal bank system.

Nonprofit
An organization that has no shareholders, does not distribute profits, and is without federal and state tax liabilities.

Norms
See Financial ratios

North American Free Trade Agreement (NAFTA)
Passed in 1993, NAFTA eliminates trade barriers among businesses in the U.S., Canada, and Mexico.

NYSE
See New York Stock Exchange

Occupational Safety & Health Administration (OSHA)
Federal agency that regulates health and safety standards within the workplace.

Optimal firm size
The business size at which the production cost per unit of output (average cost) is, in the long run, at its minimum.

Organizational chart
A hierarchical chart tracking the chain of command within an organization.

OSHA
See Occupational Safety & Health Administration

Overhead
Expenses, such as employee benefits and building utilities, incurred by a business that are unrelated to the actual product or service sold.

Owner's capital
Debt or equity funds provided by the owner(s) of a business; sources of owner's capital are personal savings, sales of assets, or loans from financial institutions.

P & L
See Profit and loss statement

Part-time workers
Normally, those who work less than 35 hours per week. The Tax Reform Act indicated that part-time workers who work less than 17.5 hours per week may be excluded from health plans for purposes of complying with federal nondiscrimination rules.

Part-year workers
Those who work less than 50 weeks per year.

Partnership
Two or more parties who enter into a legal relationship to conduct business for profit. Defined by the U.S. Internal Revenue Code as joint ventures, syndicates, groups, pools, and other associations of two or more persons organized for profit that are not specifically classified in the IRS code as corporations or proprietorships.

Patent
A grant made by the government assuring an inventor the sole right to make, use, and sell an invention for a period of 17 years.

PC
See Professional corporation

Peak
See Cyclical peak

Pension
A series of payments made monthly, semiannually, annually, or at other specified intervals during the lifetime of the pensioner for distribution upon retirement. The term is sometimes used to denote the portion of the retirement allowance financed by the employer's contributions.

Pension fund
A fund established to provide for the payment of pension benefits; the collective contributions made by all of the parties to the pension plan.

Performance appraisal
An established set of objective criteria, based on job description and requirements, that is used to evaluate the performance of an employee in a specific job.

Permit
See Business license

Plan
See Business plan

Pooling
An arrangement for employers to achieve efficiencies and lower health costs by joining together to purchase group health insurance or self-insurance.

PPO
See Preferred provider organization

Preferred lenders program
See SBA special lending institution categories

Preferred provider organization (PPO)
A contractual arrangement with a health care services organization that agrees to discount its health care rates in return for faster payment and/or a patient base.

Premiums
The amount of money paid to an insurer for health insurance under a policy. The premium is generally paid periodically (e.g., monthly), and often is split between the employer and the employee. Unlike deductibles and coinsurance or copayments, premiums are paid for coverage whether or not benefits are actually used.

Prime-age workers
Employees 25 to 54 years of age.

Prime contract
A contract awarded directly by the U.S. Federal Government.

Private company
See Closely held corporation

Private placement
A method of raising capital by offering for sale an investment or business to a small group of investors (generally avoiding registration with the Securities and Exchange Commission or state securities registration agencies). Also known as Private financing or Private offering.

Pro forma
The use of hypothetical figures in financial statements to represent future expenditures, debts, and other potential financial expenses.

Proactive
Taking the initiative to solve problems and anticipate future events before they happen, instead of reacting to an already existing problem or waiting for a difficult situation to occur.

Procurement
A contract from an agency of the federal government for goods or services from a small business.

Prodigy
An online service which is accessible by computer modem. The service features Internet access, bulletin boards, online periodicals, electronic mail, and other services for subscribers.

Product development
The stage of the innovation process where research is translated into a product or process through evaluation, adaptation, and demonstration.

Product franchising
An arrangement for a franchisee to use the name and to produce the product line of the franchisor or parent corporation.

Production
The manufacture of a product.

Production prototype
See Prototype

Productivity
A measurement of the number of goods produced during a specific amount of time.

Professional corporation (PC)
Organized by members of a profession such as medicine, dentistry, or law for the purpose of conducting their professional activities as a corporation. Liability of a member or shareholder is limited in the same manner as in a business corporation.

Profit and loss statement (P & L)
The summary of the incomes (total revenues) and costs of a company's operation during a specific period of time. Also known as Income and expense statement.

Proposal
See Business plan

Proprietorship
The most common legal form of business ownership; about 85 percent of all small businesses are proprietorships. The liability of the owner is unlimited in this form of ownership.

Prospective payment system
A cost-containment measure included in the Social Security Amendments of 1983 whereby Medicare

payments to hospitals are based on established prices, rather than on cost reimbursement.

Prototype
A model that demonstrates the validity of the concept of an invention (laboratory prototype); a model that meets the needs of the manufacturing process and the user (production prototype).

Prudent investor rule or standard
A legal doctrine that requires fiduciaries to make investments using the prudence, diligence, and intelligence that would be used by a prudent person in making similar investments. Because fiduciaries make investments on behalf of third-party beneficiaries, the standard results in very conservative investments. Until recently, most state regulations required the fiduciary to apply this standard to each investment. Newer, more progressive regulations permit fiduciaries to apply this standard to the portfolio taken as a whole, thereby allowing a fiduciary to balance a portfolio with higher-yield, higher-risk investments. In states with more progressive regulations, practically every type of security is eligible for inclusion in the portfolio of investments made by a fiduciary, provided that the portfolio investments, in their totality, are those of a prudent person.

Public equity markets
Organized markets for trading in equity shares such as common stocks, preferred stocks, and warrants. Includes markets for both regularly traded and nonregularly traded securities.

Public offering
General solicitation for participation in an investment opportunity. Interstate public offerings are supervised by the U.S. Securities and Exchange Commission (see separate citation).

Quality control
The process by which a product is checked and tested to ensure consistent standards of high quality.

Rate of return
The yield obtained on a security or other investment based on its purchase price or its current market price. The total rate of return is current income plus or minus capital appreciation or depreciation.

Real property
Includes the land and all that is contained on it.

Realignment
See Resource realignment

Recession
Contraction of economic activity occurring between the peak and trough (see separate citations) of a business cycle.

Regulated market
A market in which the government controls the forces of supply and demand, such as who may enter and what price may be charged.

Regulation D
A vehicle by which small businesses make small offerings and private placements of securities with limited disclosure requirements. It was designed to ease the burdens imposed on small businesses utilizing this method of capital formation.

Regulatory Flexibility Act
An act requiring federal agencies to evaluate the impact of their regulations on small businesses before the regulations are issued and to consider less burdensome alternatives.

Research
The initial stage of the innovation process, which includes idea generation and invention.

Research and development financing
A tax-advantaged partnership set up to finance product development for start-ups as well as more mature companies.

Resource mobility
The ease with which labor and capital move from firm to firm or from industry to industry.

Resource realignment
The adjustment of productive resources to interindustry changes in demand.

Resources
The sources of support or help in the innovation process, including sources of financing, technical evaluation, market evaluation, management and business assistance, etc.

Retained business earnings
Business profits that are retained by the business rather than being distributed to the shareholders as dividends.

Revolving credit
An agreement with a lending institution for an amount of money, which cannot exceed a set maximum, over a specified period of time. Each time the borrower repays a portion of the loan, the amount of the repayment may be borrowed yet again.

Risk capital
See Venture capital

Risk management
The act of identifying potential sources of financial loss and taking action to minimize their negative impact.

Routing
The sequence of steps necessary to complete a product during production.

S corporations
See Sub chapter S corporations

SBA
See Small Business Administration

SBA direct loans
Loans made directly by the U.S. Small Business Administration (SBA); monies come from funds appropriated specifically for this purpose. In general, SBA direct loans carry interest rates slightly lower than those in the private financial markets and are available only to applicants unable to secure private financing or an SBA guaranteed loan.

SBA 504 Program
See Certified development corporation

SBA guaranteed loans
Loans made by lending institutions in which the U.S. Small Business Administration (SBA) will pay a prior agreed-upon percentage of the outstanding principal in the event the borrower of the loan defaults. The terms of the loan and the interest rate are negotiated between theborrower and the lending institution, within set parameters.

SBA loans
See Disaster loans; SBA direct loans; SBA guaranteed loans; SBA special lending institution categories

SBA Management Assistance Programs
Classes, workshops, counseling, and publications offered by the U.S. Small Business Administration.

SBA special lending institution categories
U.S. Small Business Administration (SBA) loan program in which the SBA promises certified banks a 72-hour turnaround period in giving its approval for a loan, and in which preferred lenders in a pilot program are allowed to write SBA loans without seeking prior SBA approval.

SBDB
See Small Business Data Base

SBDC
See Small business development centers

SBI
See Small business institutes program

SBIC
See Small business investment corporation

SBIR Program
See Small Business Innovation Development Act of 1982

Scale economies
The decline of the production cost per unit of output (average cost) as the volume of output increases.

Scale efficiency
The reduction in unit cost available to a firm when producing at a higher output volume.

SCORE
See Service Corps of Retired Executives

SEC
See Securities and Exchange Commission

SECA
See Self-Employment Contributions Act

Second-stage financing
Working capital for the initial expansion of a company that is producing, shipping, and has growing accounts receivable and inventories. Also known as Second-round financing.

Secondary market
A market established for the purchase and sale of outstanding securities following their initial distribution.

Secondary worker
Any worker in a family other than the person who is the primary source of income for the family.

Secondhand capital
Previously used and subsequently resold capital equipment (e.g., buildings and machinery).

Securities and Exchange Commission (SEC)
Federal agency charged with regulating the trade of securities to prevent unethical practices in the investor market.

Securitized debt
A marketing technique that converts long-term loans to marketable securities.

Seed capital
Venture financing provided in the early stages of the innovation process, usually during product development.

Self-employed person
One who works for a profit or fees in his or her own business, profession, or trade, or who operates a farm.

Self-Employment Contributions Act (SECA)
Federal law that governs the self-employment tax (see separate citation).

Self-employment income
Income covered by Social Security if a business earns a net income of at least $400.00 during the year. Taxes are paid on earnings that exceed $400.00.

Self-employment retirement plan
See Keogh plan

Self-employment tax
Required tax imposed on self-employed individuals for the provision of Social Security and Medicare. The tax must be paid quarterly with estimated income tax statements.

Self-funding
A health benefit plan in which a firm uses its own funds to pay claims, rather than transferring the financial risks of paying claims to an outside insurer in exchange for premium payments.

Service Corps of Retired Executives (SCORE)
Volunteers for the SBA Management Assistance Program who provide one-on-one counseling and teach workshops and seminars for small firms.

Service firm
See Business service firm

Service sector
Broadly defined, all U.S. industries that produce intangibles, including the five major industry divisions of transportation, communications, and utilities; wholesale trade; retail trade; finance, insurance, and real estate; and services.

Set asides
See Small business set asides

Short-haul service
A type of transportation service in which the transporter supplies service between cities where the maximum distance is no more than 200 miles.

Short-term debt
An obligation that matures in one year.

SIC codes
See Standard Industrial Classification codes

Single-establishment enterprise
See Establishment

Small business
An enterprise that is independently owned and operated, is not dominant in its field, and employs fewer than 500 people. For SBA purposes, the U.S. Small Business Administration (SBA) considers various other factors (such as gross annual sales) in determining size of a business.

Small Business Administration (SBA)
An independent federal agency that provides assistance with loans, management, and advocating interests before other federal agencies.

Small Business Data Base
A collection of microdata (see separate citation) files on individual firms developed and maintained by the U.S. Small Business Administration.

Small business development centers (SBDC)
Centers that provide support services to small businesses, such as individual counseling, SBA advice, seminars and conferences, and other learning center activities. Most services are free of charge, or available at minimal cost.

Small business development corporation
See Certified development corporation

Small business-dominated industry
Industry in which a minimum of 60 percent of employment or sales is in firms with fewer than 500 employees.

Small Business Innovation Development Act of 1982
Federal statute requiring federal agencies with large extramural research and development budgets to allocate a certain percentage of these funds to small research and development firms. The program, called the Small Business Innovation Research (SBIR) Program, is designed to stimulate technological innovation and make greater use of small businesses in meeting national innovation needs.

Small business institutes (SBI) program
Cooperative arrangements made by U.S. Small Business Administration district offices and local colleges and universities to provide small business firms with graduate students to counsel them without charge.

Small business investment corporation (SBIC)
A privately owned company licensed and funded through the U.S. Small Business Administration and private sector sources to provide equity or debt capital to small businesses.

Small business set asides
Procurement (see separate citation) opportunities required by law to be on all contracts under $10,000 or a certain percentage of an agency's total procurement expenditure.

Smaller firms
For U.S. Department of Commerce purposes, those firms not included in the Fortune 1000.

SMSA
See Metropolitan statistical area

Socially and economically disadvantaged
Individuals who have been subjected to racial or ethnic prejudice or cultural bias without regard to their qualities as individuals, and whose abilities to compete are impaired because of diminished opportunities to obtain capital and credit.

Sole proprietorship
An unincorporated, one-owner business, farm, or professional practice.

Special lending institution categories
See SBA special lending institution categories

Standard Industrial Classification (SIC) codes
Four-digit codes established by the U.S. Federal Government to categorize businesses by type of economic activity; the first two digits correspond to major groups such as construction and manufacturing, while the last two digits correspond to subgroups such as home construction or highway construction.

Standard metropolitan statistical area (SMSA)
See Metropolitan statistical area

Start-up
A new business, at the earliest stages of development and financing.

Start-up costs
Costs incurred before a business can commence operations.

Start-up financing
Financing provided to companies that have either completed product development and initial marketing or have been in business for less than one year but have not yet sold their product commercially.

Stock
A certificate of equity ownership in a business.

Stop-loss coverage
Insurance for a self-insured plan that reimburses the company for any losses it might incur in its health claims beyond a specified amount.

Strategic planning
Projected growth and development of a business to establish a guiding direction for the future. Also used

to determine which market segments to explore for optimal sales of products or services.

Structural unemployment
See Unemployment

Sub chapter S corporations
Corporations that are considered noncorporate for tax purposes but legally remain corporations.

Subcontract
A contract between a prime contractor and a subcontractor, or between subcontractors, to furnish supplies or services for performance of a prime contract (see separate citation) or a subcontract.

Surety bonds
Bonds providing reimbursement to an individual, company, or the government if a firm fails to complete a contract. The U.S. Small Business Administration guarantees surety bonds in a program much like the SBA guaranteed loan program (see separate citation).

Swing loan
See Bridge financing

Target market
The clients or customers sought for a business' product or service.

Targeted Jobs Tax Credit
Federal legislation enacted in 1978 that provides a tax credit to an employer who hires structurally unemployed individuals.

Tax number
A number assigned to a business by a state revenue department that enables the business to buy goods without paying sales tax.

Taxable bonds
An interest-bearing certificate of public or private indebtedness. Bonds are issued by public agencies to finance economic development.

Technical assistance
See Management and technical assistance

Technical evaluation
Assessment of technological feasibility.

Technology
The method in which a firm combines and utilizes labor and capital resources to produce goods or services; the application of science for commercial or industrial purposes.

Technology transfer
The movement of information about a technology or intellectual property from one party to another for use.

Tenure
See Employee tenure

Term
The length of time for which a loan is made.

Terms of a note
The conditions or limits of a note; includes the interest rate per annum, the due date, and transferability and convertibility features, if any.

Third-party administrator
An outside company responsible for handling claims and performing administrative tasks associated with health insurance plan maintenance.

Third-stage financing
Financing provided for the major expansion of a company whose sales volume is increasing and that is breaking even or profitable. These funds are used for further plant expansion, marketing, working capital, or development of an improved product. Also known as Third-round or Mezzanine financing.

Time deposit
A bank deposit that cannot be withdrawn before a specified future time.

Time management
Skills and scheduling techniques used to maximize productivity.

Trade credit
Credit extended by suppliers of raw materials or finished products. In an accounting statement, trade credit is referred to as "accounts payable."

Trade name
The name under which a company conducts business, or by which its business, goods, or services are identified. It may or may not be registered as a trademark.

Trade periodical
A publication with a specific focus on one or more aspects of business and industry.

Trade secret
Competitive advantage gained by a business through the use of a unique manufacturing process or formula.

Trade show
An exhibition of goods or services used in a particular industry. Typically held in exhibition centers where exhibitors rent space to display their merchandise.

Trademark
A graphic symbol, device, or slogan that identifies a business. A business has property rights to its trademark from the inception of its use, but it is still prudent to register all trademarks with the Trademark Office of the U.S. Department of Commerce.

Translation
See Product development

Treasury bills
Investment tender issued by the Federal Reserve Bank in amounts of $10,000 that mature in 91 to 182 days.

Treasury bonds
Long-term notes with maturity dates of not less than seven and not more than twenty-five years.

Treasury notes
Short-term notes maturing in less than seven years.

Trend
A statistical measurement used to track changes that occur over time.

Trough
See Cyclical trough

UCC
See Uniform Commercial Code

UL
See Underwriters Laboratories

Underwriters Laboratories (UL)
One of several private firms that tests products and processes to determine their safety. Although various firms can provide this kind of testing service, many local and insurance codes specify UL certification.

Underwriting
A process by which an insurer determines whether or not and on what basis it will accept an application for insurance. In an experience-rated plan, premiums are based on a firm's or group's past claims; factors other than prior claims are used for community-rated or manually rated plans.

Unfair competition
Refers to business practices, usually unethical, such as using unlicensed products, pirating merchandise, or misleading the public through false advertising, which give the offending business an unequitable advantage over others.

Unfunded accrued liability
The excess of total liabilities, both present and prospective, over present and prospective assets.

Unemployment
The joblessness of individuals who are willing to work, who are legally and physically able to work, and who are seeking work. Unemployment may represent the temporary joblessness of a worker between jobs (frictional unemployment) or the joblessness of a worker whose skills are not suitable for jobs available in the labor market (structural unemployment).

Uniform Commercial Code (UCC)
A code of laws governing commercial transactions across the U.S., except Louisiana. Their purpose is to bring uniformity to financial transactions.

Uniform product code (UPC symbol)
A computer-readable label comprised of ten digits and stripes that encodes what a product is and how much it costs. The first five digits are assigned by the Uniform Product Code Council, and the last five digits by the individual manufacturer.

Unit cost
See Average cost

UPC symbol
See Uniform product code

U.S. Establishment and Enterprise Microdata (USEEM) File
A cross-sectional database containing information on employment, sales, and location for individual

enterprises and establishments with employees that have a Dun & Bradstreet credit rating.

U.S. Establishment Longitudinal Microdata (USELM) File

A database containing longitudinally linked sample microdata on establishments drawn from the U.S. Establishment and Enterprise Microdata file (see separate citation).

U.S. Small Business Administration 504 Program

See Certified development corporation

USEEM

See U.S. Establishment and Enterprise Microdata File

USELM

See U.S. Establishment Longitudinal Microdata File

VCN

See Venture capital network

Venture capital

Money used to support new or unusual business ventures that exhibit above-average growth rates, significant potential for market expansion, and are in need of additional financing to sustain growth or further research and development; equity or equity-type financing traditionally provided at the commercialization stage, increasingly available prior to commercialization.

Venture capital company

A company organized to provide seed capital to a business in its formation stage, or in its first or second stage of expansion. Funding is obtained through public or private pension funds, commercial banks and bank holding companies, small business investment corporations licensed by the U.S. Small Business Administration, private venture capital firms, insurance companies, investment management companies, bank trust departments, industrial companies seeking to diversify their investment, and investment bankers acting as intermediaries for other investors or directly investing on their own behalf.

Venture capital limited partnerships

Designed for business development, these partnerships are an institutional mechanism for providing capital for young, technology-oriented businesses. The investors' money is pooled and invested in money market assets until venture investments have been selected. The general partners are experienced investment managers who select and invest the equity and debt securities of firms with high growth potential and the ability to go public in the near future.

Venture capital network (VCN)

A computer database that matches investors with entrepreneurs.

WAN

See Wide Area Network

Wide Area Network (WAN)

Computer networks linking systems throughout a state or around the world in order to facilitate the sharing of information.

Withholding

Federal, state, social security, and unemployment taxes withheld by the employer from employees' wages; employers are liable for these taxes and the corporate umbrella and bankruptcy will not exonerate an employer from paying back payroll withholding. Employers should escrow these funds in a separate account and disperse them quarterly to withholding authorities.

Workers' compensation

A state-mandated form of insurance covering workers injured in job-related accidents. In some states, the state is the insurer; in other states, insurance must be acquired from commercial insurance firms. Insurance rates are based on a number of factors, including salaries, firm history, and risk of occupation.

Working capital

Refers to a firm's short-term investment of current assets, including cash, short-term securities, accounts receivable, and inventories.

Yield

The rate of income returned on an investment, expressed as a percentage. Income yield is obtained by dividing the current dollar income by the current market price of the security. Net yield or yield to maturity is the current income yield minus any premium above par or plus any discount from par in purchase price, with the adjustment spread over the period from the date of purchase to the date of maturity.

Index

Listings in this index are arranged alphabetically by business plan type, then alphabetically by business plan name. Users are provided with the volume number in which the plan appears.

Academic Testing Improvement Service
Academic Assistance, 14

Accounting Service
Marcus Accounting LLC, 7

Accounting Systems Consultants
Accounting Management Systems, 1

Adventure Travel Lodging Company
Cobra Travel Adventure Group, 11

Advertising Agency
BlueIsland.com, 8

Advertising Brokerage Firm
Cover Art Advertising, 13

Aerospace Supplier
Flatland Manufacturing, Inc., 1

Aftermarket Internet Applications
AutoAftermarket.com, 8

Aftermarket Skate Store
Pegasus Sports International, 8

Air Brushing Services
Workz of Art, 15

Airlines
Puddle Jumpers Airlines, Inc., 6
SkyTrails Airlines, Ltd., 9

Airport Shuttle
Prestige Car Service, 26

Ambulance Service
CareOne Ambulance Service, 20

Apartment Complex
Olde Towne Apartments, 20

Apparel Manufacturer
TTK Outdoor Apparel Company, 17

Architecture Firm
Smith Architecture Firm, Inc., 17

Arts and Crafts Company
3 Sister Crafts, 25

Art Easel Manufacturer
Art Easels and Supplies, Inc., 15

Art Gallery
Cooke Gallery, 14

Art Glass Studio
Phyllis Farmington Art Glass, 6

Assisted Living Facility
Home Again Assisted Living, 19

Audio Production Service
Jack Cornwall Productions, 4

Auto Accessories and Detailing
Auto Accessories Unlimited, 3
J.E.M. Ventures, Inc., 3

Auto Detailing
Hands-On Car Wash & Detail Center Inc., 23
Johnson's Mobile Detail, 19

Automated Teller Machines (ATMs)
Quick Cash Services, 16

Automobile Advertising
Carvertising, 18

Automobile Assembly
Dream Cars, 2

Automotive Dealer
Pompei-Schmidt Auto Dealers Inc., 4
Pallisimo Motors, 19

Automotive Repair Service
Collision Experts Inc., 10
LR Automotive, 4 and 19

Auto Sales Company
Mountain View Lease, LLC, 7

AV Equipment Rental Business
Galaxy Equipment Works Inc., 21

Baby Furniture Rental
Baby, Baby, 26

Bagel Shop
USA Bagels, 5

Banquet Facility
Pier 43, Inc., 24
Sycamore Hills Banquet Center, 26

Barbecue Sauce Manufacturer
Flamethrower Barbecue Sauce, 13

Barber School
Norm's School of Barbering, 24

Barbershop
D'Angelo's Choice Cut Barbershop Inc., 20

Beauty Salon
Salon Flora, 12

Bed & Breakfast
Aphrodite's Dream Bed & Breakfast, 6
Home Again Bed & Breakfast, 17
Red Barron Bed & Breakfast, 1
Rocheport Bed and Breakfast, 16
Victoria Bed & Breakfast, 4

Beekeeping Business
B. Strand's Bees, 16

Bicycle Shop
Wheelies, 15

Biobased Metalworking Fluids Company
Ecolubes, 23

Bioterrorism Prevention Organization
Bioterrorism & Infections Prevention Organization, 10

Biscotti Bakery
Italian Eatery, The, 1

Bistro and Wine Bar
Wine Bistro, The, 10

Bookkeeping Practice
Kohn Bookkeeping Practice, 17

Bookstore
Betty's Books, 18

Bottled Water Manufacturer
Sparkling Horizon Bottled Water, 4

Bowling Alley
Family Bowl, The, 7
Strikers Lanes, 19

Bread Bakery
Breadcrafter, 5

Brewpub
Hopstreet Brewery, 11

Bridal Salon
Megan's Bridal Boutique, 6

Broker
Marshall Financial Services, 23

Burger Stand
Bob's Burger Shack, 22

Business Consulting
Blake & Associates, 1, 21
Cartwright Business Consultants, LLC, 23
Koshu, 1

Business Development Firm
NKR Consulting, Inc., 9

Business Valuation Expert
Carlisle & Associates, 24

Cafe and Gas Station
Troon Cafe and Gas Station, 14

Campground
California RV & Campgrounds, 12

Campus Apartment Complex
Fourwinds Apartments, 13

Car Service
The Personal Touch Car Service, 18

Car Wash
ABC, Inc., 7
Dirt Buster, The, 1
J&A Ventures, Inc., 5
Platinum Carwash, 12

Car Wash and Car Detailing Business
Wash and Go, 16

Caribbean Café
Calypso Café, 6

Carpet Cleaning Service
Carpet Chem Corporation, 3

Catering Service
Creative Catering, 26

Caviar Company
Caviar Delights, 9

Charity Youth Hockey Tournament
Lucky Pucks, 8

Chemical Manufacturer
Chemalyze, Inc., 8

Child Transportation Service
Kid Cart, 4
Trusted Transport Inc., 25

Children's Bookstore
Under the Shade Tree, 17

Children's Catering Business
Katering2Kidz Inc., 18

Children's Hair Salon
Kool Kidz, 26

Children's Indoor Recreation Center
Interactive Garden, 13

Chiropractic Office
Cole's Care Chiropractic, 6

Christmas Ornament Company
Scriptures for You, Inc., 6

Church
New Beginnings Ministry, 22

Cigar Company
Smokescreen Cigars, 11

Cigar Shop
Holy Smokes, 5

Climbing Outfitter
Rockhound Outfitters, 5

Cloud Computing Business
Premier Cloud Infrastructure, Inc., 23
Beecham Consulting, 24

Coatings Inspection Company
Professional Coatings Services, Inc. 10

Coffee Bean Plant/Exporter
Silvera & Sons Ltda., 7, 24

Coffee House
Coffee Circus, 4

Coffee Roaster
Venezia Coffee Roasters, 4

Combination Coffeehouse/Play Spot
JavaJumpz LLC, 18

Comedy Club
The Comedy Corner, 15

Commercial Bank
Bronx Community Bank, 23

Commercial Diving Service
Working Diver & Marine Services, 22

Commodities Trading Firm
Admirian Commodities, 19

Computer Reseller
Computech Management, 5, 25
Ellipse Technologies, Inc., 5

Computer Training Service Business
Enhanced Occupations Center, 9

Concierge Service
Business Errands, 25

Concert Promotions Company
Good Vibrations, Inc., 9

Concession Equipment Rental Business
ConcessionMaster Enterprises LLC, 22

Concrete Coating Company
Techno–Coatings USA, 12

Condiment Manufacturer
Salvador Sauces, Inc., 6

Consignment Shop
Upscale Resale, 26

Construction Development & Real Estate Firm
Black Pearl Development and Real Estate LLC, 11

Construction and Home Rehabilitation Company
Pedro's Construction, 11

Convenience Store & Bait Shop
The Dock Store, 8

Cookie Shop
Grandma Miller's Cookies and Muffins, 6

Copy Shop
Pronto Printing, 26

Corner Store
Martin General Store, 13

Cosmetics Manufacturer
Glamour Girl Cosmetics, 22

Counseling Center
Juniper Counseling Center, 9

Counseling Practice
Roper Counseling Services Inc., 16

Courier Service
Corporate Courier, 14

Crane Service
Chesterfield Crane Service, 1

Creative Agency
Oceania Creative Print & Interactive, 8

Currency Trading
Fundex Currency Trading Co. Inc., 17

Custodial Cleaning Company
Spic and Span, 12

Custom Carpentry Shop
Choice Cut Carpentry Inc., 16

Custom Denim Retailer
Patch Denim Company, 18

Custom Paint and Body Shop/ Classic Car Restorations
Racing Stripes, 26

Dance and Skate Outfitter
Arabesque Dance & Skate Shop, 3

Dance Studio
Dancing Divas, 26
New Baltimore Dance Academy, 25

Day Camp Organizer
Camp in the Park, 16

Daycare Facility
Childhood Dreams Inc. , 12
Rachel's Clubhouse, 11
Ziggle Zag Zip Daycare/Childcare, 12

Daycare/Preschool
Little Lambs Daycare and Preschool, 18

Day Spa
Temple Creek Day Spa, 21

Debt Collection Agency
Zerri Collection Agency, 23

Dentist
Fremont Dental Office, 12
Stanley M. Kramer, DDS, LLC, 8

Desktop Publishing Company
Power Desk Top Publishing, Inc., 7

Detective Agency
Barr Detective Agency, 5

Dial-It Service
Callmaster, Inc., 3

Diaper Delivery
Diapers 'n More, 1 and 19

Digital Asset Management Consultant
Stephen Jacobson LLC, 25

Digital Presentations
Martin Productions, 19

Diner
Shoestrings, 16

Direct Mail Outlet
Post Direct, 4

Discount Consumer Electronics Retailer
JBN Elektronix, Inc., 24

Discount Internet Securities Broker
E-Best-Trade.com, 8

Dispatched Trucking Company
Preferred Trucking, 23

Display Technology Company
TouchTop Technologies, Inc., 7

DJ Service
MID-MO MUSIC, 21

Dog Training Business
A-1 Dog Training & Behavior LLC, 17

Dollar Store
Dollar Daze, 9, 26

Domestic Services Provider
Helping Hands Personal Services LLC, 16

Dry Cleaner
A.Z. Ventures/Expert Cleaning, 3

DVD Kiosk Rental Business
Movies To Go, Inc., 22
Rent DVDs Now, 15

Early Childhood Program
RYC Early Childhood Center, 24

E–Commerce Website Producer
Internet Capabilities, 12

Editorial Services & Consulting
Hilton & Associates, 1

Elder Care
Summer Gardens Residential Care Facility for the Ambulatory Elderly, 1 and 20

Electronic Document Security Company
GoldTrustMark.com, 9

Emu Ranch
Southwestern Emu Ranch, 4

Energy Consultant
Jacobs Consulting, 15

Energy Efficiency Auditing Firm
Energy Physicians, 16

Energy Solutions Company
Abaka Energy Solutions, 8, 23

Engineering Management Consultant
Herman Livingston Consultants, 4

Entertainment Production, Distribution, and Performance Company
Mentonic Hero Inc. , 12

Environmentally–Friendly Greenhouse
Green Greenhouse, 15

Environmentally–Minded Residential Construction Company
Green Earth Construction, 13

Equipment Rental
Rich Rentals, 1

Ethanol Fuel Production
Ontario Ethanol Supply, 14

Ethnic Food Supplier
World Cuisine, 13

Event Photography Service
brightroom, Inc., 10

Event Planning Company
Occasions, The Event Planning Specialists, 7
Unforgettable Event Partners LLC, 25

Family Entertainment Center
FunXplosion LLC, 18

Fantasy Book & Memorabilia Store
Wizard and Warlock Books, 14

Farm
Gilmore Farms, 19

Fast Food
Pasta Express, 3
Pasta Now!, 3

Fertilizer & Commodity Chemicals Company
Agronix Organics, Inc., 10

Financial Services Company
Diamond Strategic Services, 7
Prisma Microfinance, Inc., 9

Fire Equipment Retailer
Gallagher's Fire Service, 5

Fitness Center
Woodland Gym Ltd., 13

Food and Beverage Vending Company
Paco Bello Vending, 14

Food, Diet, & Nutrition Company
Think Thin Weight Loss Corporation, 10

Food Processor
Rio Grande, 3

Food Truck
Eddie's Edibles Mobile Food, 21
Suerte Cuban Cuisine, 26

Framing/Antiques Store
Flora's Frames & Antiques, 1

Franchise Postal Service
Express Postal Center, 5

Freelance Children's Librarian
Storytime Alternatives, 23

Freelance Editor
Scrivener, The, 2
Word for Word, 2

Freight Expediting
Gazelle Expediting Inc., 5

Furniture Resale Shop
Furniture Finds, 15

Furniture Restoration Company
Furniture Restoration Business, 15

Furniture Store
Collins Furniture, 19

Gas Station
Rapid Roger's Gas Station, 19

General Contracting Company
HandyWoman Services, 25
Smith Contracting Company, 7

General Staffing Company
GENRX LLC, 12, 26

Gift Basket Service
Sunrise Gift Baskets, 26

Gift Shop
The Busy Bee, 16

Gift Store
Crystal Creek Gifts, 5
Little Treasures Gift Shop, 13

Giftware Company
Jenni Frey Gifts, 11

Go–Cart Designer and Supplier
Speedy Go–Cart, 12

Go Kart Track
Supersonic Racing, 21

Gold Mining
Davis Gold Mining, 21

Golf Driving Range
Mountain Cedar Golf Club, 9

Golf Grip Manufacturer
ProGrip, 10

Golf-Themed Restaurant and Conference Facility
The Golf Garden at Sandy Rock Inc., 25

Gourmet Foods Company
Good Earth Foods Company, 8

Graffiti Removal Service
Graffiti, Inc., 3

Grant Writer
Landon Consulting, 22
Whitfield Resources LLC, 18

Green/Sustainability Consulting Firm
Ward & O'Neil LLC, 18

Greenhouse and Flower Shop
Little Greenie Shop, 14

Grocery Store
Viking Grocery Stores, 9

Hair Salon
Epiphany Salon, 6

Handmade Greeting Card Company
Heartsongs, 11

Handmade Writing Instruments & Accessories Business
StanMark Gifts Inc., 26

Handyman Service
"I'm the Man!" Handyman Services, 11

Health Advocacy Business
Medical Navigation Services Inc., 17

Healthcare Marketing Agency
Johnson & Brooks LLC, 15

Healthcare Software Company
QuikMed Info., 7

Healthcare Translation & Interpretation Business
Cross–Cultural Communications Inc., 17

Health Communications Consultant
Stanton Health Communications LLC, Inc., 25

Health Insurance Company
Southeast Healthplans, Inc., 6

Hedge Fund
Oxford Advisors, 26

Holistic Health Center
Holistic Choices, LLC, 10

Home Accessibility Services Provider
AccessibilityWorx Inc., 26

Home Brewing Supplies Company
Peterson's Homebrew LLC, 25

Home Décor Products Manufacturer
Burton Decor, Inc., 10

Home Furnishing Manufacturer
Castellini Manufacturing, 14

Home Inspection Company
Home Inspectors Are We, 12

Home Organization Service
Break Free Organizing, 16

Home Oxygen Delivery Service
Mercy Home Oxygen Services, 24

Home Renovation Contractor
Stephens Contracting, 13

Home Repair and Improvement Contractor
HandyGals Inc., 17

Homeless Shelter
Sister Joan of Arc Center, 11

Horse Riding School
Apple Blossom Stables, 24

Hotel Resort
Seven Elms Resort, 7

House Cleaning
Mid-Missouri Maid Service, 16

Housing Rehabilitation Company
Madison Builders, LLC, 10

Human Resources Consultant
Anders Johnson LLC, 20

Ice Cream Parlor
SonnyScoops, 16

Ice Cream Shop
Fran's Ice, 3 and 19

Import Boutique
Bellisimo Imports, Inc., 1

Import/Export Store
Central Import/Export, 9

Indoor Playground
Kid's World, 3

Indoor Softball Practice Facility
Richmond Fieldhouse, 24

Inflatable Amusement Rental Business
FunGiant Enterprises Inc., 22

Information Technology Personnel Agency
Rekve IT Staffing, 12

Infusion Therapy
Pharma Infusion Services, Inc., 22

Inn/Resort
Lighthouse Inn, The, 1

Interior Decorator
Lindsay Smith Interiors LLC, 19

Interior Design Company
Gable & Nash LLC, 19
Make It Your Own Space Inc., 11

Interior Painting Service
Eyecatching Interiors LLC, 11

Interior Renovation Company
Addams Interiors, 14

Internet & Network Security Solution Provider
Safety Net Canada, Inc., 10

Internet Bid Clearinghouse
Opexnet, LLC, 5

Internet Cafe
Wired Bean, 5, 24

Internet Communications Service Provider
Appian Way Communications Network, Ltd., 9

Internet Consultant
Allen Consulting, 3
Worldwide Internet Marketing Services, 3

Internet Loyalty Program
Tunes4You, 11

Internet Marketplace
ABC Internet Marketplace, Inc., 8

Internet Services Portal Site
Net Solutions, 11

Internet Software Company
Poggle, Inc., 9

Internet Travel Agency Business
Memory Lane Cruises, 9

Investor Trading Software Company
Investor Trends, Inc., 6

iPhone App Developer
AppStar, 22

IT Network Installer
Misch Computer Network Services, 22

Jewelry Designer
Oswipi Custom Costume Jewelry Designs, 18

Junk Removal Business
Harry's Haul-Away Service Inc., 21

Kennel
Best Friend Kennel, 2

Ladder Company
Jacks' Ladder Inc., 1

Landscaping Service
G & D Landscaping, 20
Greenscapes Lawn Care, 25
Helping Hand, Inc., 13

Laundromat
Duds and Suds Laundry Mat, 19

Leasing Company
Leasing Group, 8

Leather Accessory Manufacturer
Safari Leatherworks, 13

Limited Liability Company
Northern Investments, LLC, 7

Litigation Services Company
Acme Litigation Company, 10

Low–Cost Home Decorating Service
Your Home Stylists, 15

Magazine Publisher
GRAPEVINE, 1

Mailing List Service
Forest Mail Service, 3

Management Consulting Service
Salmon & Salmon, 3

Manufacturing Business
Fiber Optic Automation, Inc., 3

Marble Quarry
Vomarth Marble Quarry, 9

Marina
The Bayshore Marina, 19

Marketing Communications Firm
Cornelius Marketing, 4
Meridian Consulting, 5, 25
Simmons Marketing Associates, 3
TargetPoint Consulting LLC, 20

Massage Therapists
Healing Hands Massage Therapy LLC, 25
MASSAGEWORKS, 11

Maternity Aid
Nest in Comfort, 2

Meal Facilitation and Preparation Company
Kitchen Helper, LLC, 13

Meat Market
A Cut Above Meats, 24

Media Conversion Company
The Memory Keeper, 18

Media Duplication & Transferring Business
DupliPro Inc., 21

Media Producer
Dynamic Video, 2
Dynamic Video (Revised), 2
Shalimar Films, Inc., 2

Medical Billing Company
Physicians 1st Billing and Claims, 7

Medical Equipment Producer
Mediquip, Inc., 6
Premium Therapy, LLC, 10

Medical Practice
North Oakland Medical Associates, 22

Men's Clothing Retailer
Van Schaack, 4

Mentally Disabled Care Facility
Welcome Home Organization, 11

Messenger Service
Legal Deliveries, 25

Metal Shop
Krosnow Metal Works, 5

Microbrewery
Harbor Brewing Company, 2
Juniper Brewing Company, 2
Smith Microbrewery, Inc., 17

Mobile App Development Business
AppStax LLC, 21

Mobile Oil Change Business
LocationLube Inc., 22

Mobile Pizza Kitchen Business
Pizza2go–go Inc., 19

Mobile Studio
CRS Mobile Studio, 2

Mobile Veterinary Practice
PetWheelz Inc., 17

Montessori School
Edison Park Montessori, 20

Mortgage Company
National Mortgage, Inc., 7
Stiles Mortgage Banking Firm, Inc., 17

Motorcycle Dealership and Racetrack
Zoom Motors, 11

Multilevel Marketing
RFM Enterprises, 3

Mural Company
Smith Ray Design, 10

Music Lessons Business
MelodyWorx Inc., 21

Music Store
The Fret Board, 15

Musical Festival Promotion
Metropolitan Entertainment Promotions, Inc., 24

Natural Gas Home Filling Station Provider
Green Fuel Stations, 15

Nature Photography Business
Shutterbugs Inc., 16

Network Game Centers
PowerPlay Gaming, LLC, 10

Newsletter
Network Journal, 2
Network Journal (Revised), 2

Nightclub
Wild Oasis, 7

Non-Medical Assistance
Helping Hands Companion Service, 20

Nonprofit Concession Stand Business
RGFA Concession Stand, 22

Nonprofit Pharmaceutical Research Center
The Center, 23

Nonprofit Youth Outreach Ministry
Life Works Cincinnati, 9

Novelty Shop
Great Pretender, The, 5

Nursery
Wonderland Nursery, 7

Office Furniture
Powerline of Northern Minnesota, 5

Oil and Gas Manufacturing and Services Co.
Russel Oil and Gas Valves Co. Inc., 17

Online Consulting
Borderline Transmissions, Inc., 1

Online Customer Service Support
live e-care, Inc., 10

Online Dating/Matchmaking Service
Matchmate, Inc., 3, 23

Online Government Contract Service
U.S.Consulting - GOV.COM, 4

Online Hospitality Service
Tinner Corp., 4

Online Job Service
CareerConnections.com, 8, 22
The Job Authority, Inc., 23

Online Merchant
E-Return Solutions, 8

Online Mortgage Company
Valuable Mortgage, 11

Online Outdoor Company
Outdoorsman.com, 8

Online Party–Planning Company
Theme Party in a Box, 16

Online Payment Services
Exactor Technologies, LLC, 12

Online Publishing System
Moonbeam Publishing, 9

Online Woodworking Manufacturing & Retailing
U–nique Woodworking, 12

Organic Cleaning Supplies
Green Home Care Solutions, 16

Organic Food Store
Earth's Bounty Organic Foods, 20

Organic Grower and Supplier
Great Lakes Organics, 14

Organic Lawn Care Services
Evergreen Organic Lawn Care Services, 17

Outdoor Adventure Travel Company
RAD-Venture, 4

Paint Distributor
Eartham Distributors, 4

Paintball Sport Company
Paintball Sport Palace, 6

Paintball Store and Field
X-Treme Paintball, 26

Painting Company
Ko-Bas Painting Company, 10

Parts Manufacturer
Zemens Metal Corporation, 5

Party Planning
Perfect Party, 18

Party Supply Store
Celebrations, 5

Pasta Franchise
Pasta Express, 5

Personal Loan Company
Marshall Personal Loan Services, 22

Personal Organizing Consultant
All In Place Inc., 21

Pest Control Service
Quality Pest Control Service, 24

Pet Sitting Service
Pet Care People, 14
Pet Watchers Inc., 20

Pet Waste Removal Business
The Scoop, 20

Pharmaceutical Company
Pain Away, Inc., 3

Photo Framing
Talking Photo Technology, 2

Photography Studio
Midwest Studios, 15

Physical Therapy Practice
Healing Hands Physical Therapy Inc., 16

Pipeline Fracture Testing Service
ADSL Pipeline Services Inc., 17

Pizza & Pasta Restaurant
Geno's Pizza & Pasta Restaurant, 18

Pizzeria
Coastal Pizza, 11
Pizza to Go, Inc., 6

Plant Nursery
Village Garden Center, 21

Plastic Drum Company
River City Drum, Inc., 7

Plumbing Service
Jax Plumbing, 3
Matt's Plumbing and Air Conditioning, 12

Plus–Sized Children's Clothing Store
Jennifer's Clothing Corner, 15

Powder Coating Manufacturer
Brudder Coating Systems Inc., 4
Innovative Over Coat, 4

Pressure Washing Business
ABC PressureClean Inc., 22

Printing Company
Big Picture Press Inc., 21
Master Printer and Partners Printing, 1
Printer Perfect, 1

Private Investigator
FBEyes, 11
Ferguson Investigation LLC, 18

Private Label Food Manufacturer
Clarence Pratt Enterprises, Inc., 6

Process Serving Business
Morgan Legal Services, 23

Produce and Flower Market
Richmond Farmer's Market, 25

Producer and Supplier of Plants and Flowers
Bountyfull Farms, 13

Product Assembly Business
AssemblyPro LLC, 23

Professional Organizing Consultant
Marilyn Ruby Inc., 21

Public Relations Firm
SHP & Associates Business Communications, 2
Hampton Public Relations LLC, 24

Publisher
Group Publishing, The, 6
Infoguide Inc., 1

Racing Parts Store
Southeast Racing Parts, 8

Real Estate Brokerage
Thomasson Real Estate, 15

Real Estate Company
MSN Real Estate, 7

Real Estate Investment Company
Schroeder Real Estate, 26
Wolfe Partners, 6

Real Estate Renovation Company
ABC Corp., 6

Real Estate Renovation and Resale
HouseFlipperz, 15

Record Company
Reed Entertainment Corp., 4
Stone Records, 22

Record Store
Hidden Treasure Records L.C., 6

Refrigerant Recovery
Road Runner Refrigerant Recovery System, 3

Rental Defibrillator Service
Heartsong Defibrillator, LLC, 15

Resale Clothing Store
New to You Resale Clothing Store, 18

Residential and Commercial Painting Service
Color My World, Inc., 14

Restaurant
American Diner, 1
Butcher Hollow Bar BQ, 7
Cafe Fresco, 13
The Fry House, 24
Kelly House Inn, 5
Peach Blossom Diner, 1
Rock Island Tavern, 5
Tokyo Sun, 13

Whistle Shop, The, 4

Restaurant (Nonprofit)
McMurphy's Grill, 1
Murphy's Grill, 2
Murphy's Grill (Revised), 2

Restaurant Franchise
The Chophouse, 24
Reuben's Deli, 2

Restaurant/Bar
Plugged Nickel, The, 2
Watering Hole, The, 2

Restaurant/Microbrewery
Homesteaders' Pub & Grub, 5

Resume Writing Business
Nieberger Career Consulting, LLC, 26

Retail Accessories and Art Store
Found Treasures, 24

Retail & Commercial Design Firm
Future Designs, 4

Retail Art Furnishings Business
Wood Designs Gallery, 6

Retail Business Incubator
Acme Incubators, 9

Retail Clothing
Boston Rags Clothing Store, 9
Clothes as Art Inc., 1 and 20

Retail Florist
Designs by Linda, 1

Retail Popcorn Stand
Franklin's Popcorn Works, 25

Retail Tobacco/Magazines
Standard Tobacco & News, 1

Retro Gaming Systems
Fist Full of Quarters Gaming Systems, 25

Rock Climber's Store & Cafe
The Boulder Stop, 8

Roller Rink
Dancing Wheels Roller Rink, 19
Santiago Roller Rink, 7

Routing/Navigation Software Company
PATH Systems, Inc., 10

Rubber Adhesive Manufacturer
Shake Proof, 4

RV Park
Eastchester Bay RV Park, 24

Safety Consulting Firm
Peters, Marsh & McLellan LLC, 17

Salad Packaging
Lyons & Coyne, Inc., 1

Sandwich Shop
Romastrano Incorporated, 3

School Store
The Devil's Den, 25

Science Information Website Company
e-Science Technologies, Inc., 9

Screen Print Drying Company
DLP, Inc., 7

Search Service
Searchers, The, 2

Self–Defense/Anti–Bullying Training Company
Safe Zone Personal Defense LLC, 18

Self Service Laundry Business
Wash 'N Go, 17

Self Storage Business
Tulsa StorageMaster Inc., 22

Senior Care Facility
Hearts and Hopes Senior Home, 12

Senior Relocation Service
A New Day, 23

Sharpening Service
The Razor's Edge LLC, 21

Shave Ice Business
Ice Dreams, 6

Shoe Store
Thomasson Shoes, 14

Ski Resort
Mounjoy, LLC, 8

Skin Cream Formulator
LaBelle Industries, Inc., 9

Smoothie and Juice Shop
Suzie's Smoothies, 14

Soap Making Business
Felson's Homemade Soaps Inc., 21

Software Developer
Data Technologies Corporation, 1

Software Engineering & Management Company
Swiss Issue WebTools, 7

Solar Energy Farm
Ward Solar Energy Farm, Inc., 17

Solar Panel Installation Service
Living Green Energy Services, 26

Special Needs Clothing Store
You Can Do It!, 7

Specialty Bakery
Creative Cupcakes, 20
Kate's Cupcakery, 21

Specialty Food Manufacturer
TOFU Beanery, LLC, 23

Sports Bar
Stone Oak Sports Bar & Grille, 12
Take Five Sports Bar & Grill, 6

Sports Collectibles
Diamond Collection, Inc., 2

Sports Tournament Organizer
Scramble Sports Tournament Series, 12

Stable
Miller Stables, 16

Stained Glass Business
Rose's Colored Glass, 19

Steak House
1845 Steakhouse, 20

Structural Engineering Consulting Firm
StructureAll Ltd., 8

Structural Genomics Software Provider
Pharmatech Genomics, 10

Student Advocate
Student Support Services, LLC, 25

Student Art Gallery
Pozzo Gallery, 23

Student Services Consulting Firm
Grad Student Exchange Consultants International, 8

Tattoo & Body Piercing
Chapel Hill Tattoo, 14

Tattoo Studio/Art Gallery
LivingArts Inc., 23

Taxi Service
Lakeview Taxi, 5

Tea Shop
Cuppa!, 18

Teacher Continuing Education
The Institute for the Advancement of
Teacher Education (IATE), 20

Technology Solutions Provider
Exceed Expectations, 13

Teen Night Club
Ventures, 8

Television Childproofer
Television for Kids, 2

Toiletry Company
Verde, 1

Toy Company
Toys for a New Generation Inc., 1

Toy Rental Company
Granny's Attic, 23

**Trademarked Resort Wear
Distributor**
Muskrat Bluffs Apparel, 13

Transcription Business
Speedy Transcription Services LLC, 21

Travel Agency
International Business Tours, 4

Travel Information Service
Traveling U.S. Inc., 4

Tutoring Service
Ellen's English Tutoring Service, 18
Stuart Tutoring, 20

Used Car Business
Budget Cars, 6, 22

**Used Clothing, Furniture, and
Antique Store**
Rebecca's Shoppe, 14

Used Furniture Business
Furniture xCHANGE, 20

**Used Records & Collectibles
Business**
Rudy's Record Shop, 21

Utilities Reclamation Services
Hydro Power Lines Reclamation Services Inc., 17

Vegetarian Fast Food Restaurant
Benny & Dell's, 18

Veterinary Practice
Four Legged Friends Clinic, 13

**Video Production & Distribution
Company**
Kitamon Productions, 9

Video Service
Express Video Service, 3

Virtual Assistance
AdminiStar Services, 20

Virtual Reality
Building Aids Inc., 1
CineMedia Studios, Inc., 1

Virtual Shopping
Click'n Shop Inc., 2

Waste Management
Waste Removal Serivces, Inc., 21

**Water Purification System
Distributor**
Fresh Faucet Distribution, 14

Website Designer
Portal Code, Inc., 14
Web Wizards, 19

Wedding Planning Service
Together Forever Wedding Planners, 20

Windmill Distributor
Pierson Windmills, 15

**Wine Merchant and Storage
Facility**
Wine Seller Cellar, 13

Wine Storage
Wine Portfolio Inc., 16

Wireless Internet Service
Superior XL Internet, 7

Wireless Systems Integrator
SpongeShark, LLC, 9

**Wooden Furniture Manufacturer
and Supplier**
Nashville Furniture, 14

X-Ray Imaging Center
Alliance X-Ray Imaging, 24

Yoga Studio
Namaste Family Yoga Studio, 15